Handbook of Marketing Decision Models

Recent titles in the **INTERNATIONAL SERIES IN OPERATIONS RESEARCH & MANAGEMENT SCIENCE**

Frederick S. Hillier, Series Editor, *Stansford University*

* A list of the early publications in the series is at the end of the book*

Berend Wierenga
Editor

Handbook of Marketing
Decision Models

 Springer

Editor
Berend Wierenga
Erasmus University
Rotterdam
The Netherlands
bwierenga@fbk.eur.nl

ISBN: 978-0-387-78212-6   ·   e-ISBN: 978-0-387-78213-3
DOI: 10.1007/978-0-387-78213-3

Library of Congress Control Number: 2008920719

Printed on acid-free paper

springer.com

Preface

This handbook presents the state of the art in marketing decision models. The book deals with new modeling areas such as customer relationship management, customer value and online marketing, but also describes recent developments in other areas. In the category of marketing mix models, the latest models for advertising, sales promotions, sales management, and competition are dealt with. New developments are presented in consumer decision models, models for return on marketing, marketing management support systems, and in special techniques such as time series and neural nets. Not only are the most recent models discussed, but the book also pays attention to the implementation of marketing models in companies and to applications in specific industries.

The reader can find short content descriptions of the different chapters of the book in the first chapter.

I am very pleased that we can offer this book. Marketing decision models are important and relevant for everyone in the field of marketing, including those with no specific expertise on this topic. Several subsets of readers can be distinguished for this book (partly overlapping): builders of marketing models, users of marketing models, academics in marketing departments of business schools (and in related departments such as decision sciences and strategy), PhD students, marketing researchers, and consultants.

The book is also designed to cover the substantive content in marketing models courses at the PhD and masters level.

At the completion of this book, my greatest thanks go to the authors of the different chapters. They are world renowned specialists in their areas, people with very busy schedules, and they have taken the time and effort to write their chapters. In this way they provide the opportunity to others to share their expertise. This is a great service to the field.

Second, I want to thank the reviewers. Each chapter was reviewed by two expert-colleagues, and the authors have benefited a lot from their comments and recommendations. A list with the names of the reviewers can be found as an Appendix to this preface.

Next, I want to thank the colleagues who have helped with advice and support during the preparation of this book. There were many of them, but I want to specially thank Gary Lilien (Pennsylvania State University) who has a lot of experience with writing books on marketing models himself, and Gerrit van Bruggen, my colleague at Rotterdam School of Management, Erasmus University. Both of them were excellent sounding board for ideas. I also want to thank the secretaries of the marketing department at RSM, Annette Bartels and Jolanda Lenstra for their invaluable support during the whole process.

Before setting out to write their chapters for this book, the authors got together in the "Workshop on Advances in Marketing Decision Models" which was held on May 27th, 2006, in Athens (Greece). I want to thank the Marketing Science Institute (Dominique Hanssens, then Executive Director) and the Greek Marketing Academy (George Avlonitis, President) for their support in organizing this workshop.

Finally, I want to mention the excellent cooperation with Fred Hillier, the Editor of the Springer International Series on Operational Research and Management Science, and with all the persons at Springer who put a lot of effort in the preparation, production and marketing of this book: Gary Folven, Carolyn Ford and many others.

The field of marketing decision models started almost fifty years ago and has been booming ever since. I hope that this book will be a useful guide for the next phase of its life cycle, and a source of inspiration for everyone who reads it.

Rotterdam, The Netherlands   Berend Wierenga

Appendix: Reviewers of the chapters for the Handbook of Marketing Decision Models

Kusum Ailawadi, Tuck School of Business, Dartmouth College, USA
Eric Bradlow, The Wharton School, University of Pennsylvania, USA
René Darmon, ESSEC Business School, France
Jehoshua Eliashberg, The Wharton School, University of Pennsylvania, USA
Rajdeep Grewal, Pennsylvania State University, USA
Sunil Gupta, Harvard Business School, USA
Manfred Krafft, University of Münster, Germany
V. Kumar, University of Connecticut, USA
Peter Leeflang, University of Groningen, The Netherlands
Donald Lehmann, Columbia University, USA
Gary Lilien, Pennsylvania State University, USA
John Little, Massachusetts Institute of Technology, USA
John Lynch, Duke University, USA
Carl Mela, Duke University, USA
Prasad Naik, University of California, Davis, USA
Scott Neslin, Tuck School of Business, Dartmouth College, USA
Vincent Nijs, Kellogg School of Management, Northwestern University, USA
Leonard Parsons, Georgia Institute of Technology, USA

Arvind Rangaswamy, Pennsylvania State University, USA
David Reibstein, The Wharton School, University of Pennsylvania, USA
John Roberts, University of New South Wales, Australia
Gerrit van Bruggen, RSM Erasmus University, The Netherlands
Dirk van den Poel, University of Gent, Belgium
Harald van Heerde, Waikato Management School, New Zealand
Fred Zyfryden, University of Southern California, USA

Contents

Part I

Introduction

Chapter 1
The Past, the Present and the Future of Marketing Decision Models

Introduction to the Handbook

Berend Wierenga

1.1 Introduction

The idea that marketing decisions can be supported with analytical, mathematical models took off in the sixties of the last century. Before that time, marketing decisions were mainly based on judgment and experience. This does not mean that there was no marketing analysis. For example, in the United Stated, by 1960 systematic marketing research was already more than 50 years old. But the emphasis was much more on collecting facts than on analyzing these facts in a way that is helpful for executive decision making (Alderson 1962).

In the first half of the 1960s, change was in the air. Within a short time interval, three books on marketing models were published by prominent marketing academics: Bass et al. (1961), Frank et al. (1962), and Buzzel (1964). These books introduced the concept of marketing models, discussed their advantages, and gave examples of how marketing models can be implemented and used in marketing domains such as advertising, media planning, pricing, sales force allocation, forecasting and inventory control. They marked the beginning of an explicit analytical approach to marketing decision making.

Three factors explain why this happened precisely at that time. First, in the early sixties computers (mainframes) were entering organizations. Although these computers were initially used for supporting primary processes and administrative procedures, such as production, operations, payrolls, and accounting, it was not long until marketers also recognized the potential of information technology for their work. An important effect of information technology was that much more marketing data became available in companies. Data act as a catalyst for analysis, and analysis requires appropriate tools. So, this increased data availability created the demand for marketing models. Second, the field of management was going through a transition towards a more science-based field, with increased attention for the behavioral sciences, social sciences, statistics and even experimentation. The famous recommendations of the Carnegie

B. Wierenga
RSM Erasmus University, Rotterdam, The Netherlands
e-mail: bwierenga@rsm.nl

B. Wierenga (ed.), *Handbook of Marketing Decision Models*,
DOI: 10.1007/978-0-387-78213-3_1, © Springer Science+Business Media, LLC 2008

Foundation[1] and the Ford Foundation[2] reports to bring more research rigor in business schools had also a major impact on marketing. It stimulated a more analytical approach to marketing, which favored the use of models. Third, the sixties were the heydays of Operation Research (OR), also called Management Science (MS). Operation Research started as a field that developed mathematical tools to support military operations in the Second World War (especially for logistics and transportation), and later became a modeling and optimization field with applications in virtually all areas of society. OR/MS became particularly important in the domain of business. A few years ago, the field of OR celebrated its 50th anniversary (ORSA and TIMS, the predecessors of the current professional association INFORMS, were founded in 1952 and 1953, respectively). The field of marketing models started about ten years later, and is now in its 5th decade.

In the 50 years of its existence the field of marketing decision models has developed into one of the main areas of marketing. The Chapters 2–17 of this "Handbook of Marketing Decision Models" describe the most recent advances in this field. In this first chapter we start with a brief sketch of the developments in marketing decision models over the past decades and see how this has led to the state of the art of today. Then we discuss the topics of the different chapters of this book, and we conclude with a short reflection on the future of marketing decision models.

1.2 Five Decades of Marketing Decision Models

We will give a sketch of the developments in marketing decision models by formulating per decade the most prominent approaches, together with examples of these approaches. The overview is summarized in Table 1.1. By necessity, such a characterization has a subjective element, but we trust that the overall picture is reasonably valid. Below we briefly discuss the five decades.

1.2.1 The Sixties: The Beginning

The first mathematical approaches to marketing problems can be found in the micro-economics literature. Of the key references given in Table 1.1, perhaps the Dorfman and Steiner paper (1954), with their theorem for marketing mix optimization, is the most famous one. Later in the sixties, the application of OR techniques to marketing problems became in vogue. Optimization methods (for example linear programming and goal programming), Markov models, simulation techniques, and game theory were applied to marketing problems

---

[1] Pierson (1959)
[2] Gordon and Howell (1959)

Table 1.1 Marketing decision models in 5 decades

Period	Prominent approaches	Representative examples/references
1960–1969 *The Beginning*	• Micro-economic approaches to marketing problems	• Dorfman and Steiner (1954); Nerlove and Arrow (1962); Vidale and Wolfe (1957)
	• Marketing problems formulated as known operation research (OR) problems	• Engel and Warshaw (1964); Montgomery and Urban (1969; 1970)
1970–1979 *The Golden Decade*	• Stochastic Models	• Massy et al. (1970);
	• Models for marketing instruments	• Kotler (1971);
	• Market response models	• Clarke (1976); Little (1979a);
	• Labeled marketing decision models	• CALLPLAN (Lodish 1971); ASSESSOR (Silk and Urban 1978) ADMOD (Aaker, 1975);
	• Marketing decision support systems	• Little (1979b)
1980–1989 *Towards Generalizations and Marketing Knowledge*	• Meta-analyses of the effects of marketing instruments	• Asmus et al. (1984); Tellis (1988)
	• Knowledge-based models and expert systems	• PROMOTER (Abraham and Lodish 1987); ADCAD (Burke et al. 1990); McCann and Gallagher (1990)
	• Conjoint analysis models	• Green et al. (1981)
1990–1999 *The Marketing Information Revolution*	• Scanner-data-based consumer choice modeling	• Neslin (1990); Chintagunta et al. (1991); Abraham and Lodish (1993);
	• Neural nets and data mining	• Hruschka (1993); West et al. (1997)
	• Stylized theoretical modeling	• Moorthy (1993); Choi (1991); Kim and Staelin (1999)
2000- *The Customer-centric Approach*	• Customer Relationship Management (CRM) models	• Reinartz and Kumar (2000); Reinartz et al. (2005); Hardie et al. (2005)
	• Customer Life-Time Value (CLV) models	• Gupta et al. (2004)
	• Electronic Commerce Models	• Chatterjee et al. (2003): Ansari and Mela (2003); Bucklin and Sismeiro (2003); Moe and Fader (2004)

(Montgomery and Urban 1969, 1970). Interestingly, in these early days, the OR approach to marketing problems was often combined with concepts from the (Bayesian) theory of decision making under uncertainty (Pratt et al. 1965). In subsequent decades we have not seen much of Bayesian concepts in marketing (decision) models, but very recently, stimulated by the immensely increased capacity of computers, Bayes has returned to marketing in the form of the Bayesian estimation techniques which have become very popular (Rossi et al. 2005).

1.2.2 The Seventies: The Golden Decade of Marketing Models

If there has ever been a "Golden Decade" for marketing decision models, these were the seventies of the previous century. In this decade, the field of marketing models grew exponentially and, what is perhaps more important, developed an identity of its own. The modeling of marketing phenomena and marketing problems became interesting in itself, irrespective of whether or not they could be solved with a known OR technique. In the sixties it was often a matter of a technique seeking for a task, whereas now the marketing problems as such became the point of departure. Researchers started to realize that OR algorithms can be too much of a straightjacket for real world marketing problems. Sometimes marketing problems had to be "mutilated" in order to fit them to an existing OR technique (Montgomery and Weinberg 1973). The most conspicuous example is the application of linear programming to media planning (Engel and Warshaw 1964). Media-planning problems are not really linear, but were forced to be so, in order to solve them with linear programming. The development of marketing models as an independent field from OR has continued since then. Although this very Handbook of Marketing Decision Models is published in the "Series in Operations Research and Management Science", one glance through its content makes immediately clear that the overlap with OR/MS is limited.

As Table 1.1 shows, the seventies saw a rich variety of modeling approaches to marketing. In the first half of the decade, stochastic models, especially consumer brand choice models, attracted a lot of attention from researchers. In later decades, stochastic models had a modest place in the marketing models domain, but they became more prominent again in the recent work on the modeling of individual customer behavior in the CRM context (see Chapters 9 and 10 of this Handbook).

Most attention in the seventies was devoted to models for marketing mix instruments (for example models for advertising, price, and personal selling). The issue was how to model the relationship between a particular marketing instrument and sales, i.e., to specify so-called marketing response models, with much attention for the mathematical form of this relationship (e.g., linear, concave, or S-shaped (Kotler 1971). The next issue was how to estimate these response functions from empirical data. This is where econometrics came in (Naert and Leeflang 1978).

In the seventies we also saw the take-off of "labeled models". A labeled model typically works in three steps: (i) a specific mathematical structure (model) for a particular marketing phenomenon is proposed; (ii) this model is coded in a computer program, and (iii) this program is used for marketing decision making, e.g., for predicting the outcomes of alternative marketing actions or for optimizing marketing efforts. It became fashionable to give a specific label or name to such a model, often an acronym that expressed its purpose. Well-known examples are: CALLPLAN (Lodish 1971) for the planning of sales call decisions, ADMOD (Aaker 1975) for media planning in advertising, and ASSESSOR (Silk and Urban 1978) for new product decisions. There are many more of these labeled models, some of them published before or after the seventies. Many of these labels have become "icons" in the marketing models field.

Another significant development in the seventies was the emergence of the concept of "Marketing Decision Support Systems" (MDSS) (Little 1979b). The purpose of MDSS is to bridge the distance between the (often) abstract marketing models and the reality of marketing decision making in practice. Practical marketing problems often are not very well structured, and MDSS are particularly suitable for dealing with less- or semi-structured problems (for example decisions about new products). The first papers on marketing decision support systems in the seventies were followed by a lot of subsequent work on the issue of how marketing models can really have an impact on marketing decision making in practice (see Chapters 16 and 17 of this Handbook).

1.2.3 The Eighties: Marketing Generalizations and Marketing Knowledge

By the eighties the work on marketing response models had produced a sufficiently large number of empirical studies in order to make generalizations. This gave rise to meta-analyses for several marketing instruments. Often-cited studies are the meta-analyses for advertising (Asmus et al. 1984) and for price (Tellis 1988). This work had a follow-up in the nineties with the Special Issue of Marketing Science on Empirical Generalizations in Marketing (Bass and Wind 1995).

Generalizations have the purpose of summarizing what we *know* about a particular subject or area. In the second half of the eighties, marketing knowledge as such became a popular topic. Using techniques from the fields of artificial intelligence (AI) and computer science, it became possible to "store" marketing knowledge in computers and make it available for decision making. This gave rise to the development of knowledge-based systems and expert systems. In marketing most of these systems were developed for advertising and sales promotions.

As a separate development, in this decade, conjoint analysis models became quite prominent. Interestingly conjoint analysis models the decision making of individuals (customers for example), but its results can be used as input for marketing decision makers, for example for the design of new products. Conjoint analysis has its roots in psychology. The first work on conjoint analysis in marketing appeared in the seventies (Green and Srinivasan 1978) and it has remained a very important area until today (see Chapter 2 of this Handbook).

1.2.4 The Nineties: The Marketing Information Revolution

The nineties is the decade in which (point-of-purchase) scanner data became available on a large scale. This "marketing information revolution" (Blattberg et al. 1994) was a major stimulating factor behind a surge in consumer choice modeling, especially in the area of sales promotions. Multinomial logit models (Guadagni and Little 1983) were used as the most prominent tool to carry out these analyses. The topics that were studied included the construction of baseline sales levels, the effects of different sales promotion instruments on sales, the effects of heterogeneity in the consumer population and the decomposition of the sales promotion "bump" into components, such as brand switching, purchase time acceleration, and stockpiling (Gupta 1988).

The quickly growing amounts of data also made it possible to employ new techniques from artificial intelligence and computer science: inductive techniques (e.g., artificial neural nets) that can find regularities in large data bases, and in this way "extract" knowledge from data. These methods, often referred to as "data mining", started to emerge in marketing in the nineties, and with the ever growing power of computers and the ever larger size of databases, they can be expected to become even more important in the future (see also Chapter 12 of this Handbook).

Quite different is another approach that became popular in the nineties: theoretical modeling, also called "stylized" theoretical modeling. In theoretical modeling, a marketing phenomenon or marketing problem is described by a number of mathematical equations. These equations are based on assumptions about the underlying process, for example the behavior of actors in the market place. This deductive approach (starting with assumptions and deriving managerially relevant implications) follows the tradition from micro-economics. "What-if" questions are answered by carrying out mathematical manipulations ("logical experiments"). This approach can, in principle, be applied to every marketing problem. No data is needed. Applications have been published in areas such as sales force compensation, pricing, and channel decisions (see references in Table 1.1).

1.2.5 The First Decade of the New Millennium: Individual Customer Models

The most important development of the recent years is that the individual customer has become the unit of analysis. Enabled by the increased capacity of information technology, companies have set up (often huge) databases with records of individual customers. Mostly, these databases are part of Customer Relationship Management (CRM) systems. This customer-centric approach has given rise to new species of marketing models (CRM models), for example models for the acquisition and retention of customers, models for predicting churn (customers who leave the company), and models that help to select customers for specific marketing campaigns. A major concept in such a customer-centric approach is the value of an individual customer. This has led to the development of Customer Life-time Value (CLV) models.

The emphasis on individual customers has been amplified by the advent of e-commerce or online marketing. Online marketing has dramatically changed the way suppliers interact with their customers. Here also a new category of models is emerging: electronic commerce models, for example models for the attraction of visitors to a site, models for banner ad response, and models for paid search advertising. The movement towards the individual customer and online marketing has again generated enormous amounts of new data: CRM data, clickstream data, and electronic commerce data. We can easily speak here of a "second marketing information revolution". This data requires new kinds of models. The Chapters 8, 9 and 10 of this Handbook deal with the new breed of customer-centric marketing models.

This concludes our discussion of the history of marketing decision models. We add three comments: on additional literature, on the application of marketing models in practice, and on model implementation.

In this overview, we have only been able to highlight the most important developments in marketing decision models. Readers interested in a more complete picture of the developments in marketing (decision) models over the previous decades can be referred to a sequence of books that appeared during this period: Kotler (1971), Lilien and Kotler (1983), Lilien et al. (1992), and Eliashberg and Lilien (1993).

The current Handbook of Marketing Decision Models, which offers the state of the art in marketing decision models in 2008, appears about fifteen years after its most recent predecessor.

In our overview we have concentrated on the substantive issues that marketing (decision) models have dealt with. We did not pay much attention to the methodologies that were used, such as data collection, measurement, and data analysis. For more information about the technical and methodological aspects of marketing models (e.g., model specification, estimation, forecasting, optimization), we refer the reader to books such as Naert and Leeflang (1978), Hanssens et al. (2001) and Leeflang et al. (2000).

Although there was a lot of initial optimism, it turned out that the availability of marketing models does not automatically imply that these models are actually used for marketing decision making in practice. The acceptance and use of marketing decision models has been a continuing problem. This has created a stream of research on the bottlenecks for the implementation and use of marketing models in practice and how to overcome them, starting with Little (1970). The reader is referred to Wierenga and Van Bruggen (2000) and Lilien and Rangaswamy (2004) for accounts of the issues involved. The Chapters 16 and 17 of this Handbook present the most recent insights on this topic.

1.3 The Chapters in this Handbook

At several places in the previous discussion we have linked earlier work in marketing decision models to the content of the chapters in this Handbook. We will now give a more systematic account of the content of the book. In doing so, we follow the sections of the Handbook.

1.3.1 Consumer Decision Making Models

Although traditionally marketing models have been more focused on managerial decision making than on consumer decision making, consumer decisions are the most important inputs to any marketing decision. Therefore, the Handbook starts with models for consumer decision making.

- Chapter 2, *"Developments in Conjoint Analysis"* (Rao) deals with a modeling technology that that is tremendously rich, both from a methodological point of view and from the perspective of practical applications. Conjoint analysis is particularly fruitful for the design of new products that fit with the preferences of customers. By mid-1994, over 1760 commercial applications were already reported (Wittink et al. 1994), and this number probably has risen exponentially since then. As can be seen from Table 1.1, conjoint analysis was already fully blooming in the eighties, but its methodology has been developing ever since. This Handbook chapter deals with the most recent advances in research design, new estimation methods (e.g., Hierarchical Bayes), and the handling of large numbers of attributes.
- The topic of Chapter 3, *"Interactive Consumer Decision Aids"* (Murray and Häubl), is of much more recent origin, and did not receive attention in earlier books on marketing models. Modern consumers are confronted with a vast array of choice possibilities and computer technology has made it possible to help them with interactive decision aids. Interactive Consumer Decision Aids (ICDA's) combine insights from consumer behavior research with knowledge about choice models (e.g., conjoint analysis models), and internet technology. ICDA's can be considered as decision support systems for consumers and can also act as "agents" on behalf of the consumers.

1.3.2 Marketing Mix Models

As we have seen, the work on marketing instruments started in the seventies, and this remained a core area of marketing models ever since. In the chapters of this section, new development are presented in the areas of advertising, sales promotions, sales management and competition.

Chapter 4 *"Advertising Models"* (Danahar) takes its departure in the advertising response models from the mid-seventies, and then moves on to topics such as media exposure on the Internet, Internet advertising models, and models for media channel selection. The Internet is becoming very important as an advertising channel, and there is a great need for models that can help advertisers to support their media decisions in the interactive era that we experience today.

- Chapter 5 "*Sales Promotion Models*" (van Heerde and Neslin) presents the newest insights on how to model and measure sales promotion effects. The scanner information revolution was needed before it became possible to precisely analyze the effects of a sales promotion. This chapter shows how to make a sophisticated decomposition of the "sales bump" during a sales promotion (with elements such acceleration, deceleration, cannibalization, and store switching). Also models are presented for forward buying and pass-through, which can help decision makers to optimize their sales promotion decisions, both at the level of the manufacturer and the retailer.
- Chapter 6, "*Models for Sales Management Decisions?*" (Albers and Mantrala) deals with a classical domain of marketing decision models. Since the publication of "CALLPLAN" in the early seventies (Lodish 1971), there has been a constant stream of work in this area with ongoing improvements, both in the estimation methods of sales response functions and in the optimization methods for sales planning. Sales management models represent the area of marketing decision models with probably the highest implementation rate (especially in the pharmaceutical industry). Chapter 6 deals with the progress in this field since 1996, discusses new approaches for the estimation of sales response functions, and discusses advances in decision models for sales resource allocation, sales territory design, and sales force structure.
- Chapter 7 "*Modeling Competitor Responsiveness*" (Leeflang) is also about market response models, but not the response of the sales to the (own) marketing instruments, but about competitive response. This can be the competitors' response to the marketing actions of the focal firm, but also the response of the own sales to marketing mix decisions of competitors. This chapter shows how to model the complex set of interdependent phenomena that we have here and also presents emerging insights from empirical research on short-term and long-term reaction functions.

1.3.3 Customer-Centric Marketing Models

The chapters in this section deal with completely new types of models. These models were developed as a consequence of the focus on individual customers which is increasingly common in today's marketing. We have discussed this earlier as the defining characteristic of marketing models in the current decade.

- Chapter 8 "*Models of Customer Value*" (Gupta and Lehmann) deals with the value of a customer for a company. In customer-centric marketing, individual customers are the targets of marketing strategies. Companies want to know how much they should spend on particular customers. In this context, the concept of customer lifetime value (CLV) has become very important. Chapter 8 discusses methods for determining the value of a customer (based on current and expected purchase behavior) and also deals with the factors that drive CLV.

- In Chapter 9 *"Decision Models for Customer Relationship Management (CRM)"*, Reinartz and Venkatesan start with the concept of CLV and then focus on CRM processes such as acquisition, retention, and win-back. They present a comprehensive set of models for (1) customer selection (which customers to acquire, to retain, or to focus on growing) and (2) the management of selected customers (allocation of resources to acquisition, retention and growth). Their chapter also gives an excellent account of the recent literature in this booming area.

- The final chapter in this section is Chapter 10: *"Marketing Models for Electronic Commerce"* (Bucklin). Online marketing is growing dramatically as a vehicle for facilitating commerce. This type of marketing has created the need for a new breed of marketing models. This chapter probably is the first review of this kind and deals with models for attracting website traffic, predicting online purchases, response to banner ads, paid search advertising, and electronic word of mouth.

1.3.4 Special Model Approaches

In this section the Handbook deals with modeling approaches that have not been specifically developed for marketing, but that have great potential for this field.

- Chapter 11 *"Time-Series Models in Marketing"* (Dekimpe, Franses, Hanssens, and Naik) deals with methods for the analysis of observations that are ordered over time. This type of observations ("time-series data") occurs very often in marketing, but only recently time-series methods are getting serious attention in the field. The focus of this chapter is on two important domains in time-series: (1) persistence modeling for making long-run inferences; and (2) state-space models, which can be used to integrate econometric analysis with normative decision problems (e.g., to determine the optimal media budget).

- The methods discussed in Chapter 12 *"Neural Nets and Genetic Algorithms in Marketing"* (Hruschka) were developed in the context of large databases. Large databases offer the possibility to search, in an inductive way, for patterns that give information about relationships in the data. In marketing, the size of the databases is growing exponentially, which makes it possible to benefit from (data-mining) techniques such as neural nets and genetic algorithms. In this chapter, special attention is given to the use of neural nets for estimating market response functions.

1.3.5 Industry-Specific Models

Although marketing models in principle are suitable for any industry, it is instructive to look with some depth at the contribution of marketing models to decision making in specific sectors. Whereas most work on marketing models has been carried out in the area of fast moving consumer goods (or "consumer packaged goods"), we have chosen two different industries for this purpose.

- Chapter 13 *"Decision Models for the Movie Industry"* (Eliashberg, Weinberg, and Hui) deals with the motion picture industry. This is a very interesting industry because of its tradition of intuitive, rather than analytical decision making. This chapter shows that there are plenty of opportunities here for supporting decision making with marketing models. Examples are: forecasting models of theatrical performance, models for theatrical release timing, models for local cinema competition, movie scheduling algorithms, and models for home video release timing.
- Chapter 14 *"Strategic Marketing Decision Models for the Pharmaceutical Industry"* (Shankar) discusses the use of marketing models in a completely different sector. In pharmaceuticals, a lot of emphasis is put on models for R&D and New Product Development (NPD). Also models are discussed for entry, growth and defensive strategies.

1.3.6 Return on Marketing Models

There is an increasing interest in the contribution of marketing to the overall performance of the company. This is related to the issue of marketing accountability.

- In Chapter 15 *"Models for the Financial-Performance Effects of Marketing"*, Hanssens and Dekimpe focus on the issue of how marketing efforts ultimately relate to the creation of cash flows for the company. The sales-response model, which has been the backbone of marketing models since the seventies, is also the core element of their model of how marketing efforts ultimately drive company results. Flow and stock metrics are very important in this context. Through the important stock metric of customer equity, an interesting link is made with the work on CLV in other chapters of the Handbook.

1.3.7 Implementation, Use, and Success of Marketing Models

Since the origination of marketing decision models, the implementation and use of these models in companies for actual decision making has been a major and continuing concern. This is the topic of the last two chapters.

- Chapter 16 *"Marketing Engineering: Models that Connect with Practice"* (Lilien and Rangaswamy) discusses the impact that marketing models have on practice. There is a measurable impact, but at the same time there is a gap between realized and actual potential for applications. The "marketing engineering" approach is a systematic approach towards technology-enabled, model-supported decision making. The chapter also provides a look ahead for marketing engineering in the light of developments in IT infrastructures and communication networks.

- The last chapter *"Advances in Marketing Management Support Systems"* (Wierenga, Van Bruggen and Althuizen) describes the improvements in the quality of marketing management support systems (MMSS) that have taken place over time. It also deals with the systematic insights that have been gathered with respect to the factors that drive the adoption and use of MMSS in companies. These insights can be used to make MMSS a greater success. Furthermore, this chapter pays attention to a new breed of marketing management support systems. Whereas most MMSS so far have been dealing with relatively structured decisions, Chapter 17 discusses approaches for decision making in weakly-structured areas, such as the design of a sales promotion campaigns.

1.4 The Past, the Present, and the Future of Marketing Decision Models

We can compare the field of marketing decision models with a river, which started as a tiny creek in the sixties of the last centuries, fed by the drops that trickled down from upstream areas such as economics and operations research. During the seventies this creek formed a bedding of its own. From then on it has continuously broadened itself by incorporating a variety of new confluents over time (enumerated in Table 1.1). By now it is an impressive current.

Figure 1.1 shows the field of marketing decision models in its upstream and downstream context. Marketing decision models (the centerpiece of the picture) is positioned within its direct environment, the field of marketing. Upstream, we see the important supplier disciplines to marketing decision models: economics, psychology, econometrics, operations research, information technology and artificial intelligence. Downstream from marketing decision models, we see where results of the work in marketing decision models go: to the marketing science literature and to the practice of marketing management.

The field of marketing decision models emerged when researchers started to use models as a means for understanding marketing processes and marketing phenomena and to solve marketing problems. In this process, marketing decision models (or briefly: marketing models), became a field in itself. Somewhat later the term "marketing science" became in vogue, as a close synonym to marketing models.

These developments took place at the time that marketing was becoming a core field of management, with the marketing mix as its focal paradigm. Therefore, it is no coincidence that the field of marketing models started (in the seventies) with a lot of attention for marketing mix models and marketing response functions. Although in later decades the scope of marketing has

Fig. 1.1 Marketing Decision
Models in its upstream and
downstream context

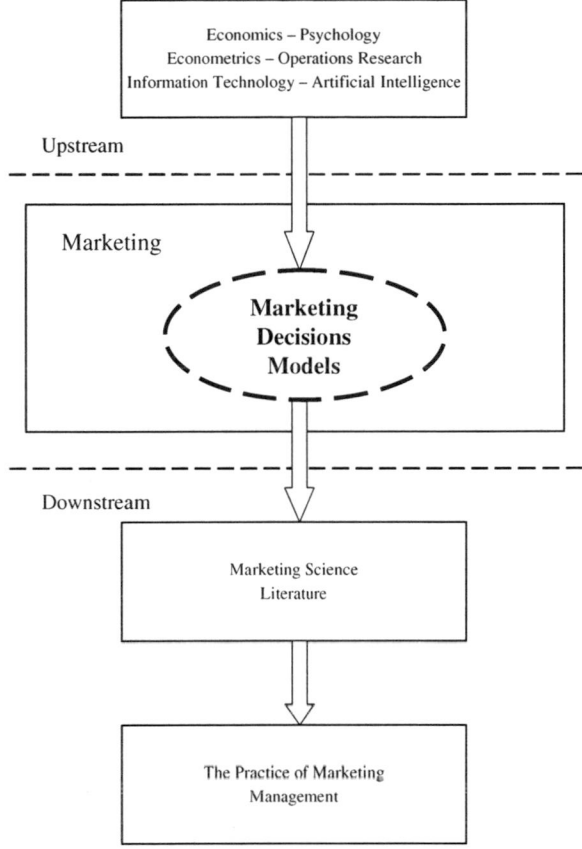

widened to many more marketing instruments than the 4 P's, and also to other
industries than the fast-moving-consumer-goods (where it originated), the
marketing modeling approach has basically remained the same. We still try to
model marketing processes and the working of marketing instruments. Once we
have specified the model, we estimate the effects of the different variables from
observed data. And when we have measured those effects, we use the results to
optimize marketing policy. Over the years, this work has accumulated a substantial amount of knowledge about marketing phenomena and how to model
them. Except for theoretical modeling, there always has been a strong emphasis
on empirical research in marketing science. The recent work reported in this
volume is fully in this tradition.

1.4.1 The Future of Marketing Decision Models

What does the future hold for marketing decision models? Many of the developments in marketing decision models over time were driven by changes in the

upstream. For example, the availability of more sophisticated econometric methods has significantly improved our ability to measure the effects of marketing instruments. (Think of the evolution from least-squares estimation to maximum-likelihood estimation to Bayesian estimation). Advances in information technology have led to quantum leaps in the amounts of available data and have also changed the nature of this data (from accounting data, to scanner data, to click-stream and e-commerce data). Progress in artificial intelligence has made it possible to capture marketing knowledge and make it available through computers.

Advances in the upstream (new methods, advances in information technology, new insights from economics and psychology) will keep the field of marketing decision models moving forward. But also developments in the field of marketing itself will be drivers of progress in marketing decision models. Often, it will be a combination of the two. A good example is the recent surge of CRM and online marketing, which is a development in marketing, but strongly stimulated by the growing capabilities of information technology. For the near future, we expect a significant further development in this area, i.e. in the work on models of individual customers. There is a clear managerial *demand* for this work. Marketers need tools to determine which customers in their databases they need to acquire, retain, or dispose of. Also they need to know how to obtain the best match between the customer's profile (e.g., purchase history) and the offer that the company is going to make. On the *supply* side, the field of marketing models has the proper econometric and optimization tools available for dealing with these issues. So, this is a winning combination. At one point, Kotler (1971, pp. 16–19) formulated marketing management as a "marketing programming problem". That is, once we have (i) a model describing the effects of marketing variables, (ii) a set of goal variables and (iii) a set of constraints, a computer can find the optimal solution. Almost 40 years later, this stage has been reached now in the CRM context where marketing mix decisions for individual customers are optimized and automated. Interestingly this marketing automation did not take place in the industry where it was first expected, i.e. the fast-moving consumer goods (Bucklin et al. 1998), but in very different industries. Examples of industries where CRM is very strong are: financial services, telecommunications, utilities, leisure and travel. We expect that this development of optimizing the marketing efforts for individual customers will continue, also favored by the quick increase of online marketing.

For the somewhat distant future one can speculate about the drivers of change in marketing decision models. Will this, for example, be triple play, viral marketing, RFID, or fMRI, to mention a few? Triple play (the integration of telephone, TV and PC/Internet in households) will generate enormous quantities of new marketing data, especially on media use and the exposure to (interactive) advertising. With viral marketing, organizations use networks of customers and Internet-based communication platforms to spread their messages (Van der Lans et al., 2008). This eWOM (electronic word-of-mouth) which is becoming very popular, requires new marketing models. The Radio

Frequency Identification (RFID) technique (which makes objects recognizable at a distance by means of placing minuscule tags on them) also has the potential of generating lots of new data. For marketing this becomes particularly interesting when such tags are put on consumer products in stores (e.g. supermarkets). Functional magnetic resonance imaging (fMRI) is a technique from neuroscience which makes it possible to monitor brain activities during decision making processes. There is great potential for the application of this technique in marketing (Shiv et al. 2005). This will create a demand for yet another type of new marketing models.

The four developments just mentioned are already visible. Other causes of change may still be under the surface. We can be sure that the field of marketing decision models will progress further, but there are many different directions possible. It is clear, however, that there will be plenty of interesting challenges for model builder in marketing for the years to come.

Finally, let's look at the downstream part of Fig. 1.1. Typically, the results from the work in marketing decision models first go to the marketing science literature. This flow seems to be in excellent shape. The volume of publications about marketing models is growing exponentially. We not only refer here to the journal with the name "Marketing Science" but also to marketing model publications in journals such as Journal of Marketing Research, Journal of Marketing, International Journal of Research in Marketing, Management Science, Operations Research, and several others. Some of these journals have recently enlarged their volumes (more issues per year) and a few years ago the set of journals in the field of marketing decision models has been expanded with a new journal: Quantitative Marketing and Economics. There can be no doubt that the (academic) literature on marketing models is booming and will do so for the years to come.

However, when we get to the second downstream flow in Fig. 1.1, from marketing science to marketing practice, the picture is much less cheerful. Sure, a lot of marketing models are being implemented, but this could be much more. This adoption and use of marketing models is continuing concern, as we have seen earlier. An augmented view of the field is needed and besides model building, implementation issues should get a lot of attention. We agree with Lilien and Rangaswamy (2000)'s statement: "Marketing modeling should not be restricted to faithfully capturing marketing phenomena. That will not bring a vibrant future for our field."(p. 234). Clearly, much more work is needed here. A future where marketing managers are eager to snatch the most recent marketing models from the researchers because they are convinced that these models help them to perform better, is so much more attractive than one where the models remain in the ivory towers of academia, however sophisticated they may be.

Today's marketers work in an environment where the computer is completely integrated in their work. They use all kind of databases and spreadsheet programs to monitor the market and to plan marketing actions. Whereas in the past many marketing models where "stand-alone" models (remember the labeled models discussed earlier), future marketing models will often be "embedded" models, integrated with larger systems of models in a company (Lilien and Rangaswamy 2000).[3] The integration of models in the manager's IT infrastructure makes it much easier to get marketers to use them on a day-to-day basis, which is a favorable condition for the adoption and use of marketing models in practice. We hope that model builders will take advantage of this opportunity and that in the next decade marketing models will become and integrated element in the decision processes of many marketing managers.

This concludes the introductory chapter of this book. We hope that it has whetted the appetite of the reader for the exciting sagas about marketing decision models in the next sixteen chapters.

References

Aaker, D.A. 1975. ADMOD: An Advertising Decision Model. *Journal of Marketing* **12**(1) 37–45.

Abraham, M.M., L.M. Lodish. 1987. PROMOTER: An Automated Promotion Evaluation System. *Marketing Science* **6**(2) 101–123.

Abraham, M.M., L.M. Lodish. 1993. An Implemented System for Improving Promotion Productivity Using Store Scanner Data. *Marketing Science* **12**(3) 248–269.

Alderson, W. 1962. Introduction in Frank., R.E., A.A. Kuehn, and W.F. Massy, eds. *Quantitative Techniques in Marketing Analysis*. Irwin, Homewood, IL, (xi–xvii).

Ansari, A., C.F. Mela. 2003. E-Customization. *Journal of Marketing Research* **40**(2) 131–45.

Asmus, G., J.U. Farley, D.R. Lehmann. 1984. How Advertising Affects Sales: Meta-Analysis of Econometric Results. *Journal of Marketing Research* **21**(1) 65–74.

Bass, F.M., R.D. Buzzel, M.R. Greene et al., Eds. 1961. *Mathematical Models and Methods in Marketing*. Homewood, Irwin, IL.

Bass, F.M., J. Wind. 1995. Special Issue: Empirical Generalizations in Marketing. *Marketing Science* **14**(3, Part 2 of 2).

Blattberg, R.C., R. Glazer, J.D.C. Little, Eds.1994. *The Marketing Information Revolution*. Harvard Business School Press, Boston, MA.

Bucklin, R.E., D.R. Lehmann, J.D.C. Little. 1998. From Decision Support to Decision Automation: A 2020 Vision. *Marketing Letters* **9**(3) 235–246.

Bucklin, R.E., C. Sismeiro. 2003. A Model of Web Site Browsing Behavior Estimated on Clickstream Data. *Journal of Marketing Research* **40**(3) 249–67.

Burke, R.R., A. Rangaswamy, Y.Wind, J. Eliashberg. 1990. A Knowledge-Based System for Advertising Design. *Marketing Science* **9**(3) 212–229.

Buzzel, R.D. 1964. *Mathematical Models and Marketing Management*. Harvard University, Division of Research, Boston, MA.

Chatterjee, P.D., L. Hoffman, T.P. Novak. 2003. Modeling the Clickstream: Implications for Web-Based Advertising Efforts. *Marketing Science* **22**(4) 520–41.

Chintagunta, P.K., D.C. Jain, N.J. Vilcassim. 1991. Investigating Heterogeneity in Brand Preferences in Logit Models for Panel Data. *Journal of Marketing Research* **28**(4) 417–428.

Choi, S.C. 1991. Price Competition in a Channel Structure with a Common Retailer. *Marketing Science* **10**(4) 271–296.

Clarke D.G. 1976. Economic Measurement of the Duration of Advertising Effects on Sales. *Journal of Marketing Research* **18**(4) 345–357.

---

[3] See also Chapter 16 of this Handbook

Dorfman, R., P.O. Steiner. 1954. Optimal Advertising and Optimal Quality. *American Economic Review* **44** 826–836.

Eliashberg, J., G.L. Lilien. 1993. *Handbooks in Operations Research and Management Science. Volume 5: Marketing.* Elsevier Science Publishers, Amsterdam.

Engel, J.F., M.R. Warshaw. 1964. Allocating Advertising Dollars by Linear Programming. *Journal of Advertising Research* **4** 42–48.

Frank, R.E., A.A. Kuehn, W.F. Massy, Eds. 1962. *Quantitative Techniques in Marketing Analyses.* Irwin, Homewood, IL.

Gordon, R.A., J.E. Howell. 1959. *Higher Education for Business.* Columbia University Press, New York, NY.

Green, P.E., J.D. Caroll, S.M. Goldberg. 1981. A General Approach to Product Design Optimization via Conjoint Analysis. *Journal of Marketing* **45**(3), 17–37.

Green, P.E., V. Srinivasan. 1978. Conjoint Analysis in Consumer Research: Issues and Outlook. *Journal of Consumer Research* **5**(2) 103–123.

Guadagni, P.M., J.D.C. Little. 1983. A Logit Model of Brand Choice Calibrated on Scanner Data. *Marketing Science* **2**(3) 203–238.

Gupta, S. 1988. Impact of Sales Promotions on When, What, and How Much to Buy. *Journal of Marketing Research* **259**(4) 342–355.

Gupta, S., D.R. Lehmann, J.A. Stuart. 2004. Valuing Customers. *Journal of Marketing Research* **51**(1) 71–8.

Hanssens, D.M., L.J. Parsons, R.L. Schultz. 2001. *Market Response Models: Econometric and Time Series Analysis*(2 nd ed.). Kluwer Academic Publishers, Boston.

Hardie, G.S., K.L. Lee, P.S. Fader. 2005. Counting Your Customers the Easy Way: An Alternative to the Pareto/NBD Model. *Marketing Science* **24**(2) 275–284.

Hruschka, H. 1993. Determining Market Response Functions by Neural Network Modeling: A Comparison to Econometric Techniques. *European Journal of Operations Research* **66** 27–35.

Kim, S.Y., R. Staelin. 1999. Manufacturer Allowances and Retailer Pass-Through Rates in a Competitive Environment. *Marketing Science* **18**(1) 59–76.

Kotler, P.H. 1971. *Marketing Decision Making: A Model Building Approach.* Holt, Rinehart, and Winston, New York, NY.

Leeflang, P.S.H., D.R. Wittink, M. Wedel, P.A. Naert. 2000. *Building Models for Marketing Decisions.* Kluwer Academic Publishers, Boston, MA.

Lilien, G.L., P.H. Kotler. 1983. *Marketing Decision Making: A Model-Building Approach.* Harper & Row, New York, NY.

Lilien, G.L., P.H. Kotler, K.S. Moorthy. 1992. *Marketing Models.* Prentice Hall, Englewood Cliffs, NJ.

Lilien, G.L., A. Rangaswamy. 2000. Modeled to Bits: Decision Models for the Digital Networked Economy. *International Journal of Research in Marketing* **17**(2–3) 227–235.

Lilien, G.L., A. Rangaswamy. 2004. *Marketing Engineering: Computer Assisted Marketing Analysis and Planning.* (2 nd ed.). Prentice Hall, Upper Saddle River, NJ.

Little, J.D.C. 1970. Models and Managers: The Concept of A Decision Calculus. *Management Science* **16** B466–B485.

Little, J.D.C. 1979a. Aggregate Advertising Models: The State of the Art. *Operations Research,* **27**(4) 629–667.

Little, J.D.C. 1979b. Decision Support Systems for Marketing Managers. *Journal of Marketing* **43**(3) 9–26.

Lodish, L.M. 1971. CALLPLAN: An Interactive Salesman's Call Planning System. *Management Science* **18**(4 Part II) 25–40.

Massy, W.F., D.B. Montgomery, D.G. Morrison. 1970. Stochastic Models of Buying Behavior. M.I.T. Press, Boston, MA.

McCann, J.M., J.P. Gallagher. 1990. *Expert Systems for Scanner Data Environments.* Kluwer Academic Publishers, Boston MA.

Moe, W.W., P.S. Fader. 2004. Dynamic Conversion Behavior at e-Commerce Sites. *Management Science* **50**(3) 326–35.

Moorthy, K.S. 1993. Theoretical Modeling in Marketing. *Journal of Marketing* **57**(2) 92–106.

Montgomery, D.B., G.L. Urban.1969. *Management Science in Marketing*. Prentice Hall, Englewood Cliffs, NJ.

Montgomery, D.B., G.L. Urban, Eds. 1970. *Applications of Management Sciences in Marketing*. Prentice Hall, Englewood Cliffs, NJ.

Montgomery, D.B., C.B. Weinberg. 1973. Modeling Marketing Phenomena: A Managerial Perspective. *Journal of Contemporary Business*, Autumn, 17–43.

Naert, P.A., P.S.H. Leeflang, 1978. *Building Implementable Marketing Models*. Leiden: Martinus Nijhoff.

Nerlove, M., K.J. Arrow. 1962. Optimal Advertising Policy under Dynamic Conditions. *Econometrica*, 29 (May), 129–142.

Neslin, S.A. 1990. A Market Response Model for Sales Promotion. *Marketing Science*, **9**(2), 125–145.

Pierson, F.C. 1959. *The Education of American Businessmen*. McGraw Hill, New York, NY.

Pratt, J., H. Raiffa, R. Schlaifer. 1965. *Introduction to Statistical Decision Theory*. Mc-Graw-Hill, New York, NY.

Reinartz, W.J., V. Kumar. 2000. On the Profitability of Long-Life Customers in a Noncontractual Setting: An Empirical Investigation and Implications for Marketing. *Journal of Marketing*, **64**(4) 17–35.

Reinartz, W., J.S. Thomas, V. Kumar. 2005. Balancing Acquisition and Retention Resources to Maximize Customer Profitability. *Journal of Marketing*, **69**(1) 63–79.

Rossi, P.E., G.M. Allenby, R. McCulloch. 2005. *Bayesian Statistics and Marketing*. John Wiley, Chichester, UK.

Shiv, B., A. Bechara, I. Levin, J.W. Alba, J.R. Bettman, L. Dube, A. Isen, B. Mellers, A. Smidts, S.J. Grant, A.P McCraw. 2005. Decision Neuroscience. *Marketing Letters* **16**(3/4) 375–386.

Silk, A.J., G.L. Urban. 1978. Evaluation of New Packaged Goods: A Model and Measurement Methodology. *Journal of Marketing Research* **15**(2) 171–191.

Tellis, G.J. 1988. The Price Elasticity of Selective Demand: A Meta-Analysis of Econometric Models of Sales. *Journal of Marketing Research* **25**(4) 331–341.

Van der Lans, R., G.H. Van Bruggen, J. Eliashberg, B. Wierenga. 2008. A Viral Branching Model for Predicting the Spread of ElectronicWord-of-Mouth in Viral Marketing Campaigns. Working paper RSM Erasmus University, 2008.

Vidale, M.L., H.B. Wolfe. 1957. An Operations-Research Study of Sales Response to Advertising. *Operations Research* **5**(3) 370–81.

West, P.M., P.L. Brocket, L. Golden 1997. A Comparative Analysis of Neural Networks and Statistical Methods for Predicting Consumer Choice. *Marketing Science* **16**(4) 370–391.

Wierenga, B., G.H. Van Bruggen. 2000. *Marketing Management Support Systems: Principles, Tools, and Implementation*. Kluwer Academic Publishers, Boston, MA.

Wittink, D.R., M. Vriens, W. Burhenne. 1994. Commercial Use of Conjoint Analysis in Europe: Results and Critical Reflections. *International Journal of Research in Marketing* **11**(1) 41–52.

Part II

Consumer Decision Making Models

Chapter 2
Developments in Conjoint Analysis

Vithala R. Rao

2.1 Introduction

Since the introduction some thirty five years ago of conjoint methods in marketing research (Green and Rao 1971), research on the methodology and applications of conjoint analysis has thrived extremely well. Researchers continue to explore both theoretical issues and problems encountered in practice. Academic research on conjoint methods is quite alive and well. It is not an exaggeration to say that "conjoint analysis is a journey and not a destination". A recent paper on this topic (Hauser and Rao 2003) reviewed the origins of the methodology, and research approaches used in data collection and estimation. Another paper (Green et al. 2003) reviews issues of how estimates of partworths from conjoint methods can be used to identify market segments, identify high-potential product designs, plan product lines, and estimate sales potential.

My primary focus of this chapter is to review selected recent developments[1] in conjoint analysis research. I will organize this chapter into seven sections. In the second (and next) section, I will quickly describe various topics to set the stage; these include the origins of conjoint analysis, various approaches employed in the literature, an overview of designing and implementing a conjoint study, and selected applications that made significant impact. In the third section, I will review developments in research design for the construction of profiles (for ratings-based conjoint methods) and choice sets (for choice-based conjoint methods). In addition, I will describe in this section research on partial profiles, incentive-aligned data collection methods, and self-explicated methods. I will devote the fourth section to developments in analysis/estimation

V.R. Rao
Cornell University, Ithaca, NY, USA
e-mail: vrr2@cornell.edu

[1] I will not delve into simulation methods in this chapter; readers are referred to the article by Green et al. (2003). Likewise, I will not delve into the advances in the conduct of conjoint analysis using the web-based administration and the use of visual and sensory characteristics of stimuli, and configurators; readers are referred to the paper by Hauser and Rao (2003).

B. Wierenga (ed.), *Handbook of Marketing Decision Models*,
DOI: 10.1007/978-0-387-78213-3_2, © Springer Science+Business Media, LLC 2008

methods, namely, polyhedral estimation methods, hierarchical Bayesian estimation methods, and their generalizations, including some results on their validation. In the fifth section, I will describe some emerging approaches for handling a large number of attributes in conjoint research. I will devote the sixth section to three recent developments to illustrate the current progress in conjoint methods: a method to estimate the market value of an improvement in an attribute of a product, measuring reservation prices for products and bundles, and a choice model bundle of items from heterogeneous product categories that considers the interactions between attributes the of bundle. Finally, in the seventh section, I will summarize my perspective on various developments in conjoint research and identify a few research possibilities.

2.2 A Brief Overview of Conjoint Analysis

It is fair to say that the methods of conjoint analysis[2] became prominent to tackle the problem of reverse mapping in multidimensional scaling applications (i.e., determining values of objective/physical characteristics of a product to yield a predetermined position in the space of perceptual dimensions). The main issue is how to design a new product's attributes (mainly physical characteristics) relevant to a specific location in a positioning map. This problem is quite complicated due the potential for multiple solutions (see DeSarbo and Rao 1986). However, the researcher can determine a function that relates physical characteristics to preference (or perceptions) for a new product with relative ease. With the knowledge of the preference function, a researcher can determine, the attributes of a product to reach a given preference level using simulation or optimization methods. Given this relative ease, the methodology of conjoint analysis has become quite popular in marketing research.[3] In this methodology, a utility function for a choice alternative is directly specified in terms of attributes and estimated with appropriate methods; accordingly, no reverse mapping is necessary.

2.2.1 Basics of Conjoint Analysis

Conjoint methods are intended to "uncover" the underlying preference function of a product in terms of its attributes.[4] A general product profile defined on

---

[2] The differences between conjoint measurement (with its psychometric origins and axioms) and conjoint analysis (a more pragmatic methodology) are important from a theoretical perspective. But, I will not delve into them here. See Rao (1976) for a discussion of conjoint measurement.

[3] This point was discussed at the Conference to honor Paul E. Green held at the University of Pennsylvania in May 2002.

[4] For an introduction to the subject matter of conjoint analysis, see Orme (2006).

r attributes can be written as $(x_{j1}, x_{j2},\ldots,x_{jr})$ where x_{jt} is the level for the j-th profile on the t-th attribute a product profile. While there exist several ways for specifying the preference functions in conjoint analysis, researchers usually start with an additive conjoint model. With an additive conjoint model, the preference score[5] for the j-th product profile, y_j for one respondent is modeled as $y_j = U_1(x_{j1}) + U_2(x_{j2}) + \ldots + U_r(x_{jr})$ where U_t $(\cdot)$ is the component utility function specific to the t-th attribute (also called part-utility function or part-worth function). No constant term is specified, but it could be included in any one of the U-functions or assumed to be zero (without any loss of generality.) The specification of the U-function for any attribute will depend upon its type (categorical and quantitative). In practice, a conjoint study may contain both types of attributes.

Brand names or verbal descriptions such as high, medium or low are examples of a categorical attribute; here the levels of the attribute are described by words. A quantitative attribute is one measured by either an interval scale or ratio scale; numbers describe the "levels" of such an attribute; examples are the weight of a laptop and speed of the processor.

The levels of a categorical attribute can be recoded into a set of dummy variables (one less various than the number of levels) and a part-worth function is specified as a piecewise linear function in the dummy variables. In this case, the component-utility function for a categorical attribute (t-th for example) will be:

$$U_t(x_{jt}) = D_{t1}U_{t1} + D_{t2}U_{t2} + \ldots + D_{tr_t}U_{tr_t} \tag{2.1}$$

Where r_t is the number of discrete levels for the t-th attribute (resulting from the construction of the profiles or created ex post); D_{tk} is a dummy variable taking the value 1 if the value x_{it} is equivalent to the k-th discrete level of x_t and 0 otherwise; and U_{tk} is the component of the part-worth function for the k-th discrete level of x_t.

In practice, only (r_t-1)—one less the number of discrete levels of the attribute—dummy variables are necessary for estimation.

A quantitative attribute can be used in a manner similar to a categorical attribute by coding its values into categories or used directly in the specification of the part-worth function for the attribute. In the latter case, the function can be specified as linear (vector model) or nonlinear; one example of a nonlinear function is the ideal point model. Mathematically, the component-utility function can be specified as:

---

[5] For exposition purposes, I am considering a ratings-based conjoint analysis where respondents provide preference ratings for a number of product profiles. Later in the chapter, I will describe choice-based conjoint methods as well. In a choice-based conjoint analysis, a respondent is presented several choice sets, each choice set consisting of a small number, four or five, profiles and is asked to make a choice among the alternatives for each choice set.

$$U_t(x_{jt}) = \begin{cases} w_t x_{jt} & \text{for the vector model; and} \\ w_t(x_{jt} - x_{0t})^2 & \text{for the ideal point model;} \end{cases} \qquad (2.2)$$

Where w_t is a weight (positive or negative); and x_{0t} is the ideal point on the t-th attribute.

A linear function is appropriate for an attribute deemed to be desirable (e.g. speed of a laptop computer) or undesirable (e.g., weight of a laptop computer); such a function is called a vector model for which the utility increases (or decreases) linearly with the numerical value of the attribute. An ideal point model is appropriate for such attributes as sweetness of chocolate where the utility function is an inverse U-shaped and it is highest at the ideal value of the attribute. For some attributes such as temperature of tea, the utility is lowest at the ideal value and it is called the negative ideal point model.

With suitable redefinitions of variables, the preference function can be written as $y = X\beta + \varepsilon$; where ε is the random error of the model assume to be normally distributed with zero mean and variance of σ^2 and y is the rating on given profile and X is the corresponding set of p dummy (or other) variables. The β is a px1 vector of partworths for the levels of attributes.

2.2.2 Conjoint Analysis in Practice

Since its introduction, conjoint methods[6] have been applied in a large number of applied marketing research projects. There is no recent estimate[7] of the number of applied studies but its use is increasing tremendously. The method has been applied successfully for tackling several marketing decisions such as optimal design of new products, target market selection, pricing a new product, and studying competitive reactions. Some high profile applications of these techniques include the development of Courtyard Hotels by Marriott (Wind et al. 1989) and the Design of the E-Z Pass Electronic Toll Collection System in New Jersey and neighboring States in the US (Green et al. 1997). A significant advantage of the conjoint method has been the ability to answer various "what if" questions using market simulators; these simulators are based on the results of an analysis of conjoint data collected on hypothetical and real choice alternatives.

Conjoint analysis has five features: (i) it is a measurement technique for quantifying buyer tradeoffs and attribute values (or partworths); (ii) it is an

---

[6] It will be useful to review some terms used in conjoint analysis. Attributes are (mainly) physical characteristics that describe a product; levels are the number of different values an attribute takes; profile is a combination of attributes, each attribute at a particular level, presented to a respondent for an evaluation (or stated preference); choice set is a pre-specified number of profiles presented to a respondent to make a pseudo-choice (stated choice).

[7] Wittink and Cattin (1989) and Wittink et al. (1994) arrived at an estimate of over 1,760 commercial applications of conjoint analysis in US and Europe during the five year period, 1986–1991.

analytical technique for predicting buyers' likely reactions to new products/ services; (iii) it is a segmentation technique for identifying groups of buyers who share similar tradeoffs/values; (iv) it is a simulation technique for assessing new product service ideas in a competitive environment; and (v) it is an optimization technique for seeking product/service profiles that maximize a pre-specified outcome measure such as share or rate of return. One may attribute these versatile features to the popularity of the methodology and the diversity of the domains (marketing and elsewhere) of applications of conjoint analysis.

As mentioned earlier, there are essentially two types of conjoint studies[8]; these are ratings-based and choice based. A typical conjoint analysis project consists of four main steps: (i) development of stimuli based on a number of salient attributes (hypothetical profiles or choice sets); (ii) presentation of stimuli to an appropriate sample of respondents: (iii) estimation of part-worth functions for the attributes as well as any heterogeneity among the respondents; and use of the estimates in tackling any managerial problems (e.g., forecasting, pricing, or product design). Figure 2.1 shows the steps involved in implementing a conjoint study.

Current approaches for implementing a conjoint analysis project differ in terms of several features; some main features are: stimulus representation, formats of data collection, nature of data collection, and estimation methods. Table 2.1 lays out some alternatives for these features. The approaches that are more commonly used are: Ratings-based (or Full-profile) Conjoint Analysis; Choice-based Conjoint Analysis; Adaptive Conjoint Analysis; Self-explicated Conjoint Analysis. I described in footnote 5 the distinction between the ratings-based and choice-based methods.

Adaptive methods involve developing questions in a sequential manner depending upon the responses from a respondent to previous questions; these methods are essentially subset of either ratings or choice-based methods. All of these three methods are called decompositional because, the partworths are estimated from data on ratings for a number of profiles or choices made for a number of choice sets, where alternatives are described in terms of attributes.

Self-explicated methods on the other hand are called compositional because both attribute importances and desirability of levels within each attributes are directly obtained from respondents and the utility value for an alternative is composed from these data specified as a weighted sum of importances and desirability values. There are obvious advantages and disadvantages of these approaches. One main factor is that procedures used for design of profiles or choice sets become quite critical and complicated in the use of ratings or choice-based methods. Self-explicated methods are relatively easy to implement and are shown to be quite robust (Srinivasan and Park 1997).

One important issue in conjoint analysis is how heterogeneity among respondents is taken into account; while earlier methods strive to collect ample data to

---

[8] As conjoint studies are implemented in practice, various other forms have emerged; these include self-explicated methods, adaptive methods and so on. See Hauser and Rao (2003) for details.

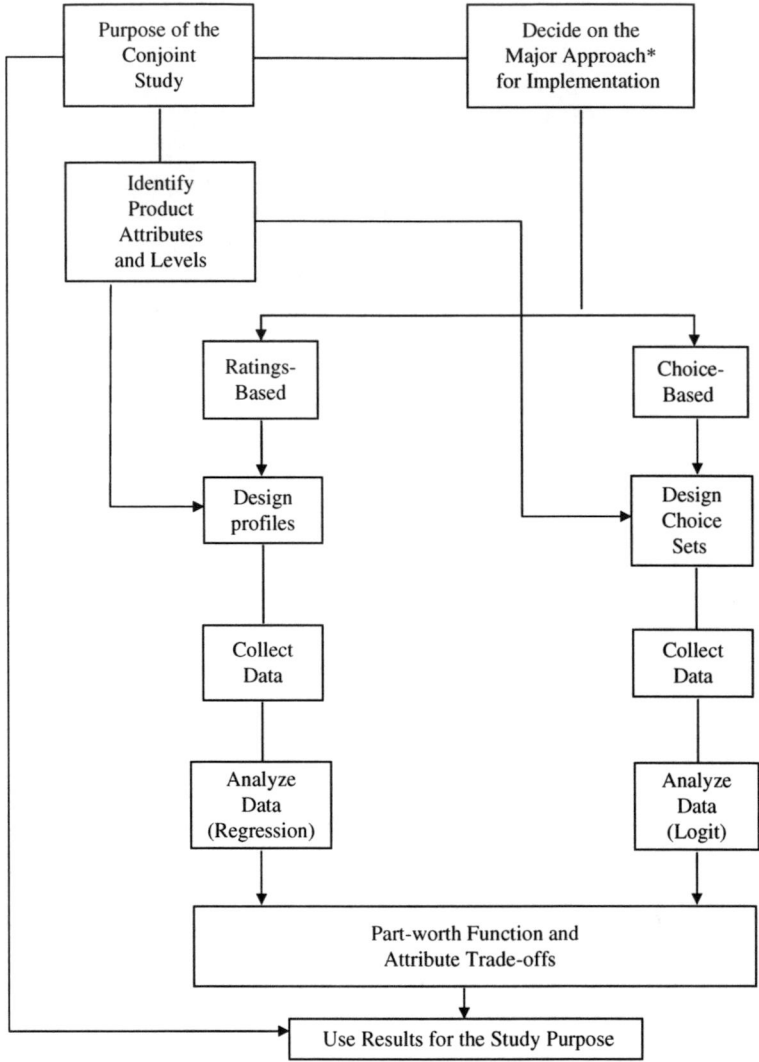

Fig. 2.1 Major steps in a conjoint study
*Several alternatives exist here; two are highlighted.

obtain estimates for each individual in the sample, newer approaches utilize hierarchical Bayesian methods for obtaining individual-level estimates even with sparse data from respondents; I will discuss these later in the chapter. I refer the reader to Green and Srinivasan (1978, 1990), Carroll and Green (1995), and Hauser and Rao (2003) for various details of these approaches.

Typically, a linear, additive model is used to describe the evaluations (preferences) in a ratings-based conjoint study while a multinomial logit model is used to model the probability of choice of a profile for the choice-based conjoint

Table 2.1 Alternatives for Selected Features of Conjoint Analysis

Representation of Stimuli	Formats of data collection	Nature of data collection	Estimation methods
Verbal descriptions	Full profile Evaluations	One-shot	Regression-based Methods
		Adaptive	
Pictorial descriptions	Partial profile Evaluations	Multiple times*	Random Utility Models
Videotapes and supporting materials	Stated preferences		Direct Computation based on Self-Explicated Importances
Virtual proto-types	Self-explicated Methods		Hierarchical Bayes Estimation*
Combinations of physical models, photographs and verbal descriptions	Configurators*		Methods Based on New Optimization Methods* Analytic center estimation, Support-vector machines, Genetic algorithms

* These are newer methods; I will briefly describe them later in this chapter.
Source: Adapted from Hauser and Rao (2003)

studies. Undoubtedly, there are several variations of these basic models used in practice. Against this brief background of the methodology of conjoint analysis, I will now review some recent developments.

2.3 Developments in Research Design

As can be seen from Figure 2.1, any conjoint analysis study will almost invariably depend upon the design of stimuli (either profiles or choice sets). This aspect of study design draws much from the theory of experimental design, where procedures for constructing subsets of combinations of all attribute levels are developed. This aspect of research design has received much focus since the beginning of conjoint analysis; for simplicity, we call this "Research Design"; data collection methods depend on the specific approach employed in research design of the study.

When one concatenates levels of all attributes, the set of profiles will in general be very large; the corresponding design is called full-factorial design. Use of a full factorial design (all profiles) will place an undue burden on respondent for providing evaluations. Therefore, researchers utilize fractional factorial designs or a subset of all profiles. Usually orthogonal arrays are employed for designing profiles for the ratings based approach and for designing choice sets for the choice-based conjoint methods. The orthogonal arrays are derived out of the complete factorial of all attribute combinations. If there are n attributes in a conjoint study with there are l_k levels for the k-th attribute, the total number of profiles will be $\prod l_k$. This number can become very large as the number of attributes or their levels increases and researchers generally construct fractional designs (For example, for a study with five attributes each at 4 levels, the total number of profiles will be $4^5 = 1024$.) While such designs continue to be the mainstay in applied conjoint analysis, various developments have occurred in the recent years in this area of experimental designs useful for conjoint analysis. However, the effective number of partworth parameters to be estimated from conjoint data $m = \Sigma (l_k - 1)$.

2.3.1 Designs for Ratings-Based Methods

Orthogonal arrays are categorized by their *resolution*. The resolution[9] identifies which effects, possibly including interactions, are confounded and which ones are estimable. For example, resolution III designs enable the estimation of all main effects free of each other, but some of them are confounded with two-factor interactions. For resolution V designs, all main effects and two-factor interactions are estimable free of each other. Higher resolution designs require larger number of profiles and therefore a larger number of full profiles to be administered to respondents. Resolution III designs (or orthogonal arrays) are most frequently used in marketing conjoint studies and there are very few studies with designs of a higher order resolution.

Orthogonal arrays can be either balanced or unbalanced in terms of levels of attributes. The property of level balance implies that each level of an attribute occurs an equal number of times within each attribute in the design. An unbalanced design gives larger standard errors the parameter (partworth) estimates for those attributes that are less frequently administered. An additional property of an orthogonal design is the proportionality criterion; this implies that the joint occurrence of any two levels of different attributes is proportional to the product of their marginal frequencies. Designs can satisfy the proportionality criterion yet fail the level balance criterion.

Various measures for discussing the efficiency of an experimental design can be described as follows for the linear model (Kuhfeld et al. 1994), $Y = X\beta + \varepsilon$; where β is a p×1 vector of parameters, X is an n×p design matrix, and ε is random error. With the usual assumption on errors, the least squares estimate of β is given by $(X'X)^{-1}X'Y$. The variance-covariance matrix of the parameter estimates (or partworths) of the attributes is proportional to $(X'X)^{-1}$. The efficiency of a design is based on the information matrix $X'X$. An efficient design will have a smaller variance matrix and the eigenvalues of $(X'X)^{-1}$ provide measures of the size of the matrix. Three efficiency measures (all based on the eigenvalues) are:

---

[9] "Resolution" describe the degree to which estimated main effects are confounded with estimated higher-order level interactions (2, 3, 4, or more) among the attributes; it is usually one more than the smallest order interaction that some main effect is confounded with. In a Resolution-III design, some main effects are confounded with some 2-level interactions.

$$\text{A-efficiency: } 1/(n \text{ trace } ((X'X)^{-1}/p)); \tag{2.3}$$

$$\text{D-efficiency: } 1/(n|(X'X)^{-1}|^{1/p}); \text{ and} \tag{2.4}$$

$$\text{G-efficiency: } \sqrt{p/n}/\sigma_M, \tag{2.5}$$

where σ_M is the minimum standard error possible.

The minimum standard error is attained when a full factorial design is used and any fractional design will have efficiency less than 1. These three measures are useful for making comparisons of efficiency of designs used for a given situation. Orthogonal designs for linear models are generally considered to be efficient because their efficiency measure is close to 1. Kuhfeld et al. (1994) show that the OPTEX procedure (Kuhfeld 2005) can produce more efficient designs while achieving neither perfect level balance nor the proportionality criteria. More recently, the criterion of managerial efficiency (M-efficiency) is introduced by Toubia and Hauser (2007).

2.3.2 Design for Choice-Based[10] Conjoint Methods

The probability of choosing an alternative in a choice-based conjoint study is generally modeled as a logit function in terms of the attribute differences of the item with respect to a base alternative in the choice set. Thus, the underlying model for a choice-based conjoint experiment is nonlinear and the considerations of choosing a design for a choice-based study are different than those for a ratings-based study. Two additional properties come into play; these are minimal level overlap and utility balance (Huber and Zwerina 1996).

2.3.3 Minimal Overlap

Minimal level overlap means that the probability that an attribute level repeats itself in each choice set should be as small as possible; this is important because the contrasts between the levels of an attribute are used in the calibration of the logit model. If the same level is repeated several times within the choice set, the choices made in that choice set do not contribute any information on the value of that attribute.

2.3.4 Utility Balance

The property of utility balance implies that the utilities of the alternatives in a choice set are approximately equal. When a design is utility balanced, the variance of the probabilities of choice of alternatives within a choice set will be reduced. Huber and Zwerina show that achieving such utility balance

---

[10] For a discussion of formal choice models, see Corstjens and Gautchi (1983).

increases the efficiency of a design to the tune of 10–50%. The process of swapping and relabeling attribute levels of alternatives in an initial choice set accomplishes this objective.

The initial choice sets are developed any number of ways; these include: orthogonal arrays, availability designs, and D-efficient (possibly non-orthogonal) designs developed by the OPTEX procedure of Kuhfeld (2005), available in the SAS system. It is worth noting that a non-orthogonal design will enable estimation of cross-effects among attributes as well as direct effects; see Kuhfeld et al. (1994) for an illustration.

2.3.5 Other Approaches for Choice Designs

If there is prior information on the part-worth estimates, Bayesian methods can be used to create more efficient designs for choice-based conjoint experiments. Building on the ideas of Huber and Zwerina (HZ) for MNL models, Sandor and Wedel (2001) develop methods for creating designs when prior information is available. Their procedure involves finding a design (or X-matrix) that minimizes the expected value of the errors of parameters. Their algorithm for the design development uses the tools of relabelling, swapping, and cycling; GAUSS codes for this are available from the authors. Their method is shown to yield lower standard errors than the HZ method with higher predictive validity. These authors also developed procedures for designing choice experiments for mixed logit models; see Sandor and Wedel (2002).

Kanninen (2002) derives choice sets for binary and multinomial choice experiments that maximize the D-optimal criterion (or D-efficiency defined above) through algebraic manipulation and numerical optimization. She points out that the designs developed by Huber and Zwerina (1996) and Sandor and Wedel (2001) may not be fully efficient due to the search procedures employed.

One issue that is worth considering is the specific criterion for the design of choice-based conjoint experiments. While the advances seem to be in terms of lower standard errors of the parameters, one may consider other criteria such as better prediction of market shares of profiles; some work in this direction is being done by Bodapati (2006).

An additional development is the method due to Burgess and Street (2003, 2005) for constructing "good" designs for choice experiments. Their method essentially constructs choice set designs for forced choice experiments (i.e., that exclude the no choice option) for binary attributes based on the multinomial logit (MNL) model for choice. Their designs can be useful for a choice experiment for testing main effects and for testing main effects and two-attribute interactions. Their methods will lead to optimal and near-optimal designs with small numbers of choice sets for 2^k choice experiments. Street and Burgess (2004) and Street et al. (2005) compare a number of common strategies for design of choice sets for stated choice experiments and conclude that their method is superior to designs based on extant methods. Readers may refer to a recent book by Street and Burgess (2007) for a detailed exposition of these designs.

2.3.6 Selected Data Collection issues

2.3.6.1 Partial Profiles

When respondents are presented with partial profiles (i.e. information on some attributes is missing) in a ratings-based conjoint experiment, they tend to impute values for the missing attributes. The process of such imputation can have an effect on the part-worth values estimated from data. Bradlow et al. (2004) developed a mathematical model based on Bayesian learning and investigated the effects of such imputations. Their model of imputation yields probabilities that the missing attribute takes one of two levels and is a generalization of extant methods. Specifically, they found that learning in fact occurs and that the relative importance of attribute partworths can shift when subjects evaluate partial profiles and the relative partworths are sensitive to the order in which partial profiles are presented. They also found that the imputation process is sensitive to the available prior information on the product category. This research has significance for conjoint studies with a large number of attributes.

In a comment on this article, Alba and Cooke (2004) suggested the opportunity for behavioral researchers, modelers, and conjoint practitioners to come together to formulate psychologically grounded conjoint models and procedures for practice. I believe that there is a significant benefit from such collaboration. As I see it, conjoint modelers have largely been concerned with predictive accuracy. There has been limited effort to develop conjoint models to incorporate the learning from behavioral research on information processing and choice. A shift toward models that depict the choice process well can only help prediction. An illustration of this possibility is Gilbride and Allenby (2004), who model attribute thresholds and screening rules of consumer choices in conjoint context.

2.3.6.2 Incentive-Aligned Methods

An issue in the data collection in conjoint studies is whether respondents experience strong incentives to expend their cognitive resources (or devote adequate time and effort) in providing responses (ratings or choices) to hypothetical stimuli presented as profiles or in choice sets. The literature on experimental economics suggests that data collected without such incentive-compatibility may be inconsistent, erratic, and possibly, untrustworthy. Incentive compatibility can be implemented using the BDM procedures (Becker et al. 1964). In a recent paper, Ding et al. (2005) provide experimental evidence to strongly indicate that conjoint data collected which are incentive-aligned[11] outperform those without

---

[11] In this paper, the authors conducted a comprehensive field experiment in a Chinese restaurant during dinnertime using Chinese dinner specials as the context. The study

such alignment in terms of out-of-sample predictive power. In fact, Wertenbroch and Skiera (2002) also show that willingness to buy estimates for products using contingent evaluation procedures are lower when the incentive-compatibility constraint is not imposed. This stream of research has obvious implications for collecting conjoint data in practice. See Ding (2007) for a more complete discussion of a truth-telling mechanism for conjoint applications.

2.3.6.3 Adaptive Self-Explicated Methods

Srinivasan and Park (1997) show surprising robustness of self-explicated methods. More recently, Netzer and Srinivasan (2007) propose a web-based adaptive self-explicated procedure for eliciting attribute importances conjoint studies with large number of attributes and demonstrate higher predictive validity for the adaptive procedure. Given the advances of the self-explicated methods, one needs to evaluate the practical benefits of the additional effort in conducting conjoint studies (ratings-based or choice-based). In my view, this is an open research issue.

2.3.6.4 Configurators

Configurators represent a newer form of collecting conjoint data; in this approach, the respondent will choose a level for each attribute in order to design the best product from his perspective (under the budget and other situational factors). This method also is useful for product customization. An example of this is the order/purchase of a laptop using the Dell.com website. Implicitly, all other combinations are dominated by the chosen alternative. Examples include Liechty et al. (2001) and Urban and Hauser (2002).

2.4 Developments in Estimation Methods

2.4.1 Hierarchical Bayesian (HB) Methods

One of the challenges in conjoint analysis is to get sufficient data to estimate partworths at the individual level with relatively few questions. This issue is handled in the experimental design used to construct the profiles for evaluation;

---

compared hypothetical choice-conjoint method with incentive-aligned choice conjoint method and incentive-aligned contingent evaluation method. In the hypothetical choice conjoint method, the restaurant served the meal chosen by the subject in the holdout choice task and the cost was deducted from the compensation given to the subjects. In the incentive-aligned method, the Chinese dinner special for any subject was randomly chosen from the choices made in the main task of evaluating 12 choice sets at the posted price. This random lottery procedure is widely used in experimental economics and it minimizes the effect of reference point and wealth.

nevertheless there is some tradeoff in the choice of designs between the need for a large number of questions (or profiles) and respondent fatigue, which makes the responses less reliable. Further, with standard methods of estimation used for ratings at the individual level, it is not uncommon to obtain partworth estimates with the wrong sign.[12] This problem can also occur when choice data are analyzed at the level of a segment or the full sample.

One way to deal with these issues is to utilize information about the partworths of all the respondents in the sample and employ Hierarchical Bayesian (HB) methods for estimation of partworths.[13] For this purpose, each respondent's partworths are characterized by a known distribution to describe the uncertainty in the partworths. Next, the parameters of that distribution are assumed to be different across the population (or the sample). Prior distributions (beliefs) are specified for the parameters, which are updated by data using the Bayes theorem. Given that two stages are specified, the procedure becomes a Hierarchical Bayesian approach. The resulting equations for estimating the parameters are not amenable to analytical solution. Therefore, individual parameters are estimated by the use of sophisticated Monte Carlo simulation techniques such as the Gibbs sampling and Metropolis-Hastings algorithms. In these methods, restrictions on partworths can also be incorporated with ease.

There exist at least three types of HB methods: a random coefficients Bayesian model, a linear hierarchical Bayesian model, and linear hierarchical Bayesian model with mixture of distributions. In the first model, respondent heterogeneity is assumed to be randomly distributed while in the second, the heterogeneity is governed by some covariates measured at the individual level. The third model is an extension of the second and it assumes that the individual-level data arise from a mixture of distributions (usually referred to as latent segments).

---

[12] For example, the partworth function for price can sometimes be upward sloping contrary to expectations. This may be due to the information role of price versus its allocative role. One approach to correct this is discussed in Rao and Sattler (2003); this method calls for collecting two sets of preferences for profiles without and with a budget constraint.

[13] An alternative way to estimate individual-level partworths is to specify heterogeneity using finite mixture (FM) models and to estimate mixture (or segment) level parameters and recover individual-level parameters using posterior analysis (DeSarbo et al. 1992). In comparison using simulated data in the context of ratings-based conjoint analysis, Andrews et al. (2002a and b) found that both the methods (HB and FM) are equally effective in recovering individual-level parameters and predicting ratings of holdout profiles. Further, HB methods perform well even when the individual partworths come from a mixture of distributions and FM methods yield good individual partworth estimates. Both methods are quite robust to underlying assumptions. Given the recent popularity of HB methods, I focus on them in this review chapter. See Rossi et al. (2005) for an exposition of Bayesian methods in marketing.

2.4.1.1 Ratings-Based Approach

The conjoint model for ratings data can be written generally as: $y = X\beta + \varepsilon$; where ε is the random error of the model assume to be normally distributed with zero mean and variance of σ^2 and y is the rating on given profile and X is the corresponding set of variables (dummy or other). The β is a px1 vector of partworths. The ratings from the sample of n individuals are stacked in the column of y. If one estimates this model using OLS, the estimates of the β-parameters will be used to compute the average partworths of the model.

The hierarchical Bayesian estimation method for the random coefficients model involves specifying prior distributions for the parameters, $\theta = (\beta$ and $\sigma^2)$ of the above model. These priors are chosen so that the posterior distributions can be easily derived (or in other words, they are conjugate distributions). Given that the model errors are assumed to be normal, a natural conjugate prior[14] is also normal for the β-vector with mean βbar and covariance matrix A^{-1} and inverted chi-squared for σ^2 with g degrees of freedom and prior precision G. Further, the prior distributions for β and σ^2 are assumed to be independent. With these assumptions, the HB approach involves deriving conditional distributions for each set of parameters and employing Gibbs sampling (a series of random draws) to obtain estimates of the parameters and their posterior distributions. Confidence intervals (e.g., 95%) can be computed from these posterior distributions.

When covariates are employed to govern heterogeneity, the conjoint model for the i- th individual level is written as: $Yi = Xi \beta i + \varepsilon i$; for $i = 1,\ldots, n.$, where Yi = is a vector of mi responses (ratings); note that the number of responses can vary over individuals (due to such reasons as incompleteness of data). Further, the subjects' partworths are described in terms of a set of covariates (usually background variables) as $\beta i = \Theta zi + \delta i$ for $i = 1,\ldots, n.$

Here, z_i is a qx1 vector of covariates and Θ is a (pxq) matrix of regression coefficients which represent the relationships between the partworths and subject covariates.

The error terms $\{\varepsilon_i\}$ and $\{\delta_i\}$ are assumed to be mutually independent and distributed as multivariate normal with zero means and covariance matrices $\{\sigma_i^2 I\}$ and Λ respectively, where Λ is a pxp matrix. The error variances $\{\sigma_i^2\}$ are assumed to have prior distributions of inverse gamma distribution. Using these assumptions, one can work out the posterior distributions for the β_i –parameters. The various parameters are estimated using the MCMC method and the Metropolis algorithm. The third model with latent segments is a simple extension of the second model.

---

[14] 1 If the analyst wishes to incorporate no prior information, one sets the initial βbar and A-matrix equal to zero. In that case, the HB estimates will be asymptotically the same as the OLS results. In a similar manner, constraints on signs or order of partworths (therefore the β-parameters) are incorporated directly in the posterior distribution of the β-vector.

2.4.1.2 Choice-Based Approach

When the data are collected via choice-based conjoint study, the procedure of estimating parameters using HB methods is quite similar. First, a model for the probability of choice is specified; it is usually a logistic one such as:

$$\text{Prob (choosing } j \, \varepsilon \, C) = \text{Pr}_j = \exp(yj) / \sum_{j \varepsilon C} \exp(yj) \qquad (2.6)$$

where C is the choice set and the summation in the denominator is taken over all the elements of the choice set C.

Let N denote the multinomial outcome with the j-th element equal to one if the j-th alternative is chosen and 0 otherwise. The observed choices are now related to the attributes, X via the model for the probabilities of choice. The likelihood will then be:

$$[N|y] \, [y|X, \beta, \sigma^2] \, [\beta] \, [\sigma^2]. \qquad (2.7)$$

The model, [N|y] relates the latent ys to the discrete outcomes. This is an additional step in the Gibbs sampling procedure; this step involves drawing a sample of ys from the conditional distribution of y given X, β, and σ^2 ; the value of y_j is chosen with the probability equal to the choice probability using the method of rejection sampling. Details are available in See Allenby and Lenk (1994).

The recent literature on conjoint analysis is quite replete with examples of applications of HB methods and implications for designing conjoint studies. I will highlight two implications:

(i) The HB methods seem to have the advantage of being able to work with fewer profiles (or questions in a conjoint study); this was demonstrated by Lenk et al. (1996) based on simulation and an applied study of personal computers; and

(ii) Constraints on part-worth functions for attributes such as price can be incorporated while using HB methods. In an application for alkaline batteries, Allenby et al. (1995) shows that the hierarchical Bayes estimation method with constraints yields part-worth estimates for each individual with higher predictive validity.

2.4.1.3 A Comparison of Bayesian and Classical Estimation Methods

In a recent study, Huber and Train (2001) compared the estimates obtained from Hierarchical Bayesian methods with those from classical maximum simulated likelihood methods in a conjoint study of electricity suppliers, each supplier described on five attributes. In both the methods, the partworths at the individual level are assumed to follow a normal distribution and the probability of choice of an alternative is derived from the multinomial logit function.

The authors found the average of the expected partworths for the attributes to be almost identical for both methods of estimation. They also found the prediction of a holdout choice to be almost identical for the two methods (with hit rates of 71 and 72% for the Bayesian and classical methods). This empirical research is useful in determining which approach is best suited to a given problem. When there is a large number of partworths to be estimated, the likelihood function for the classical approach may have multiple maxima and can use up large number of degrees of freedom; in such a case the Bayesian approach can be very useful; Bayesian methods yield not only point estimates of part-worth parameters but also the entire distribution that is available from the sampling procedures.

2.4.2 Polyhedral Estimation

Recently, Toubia et al. (2003) have developed an adaptive conjoint analysis method[15] that reduces respondent burden while simultaneously improving accuracy. The answer to a question in the adaptive conjoint analysis (i.e., a question on choice between two pairs) places a constraint on the possible values that the partworths can take. They use "interior point" developments in mathematical programming which enable one to select questions that narrow the range of feasible partworths as fast as possible. This method is called Fast Polyhedral Adaptive Conjoint Estimation, with the acronym FastPACE. Once the responses to selected questions are obtained, they use the method of analytic center estimation to estimate partworths; the analytic center is the point that minimizes the geometric mean of the distances to the faces of the polyhedron (this method yields a close approximation to the center of a polyhedron and is computationally more tractable than computing the true center). The authors compared the polyhedral estimation methods against efficient (fixed) designs and Adaptive Conjoint Analysis using a Monte Carlo simulation study. The context for this simulation is that of a Product Development team interested in learning about the incremental utility of ten product features (each at two levels indicating presence or absence of the feature). The simulation indicated that no method dominates in all situations. But, the polyhedral algorithms are shown to hold significant potential when (a) profile comparisons are more accurate than the self-explicated importance measures used in ACA, (b) when respondent wearout is a concern, and (c) when the product development and marketing teams wish to screen many features quickly.

To validate the polyhedral approach, Toubia et al. (2003) conducted a conjoint study on an innovative new laptop computer bag that includes a removable padded sleeve to hold and project a laptop computer. The bag includes a range of separable product features and the study focused on nine

---

[15] See Toubia et al. (2004) for a discussion of this adaptive approach for choice-based conjoint analysis.

product features, each at two levels (presence or absence); the features are: size, color, logo, handle, holders for a PDA and a mobile-phone, mesh pocket holder, sleeve closure, and boot. The tenth attribute was price between $70 and $100. They used an across-subjects research design among 330 first-year MBA students to provide both internal and external validity for the polyhedral approach (two versions of FastPACE method, FP1 with ratings questions and no self-explicated questions and FP2 with self-explicated questions and paired comparisons) against a fixed efficient design (as in the full-profile method) and ACA (adaptive conjoint analysis). Different methods of estimation were employed in the analysis. In addition to self explicated questions (where necessary), respondents answered 16 questions. The authors also examined the sensitivity of results for using data with 8 and 16 questions.

The authors tested the internal validity of various methods using four hold-out questions (metric or paired-comparison) beyond the 16 questions of the main conjoint tasks using the measure of correlation between observed and predicted responses. To test the external validity of the methods, respondents were told that they had $100 to spend and were asked to choose between five bags drawn randomly from an orthogonal fractional factorial design of sixteen bags. The respondents were instructed that they would receive the bag that they chose. Using the notion of unavailability of a chosen bag, a complete ranking of all the five bags was also obtained. At the end of the study, the respondents were given the bag chosen along with any cash difference (if any) between the price of the chosen bag and $100. Two measures of external validity were used: (i) correlation between observed and predicted rankings was used as one measure of external validity and (ii) percent correct predictions of the chosen bag. The main results of this study were: (i) The polyhedral approach FP method was superior to the fixed efficient design in both internal and external validity; and (ii) The FP method is slightly better over the ACA method in internal and validity and one measure of external validity.

In a recent study Vadali et al. (2006) developed an approach that frames the FastPACE method in terms of a Hierarchical Bayes specification and demonstrate the that their approach (called GENPACE) performs at least as well as both the FastPACE method and the constrained version of a HB regression model. GENPACE is shown to outperform FastPACE under certain conditions. This is an example of continuous developments in conjoint analysis research.

2.4.3 Support Vector Machines

A recently developed method for specifying the preference function for attributes offers promise (Evgeniou et al. 2005). This method is based on ideas from statistical learning theory and support vector machines.[16] The method can be

---

[16] A tutorial on support vector machines is found in Burgess (1998).

described as follows. Assume that one has choice data for a set of product profiles and that the underlying utility function is linear. The choice data can be recast as a set of inequalities that compare the utility of the chosen item to each of the utilities of the remaining items. The method then involves minimizing a function defined as the sum of the errors for the inequalities and the sum of squares of the weights in the utility function, multiplied by a parameter, λ. The parameter λ controls the tradeoff between the fitting the data (or the sum of errors) and the complexity of the model and it can be tuned using cross valida-tion of the utility model. They utilize the theory of dual optimization and solve for a number of parameters equal to the number of utility inequalities indepen-dent of the number of parameters (or dimensionality) of the utility function. It involves creation of new variables for attribute interactions and nonlinearities but retaining the preference function linear in parameters. Based on simulation experiments, the authors compare their method with standard logistic regres-sion, hierarchical Bayes, and polyhedral methods. They show that their method handles noise significantly better than both logistic regression and the polyhe-dral methods and is never worse than the best method among the three methods compared to.

2.5 Selected Methods for Handling Large Number of Attributes

As conjoint analysis became popular in industry, one nagging issue that arose is how to handle large number of attributes in a product category. It is easy to see that the total number of profiles explodes as the number of attributes and levels in an attribute; for example, if one has 12 attributes, each at 2 levels, the number is 2^{12} or 4,096. Even with fractional factorial designs, one has to present a large number of profiles to a respondent (either singly or in choice sets) to obtain data that will yield reasonable partworth estimates. Some methods that have been in vogue are the hybrid conjoint analysis (Green 1984), adaptive conjoint analysis (Johnson 1991), and self-explicated methods (Srinivasan 2006). Some newer methods include upgrading and the use of meta-attributes. I have described the self-explicated method earlier in the chapter. I will describe the other methods briefly.

2.5.1 Hybrid Methods

Hybrid methods have been developed to deal with the problem of handling large number of attributes (and levels) in a conjoint study. It is obvious that no one respondent has the desire or time to evaluate a large number of profiles. This problem was tackled by combining the two approaches of the self-expli-cated method and the full profile approach. Essentially, the hybrid approach involves two phases. In Phase I, the respondent is asked to provide data on attribute desirabilities and attribute importances in a manner quite similar to the self-explicated approach. In Phase II, the respondent is given a limited number of profiles for evaluation rather than administering all profiles as done in a full profile approach. The limited number of profiles administered is drawn from a master design, constructed according to an orthogonal main effects plan or some other experimental design. The final estimation of part-worth functions in this approach is at the level of a subgroup. The software need to be tailor-made specific to the situation on hand.

2.5.2 Adaptive Methods

It is easy to argue that if one designs additional questions on the basis of some preliminary idea of the part-worth functions, the final estimates of the part-worth functions will be more indicative of the true underlying utility of the individual. The adaptive methods are essentially based on this premise. In one sense, the approach is quite consistent with Bayesian statistical analysis. The most popular implementation of the adaptive conjoint methods is through the interactive computer software called Adaptive Conjoint Analysis (ACA) and we focus our discussion on this particular method. This discussion is based on Sawtooth Software's published materials;[17] (see www.sawtoohsoftware.com)

The ACA procedure consists of four phases (Version II of the software). In the first phase, each respondent ranks one's preferences for each level of each attribute of the study in turn. The second phase consists of having the respondent rate the attributes in terms of their importance on a 1–4 equal-interval rating scale where 4 denotes the highest importance. In the third phase, the respondent receives a set of paired partial profiles (designed by the software using the information collected in the first two phases) and makes a preference judgment on a nine point equal interval scale. The objective is to get an assessment of which profile is preferred over the other and by how much; these are called graded paired comparisons. In the last phase, the respondent receives 2–9 profiles composed of at most 8 attributes. These calibration concepts are chosen by the software so as to progress from highly undesirable to highly desirable. The respondent rates these on a 0–100 likelihood of purchase scale.

The procedure in the third phase is at the heart of the ACA methodology. The procedure is adaptive in the sense that each paired comparison is constructed so as to take advantage of the information collected about the respondent's part-worths in the previous steps.

The ACA approach clearly has several advantages. It is a highly visible way to elicit an individual's preference functions. It is quite versatile and can be adapted to almost any situation. From the respondent's perspective it is easy to learn and use and can even be fun. In an evaluative study of this technique,

---

[17] Johnson, R.M. (1987) and Green et al. (1991).

Green et al. (1991) found some weaknesses of the approach. First, they found a weakness in forcing equal subjective scales and ranges for all attributes in Phase I. They deemed the scale used in Phase II to be too coarse. Although the data collected in Phase III are the major component of the method, they found a lack of consistency between the way profiles are designed to be indifferent and the use of a 9 point scale for assessment. Finally, the software needs to utilize commensurate scales in all the four phases. The authors indicated ways to improve the ACA system such as providing of an option for including a part-worth updating feature that does not require commensurate units between phases and a formal procedure for finding commensurate units between Phase I/II and Phase III. The Sawtooth software has been modified since to handle these problems.

2.5.3 Other Approaches

Recently, my colleagues and I developed alternate methods to deal with the large number of attributes problem. One of these is the Upgraded Conjoint Method (Park et al. forthcoming), which is a new incentive-aligned approach for eliciting attribute preferences about complex products that combines the merits of self-explicated approach and conjoint analysis. The approach involves asking a subject to bid to upgrade from one product profile to a more desirable one. The data on monetary bids for upgrading are used to calibrate a HB logit model to determine the partworths of various attributes. This procedure is shown to significantly improve predictive validity in an empirical implementation with digital cameras.

The second method uses the concept of Meta-Attributes (Ghose and Rao 2007). This relies on the concept that individuals may rely on meta-attributes in the evaluation of alternatives with a large number of attributes. Meta-attributes are typically fewer in number than the number of product characteristics. Their initial empirical work on meta-attributes focusing on product design in an existing category suggests that there are significant benefits with the meta-attributes approach.

2.6 Some Other Developments

I will now describe four recent developments to illustrate the current progress in conjoint methods. The first is a way to estimate the market value of an improvement in an attribute of a product. The second is a procedure to estimate heterogeneous reservation prices for products and bundles; this procedure is an application of the hierarchical Bayesian methods described above. The third is an attempt at understanding the stability of preference structures in conjoint analysis, which I will call "Dynamic Conjoint Analysis". The fourth is a model that describes the choice of a bundle of items from heterogeneous product categories; this model is estimated using a mixture multinomial logit with hierarchical Bayesian methods. I should add that the bundling models generalize the single item choice problems normally handled with conjoint methods.

2.6.1 Market Value of an Attribute Improvement (MVAI)

As firms improve the attributes of their products, a question that arises is whether the attribute improvement measured in terms of profitability is worth the cost. This question can be answered with the help of conjoint results as shown by Ofek and Srinivasan (2002). I now describe their approach in some detail.

It is possible to derive a mathematical expression for the market value of an attribute improvement. For this purpose, consider a market consisting of J firms, each offering one product in a category. Each product has K attributes in addition to its price. Let x_{jk} be the value of the k-th attribute for the j-th product and let p_j be the price of the j-th product. Consumers have the choice of buying any one of the J products or not buying at all. Let m_j denote the market share for the j-th product ($j = 1, \ldots, J$) and m_0 be the market share of the no purchase option. Further[18] let c_{jk} be the change in the cost of the j-th product for a unit change in the k-th attribute. The authors consider the ratio of the change in market share due to the improvement (positive change) in an attribute to the ratio of decrease (negative change) in market share due to change in price as the market value of an attribute improvement. Mathematically,

$$\mathrm{MVAI} = -(\partial m_j / \partial x_{jk}) / (\partial m_j / \partial p_j) \qquad (2.8)$$

It would be worthwhile for the firm to undertake the attribute improvement if this quantity exceeds the cost of attribute improvement (c_{jk}). Naturally, the market share of a brand depends upon the choice set, competitive reactions, heterogeneity of the sample of individuals whose responses are used to calibrate the conjoint model, and the particular specification used for the conjoint model, and the rule used to translate utilities into probabilities of choice. If there is no heterogeneity and if a vector model is used to specify the partworths, the model is additive and a logit choice rule is used, then the MVAI will simply be the ratio of the weights for the k-th attribute and price in the conjoint model. But,

---

[18] While the authors developed their theory using continuous changes in the attributes, discrete changes are used here for the purposes of exposition. See their paper for complete theoretical analysis.

averaging such ratios across a heterogeneous sample of people will yield a biased estimate of MVAI.

The changes in market share can be estimated using a conjoint study. This is what Ofek and Srinivasan used to empirically evaluate attribute improvements in a product under two scenarios of no reaction by competition and when competitors react to the change by making appropriate changes in their own products. They used a logit model to specify the probabilities of choice at the individual level and aggregate them to obtain market shares at the aggregate level.

We use the authors' example to illustrate the approach. The product category for this example is portable camera mount products. The set of competing products consists of UltraPod, Q-Pod, GorillaPod, Camera Critter, and Half Dome; the third product is a hypothetical one under development. These products are described on five attributes: weight, size, set up time in minutes, stability, and positioning flexibility for adaptation to different terrains and angles. In the conjoint study, each attribute was varied at three levels and 302 subjects ranked 18 full profiles. The authors estimated the MVAI for each of the five attributes when changes are made in each of the three products. Their results show that the benefits from improving all attributes except set up time exceed the cost of making the improvement. Further, the authors found that the attribute values calculated using a commonly used approach of averaging the ratio of weights of attribute and price across the individuals in the sample to be considerably upward biased as compared to the MVAI values. Further, the profitability of different attribute improvements are much lower when competitive reactions are considered in the computations. (I should also note that such calculations are possible with simulations in conjoint studies.)

2.6.2 Estimation of Heterogeneous Reservation Prices

Jedidi and Zhang (2002) developed a method to estimate reservation prices for products which are multi-attributed using the methods of preference estimation a la conjoint analysis and economic theory of consumer choice. I will describe it at the level of one individual. First, an individual's utility is specified as $U(X, y)$ where X is the multi-attribute profile of the good under consideration to be purchased and y denotes the composite good consisting of all other purchase, measured in the individual-specific purchase basket. Assuming an income of B for the individual, the budget constraint becomes $p^y y + p = B$, where p^y is the price for the composite good and p is the price of the product under consideration. Then the indirect utility for the individual is $U(X, (B-p)/p^y)$ if the individual purchases the product and $U(0, B/p^y)$ if the individual does not purchase the product. Then, the individual's reservation price for the product profile X, denoted by $R(X)$, is given by: $U(X, (B-p)/p^y) - U(0, B/p^y) = 0$. Now, the authors specify the utility for the product in terms of its attributes and price as $u(X) = \beta_0 + \Sigma\beta_k x_k - \beta_p p$ where the βs are parameters and xs are the specific values of the attributes and summation taking place over all the r attributes of the product. Here β_p is the weight given to price of the product. Further, they specify the U (X, y) function as quasi-linear as: $u(X) + \alpha (B-p)/ p^y$, where α is a parameter that compares the utility of composite good to that of the product under question. With these specifications, one can easily derive the reservation price for the product, X as $R(X) = \Sigma\beta_k x_k / \beta_p$. Thus the reservation price pf a product can be estimated once the conjoint utility function is estimated from data collected by any of the conjoint methods described earlier in the chapter. While this approach is impressive, it is important that there is no correlation between the product attributes and price and that price does not play any informative role[19] in the conjoint function. Jedidi and Zhang used this approach to model a consumer's decision of not only which of the alternatives in a product category to buy, and whether to buy in the category at all. They demonstrate the predictive validity of this approach using data from a commercial study of automobile brands.

Utilizing the essence of the procedure just described, Jedidi et al. (2003) developed a model to capture continuous heterogeneity among respondents in the reservation prices for products and bundles of products. The context is mixed bundling where a firm offers both individual products as well as the bundle for sale. They model the heterogeneity both within the individual and across individuals using multivariate normal distributions. Using these distributions, they derive expressions for a typical consumer to decide not to buy in the category, to buy any one of the products, or to buy the bundle of all products. They estimate the model using HB methods with choice data collected for mixed bundles and show that their method yields less-biased results compared to direct elicitation of reservation prices.

2.6.3 Dynamic Conjoint Analysis

One issue that is of interest to conjoint analysis estimation is the stability of preference structure. The issue is whether the individual's underlying preferences change during the course of a conjoint study involving responses on multiple profiles or choice sets used in the data collection. Preferences may change due to a variety of factors such as learning, fatigue, boredom etc. Liechty et al. (2005) investigated this issue using simulated data and suggest that one should utilize statistical models that capture dynamics and accommodate heterogeneity.

I think that the issue of dynamics is much broader than the changes within the same data collection episode. While utilizing a conjoint simulator, the

---

[19] The problem of separating the informative and allocative roles of price is not trivial. See Rao and Sattler (2003) for an approach and empirical results.

analyst makes the assumption that individuals have complete information on the levels of attributes of the new product; the resulting estimates of sales or market share may be deemed "stable" values for the new product. But, it is important to be able to predict the diffusion pattern of the new product long before it is launched.[20] One should consider continuous (multi-period) conjoint analysis studies to capture the effects of dynamics of diffusion of attribute information among the individuals. This issue is identified as future research topic in Hauser and Rao (2003). A recent application of this idea is found in Su and Rao (2006); they conduct several choice conjoint studies among a sample of individuals and provide varying sets of product attribute information between each successive study (on the lines of information acceleration methodology). They utilize these "dynamic" conjoint studies to estimate the adoption behavior over time with good results. See also Wittink and Keil (2003) for an interesting application that explores dynamics of consumer preferences for common stock investments.

2.6.4 Bundle Choice Models

A bundle consists of a number of products (components) offered for sale by a supplier. Bundle choices by consumers can be modeled in two main ways: using the components directly (see Green et al. 1972) or using the attributes of the components. A bundle choice model in terms of attributes will be more useful from a bundle design perspective. The balance model of Farquhar and Rao (1976) is suitable for describing the utility of a bundle of items drawn from a homogeneous product category (e.g., bundle of magazines); this model includes means and dispersions among the items in the bundle for each of the attributes. A hierarchical Bayes version of the balance model was developed by Bradlow and Rao (2000);

Against this background, Chung and Rao (2003) have developed a general choice model that extends the balance model to accommodate different types of bundles drawn from either homogeneous products or heterogeneous product categories (e.g. a bundle of computer, printer and monitor). Their COBA Model (COmparability-based BAlance model) is a generalization of the balance model applicable to the case of bundles drawn from heterogeneous product categories; it uses the construct of "comparability" of attributes. The utility function for the bundle in the COBA model consists of terms for "fully comparable" attributes, "partially comparable" attributes and "noncomparable" attributes. It incorporates heterogeneity among individual weights for the attribute terms (means and dispersions) and price of the bundle. The model for the value that individual i places on bundle b in terms of attributes in the COBA model (suppressing the subscript i) is:

---

[20] The Bass Diffusion Model (Bass 1969) is not particularly useful for this purpose because it is based on sales data obtained for a first few periods after the launch of the new product.

$$BV_b = \alpha_0 + \sum_{p_1 \in A^1} \left[\beta_{p_1} S_{p_1}^b + \gamma_{p_1} D_{p_1}^b \right] + \sum_{p_2 \in A^2} \left[\beta_{p_2} S_{p_2}^b + \gamma_{p_2} D_{p_2}^b \right] + \sum_{p_3 \in A^3} \alpha_{p_3} C_{p_3}^b \quad (2.9)$$

where A^1, A^2, and A^3 are the sets of fully comparable, partially comparable and noncomparable attributes; S and D are sum and dispersion measures for the fully and partially comparable attributes, and C is a component score for the noncomparable attributes. The parameters in the model are the αs, βs, and γs. The bundle utility, V_b is written as:

$$V_b = BV_b + \alpha_{BP} BP_b \quad (2.10)$$

Where BP_b is the bundle price and α_{BP} is the coefficient of price in the utility for the bundle. The choice of a bundle is modeled as a nested logit function with the inclusion of the "no purchase" option.

They implement this model using a set of choice data collected from a sample of students for choices made among computer systems (consisting of computer, printer and monitor) using a mixed logit model and estimate it using Hierarchical Bayesian methods. They show that the mixed logit model for two segments case is superior to other bundle choice models (mostly special cases of the COBA model) in terms of both in-sample and out-of-sample fit. Further, they show how their model can be employed to determine reservation prices for bundles.

2.7 Summary and Future Outlook

In this chapter, I reviewed several recent developments in the design and analysis of conjoint studies (both ratings-based and choice based approaches). These methods included new methods for design of profiles and choice sets based on such criteria as non-orthogonality, utility balance and reduction of error in estimating partworths. I also described methods that utilize prior knowledge of partworths in the design of choice sets. These new approaches result in designs that are more efficient than the traditional methods such as the orthogonal arrays or fractional factorial designs.

Further, I reviewed advances in conjoint estimation methods. These included hierarchical Bayesian (HB) methods that enable estimation of individual partworths with limited data from each respondent (individual partworths cannot be estimated with such limited data under traditional techniques). While these HB methods require advanced knowledge of statistical methodology, they are worth considering in applied studies. At the aggregate level, one study found that the difference between the HB methods and traditional methods is quite small.

A promising new technique is that of polyhedral methods which are useful not only for design of questions in an adaptive conjoint analysis but also offer a new approach to estimating partworths. These methods utilize advanced techniques called analytic center estimation. Simulations and one empirical study showed that the polyhedral techniques can be superior in both internal and external validity. Another development for estimation is the use of robust methods based on support vector machines.

While there are several substantive developments, I focused on four of these. One is the development of a method to estimate the market value of improvement in an attribute in product design; this is an important problem for research and development. Other developments are estimation of reservation prices and continuous conjoint analysis. I also covered a general choice model for bundles made up of items drawn from different product categories. This general model subsumes extant choice models for bundles and is shown to be more valid in both fit and for holdout predictions.

Several promising research directions exist in this vibrant methodology of conjoint analysis.[21] In one sentence, I should say that conjoint analysis is alive, well, and growing. The preceding discussion of recent developments is an indication of the potential future for conjoint analysis. Theory and practice have exploded to address a myriad of issues. As this field continues to be vibrant for many years to come, new challenges will appear. Hauser and Rao (2003) identified a set of research challenges under three categories – pragmatic issues, conceptual issues, and methodological issues. Pragmatic issues involve an analysis of tradeoffs between complexity of method, cost, and managerial application. Conceptual issues relate to the development of suitable conjoint models that include roles of price, diffusion of information on attributes, and competition, while methodological issues involve the development of newer methods of data collection and estimation. Further, I expect future conjoint studies to go beyond individual or organizational consumers and be employed for other stakeholder groups, such as stockholders, employees, suppliers, and governmental organizations.

As a summary, I may suggest that the following eight developments in conjoint analysis are significant from my perspective.

1. *Shift from ratings-based methods to choice-based conjoint methods*: It is becoming quite common to utilize choice-based conjoint analysis in most situations; this is due to various reasons including the appeal of dealing with choice rather than preference. Even when one deals with preference data, it becomes necessary to convert utility estimates into probability of choice.

---

[21] Eric Bradlow (2005) presents a wish list for conjoint analysis such as within task learning/variation, embedded prices, massive number of attributes, non-compensatory decision rules, integration of conjoint data with other sources, experimental design (from education literature), getting the right attributes and levels, mix and match, and product-bundle conjoint. There is a considerable overlap between this list and mine described below.

This step is essentially eliminated in the choice-based methods. However, the choice-based methods may not have the same flexibility as ratings-based methods.

2. *Shift from regression methods to hierarchical Bayesian regression methods:* Independent of which approach is used for collecting conjoint data (ratings or choices), there is a trend to utilize hierarchical Bayesian methods for estimation. As we have seen, the HB methods enable incorporating hetero-geneity and yield individual-level estimates of partworths.

3. *Tendency to utilize adaptive conjoint analysis methods:* Given the availability of commercial software for implementing conjoint analysis, applied studies in industry seem to utilize adaptive conjoint methods.[22] Such software is available from Sawtooth Software (http://www.sawtoothsoftware.com).

4. *Beginnings of multi-period (dynamic) conjoint studies:* As conjoint analysis is used for a diversity of problems, the issue of understanding dynamics of consumer choice behavior will become significant. The idea of estimating demand for new products even before they diffuse in the marketplace becomes important for both practice and research. The concepts of information acceleration can be utilized for such estimation problems. It is at least in this context I think that dynamic conjoint studies will become extremely essential.

5. *Shift from focus on prediction to focus on understanding of choice process:* The primary focus in conjoint analysis has so far been on developing models and procedures that enhance predictive ability. As noted in the discussion on partial profiles, there is some shift toward incorporating some postulates of choice process. I expect that this will become more significant as conjoint modelers begin to incorporate learnings from behavioral research on information processing and choice. I also think that such a shift will be highly worthwhile. An application of this is by Yee et al. (2005) who infer non-compensatory decision rules using greedoid algorithms. Another approach is due to Gilbride and Allenby (2004), who utilize data augmentation methods to estimate thresholds and discontinuities in the conjoint preference function.

6. *Pragmatic approaches to theoretically sound methods (e.g. incentive-aligned):* Despite the fact that the origins of conjoint analysis were in the axiomatic development of conjoint measurement, current practice seems to have largely been on developing pragmatic approaches for data collection and

---

[22] The adaptive conjoint analysis (ACA) approach involves presenting two profiles that are as nearly equal as possible in estimated utility measured on a metric scale and developing new pairs of profiles sequentially as a respondent provides response to previous questions. There has been considerable amount of research on this approach. In a recent paper, Hauser and Toubia (2005) found that the result of the metric utility balance used in ACA leads to partworth estimates to be biased due to endogeneity. The author also found that these biases are of the order of response errors and suggest alternatives to metric utility balance to deal with this issue. See also, Liu et al. (2007) who suggest using the likelihood principle in estimation to deal with the endogeneity bias in general.

estimation. However, recent trends indicate that conjoint researchers are concerned about theoretical bases of the data collected in conjoint studies. An example of this is the development of incentive-aligned methods for data collection. I expect that this trend to continue and that future data collection efforts will begin to incorporate assumptions normally made to develop consumer utility functions (e.g., budget constraints and separability).

7. *Simpler models to richer methods and models:* The trend toward technically advanced methods of estimation and data collection is here to stay. In particular, the hierarchical Bayesian methods will continue to be part of standard arsenal of a conjoint analyst.

8. *Mainly product design domain to varied domains:* A general application of conjoint analysis has been product/service design. The methods are now being applied to a varied set of domains such as tourism, healthcare, corporate acquisitions and the like. This trend is likely to continue.

References

Alba, J.W., A.D.J. Cooke. 2004., When Absence Begets Inference in Conjoint Analysis. *Journal of Marketing Research*, **41**(November) 382–387.

Allenby, G.M., N. Arora, J. L. Ginter. 1995. Incorporating Prior Knowledge into the Analysis Of Conjoint Studies. *Journal of Marketing Research*, **37**(May) 152–162.

Allenby, G.M., P.J. Lenk. 1994. Modeling Household Purchase Behavior with Logistic Normal Regression. *Journal of the American Statistical Association*, **89**(December) 1218–1231.

Andrews, R.L., A. Ansari, I. Currim. 2002a, Hierarchical Bayes Versus Finite Mixture Conjoint Analysis Models: A Comparison Of Fit, Prediction, And Partworth Recovery. *Journal of Marketing Research*, **39**(February) 87–98.

Andrews, R.L., A. Ainslie, I. Currim. 2002b, An Empirical Comparison Of Logit Choice Models with Discrete Versus Continuous Representations of Heterogeneity. *Journal of Marketing Research*, **39**(November) 479–487.

Bass, F. 1969. A New Product Growth Model for Consumer Durables. *Management Science*, **15**(January), 215–227.

Becker, G.M., M.H. DeGroot, J. Marschak.1964. Measuring Utility By A Single-Response Sequential Method. *Behavioral Science* **9**(July), 226–32.

Bodapati, A. 2006. Personal communication.

Bradlow, E.T. 2005. Current Issues and a 'wish list' for Conjoint Analysis. *Applied Stochastic Models in Business and Industry* **21**, 319–323.

Bradlow, E.T., V.R. Rao. 2000. A Hierarchical Bayes Model For Assortment Choice. *Journal of Marketing Research* **37**(May), 259–268.

Bradlow, E., Y. Hu, T.-H. Ho. 2004., A Learning-Based Model Fro Imputing Missing Levels in Partial Conjoint Profiles. *Journal of Marketing Research* **41**(November), 369–381.

Burgess, C.J.C. 1998. A Tutorial On Support Vector Machines For Pattern Recognition. *Data Mining and Knowledge Discovery* **2** 121–167.

Burgess, L., D. Street. 2003. Optimal Designs for 2ok Choice Experiments. *Communications in Statistics: Theory and Methods*, **32** (11) 2185–2206.

Burgess, L., D. Street. 2005. Optimal Designs for Choice Experiments with Asymmetric Attributes. *Journal of Statistical Planning and Inference* **134** 288–301.

Carroll, J.D., P.E. Green. 1995. Psychometric Methods in Marketing Research: Part I, Conjoint Analysis. *Journal of Marketing Research* **32**(November) 385–391.

Chung, J., V.R. Rao. 2003. A General Choice Model for Bundles with Multiple Category Products: Application To Market Segmentation and Optimal Pricing for Bundles. *Journal of Marketing Research* **40**(May) 115–130.

Corstjens, M., D.A. Gautschi. 1983. Formal Choice Models in Marketing. *Marketing Science*, **2**(1), 19–56.

DeSarbo, W.S., V.R. Rao. 1986. A Constrained Unfolding Methodology For Product Positioning. *Marketing Science* **5**(1) 1–19.

DeSarbo, W.S., W.M. Vriens, V. Ramaswamy. 1992. Latent Class Metric Conjoint Analysis. *Marketing Letters* **3**(3) 273–288.

Ding, M.. 2007. An Incentive-Aligned Mechanism For Conjoint Analysis. *Journal of Marketing Research* **44**(May) 214–223.

Ding, M., R. Agarwal, J. Liechty. 2005. Incentive-Aligned Conjoint Analysis. *Journal of Marketing Research* **42**(February) 67–82.

Evgeniou, T., C. Boussios, G. Zacharia. 2005. Generalized Robust Conjoint Estimation. *Marketing Science* **24**(3) 415–429.

Farquhar, P.H.. V.R. Rao. 1976. A Balance Model For Evaluating Subsets of Multiattributed Items. *Management Science* **22**(January) 528–539.

Gilbride, T.J., G.M. Allenby. 2004. A Choice Model with Conjunctive, Disjunctive, and Compensatory Screening Rules. *Marketing Science* **23**(2) 391–406.

Ghose, S., V.R. Rao. 2007. A Choice Model of Bundles Features and Meta-Attributes: An Application to Product Design. *Working paper*, Cornell University.

Green, P.E. 1984. A Hybrid Models For Conjoint Analysis: An Expository View. *Journal of Marketing Research* **21**(May) 33–41.

Green, P.E., V.R. Rao. 1971. Conjoint Measurement for Quantifying Judgmental Data. *Journal of Marketing Research* **8**(August) 355 363.

Green, P.E., V. Srinivasan. 1978. Conjoint Analysis in Consumer Research: Issues and Outlook. *Journal of Consumer Research* **5**(September) 103–123.

Green, P.E., V. Srinivasan. 1990. Conjoint Analysis in Marketing: New Developments with Implications for Research and Practice. *Journal of Marketing* **54**(October) 3 19.

Green, P. E., A. M. Krieger, M. K. Agarwal. 1991. Adaptive Conjoint Analysis: Some Caveats and Suggestions. *Journal of Marketing Research* **28**(May) 215–222.

Green, P.E., A. Krieger, T.G. Vavra. 1997. Evaluating New Products. *Marketing Research* **9**(4) 12–19.

Green, P.E., A. Krieger, Y. Wind. 2003. Buyer choice Simulators, Optimizers, and Dynamic Models. Wind Y., Paul E. Green, *Marketing Research and Modeling: Progress and Prospects: A Tribute to Paul E. Green.* Kluwer Academic Publishers, Norwell, MA.

Green, P.E., Y. Wind, A.K. Jain. 1972. Preference Measurement of Item Collections. *Journal of Marketing Research* **9**(November) 371–377.

Hauser, J.R.. V.R. Rao. 2003. Conjoint Analysis, Related Modeling, and Applications. Wind, Y., P.E. Green, *Marketing Research and Modeling: Progress and Prospects: A Tribute to Paul E. Green*, Kluwer Academic Publishers, Norwell, MA.

Hauser, J.R., O. Toubia. 2005. The Impact of Utility Balance and Endogeneity in Conjoint Analysis. *Marketing Science*, **24**(3) 498–507.

Huber, J., K. Train. 2001. On the Similarity of Classical and Bayesian Estimates of Individual Mean Partworths. *Marketing Letters* **12**(3) 259–269.

Huber, J., K. Zwerina. 1996. On the Importance of Utility Balance in Efficient Designs. *Journal of Marketing Research*,**33**(August), 307–317.

Jedidi, K., Z.J. Zhang. 2002. Augmenting Conjoint Analysis to Estimate Consumer Reservation Price. *Management Science*, **48**(10), 1350–1368.

Jedidi, K., S. Jagpal, P. Manchanda. 2003. Measuring Heterogeneous Reservation Prices for Product Bundles. *Marketing Science* **22**(1), 107–130.

Johnson, R.M. 1987. Adaptive Conjoint Analysis. *Sawtooth Software Conference on Perceptual Mapping, Conjoint Analysis, and Computer Interviewing.* Sawtooth Software, Inc., Ketchum, ID, 253–265.

Johnson, R.M. 1991 Comment on "Adaptive Conjoint Analysis": Some Caveats and Suggestions. *Journal of Marketing Research,* **28**(May), 223–225.

Kanninen, B.J. 2002. Optimal Designs For Multinomial Choice Designs. *Journal of Marketing Research,* **39**(May), 214–227.

Kuhfeld, W.F. 2005. Marketing Research Methods in SAS. *Experimental Design, Choice, Conjoint, and Graphical Techniques.* SAS 9.1 Edition, TS-722, SAS Institute Inc., Cary, NC

Kuhfeld, W.F., R.D. Tobias, and M.Garratt. 1994. Efficient Experimental Designs with Marketing Research Applications. *Journal of Marketing Research,* **31**(November), 545–557.

Lenk, P.J., W.S. DeSarbo, P.E. Green and M.R. Young. 1996. Hierarchical Bayes Conjoint Analysis: Recovery of Partworth Heterogeneity from Reduced Experimental Designs. *Marketing Science* **15**(2), 173–191.

Liechty, J., V. Ramaswamy, S. H. Cohen. 2001. Choice Menus for Mass Customization: An Experimental Approach for Analyzing Customer Demand with an Application to a Web-Based Information Service. *Journal of Marketing Research,* **38**(2), 183–196.

Liechty, J.C., D.K.H. Fong and W.S. DeSarbo. 2005. Dynamic Models Incorporating Individual Heterogeneity: Utility Evolution in Conjoint Analysis. *Marketing Science* **24**(2), 285–293.

Liu, Q., T. Otter, and G.M. Allenby. 2007. Investigating Endogeneity Bias in Marketing. *Marketing Science,* **26**(5), 642–650.

Oded N., V. Srinivasan. 2007. Adaptive-Self Explication of Multi-Attribute Preferences. *Working Paper,* Stanford, CA: Graduate School of Business, Stanford University

Ofek, E. and V. Srinivasan. 2002. How Much Does the Market Value an Improvement in a Product Attribute?. *Marketing Science* **22**(3) 398–411.

Orme, B. (2006) Getting Started with Conjoint Analysis: Strategies for Product Design and Pricing Research. Research Publishers LLC, Madison, WI.

Park, Y.-H., M. Ding, V.R. Rao. Forthcoming. Eliciting Preference for Complex Products: A Web-Based Upgrading Method. *Journal of Marketing Research.*

Rao, V.R. 1976. Conjoint Measurement in Marketing Analysis. Sheth, J.N. *Multivariate Methods for Market and Survey Research,* American Marketing Association.

Rao, V.R., H. Sattler. 2003. Measurement of Price Effects with Conjoint Analysis: Separating Informational and Allocative Effects of Price. Gustafsson, A., A. Herrmann, F. Huber, *Conjoint Measurement: Methods and Applications,* 3rd edition, Springer, Berlin

Rossi, P.E., G.M. Allenby, R. McCulloch. 2005. *Bayesian Statistics and Marketing,*John Wiley & Sons Ltd., West Sussex, England.

Sandor, Z., M. Wedel. 2001. Designing Conjoint Choice Experiments using Managers' Beliefs. *Journal of Marketing Research,* **38**(November) 430–444.

Sandor, Z., M. Wedel. 2002. Profile Construction in Experimental Choice Designs for Mixed Logit Models. *Marketing Science,* **21**(4) 455–475.

Srinivasan, V., C.S. Park. 1997. Surprising Robustness of Self-Explicated Approach to Customer Preference Structure Measurement. *Journal of Marketing Research,* **34**(2) 286–291.

Street, D.J., L. Burgess. 2004. Optimal and Near-Optimal Pairs for the Estimation of Effects in 2-Level Choice Experiments. *Journal of Statistical Planning and Inference,* 118, 185–199.

Street, D.S., and L. Burgess. 2007. *The Construction of Optimal Stated Choice Experiments: Theory and Methods.* Hoboken, NJ: Wiley-Interscience, A John Wiley & Sons, Inc. Publication.

Street, D.J., L. Burgess, J.J. Louviere. 2005. Quick and Easy Choice Sets: Constructing Optimal and nearly Optimal Stated Choice Experiments. *International Journal of Research in Marketing,* **22** 459–470.

Su, M. V.R. Rao. 2006. A Continuous Conjoint Analysis for Preannounced New products with Evolutional Attributes. *Working Paper*, Johnson School, Cornell University.

Toubia, O., J.R. Hauser. 2007. On Managerially Efficient Experimental Designs. *Marketing Science*. **26**(6), 850–858.

Toubia, O., J.R. Hauser, D.I. Simester. 2004., Polyhedral Methods for Adaptive Conjoint Analysis. *Journal of Marketing Research*, **42**(February) 116–131.

Toubia, O., D.I. Simester, J.R. Hauser, E. Dahan. 2003. Fast Polyhedral Adaptive Conjoint Estimation. *Marketing Science*, **22**(3), 273–303.

Urban, G.L. and J.R. Hauser. 2002. 'Listening in' to find consumer needs and solutions, Working Paper, Cambridge, MA: Center for Innovation in Product Development, MIT (February).

Vadali, S., J. Liechty, A. Rangaswamy. 2006. Generalized Hierarchical Bayes Estimation for Polyhedral Conjoint Analysis. *Working Paper*, Penn State University.

Wertenbroch, K., B. Skiera. 2002. Measuring Consumers' Willingness to Pay at the Point of Purchase. *Journal of Marketing Research*, **39**(May) 228–241.

Wind, Y, P.E. Green, D. Shifflet, and M. Scarbrough. 1989. Courtyard by Marriott: Designing a Hotel with Consumer-based marketing. *Interfaces*, **19**(January–February) 25–47.

Wittink, D.R., P. Cattin. 1989. Commercial Use of Conjoint Analysis: An Update. *Journal of Marketing*. **53**(July), 91–96.

Wittink, D.R., S.K. Keil. 2003. Continuous Conjoint Analysis. Gustafsson, A., A. Herrmann, F. Huber. *Conjoint Measurement Methods and Applications*, . 3rd Edition, Springer, New York.

Wittink, D.R., M. Vriens, W. Burhenne. 1994. Commercial Use of Conjoint Analysis in Europe: Results and Critical Reflections. *International Journal of Research in Marketing*, **11** 41–52.

Yee, M., E. Dahan, J.R. Hauser, J. Orlin. 2005. Greedoid-Based Noncompensatory Inference. *Marketing Science* **26** 532–549.

Chapter 3
Interactive Consumer Decision Aids

Kyle B. Murray and Gerald Häubl

3.1 Too Much Choice for Consumers?

Today's consumers are faced with a vast and unprecedented breadth and depth of product alternatives: a Wal-Mart Supercenter stocks over 100,000 items (Yoffie 2005), Home Depot more than 50,000 (Murray and Chandrasekhar 2006), and the typical grocery store more than 30,000 (Schwartz 2005). The advent of online shopping has further increased the choices that are available to consumers; both eBay.com and amazon.com offer literally millions of unique products, from thousands of product categories, for sale through their websites. If deciding among all of these alternatives gives consumers a headache, a trip to the local pharmacy does little to relieve the pain. Even in product categories that one might consider relatively simple and straightforward, such as analgesics, it is common to find in excess of 60 different varieties side-by-side on the shelf (Schwartz 2005). The consumer is asked to select the chemical composition (ibuprofen, acetaminophen, acetylsalysic acid, etc.), decide between brand names (Advil, Tylenol, Aspirin, etc.) and generics, and choose from numerous features ("cool burst," coated, time release, etc.), packaging (liquid gel, tablet, caplet, as well as the number of pills, etc.) and concentrations (regular, extra strength).

For the consumer, there is a cost to processing information, and that cost rises as the complexity of the decision increases (Shugan 1980). As a result, making decisions in a world with an ever-growing variety of products and product categories is increasingly taxing. Traditionally, humans have been able to effectively adapt to complex environments by adjusting their decision making strategies to the situation they are faced with (Payne et al. 1993), employing heuristics to lighten the cognitive load (e.g., Kahneman and Tversky 1984), or simply doing what they did last time (Hoyer 1984; Murray and Häubl 2007; Stigler

K.B. Murray
Western Ontario University's, Richard Ivey School of Business, London, Ontario
e-mail: kmurray@ivey.uwo.ca

B. Wierenga (ed.), *Handbook of Marketing Decision Models*,
DOI: 10.1007/978-0-387-78213-3_3, © Springer Science+Business Media, LLC 2008

and Becker 1977) to arrive at a satisfactory, if occasionally suboptimal, decision (Simon 1955, 1957).

In fact, we are relatively adept at trading off the effort we expend to produce the results we require. Nevertheless, as the number of choices and decision complexity increase, our ability to efficiently make good decisions is compromised. The additional constraints of time pressure and the many demands upon us beyond consumption decisions (e.g., work, family, etc.) only exacerbate the problem (Perlow 1999; Perlow et al. 2002). In fact, there is growing evidence that the cumulative effect of all the choices that must be made on a regular basis cause consumers substantial (di)stress (Schwartz 2005; Mick et al. 2004). In this chapter, we examine the current state of a set of tools that have the potential to assist consumers in their decision making by improving the quality of the choices they make while simultaneously reducing the effort required to make those decisions. We refer to these tools as *interactive consumer decisions aids* (ICDAs).

3.1.1 The Paradox of Choice

Decades of psychological research have demonstrated that having a choice among alternatives is better than having no choice at all. Specifically, we know that the freedom to choose increases intrinsic motivation, perceived control, task performance, and life satisfaction (Deci 1975, 1981; Deci and Ryan 1985; Glass and Singer 1972a, b; Langer and Rodin 1976; Rotter 1966; Schulz and Hanusa 1978; Taylor 1989; Taylor and Brown 1988). In addition, it appears that consumers are more attracted to vendors that offer more choice through a greater variety of products (Iyengar and Lepper 2000) and products with more features (Thompson et al. 2005).

However, recent research has revealed that too much choice can, in fact, have adverse consequences. This work suggests that choosing from among a large number of alternatives can have negative effects, including increased regret, decreased product and life satisfaction, lower self-esteem, and less self-control (e.g., Baumeister and Vohs 2003; Carmon et al. 2003; Schwartz et al. 2002).

For example, in a series of field and laboratory experiments, Iyengar and Lepper (2000) compared the effects of choosing from a small versus a large number of alternatives. All else being equal, they found that shoppers were significantly more likely to stop to sample products when 24 were on display (60%) than when only 6 were on display (40%). However, when it came to actually making a purchase, only 3% of those in the extensive choice condition (24 products) bought one of the products, while 30% of those in the limited-choice condition (6 products) made a purchase. In a follow-up study examining chocolate consumption, the same authors replicated previous research when they found that consumers prefer to have the freedom to choose what they are consuming. Specifically, they found that people are more satisfied with the chocolate they eat when they are able to select it themselves, as compared to being given a chocolate randomly selected from the same assortment. However, they also found that people choosing a chocolate from a limited selection (6) were significantly more satisfied with their choice than those choosing from an extensive selection (30). It seems that, although people like to have the freedom to choose what they consume, and are attracted to larger product assortments, they are more likely to make a purchase and be satisfied with it when the choice is made from a limited number of alternatives.

Similar results have been found by researchers studying the optimal number of product features. Advances in technology have not only allowed retailers to offer consumers an ever-increasing number of products, they have also allowed manufacturers to load products with a growing number of features. Take, for example, today's cell phones that include the capabilities of a gaming console, text messaging device, wireless internet, calendar, contact organizer, digital camera, global positioning system, and MP3 player; in addition to its multiple telephone functions. Although each of these features are individually useful, when combined in large numbers they can result in an effect known as "feature fatigue" (Rust et al. 2006; Thompson et al. 2005). When consumers are deciding which product to buy, they tend to focus on the capabilities of the product (i.e., what it can do); however, their satisfaction with the product, once it has been purchased, is driven mostly by how easy it is to use (Thompson et al. 2005). Ironically, consumers prefer to buy products that have many features and, as a result, they are less satisfied with their choices. Consequently, this dissatisfaction decreases the vendor's long-term profitability (Rust et al. 2006).

Interestingly, Schwartz et al. (2000) find that the negative effects of too much choice are most acute when people attempt to find an optimal product – i.e., when they act as maximizers. For example, a consumer looking for the perfect cell phone will tend to be less happy, less optimistic and less satisfied, as well as lower in self-esteem, than someone who is just looking for an adequate phone. Even at a more general (societal) level, there is evidence to suggest that too much choice is decreasing happiness, increasing incidents of depression, and potentially having a negative impact on moral development (Botti and Iyengar 2006; Mick et al. 2004; Schwartz 2005).

It seems counter-intuitive that fewer choices are better. Why would we want to limit our options and opportunities? Yet, it is becoming apparent that there are benefits to having some constraints on the number and complexity of the choices that consumers have to make. Do we really need (or want) to choose from more than 60 types of pain relievers, 175 varieties of salad dressing or 85 different home telephones (Schwartz 2005)? Maybe not. Yet, when we have a headache, it would be nice to have pain relief that was the best available for our own unique physiology. In fact, although people generally do not want to sort through a vast selection of salad dressings or telephones (or, for that matter, most products), rarely would consumers object to having a small number of options that are ideally suited to their particular preferences. Similarly, we would like to buy products with the capabilities that we need, and avoid the features that add complexity without increasing usefulness. In other words, most consumers would like to make better decisions with less effort. This is the promise of ICDAs.

3.1.2 Building Interactive Consumer Decision Aids (ICDAs)

We define ICDAs broadly as technologies that are designed to interact with consumers to help them make better purchase decisions and/or to do so with less effort. Fortunately, recent advances in information technology have made the development and implementation of such tools a realistic ambition. In fact, examples of effective ICDAs are becoming a part of everyday life for many people. Take, for instance, internet search engines, in-car navigation systems, personal video recorders (e.g., TiVo), and RSS feeds (e.g., for news and coupons). In fact, it has been argued that humans are at the beginning of a transition to a world of augmented reality – wherein the real world is augmented by computer-generated ("virtual") stimuli – that offers substantial assistance anywhere at any time (Abowd et al. 2002; Weiser 1991, 1993). For example, together with the physical traffic environment, the electronic maps and context-sensitive assistance built into a vehicle's navigation system can be viewed as creating an augmented driving reality.

Unfortunately, these (emerging) technologies have not been harnessed for the purpose of consumer decision support. Early attempts at creating ICDAs, in the form of electronic recommendation agents (Häubl and Trifts 2000), such as personalogic.com, were unsuccessful, and they may even have incited some resentment on the part of consumers (Fitzsimons and Lehmann 2004). Currently, the vast majority of systems that could be considered ICDAs are aimed exclusively at personalization in an e-commerce setting (e.g., amazon.com's Gold-box) or are focused on price search (e.g., mysimon.com, pricegrabber.com or shopzilla.com). Although useful under some conditions, these tools are highly constrained and fail to live up to the full promise of ICDAs. In the sections that follow, we review the research that has led us to our current understanding of the significant potential of ICDAs to assist consumers in their decision making, and we discuss a number of reasons why this potential remains unrealized.

3.1.3 Interactive Shopping: Agent's to the Rescue?

The development and adoption of new technologies, such as the internet, has opened the door to new kinds of exchanges between buyers and sellers. For example, buyers have fewer constraints on search and comparison shopping. Rather than drive across town to obtain some information about a particular product (e.g., its price), consumers are able to access a wealth of information at the click of a mouse. In the extreme, such a marketplace has the potential to spark a dramatic rise in the amount of search that consumers undertake before making a purchase decision, which could result in substantial downward pressure on prices (Bakos 1997).

Alba et al. (1997) suggested that, for this type of search to be feasible, a number of conditions would have to be met: (1) product information would have to be faithfully provided to consumers; (2) the set of available products would have to be substantially expanded beyond what local or catalogue shopping offered; and (3) search across stores and brands would have to be unimpeded. Importantly, these authors emphasized screening as the most critical determinant of the adoption of online shopping (see also Diehl et al. 2003). By and large, the first and second conditions appear to have been fulfilled. Although the internet has created its share of new forms of fraud, online product information appears to be at least as reliable as its offline counterpart. In fact, the growth of online shopping has also seen a rise in novel methods of providing consumers with information about information; including website certifications and verifications (e.g., Verisign, Truste, etc.), reviews from other consumers that have experienced the product (e.g., Amazon, Bizrate, etc.) or ratings of buyers' and sellers' past performance (e.g., eBay, Better Business Bureau, etc.). It is also true that for most (if not all) consumers, online shopping makes substantially more products available than can be found locally or through catalogue shopping.

However, search across stores and brands appears to be "stickier" than originally anticipated (Johnson et al. 2004). Although, some pundits initially saw online shopping as the death of the brand,[1] it has become apparent that consumers are at least as loyal online as they are offline (Johnson et al. 2003; Brynjolfsson and Smith 2000). In addition, even though competition is "only a click away," that is a distance many consumers are unwilling to travel (Johnson et al. 2003). In fact, research indicates that once shoppers have learned to use one store's electronic interface, they are very reluctant to switch to other stores (Murray and Häubl 2007).

Consequently, the evolution of online shopping has underscored the need for something akin to a "personal electronic shopper" (Alba et al. 1997). Large volumes of relevant information are available to shoppers, who are limited in their capacity to process that information, and indeed hesitant to switch between different electronic interfaces to collect it in the first place. Current technology can provide tools that excel at searching and sorting information, and providing the results to consumers through a consistent interface.

However, it is worth noting that the need for such tools is not limited to the online world. As we have already discussed, big box stores and improvements in manufacturing technology have generated staggering assortments in traditional

---

[1] For example: "The internet is a great equalizer, allowing the smallest of businesses to access markets and have a presence that allows them to compete against the giants of their industry." Borland (1998); "The cost of switching from Amazon to another retailer is zero on the internet. It's just one click away." Friedman (1999); "Shopbots deliver on one of the great promises of electronic commerce and the internet: a radical reduction in the cost of obtaining and distributing information." Greenwald and Kephart (1999).

retail settings for even the most mundane product categories. At the same time, current technology can place the necessary tools in the palm of the consumer's hand. In doing so, the shopper's reality becomes augmented. In addition to the shelves and aisles in front of consumers, small portable devices can provide access to a virtual world of information and advice. Such a scenario has led consumer researchers to try to answer a number of important questions, not the least of which are: What role can (and should) ICDAs play in the buying and consumption process, and how should these tools be designed?

3.1.4 Four Potential Roles for ICDAs

West et al. (1999) mapped out a useful preliminary framework for thinking about the role of ICDAs in consumer decision making. They suggested that there are four key decision making tasks in which an ICDA could assist consumers. In some cases, ICDAs are already fulfilling these roles. For example, the internet offers a number of price search engines that scour the web for the lowest price on a particular set of products. However, others remain largely theoretical at the present time. Below, we will consider each of these potential roles of ICDAs.

3.1.4.1 Clerking

First, the ICDA could act as a *clerk*, assisting consumers in their search for product information and alternatives. ICDAs acting as rudimentary clerks are relatively common on the internet today. For example, there are a number of "shopbots" that search for the lowest price on a specific product. Sites such as mysimon.com, shopzilla.com and froogle.google.com gather up-to-date information on tens of millions of products from thousands of stores.[2] You tell the site what you are looking for, and it provides you with a list of vendors that have it in stock, along with their prices. In some instances, sellers pay a fee to be listed at the top of the search results. In most cases, the shopper is also able to customize the list alphabetically by store, by price, by consumer ratings or other means. These shopbots do not actually sell or ship anything, they simply provide product information.

Other ICDA clerks are specialists that work in a particular product category. For example, Amazon's bibliofind.com searches millions of rare, used and out-of-print books to help consumers locate hard-to-find titles from a community of third-party book sellers. Similarly, computershopper.com, specializes in computers and related accessories. There are other sites, often called "infomediaries," that provide third-party product information and/or consolidate product

---

[2] Even more common are general information search engines – e.g., Google, Live.com, Yahoo search, Ask.com, etc. – which could also be classified under a liberal definition of clerking.

information to assist consumers in their decision making. Examples of such sites include bizrate.com, cnet.com, and consumerreports.org.

Other examples include ICDA clerks that vigilantly watch for sales, or send coupons, relevant to products that an individual consumer has expressed an interest in. Early implementations of this idea are being tested using Really Simple Syndication (RSS) feeds, and related technology, to deliver coupons (and other information on product discounts) to consumers. Examples of such websites include monkeybargains.com, dealcatcher.com, and couponsurfer.com.

In the bricks-and-mortar world, robots using RFID (radio frequency identification) technology are being tested that could serve in a similar role. In Japan, NTT Communications has teamed up with Tmsuk to test an RFID-driven "shopping assistant robot" in a mall in Fukuoka (NTT 2006). When at the mall, shoppers choose a store that they are interested in visiting using a touch screen mounted on the robot, who then navigates its way there. However, consumers also have the option of directing the robot over the internet from their homes (or elsewhere). For the remote consumer, the robot provides a view of the in-store environment using a camera and connects the shopper to the store's human clerks via videoconferencing. When the shopper selects a product or a human clerk makes a recommendation, the robot reads the product's RFID tag and displays the relevant information (including price, features, options, etc.). The robot is also able to carry shopping bags and lock valuables up inside its safe.

3.1.4.2 Advising

Another role for an ICDA is that of an *advisor* that provides expert personalized opinions based on the decision aid's knowledge of the consumer's preferences. The critical distinction between the role of clerk and that of advisor is the degree to which the information and recommendations provided by the ICDA are personalized (i.e., driven by the tool's understanding of the consumer's personal preferences). A pioneer in this area is Amazon.com. Its website has built-in capabilities to make recommendations to consumers based on their past behavior (and the behavior of people like them). Repeat customers at Amazon are greeted with a list of product recommendations based on previous searches and purchases at the website. Moreover, regular customers have a tab designated as their own "store" that is populated with additional recommendations, as well as links to online communities, commentary and more, all personalized on the basis of the profile Amazon has developed for each individual customer. By default, Amazon records the behavior of each shopper and uses that information to make recommendations. However, the site also offers users the option of editing their profile by providing additional information on products that they own, products that they have rated and products that they are not interested in.

Another type of advisor ICDA is not associated with any particular store and shares some of the features of a clerk. These tools are similar to ICDA clerks in that they provide consumers with a list of products based on what the shopper tells the ICDA. However, the advisor elicits much more detailed input and, rather than simply supplying a list of available products, it makes recommendations that are personalized based on the preference information that the consumer has provided to it (myproductadvisor.com is an example of such a website). After arriving at the site, consumers are asked to select an advisor by product category (e.g., new cars, televisions, cell phones, digital cameras, etc.) and to respond to a series of questions about their personal preferences within that category. The advisor then provides the consumer with a list, complete with the latest product specifications and comparison information, which ranks products in order of attractiveness to that individual.

In the realm of augmented reality, the Metro Group is experimenting with a "store of the future" (future-store.org) that can adapt a bricks-and-mortar environment into a personalized shopping experience. Using RFID tags to identify individual shoppers and products, these stores employ technology to assist consumers in finding the products on their shopping list (like a clerk), as well as recommending products (e.g., wine to go with dinner, like an advisor).

3.1.4.3 Banking

West et al. (1999) also envisioned an ICDA that could act as a *banker*, negotiating on the consumer's behalf and facilitating the ultimate transaction. The Automated Teller Machine (ATM) is a familiar technology that assists consumers by providing banking information and allowing users to complete transactions without human assistance. However, this type of technology would not meet our definition of an ICDA, because it is not intended as a tool that can help consumers make better decisions with less effort.

In fact, there are few real-world examples of the ICDA as a banker. One notable exception is the automation of bidding in the realm of online auctions. Here, the tool helps to reduce the effort required to make good purchase decisions in a consumer auction. For example, eBay's "proxy bidding" system automatically places bids on a consumer's behalf, up to a certain price. Consumers are able to enter the maximum amount that they are willing to pay for an item when they begin the bidding process. This information is not shared with the market (i.e., other buyers and sellers); however, it is used by eBay to compare the consumer's bid to that of others bidding for the same product. The system then automatically places bids on the consumer's behalf, out-bidding others by a small increment, until the product is purchased or bidding exceeds the consumer's maximum willingness to pay.

In general, ICDAs are only beginning to test their potential as bankers. The current implementations are very rudimentary versions of what they could be. For example, ongoing research is investigating marketplaces composed entirely of ICDAs acting on behalf of their human masters to complete transactions from need identification through product brokering, negotiation, payment, delivery and post-purchase support and evaluation (e.g., Maes et al. 1999). In the future, such tools may be capable of creating dynamic relationships, forming buying coalitions to leverage economies of scale and/or seeking out new suppliers who are willing to manufacture products demanded by the consumers that the ICDAs are working for.

3.1.4.4 Tutoring

Another potential role for ICDAs is that of a *tutor* who assists consumers in preference construction and discovery (West et al. 1999). For example, an ICDA might teach the shopper about the important attributes within a product category and/or help the consumer "uncover" his or her preferences within a particular domain. Note the important distinction between a tutor and an advisor: the advisor uses consumers' preferences to make product recommendations; the tutor helps the consumer form his or her preferences. In other words, when acting as a tutor, the ICDA does not assume that the consumer has a detailed knowledge of his or her own preferences and, instead, helps the individual determine what these preferences are (e.g., Hoeffler et al. 2006).

Current examples of this type of ICDA are quite rudimentary. One exception is the website pandora.com. This website was created by the Music Genome Project^{TM}; a group that has assembled hundreds of musical attributes (or "genes") into a database that breaks songs down by everything from melody, harmony and rhythm to instrumentation, lyrics and vocal harmony. You begin by entering an artist or song that you like. Say, for example, that you start with Jack Johnson, which Pandora classifies as mellow rock instrumentation, folk influences, a subtle use of vocal harmony, mild rhythmic syncopation and acoustic sonority. Pandora plays a song by the selected artist (Johnson) and then moves on to other artists/songs that are similar. For any song that Pandora selects, the user can respond in a number of ways, including clicking links such as: (1) I really like this song – play more like it; (2) I don't like it – it's not what this station should play; or (3) I'm tired of this song – don't play it for a month. This input is used to refine the playlist going forward. The user can also guide Pandora by entering other artists and songs that s/he enjoys. With extended use, the ICDA learns about the user, but it also teaches the user about his or her own preferences. The tool exposes consumers to product alternatives that they may not have been previously aware of, yet are likely to be interested in buying, all based on the consumer's personal preferences. Clearly, this is a role for ICDAs that is still in its infancy. Nevertheless, given the large percentage of decisions for which people do not have well-defined preferences (Bettman et al. 1998; Mandel and Johnson 2002; Payne et al. 1999), it is an area ripe with opportunity for additional research and application.

3.1.5 Agent Algorithms

Having mapped out a set of roles that an ICDA can fulfill, it is useful to take a moment to discuss some of the approaches and algorithms that a designer might employ to create an effective decision aid. Potentially, ICDAs could be developed on the basis of a wide variety of techniques ranging from consumer-centric formats for displaying information to search engines to sophisticated preference models. At a general level, ICDAs face a fundamental tradeoff in the design of their underlying algorithms. Specifically, these tools aim to: (1) work effectively in real-time environments; and, (2) develop a deep understanding of the needs and/or preferences of individual consumers either by directly eliciting this information or unobtrusively observing their behavior over time. To the extent that the ICDA is designed to perform in real-time, complex and detailed algorithms that operate on comprehensive databases are (currently) unrealistic. Therefore, when designing such tools, developers must balance the efficacy of the algorithm with its need to react quickly during interactions with consumers. Below, we discuss a few common approaches and algorithms; however, an exhaustive account of ICDA designs is beyond the scope of this chapter.[3]

At a simple level, an interactive decision aid could be a list or matrix of product information that the consumer is able to interact with by changing the way that the list is sorted or the matrix is organized. The previously discussed mysimon.com allows for this type of functionality. Another example would be Apple's iTunes music store that provides a list of the day's top downloaded songs, which the user can refine by genre. The shopping carts used by most online stores would also fall into this category of simple ICDAs. At a more general level, the comparison matrix used in Häubl and Trifts' (2000) experimental shopping environment is an example of this type of decision aid.

More sophisticated ICDAs attempt to develop an understanding of a particular consumer's preferences and make recommendations to him or her based on that understanding. There are many potential approaches to modeling consumers' preferences for the purpose of identifying products that match these preferences. In general terms, we can classify these methods as having either an individual or collaborative consumer focus (Ariely et al. 2004). In both cases, ICDA designers employ models that are aimed at maximizing the attractiveness (i.e., utility) of the recommended products to the consumer (Murthi and Sarkar 2003). Those ICDAs that focus primarily on the *individual consumer* use behavioral observations (e.g., click-stream search data or purchase histories) and/or explicitly elicited responses (e.g., attribute rankings or ratings) to develop a model of a consumer's preferences. In these cases, the ICDA makes its recommendations based on an underlying multi-attribute utility function of the target consumer without (necessarily) taking into account the preferences of other consumers. Statistical methods that are common to this type of ICDA include conjoint analysis, ideal point models, and regression models (including logit models), among others. Myproductadvisor.com, which operates on the basis of the individual responses to a series of questions that are designed to elicit relevant attribute preference information, is one example of this type of

---

[3] Readers interested in more detailed descriptions of different types of ICDAs, recommendation agents and recommender systems are directed, as a starting point, to Adomavicius and Tuzhilin (2005) and Montaner et al. (2003).

approach. For an offline example, we can look to the Metro Group's store of the future, which makes wine recommendations based on food selected by the shopper and its database of well-matched wine-food pairings.

Another general category of approaches to ICDA design is known as *collaborative filtering*. This technique works by comparing information about the target consumer to other consumers that are similar based on previous behavior and/or stated preference information. Recommendations can then be made by identifying products that similar consumers have purchased (or searched for) and that the target consumer has not purchased (or searched for). Amazon.com's personalized recommendations are based on such a process. In a simple collaborative filtering approach, the recommendation will be generated using a weighted sum of similar people's preferences, with similar people identified through a cluster analysis. In a more advanced form, the underlying model may use sophisticated statistical techniques (e.g., Bayesian preference models, neural networks, latent class segmentation, classification and regression trees, etc.) and include a broader set of input information (e.g., stated preferences, preferences of similar consumers, expert evaluations, attribute information, etc.; see, e.g., Ansari et al. 2000).

3.1.6 Goals for Agent Design

Regardless of the underlying preference architecture of the ICDA, or the role that it is playing, West et al. (1999) argued that agents should be designed with three goals in mind: (1) to improve decision quality; (2) to increase customer satisfaction; and (3) to develop trust by acting in the best interest of the consumer. Initial research results suggest that ICDAs have the potential to successfully achieve each of these objectives.

3.1.6.1 Improving Decision Quality

A traditional axiom in consumer decision making research has been that to improve decision making quality, one has to increase the amount of effort expended. However, it has been demonstrated that, with ICDA assistance, consumers are often able to increase the quality of the decisions that they make while simultaneously decreasing the effort required to make these decisions (Todd and Benbasat 1999; Diehl et al. 2003; Häubl and Trifts 2000). For example, Häubl and Trifts (2000) conducted a large-scale experiment to examine the benefits to consumers of using an ICDA to shop for a backpacking tent and a mini stereo system in an online store.

These authors used two measures of decision quality. First, the share of consumers who chose one of six products that had been designed to be objectively superior to all other available products was 93 percent when an ICDA was available and only about 65 percent without such assistance. The second measure of decision quality was based on a switching task. After completing their shopping trips, subjects were given an opportunity to switch from their original choice in each product category to one of several attractive alternatives, all of which had already been available on the preceding shopping trip. Switching was taken as an indication of the (poor) quality of a subject's initial purchase decision. While 60 percent of the consumers who had shopped without ICDA assistance changed their choice of product, only 21 percent of those who had received ICDA assistance switched.

In addition, research suggests that the presence of personalized product recommendations enables consumers to make purchase decisions with significantly less effort than would be required otherwise. Häubl and Trifts (2000) measured consumers' search effort on a shopping trip as the number of products for which a detailed description was inspected. They found that, on average, consumers looked at the detailed descriptions of only 6.6 products when they were assisted by an ICDA, while those who shopped without such assistance inspected an average of 11.7 alternatives. This finding is consistent with the notion that reducing the effort required to make a decision is a primary motivation for using a recommendation agent, which has become widely accepted both in the field of consumer research (e.g., Alba et al. 1997; Diehl et al. 2003; Swaminathan 2003; West et al. 1999) and more generally in the literature on decision support systems (e.g., Todd and Benbasat 1999).

3.1.6.2 Increasing Consumer Satisfaction

A second goal for ICDAs that assist human shoppers is to improve consumer satisfaction. One way to do this is to create a system that is responsive to the consumer's personal preferences, and that can create or identify products that closely match these preferences (West et al. 1999). This notion fits well with the desire of marketers to interact with customers on a one-to-one basis (Blattberg and Deighton 1991; Haeckel 1998; Peppers et al. 1999). The potential to leverage the internet, and large databases of customer information, to provide personalized products and services promises a new level of intimacy between buyers and sellers (Alba et al. 1997; Häubl et al. 2003; Wind and Rangaswamy 2001; West et al. 1999). In terms of consumer satisfaction, Bechwati and Xia (2003) provided empirical evidence that interacting with an ICDA can have a positive influence. Specifically, these authors demonstrated that consumers' satisfaction with the search process is positively associated with their perception of the amount of effort that an ICDA is able to save them.

Another important component of increasing satisfaction with the buying process is limiting the monotonous or menial tasks associated with making a purchase and increasing the pleasure that consumers associate with using an ICDA. Again, the empirical evidence suggests that ICDAs are capable of improving consumers' level of enjoyment during the purchase process (Urban and Hauser 2003). Related results indicate that ICDAs are capable of automating many aspects of decision making that consumers prefer to avoid – e.g., tasks that are tedious or otherwise unpleasant – during the process of buying or selling (e.g., Häubl and Trifts 2000; Maes et al. 1999; West et al. 1999). In other words, a well-designed ICDA not only improves the quality of consumer decision outcomes, but it also makes the process of deciding a more pleasurable one.

3.1.6.3 Developing Trust

The ability to engender consumer trust is another important design component for ICDAs. To be effective, it is commonly believed that ICDAs should become trusted advisors (e.g., Häubl and Murray 2006; Trifts and Häubl 2003; Urban, Sultan and Qualls 2000; West et al. 1999). Initial evidence suggests that consumers are willing to place a considerable amount of trust in an ICDA. For example, in a recent study, consumers who received product recommendations from an ICDA were twice as likely to choose the recommended product as consumers who shopped without such assistance (Senecal and Nantel 2004). Moreover, these authors found that product recommendations by ICDAs were more influential than those provided by human experts.

Similarly, Urban and Hauser (2003) found that customers trusted a virtual advisor that assisted them in making automobile purchase decisions by an 8-to-1 margin over automobile dealers, and that they would be more likely to purchase a vehicle recommended by an ICDA by a 4-to-1 margin over one recommended by an automobile dealer. Moreover, in the same study, consumers indicated that they would be willing to pay for the advice provided by an ICDA over and above the cost of the car. As was the case with the goals of decision quality and consumer satisfaction, empirical evidence has emerged to suggest that ICDAs are capable of becoming trusted advisors.

3.1.6.4 Other Benefits of Interactive Consumer Decision Aids

In addition to demonstrating that ICDAs are capable of meeting the initial goals of improving decision quality and customer satisfaction, as well as engendering consumer trust, a number of articles have reported other benefits of such assistance. For example, it is possible for ICDAs to lead consumers to pay lower prices (Diehl et al. 2003). In practice, an internet shopbot that searches for the lowest price for a particular product or service is a common form of ICDA.

It has also been shown that ICDAs that allow a company to "listen in" during the consumer decision making process have the potential to benefit both the firm providing the ICDA and the consumer using the ICDA. This process involves the firm recording and analyzing the conversation between the ICDA and the consumer as a purchase decision is being made. Research in this area indicates that listening in can provide companies with a substantial advantage in the product development process by improving their understanding of consumers' preferences and identifying "new high-potential unmet-need segments" (Urban and Hauser 2003). Similarly, it has been argued that firms should be able to substantially improve their relationships with consumers if they can use technology to become advocates for their customers (Trifts and Häubl 2003; Urban 2004) and provide products that better match customers' preferences (e.g., Wind and Rangaswamy 2001).

3.2 Barriers to the Successful Adoption of ICDA Technology

The initial visions for a new world of buyer-seller interaction have yet to materialize. While it has been demonstrated that ICDAs are capable of providing valuable assistance to consumers in terms of improving decision quality, increasing satisfaction, developing trust, lowering price, improving product design, and reducing decision making effort (even automating portions of the process), ICDAs have not come to dominate internet shopping and they have almost no presence in the offline world. It seems that the initial consumer response to much of what ICDAs have to offer has been: "No Thanks" (Nunes and Kambil 2001). Although somewhat surprising given the benefits of ICDAs discussed above, this finding is consistent with the more general consensus that decision support systems tend to be used far less often than anticipated by their proponents (Adelman 1992; McCauley 1991). In addition, ICDAs have been far less effective in real-world settings than laboratory tests would have predicted (O'Connor et al. 1999; Yates et al. 2003). As a starting point, it is likely that the successful adoption of these tools will require consumers to perceive that ICDAs offer a clear advantage relative to unassisted decision making.

One reason that ICDA adoption has not lived up to its potential may be that the criteria that a consumer uses to assess the quality of a decision are different from the criteria used by the ICDA. For instance, the ICDA and the consumer do not necessarily agree on what constitutes a good decision. In fact, research suggests that consumers define decision quality in multi-faceted ways, which differ between people and within the same people at different times (Yates et al. 2003). ICDAs, on the other hand, tend to define decision quality the same way, or in a highly constrained set of ways, for all decisions and decision makers. Therefore, while the system makes recommendations or provides information consistent with a good decision, where decision quality is defined by, say, X+Y, decision makers will sometimes use X+Y and sometimes just X, or Y+Z, or just Z. As a result, although the system is "assisting" in a manner that is consistent with the outcome it believes the consumer desires, the consumer will often be looking for a different outcome and find assistance that is inconsistent with that outcome unhelpful.

This can be especially problematic to the extent that the ICDA makes recommendations that clearly contradict the consumer's preferences. Under such circumstances, the consumer may not only reject the recommendation, but may react against the recommender. When this happens consumers are more likely to be dissatisfied with the process, and possibly the ICDA, and they are more likely to choose something different from the recommended alternative than if they had received no recommendation at all (Fitzsimons and Lehmann 2004).

Another problem, recently articulated by Simonson (2005), is that because preferences tend to be highly context dependent and constructive in nature (Bettman et al. 1998), it is difficult to elicit reliable information that can be used to make effective recommendations. If the preference information that the ICDA bases its recommendations on is unstable and/or unreliable, the ability of the ICDA to be effective is reduced considerably.

The lack of compelling incentives – perceived or real – for consumer to use ICDA systems, and for firms to create such tools, is also a barrier to the wide-spread adoption of ICDA technologies. For consumers, there are two major issues. The first of these is *privacy*. To make intelligent individual-level recommendations, the ICDA has to know something about the consumer. This means that the tool must compile some information about the consumer by observing (and recording) behavior, and/or it must explicitly elicit information from the consumer about his or her preferences. Ignoring, for the moment, the fact that there is some doubt that the tool is able to effectively elicit preferences (Simonson 2005), it is not clear that consumers are willing to provide accurate preference information even if they could.

Of course, the ability of the ICDA to engender trust may, to some degree, alleviate this problem. However, it is likely that in any particular instantiation of an ICDA, the tool will be a "double agent" (Häubl and Murray 2006). That is, the tool works on behalf of the consumer based on the parameters built into it by its designers (e.g., Alba et al. 1997; Lynch and Ariely 2000). The objectives, and economic incentives, of these designers – many of whom may themselves be vendors – are not necessarily aligned with those of the consumer. To the extent that this leads to suboptimal or unsatisfactory decisions, the ICDA is likely to lose credibility and consumer trust (Fogg 2003). If this, in turn, results in a decrease in the consumer's willingness to share personal information, then the ability of the ICDA to perform effectively will be reduced further.

The second major concern for consumers is *ease of use*. According to the Technology Acceptance Model (Davis 1989), there are two key determinants of information technology acceptance: perceived usefulness and perceived ease of use. Usefulness is defined as the extent to which a technology is viewed as being advantageous in some way. For example, a car navigation system is useful if it helps drivers find their destination and a price search engine is useful if it helps consumers find the lowest price for a product they desire. However, even if people believe that a technology will substantially improve their performance, they will still not adopt it if it is too difficult to use. In other words, if the costs of using a technology outweigh the benefits, the technology will not be accepted.

The incentives for firms can be equally controversial as many current ICDAs are, in essence, price search engines. As a result, participating by providing information to the ICDA may not be very attractive. If cooperating with an ICDA means that the firm is forced to compete primarily on price, there may be a strong incentive to avoid such cooperation. In addition, it is not clear that all products are designed to compete in a marketplace where consumers are able to efficiently and effectively match their preferences to the available products.

In fact, some products may benefit from consumers' inability to accurately screen and evaluate the available alternatives.

Consumer decisions about investment and savings products are an example of this. Research suggests that most consumers struggle to understand even the most basic criteria for choosing between the different financial products that are available to them. For example, Benartzi and Thaler (2001) demonstrated that a common strategy for making investment allocation decisions is to use what they call "naïve diversification" or a "1/n" strategy. Investors using this approach divide their investments equally among the alternatives available to them – e.g., if there are ten funds available in their pension plan, 10% will be allocated to each one. Therefore, the proportion of their portfolio that is allocated to stocks depends on how many stock funds are part of the plan, rather than how much an investor should put into equities to achieve the outcome s/he desires.

Furthermore, many of the investment products that are purchased by consumers are dominated by superior alternatives. For example, the vast majority of mutual funds that are sold to consumers underperform – i.e., provide returns lower than – a corresponding index fund (Bazerman 2001; Bogle 1994). Yet, "the mutual fund industry is among the most successful recent financial innovations. In aggregate, as of 2001, mutual funds held assets worth $11.7 trillion or 17% of our estimate of the 'primary securities' in their national markets" (Khorana et al. 2005, p. 145). According to Bazerman (1999, 2001), much of this success has been driven by the fund industry's ability to capitalize on "investor biases – including overconfidence, optimism, failure to understand regression to the mean, and vividness (2001, p. 502)." To the extent that an ICDA would eliminate, or at least reduce, such biases in consumer decision making, and lead consumers away from underperforming or dominated products, some sellers would have a disincentive to participate.

Another set of problems arises when consumers are faced with the choice of which decision aid to use. Even if consumers and firms are willing and able to effectively provide useful information to an ICDA, and individually the tools are easy to use, choosing a decision aid adds another level of complexity to the decision process. Now the consumer not only has to make a purchase decision, s/he must also decide which decision aid to use to do so. Moreover, selecting the wrong ICDA can result in poor product choices (Gershoff et al. 2001).

The empirical evidence on ICDAs suggests that such tools have the potential be very advantageous to consumers in a number of ways that are generally considered to be important in the buying decision process – i.e., they have the potential to be very useful. However, they may not be useful to the extent that the human and the ICDA have different notions of what constitutes a good decision, or if the tool is unable to develop a meaningful understanding of the consumer's preferences. In addition, the tool may not be perceived as easy to use if the recommendations incite psychological reactance, or if obtaining assistance requires an additional decision of what tool to use, or if using the tool itself is more difficult than making an unassisted decision. In fact, viewed through this lens, it is clear that, although there is great potential for ICDAs, better theory and principles for design are required to make them acceptable to, and adoptable by, consumers. In the remainder of this chapter, we will briefly outline areas for new ICDA research that we believe have the potential to alleviate (or solve) many of the problems that have been identified, and in so doing substantially improve the probability that the next generation of ICDAs will be accepted by consumers.

3.3 Building Better ICDAs: Opportunities for Future Research

The accuracy and effectiveness of the assistance provided by an ICDA is directly affected by the quality of the information provided to it. For instance, if the tool's algorithm bases its recommendations on the preference information it elicits from the consumer, the quality of the advice depends critically on the quality of that input. Therefore, we suggest that the next generation of ICDAs consider incorporating a broader range of information. In this regard, it may help to elicit more than merely preference information, and to incorporate other, potentially more stable and reliable consumer inputs. For example, research has suggested that incorporating information on consumers' under-lying values may lead to better recommendations and decisions (Keeney 1994). ICDAs may also need to take a more active tutor role and teach consumers how to make good decisions (Keeney 2004; West et al. 1999). By doing so, these tools may be able to improve the quality of the inputs they collect and, as a result, the efficacy of the assistance they provide. Whether (and how) ICDAs can fulfill this role is a potentially fruitful area for future research.

In addition, it may be helpful to design ICDAs that are capable of long-term interactions with individual consumers. Building tools that provide recommenda-tions to millions of consumers using a single approach, and expecting all (or even most) of those people to be satisfied with the output, may be unrealistic. Instead, we suggest that creating ICDAs that learn from their experiences with a particular consumer over time, and adapt their approach based on this learning, may improve the quality of their recommendations to that individual. Initial evidence in this area indicates that different algorithms can be either more or less effective under different conditions, and that feedback is an important component of ICDA effectiveness (Ariely et al. 2004). Nevertheless, much more research is needed that examines the potential for interactions between ICDAs and humans over extended periods of time. It would be especially interesting to better under-stand how long-term interaction might help alleviate some of the other problems with ICDAs identified in this chapter – e.g., input solicitation and preference discovery, incentives for consumers (privacy concerns), and minimizing psycho-logical reactance against unsolicited or inappropriate recommendations.

It is also worth noting that our current definitions of ICDA effectiveness, including what constitutes the quality of the assistance provided, are relatively crude and could benefit from further refinement. Establishing measures of how well an ICDA is performing would go a long way towards building trust with consumers and providing an incentive for participation. As a starting point, it may be useful to consider metrics that measure consumer satisfaction, decision quality, decision efficiency, frequency of use and the importance of decisions that the ICDA is relied upon to assist the consumer with. From the firm's perspective, it would be worth knowing what consumers are willing to pay for ICDA support. In addition, sellers would be interested in financial metrics such as the return on investment of building, or providing information to, an ICDA. While the impact of search-cost-reducing technology on consumer price sensitivity has received some attention in the literature (e.g., Diehl et al. 2003; Iyer and Pazgal 2003; Lynch and Ariely 2000), the factors that affect sellers' incentives to participate in ICDAs are not well understood at this time.

A related area that can benefit significantly from additional rigorous research is the "design space" for ICDAs – i.e., what are the critical dimensions that we need to focus on when constructing effective decision support systems for consumers? For example, at what level of specificity should the understanding of consumers' preferences be represented? Is there (sufficient) value in ICDAs knowing an individual consumer's values, lifestyle, personal goals, budget constraints, etc. to justify collecting and storing such information? There are many opportunities for technology-based systems to provide assistance to consumers – e.g., the automated gathering, filtering, analysis, presentation, and storage of information about market offerings, as well as the provision of interactive decision assistance and expert advice, to name just a few. However, an important question is what the critical areas are in which consumers require and/or desire such assistance the most?

Similarly, we currently know very little about how consumers would like to interact with ICDAs. For example, to what extent should such systems act autonomously and when should they interact with consumers? The development of "interaction protocols," or an ICDA "etiquette," based on sound principles from decision research and human-computer interaction, might significantly enhance both the actual and the perceived usability of these tools. Along the same lines, there is an interesting body of research that examines the social nature of the interactions between humans and computers that has the potential to inform the design of ICDAs for long-term relationships with consumers (e.g., Moon and Nass 1996; Nass et al. 1996). To the extent that consumers' interactions with ICDAs are less like market research surveys (or, worse, interrogations) and more like conversations with a friend or trusted advisor, the easier they will be to use. In turn, as the ease of use of ICDAs increases, consumers will become more likely to adopt such technologies (Davis 1989). Most of the work in this area to date has focused on laboratory studies that require a participant to use an ICDA, which has allowed researchers to examine the consequences of human-ICDA interaction. Further research aimed at examining the decision to use (or not use) an ICDA in the first place, as well as the key determinants of consumers' ICDA choices, is clearly warranted.

More effective, successful and widely adopted ICDAs may also require a change in the approach that firms take to their relationships with consumers. Persuading consumers to buy the firm's products, whether or not they represent the best fit to their personal preferences, will be much more challenging in a world where ICDAs filter out alternatives that do not closely match a consumer's preferences. Instead, firms may have to play more of an advocate role. For example, Urban (2004) argues that in response to increasingly knowledgeable consumers, innovative companies will have to try a non-traditional approach: they will have to "provide customers with open, honest, and complete information – and then find the best products for them, even if those offerings are from competitors ... if a company advocates for its customers, they will reciprocate with their trust, loyalty and purchases – either now or in the future (p. 77). " This perspective is very consistent with the broader notion that "marketing should be less about representing the company to the customer and more about representing the customer to the company" (Sheth and Sisodia 2005, p. 161). What we have proposed in this chapter, in terms of the design of advanced decision aids for consumers and the ensuing transformation of how firms and consumers interact with each other, is clearly an ambitious agenda. However, it is one that we believe offers a number of exciting areas for future research in marketing decision modeling.

Acknowledgments The authors gratefully acknowledge the research funding provided by the Social Sciences and Humanities Research Council of Canada. This work was also supported by the F.W.P. Jones Faculty Fellowship held by Kyle B. Murray and the Canada Research Chair in Behavioral Science and the Banister Professorship in Electronic Commerce held by Gerald Häubl.

References

Abowd, G.D., E.D. Mynatt, T. Rodden. 2002. The Human Experience [of ubiquitous computing]. *Pervasive Computing* **1**(1) 48–57.

Adelman, L. 1992. *Evaluating Decision Support and Expert Systems*. Wiley, New York, NY.

Adomavicius, G., A. Tuzhilin. 2005. Toward the Next Generation of Recommender Systems: A Survey of the State-of-the-Art and Possible Extensions. *IEEE Transactions on Knowledge and Data Engineering* **17**(6), 734–749.

Alba, J., J.G. Lynch, B. Weitz, C. Janiszewski, R. Lutz, A. Sawyer, S. Wood. 1997. Interactive Home Shopping: Consumer, Retailer, and Manufacturer Incentives to Participate in Electronic Marketplaces. *Journal of Marketing* **61**(3) 38–53.

Ansari, A., S. Essegaier, R. Kohli. 2000. Internet Recommendation Systems. *Journal of Marketing Research* **37**(3) 363–375.

Ariely, D., J.G. Lynch, M. Aparicio. 2004. Learning by Collaborative and Individual-Based Recommendation Agents. *Journal of Consumer Psychology* **14**(1&2) 81–95.

Bakos, J.Y. 1997. Reducing Buyer Search Costs: Implications for Electronic Marketplaces. *Management Science* **43**(12) 1676–1692.

Baumeister, R., K. Vohs. 2003. Willpower, Choice and Self-Control. G. Loewenstein, D. Read, R. Baumeister, *Time and Decision*. Russell Sage Foundation, New York, NY.

Bazerman, M.H. 1999. *Smart Money Decisions*. Wiley, New York, NY.

Bazerman, M.H. 2001. Consumer Research for Consumers. *Journal of Consumer Research* **27**(4) 499–504.

Bechwati, N.N., L. Xia. 2003. Do Computers Sweat? The Impact of Perceived Effort of Online Decision Aids on Consumers' Satisfaction with the Decision Process. *Journal of Consumer Psychology* **13**(1&2) 139–148.

Benartzi, S., R.H. Thaler. 2001. Naïve Diversification Strategies in Defined Contribution Saving Plans. *American Economic Review* **91**(1) 79–98.

Bettman, J.R., M.F. Luce, J.W. Payne. 1998. Constructive Consumer Choice Processes. *Journal of Consumer Research* **25**(3) 187–217.

Blattberg, R.C., J. Deighton. 1991. Interactive Marketing: Exploiting the Age of Addressability. *Sloan Management Review* **22**(1) 5–14.

Bogle, J.C. 1994. *Bogle on Mutual Funds*. Irwin, New York, NY.

Borland, J. 1998. Move Over Megamalls, Cyberspace is the Great Retailing Equalizer. *Knight Ridder/Tribune Business News*. April 13, 1998.

Botti, S., S.S. Iyengar. 2006. The Dark Side of Choice: When Choice Impairs Social Welfare. *Journal of Public Policy & Marketing* **25**(1) 24–38.

Brynjolfsson E., M.D. Smith. 2000. Frictionless Commerce? A Comparison of Internet and Conventional Retailers. *Management Science* **46**(4) 563–585.

Carmon, Z., K. Wertenbroch, M. Zeelenberg. 2003. Option Attachment: When Deliberating Makes Choosing Feel like Losing. *Journal of Consumer Research* **30**(1) 15–29.

Davis, F.D. 1989. Perceived Usefulness, Perceived Ease of use, and User Acceptance of Information Technology. *MIS Quarterly* **13**(3) 319–340.

Deci, E.L. 1975. *Intrinsic Motivation*. Plenum Press, New York, NY.

Deci, E.L. 1981. *The Psychology of Self-Determination*. Heath, Lexington, MA.

Deci, E.L., R.M. Ryan. 1985. *Intrinsic Motivation and Self-Determination in Human Behavior*, Plenum Press, New York, NY.

Diehl, K., L.J. Kornish, J.G. Lynch. 2003. Smart Agents: When Lower Search Costs for Quality Information Increase Price Sensitivity. *Journal of Consumer Research* **30**(1) 56–71.

Fitzsimons, G.J., D.R. Lehmann. 2004. Reactance to Recommendations: When Unsolicited Advice Yields Contrary Responses. *Marketing Science* **23**(1) 82–94.

Fogg, B.J. 2003. *Persuasive Technology: Using Computers to Change What we Think and Do*. Morgan Kaufmann Publishers, San Francisco, CA.

Friedman, T.L. 1999. Amazon.You. *New York Times*, February 26, p. A21.

Gershoff, A.D., S.M. Broniarczyk, P.M. West. 2001. Recommendation or Evaluation? Task Sensitivity in Information Source Selection. *Journal of Consumer Research* **28**(3) 418–438.

Glass, D.C., J.E. Singer. 1972a. *Stress and Adaptation: Experimental Studies of Behavioral Effects of Exposure to Aversive Events*. Academic Press, New York, NY.

Glass, D.C., J.E. Singer. 1972b. *Urban Stress*. Academic Press, New York, NY.

Greenwald, A.R., J.O. Kephart. 1999. Shopbots and Pricebots. *Proceedings of the 16th International Joint Conference on Artificial Intelligence (IJCAI-99)*.

Haeckel, S.H. 1998. About the Nature and Future of Interactive Marketing. *Journal of Interactive Marketing* **12**(1) 63–71.

Häubl, G., K.B. Murray. 2006. Double Agents: Assessing the Role of Electronic Product-Recommendation Systems. *Sloan Management Review* **47**(3) 8–12.

Häubl, G., K.B. Murray, V. Trifts. 2003. Personalized Product Presentation: The Influence of Electronic Recommendation Agents on Consumer Choice. A. Rangaswamy, N. Pal, *The Power of One: Gaining Business Value from Personalization Technologies*, Trafford, Victoria, BC, 144–163.

Häubl, G., V. Trifts. 2000. Consumer Decision Making in Online Shopping Environments: The Effects of Interactive Decision Aids. *Marketing Science* **19**(1) 4–21.

Hoeffler, S, D. Ariely, P. West, R. Duclos. 2006. Preference Exploration and Learning: The Role of Intensiveness and Extensiveness of Experience. *Organizational Behavior and Human Decision Processes* **101**(2) 215–229.

Hoyer, W.D. 1984. An Examination of Consumer Decision Making for a Common Repeat Purchase Product. *Journal of Consumer Research* **11**(3) 822–829.

Iyengar, S.S., M.R. Lepper. 2000. When Choice is Demotivating: Can One Desire too Much of a Good Thing? *Journal of Personality and Social Psychology* **79**(6) 995–1006.

Iyer, G., A. Pazgal. 2003. Internet Shopping Agents: Virtual Co-location and Competition. *Marketing Science* **22**(1) 85–106.

Johnson, E.J., S. Bellman, G.L. Lohse. 2003. Cognitive Lock-in and the Power Law of Practice. *Journal of Marketing* **67**(2) 62–75.

Johnson, E.J., W.W. Moe, P.S. Fader, S. Bellman, G.L. Lohse. 2004. On the Depth and Dynamics of Online Search Behavior. *Management Science* **50**(3) 299–308.

Kahneman, D., A. Tversky. 1984. Choices, Values, and Frames. *American Psychologist* **39** 341–350.

Keeney, R.L. 1994. Creativity in Decision Making with Value-Focused Thinking. *Sloan Management Review* **35**(4) 33–41.

Keeney, R.L. 2004. Making Better Decision Makers. *Decision Analysis* **1**(4) 193–204.

Khorana, A., H. Servaes, P. Tufano. 2005. Explaining the Size of the Mutual Fund Industry Around the World. *Journal of Financial Economics* **78**(1) 145–185.

Langer, E.J., J. Rodin. 1976. The Effects of Choice and Enhanced Personal Responsibility for the Aged: A Field Experiment in an Institutional Setting. *Journal of Personality and Social Psychology* **34**(2) 191–198.

Lynch, J.G., D. Ariely. 2000. Wine Online: Search Costs Affect Competition on Price, Quality and Distribution. *Marketing Science* **19**(1) 83–103.

Maes, P., R.H. Guttman, A.G. Moukas. 1999. Agents that Buy and Sell. *Communications of the ACM* **42**(3) 81–91.

Mandel, N., E.J. Johnson. 2002. When Web Pages Influence Choice: Effects of Visual Primes on Experts and Novices. *Journal of Consumer Research* **29**(2) 235–245.

McCauley, C. 1991. Selection of National Science Foundation Graduate Fellows: A Case Study of Psychologists Failing to Apply what they know About Decision Making. *American Psychologist* **46** 1287–1291.

Mick, D.G., S.M. Broniarczyk, J. Haidt. 2004. Choose, Choose, Choose, Choose, Choose, Choose, Choose, Choose: Emerging and Prospective Research on the Deleterious Effects of Living in Consumer Hyperchoice. *Journal of Business Ethics* **52**(2) 207–211.

Montaner, M., B. Lopez, J.L. de la Rosa. 2003. A Taxonomy of Recommender Agents on the Internet. *Artificial Intelligence Review* **19**(4) 285–330.

Moon, Y., C. Nass. 1996. How 'Real' are Computer Personalities? Psychological Responses to Personality Types in Human-Computer Interaction. *Communication Research* **23**(6) 651–674.

Murray, K.B., R. Chandrasekhar. 2006. Home Depot Canada: Renovating strategy. Ivey Business School Case Study. Ivey Publishing, London, ON.

Murray, K.B., G. Häubl. 2007. Explaining Cognitive Lock-In: The Role of Skill-Based Habits of Use in Consumer Choice. *Journal of Consumer Research* **34**(1) 77–88.

Murthi, B.P.S., S. Sarkar. 2003. The Role of the Management Sciences in Research on Personalization. *Management Science* **49**(10) 1344–1362.

Nass, C., B.J. Fogg, Y. Moon. 1996. Can Computers be Teammates? *International Journal of Human-Computer Studies* **45**(6) 669–678.

NTT. 2006. Press Release: Actual proof experiment of the Autonomous Operational type Service Robot [http://www.ntt.com].

Nunes, P.F., A. Kambil. 2001. Personalization? No Thanks. *Harvard Business Review* **79**(4) 109–112.

O'Connor, A.M., A. Rostom, V. Fiset, J. Tetroe, V. Entwistle, H. Llewellyn-Thomas, M. Holmes-Rovner, M. Barry, J. Jones. 1999. Decision Aids for Patients Facing Health Treatment or Screening Decisions: Systematic Review. *British Medical Journal* **319** 731–734.

Payne, J.W., J.R. Bettman, E.J. Johnson. 1993. *The Adaptive Decision Maker*. Cambridge University Press, Cambridge, UK.

Payne, J.W., J.R. Bettman, D.A. Schkade. 1999. Measuring Constructed Preferences: Towards a Building Code. *Journal of Risk and Uncertainty* **19**(1–3) 243–270.

Peppers, D., M. Rogers, B. Dorf. 1999. Is your Company Ready for One-to-One Marketing? *Harvard Business Review* **77**(1) 151–160.

Perlow, L.A. 1999. The Time Famine: Toward a Sociology of Work Time. *Administrative Science Quarterly*, **44**(1) 57–81.

Perlow, L.A., G.A. Okhuysen, N.P. Repenning. 2002. The Speed Trap: Exploring the Relationship Between Decision Making and Temporal Context. *Academy of Management Journal* **45**(5) 931–955.

Rotter, J.B. 1966. Generalized Expectancies for Internal Versus External Locus of Control of Reinforcement. *Psychological Monographs* **80** 1–28.

Rust, R.T., D.V. Thompson, R.W. Hamilton. 2006. Defeating Feature Fatigue. *Harvard Business Review* **84**(2) 98–107.

Schulz, R., B.H. Hanusa. 1978. Long-Term Effects of Control and Predictability-Enhancing Interventions: Findings and Ethical Issues. *Journal of Personality and Social Psychology* **36**(11) 1194–1201.

Schwartz, B. 2005. *The Paradox of Choice: Why More is Less*. Harper Collins, New York, NY.

Schwartz, B., A. Ward, J. Monterosso, S. Lyubomirsky, K. White, D. Lehman. 2002. Maximizing Versus Satisficing: Happiness is a Matter of Choice. *Journal of Personality and Social Psychology* **83**(5) 1178–1197.

Senecal, S., J. Nantel. 2004. The Influence of Online Product Recommendations on Consumers' Online Choices. *Journal of Retailing* **80**(2) 159–169.

Sheth, J.N., R.S. Sisodia. 2005. A Dangerous Divergence: Marketing and Society. *Journal of Public Policy & Marketing* **24**(1) 160–162.

Shugan, S.M. 1980. The Cost of Thinking. *Journal of Consumer Research* **7**(2) 99–111.

Simon, H.A. 1955. A Behavioral Model of Rational Choice. *Quarterly Journal of Economics* **69**(1) 99–118.

Simon, H.A. 1957. *Models of Man*. Wiley, New York, NY.

Simonson, I. 2005. Determinants of Customers' Responses to Customized Offers: Conceptual Framework and Research Propositions. *Journal of Marketing* **69**(1) 32–45.

Stigler, G.J., G.S. Becker. 1977. De gustibus non est disputandum. *American Economic Review* **67**(2) 76–90.

Swaminathan, V. 2003. The Impact of Recommendation agents on Consumer Evaluation and Choice: The Moderating Role of Category Risk, Product Complexity, and Consumer Knowledge. *Journal of Consumer Psychology* **13**(1&2) 93–101.

Taylor, S. E. 1989. *Positive Illusions: Creative Self-Deception and the Healthy Mind*. Basic Books, New York, NY.

Taylor, S.E., J.D. Brown. 1988. Illusion and Well-Being: A Social Psychological Perspective on Mental Health. *Psychological Bulletin* **103**(2) 193–210.

Thompson, D.V., R.W. Hamilton, R.T. Rust. 2005. Feature Fatigue: When Product Capabilities Become too Much of a Good Thing. *Journal of Marketing Research* **42**(4) 431–442.

Todd, P., I. Benbasat. 1999. Evaluating the Impact of DDS, Cognitive Effort, and Incentives on Strategy Selection. *Information Systems Research* **10**(4) 356–374.

Trifts, V., G. Häubl. 2003. Information Availability and Consumer Preference: Can Online Retailers benefit from Providing Access to Competitor Price Information? *Journal of Consumer Psychology* **13**(1&2) 149–159.

Urban, G. L. 2004. The Emerging Era of Customer Advocacy. *Sloan Management Review* **45**(2) 77–82.

Urban, G.L., J.R. Hauser. 2003. 'Listening in' to Find Unmet Customer Needs and Solutions. *MIT Sloan School Working Paper No. 4276–03* [available at SSRN: http://ssrn.com/abstract=373061 or DOI: 10.2139/ssrn.373061].

Urban, G.L., F. Sultan, W.J. Qualls. 2000. Placing Trust at the Center of Your Internet Strategy. *Sloan Management Review* **42**(1) 39–48.

Weiser, M. 1991. The Computer for the 21st Century. *Mobile Computing and Communications Review* **3**(3) 3–11.

Weiser, M. 1993. Some Computer Science Issues in Ubiquitous Computing. *Communications of the ACM* **36**(7) 75–84.

West, P.M., D. Ariely, S. Bellman, E. Bradlow, J. Huber, E.J. Johnson, B. Kahn, J. Little, D. Schkade. 1999. Agents to the Rescue? *Marketing Letters* **10**(3) 285–300.

Wind, J., A. Rangaswamy. 2001. Customerization: The Next Revolution in Mass Customization. *Journal of Interactive Marketing* **15**(1) 13–32.

Yates, J.F., E.S. Veinott, A.L. Patalano. 2003. Hard Decisions, Bad Decisions: On Decision Quality and Decision Aiding. S.L. Schneider, J. Shanteau, *Emerging Perspectives on Judgment and Decision Research*. Cambridge University Press, Cambridge, 13–63.

Yoffie, D.B. 2005. Wal-Mart 2005. *Harvard Business School Case*. Harvard Business School Publishing, Boston, MA.

Part III

Marketing Mix Models

Chapter 4
Advertising Models

Peter J. Danaher

4.1 Introduction

Advertising is ubiquitous in our society. Television, newspaper, magazine, radio and internet advertisements of commercial messages are part of our daily lives. Moreover, not all advertisements contain commercial messages. There are also public service announcements, in particular, for not-for-profits like World Vision and the Red Cross. Event sponsorship and direct marketing through the mail are also methods used to reach and influence consumers. All these forms of advertising have received attention by modelers in the past 40 years. Early work focused on how advertising affects sales or market share, and the relative importance of advertising in the marketing mix (see Leeflang et al. 2000 for a review). No doubt this was motivated by anxiety that advertising might have no effect on sales. Having verified that advertising can positively influence sales (Clarke 1976; Leone and Schultz 1980), subsequent effort when into developing models that could optimize the allocation of an advertising budget. Early efforts in media selection decisions drew heavily from the operations research field, with models using linear, goal and dynamic programming methods (see a review by Rust 1986). As the number of media vehicles in television, print and radio increased, models were developed to assist with media scheduling decisions. Issues here include the placement and length of ads, whether they should be pulsed, flighted or continuous (Mahajan and Muller 1986; Naik et al. 1998; Simon 1982).

With the widespread availability of scanner data in the grocery industry in the past 20 years, advertising effects were revealed to be much smaller than those observed for price promotions (Cooper and Nakanishi 1988, pp. 178–180; Hanssens et al. 2001, pp. 210–211; Tellis 1988). A huge shift in marketing budgets led to more funds being allocated 'below the line' to trade promotions rather than 'above the line' advertising. In the past 10 years, however, a number

P.J. Danaher
Coles Myer Chair in Marketing and Retailing, Melbourne Business School,
University of Melbourne, Australia
e-mail: p.danaher@mbs.edu

B. Wierenga (ed.), *Handbook of Marketing Decision Models*,
DOI: 10.1007/978-0-387-78213-3_4, © Springer Science+Business Media, LLC 2008

of studies (e.g., Ehrenberg et al. 1994; Mela et al. 1997) have shown that price promotions have strong short term effects, inducing brand switching and category expansion (Van Heerde et al. 2003), but the brand switching effects do not result in long-term changes in brand loyalty. In contrast, Mela et al. (1997) show that advertising has a small short-term effect, but a much larger long-term effect on brand loyalty. This finding, combined with the widespread belief that firms must invest in brand building (Keller 1998), has resulted in the pendulum swinging back towards advertising, especially in the past 5 years. Furthermore, in the last 8 years, the new internet medium has gained ground as a legitimate advertising medium, but some issues remain in terms of it comparability with existing media (Smith 2003). So, as with most economic cycles, advertising has had its ups and downs in the past. In the last three years there has been steady growth in advertising spend, following a slump in advertising subsequent to the internet stock market crash of 2000 (Demers and Lev 2001).

A number of concerns about advertising exist today, and will worsen over the next decade, that impact on advertising effectiveness and therefore the relevant modeling agenda. These concerns are:

1. accurately gauging the effectiveness of advertising at generating sales or market share response
2. decreasing television viewing to major networks which reduces the ability to reach a mass audience
3. increasing advertising avoidance by consumers
4. an increasing number of available marketing communication channels.

In a business environment where many industries are maturing domestically and facing increased competition globally, firms are looking to save costs wherever they can. Recently, the spotlight has fallen on advertising due to the difficulty of measuring its effectiveness and ROI (Srivastava and Reibstein 2005). Part of this stems from an old-fashioned view that advertising's sole purpose is to generate sales or increase market share. However, Allenby and Hanssens (2004) comment that advertising works on many levels besides sales response. Other relevant criteria are offsetting the effects of competitors' advertising, protecting or enhancing price premiums, increasing sales call effectiveness, building distribution, motivating employees, increasing stock price, signaling intentions to competitors and brand equity building. Nonetheless, there is an implicit belief that advertising works (somehow), but managers outside the marketing domain are seeking stronger assurances than they've received in the past. In this challenging environment for advertising, rigorous models demonstrating the effectiveness of advertising are needed more than ever.

The three broad areas where models have been used for business decision making in advertising are: response models; media planning and advertising scheduling and media selection. In this brief chapter we cannot reasonably cover these large topics in depth. Fortunately, there are some very good literature reviews of these topics already, so there is no need to exhibit the entire history of advertising models. Instead, we give brief reviews of key previous models then concentrate on possible models to deal with the new and emerging issues listed above. For example, a new area of growing importance is the selection of media channel(s) in which to advertise.

4.2 Advertising Response Models

Models have been applied to advertising primarily to gauge the sales or market share response to advertising. This is a natural starting point, since advertising expenditures are often large and firms want to be able to assess whether their advertising is successful. Although this seems like a straightforward endeavor, there is no one model that can claim to successfully capture advertising's effect on sales or market share. In this section we mention a few seminal advertising response models, and then refer the reader to several excellent books that summarize the history and breadth of this topic. We also discuss current and future directions for advertising response models.

4.2.1 Advertising in Isolation

Rather than considering advertising as just one of several components in the marketing mix, initial advertising response models considered advertising in isolation, ignoring other marketing instruments, such as price. Much of this work is reviewed by Little (1979), who summarized the following five advertising response phenomena that a model ought to capture: the steady-state response of sales to advertising is concave or S-shaped; upward response is fast, while downward response is slower (hysteresis); advertising by competitors has an impact; advertising effectiveness changes over time; response can decline even when ad spend is constant. Little's own efforts at capturing these phenomena resulted in his *ADBUDG* model (Little 1970), which has the capability to model four of the five phenomena directly. The effect of competitive advertising is captured indirectly by lowering the own-response parameter when competitors advertise. The functional form of the *ADBUDG* model is

$$MS_t = \text{long\_run\_minimum} + \text{persistence} \times [MS_{t-1} - \text{long\_run\_minimum}]$$

$$+ (a - b)\frac{\text{Adv}_t^c}{d + \text{Adv}_t^c}, \tag{4.1}$$

where MS_t is the market share of a product at time t, long_run_minimum is the share after the prolonged absence of advertising, persistence is the percentage of share retained when advertising is stopped for one period and Adv_t is the advertising level in dollars or gross rating points. Parameters a through d are determined by a method Little (1970) called 'decision calculus', whereby a manager has to make an informed judgement about sales or share for various levels of advertising, different from the current 'maintenance spend'.

Equation (4.1) is a dynamic model, having great flexibility. For example, if $0 < c < 1$, a concave response function results, but is S-shaped[1] if $c > 1$. Increased advertising by competitors can be accommodated by increasing d, which lowers the response to own-advertising.

4.2.2 Advertising as Part of a Marketing Mix Model

Considering advertising in isolation helps gain an understanding specifically of how advertising works. However, to properly model sales or market share response to advertising, a complete model that also incorporates price, promotion activities and distribution coverage is required. Three excellent books by Cooper and Nakanishi (1988), Hanssens et al. (2001) and Leeflang et al. (2000) review the numerous econometric, fully-specified, advertising response models. One of the most robust aggregate response models is Wittink et al.'s (1988) SCAN*PRO model,[2] which for data aggregated across stores within a market is

$$\text{Sales}_{it} = \left(\prod_{j=1}^{B} (\text{Price}_{jt})^{\beta_{ij}^{\text{Price}}} \right) \left(\prod_{j=1}^{B} (\text{Adv}_{jt})^{\beta_{ij}^{Adv}} \right) \left(\prod_{k=1}^{K} (X_{ikt})^{\beta_{ik}} \right) \exp(u_{it}), \quad (4.2)$$

where Sales_{it} is the geometric mean of sales across all the stores in the market for brand i ($i = 1, \ldots, B$) in week t (i.e., $\text{Sales}_{it} = \left(\prod_{l=1}^{L} \text{Sales}_{ilt} \right)^{1/L}$, with Sales_{ilt} being the quantity sales for brand i in store l), Price_{it} is the corresponding geometric mean of price across all stores, Adv_{it} is some measure of market-level advertising, $(X_{i1t}, \ldots, X_{iKt})$ are a set of K promotion covariates, such as the occurrence of feature and display activity and u_{it} is a random disturbance term.

A very attractive feature of this model is that the own and cross elasticities are obtained directly from the regression coefficients $\beta_{ij}^{\text{Price}}$, β_{ij}^{Adv} and β_{ik}. For instance, β_{ii}^{Adv} corresponds to the own-brand advertising elasticity for brand i. Equation (4.2) can be linearized by taking the log of both sides and then fit by OLS. Christen et al. (1997) show there is no aggregation bias when sales and price data across stores are aggregated with the geometric mean and a multiplicative model, as in Equation (4.2), is used. With the widespread availability of weekly scanner data, models such as Equation (4.2) have demonstrated that advertising elasticities are smaller than for price and promotion, by some magnitude (see Clarke 1976; Leone and Schultz 1980; Little 1975; Lodish

---

[1] A key issue imbedded in here is the shape of the advertising response curve. Is it S-shaped (implying threshold effects) or concave (implying diminishing returns)? Simon and Arndt (1980) come out in favor of concave, but recent work by Vakratsas et al. (2004) shows this may not be the case – due to a censoring effect of the observed data.

[2] The full SCAN*PRO model also allows for seasonality and data disaggregated to the store level. The model in Equation (4.2) is for data aggregated to the market level.

et al. 1995; Assmuss et al. 1984). For instance, price elasticities are of the order −2 to −3, while advertising elasticities typically range between 0.01 and 0.4. However, this does not mean that advertising is less profitable than other marketing instruments (Jones 1990; Mela et al. 1997), since price promotions may generate rapid increases in sales, but have a lower per-unit revenue.

Equation (4.2) is a good general-purpose aggregate advertising response model that uses time series data at either the store or market level. Due to its flexibility, this model has been strongly endorsed by Christen et al. (1997), Cooper and Nakanishi (1988), Telser (1962) and Wittink (1977).

With the advent of panel data in the 1980s, models using data at the individual level, such as the multinomial logit (Guadagni and Little 1983), have become popular as response models for the marketing mix. Although individual-level data might seem to be more informative, Allenby and Hanssens (2004) point out that the most managerially relevant research on advertising response is at some aggregate (usually market) level. Moreover, Allenby and Rossi (1991) find that advertising response models at the aggregate level generally do not suffer from aggregation bias. Hence, models such as Equation (4.2) are still extremely useful, despite their age.

The topic of endogeneity in marketing models has received renewed attention in recent years (see, e.g., Villas-Boas and Winer 1999). Endogeneity might arise in advertising response models due to future advertising spend depending on current or expected future sales. This issue was examined some time ago by Bass and Parsons (1969) and Parsons and Bass (1971), who used a simultaneous equation method, but with advertising examined in isolation. Danaher et al. (2008) use instrumental variables in a complete marketing mix model, where advertising is one of the instruments. Recent developments in econometrics that deal with simultaneously determined variables, such as sales response and advertising expenditure, have emerged (see, e.g., Yang et al. 2003). Such models add rigor to the advertising response modeling and will become increasingly important.

Other possible enhancements to Equation (4.2) are the inclusion of lagged dependent variables, or permitting the error term to be autoregressive. This is done to capture possible carryover effects (Rossiter and Danaher 1998), which means that advertising has both short- and long-term effects. Dekimpe and Hanssens (1995) develop a VAR model that is capable of measuring long-term advertising effects.

4.2.3 Modeling Advertising Interference

With increasing competitiveness among firms and a proliferation of media channels, consumers are being bombarded with growing levels of advertising clutter (Chunovic 2003). The irony is that advertisers' response to this has been to advertise even more, leading to escalation in advertising (Metwally 1978). Burke and Srull (1988) and Keller (1987; 1991) have shown that advertising by competitors reduces the advertising recall and purchase intentions for a focal brand. What is uncertain is how this so called 'competitive advertising interference' affects sales.

A recent study by Bonfrer et al. (2007) finds that advertising elasticity and therefore sales are attenuated by advertising interference. That is, if a focal firm is advertising and their competitors are simultaneously advertising, the lift in sales for the focal firm is lower than it would have been if it had advertised by itself. This has widespread implications for previous advertising research, much of which has examined only the focal brand's advertising and often found little or no effects (e.g., Lodish et al. 1995). The advertising may well be effective, but its *observed* effectiveness is diminished by the presence of high levels of competitive interference. Hence, models can be used to find ways to enhance the advertising effectiveness of a focal brand by scheduling ads away from their competitors' advertising. A potential game theory approach could be used here. An upshot of this is that media planners need to do a better job of avoiding advertisements by their competitors. With that in mind, we now turn to the topic of media planning.

4.2.4 Advertising Tracking Models

Due to the frequent difficulty of linking advertising to sales, an alternative measure of advertising effectiveness is ad awareness. Awareness is usually measured as the proportion of a target group who claim to have seen a particular brand's advertisement in a recent time period. Oftentimes, the product category is prompted and sometimes the actual brand name, a process known as 'aided recall'. Pioneering work by Brown (1985, 1991) shows how Millward Brown's proprietary Advanced Tracking Program (ATP) model can accurately predict the downstream awareness from an advertising campaign. Their model can be used to help managers decide what level of advertising is required to maintain or achieve a target awareness level.

Validation for using advertising awareness is provided by Hollis (1995), who shows that awareness and sales are highly correlated, but Rossiter and Percy (1997, p. 608) cast some doubt on this. Since Millward Brown's model is proprietary little is known about the actual model, but some academic work by Naik et al. (1998) and West and Harrison (1997) has used awareness tracking data. For example, Naik et al. (1998) find that awareness declines due to both copy wearout and repetition wearout, whereby ads are shown too often and for too long. Knowledge of such wearout can help managers decide when to change their ad copy as well as how to improve their media planning.

4.3 Media Planning Models

There is a long history of probability models being used for estimating media exposure distributions, particularly the television and print media (Chandon 1986; Leckenby and Kishi 1982; Rust 1986; Danaher 1992). Such models are required by media planners for audience estimates, such as *reach*, being the proportion of the target group exposed to an advertisement at least once; *frequency*, the average number of exposures among those reached; GRPs, the average number of exposure (with GRPs = reach × frequency); and the *exposure distribution* (ED), the proportion of the target audience exposed to none, just one, just two, etc., ads. Models have also been used to estimate 'reach curves' which translate GRPs into reach, that is, they estimate the reach obtained for a given GRP purchase.

Exposure distribution models fall into three classes, *ad hoc*, simulation and stochastic. Excellent literature reviews of the historical development of exposure distribution models are given by Broadbent (1966), Chandon (1986) (who compared 47 different models), Danaher (1992), Gensch (1973), Leckenby and Kishi (1982) and Rust (1986). Danaher (1989a) additionally discusses several simulation methods. Some new model-based methods are reviewed by Danaher (1992) and we will look at these in more detail below. In this section we discuss some modeling ideas for univariate through to multivariate exposure distributions.

4.3.1 Models for Vehicle Exposure

Let X_1 and X_2 denote the exposures a person has to two separate media vehicles, and let $X = X_1 + X_2$ be the total exposures to both these vehicles. Although X is a simple sum of random variables, two non-ignorable correlations make modeling it difficult (Danaher 1989b, 1992). One is the intra-vehicle correlation due to repeat reading/viewing to the same media vehicle (Danaher 1989b; Morrison 1979) and the other is inter-vehicle correlation, where there might be an overlap (i.e., duplication) in exposure to two vehicles.

Reading, listening or viewing loyalty to a media vehicle is common (Barwise and Ehrenberg 1988) and this gives rise to 'lumpiness' in the observed exposure distribution (Danaher 1992). Despite the lumpiness of many observed print media exposure distributions, in particular, the most popular model used to estimate total exposures is one based on a smooth beta-binomial distribution, commonly attributed to Metheringham (1964). The mass function of the beta-binomial distribution (BBD) is

$$f(X = x) = \binom{k}{x} \frac{\Gamma(\alpha + \beta)}{\Gamma(\alpha + \beta + k)} \frac{\Gamma(\alpha + x)}{\Gamma(\alpha)} \frac{\Gamma(k - x + \beta)}{\Gamma(\beta)}, \qquad (4.3)$$

where $X = 0, \ldots, k$ and α and β are parameters to be estimated. The advantages of the beta-binomial model are that it is relatively simple to estimate and requires only readily available survey data for model fitting. While it is an excellent model for one media vehicle (Chandon 1986; Rust 1986), Danaher (1992) demonstrates its limitations for two or more magazines due to the lumpiness mentioned earlier.

Now, generalizing to a multivariate setting, a formal statement of the exposure distribution set-up is as follows. Let X_i be the number of exposures a person has to media vehicle i, $X_i = 0, 1, 2, \ldots k_i, i = 1, \ldots, m$, where m is the number of different vehicles. The exposure random variable to be modeled is $X = \sum_{i=1}^{m} X_i$, the total number of exposures to an advertising schedule.

In the case of print media, observed empirical exposure distributions are known to be particularly lumpy due to strong intra-vehicle correlation. As a consequence, Danaher (1988, 1989b, 1991a) shows that it is necessary to firstly model the joint multivariate distribution of $(X_1, X_2, \ldots, X_m)$, from which the distribution of total exposures can be derived. This is less of a problem with television exposure distributions (Rust 1986) where loyalty from episode to episode is generally moderate, with intra-exposure duplication factors of the order 0.28 (Ehrenberg and Wakshlag 1987). In addition, for the television environment there are more vehicle choices than for the print medium (Krugman and Rust 1993) and this helps to reduce both intra- and inter-vehicle correlation. As a result, models for just X, like the beta-binomial, rather than the full multivariate $(X_1, X_2, \ldots, X_m)$ are often adequate for television exposure distributions, which tend to be smooth (Rust and Klompmaker 1981).

A reasonably robust model for multivariate exposure distributions that captures both the intra- and inter-vehicle correlations is Danaher's (1991a) canonical expansion model. It is a generalization of Goodhardt and Ehrenberg's (1969) 'duplication of viewing law', having mass function

$$f(X_1, X_2, \ldots, X_m) = \left\{ \prod_{i=1}^{m} f_i(X_i) \right\} \left[1 + \sum_{j_1 < j_2} \rho_{j_1, j_2} \frac{(x_{j_1} - \mu_{j_1})(x_{j_2} - \mu_{j_2})}{\sigma_{j_1} \sigma_{j_2}} \right], \qquad (4.4)$$

where $f_i(X_i)$ is the univariate distribution for vehicle i, which could be a beta-binomial distribution, ρ_{j_1, j_2} is the correlation between any pair of vehicles, and μ_j and σ_j are the mean and standard deviation of the number of exposures for vehicle j. The final model for the total number of exposures is obtained from the multivariate model in the following way:

$$f_X(x) = \sum_{\{(x_1, \ldots, x_m): x_1 + \cdots + x_m = x\}} f(X_1, X_2, \ldots, X_m), \qquad x = 0, 1, 2, \ldots k_T. \qquad (4.5)$$

Danaher (1991a) demonstrates that the canonical expansion model predicts better than all other models across a range of media vehicles. We also give an example in Section 4.4.2

4.3.2 Media Exposure Models for the Internet

In this subsection we review the relatively few previous efforts at developing media exposure models in the online environment. With the availability of large panels of internet users, it is unclear that models are even required for internet ad campaigns. Hence, we also justify why and where advertising models are required for online media.

4.3.2.1 Previous Page View and Internet Advertising Models

We note at the outset that it is important to distinguish between banner ads and a rapidly growing form of online advertising revenue, namely, paid search advertising (IAB 2006). Paid search advertising is the primary source of revenue for Google.com and Yahoo.com, for example. Current internet models thus far are best suited to the situation where banner ads are placed on a website, but can accommodate sponsored links, since they are conveyed by pages served up to web users, who may view the links then click on them. The platform for a model of internet advertising reach and frequency is a model for website page views. To the best of our knowledge, only two page view models exist, the first being a multivariate discretized version of the Tobit model, developed by Li et al. (2002). Their use of the Tobit model is justified because a large proportion of web users do not visit particular sites, creating a 'spike' at zero page views for each website. In addition, page views are nonnegative integers, so the Tobit must be 'discretized'. Lastly, Li et al. (2002) recognize the need to allow for correlations in page views across different website categories so they generalize the univariate Tobit model to one that has a multivariate normal distribution. They apply their model to page views of comScore Media Metrix data, but their primary purpose is to uncover patterns in browsing behavior across categories of websites like auction and portal sites and test the effects of user demographics on such browsing, rather than predicted the audience for an online ad campaign. Still, their model can be adapted to predicting internet reach and frequency if required.

The second page view model is one developed by Danaher (2007). As will be seen later, Danaher (2007) shows that for a single website an appropriate model is the negative binomial distribution (NBD). For more than one website, Danaher (2007) uses a Sarmanov distribution (Park and Fader 2004) to create a multivariate NBD (MNBD). Details on the Sarmanov distribution and how it can combine several univariate models into a combined multivariate model are given in Section 4.5.1. In a rigorous validation exercise, Danaher's (2007) MNBD model performs extremely well, doing better than proprietary commercial models in terms of prediction accuracy. It also performs better than Li et al. (2002) multivariate discretized Tobit model.

4.3.2.2 Internet Advertising Models

To date only two proprietary and two nonproprietary models have been developed specifically for online advertising. Each has its shortcomings, being either a lack of accuracy or the model does not address factors unique to the internet that do not arise in traditional media.

The first proprietary model for reach and frequency prediction is Nielsen/ Netratings' WebRF model, which uses individual-level data from their netratings panel to build an empirical exposure distribution (www.netratings.com). Telmar have a very similar model, named WebPlanner, that uses comScore instead of Nielsen panel data (www.us.telmar.com). The second proprietary model is one developed by Atlas DMT (www.atlasdmt.com), which combines site centric ad server information with comScore Media Metrix panel data (Smith 2003). No technical details about this model are available, except that it is based on a simulation method, although Chandler-Pepelnjak (2004) reports that the average prediction error for reach for this model is 20%. Danaher (2007) demonstrates that this is much higher than the 5% average prediction error for his MNBD model.

Of the two previous nonproprietary studies of internet advertising models, the most comprehensive is Leckenby and Hong's (1998) study, with Wood's (1998) model essentially being a curve-fitting method rather than a formal model. Leckenby and Hong compare some well known models from offline media, such as the beta-binomial distribution (BBD) (Metheringham 1964), the Dirichlet-multinomial (Leckenby and Kishi 1984) and Hofmans' (1966) model, with some lesser-known models, like the Kim (1994) correlated BBD and the sequential aggregation model (Chandon 1986). To use these models Leckenby and Hong (1998) had to artificially aggregate the panel-based website exposure data in such a way so as to force it into the same format as that used in offline media. For example, over a two-week period Leckenby and Hong (1998) aggregate the exposure data into two successive one-week periods and panelists are classified as being potentially exposed just once, twice or not at all across the 2 weeks. Hence, if someone visits the same site every day in the 2-week period (as might happen with their internet service provider), they are classified as having been exposed just twice instead of 14 times. Indeed, in a 2 week period a person can visit the same site any number of times, so it is somewhat unnatural to enforce a 'one week rule' where multiple exposures to the same site are counted only once.

Rather than restricting the number of exposures to coincide with a pre-specified time period, a more appropriate model should allow each person's exposure level to range from zero to infinity. Such a requirement is demanded by the internet, where there is varying exposure opportunity per website visitor. This exposure variation does not occur for offline media, where the broad-caster/publisher has control over the exposure delivery. For this reason, Danaher (2007) suggests using a univariate NBD for a single website, and then makes use of the Sarmanov (1966) distribution to combine several NBDs to handle the multivariate situation.

In recent years, Nielsen/Netratings and comScore Media Metrix have enlarged their panels to the point where a model is seemingly redundant. In particular, the comScore Media Metrix dataset now comprises one million panelists, which allows an advertiser to accurately compile an empirical expo-sure distribution to an internet ad campaign, comprising the entire panel as well as demographic subgroups. Indeed, empirical distributions are the basis of Nielsen's WebRF and Telmar's WebPlanner models. Danaher (2007) shows that the *real* challenge for internet media models is not to estimate the reach and frequency for a historical dataset, since the availability of large panels enables reach and frequency to be estimated empirically with high accuracy. Instead, the pertinent problem is to *predict* the reach and frequency for a time period in the future, based on historical data. None of the models considered by Leckenby and Hong (1998), for example, are adaptable to the predictive environment. Furthermore, Danaher (2007) demonstrates that simple, yet robust, empirical estimates of reach and frequency based on historical data do not perform as well as his MNBD model when predicting future audience sizes. We now detail the subtle challenges that arise in online reach and frequency prediction that do not arise with offline media, thereby demonstrating the need for a model.

4.3.2.3 Why Is a Model Necessary for Internet Ad Exposure?

For online media to be accepted by advertisers and advertising agencies, online publishers must also be able to apply traditional media language, particularly GRPs, to their medium (Meskauskas 2003). However, when it comes to online advertising there is a fundamental difference between the way advertising space is bought compared with offline media. The primary difference is that online campaigns are often purchased on the basis of 'ad impressions'. An online ad impression is some form of advertisement (e.g., banner, interstitial, pop-up, etc.) that is served to a website's user during the course of their visit. A typical online ad campaign might comprise 50,000–200,000 ad impressions (http://computer.howstuffworks.com/banner-ad.htm). While a user is surfing a particular website they download different pages depending on the links they click. As each page is assembled, advertisements are added to the page by the site's server. Each page served could have different ads embedded within it. However, the more pages a user requests the more likely they are to receive several exposures to the same ad, especially if they visit the site multiple times over several weeks.

To illustrate the difference between reach and frequency for traditional and online media, Table 4.1 gives a hypothetical example for a television commercial that is broadcast three times during a 1-hour period of *Monday Night Football*. Consider a small sample of ten people, some of whom watch *Monday Night Football* for this one-hour period. Assume that if they are watching the game then they are exposed to all three insertions (or, more precisely, have the opportunity to see each insertion). The online campaign has a banner ad placed on ebay.com for 1 week. The banner ad is served up for every 6th page viewed by a user. Hence, someone who views 30 pages on ebay.com is potentially exposed to the banner ad 5 times. Table 4.1 gives the banner ad exposure pattern for a different sample of 10 people.

Table 4.1 Hypothetical example of exposure pattern to separate TV and internet ad campaigns

TV Campaign		Internet Campaign	
Person	Ads seen	Person	Ad impressions
1	3	1	
2		2	
3		3	2
4	3	4	
5		5	
6		6	7
7		7	
8	3	8	
9		9	
10		10	
Reach = 3/10 = 30%		Reach = 2/10 = 20%	
Frequency = (3+3+3)/3 = 3		Frequency = (2+7)/2 = 4.5	
GRPs = (3/10)*(3)*100 = 90		GRPs = (2/10)*(4.5)*100 = 90	

The difference between the TV and web campaigns is that for TV each person reached has exactly the same number of exposures (namely, 3), whereas web users differ in their ad consumption (being 2 and 7 for the two people that visit the site). For television, the network controls the frequency of advertisement delivery, while for online campaigns the delivery frequency is determined by the user. Notice that both campaigns have GRPs of 90, but the TV campaign has higher reach, at 30%. By contrast, the online campaign has lower reach (20%) but higher frequency, at 4.5 ads per person reached.

An advertiser delivering 3 insertions to those watching a TV show, for a total of 90 GRPs, can correctly calculate the reach to be $90/3 = 30\%$ (since GRPs = reach × frequency). However, an online advertiser buying 9 ad impressions (the equivalent of 90 GRPs for the example in Table 4.1) has no idea what proportion of people will be reached because visitors to the site do not have the same number of ad impressions. For instance, one person might receive all 9 impressions, resulting in a reach of 10%, or 9 people might receive 1 impression each, for a campaign reach of 90%. That is, there is variation in the impression frequency at the individual level. Therefore, for a purchase of a fixed number of internet GRPs there is no way of accurately determining reach, since the frequency is not fixed for each person. A model is required to firstly capture this variation in frequency and secondly to enable a media planner to predict the reach and frequency for alternative GRP levels. For instance, suppose in Table 4.1 that we want the campaign to have 120 GRPs instead of 90. For TV all that is required is to increase the number of insertions from 3 to 4 and the reach stays at 30%. For an internet campaign with a purchase of 12 ad impressions (i.e., 120 GRPs), there are many possible combinations of impressions at the individual level that can result in 120 total GRPs, but most have a different reach from the original campaign. One possibility is that

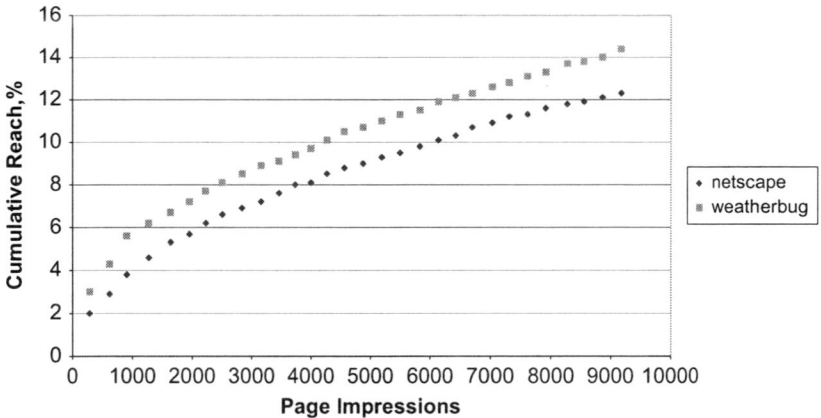

Fig. 4.1 Cumulative Reach for Netscape.com and Weatherbug.com

person 1 has five impressions where they previously had none. In this case the reach increases from 20 to 30%, while the frequency decreases to 4.

Figure 4.1 further illustrates this problem for two actual websites, weatherbug.com and netscape.com. It shows the build in reach for a sample of 5000 comScore Media Metrix panelists for the month of September 2002. It is evident that for the same level of page impressions, the cumulative reach for weatherbug.com is always higher than for netscape.com. This is consistent with what is expected of visitors to a weather site, who typically check the weather at approximately regular intervals, viewing only one or two pages each time. In this case a page served up to a visitor has a good chance of hitting a new user, thereby enhancing reach. On the other hand, the portal, netscape.com, probably has a moderate-sized group of loyal users who consume a disproportionate number of page impressions. The average number of page impressions among visitors to weatherbug.com and netscape.com are, respectively, 1.8 and 3.0, which is consistent with weatherbug.com attracting 'shallow' visitors, while netscape.com's unique visitors are fewer in number, but they view more pages.

Estimating the audience for an internet advertising campaign is further complicated by issues such as possibly having multiple ads per page, ads on just the homepage and frequency capping, whereby websites limit the number of ads served to a computer by using cookies. Handling these issues requires data not just from the page server, but also the ad server. User centric web browsing data (such as the comScore Media Metrix used by Li et al. 2002 and Danaher 2007) has only page views and no record of ads served. Hence, Danaher (2007) models page views/impressions, which are conceptually similar to ad impressions, since all ads are served on web pages. If an advertiser is fortunate enough to additionally have data on the advertising regime, then the 'ad view data' simply replaces the page view data. For example, suppose an advertiser arranges for their ad to be displayed on every third page served to a website visitor. If a visitor is served 18 pages on their domain visit we can adjust the raw data from 18 page views to 6 ad views. Danaher's (2007) model is flexible enough to accommodate ad views/impressions, page views and even clicks, where clicks on banner ads are counted rather than page views or advertising impressions.

A further reason for developing a model is to help optimize media spend. As with other media, advertisers often want to maximize reach or some function of the ED for a fixed budget (Little and Lodish 1969; Rust 1986). It is usually much quicker to employ a model to estimate the reach for millions or billions of alternative advertising schedules than to conduct a complete enumeration by obtaining a reach estimate from the raw data for each schedule. We look at media exposure optimization in Section 4.4.

4.3.3 Advertising Exposure Model

Up until now, media planners have implicitly assumed that an exposure to a media vehicle implies exposure to the advertisements carried by the vehicle. Of course, this is highly unlikely, so a common terminology used in the advertising industry, in particular for television, is that an advertisement carried by a media vehicle offers an opportunity to see (OTS). With the increasing prevalence of ad avoidance technology like TiVo, future media planning models will have to handle *advertising* exposure instead of *vehicle* exposure (Danaher 1995). To date, no such models have been developed. We now consider how such a model might be developed.

4.3.3.1 Single-Vehicle Ad Exposure Model

Consider for the moment a single media vehicle and let X be the number of vehicle exposures, or OTS's, $X = 0, 1, 2. \ldots, k$. Now denote Y as the number of *advertising* exposures $Y = 0, 1, 2. \ldots, k,$ *and* $Y \leq X$. The motivation for the BBD vehicle-exposure model is that each person in the population has a personal probability of an OTS, denoted as P, and P has a beta distribution. Now, $X|P = p \sim bin(k, p)$ is a reasonable assumption for the conditional distribution of the number of exposures given a person's probability of exposure (Sabavala and Morrison 1977). Compounding the binomial and the beta distribution gives rise to the BBD, as given in Equation (4.3).

For advertising, as opposed to vehicle, exposure we might equally assume that each person has a probability P^* of advertisement exposure given vehicle exposure. Then, conditional on P^* and $X = x$ vehicle exposures, $Y|(P^* = p^*, X = x) \sim bin(x, p^*)$. The distribution of $Y|X = x$ is then also BBD if we (reasonably) assume that P^* also has a beta distribution but with different parameters α^* and β^*. Hence, a distribution for advertising exposures is

$$f(Y = y) = \sum_{x=0}^{k} f(Y|X = x) f_X(x), \tag{4.6}$$

where $f_X(x)$ is the BBD in Equation (4.3) and $f(Y|X = x)$ is a BBD with parameters α^* and β^*. This is a reasonably straightforward model. The marginal distribution $f_X(x)$ is easy to estimate, as it is just the usual BBD. The conditional distribution $f(Y|X = x)$ is a bit more challenging since it requires an observed distribution of Y for each level of $X = x$. For example, if $X = 0$ then $Y = 0$ with certainty. If $X = 1$ then $Y = 0$ or $Y = 1$, with respective probabilities $\beta^*/(\alpha^* + \beta^*)$ and $\alpha^*/(\alpha^* + \beta^*)$, and so on.

Using the double expectation formula it is easy to show that for the probability model in Equation (4.6),

$$E[Y] = \frac{k\alpha}{(\alpha + \beta)} \frac{\alpha^*}{(\alpha^* + \beta^*)}, \tag{4.7}$$

In addition, the probability at $Y = 0$ (using Equation (4.6)) is

$$f(Y = y) = \sum_{x=0}^{k} \frac{\Gamma(\alpha^* + \beta^*)}{\Gamma(\alpha^* + \beta^* + x)} \frac{\Gamma(x + \beta^*)}{\Gamma(\beta^*)} f_X(x). \tag{4.8}$$

Now, $f(Y = y)$ can be fit by the method of means and zeros (Anscombe 1950; Goodhardt et al. 1984) using Equations (4.7) and (4.8) or by the method of moments, by equating the sample mean and variance to the parametric formulas (as for $E[Y]$ in Equation (4.7) and var(Y)).

The conditional distribution $f(Y|X = x)$ might require some modifications, since it is conceivable that the more often a person is exposed to a media vehicle carrying the same advertisement, consumer attention wears out (Naik et al. 1998; Rossiter and Danaher 1998). In this situation, ad exposure decreases as vehicle exposure increases, and so P^* depends on X, whereas in model (4.6), it does not.

To obtain a multivariate model for advertising exposure, the Sarmanov distribution can be employed, using the univariate model in Equation (4.6) for each separate media vehicle. The Sarmanov distribution will be discussed in more detail in Section 4.5.

4.4 Advertising Scheduling/Media Selection Models

The media planning models discussed above focus on estimation of the exposure distribution. This is an important first step in media planning. A subsequent step is the allocation of advertising time across different vehicles.

4.4.1 Set Up for Media Scheduling

A typical mathematical set up of an advertising scheduling problem is to maximize target audience reach, subject to a budget constraint. Formally this can be written as follows.

$$\text{Maximize } 1 - f(X = 0), \text{ subject to } 0 \leq X_i \leq k_i \quad \text{and} \quad \sum_{i=1}^{m} c_i X_i \leq B, \quad (4.9)$$

where $X = \sum_{i=1}^{m} X_i$, k_i is a possible upper limit on the number of ad insertions in media vehicle i, c_i is the cost per advertising insertion and B is the total budget.

Initial efforts to solve this problem used operations research methods such as linear programming (Lee and Burkhart 1960; Lee 1962; 1963; Day 1962; Ellis 1966; Brown and Warshaw 1965; Bass and Lonsdale 1966), dynamic programming (Maffei 1960), goal programming (Charnes et al. 1968) and simulation methods (Gensch 1969). The first serious model for combining media planning with advertising scheduling that can be used for decision support was Little and Lodish's (1969) MEDIAC model. Later developments were made by Aaker's (1975) ADMOD and Rust's (1985) VIDEAC models. Also see Danaher's (1991b) review of operations research methods for optimal media placement. Internet media scheduling has been tackled by Lee and Kerbache (2005). All of these models maximize reach or some advertising response function while keeping within an overall advertising budget, as in Equation (4.9). Heuristic optimization methods, like the so-called 'greedy algorithm', have proven popular and surprisingly accurate for optimizing media allocation (Rust 1986; Danaher 1991b).

There have been a number of proprietary commercial software packages developed to optimize advertising scheduling. These include SuperMidas and X-pert (www.wpp.com). None of the proprietary methods have been benchmarked against the published methods, but the widespread uptake of commercial software is evidence that the advertising industry views them as extremely useful (Ephron 1998).

In addition to allocation across media vehicles, Naik et al. (1998) and Dubé et al. (2005) examine optimal timing and placement of commercials, to answer questions regarding flighting, pulsing or continuous advertising. This remains a fruitful area where models can be very useful.

4.4.2 An Example Media Schedule with Optimization

We now give a short example of a media plan. A common target demographic for packaged goods is a household shopper, defined to be the person who does the bulk of the grocery buying in a home. Suppose the advertiser is 'Tide' liquid laundry detergent and they have a budget of $300,000 to spend in the Houston

Table 4.2 Audience and Cost Information for the Example Media Plan*

Program	Rating, %	Cost/Ins, $	CPM
Gray's Anatomy	15.1	35,000	2.3
The Sopranos	14.0	28,000	2.0
Desperate Housewives	14.7	33,000	2.2
American Idol	12.1	27,000	2.2
Lost	9.6	26,000	2.7
ER	14.9	33,000	2.2
Sex and The City	8.2	21,500	2.6
CSI	14.5	33,000	2.3
Boston Legal	6.6	22,000	3.3
Scrubs	4.0	17,000	4.3

* These are realistic but not actual ratings and costs - they are for illustration only.

network television market over a four week period. An initial comparison of the television ratings among all people and those who are household shoppers creates an index showing the suitability of program for a particular target audience (Assael and Poltrack 1991). All of the ten programs in Table 4.2 have indices above 125%, indicating they are suitable for the target audience.

Table 4.2 shows that *Gray's Anatomy* is the top rating program among those eligible for advertising, with *ER* a close second. It also give costs per 30 second commercial slot for each of these programs, from which the cost per thousand (CPM) can be calculated. On a CPM basis, *The Sopranos* and *ER* are the most cost efficient programs, having the lowest CPM. Table 4.2 does not show the duplications among each of the programs, but we can report that many of the pairs of programs do have overlapping audiences, such as *American Idol* and *Lost*. Such pairwise duplications have important implications for determining schedules with high reach or frequency. For instance, higher reach is achieved by selecting vehicles that do not overlap much and vice versa for high frequency schedules (Rossiter and Danaher 1998).

Having selected the initial set of programs it is now necessary to find the mix of programs that maximizes reach or frequency, while keeping within the total budget. For this example we use a simple media model software package, called Media Mania, which is reported in more detail in Rossiter and Danaher (1998). It uses the rating for one episode and the reach over two episodes for each program, plus the pairwise duplications as input to Danaher's (1991) Canonical Expansion model described above.

In this example we employ a feature of the Media Mania software which maximizes the reach or the effective frequency at the 3+ level (i.e., 3 or more exposures), while staying within the budget. Table 4.3 shows the number of insertions that should be in each program to maximize either reach or frequency at the 3+ level (sometimes referred to as effective reach). The difference between the two media plans is very apparent. The reach strategy spreads the commercials over 8 different shows, with no program having more than 2 insertions.

Table 4.3 Optimal media plans for reach and frequency strategies

Program	Reach Strategy Insertions	Frequency Strategy Insertions
Gary's Anatomy	1	5
The Sopranos	1	4
Desperate Housewives	1	0
American Idol	1	0
Lost	1	0
ER	2	0
Sex and The City	0	0
CSI	2	0
Boston Legal	0	0
Scrubs	1	0
Reach at 1+	66.0%	37.9%
Reach at 3+	17.2%	25.0%
Total Cost	$298,000	$287,000
GRPs	128	132

By contrast, the frequency strategy concentrates its commercials into just two programs, with each having multiple insertions.

Figure 4.2 shows a bar chart of the full frequency distribution resulting from the media plans in Table 4.3. It clearly shows that the reach strategy has a much higher 1+ reach, but this switches over at the 3+ frequency level, where the frequency strategy then has a higher audience. The choice between these two media plans depends on the marketing and media objectives. High reach would be desired when the intention is to expose a lot of people just once or twice, with a view to increasing or maintaining awareness. High frequency might be more suitable when the objective is to counter a competitor who is advertising heavily or when the goal is to induce brand switching among those presently loyal to another brand (Rossiter and Danaher 1998).

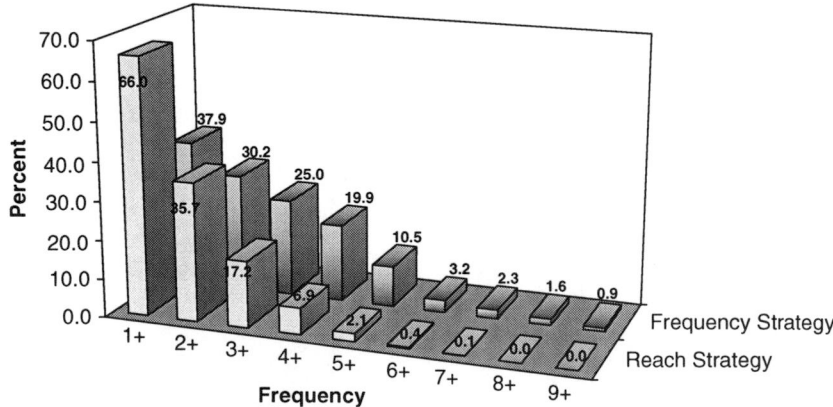

Fig. 4.2 Frequency Distribution for Reach and Frequency Strategies

4.5 Models for Media Channel Selection

Over the past decade there has been a rapid increase in the number of media channels. Even within the television environment, the dominance of the networks has eroded considerably in the face of numerous cable stations (Krugman and Rust 1993). Audiences have fragmented as a result, and this has reduced the ability of TV networks to deliver a mass audience quickly, as they were previously able to. Even more rapid than television channel proliferation, has been the rise of the internet. While advertisers were initially unsure about the effectiveness of the internet (Smith 2003), today ad spend on the web is substantial and sustained (IAB 2006). Other digital communication channels, such as SMS text messaging, have also emerged as possible advertising media.

Up until 10 years ago, it was relatively easy to reach a mass audience with just one medium, but this is becoming increasingly difficult. As a consequence, one of the most pressing advertising issues for today is which portfolio of media is best to achieve maximum effectiveness. To cope with this growing issue, models are required that can assess the relative effectiveness of alternative media, in much the same way that a marketing mix model can assess the relative importance of alternative marketing instruments. To date, very few models have attempted to combine different media. A notable exception is Rust and Leone's (1984) Dirichlet model for combined TV and magazine schedules.

4.5.1 A Model for Mixed Media

A promising model for handling multimedia applications, for media planning at least, is based on the Sarmanov (1966) distribution. The general form of the Sarmanov bivariate distribution for (X_1, X_2) is

$$f(X_1, X_2) = f_1(X_1)f_2(X_2)[1 + \omega\phi_1(x_1)\phi_2(x_2)], \qquad (4.10)$$

where $f_i(X_i)$ is the marginal distribution for random variable X_i and $\phi_i(x_i)$ are called 'mixing functions', with the requirement that $\int\phi_i(t)f_i(t)dt = 0$. Notice that the general form of this bivariate distribution is the product of the marginal distributions, with a 'correction factor' to allow for correlation. Lee (1996) gives a general expression for the correlation between random variables in the Sarmanov distribution. Depending on the marginal distributions, this correlation can be used to estimate ω.

Park and Fader (2004) use the Sarmanov distribution in Equation (4.10) to model the bivariate visit-time distribution between two websites. Danaher (2006) employs the Sarmanov distribution to model web page views across multiple websites. An extraordinary feature of the Sarmanov distribution that makes it suitable in a multimedia environment is that the $f_i(X_i)$ marginal distributions do not have to be the same. For example, to model exposure to websites and TV, $f_1(X_1)$ can be an NBD

(Danaher 2006), while $f_2(X_2)$ can be a BBD (Rust and Klompmaker 1981). The only remaining challenge is to collect data from website/TV pairs to estimate ω. For many disparate media, an assumption of independence might be reasonable, but ought to be tested empirically first. Certainly within the same media, some correlation is expected (Danaher 1992; Ehrenberg and Wakshlag 1987), but across separate media, independence might be reasonably assumed.

For multiple media, the Sarmanov distribution generalizes to

$$f(X_1, X_2, \ldots, X_m) = \left\{ \prod_{i=1}^{m} f_i(X_i) \right\} \left[1 + \sum_{j_1 j_2} \omega_{j_1, j_2} \phi_{j_1}(x_{j_1}) \phi_{j_2}(x_{j_2}) + \ldots \right.$$

$$\left. + \omega_{1,2,\ldots,m} \prod \phi_i(x_i) \right]. \tag{4.11}$$

Equation (4.11) is a series expansion of bivariate, trivariate, up to m-variate terms. Estimating parameters for such a model would require observed multivariate duplications among the m websites. To reduce the number of terms in the multivariate Sarmanov model it is best to truncate Equation (4.11) after just the bivariate or trivariate terms (Danaher 2006). This gives an approximation to the full Sarmanov expansion, with accuracy up to second or third order terms. Expanding only up to the second order means that a multimedia distribution can be estimated with just bivariate (pairwise) information.

4.5.2 Industry Initiatives for Media Channel Selection

The demand for multimedia channel selection methods has primarily come from industry, where marketing managers and advertisers are struggling to reach target consumers and are unsure how to allocate existing marketing budgets across old and new media. Two approaches have been developed thus far. The first was developed in Japan by Video Research Limited (2006). Their model combines different media and estimates the multivariate exposure distribution using Danaher's (1991) canonical expansion model. The canonical expansion model has the capability to juxtapose different media, in much the same way we describe above for the Sarmanov distribution.

The second approach is an empirical method called 'Compose' (Foley et al. 2005). The essence of this technique is to have a large sample of consumers rate seven brand attributes on how important they are when purchasing a product from one of 28 categories, ranging from soda to computer hardware. In turn, each of 26 marketing communication channels are evaluated on the same brand attributes. For example, if trust is a brand attribute that consumers seek when purchasing financial products, then 'Compose' will search through the 26 media channels to determine their ranking on the trust attribute. This is a simple, but intuitively appealing, empirical method for determining channel appropriateness. Further embellishments where models could be employed are channel rankings that incorporate cost, audience size and speed of delivery of the advertising message.

A recent study by Danaher and Rossiter (2006) compares 11 different media in terms of 14 attributes (e.g., trustworthy, reliable, annoying and objectionable). Moreover, it uses hypothetical selling propositions to assess whether or not the advertising channel has any impact on downstream purchase intentions. The results show that products and services advertised via traditional mass media (TV, radio and print), plus paper-based direct media (personally-addressed mail, catalogs and brochures) have higher purchase intentions than when advertised by telephone, email and text messaging. This is true even among young people, who also appear to be conservative in their preferences of media for receiving marketing communications.

4.6 Conclusion

As can be seen from this overview of past and current models used in advertising, there has been much activity. Managers clearly see a use for models and have shown enthusiasm for making them part of their working lives. The topic of advertising response has received the most attention historically and has matured to the point where we can confirm that advertising is generally effective, but does not have as strong an effect as price promotions. Advertising, however, is ideal for long-term growth of a brand. Much of the previous work on advertising response has used data from the grocery industry, particularly scanner data. Models applied to data from the many service industries, such as telecommunications, banks, hotels and airlines would be welcome for future work. When observational studies prove difficult, field experiments should be conducted (e.g., Lodish et al 1995).

Media planning has always required the use of models and the rise of the internet has placed additional demands on models for use in this new medium. The increasing number of media channels has also forced managers and academics to think about the relative importance of different media in achieving advertising objectives. This impacts on advertising budget setting, where the work of Broadbent (1988; 1999) and Lodish (1971) needs to be extended to today's media-rich environment. We can be sure that models will continue to be important in the advertising industry, and academics need to look to industry concerns to help generate a managerially-relevant research agenda.

References

Aaker, D.A. 1975. ADMOD: An Advertising Decision Model. *Journal of Marketing Research* February 37–45.

Allenby, G., D.M. Hanssens. 2004. MSI Advertising Response Steering Group: Discussion Paper", presented at MSI Conference on Future Research Agenda, Atlanta, May 2004.

Allenby, G., P.E. Rossi. 1991. There is No Aggregation Bias: Why Macro Logit Models Work. *Journal of Business and Economic Statistics* **9**(1, January) 1–14.

Anscombe, F.J. 1950. Sampling Theory of the Negative Binomial and Logarithmic Distributions. *Biometrika* **37**(^{3}/$_4$) 358–382.

Assael, H., D.F. Poltrack. 1991. Using Single Source Data to Select TV Programs Based on Purchasing Behavior. *Journal of Advertising Research* **31**(4) 9–17.

Assmus, G., J.U. Farley, D.R. Lehmann. 1984. How Advertising Affects Sales: Meta-Analysis of Econometric Results. *Journal of Marketing Research* **21**(February) 65–74.

Barwise, T.P., A.S.C. Ehrenberg. 1988. *Television and Its Audience*. Sage, London, UK.

Bass, F.M. 1969. A Simultaneous-Equation Regression Study of Advertising and Sales of Cigarettes. *Journal of Marketing Research* **6**(August) 291–300.

Bass, F.M., R.T. Lonsdale. 1966. An Exploration of Linear Programming in Media Selection. *Journal of Marketing Research* May 179–188.

Bass, F.M., L.J. Parsons. 1969. Simultaneous-Equation Regression Analysis of Sales and Advertising. *Applied Economics* **1** 103–124.

Broadbent, S.R. 1966. Media Planning and Computers: A Review of the Use of Mathematical Models in Media Planning. *Applied Statistics* November 240–241.

Broadbent, S.R. 1988. *The Advertiser's Handbook for Budget Determination*. Lexington Books, Lexington, MA.

Broadbent, S.R. 1999. *When to Advertise*. Admap Publications, Henley-on-Thames, Oxfordshire, U.K.

Brown, D.B., M. Warshaw. 1965. An Exploration of Linear Programming in Media Selection. *Journal of Marketing Research* February 83–88.

Brown, G. 1985. Tracking Studies and Sales Effects: A U.K. Perspective. *Journal of the Advertising Research* **25**(1) 52–64.

Brown, G. 1991. Modelling Advertising Awareness. *ADMAP*, April, **1** 25–29.

Burke, R.R., T.K. Srull. 1988. Competitive Interference and Consumer Memory for Advertising. *Journal of Consumer Research* **15**(June) 55–68.

Chandler-Pepelnjak, J. 2004. Forecasting Reach, Frequency and GRPs on the Internet. Atlas Digital Marketing Technologies, www.atlasdmt.com.

Chandon, J.-L.J. 1986. *A Comparative Study of Media Exposure Models*. Garland, New York, NY.

Charnes, W.W., J.K. Cooper, D.B. De Voe, W. Reinecke. 1968. A Goal Programming Model for Media Planning. *Management Science* April 423–430.

Christen, M., S. Gupta, J.C. Porter, R. Staelin, D.R. Wittink. 1997. Using Market-Level Data to Understand Promotion Effects in a Nonlinear Model. *Journal of Marketing Research* **34**(August) 322–334.

Chunovic, L. 2003. Clutter Reaches All-Time High. *Television Week*, May 12, **22**(19) 19.

Clarke, D.G. 1976. Econometric Measurement of the Duration of Advertising Effects on Sales. *Journal of Marketing Research* **18** 345–357.

Cooper, L.G., M. Nakanishi. 1988. *Market Share Analysis: Evaluating Competitive Marketing Effectiveness*. Kluwer Academic Publishers, Boston, MA.

Danaher, P.J. 1988. A Log-Linear Model for Predicting Magazine Audiences. *Journal of Marketing Research* **25**(4, November) 356–362.

Danaher, P.J. 1989a. Simulating Media Exposure Distributions. *Communications in Statistics: Simulation and Computation* **B18**(4) 1381–1392.

Danaher, P.J. 1989b. An Approximate Log-Linear Model for Predicting Magazine Audiences. *Journal of Marketing Research* **26**(4, November) 473–479.

Danaher, P.J. 1991a. A Canonical Expansion Model for Multivariate Media Exposure Distributions: a Generalization of the Duplication of Viewing Law. *Journal of Marketing Research* **28**(3, August) 361–367.

Danaher, P.J. 1991b. Optimizing Response Functions of Media Exposure Distributions. *Journal of the Operational Research Society* **42**(7) 537–542.

Danaher, P.J. 1992. Some Statistical Modeling Problems in the Advertising Industry: A Look at Media Exposure Distributions. *The American Statistician* **46**(4) 254–260.

Danaher, P.J. 1995. What Happens to Television Ratings During Commercial Breaks? *Journal of Advertising Research* **35**(1) 37–47.

Danaher, P.J. 2007. Modeling Page Views Across Multiple Websites With An Application to Internet Reach and Frequency Prediction. *Marketing Science* **26**(3, May/June) 422–437.

Danaher, P.J., J.R. Rossiter. 2006. A Comparison of the Effectiveness of Marketing Communication Channels: Perspectives from Both Receivers and Senders in Consumer and Business Markets, accessed at http://staff.business.auckland.ac.nz/pdanaher.

Danaher, P.J., A. Bonfrer, S. Dhar. (2008). The Effect of Competitive Advertising Interference on Sales for Packaged Goods. *Journal of Marketing Research* **45**(2, May), 211–225.

Day, R.L. 1962. Linear Programming in Media Selection. *Journal of Advertising Research* June 40–44.

Dekimpe, M., D.M. Hanssens. 1995. The Persistence of Marketing Effects on Sales. *Marketing Science* **14**(1) 1–21.

Demers, E., B. Lev. 2001. A Rude Awakening: Internet Shakeout in 2000. *Review of Accounting Studies* **6**(August) 331–359.

Dubé, J.-P., G.J. Hitsch, P. Manchanda. 2005. An Empirical Model of Advertising Dynamics. *Quantitative Marketing and Economics* **3** 107–144.

Ehrenberg, A.S.C., K. Hammond, G.J. Goodhardt. 1994. The After-Effects of Price-Related Consumer Promotions. *Journal of Advertising Research* July/August 11–21.

Ehrenberg, A.S.C., J. Wakshlag. 1987. Repeat-Viewing with People-Meters. *Journal of Advertising Research* February 9–13.

Ellis, D.M. 1966. Building up a Sequence of Optimum Media Schedules. *Operational Research Quarterly* **13**(3) 413–424.

Ephron, E., 1998. Optimizers and Media Planning. *Journal of Advertising Research* **38**(4 (July/August) 47–56.

Foley, T., P. Engelberts, G. Wicken. 2005. Compose: The Art of Channel Planning. *Admap* **467**(December) 3–8.

Gensch, D. H. 1969. A Computer Simulation Model for Selecting Advertising Schedules. *Journal of Marketing Research* May 203–214.

Gensch, D.H. 1973. *Advertising Planning: Mathematical Models in Advertising Media Planning, Amsterdam.*Elsevier Scientific Publishing Company.

Goodhardt, G.J., A.S.C. Ehrenberg. 1969. Duplication of Television Viewing Between and Within Channels. *Journal of Marketing Research* **6**(May) 169–178.

Goodhardt, G.J., A.S.C. Ehrenberg, C. Chatfield. 1984. The Dirichlet: A Comprehensive Model of Buying Behavior. *Journal of the Royal Statistical Society A* **147**(5) 621–655.

Guadagni, P.M., J.D.C. Little. 1983. A Logit Model for Brand Choice Calibrated on Scanner Data. *Marketing Science*, **2**(3 (Summer)) 203–238.

Hanssens, D.M., L.J. Parsons, R.L. Schultz. 2001. *Market Response Models: Econometric and Time-Series Analysis*, 2nd ed., Kluwer Academic Press, Boston, MA.

Hofmans, P. 1966. Measuring the Net Cumulative Coverage of Any Combination of Media. *Journal of Marketing Research* **3**(3) 269–278.

Hollis, N.S. 1995. Like it or Not, Liking is not Enough. *Journal of Advertising Research* September 7–16.

IAB 2006. IAB/PwC Release Full Year 2005 Internet Ad Revenue Figures, 20 April 2006, http://www.iab.net/news/pr_2006_04_20.asp

Jones, J.Philip.1990. The Double Jeopardy of Sales Promotions. *Harvard Business Review* **68**(5) 145–152.

Keller, K.L. 1987. Memory Factors in Advertising: The Effect of Advertising Retrieval Clues on Brand Evaluation. *Journal of Consumer Research* **14**(December) 316–333.

Keller, K.L. 1991. Memory and Evaluation Effects in Competitive Advertising Environments. *Journal of Consumer Research* **17**(March) 463–476.

Keller, K.L. 1998. *Strategic Brand Management: Building, Measuring and Managing Brand Equity*. Prentice Hall, Upper Saddle River, N.J.

Kim, H. 1994. A Conditional Beta Distribution Model for Advertising Media Reach/Frequency Estimation, unpublished doctoral dissertation, University of Texas at Austin.

Krugman, D.M., R.T. Rust. 1993. The Impact of Cable and VCR Penetration on Network Viewing: Assessing the Decade. *Journal of Advertising Research* **33**(January) 67–73.

Leckenby, J.D., J. Hong. 1998. Using Reach/Frequency for Web Media Planning. *Journal of Advertising Research* **38**(January) 7–20.

Leckenby, J.D., S. Kishi. 1982. How Media Directors View Reach/Frequency Estimation. *Journal of Advertising Research* **22**(June) 64–69.

Leckenby, J.D., and S.Kishi. 1984. The Dirichlet-Multinomial Distribution as a Magazine Exposure Model. *Journal of Marketing Research* **21** 100–6.

Lee, A.M. 1962. Decision Rules for Media Scheduling: Static Campaigns. *Operational Research Quarterly* **13**(3) 229–242.

Lee, A.M. 1963. Decision Rules for Media Scheduling: Dynamic Campaigns. *Operational Research Quarterly* **14**(4) 365–372.

Lee, A.M., A.J. Burkhart. 1960. Some Optimization Problems in Advertising. *Operational Research Quarterly* **11**(3) 113–122.

Lee, J., L. Kerbache. 2005. Internet Media Planning: A Optimization Model, Working paper, HEC School of Management, Paris, France.

Lee, M.-L.T. 1996. Properties and Applications of the Sarmanov Family of Bivariate Distributions. *Communications in Statistics: Theory and Methods* **25**(6) 1207–1222.

Leeflang, P.S.H., D.R. Wittink, M. Wedel, P.A. Naert. 2000. *Building Models for Marketing Decisions*. Kluwer Academic Publishers, Boston, MA.

Leone, R.P., R.L. Schultz. 1980. A Study of Marketing Generalizations. *Journal of Marketing* **44**(Winter) 10–18.

Li, S., J.C. Liechty, A.L. Montgomery. 2002. Modeling Category Viewership of Web Users with Multivariate Count Models. GSIA Working Paper #2003-E25, Carnegie Mellon University, http://www.andrew.cmu.edu/user/alm3

Little, J.D.C. 1970. Models and Managers: The Concept of a Decision Calculus. *Management Science* **16**(8), April B466–B485.

Little, J.D.C. 1975. BRANDAID: A Marketing-Mix Model, Part 2: Implementation, Calibration and Case Study. *Operations Research* **23** 656–673.

Little, J.D.C. 1979. Aggregate Advertising Models: the State of the Art. *Operations Research* **27**(4) July–August 629–667.

Little, J.D.C., L.M. Lodish. 1969. A Media Planning Calculus. *Operations Research* **17**(1), January-February, 1–35.

Lodish, L.M. 1971. Considering Competition in Media Planning. *Management Science* **17**(6) B293–306.

Lodish, L.M., M. Abraham, S. Kalmenson, J. Livelsberger, B. Lubetkin, B. Richardson, M.E. Stevens. 1995. How T.V. Advertising Works: A Meta-Analysis of 389 Real World Split Cable T.V. Advertising Experiments. *Journal of Marketing Research* **32**(May) 125–139.

Maffei, R. B. 1960. Planning Advertising Expenditures by Dynamic Programming Methods. *Management Technology* December 94–100.

Mahajan, V., E. Muller. 1986. Reflections on Advertising Pulsing Policies for Generating Awareness for New Products. *Marketing Science* **5**(2) 89–111.

Mela, C.F., S. Gupta, D.R. Lehmann. 1997. The Long-Term Impact of Promotion and Advertising on Consumer Brand Choice. *Journal of Marketing Research* **34**(May) 248–261.

Meskauskas, J. 2003. Reach and Frequency – Back in the Spotlight. iMedia Connection, www.imediaconnection.com, 5 November.

Metheringham, R.A. 1964. Measuring the Net Cumulative Coverage of a Print Campaign. *Journal of Advertising Research* **4**(December) 23–28.

Metwally, M.M. 1978. Escalation Tendencies of Advertising. *Oxford Bulletin of Economics and Statistics* **40**(May) 153–163.

Morrison, D.G. 1979. Purchase Intentions and Purchasing Behavior. *Journal of Marketing* **43**(Spring) 65–74.

Naik, P.A., M.K. Mantrala, A.G. Sawyer. 1998. Planning Media Schedules in the Presence of Dynamic Advertising Quality. *Marketing Science* **17**(3) 214–235.

Park, Y.-H., P.S. Fader. 2004. Modeling Browsing Behavior at Multiple Websites. *Marketing Science* **23**(3 (Summer)) 280–303.

Parsons, L.J., F.M. Bass. 1971. Optimal Advertising-Expenditure Implications of a Simultaneous-Equation Regression Analysis. *Operations Research* **19**(3) 822–831.

Rossiter, J. R., P.J. Danaher. 1998. *Advanced Media Planning*. Kluwer Academic Publishers, Norwell, MA.

Rossiter, J.R., L. Percy. 1997. *Advertising Communications and Promotion Management*, 2nd ed., McGraw-Hill, New York, NY.

Rust, R.T. 1985. Selecting Network Television Advertising Schedules. *Journal of Business Research* **13** 483–494.

Rust, R.T. 1986. *Advertising Media Models: A Practical Guide*. Lexington Books, Lexington, MA.

Rust, R.T., J.E. Klompmaker. 1981. Improving the Estimation Procedure for the Beta Binomial TV Exposure Model. *Journal of Marketing Research* **18**(November) 442–448.

Rust, R.T., R.P. Leone. 1984. The Mixed-Media Dirichlet-Multinomial Distribution: A Model for Evaluating Television-Magazine Advertising Schedules. *Journal of Marketing Research* **21**(February) 89 99.

Sabavala, D.J., D.G. Morrison. 1977. A Model of TV Show Loyalty. *Journal of Advertising Research*. **17**(6) 35–43.

Sarmanov, O.V. 1966. Generalized Normal Correlations and Two-Dimensional Frechet Classes. *Doklady (Soviet Mathematics)* **168** 596–599.

Simon, H. 1982. ADPLUS: An Advertising Model with Wearout and Pulsation. *Journal of Marketing Research* **19**(August) 352–363.

Simon, J.L., J. Arndt. 1980. The Shape of the Advertising Response Function. *Journal of Advertising Research* **20**(August) 11–28.

Smith, D. L. 2003. Online Reach and Frequency: An Update. April, http://www.mediasmithinc.com/white/msn/msn042003.html.

Srivastava, R., D. Reibstein. 2005. Metrics for Linking Marketing to Financial Performance. Marketing Science Institute Report No. 05-200.

Tellis, G.J. 1988. The Price Elasticity of Selective Demand: A Meta-Analysis of Econometric Models of Sales. *Journal of Marketing Research* **25**(November) 331–341.

Telser, L.G. 1962 Advertising and Cigarettes. *Journal of Political Economy*. **70**(October) 471–499.

Vakratsas, D., T. Ambler. 1999. How Advertising Works: What Do We Really Know? *Journal of Marketing* **63**(January) 26–43.

Vakratsas, D., F.M. Feinberg, F.M. Bass, G. Kalyanaram. 2004. The Shape of the Advertising Response Functions Revisited: A Model of Dynamic Probabilistic Thresholds. *Marketing Science* **23**(1) 109–119.

Van Heerde, H.J., S. Gupta, D.R. Wittink. 2003. Is 75% of the Sales Promotion Bump Due to Brand Switching? No, Only 33% Is. *Journal of Marketing Research* **40**(November) 481–491.

Video Research Limited. 2006. Service and Products. http://www.videor.co.jp/eng/products/index.html#analysis.

Villas-Boas, M.J., R.S. Winer. 1999. Endogeneity in Brand Choice Models. *Management Science* **45**(10) 1324–1338.

West, M., J. Harrison. 1997. Bayesian Forecasting and Dynamic Models. Springer, New York, NY.

Wittink, D.R. 1977. Exploring Territorial Differences in the Relationship Between Marketing Variables. *Journal of Marketing Research* **14**(May) 145–155.

Wittink, D.R., M.J. Addona, W.J. Hawkes, J.C. Porter. 1988. SCAN*PRO: The Estimation, Validation and Use of Promotional Effects Based on Scanner Data. Working Paper, Cornell University.

Wood, L. 1998. Internet Ad Buys – What Reach and Frequency Do They Deliver? *Journal of Advertising Research* **38**(January) 21–28.

Yang, S., Y. Chen, G.M. Allenby. 2003. Bayesian Analysis of Simultaneous Demand and Supply. *Quantitative Marketing and Economics* **1** 251–304.

Chapter 5
Sales Promotion Models

Harald J. van Heerde and Scott A. Neslin

Firms spend a significant part of their marketing budgets on sales promotions. The Trade Promotion report (2005) indicates that during 1997–2004, promotion accounted for roughly 75% of marketing expenditures for US packaged goods manufacturers; the other 25% was for advertising. In 2004, 59% of the budget was spent on promotion to the trade (i.e., from manufacturers to retailers), and 16% on manufacturer promotions to consumers. Since the impact of promotions on sales is usually immediate and strong (Blattberg et al. 1995), promotions are attractive to results-oriented managers seeking to increase sales in the short term (Neslin 2002). In a recent meta-analysis, Bijmolt et al. (2005) report that the average short-term sales promotion elasticity is –3.63, which implies that a 20% temporary price cut + leads to a 73% rise in sales.[1] There are few, if any, other marketing instruments that are equally effective. Because of this, coupled with the availability of scanner data, marketing researchers have been very active in developing models for analyzing sales promotions.

This chapter discusses models for measuring sales promotion effects. Part I (Sections 5.1–5.9) focuses on descriptive models, i.e. models that describe, analyze, and explain sales promotion phenomena. We start by discussing promotions to consumers. Sections 5.1 through 5.5 focus on models for analyzing the immediate impact of promotions and decomposing the resulting sales promotion bump into a variety of sources. Section 5.6 examines what happens after the immediate bump, and describes models for measuring feedback effects, reference price effects, learning effects, permanent effects, and competitive reactions. Next we turn to descriptive models for promotions aimed at retailers ("trade promotions") in Section 5.7, and discuss key issues and models concerning forward buying (6.8) and pass-through (Section 5.9).

H.J. van Heerde
Waikato Management School, Hamilton, New Zealand
e-mail: heerde@mngt.waikato.ac.nz

---

[1] This figure holds for temporary price cuts without feature or display support. A feature or display may increase the sales effect up to a factor 9 (Narasimhan et al. 1996).

B. Wierenga (ed.), *Handbook of Marketing Decision Models*,
DOI: 10.1007/978-0-387-78213-3_5, © Springer Science+Business Media, LLC 2008

In Part II we discuss normative models, i.e. models that tell the decision maker what is the best (profit maximizing) decision for sales promotion activities. Section 5.10 covers models for planning promotions to consumers, Section 5.11 provides decision models on trade promotions for manufacturers, and Section 5.12 describes normative retailer models for optimal forward buying and pass-through. Part III concludes this chapter with a summary (Section 5.13), practical model guidelines (Section 5.14), and directions for future research (Section 5.15).

Part I: Descriptive Models

5.1 Promotions to the Consumer – Introduction

Promotions to the consumer include coupons, rebates, in-store temporary price cuts, feature advertising, and in-store displays. The impact of these promotions can be divided into two categories – the immediate sales promotion bump (Sections 5.1–5.5), and effects beyond the immediate bump (Section 5.6). Each aspect presents its own modeling challenges. Table 5.1 lists the phenomena relevant to each aspect.

The ultimate goal in modeling the immediate promotion bump is to allocate the increase in sales that occurs in period *t* to one or more of the sources listed in the second column of Table 5.1. These sources can be classified in three areas: The first is "Industry Growth", which means that the consumer buys more of the promoted item, but this does not come at the expense of other products or stores within the industry, or sales in other time periods. Industry growth may be caused by two phenomena. First, promotion-induced purchase acceleration causes the household to carry extra inventory, which is consumed at a higher rate. For example, a promotion on potato chips may increase household inventory and cause the household to consume more food. Second, the

Table 5.1 The impact of promotions to the consumer

The immediate promotion bump (Sections 5.1–5.5)		Strategic impact – beyond the immediate sales bump (Section 5.6)
Industry Growth	Increased Consumption Rate	Purchase-Event Feedback
	Drawn from Outside Industries	Reference Prices
		Consumer Learning
		Permanent Effects
		Competitive Response
Within-Industry Contemporaneous Effects	Cannibalization	
	Brand Switching	
	Category Switching	
	Store Switching	
Within-Industry Timing Effects	Acceleration	
	Deceleration	

promotion creates an extra purchase not drawn from another product in the industry. For example, a promotion for a High Definition TV results in increased expenditures on consumer electronics. In both cases, the extra expenditures on the promoted product come from household savings or another industry.

The second area consists of within-industry contemporaneous sources, i.e., the purchase draws from within the industry, in the same time period. These effects include:

- Cannibalization: the consumer switches from SKU j' of brand b to SKU j of brand b;
- Brand switching: the consumer switches from brand b' to brand b;
- Category switching: the consumer switches from a product from another category to brand b;
- Store switching: the consumer switches from another store s' to store s to buy brand b;

The third area consists of within-industry temporal sources, i.e. substitution from the period before the promotion (deceleration) or after (acceleration). Deceleration means the consumer postpones the category purchase to week t, because the consumer expects a promotion in week t. Deceleration implies there is purchase displacement from the past ($<t$) to now. Acceleration takes the form of purchase timing acceleration – the consumer buys the category in week t rather than later, or quantity acceleration – the consumer buys more of the category than usual. Both timing and quantity acceleration lead to higher household inventories, and both lead to a purchase displacement from the future ($>t$) to now (t). Importantly, in defining acceleration we assume that the *postpromotion consumption rate does not increase*. If it does, we are in the case of Industry Growth, and there is no purchase displacement.

Table 5.2 lists all possible effects derivable from Table 5.1. We first list Industry Growth. Then, within-industry substitution can come from four types of products (the item itself in another time period, other items within the same brand, other brands, and other categories), from two places (within the same store, from other stores) and from three time periods (before, during, and after the promotion). Hence in total there are 4*2*3 = 24 combinations, of which one drops out since a promoted product can not substitute its own sales in the same period and store. These 23 combinations all imply some form of substitution, as we show in Table 5.2 (listings 2–24). For example, a brand- and store switch (source 7) implies that brand b' in store s' loses sales. The combination of store switching and acceleration (source 17) is sometimes referred to as indirect store switching (Bucklin and Lattin 1992): the consumer visits both stores, but, because of the promotion in store s, she buys the promoted product in store s whereas otherwise she would have bought a product in store s'. Hence a current purchase in store s pre-empts a future purchase in store s'.

Table 5.2 shows where each of the 24 combinations (the 23 within-industry combinations plus Industry Growth) draws from and also whether category

Table 5.2 The 24 decomposition effects from manufacturer and retailer perspectives

#	Effect	Promotion of focal SKU of a brand in focal store in focal time period draws sales from...	Increased Category Consumption	Net unit sales effect for manufacturer	Net unit sales effect for retailer
Industry Growth					
1	Faster Consumption or Industry Substitution	Household Budget; External industry	Yes	+	+
Within-Industry Contemporaneous					
2	Cannibalization	Other SKUs from the same brand, in same store and same period	No	0	0
3	Brand switching	Other brands in same store in same period	No	+	0
4	Category switching	Other categories in same store in same period	Yes	+	0
5	Store switching	Same SKU in other stores same store in same period	No	0	+
6	Cannibalization & store switching	Other SKUs from the same brand, in other stores in same period	No	0	+
7	Brand switching & store switching	Other brands in other stores in same period	No	+	+
8	Category switching & store switching	Other categories in other stores in same period	Yes	+ or 0[a]	+
Within-Industry Timing					
9	Acceleration	Same SKU in same store in future periods	No	0	0
10	Deceleration	Same SKU in same store in earlier periods	No	0	0
11	Cannibalization & acceleration	Other SKUs from the same brand, in same store and future periods	No	0	0
12	Cannibalization & deceleration	Other SKUs from the same brand in earlier periods	No	0	0
13	Brand switching & acceleration	Other brands in same store in future periods	No	+	0

Table 5.2 (continued)

#	Effect	Promotion of focal SKU of a brand in focal store in focal time period draws sales from…	Increased Category Consumption	Net unit sales effect for manufacturer	Net unit sales effect for retailer
14	Brand switching & deceleration	Other brands in same store and earlier periods	No	+	0
15	Category switching & acceleration	Other categories in same store in future periods	Yes	+ or 0^a	0
16	Category switching & deceleration	Other categories in same store and earlier periods	Yes	+ or 0^a	0
17	Store switching & acceleration	Same SKU in other stores in future periods	No	0	+
18	Store switching & deceleration	Same SKU in other stores in earlier periods	No	0	+
19	Cannibalization, store switching &acceleration	Other SKUs from same brand in other stores in future periods	No	0	+
20	Cannibalization, store switching & deceleration	Other SKUs from same brand in other stores in earlier periods	No	0	+
21	Brand switching, store switching & acceleration	Other brands in other stores in future periods	No	+	+
22	Brand switching, store switching & deceleration	Other brands in other stores in earlier periods	No	+	+
23	Category switching, store switching & acceleration	Other categories in other stores in future periods	Yes	+ or 0^a	+
24	Category switching, store switching & deceleration	Other categories in other stores in earlier periods	Yes	+ or 0^a	+

[a] If the manufacturer produces the product in the other category that is being substituted, s/he does not benefit from the category switch (0); otherwise s/he does (+).

consumption increases. This is certainly the case for Industry Growth. Category consumption also increases when the contributing source involves category switching (#4, 8, 15, 16, 23, 24).

The effects listed in Table 5.2 are important because each has distinctive managerial implications in terms of unit sales impact. For example, brand switching benefits manufacturers but not stores; store switching benefits retailers but not manufacturers; industry growth benefit both manufacturers and retailers; category switching is neutral for retailers and may or may not be neutral for manufacturers, depending on whether the manufacturer has products in both categories. The rightmost two columns of Table 5.2 show that some combinations show a "+" for both manufacturers and retailers. So there is potential for conflict as well as "win-win" between manufacturers and retailers (see Van Heerde and Gupta 2006). Further complicating matters is that the profit margins, both to the retailer and manufacturer, may differ. So a brand switch might actually benefit the retailer if the switched-to brand has higher margin. This motivates the retailer to demand a trade deal discount so that the retailer can "pass through" some of the discount to promoting the brand, while at the same time increasing the margin on that brand. We discuss this in more detail in Section 5.9.

In sum, it is crucial to measure how the immediate impact of promotion is decomposed into the components shown in Table 5.2. Consequently, the decomposition of the sales promotion bump has gained considerable attention in the literature, and we summarize empirical generalizations in Section 5.5. First, however, we discuss the models necessary for measuring the decomposition. We start with individual-level incidence, choice, and quantity models in Section 5.2. Note that these models can be used for decomposition purposes but also for others, e.g., exploring brand loyalty issues. In Section 5.3 we discuss individual-level models for store switching, category switching, cannibalization, and deceleration. In Section 5.4 we present aggregate models for promotion effects.

5.2 Customer-Level Models – Incidence, Choice, and Quantity

Promotions can influence category incidence, brand choice, and purchase quantity, and historically, these decisions have received the most attention. The models for these household-level decisions are based on household panel scanner data, as are the models discussed in Section 5.3. The models in Section 5.4 are based on aggregate- (store- or higher) level data. Table 5.4 provides a comparison of household and store data.

The probability that household h buys q_{bt}^h units of brand b at shopping trip t is the product of three probabilities:

$$P(Q_{bt}^h = q_{bt}^h) = P(I_t^h = 1) * P(C_t^h = b | I_t^h = 1) * P(Q_{bt}^h | I_t^h = 1, C_t^h = b) \quad (5.1)$$

where

$$P(I_t^h = 1) \quad \text{is the probability that household } h \text{ buys the category at trip } t \text{ (incidence),}$$

$$P(C_t^h = b | I_h^t = 1) \quad \text{is the probability that, conditional on incidence at } t, \text{ household } h \text{ buys brand } b, \text{ and}$$

$$P(Q_{bt}^h = q_{bt}^h | I_h^t = 1, C_t^h = b) \quad \text{is the probability that, conditional on a choice to buy brand } b \text{ at trip } t, \text{ the household buys } q_{bt}^h \text{ units.}$$

5.2.1 Category Incidence Models

Category incidence is often modeled as a binary logit (e.g., Bucklin, Gupta, and Siddarth 1998):

$$P(I_t^h = 1) = \frac{1}{1 + e^{-(\gamma_0 + \gamma_1 CV_t^h + \gamma_2 I_{t-1}^h + \gamma_3 \bar{C}^h + \gamma_5 INV_t^h)}} \tag{5.2}$$

where CV_t^h is the "inclusive value", which in a nested logit framework is the maximum expected utility available to household h from buying a brand in the category at time t. It is given by the log of the denominator of the brand choice probability: $CV_t^h = \ln \left(\sum_{b'=1}^{B} \exp(u_{b'} + \beta X_{b't}^h) \right)$ (see Section 5.2.2).[2] I_{t-1}^h is a lagged purchase incidence dummy (Ailawadi and Neslin 1998), and $\bar{C}^h$ is the household's average daily consumption computed from an initialization sample. INV_t^h represents the inventory carried by household h at the beginning of shopping trip t. The standard approach to operationalize INV_t^h is:

$$INV_t^h = INV_{t-1}^h + PurQty_{t-1}^h - \bar{C}^h,$$

where $PurQty_{t-1}^h$ is the quantity (in ounces) purchased by household h during trip $t-1$. Inventory should be mean-centered over time for a given household to remove household differences.

The most common assumption is that $\bar{C}^h$ represents the constant consumption rate of household h. However, Ailawadi and Neslin (1998) propose that the consumption rate for household h at time t ($Consumpt_t^h$) flexibly varies over time as a function of inventory:,

$$Consumpt_t^h = INV_t^h \left[\frac{\bar{C}^h}{\bar{C}^h + (INV_t^h)^f} \right]. \tag{5.3}$$

---

[2] The derivation of CV and its place in the purchase incidence models can be derived from a "nested" logit framework (e.g., see Bucklin et al. 1998).

This means that promotion-induced stockpiling can increase category consumption (Effect #1 in Table 2; see also Sun 2005).

5.2.2 Brand Choice Model

The probability that household h buys brand b at time t, conditional on buying in the category, is often given by a multinomial logit model[3] (Guadagni and Little 1983):

$$P(C_t^h = b | I_t^h = 1) = \frac{\exp(u_b + \beta X_{bt}^h)}{\sum\limits_{b'=1}^{B} \exp(u_{b'} + \beta X_{b't}^h)}, \tag{5.4}$$

where B is the number of brands and V_{bt}^h is the "deterministic component" of the utility of household h for brand b at time t (Guadagni and Little 1983). A typical formulation would be:

$$V_{bt}^h = u_b + \beta X_{bt}^h = u_b + \beta_1 PRICE_{bt} + \beta_2 FEAT_{bt} + \beta_3 DISP_{bt} + \beta_4 BL_b^h + \beta_5 LAST_{bt}^h, \tag{5.5}$$

where u_b is a brand-specific intercept, X_{bt}^h is a vector of marketing and household-specific covariates; and β is a vector of response coefficients. The components of X_{bt}^h might include $PRICE_{bt}$, the net price of brand b at time t, $FEAT_{bt}$ and $DISP_{bt}$ as feature and display indicators for this brand, and BL_b^h is the intrinsic loyalty or preference for brand b, calculated as the within-household h market share of brand b in an initialization period and assumed constant over time (Bucklin et al. 1998). The BL term can be eliminated if differences in customer preference (μ_b) are modeled as unobserved heterogeneity (see Section 5.2.5). The term $LAST_{bt}^h$ is a dummy that is 1 in case brand b was bought last time by household h, and zero else. It captures purchase-event feedback or "state dependence" (see Section 5.6.1 for more discussion).

5.2.3 Purchase Quantity Model

Given store choice, purchase incidence and choice of brand b, the probability that household h buys $q_{bt}^h = 1, 2, \ldots, n$ units on a store visit at time t is captured by a Poisson model with a truncation at the zero outcome (Bucklin et al. 1998). This can be written as:

---

[3] Multinomial probit is an alternative to the logit (e.g., see Jedidi et al. (1999). The advantage of the probit model is that it avoids the independence of irrelevant alternatives (IIA) assumption of logit models (see Guadagni and Little 1983). However, it does not produce a closed form for the probability of consumer choice.

$$P(Q^h_{bt} = q^h_{bt}|I^h_t = 1, C^h_t = b) = \frac{\exp(-\lambda^h_{bt})(\lambda^h_{bt})^{q^h_{bt}}}{[1 - \exp(-\lambda^h_{bt})]q^h_{bt}}, \quad (5.6)$$

where λ^h_{bt} is the purchase rate of household h for brand b at time t. This parameter is a linear function of (mean-centered) inventory, the average number of units purchased by the household, and the size, price, and promotion status of the selected brand:

$$\lambda^h_{bt} = \exp\Big(\theta_0 + \theta_1(Inv^h_t - \overline{Inv}^h_.) + \theta_2\bar{Q}^h + \theta_3 SIZE_b + \theta_4 PRICE_{bt}$$

$$+\theta_5 FEAT_{bt} + \theta_6 DISP_{bt}\Big)$$

5.2.4 Estimation

The likelihood function for incidence, choice, and quantity is given by:

$$L = \prod_{h=1}^{H}\prod_{t=1}^{T}\prod_{b=1}^{B}\Big(P(I^h_t = 1)^{Y^h_t}(1 - P(I^h_t = 1))^{1-Y^h_t} P(C^h_t = b|I^h_t = 1)^{Z^h_{bt}}$$

$$P(Q^h_{bt} = q^h_{bt}|I^h_t = 1, C^h_t = b)^{Z^h_{bt}}\Big)$$

where:

Y^h_t = Category purchase indicator, equals 1 if household h purchased the category on shopping trip t; 0 otherwise.

Z^h_{bt} = Brand purchase indicator, equals 1 if household h purchased brand b on shopping trip t ; 0 otherwise.

Methods used to estimate the model include maximum likelihood, simulated maximum likelihood (Train 2003), and Bayesian "MCMC" estimation (Rossi et al. 2005). Once the incidence, choice, and quantity models have been estimated, we can calculate the incidence elasticity, $\eta_I = \frac{\partial P(I)}{\partial PRICE}\frac{PRICE}{P(I)}$; the choice elasticity, $\eta_{C|I} = \frac{\partial P(C|I)}{\partial PRICE}\frac{PRICE}{P(C|I)}$; and the quantity elasticity, $\eta_{Q|I,C} = \frac{\partial E(Q)}{\partial PRICE}\frac{PRICE}{E(Q)}$, where $E(Q)$ is the expected purchase quantity.[4] Gupta (1988) decomposes the total sales elasticity η_S into a part due to purchase incidence (η_I), brand switching ($\eta_{C|I}$) and purchase quantity ($\eta_{Q|I,C}$), i.e., $\eta_S = \eta_{C|I} + \eta_I + \eta_{Q|I,C}$. For example, we might find that an purchase probability elasticity of -3 with respect to promotion might be decomposed as $\underset{(100\%)}{-3} = \underset{(75\%)}{-2.25} \underset{(15\%)}{- 0.45} \underset{(10\%)}{- 0.3}$, i.e., the brand switching elasticity comprises 75% of the total elasticity, whereas the

---

[4] The full expressions for the elasticities are not shown due to space restrictions; they require taking the derivatives of Equations (5.2), (5.4), and (5.6) (see Gupta 1988).

incidence elasticity is 15% and the quantity elasticity is 10%. We refer to Section 5.5 for a more in-depth discussion on how (not) to interpret this result.

5.2.5 Heterogeneity

Consumers are naturally heterogeneous in their brand preferences, responsiveness to marketing actions, and how much they learn from the product usage experience. As a result, the parameters of the choice, incidence, and quantity models (Equations 5.2–5.6) should be modeled to vary across consumers. For example, Equation (5.5) could be written as:

$$V_{bt}^h = u_b^h + \beta^h X_{bt}^h = u_b^h + \beta_1^h PRICE_{bt} + \beta_2^h FEAT_{bt} + \beta_3^h DISP_{bt}$$
$$+ \beta_4^h BL_b^h + \beta_5^h LAST_{bt}^h \tag{5.7}$$

The brand-specific intercept from Equation (5.4) is now household-specific (u_b^h) meaning that households can differ in their preferences for various brands. The response coefficients for variable k (β_k^h) also differ across households.

Modeling heterogeneity adds much complexity to choice, incidence, and quantity models. It is worthwhile to make clear why modeling heterogeneity is important:

- *Aggregation Bias:* In a linear model, it is well-known that if observations have observation-specific parameters yet the data are pooled and only one parameter estimated, that estimated parameter is biased in that it does not represent the average parameter across observations (see Hsiao 1986). The same would be expected to hold for nonlinear models. The implication is that the estimates we obtain for the brand choice constants and market response in a homogeneous model are misleading.
- *Spurious State Dependence:* In a homogeneous model, the state dependence parameter (β_5^h) would be over-stated because it soaks up the variation due to heterogeneous preference as well as dynamically changing preferences (see Keane 1997a; also Abramson et al. 2000).
- *Segmentation:* Marketing is about segmentation. By learning about heterogeneity, we make our models more useful because we can segment the market based on preference or response.
- *Avoid Independence of Irrelevant Alternatives (IIA):* As mentioned earlier, logit models are open to the IIA criticism (see Guadagni and Little 1983). Modeling heterogeneity eliminates IIA problems at the aggregate level, although it still exists at the level of each household.
- *Better Prediction:* Incorporating heterogeneity means that our models incorporate more information; hence they should be expected to predict better.

Researchers face a myriad of decisions in how to model heterogeneity. Following are six of those decisions:

- *Distribution of the Individual Parameters:* The distribution of individual-level parameters can be considered to be continuous (Chintagunta et al. 1991), discrete (Kamakura and Russell 1989), or finite mixture (Varki and Chintagunta 2004; Allenby et al. 2002; Wedel and Kamakura 1998).
- *Parameters to be Considered Heterogeneous:* The parameters to model heterogeneously can include preference, most coefficients, or all coefficients.
- *Joint Distribution of the Parameters:* The distribution of the heterogeneous parameters can be considered to be uncorrelated, correlated, or no assumption made.
- *Incorporation of Observed Heterogeneity:* Heterogeneity can be thought of as "observed" vs. "unobserved." Observed heterogeneity means that the heterogeneity in any parameter can be captured by measurable variables such as demographics or initialization-period preference (BL_b^h). Observable heterogeneity is easy to incorporate by including main effects and interactions between the observed sources of heterogeneity and the variables in the model. The concern is that these measures do not capture all the heterogeneity, and so researchers often model unobserved heterogeneity (possibly in addition to observed heterogeneity).
- *Choice Set Heterogeneity:* The model in Equation (5.4) assumes that each household considers the same brands when making a choice. Researchers such as Siddarth et al. (1995) have questioned this assumption, and argue that households are heterogeneous in the brands they consider.
- *Estimation:* Maximum Likelihood (ML), Simulated Maximum Likelihood (SML), and Bayesian are possible ways to estimate the model.

The above choices give rise to $3 \times 3 \times 3 \times 2 \times 2 \times 3 = 324$ possible ways to handle heterogeneity. No one route has emerged as most popular. Table 5.3 gives a summary of how a few papers have handled heterogeneity.

While no one single method has been shown to be superior, and sometimes the differences across various approaches are not crucial (e.g., Andrews et al. 2002; Andrews et al. 2002), the general conclusion is that it is crucial to include some form of unobserved heterogeneity in the model, at a minimum, in the brand-specific intercept. The reasons are (1) Heterogeneity improves fit and prediction (e.g., see Chintagunta et al. 1994), (2) Heterogeneity changes the coefficients of other variables (e.g., see Chintagunta et al. 1994), although Ailawadi et al. 1999 note that aggregate price elasticities may not change, (3) While it is clear that even after incorporating preference heterogeneity, state dependence exists (Keane 1997a; Erdem and Sun 2001; Seetharaman 2004), state dependence can be over-stated when preference heterogeneity is not included (e.g., Keane 1997a; see also Horsky et al. 2006).[5]

---

[5] It is noteworthy that there is some evidence (Abramson et al. 2000; Chiang et al. 1999) that not including choice set heterogeneity significantly distorts parameters. However, perhaps because there have not been too many studies, choice set heterogeneity is usually not included.

Table 5.3 Ways to handle heterogeneity in household-level models (selected papers)

	Distribution of Parameters	Which Parameters Heterogeneous	Joint Distribution of Parameters	Choice Set Heterogeneity	Including Observed Heterogeneity?	Estimation
Kamakura and Russel 1989	Latent Structure	All	N/A	No	No	ML
Ailawadi et al. 2006	Continuous	Most	No stipulation	No	No	SML
Ansari et al. 2006	Continuous	Most	Correlated	No	No	Bayesian
Gupta and Chintagunta 1994	Finite Mixture	All	N/A	No	Yes	ML
Seetharaman et al. 1999	Continuous	All	Correlated	No	Yes	Bayesian
Chiang et al. 1999	Continuous	All	Correlated	Yes	No	Bayesian

5.2.6 Integrated Incidence, Choice, Quantity Models

Specialized models have been developed that expressly integrate two or more consumer decisions. The integration takes place through the utility function, correlations between error terms, or through the set of decision options. For example, Krishnamurthi and Raj (1988) develop a model that integrates brand choice and quantity decisions in a selectivity modeling framework. Nested logit integrates choice and incidence decisions (see Footnote 2 and Ben-Akiva and Lerman 1991). The incidence portion of the nested logit is what we describe in Section 5.2.1. Another set of models integrates choice and incidence through a "no-purchase" option, i.e., the consumer is assumed to choose among a set of alternatives, J-1 of which are brands; the Jth is the no-purchase option. See Chib et al. (2004) and the papers to which they refer for examples. Chiang (1991) and Chintagunta (1993) develop integrated models of incidence, choice, and quantity. Bell and Hilber (2006) investigate the relationship between incidence and quantity. They find that consumers with greater storage constraints shop more often and purchase smaller quantities per visit. While modeling the decisions in an integrated way is attractive from econometric and behavioral perspectives, the overall decomposition results do not seem to differ much from separate models. For instance, for the coffee category Gupta (1988) uses non-integrated models whereas Chiang (1991) uses integrated models, but their results on the elasticity decomposition into brand switching, incidence and quantity are almost identical (see Table 5.5 in Section 5.5).

Another approach to modeling consumer decisions is dynamic structural models. These models begin with the household utility function and include dynamic phenomena, and often allow the consumer to be "forward looking." This means that the consumer takes into account future utility in making the current period decision. Erdem and Keane (1996) develop a dynamic structural model of brand choice. Gönül and Srinivasan (1996) develop a dynamic structural model of purchase incidence. Sun, Neslin, and Srinivasan (2003) develop a dynamic structural model of incidence and choice. Erdem et al. (2003), Sun (2005), and Chan et al. (2006) develop dynamic structural models of incidence, choice, and quantity. Using structural models vs nonstructural ones seem to affect the elasticity decomposition outcomes. For instance, Sun et al. (2003) report a brand switching percentage of 56% for a dynamic structural model that accounts for forward-looking customers, whereas the percentage for the non-structural integrated model (nested logit) is 72%.

5.3 Customer-Level Models – Beyond Incidence, Choice, and Quantity

In order to enrich our understanding of promotions, we may want to extend the classical set up of incidence-choice-quantity. As we explained in Table 5.2, promotions may cause store switching, and we discuss a store choice model in

Section 5.3.1. Furthermore, consumers may switch from one category to another, and that is why we need a model that captures cross-category effects (Section 5.3.2). To allow for within-brand cannibalization effects, we need an SKU choice model, which is presented in Section 5.3.3. Finally, to capture deceleration effects we need a model that shows how expected promotions affect purchase behavior (Section 5.3.4).

5.3.1 Extension 1: Store Switching

Bucklin and Lattin (1992) propose a model that can be used to capture store switching effects. Their store choice model is given by a multinomial logit expression:

$$P_t^h(S = s) = \frac{\exp\left[\delta_{0s} + \delta_1 STLOY_s^h + \delta_2 CFEAT_{st}^h\right]}{\sum_{r=1}^{S} \exp\left[\delta_{0r} + \delta_1 STLOY_r^h + \delta_2 CFEAT_{rt}^h\right]} \tag{5.8}$$

where

$P_t^h(S = s)$ is the probability that household h chooses store s on the shopping trip at t.

$STLOY_s^h$ is the loyalty to chain s, operationalized as the within-household h market share of store s in the initialization period.

$CFEAT_{st}^h$ is the category-wide feature variable, obtained as a weighted average across brands, where the weights are the within-household shares of each brand.

One complicating factor in measuring the effects of promotions on store choice is that consumers make store choice decisions based on a host of factors (e.g., location, produce quality, waiting lines) that have little to do with an individual category's price and promotions. Another is that the standard logit model for store choice assumes that a consumer knows each store's prices and promotions, which seems unlikely. It seems more likely that there is indirect store switching: a promotional purchase in one store preempts a regular purchase in another store, as we discussed in Section 5.1. To tackle these complicating factors, increasingly sophisticated models of store choice are available (Bell and Lattin 1998; Bell et al. 1998; Rhee and Bell 2002; Bodapati and Srinivasan 2006; Singh et al. forthcoming).

5.3.2 Extension 2: Category Switching

To capture category switching, we need a model that accommodates cross-category effects. Manchanda et al. (1998) specify a model for shopping basket composition, i.e., the question which of the categories are bought on a specific shopping trip. Their multivariate probit model is specified as:

$$
P_t^h \left(\begin{pmatrix} Cat_{1t}^h \\ Cat_{2t}^h \\ \vdots \\ Cat_{Nt}^h \end{pmatrix} = \begin{pmatrix} c_{1t}^h \\ c_{2t}^h \\ \vdots \\ c_{Nt}^h \end{pmatrix} \right)
$$

$$
= \begin{pmatrix} \beta_{10}^h + \beta_{11}^h \text{Price}_{1t}^h + \beta_{12}^h PROMO_{1t}^h + \sum_{k=1}^N \beta_{13k}^h \text{Price}_{kt}^h + \beta_{14k}^h PROMO_{kt}^h \\ \beta_{20}^h + \beta_{21}^h \text{Price}_{2t}^h + \beta_{22}^h PROMO_{2t}^h + \sum_{k=1}^N \beta_{23k}^h \text{Price}_{kt}^h + \beta_{24k}^h PROMO_{kt}^h \\ \vdots \\ \beta_{N0}^h + \beta_{N1}^h \text{Price}_{Nt}^h + \beta_{N2}^h PROMO_{Nt}^h + \sum_{k=1}^N \beta_{N3k}^h \text{Price}_{kt}^h + \beta_{N4k}^h PROMO_{kt}^h \end{pmatrix} + \begin{pmatrix} \varepsilon_{1t}^h \\ \varepsilon_{2t}^h \\ \vdots \\ \varepsilon_{Nt}^h \end{pmatrix},
$$

$$(5.9)$$

where

Cat_{kt}^h (c_{kt}^h) = indicator variable for (observed) category incidence; 1 if household h buys in category k, $k = 1, \ldots, N$ on shopping trip t, 0 else;

Price_{kt}^h = category k's price for household h at shopping trip t. This is the weighted average price where the weights are the share of each brand bought by each household;

$PROMO_{kt}^h$ = category k's promotion variable for household h at shopping trip t. A brand is on promotion when it is either featured or displayed. Again, this variable is a weighted average.

The vector of error terms, $\left(\varepsilon_{1t}^h \quad \varepsilon_{2t}^h \quad \cdots \quad \varepsilon_{Nt}^h \right)'$, comes from a multivariate normal distribution. The model includes "complementarity" effects, whereas the price of one category influences sales in another category, and "coincidence" effects, whereas certain products are bought together. Complementarity is represented by the cross-category β's in Equation (5.9), whereas coincidence is represented by correlations between the ε's.

While promotions can induce category switching, they can also increase sales of other categories in the store. This is what retailers hope occurs (Lam et al. 2001). Ailawadi et al. (2006) call these positive cross-category effects halo effects, and find empirical evidence for them in a major drugstore chain.

5.3.3 Extension 3: Cannibalization

To capture cannibalization, we need to accommodate switching between SKUs of the same brand. Fader and Hardie (1996) propose a parsimonious model for SKU choice. The conditional SKU choice probability, i.e., the probability that household h buys SKU j of brand b at time t, conditional on buying in store s and buying in the category, is given by the logit model:

$$P(C_t^h = \{b,j\}|I = 1) = \frac{\exp(u_{bj} + \beta X_{bjt}^h)}{\sum\limits_{b'=1}^{B} \sum\limits_{j'=1}^{J_b} \exp(u_{b'j'} + \beta X_{b'j't}^h)},$$

(5.10)

where u_{bj} is a brand-SKU-specific intercept, X_{bjt}^h is a vector of marketing and household-specific covariates; and β is a vector of response coefficients. Suppose there are N attributes and let L_n be the number of levels associated with the nth attribute. Define the set $\{l_1, l_2, \ldots, l_N\}$ as the unique set of attribute levels for brand b, SKU j. Fader and Hardie (1996) model the SKU-specific intercept as:

$$u_{bj} = \sum_{n=1}^{N} m_{bjn} \alpha_n,$$ where m_{bjn} is an elementary row vector, the l_n^{th} element of which equals 1, and α_n is the vector of preferences over the L_n levels of attribute n. A similar approach was followed by Ho and Chong (2003) and Chintagunta and Dubé (2005). For the covariates X_{bjt}^h we may use SKU-level versions of the variables in the brand choice model Equation (5.4).

5.3.4 Extension 4: Deceleration

Deceleration means that consumers anticipate promotions, and consequently they may postpone purchases till the promotion is offered. To capture deceleration, we need a model component for the effect of an expected future promotion on current purchase behavior. Van Heerde et al. (2000) and Macé and Neslin (2004) use actual future prices in a model of brand sales to capture deceleration in a model of brand sales (more about this in Section 5.4.2). For household data, Sun et al. (2003) present a structural model for the promotion expectation process. They assume that consumers expect future promotions according to a first-order Markov model:

$$\text{Prob}(PROM_{bt} = 1|PROM_{bt-1} = 1) = \pi_{b1}, \text{ and}$$

(5.11)

$$\text{Prob}(PROM_{bt} = 1|PROM_{bt-1} = 0) = \pi_{b0},$$

(5.12)

where π_{b1} is the probability of promotion in period t, given that there was promotion in period t-1. Similarly, π_{b0} denotes the probability of promotion in period t, given that there was no promotion in period t-1. Sun et al. find that the estimated expectations conform rather well with the actual promotion schedule (see also Erdem et al. 2003).

Sun et al. (2003) also propose a reduced-form approach for measuring deceleration. They add a variable $PromTime_t^h$ to the category incidence model (see Equation (5.2)). This represents the time since the last promotion, and is meant to capture that consumers may hold out until the next promotion. To obtain $PromTime_t^h$ they calculate the average time between promotions in the category. If the time since the last promotion in the category seen by the consumer is greater than this average, $PromTime_t^h$ equals 1; otherwise it equals 0. If $PromTime_t^h$ is 1, a consumer may expect a promotion soon, and defers the current purchase. As a result, the corresponding parameter in the category incidence model is expected to be negative.

5.3.5 Discussion

While the literature provides models for each of the key consumer responses to sales promotion, there are no papers yet that combine all possible responses that are listed in Table 5.2. Van Heerde and Gupta (2006) come close by combining store switching, category incidence, brand and SKU choice, purchase quantity, increased consumption effects and deceleration effects. This allows them to identify 18 of the 24 possible sources of the sales promotion bump from Table 5.2. Since Van Heerde and Gupta (2006) do not model category choice (Section 5.3.2), they do not measure effects related to category switching.

To estimate all 24 decomposition sources, one would have to estimate a model for all pertinent consumer decisions. This would require specifying the probability for the decision to choose store s, category k, brand b, SKU j and quantity q_{skbt}^h as:

$$P(Q_{skbt}^h = q_{skbt}^h) = P(S_t^h = s) * P(Cat_{skt}^h = 1 | S_t^h = s) * P(C_{skt}^h = \{b,j\} |$$
$$Cat_{skt}^h = 1, S_t^h = s)*$$
$$P(Q_{bt}^h = q_{skbt}^h | S_t^h = s, Cat_{skt}^h = 1, C_{skt}^h = \{b,j\}) \qquad (5.13)$$

The components at the right hand side of Equation (5.13) can be modeled using Equations (5.8), (5.9), (5.10), and (5.6), respectively. In addition, it isn't clear whether one could derive an analytical formula to derive the 24-state decomposition in Table 5.2, or whether one would have to use simulation. For example, it would be difficult to distinguish between a category switch and a new category purchase that represents additional expenditures from the household's total budget.

5.4 Store-Level Models for Sales Promotion Effects

A large body of the sales promotion literature has focused on store-level models for sales promotion effects. Store-level scanner data tend to be more readily available, more representative, and easier to process than household-level

Table 5.4 Related terms in models of household- and store data

Household data	Store data
Purchase (Section 5.1)	Sales (Section 5.4.1)
Category incidence (Section 5.2.1)	Number of buyers in category
Brand switching (section 5.2.2)	Cross-brand effects (Sections 5.4.1, 5.4.3)
Acceleration (Section 5.2.1)	Postpromotion dips (Section 5.4.2)
Deceleration (Section 5.3.4)	Prepromotion dips (Section 5.4.2)

scanner data (Van Heerde et al. 2004). Table 5.4 shows that the phenomena that are studied with store-level vs household-level data are similar, but that some of the terms are different.

5.4.1 Scan*Pro Model

Perhaps the most well-known store-level model for sales promotion effects is the Scan*Pro model by Wittink et al. (1987).[6] It is a multiplicative regression model for brand sales, explained by own-brand and cross-brand prices and promotions:

$$S_{bst} = \lambda_{bs}\mu_{bt} \prod_{b'=1}^{B} \left\{ PI_{b'st}^{\beta_{b'b}} \cdot \gamma_{1b'b}^{FEATONLY_{b'st}} \cdot \gamma_{2b'b}^{DISPONLY_{b'st}} \cdot \gamma_{3b'b}^{FEAT\&DISP_{b'st}} \right\} e^{u_{bst}}, \quad (5.14)$$

where

$$
\begin{aligned}
S_{bst} &= \text{sales (in units) of brand } b \text{ in store } s \text{ in week } t \\
PI_{bst} &= \text{price index (ratio of current to regular price) of brand } b \text{ in} \\
&\quad \text{store } s \text{ in week } t \\
FEATONLY_{bst} &= \text{indicator for feature only: 1 if there is a feature without a} \\
&\quad \text{display for brand } b \text{ in store } s \text{ in week } t, 0 \text{ else} \\
DISPONLY_{bst} &= \text{indicator for display only: 1 if there is a display without} \\
&\quad \text{feature for brand } b \text{ in store } s \text{ in week } t, 0 \text{ else} \\
FEAT\&DISP_{bst} &= \text{indicator for feature \& display: 1 if there is a feature and} \\
&\quad \text{display for brand } b \text{ in store } s \text{ in week } t, 0 \text{ else}
\end{aligned}
$$

The model includes a brand-store specific intercept λ_{bs}, a brand-week specific intercept μ_{bt}, own- (β_{bb}) and cross-price ($\beta_{b'b}, b' \neq b$) elasticities, and multipliers for the own- ($\gamma_{1bb}, \gamma_{2bb}, \gamma_{3bb}$) and cross-brand ($\gamma_{1b'b}, \gamma_{2b'b}, \gamma_{3b'b}, b' \neq b$) multipliers for, respectively, feature-only, display-only, and feature & display. The model is linearized by taking logs and estimated by ordinary least squares. Van Heerde et al. (2001) propose a nonlinear version of Scan*Pro, which is estimated by nonparametric

---

[6] Another important method is "PromotionScan" (Abraham and Lodish 1993). Promotion-Scan uses a time series approach to estimating the short-term promotion bump. It is based on the "Promoter" methodology that we discuss in Section 6.8.

techniques. Their results show that the response of sales to the percentage price discount is S-shaped, i.e., there are threshold and saturation effects.

A key independent variable in the Scan*Pro model is the price index (the ratio of actual to regular price). In store data, both actual and regular prices are typically available whereas they household data tend to include actual prices only. The price index captures the effects of promotional price changes, which may be quite different from regular price effects (Mulhern and Leone 1991; Bijmolt et al. 2005). If there is sufficient variation in regular price, it can be included as a separate predictor variable as in Mulhern and Leone (1991).

Note that Equation (5.14) allows for asymmetric cross-effects between brands, i.e., the impact of promoting Brand A on sales of Brand B is not the same as the impact of promoting Brand B on sales of Brand A. This is an important feature to include when studying brand switching because asymmetric brand switching has been consistently found in the promotions literature, although its causes are not yet completely explained (Neslin 2002). A downside of modeling all cross effects without restrictions is that for N brands one needs N^2 parameters per marketing mix instrument, which can be a lot if N is high. As a result, parameter estimates can be unreliable and lack face validity. Aggregate logit models (see Section 5.4.4) overcome this problem by estimating only one parameter per instrument, from which the N^2 own- and cross effects are derived. In case a modeler wants to consider not only cross-brand effects within categories but also across category effects, the number of cross-effects may become really problematic. To handle this case, Kamakura and Kang (forthcoming) present a parsimonious solution based on a principal-component representation of response parameters.

The original Scan*Pro paper (Wittink et al. 1988) report strong differences in promotional responses across US regions. Brand managers may exploit these differences by tailoring promotions at the regional level. In the marketing literature, these spatial response differences seem to be under-explored and deserve additional attention (Lodish 2007).

5.4.2 Models for Pre- and Postpromotion Dips

Van Heerde et al. (2000) and Macé and Neslin (2004) have used store-level data to measure the aggregate effects of acceleration (i.e., postpromotion dips) and deceleration effects (i.e., prepromotion dips). The (simplified) model is of the form:

$$\ln S_t = \alpha_0 + \alpha_1 \ln PI_t + \sum_{u=1}^{S} \beta_u \ln PI_{t-u} + \sum_{v=1}^{S'} \gamma_v \ln PI_{t+v} + \varepsilon_t, \quad (5.15)$$

where

$\ln S_t$ = natural log of sales in week t
$\ln PI_t$ = natural log of price index (ratio of current to regular price) in week t.

$\beta_u = u$-week lagged effect of promotion, corresponding to post-promotion dips (acceleration). A positive β_u indicates that a price decrease is followed by a sales dip u weeks later.

$\gamma_v = v$-week lead effect of promotion, corresponding to pre-promotion dips (deceleration). A positive γ_v indicates that a price decrease in v weeks from now is preceded by a decrease in sales now.

Macé and Neslin (2004) estimate pre- and postpromotion dips based on data spanning 83 stores, 399 weeks, and 30,861 SKUs from 10 product categories. They find that 22% of the sales promotion bump is attributable to postpromotion dips, and 11% to prepromotion dips. Hence, pre- and postpromotion together are one-third of the sales promotion bump, which is remarkably close to the 32% cross-period effect reported by Van Heerde et al. (2004). Macé and Neslin (2004) find that SKU, category, and store-trading area customer characteristics all explain significant variation in pre- and postpromotion elasticities.

It is useful to clarify that models for household data and store-level data deal differently with purchase acceleration. Since typical household-level models do not incorporate a store choice model, acceleration effects manifest both *within* the same store (source 9 in Table 5.2) and *across* stores (source 17 in Table 5.2). In store-level models such as Equation (5.15), the aggregate outcome of acceleration (postpromotion dips) is only captured *within* the same store, which is source 9 in Table 5.2. As a result, one may expect acceleration effects to be larger in household-level models than in store-level models.

5.4.3 Store-Level Decomposition Model

Van Heerde et al. (2004) propose a regression-based method for decomposing own-brand effects into cross-brand (brand switching), cross-period (acceleration & deceleration), and category expansion effects. The method uses the identity that total category sales during periods t-S' through t+S (TCS) equals sales of the target brand in period t ("own-brand sales" or OBS) plus sales of other brands in period t ("cross-brand sales" or CBS) plus total category sales in period t-S' through t+S, excluding period t ("pre- and post-period category sales" or PPCS). Therefore, TCS = OBS + CBS + PPCS, or –OBS = CBS + PPBC – TCS. The method regresses these four variables on the same set of regressors:

$$-\text{OBS (own-brand sales): } -S_{bt} = \alpha^{ob} + \beta^{ob} PI_{bt} + \sum_{k=1}^{K} \gamma_k^{ob} X_{kt} + \varepsilon_{bt}^{ob}$$

$$\text{CBS (cross-brand sales): } \sum_{\substack{b'=1 \\ b' \neq b}}^{B} S_{b't} = \alpha^{cb} + \beta^{cb} PI_{bt} + \sum_{k=1}^{K} \gamma_k^{cb} X_{kt} + \varepsilon_{bt}^{cb}$$

$$\text{PPCS (cross-period sales): } \sum_{\substack{u=-S' \\ u\neq0}}^{S} \sum_{\substack{b'=1 \\ b'\neq b}}^{B} S_{b't+u} = \alpha^{cp} + \beta^{cp} PI_{bt} + \sum_{k=1}^{K} \gamma_k^{cp} X_{kt} + \varepsilon_{bt}^{cp}$$

$$-\text{TCS (total category sales): } -\sum_{u=-S'}^{S} \sum_{b=1}^{B} S_{bt+u} = \alpha^{ce} + \beta^{ce} PI_{bt} + \sum_{k=1}^{K} \gamma_k^{ce} X_{kt} + \varepsilon_{bt}^{ce}$$

where $\sum_{k=1}^{K} \gamma_k X_{kt}$ captures the effects of covariates such as cross-brand instruments, store dummies, and week dummies.

The key to the decomposition is the price index variable (PI_{bt}). If there is a promotional price discount for brand b, PI_{bt} decreases, own brand sales increases (presumably), and hence minus own brand sales decreases. Consequently, the regression coefficient β^{ob} will be positive. Similarly, a price discount for brand b decreases cross brand sales (presumably), which implies $\beta^{cb} > 0$. Furthermore, if a decrease in PI_{bt} leads to a decrease in cross-period sales (i.e., pre- and postpromotion dips) $\beta^{cp} > 0$. Finally, if the price discount for brand b manages to increase category sales, then total category sales increase and the negative decreases, and $\beta^{ce} > 0$.

Note we can restate $-\text{OBS} = \text{CBS} + \text{PPBC} - \text{TCS}$ as the following identity:

$$-S_{bt} = \sum_{b=1}^{B} S_{bt+u} + \sum_{u=-S'}^{S} \sum_{\substack{b'=1 \\ b'\neq b}}^{B} S_{b't+u} - \sum_{u=-S'}^{S} \sum_{b=1}^{B} S_{bt+u}. \text{ Assume then that we use}$$

the same set of regressors in each of the above regressions, and that we use a linear estimator such as OLS or GLS. To illustrate, the OLS estimator for a common design matrix $\mathbf{X}$ equals $\hat{\boldsymbol{\beta}} = (\mathbf{X}'\mathbf{X})^{-1}\mathbf{X}'\mathbf{y}$. Applying this to the identity, we obtain (using matrix notation):

$$(\mathbf{X}'\mathbf{X})^{-1}\mathbf{X}'(-\mathbf{S}_{bt}) = (\mathbf{X}'\mathbf{X})^{-1}\mathbf{X}\left(\sum_{b=1}^{B}\mathbf{S}_{bt+u}\right) + (\mathbf{X}'\mathbf{X})^{-1}\mathbf{X}\left(\sum_{u=-S'}^{S}\sum_{\substack{b'=1 \\ b'\neq b}}^{B}\mathbf{S}_{b't+u}\right) + (\mathbf{X}'\mathbf{X})^{-1}\mathbf{X}\left(-\sum_{u=-S'}^{S}\sum_{b=1}^{B}\mathbf{S}_{bt+u}\right),$$

or $\hat{\boldsymbol{\beta}}^{ob} = \hat{\boldsymbol{\beta}}^{cb} + \hat{\boldsymbol{\beta}}^{cp} + \hat{\boldsymbol{\beta}}^{ce}$. Taking the second element of each of these estimated coefficient vectors, we have:

$$\beta^{ob} = \beta^{cb} + \beta^{cp} + \beta^{ce}, \tag{5.16}$$

i.e., own-brand effect = cross-brand effect + cross-period effect + category expansion effect. Equation (5.16) decomposes the promoted brand's promotion bump into sales taken from other brands in the promotion week, sales taken from periods before and after the promotion, and a total increase in category sales. Equation (5.16) can be divided through by β^{ob} to provide a percentage decomposition.

Van Heerde et al. (2004) provide two extensions of Equation (5.16). One of them splits the cross-brand effect into within-brand cannibalization (β^{cbw}) and between-brand switching (β^{cbb}), i.e., $\beta^{cb} = \beta^{cbw} + \beta^{cbb}$. To obtain this split for

SKU m of brand b they run two additional regression models, one for the sales of all other SKUs within the same brand b ($\sum_{\substack{n=1 \\ n \neq m}}^{M_b} S_{bnt}$), and one for the sales of the

SKUs of all other brands ($\sum_{\substack{b'=1 \\ b' \neq b}}^{B} \sum_{n=1}^{M_{b'}} S_{b'nt}$).

The other extension splits the category expansion effect into a cross-store effect (β^{cs}) and a market-expansion effect (β^{me}) (i.e., the industry-growth effect in Tables 5.1and 5.2), i.e., $\beta^{ce} = \beta^{cs} + \beta^{me}$. To obtain this split they run two additional regression models, one for the sales of brand b in competing stores (SCS_{bt}), and one for "extended total category sales",

$$ETCS_{bt} = - \sum_{u=-S'}^{S} \sum_{b=1}^{B} S_{bt+u} - SCS_{bt},$$ i.e., minus category sales in a time window

in the focal store minus cross-store sales.

Van Heerde et al. (2004) obtain the decomposition for four types of promotional price discounts: without feature- or display support, with feature-only support, with display-only support, and with feature- and display support. To accomplish this, they use a specific set of independent variables, discussed in the appendix to this chapter.

5.4.4 Aggregate Logit Model

A frequent criticism of (log or log-log) regression models of promotion is that they are not rooted in economic theory. The aggregate logit model overcomes this issue, which is one of the reasons it is increasingly popular in marketing science. Another reason is that it accommodates own- and cross effects with an economy of parameters, which is something that does not hold for the aggregate models discussed in Sections 5.4.1–5.4.3. The aggregate logit model was introduced by Berry et al. (1995). Its logic is that individual-level consumers maximize utility and choose brands according to the multinomial logit model. Next, the individual-level logit models are aggregated across consumers. Interestingly, this leads to a relatively simple demand model at the aggregate level (Besanko et al. 1998):

$$\ln MS_{bt} = \ln MS_{0t} + \alpha_b + \beta_1 X_{bt} - \beta_2 \text{Price}_{bt} + \xi_{bt} \tag{5.17}$$

where

MS_{bt} = market share of brand b in period t.
MS_{0t} = market share of the no-purchase alternative ("outside good") in period t.
X_{bt} = vector of observable product attributes and marketing variables of brand b in period t.
ξ_{bt} = error term.

Estimation of aggregate logit models can take into account price endogeneity (Besanko et al. 1998; Villas-Boas and Winer 1999). That is, firms may set prices based on demand shocks that are observable to them but unobservable to the researcher. For instance in times of a positive demand shock, $\xi_{bt} > 0$, price is increased. To account for this phenomenon, researchers have correlated price with the error term (Besanko et al. 1998; Villas-Boas and Winer 1999). If the endogenous nature of price is ignored, its coefficient β_2 may be underestimated quite severely as was shown in a meta-analysis of price elasticity (Bijmolt et al. 2005).

To complement the demand model Equation (5.17), Besanko et al. (1998) assume a certain model of competitive conduct, and derive a supply model from that. Next, the demand and supply models are estimated simultaneously. Whereas the original aggregate logit model assumed homogenous consumers, several papers in marketing have relaxed this assumption (e.g., Chintagunta 2001; Dubé et al. 2002). Moreover, Nair et al. (2005) propose aggregate models that not only capture underlying brand choice decisions, but also incidence and quantity. Their demand elasticity breakdown shows that brand choice accounts for 65% and incidence and quantity for 35%, which is in the same ballpark as the breakdowns obtained from individual-level data (see Table 5.5 in Section 5.5).

One drawback of aggregate logit models is that it is difficult to identify unobserved heterogeneity with aggregate data (Bodapati and Gupta 2004). Another one is that it requires the specification of an outside good to account for non-incidence. This outside good has to be based on assumptions on population size and category consumption, which may be questionable. Yet another drawback of current aggregate logit models is that they typically ignore dynamic and quantity effects such as acceleration, deceleration, and purchase-event feedback. An issue that also needs further development is that the assumed competitive conduct refers to long-term stable prices instead of to Hi-Lo pricing that is the essence of promotional pricing (Neslin 2002, p. 45).

5.5 Generalizations About the Decomposition

Table 5.5 summarizes the findings of the literature on the decomposition of the sales promotion bump. For each study we indicate the product category and the percentage attributed to secondary demand effects (effects that cause substitution from other brands, i.e., brand switching) and the percentage due to primary demand effects (effects that represent same-period within-store category expansion, i.e., acceleration, deceleration, external growth, category switching, store switching). There are two fundamental approaches to calculating the decomposition, the "elasticity" approach and the "unit sales" approach. The elasticity approach is explained in Section 5.2.4, and was originated by Gupta (1988). It is

Table 5.5 Sales bump decomposition results reported in the literature

Study	Category	% Secondary Demand Effects	% Primary Demand Effects
		Elasticity Decomposition	
Gupta (1988)	Coffee	84	16
Chiang (1991)	Coffee (feature)	81	19
	Coffee (display)	85	15
Chintagunta (1993)	Yogurt	40	60
Bucklin et al. (1998)	Yogurt	58	42
Bell et al. (1999)	Margarine	94	6
	Soft drinks	86	14
	Sugar	84	16
	Paper towels	83	17
	Bathroom tissue	81	19
	Dryer Softeners	79	21
	Yogurt	78	22
	Ice Cream	77	23
	Potato Chips	72	28
	Bacon	72	28
	Liquid Detergents	70	30
	Coffee	53	47
	Butter	49	51
Chib et al. (2004)	Cola (price)	78	22
	Cola (display)	68	32
	Cola (feature)	64	36
Van Heerde et al. (2003)	Sugar	65	35
	Yogurt	58	42
	Tuna	49	51
Nair et al. (2005)	Orange juice	65	35
Average elasticity decomposition		71	29
		Unit-sales effect decomposition	
Pauwels et al. (2002)	Soup	11	89
	Yogurt	39	61
Van Heerde et al. (2003)	Sugar	45	55
	Yogurt	33	67
	Tuna	22	78
Sun et al. (2003)	Ketchup	56	44
Van Heerde et al. (2004)	Peanut butter	43	57
	Shampoo	31	69
	Tuna	31	69
	Bathroom tissue	21	79
Nair et al. (2005)	Orange juice	8	92
Sun (2005)	Tuna	42	58
	Yogurt	39	61
Average unit sales effect decomposition		32	68

based on the mathematical relationship that the elasticity of the probability of buying brand b at time t with respect to (an assumed continuous measure of) promotion equals the sum of the elasticities of brand choice, purchase incidence, and purchase quantity with respect to promotion. The unit sales composition looks at changes in actual sales of the promoted brand as well as other brands in the category. The upper part of Table 5.5 shows the elasticity decomposition, the lower part shows the unit sales decomposition. There are two important findings in Table 5.5:

1. Using the elasticity decomposition, there is a general downward trend in the percentage allocated to secondary demand, starting from about 80–85% and now at 45–70%.
2. The unit sales decomposition yields lower secondary demand effects compared to the elasticity decomposition, generally in the 10–40% range.

The reason for the general downward trend in secondary demand effects in elasticity decomposition is not clear. It could be due to treatment of heterogeneity, or simply to the use of more recent data. One speculative way of reasoning is the following (see Keane 1997b; Sun et al. 2003). Suppose there are two brands, A and B. A large segment of customers lies in wait for brand A to be on promotion, while the other segment lies in wait for brand B's promotions. When brand A is promoted, it is almost exclusively bought by the first segment. As a result, the conditional choice probability for brand A increases spectacularly when it is promoted, while the conditional choice probability for brand B approaches zero. When brand B is promoted, the reverse occurs. Such a phenomenon leads to a very strong conditional brand choice elasticity. However, actually there is very little switching between A and B, and hence there is small cross-brand sales loss in the unit sales decomposition. If this explanation holds, then models that allow for unobserved household heterogeneity should show a lower percentage brand switching than models that assume homogeneity. This could be the reason why the more recent elasticity decomposition results, which tend to be derived from heterogeneous models, show less brand switching. Since this issue is key to our understanding of promotion effects, it seems a worthwhile direction for further research.

The difference in findings for unit sales versus elasticity decompositions is detailed in Van Heerde et al. (2003). The basic intuition is that promotion of brand b draws consumers to the category, where after consideration of the brands available, may buy a non-promoted brand b'. The unit sales decomposition takes this into account, whereas the elasticity decomposition does not. More specifically, the unit sales decomposition focuses on how many sales other brands lose when the focal brand is promoted, whereas the elasticity decomposition focuses on the decrease in conditional choice probability for these brands (Van Heerde et al. 2003). Van Heerde, Gupta, and Wittink argue that this decrease has to be applied to the higher incidence probability due to the promotion. They show how to correct for this when analyzing household-level data. As a result, the actual loss in cross-brand sales is much less than what the elasticity-based secondary demand fraction suggests. This difference holds within the same category, as illustrated by the entries for orange juice (Nair et al. 2005) and sugar, yogurt and tuna (Van Heerde et al. 2003) in the top and lower parts of Table 5.5.

The brand switching fraction not only reduces when we move from an elasticity decomposition to a unit sales decomposition, but also when we move from the short- to the long term. Jedidi et al. (1999) report that while in a decomposition of the short-term elasticity, brand switching effects dominate quantity effects, in the long run the reverse is true. A related reversal of elasticity- vs unit sales results holds for the extent to which cross-brand effects are asymmetric. Based on elasticities, asymmetric switching favors high-tier brands, whereas the asymmetry vanishes when cross-effects are expressed in unit sales (Sethuraman et al. 1999).

The results in Table 5.5 are for grocery products. In a recent paper, Ailawadi et al. (2006) investigate promotion effects for drugstore products at CVS, a U.S. drug retail chain. Their unit-sales decomposition of the bump shows that 45% is due to switching within the store, 10% due to accelerating future purchases in the store, leaving a substantial 45% as incremental lift for CVS.

5.6 Strategic Impact – Beyond the Immediate Sales Bump

Promotions affect consumers beyond the immediate sales bump. Promotions may lead to purchase-event feedback effects (Section 5.6.1). Promotions may also affect reference prices, which affect subsequent purchase behavior (Section 5.6.2). Over time, consumers learn about price promotion patterns, and start acting on them (Section 5.6.3). Finally, promotions may affect long-term consumer behavior (Section 5.6.4).

5.6.1 Purchase-Event Feedback

Purchase event feedback is the degree to which current purchases affect future brand preferences. This is known as "state dependence" in the economics literature (see Roy et al. 1996), and is due to consumer learning from the outcome of the product usage experience.

To capture purchase-event feedback, researchers have included a lagged purchase indicator such as $LAST_{bt}^h$ in Equation (5.5). However, Blattberg and Neslin (1990) distinguish between the purchase effect and the promotion usage effect – the purchase-event feedback from a purchase on promotion may be different than the feedback from a regular purchase. For example, self perception theory suggests that if the consumer concludes he or she bought the brand because of the promotion rather than brand preference, purchase event feedback will be weakened (Dodson et al. 1978). Behavioral learning theory (Rothschild and Gaidis 1981) suggests promotion purchasing could enhance or detract from purchase event feedback. The effect could be positive if the promotion serves as a reward and thus encourages future purchasing, or negative if promotion merely trains consumers to buy on promotion. To investigate this, Gedenk and Neslin (1999) develop a feedback model that distinguishes whether or not the last purchase was made on promotion. They find that price promotions detract from feedback. This finding is the same as originally reported by Guadagni and Little (1983) – a promotion purchase is less reinforcing than a non-promotion purchase, but better than no purchase at all. It is also the same as found in recent work by Seetharaman (2004).

Recently, Ailawadi et al. (2007) propose yet another mechanism for feedback effects of promotions. They postulate that acceleration leads to additional purchase-event feedback because of the household consumes more of the brand over a continuous period of time. They propose the following modification of the brand choice utility function (Equation (5.5)):

$$\beta X_{bt}^h = \beta_1 PRICE_{bt} + \beta_2 FEAT_{bt} + \beta_3 DISP_{bt} + \beta_4 LAST_{bt}^h + \beta_5 LPROMO_{bt}^h$$
$$+ \beta_6 \frac{Q_{bt}^h}{\bar{Q}^h}.$$

If consumers develop higher preference for brands they consume more of, acceleration ($\frac{Q_{bt}^h}{\bar{Q}^h} > 1$) should yield more positive reinforcement. Hence $\beta_6 > 0$ and there will be more repeat purchases. On the other hand, if more consumption breeds boredom, acceleration should result in less positive purchase feedback and fewer repeat purchases ($\beta_6 < 0$). In the empirical application to yogurt and ketchup, Ailawadi et al. (2007) find that acceleration is associated with an increase in repeat purchase rates, i.e., $\beta_6 > 0$.

5.6.2 Reference Prices

The reference price is the standard to which consumers compare an observed price in order to assess the latter's attractiveness (Kalyanaram and Winer 1995). Although there are many operationalizations of reference price (Winer 1986), there is a significant body of literature to support the notion that individuals make brand choices based on this comparison. Briesch et al. (1997) conclude that a brand-specific exponentially smoothed reference price provides the best fit and prediction:

$$RP_{bt}^h = \alpha RP_{bt-1}^h + (1 - \alpha)\text{Price}_{bt-1}^h, \tag{5.18}$$

where

RP_{bt}^{h} = household h's reference price of brand b at purchase occasion t
α = carryover parameter, $0 \le \alpha \le 1$

Prospect theory (Kahneman and Tversky 1979) predicts that consumers react more strongly to price increases than to price decreases (Kalyanaram and Winer 1995). To operationalize this, Erdem et al. (2001) define *LOSS* as the difference between the actual price and the reference price, given that the reference price is lower than the actual price. Similarly, *GAIN* is the difference given that the reference price is higher than the actual price:

$$LOSS_{bt}^{h} = \max\{\text{Price}_{bt-1}^{h} - RP_{bt}^{h}, 0\}$$
$$GAIN_{bt}^{h} = \max\{RP_{bt}^{h} - \text{Price}_{bt-1}^{h}, 0\}$$

To capture the direct effect of price as well as the effects of losses and gains, the utility function in the brand choice model Equation (5.5) can be specified as (Briesch et al. 1997):

$$\beta X_{bt}^{h} = \beta_1 PRICE_{bt} + \beta_2 FEAT_{bt} + \beta_3 DISP_{bt} + \beta_4 SL_b^{h} + \beta_5 LAST_{bt}^{h} \\ + \beta_6 LOSS_{bt}^{h} + \beta_7 GAIN_{bt}^{h}. \tag{5.19}$$

In (5.19), we expect $\beta_1 < 0$, $\beta_6 < 0$, and $\beta_7 > 0$. If losses loom larger than gains, $|\beta_6| > |\beta_7|$.

Recent papers question the findings regarding loss-aversion (Bell and Lattin 2000), and whether the reference price effect itself has been significantly over-estimated (Chang et al. 1999). The Chang et al. argument is that price sensitive consumers time their purchases to promotions, so observations of purchases with low prices over-represent price sensitive consumers and over-estimate both the loss and gain aspects of reference prices. Further work is needed to take into account these points. From a modeling standpoint, these papers illustrate the subtle but important challenges in modeling household-level data.

5.6.3 Consumer Learning

Frequent exposure to sales promotions may affect consumer perceptions of promotional activity (Krishna et al. 1991) and change their response to promotion. Mela et al. (1997) study the long-term effects of promotion and advertising on consumers' brand choice behavior. They use 8 ¼ years of panel data for a frequently packaged good. Their results indicate that consumers become more price and promotion sensitive over time because of reduced advertising and increased promotions. Mela et al. (1998) conclude that the increased long-term exposure of households to promotions has reduced their likelihood of making category purchases on subsequent shopping trips. However, when households do decide to buy, they tend to buy more of a good. Such behavior is indicative of an increasing tendency to "lie in wait" for especially good promotions. This study was among the first to provide evidence of purchase deceleration (see Section 5.3.4).

Bijmolt et al. (2005) provide a meta analysis across 1851 price elasticities reported in four decades of academic research in marketing. A salient finding is that in the period 1956–1999, the average (ceteris paribus) elasticity of sales to price went from -1.8 to -3.5. The relative elasticities (i.e., choice and market share) are quite stable (i.e., no significant change). Thus, the primary demand part of the sales elasticity is increasing over time, whereas the secondary demand part is stable. This finding is consistent with "lie-in-wait" behavior reported by Mela et al. (1998), but inconsistent with an increased sensitivity of the brand choice decision to price reported by Mela et al. (1997).

5.6.4 Permanent Effects

Recently, researchers have started to investigate the permanent effects of promotions. Permanent effects are defined as permanent changes in the mean level of criterion variables (e.g. sales) caused by sales promotions. There are two primary ways of modeling the permanent effects of sales promotion: Vector Autoregressive Models with X-variables (VARX) and Vector Error-Correction Models. A two-brand VARX model for sales promotion effects could be specified as follows (cf. Nijs et al. 2001):

$$
\begin{bmatrix} \Delta \ln S_{1t} \\ \Delta \ln S_{2t} \\ \Delta \ln \text{Price}_{1t} \\ \Delta \ln \text{Price}_{2t} \end{bmatrix} = \begin{bmatrix} c_{0,S1} + \sum_{s=2}^{13} c_{s,S1} SD_{st} + \delta_{S1} t \\ c_{0,S1} + \sum_{s=2}^{13} c_{s,S1} SD_{st} + \delta_{S2} t \\ c_{0,P1} + \sum_{s=2}^{13} c_{s,P1} SD_{st} + \delta_{P1} t \\ c_{0,P1} + \sum_{s=2}^{13} c_{s,P1} SD_{st} + \delta_{P2} t \end{bmatrix}
$$

$$
+ \sum_{i=1}^{8} \begin{bmatrix} \phi_{11}^i & \phi_{12}^i & \phi_{13}^i & \phi_{14}^i \\ \phi_{21}^i & \phi_{22}^i & \phi_{23}^i & \phi_{24}^i \\ \phi_{31}^i & \phi_{32}^i & \phi_{33}^i & \phi_{34}^i \\ \phi_{41}^i & \phi_{42}^i & \phi_{43}^i & \phi_{44}^i \end{bmatrix} \begin{bmatrix} \Delta \ln S_{1t-i} \\ \Delta \ln S_{2t-i} \\ \Delta \ln \text{Price}_{1t-i} \\ \Delta \ln \text{Price}_{2t-i} \end{bmatrix}
$$

$$
+ \begin{bmatrix} \gamma_{11} & \gamma_{12} & \gamma_{13} & \gamma_{14} \\ \gamma_{21} & \gamma_{22} & \gamma_{23} & \gamma_{24} \\ \gamma_{31} & \gamma_{32} & \gamma_{33} & \gamma_{34} \\ \gamma_{41} & \gamma_{42} & \gamma_{43} & \gamma_{44} \end{bmatrix} \begin{bmatrix} \Delta FEAT_{1t} \\ \Delta DISP_{1t} \\ \Delta FEAT_{2t} \\ \Delta DISP_{2t} \end{bmatrix} + \begin{bmatrix} u_{S1t} \\ u_{S2t} \\ u_{P1t} \\ u_{P2t} \end{bmatrix}
$$

$$(5.20)$$

where

$\Delta \ln S_{bt} = \ln S_{bt} - \ln S_{bt-1}$, i.e., current minus lagged sales of brand b.

$\Delta \ln \text{Price}_{bt} = \ln \text{Price}_{bt} - \ln \text{Price}_{bt-1}$, i.e., current minus lagged price of brand b.

$SD_{st} = $ a 4-weekly seasonal dummy variable (1 during 4-week period s, 0 else)

$t = $ deterministic trend variable

$\Delta FEAT_{bt} = FEAT_{bt} - FEAT_{bt-1}$, i.e., the current minus lagged feature dummy for brand b.

$\Delta DISP_{bt} = DISP_{bt} - DISP_{bt-1}$, i.e., the current minus lagged display dummy for brand b.

Equation (5.20) is estimated by OLS or SUR (Seemingly Unrelated Regression). Once the parameters have been estimated, researchers calculate Impulse Response Functions (IRF) to track the incremental impact of a one standard deviation price promotion shock on sales in periods t, $t+1$, $t+2,\ldots\ldots$. The permanent effect of a promotion is the asymptotic value of log sales when $t \to \infty$. Figure 5.1 shows a hypothetical Impulse Response Function with a zero permanent effect of a promotion in week 1. Such a pattern corresponds to no unit root in the sales series (Dekimpe and Hanssens 1995). When sales have a unit root, there can be a nonzero permanent effect of a one-time promotion as illustrated in Fig. 5.2. The area under the curve in grey in both figures is called the "intermediate effect", or "cumulative effect".

Since the calculation of permanent effects for VARX models is somewhat involved (one has to calculate Impulse Responses Functions), Fok et al. (2006) propose a Vector-Error Correction model for the short- and long-term effects of sales promotions on *brand sales*:

$$\Delta \ln S_t = \beta_0 + \sum_{k=1}^{K} A_k^{sr} \Delta X_{kt} + \Pi \left(\ln S_{t-1} - \sum_{k=1}^{K} A_k^{lr} X_{k,t-1} \right)$$

$$+ \nu_t, \ \nu_t \sim N(0, V) \tag{5.21}$$

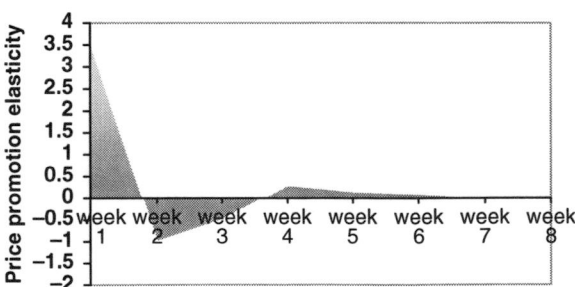

Fig. 5.1 Promotion in week 1 with a zero permanent effect

Fig. 5.2 Promotion in week 1 with a positive permanent effect

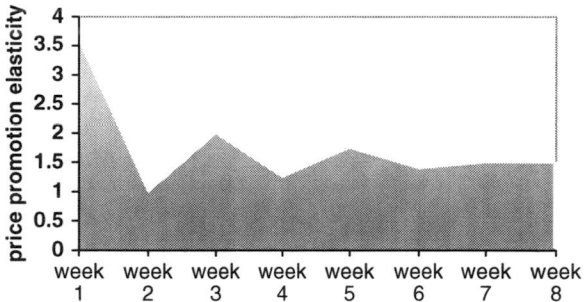

where

$\Delta =$ first difference operator: $\Delta X_t = X_t - X_{t-1}$

$S_t =$ Vector $(Bx1)$ with sales (in kilo) of brands $b = 1,..,B$ in week t

$X_{kt} =$ Vector $(Bx1)$ with marketing-mix variable k $(k = 1, ..., K)$ of brands $b = 1,...,B$ in week t

$\beta_0 =$ Vector $(Bx1)$ with intercepts of brands $b = 1,...,B$

$A_k^{sr} =$ Matrix (BxB) with short-term effects of marketing-mix variable k

$A_k^{lr} =$ Matrix (BxB) with long-term effects of marketing-mix variable k

$\Pi =$ Diagonal matrix (BxB) with adjustment effects

$\nu_t =$ Vector $(Bx1)$ of error terms of brands $b = 1,...,B$ in week t

$V =$ Variance-Covariance matrix (BxB) of the error term ν_t

The diagonal elements of A_k^{sr} and A_k^{lr} give, respectively, the short-ty and long-run effects of the k-th marketing-mix variable of each brand, while the off-diagonal elements (which need not be symmetric) capture the corresponding cross effects. The Π parameters reflect the speed of adjustment towards the underlying long-term equilibrium. We refer to Fok et al. (2006) for a formal proof of these various properties, and to Franses (1994) or Paap and Franses (2000), among others, for previous applications. Horváth and Franses (2003) provide an in-depth discussion about testing for whether Error Correction model is appropriate, and the cost of estimating an Error Correction model when it is not appropriate, and vice versa.

Using a VARX model, Nijs, Dekimpe et al. (2001) study the effects of consumer price promotions on *category sales* across 460 consumer product categories over a 4-year period. The data describe national sales in Dutch supermarkets and cover virtually the entire marketing mix. The key results are displayed in Table 5.6. Note that in 98% of the cases, there is no permanent effect of promotions on category sales, i.e., the Impulse Response Function resembles Fig. 5.1. This is a sensible result, in that one would not expect permanent category sales effects in the mature categories carried by most supermarkets. An interesting extension of this work would be to look at new categories such as MP3- or DVD players.

Steenkamp et al. (2005) use a VARX model to study the permanent effects of promotions and advertising on *brand sales* based on scanner data for the top

Table 5.6 Category-demand effects of price promotions across 460 categories

	Short term effects	Permanent effects
Positive	58%	2%
Negative	5%	0%
Zero	37%	98%

This table is based on Nijs et al. (2001).

three brands from 442 frequently purchased consumer product categories in the Netherlands. Their major results are displayed in Table 5.7. A key conclusion is that in the far majority of the cases, there are no permanent effects of sales promotions and advertising on own-brand sales. In the short term, these effects do exist, and they are more prevalent and much stronger for promotions than for advertising.[7] Interestingly, Pauwels et al. (2002) show, based on data from the canned soup and yogurt categories, that permanent promotion effects are virtually absent for brand choice, category incidence, and purchase quantity.

Fok et al. (2006) apply their VEC model (20) to seven years of U.S. data on weekly *brand sales* of 100 different brands in 25 product categories. On average, the cumulative promotional price elasticity (−1.91) tends to be smaller in absolute value than the immediate promotional price elasticity (−2.29). Hence, some of the positive effects of a price promotion are compensated in the periods following the promotion by, for example, the effects of acceleration. Actually, the implied size of the postpromotion dip is 17% (100%*((2.29−1.91)/2.29)), which is quite close to the 22% postpromotion dip calculated in Macé and Neslin (2004).[8] It is also interesting to note that the short-term

Table 5.7 Own-brand sales effects across 442 categories

	Non-significant	Positive own-sales elasticity	Negative own-sales elasticity	Mean own-sales elasticity
Short Term Effects				
Price promotions	30.96%	63.54%	5.50%	3.989
Advertising	67.00%	20.45%	12.55%	0.014
Permanent Effects				
Price promotions	94.99%	4.15%	0.86%	0.046
Advertising	98.23%	1.28%	0.49%	0.000

This table is based on Steenkamp et al. (2005).

---

[7] We note that the final version of this paper (Steenkamp et al. 2005) does not contain these results for anymore, since the journal requested the authors to focus on competitive reactions.

[8] The 22% cannot directly be calculated from Table 4 in Macé and Neslin (2004) because the elasticities reported in that table are point elasticities and therefore do not exactly correspond to the 20% price cut effects calculated in that table. However, calculations using the detailed results summarized in Macé and Neslin's Table 4, reveal that on average, 66.2% of the combined pre and post effect is due to post effects. Since the combined effect reported in Macé and Neslin's Table 4 is 33.3% of the bump (1−.667 from the last column in the table), the percentage due to postpromotion dips is .662*.333 = .2204 = 22.0%.

regular price elasticity (-0.54) is much smaller in magnitude than the short-term price promotion elasticity (-2.29).

5.6.5 Competitive Reactions[9]

Since promotions affect cross-brand sales and market shares, and they are relatively easy to replicate, competitive reactions are likely. Competitors may either retaliate or accommodate a promotion initiated by a rival brand. Moreover, they may respond in-kind with the same instrument (e.g., price cut followed by price cut) or with another instrument (e.g., price cut followed by volume-plus promotion). Leeflang and Wittink (1992, 1996) specify reaction functions that allow for the measurement of the degree and nature of competitive reactions:

$$
\ln\left(\frac{P_{bt}}{P_{b,t-1}}\right) = \alpha_i + \sum_{\substack{b=1 \\ b' \neq b}}^{B} \sum_{t*=1}^{T*+1} \beta_{bb't*} \ln\left(\frac{P_{b',t-t*+1}}{P_{b',t-t*}}\right)
$$

$$
+ \sum_{t*=2}^{T*+1} \beta_{bbt*} \ln\left(\frac{P_{b,t-t*+1}}{P_{b,t-t*}}\right) + \tag{5.22}
$$

$$
\sum_{b'=1}^{B} \sum_{t*=1}^{T*+1} \sum_{x=1}^{3} \tau_{xbb't*}\left(wx_{b',t-t*+1} - wx_{b',t-t*}\right) + \varepsilon_{bt}
$$

$\frac{P_{ib}}{P_{b,t-1}}$ = ratio of successive prices for brand b in period t

$wx_{b,t} - wx_{b,t-1}$ = first difference for the three types of promotions for brand b: $x = 1$ (feature), $x = 2$ (display), and $x = 3$ (feature and display).

The parameter $\beta_{bb't*}$ represents competitive reactions with the same instrument: the price response by brand b to a price change by brand b' that took place $t*$ periods ago. Parameter $\tau_{xbb't*}$ captures competitive reactions with different instruments: the price response by brand b to a promotion of type x by brand b' that took place $t*$ periods ago.

For the grocery category under study, Leeflang and Wittink (1992) find that competitor reactions occur quite frequently, especially using the same marketing instrument as the initiator. By studying competitive reactions based on over 400 consumer product categories over a four-year time span, Steenkamp et al. (2005) test the empirical generalizability of Leeflang and Wittink (1992, 1996). They use VARX models similar to Equation (5.20). Table 5.8 shows that the predominant reaction to a price promotion

---

[9] In this same handbook, the chapter by Leeflang (7) provides an in-depth discussion on models for competitive reactions, including structural models.

Table 5.8 Competitive reactions to price promotions

Reaction with price promotion	Short-term effect	Long-term effect
No reaction	54%	92%
Competitive reaction	30%	5%
Cooperative reaction	16%	3%

This table is based on Steenkamp et al. (2005).

attack is no reaction at all. Indeed, for 54% of the brands under price promotion attack, the average short-term promotion reaction is not significantly different from zero. Furthermore, the significant short-term promotion reactions are twice more as likely to be retaliatory than accommodating (30% versus 16%). Table 5.8 also shows that long-term reactions are very rare. In over 90% of the instances, price promotion attacks do not elicit a persistent or long-term price promotion on the part of the defending brand.

Steenkamp et al. (2005) find that absence of reaction corresponds primarily to the absence of harmful cross-sales effects. Only 118 out of 954 brands miss an opportunity in that they could have defended their position, but the chose not to. When managers do opt to retaliate, effective retaliation is prevalent (63%). In 56% of these cases the response neutralizes the competitive attack, whereas in 36% of these cases the net effect is positive for the defending brand.

An interesting perspective is provided by Pauwels (forthcoming). He finds that competitive response to promotions plays a relatively minor role in post-promotion effects. The major factor in post-promotion effects is the company's own "inertia" to continue promoting in subsequent weeks. That is, companies tend to follow up promotions in period t with more promotions in period $t+1$, etc. This is a very interesting finding in that it says companies are highly myopic when it comes to formulating promotion policy, basing the frequency of future promotions on the frequency of past promotions, rather than considering the competitive implications.

5.7 Promotions to the Trade – Introduction

Manufacturers use promotional discounts to the trade as an incentive for the trade to buy more of the brand, and to sell more to consumers by passing through at least part of the discount. The key two phenomena that determine the effectiveness of trade promotions are forward buying (Section 5.8) and pass-through (Section 5.9). In Section 5.11 we present decision models for manufacturers who want to optimize their trade promotions, and in Section 5.12 we discuss models for retailers who want to optimize pass-through and forward-buying.

5.8 Forward Buying

Trade promotions offered by manufacturers often lead to forward buying by retailers. Forward buying is essentially purchase acceleration by retailers in that retailers purchase during the promotion period to satisfy demand in future periods (Neslin 2002, p. 36). While a retailer may sell part of the extra stock to consumers at a discount, their key incentive to forward buy is to sell the other part at regular price. We show an example in Fig. 5.3a and 5.3b.

Suppose a manufacturer offers a trade deal in period t-1 in order to stimulate a retailer to promote in period t. Figure 5.3a shows how a retailer may order higher quantities in period $t-1$ than usually to benefit from the lower wholesale price offered by the manufacturer in period t. Forward buying implies that the stock bought in period $t-1$ not only satisfies the extra demand during the consumer promotion in period t (see Fig. 5.3b), but also demand sold at regular price in period $t+1$ and beyond. Figure 5.3b shows that not only the retailer forward buys but also consumers: the bump in period t is followed by a postpromotion dip in period $t+1$.

To measure the effectiveness and profitability of trade promotions, Blattberg and Levin (1987) model the interplay between manufacturer factory shipments, retailer promotions, retailer sales, and retailer inventories:

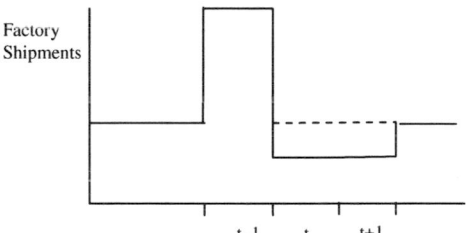

During period t–1 there is a lower wholesale price than during the other periods

Fig. 5.3a Response of ex-factory sales to trade promotion

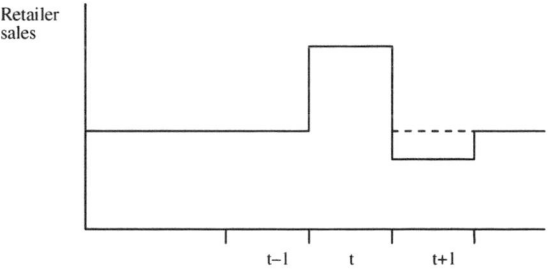

During period t there is a lower retail price than during the other periods

Fig. 5.3b Response of retailer sales to consumer promotion

$$\text{Shipments}_t = f_1(\text{Inventories}_{t-1}, \text{Trade Promotions}_t) \qquad (5.23)$$

$$\text{Consumer Promotions}_t = f_2 (\text{Trade Promotions}_t,$$
$$\text{Trade Promotions}_t, \text{Inventories}_{t-1)} \qquad (5.24)$$

$$\text{Retailer Sales}_t = f_3(\text{Consumer Promotions}_{t-1}) \qquad (5.25)$$

$$\text{Inventories}_t = f_4(\text{Inventories}_{t-1}, \text{Shipments}_t,$$
$$\text{Retailer Sales}_{t-1}) \qquad (5.26)$$

Equation (5.23) captures the effect of trade promotions and inventories on how much quantity the retailer orders. The willingness of retailers to run a consumer promotion depends on the availability of trade promotions and its own inventories (Equation (5.24)). Retail sales are driven by consumer promotions (Equation (5.25)), and Equation (5.26) shows that retail inventories are a function of its own lag, inflow (Ex-factory sales) and outflow (Retailer sales).

Another approach to evaluate the effectiveness of the trade promotion is to estimate what factory shipments would have been in the absence of the promotion (Abraham and Lodish 1987). Once we have an estimate for these baseline sales, the size of the bump can be quantified as the actual baseline factory shipments in the period with the wholesale discount (period t-1 in Fig. 5.3a) minus predicted factory shipments for the same period. To estimate baseline sales, Abraham and Lodish (1987) specify the PROMOTER model. Conceptually, it is a time series approach that tries to identify a "base" sales level by extrapolating the sales level during "normal" periods (see Abraham and Lodish 1993 for an application to retail promotions). The PROMOTER model decomposes sales into three components:

$$S_t = B_t + P_t + E_t \qquad (5.27)$$

where

$S_t =$ Factory shipments at time t
$B_t =$ Baseline at time t to be estimated
$P_t =$ Promotion effect at time t if any
$E_t =$ Noise term.

5.9 Pass-Through

The American Marketing Association defines pass-through as: "The number or percentage of sales promotion incentives offered to wholesalers or retailers by manufacturers that are extended to consumers by those channel members". For trade deals, it is the percentage of the discount that is passed on to the consumer in the form of a price reduction. Trade deals constitute close to 60% of manufacturers' marketing budgets (Trade Promotion Report 2005). Manufacturers believe that only half of their trade spending is passed through to the consumer, whereas retailers claim this percentage is substantially higher (Besanko et al. 2005). Though published numbers on pass-through range from 0% to 200% , pass-through is often less than 100% (Neslin 2002, p. 34). Besanko et al. (2005) estimate that for nine of the eleven categories studied, pass-through rates are higher than 60%.

Calculating pass-through involves some subtleties, which are directly related to forward buying. Take even a very simple situation (where cases are purchased by the retailer at the very beginning of the period, and purchased during the period by consumers), as shown in Table 5.9.

There is a trade deal in period 3. The retailer purchases 1000 cases, forward buying three periods. The retailer discounts the brand in period 3 but not in periods 4–6. What is pass-through? It appears sensible to calculate it based on the retailer's retail price in period t relative to what the retailer *paid* for the product it had available to sell in period t. In fact, Besanko et al. (2005) calculate pass through by regressing retail price versus acquisition cost of inventory (see pp. 128–129). If we do this we obtain:

$$\text{Retail\_}\hat{P}\text{rice}_t = 3.25 + 0.25 \times \text{Acquisition\_Cost}_t$$

According to this linear model, a $1 decrease in acquisition cost leads to a $0.25 decrease in Retail Price. Hence the pass-through rate is 25%.

This approach does not take into account the fact that more volume is sold when the brand is on promotion. This means pass-through increases if the retailer sells many units at the discounted price. For the data in Table 5.9, the average retail price is $4 (($4*200 + 4*200 + 4*200 + 4*200)/800$) when the inventory cost is $3, and $3.60 (($3*400 + 4*200+4*200+4*200)/1000$) when the inventory cost is $2. This would mean pass-through is $0.40. This perhaps

Table 5.9 Calculating pass-through for hypothetical data

Period	Whole-sale price	Cases purchased by retailer	Starting inventory	Value of inventory	Acquisition cost of inventory per unit	Retail price	Cases purchased by consumer
1	$3	200	200	$600	$3	$4	200
2	3	200	200	600	3	4	200
3	2	1000	1000	2000	2	3	400
4	3	0	600	1200	2	4	200
5	3	0	400	800	2	4	200
6	3	0	200	400	2	4	200
7	3	200	200	600	3	4	200
8	3	200	200	600	3	4	200

reflects a more realistic measure of pass-through since the retailer sold more units when the brand was on promotion.

Besanko et al. (2005) [BDG] find that pass-through rates vary substantially across products and across categories. Brands with larger market shares and brands that contribute more to retailer profit, receive higher pass-through. In addition, large brands are less likely than small brands to generate positive cross-brand pass-through, i.e, large brands do not induce the retailer to reduce the retail price of competing smaller products. In a critique of BDG paper, McAlister (forthcoming) argues that BDG find so many significant coefficients for cross-brand pass-through because they inadvertently inflated the number of independent observations by a factor of 15 (being the number of price zones). When she corrects for this overstatement of independent observations, McAlister (forthcoming) finds that the number of stable, significant coefficients for other brands' wholesale prices is lower than one would expect by chance.

Probably the biggest issue in pass-through research is the role of market share – does market share beget higher pass-through? Besanko et al. (2005), as well as Pauwels (forthcoming) find that it does. Walters (1989) find that market share has no impact on pass-through. A simple retailer profit model can show why a high-share brand might have difficulty achieving high pass-through. The argument is simple – a higher share brands has higher baseline sales, which means the retailer is sacrificing more margin by putting it on sale. Let:

B = baseline sales for promoted brand
B_0 = baseline sales for rest of category
M = profit margin for promoted brand
M_0 = profit margin for rest of category
D = trade deal discount
δ = pass through
η = gain in sales for promoted brand

Then: Retailer Profit with no pass through = $B(M+D) + B_0 M_0$
Retailer profit with d pass through = $B(M+D-\delta) + \eta(M+D-\delta) + (B_0 - \eta)M_0$
Difference = $-\delta B + \eta(M+D-\delta) - \eta M_0$

A high share brand has higher B and this exerts a force for decreasing δ. One could argue that higher share brands have higher η's, but that isn't good if $M_0 > M+D-\delta$, which could easily be the case if high share brands have lower regular margins for the retailer (they are stronger brands) and if the retailer passes through most of the trade deal (high δ). This leads the retailer to decrease δ, to minimize the baseline loss and make $M+D-\delta$ larger than M_0. Another approach is for the retailer to demand a steeper trade deal (large D). The manufacturer in turn might argue that promoting its high share brand grows the category through store switching, so that the η incremental units for the brand do not come completely from other brands in the category. In any case, the above analysis shows the challenges the high share brand must overcome to obtain higher pass-through.

Part II: Normative Models

In Part I we have focused on descriptive models for sales promotions, i.e. models that describe, analyze, and explain sales promotion phenomena. In Part II we discuss normative (decision) models for sales promotions, i.e. models that tell the decision maker what is the best (profit maximizing) decision on sales promotion activities. Section 5.10 focuses on models for promotions to consumers, whereas Section 5.11 zooms in on trade promotion models for manufacturers. Section 5.12 takes the perspective of a retailer who tries to optimize forward buying and pass-through in response to trade promotions offered by manufacturers.

5.10 Decision Models for Promotions to the Consumer

Tellis and Zufryden (1995) formulate a model to maximize cumulative *retailer* category profits over a finite horizon, by optimizing the depth and timing of discounts, and order quantities, for multiple brands. The model is based on an integration of consumer decisions in purchase incidence, brand choice and quantity. The retailer profit objective function is given by:

$$\max_{\{Disc_{bt}, O_{bt}, \delta_{bt}, \xi_{bt}\}} \left\{ \sum_{b,t} (M \cdot S_{bt} \cdot (\text{Price}_{bt} m_{bt} - Disc_{bt})) \right.$$

$$\left. - \sum_{b,t} (\xi_{bt} F_{bt} + h_{bt} \cdot (I_{bt} - I_{bt-1})/2 + \delta_{bt} Tag_{bt}) \right\}, \qquad (5.28)$$

where

$Disc_{bt}$	=	retailer discount level for brand b, during period t (≥ 0)
O_{bt}	=	retailer order quantity for brand b, made at beginning of period t (≥ 0)
δ_{bt}	=	integer price-change indicator ($= 1$ if a price change was made for brand b during t relative to t-1; 0 otherwise)
ξ_{bt}	=	integer order time indicator ($= 1$ if an order for brand b is placed during period t; 0 otherwise
M	=	total household market size
S_{bt}	=	average sales of brand b per customer during period t, computed as a function of causal variables (including, $Disc_{bt}$), and obtained via models for incidence, brand choice, and quantity.
$\text{Pr}ice_{bt}$	=	regular price of brand b during period t,
m_{bt}	=	regular retailer profit margin (excluding inventory costs) of brand b during period t,
F_{bt}	=	fixed costs of ordering brand b during period t

h_{bt} = cost per unit of holding inventory of brand b during period t
I_{bt} = retailer inventory for brand b during period t (this depends on orders O_{bt}, sales S_{bt}, and market size M)
Tag_{bt} = cost of retagging shelves if a price change of brand b occurs during period t

The retailer profit function (Equation (5.28)) equals the profit margin before inventory costs less inventory cost for the product category. Inventory costs include the fixed costs of placing an order, the average cost of holding inventory, and the costs for changing retail price such as retagging shelves. This optimization includes constraints that ensure that (1) inventories are updated appropriately and (2) demand is always met (see Tellis and Zufryden 1995 for details).

Natter et al. (forthcoming) present a decision support system for dynamic retail pricing and promotion planning. Their weekly demand model incorporates price, reference price effects, seasonality, article availability information, features and discounts. They quantify demand interdependencies (complements and substitutes) and integrate the resulting profit-lifting effects into an optimal pricing model. The methodology was developed and implemented at BauMax, an Austrian Do-It-Yourself (DIY) retailer. Eight pricing rounds with thousands of different Stock Keeping Units (SKUs) have each served as a testing ground for the approach. Based on various benchmarking methods, the implemented marketing decision-support system increased gross profit on average by 8.1 and sales by 2.1%.

Divakar et al. (2005) develop a sales forecasting model and decision support system that has been implemented at a major consumer packaged goods company. Managers are able to track forecast versus actual sales in a user-friendly "marketing dashboard" computing environment and drill down to understand the reasons for potential discrepancies. Based on that understanding, managers can adjust price and promotion accordingly. Divakar et al. report the company estimated that the DSS resulted in savings of $11 million on an investment of less than $1 million. The authors emphasize the importance of organization "buy-in," relevance, and diagnostics for successful real-world adoption of promotion models for decision-making.

Zhang and Krishnamurthi (2004) provide a decision-support system for planning micro-level customized promotions in online stores. Their approach provides recommendations on when to promote how much to whom. They take the perspective of a manufacturer who wants to optimize its expected gross profit from a household over three shopping trips with respect to a brand's price promotions. The corresponding objective function is:

$$\max_{\{Disc_{bt+s,s=0,1,2}\}} \left\{ \sum_{s=1}^{2} P(I_{t+s}^h = 1, C_{t+s}^h = b) \cdot E(Q_{bt+s}^h | I_{t+s}^h = 1, C_{t+s}^h = b) \right.$$

$$\left. \cdot (m_{bt+s} - Disc_{bt+s}) \right\} \qquad (5.29)$$

(all symbols have been defined previously; see Equations (5.1) and (5.28)). The optimization is subject to the constraint that discounts are nonnegative and that they do not exceed a fixed fraction of the regular price, to prevent brand equity erosion. Zhang and Krishnamurthi (2004) demonstrate that their optimization approach may lead to much higher profits, especially because it prevents wasting money by giving too deep price discounts.

5.11 Manufacturer Decision Models for Trade Promotions

Silva-Risso et al. (1999) present a decision support system that permits to search for a manufacturer's optimal trade promotion calendar. By modeling the purchase incidence (timing), choice and quantity decisions they decompose total sales into incremental and non incremental. The manufacturer's objective function is given by:

$$
\max_{\kappa_{bt}, FEAT_{bt}, DISP_{bt}} \left\{ \sum_{t=1}^{T} \rho^t \cdot M \cdot E(\Delta S_{bt}) \cdot (\text{Price}_{bt} \cdot (1 - \kappa_{bt} \cdot DSTEP) - MCOST_{bt}) \right.
$$

$$
- \sum_{t=1}^{T} \rho^t \cdot M \cdot E(B_{bt}) \cdot (\text{Price}_{bt} \cdot \kappa_{bt} \cdot DSTEP)
$$

$$
- \sum_{t=1}^{T} (\rho^t \cdot \delta_{bt} \cdot Tag_{bt} + FEAT_{bt} \cdot FCOST_{bt} \mid DISP_{bt} \cdot DCOST_{bt})
$$

$$
\left. + \sum_{t=T+1}^{T+13} \rho^t \cdot M \cdot E(\Delta S_{bt}|_{\text{nopromotion}}) \cdot (\overline{\text{Price}_b} - \overline{MCOST_b}) \right\} \qquad (5.30)
$$

Where δ_{bt} and Tag_{bt}, have been defined previously (Section 5.10), and

κ_{bt} = 0,1,2,...,10. This is the discount multiplier for brand-size b in week t. If $\kappa_{bt} = 0$, brand-size b is sold at the base price in week t. When the manufacturer offers a discount, it is computed as a multiple of a discount step level, e.g., 5%

ρ = discount rate

M = average number of category consumers that shop in the store or chain

$E(\Delta S_{bt})$ = expected number of incremental units of brand-size b in week t due to the promotion

Price_{bt} = wholesale base price of brand-size b in week t

$DSTEP$ = base discount step, e.g., 5%

$MCOST_{bt}$ = manufacturer's marginal cost of brand-size b in week t

$E(B_{bt})$ = expected number of baseline plus borrowed units of brand-size b in week t

$FCOST_{bt}$ = fixed cost charged by retailer to run a feature ad for brand-size b in week t

$DCOST_{bt}$ = fixed cost charged by retailer to set up a display for brand-size b in week t

$E(\Delta S_{bt}|_{\text{nopromotion}})$ = expected number of incremental units of brand-size b in week $t = T+1,\ldots,T+13$ due to carry-over effects from promotions in the period $t = 1,\ldots,T$.

$\overline{\text{Price}_b}$ = average wholesale base price of brand-size b

$\overline{MCOST_b}$ = average manufacturer's marginal cost of brand-size b

The objective function has four components: (1) the expected contribution from incremental units, (2) the expected opportunity cost of selling at a discount to consumers who would have bought the brand at the regular price, (3) the fixed costs associated with promotion decisions, and (4) the carry-over effects from consumption and purchase feedback over a 13-week period subsequent to the planning horizon. The objective function is maximized subject to constraints on the minimal and maximal number of promotions. Furthermore, the retailer may insist on a minimum level of category profits.

Neslin et al. (1995) develop a model that not only optimizes trade promotions but also advertising. Their dynamic optimization model considers the actions of manufacturers, retailers, and consumers. The manufacturer attempts to maximize its profits by advertising directly to consumers and offering periodic trade deal discounts in the hope that the retailer will in turn pass through a retailer promotion to the consumer. The manufacturer's objective can be written as follows:

$$\max_{MADV_t, MDISC_t} \left\{ \sum_{t=1}^{12} (MM - MDISC_t) * TRO_t - MADV_t \right\}, \quad (5.31)$$

where

$\quad\quad MM =$ per-case profit margin
$MDISC_t =$ manufacturer's trade discount in month t($/case)
$\quad TRO_t =$ total retail order in month t (cases)
$MADV_t =$ manufacturer's advertising expenditures in month t ($)

Next, Neslin et al. (1995) specify models for the retailer order and pass-through decisions, and for the effects of advertising and promotion on aggregate consumer demand. One of their findings is an intrinsic negative relationship between optimal levels of advertising and promotion. Higher advertising results in higher baseline sales, which increases the cost of promotion in the form of lost margin on baseline sales. Higher levels of promotion erode margin, thereby decreasing the incremental contribution of advertising. The result is that forces that tend to increase promotion tend to decrease advertising. These forces could be offset if more advertising results in stronger consumer response to promotions, but the point is, absent this interaction, this research suggests optimal promotion and advertising expenditures are negatively related.

5.12 Retailer Decision Models for Forward Buying and Pass-Through

Retailers may benefit from trade promotions by forward buying. Blattberg and Neslin (1990, p. 460) derive the optimal amount of forward buying:

$$W^* = \frac{52 \cdot (G \cdot P - HC)}{(PC \cdot P \cdot CC + 13 \cdot SC)} \tag{5.32}$$

where

$W^* =$ optimal number of week supply to buy forward
$G =$ gross profit dollar per case
$P =$ number of cases per pallet
$HC =$ handling cost per pallet
$PC =$ purchase cost (deal cost)
$CC =$ cost of capital
$SC =$ storage cost per pallet per month

Equation (5.32) shows that several variables influence the degree to which the retailer should forward buy. Whereas higher store-, handling-, capital-, and purchase costs lead to a lower optimal number of week supply to buy forward, gross profit dollar per case has a positive impact.

There have been a few studies that have derived the optimal level of pass-through for a retailer. In particular, Tyagi (1999) found that pass-through depends on the following function:

$$\varphi = \frac{S(\text{Price}^*)S''(\text{Price}^*)}{S'(\text{Price}^*)}, \tag{5.33}$$

where S is the demand function at the retail level, Price* is the optimal retail price, and the primes stand for the first or second derivatives of the demand function. Specifically, if $\varphi < 1$, retailer pass-through is less than 100%; if $\varphi = 1$, retailer pass-through is 100%, and if $\varphi > 1$, retailer pass-through is greater than 100%. Tyagi (1999) shows that for the linear and all concave consumer demand functions, optimal pass-through is less than 100%, However, for commonly used demand functions such as the constant elasticity demand function (e.g., the Scan*Pro model from Section 5.4.1), a rational retailer engages in greater than 100% pass-through. Moorthy (2005) generalizes Tyagi's formulation in several directions. First, besides whole price changes, Moorthy (2005) considers other cost components as well, such as inventory and labor costs. Second, Moorthy (2005) considers multiple retailers and multiple brands. Moorthy finds for example that cross-brand pass-through may be optimal, i.e., when decreasing the price of Brand A, it may be optimal to increase the price of Brand B.

Traditionally, trade promotions imply that retailers obtain a discount on the wholesale price for every unit *bought* on promotion. However, manufacturers often lose money on these deals as a result of forward-buying by retailers (Drèze and Bell 2003). Recently, a new type of trade deal has been introduced: the scan-back deal, which gives retailers a discount on units *sold* during the promotion. Drèze and Bell (2003) develop a theory to compare retailer pricing decisions and profitability under scan-back and traditional off-invoice trade deals. They derive that for a given set of deal parameters (regular price, deal size, and deal duration), the retailer always prefers an off-invoice deal (because of the benefits of forward buying), whereas the manufacturer always prefers a scan-back. However, manufacturers can redesign the scan-back to replicate the retailer profits generated by the off-invoice deal. The redesign makes the retailer indifferent between the off-invoice and the scan-back and makes the manufacturer strictly better off. The benefit of scan-back deals for retailers is that they economize on excess inventory costs, since scan-back deals do not lead to forward buying. For a redesigned scan-back in which the deal length is the same as off-invoice, but the deal depth is increased, consumer demand increases.

Part III: Conclusions

This part concludes this chapter on sales promotion models. Section 5.13 presents a summary of the key empirical findings on sales promotion effectiveness. Next, Section 5.14 offers practical guidelines in model implementation, and Section 5.15 elaborates on avenues of further research in the sales promotion realm.

5.13 Summary

This chapter has presented several models for the effects of sales promotions. In order to determine which of these models may be most relevant, we now summarize their key findings:

- Promotions to consumers lead to very strong sales promotion bumps in the short term. Hence it is essential that a model captures short-term effects.
- As a generalized finding across many categories and brands, brand switching effects expressed in unit sales are about 1/3 of the bump (Table 5.5), acceleration and deceleration effects are also 1/3 (Macé and Neslin 2004), and the remaining 1/3 is sometimes labeled "category expansion" (Van Heerde et al. 2004). Therefore it is important that any short-term model

distinguishes at least among these main sources. To obtain more detailed insight in the drivers of the bump, one can identify up to 24 different effects (Table 5.2).

- There are significant purchase-event feedback effects of promotions. That is, in the first couple of weeks after a promotion, a consumer's purchase behavior is affected by the promotion. Hence it is important to accommodate these feedback effects in models (Section 5.6.1).
- Permanent effects of promotions on brand and category sales are virtually absent (Section 5.6.4). That is, the effect of a promotion dies out after a number of weeks. Hence it may not be necessary to model these permanent effects.
- Two key factors that drive the profitability of trade promotions are pass-through and forward buying (Sections 5.8 and 5.9). Incremental sales at retail are driven by pass-through combined with consumer response to in-store promotions (Section 5.11). Any optimization model for trade dealing needs at least to include these phenomena.
- The rise of scanback deals may call for new models for pass-through and forward buying (Section 5.12).

5.14 Practical Model Guidelines

In this section we provide a number of practical guidelines for building sales promotion models. Irrespective of whether the aim is to build a descriptive model (Part I) or normative model (Part II), it is very important to first carefully screen the available data. Do they match the modeling objective? If the goal is to learn about consumer heterogeneity, data at the consumer level are required. If the goal is to understand aggregate promotion effects, data at the store-level or at a higher aggregation level are sufficient. Once the data have been collected, it is important that the most important causal drivers of the performance measure of interest are available. In other words, the independent variables in the dataset should be able to explain a significant proportion of the variation in the dependent variable. A next step is to check descriptive statistics (means, variances, time series plots) and identify (and possibly correct or delete) outliers.

The subsequent step is to specify a descriptive model. A descriptive model may be the end goal in itself or constitute the building block of a normative model. We provide in Table 5.10 a number of descriptive models, with a few (admittedly subjective) pros and cons of each. As for the individual-level models, our view is that the minimum requirements include heterogeneity (see Section 5.2.5) and purchase event feedback (see Section 5.6.1). In aggregate regression- and time series models, it is important to include dynamic effects (see Section 5.4.2). While aggregate logit models offer the benefits of (1) consistency with individual-level utility maximization and (2) parsimony in modeling cross-effects, they currently lack dynamic effects.

Table 5.10 A selection of models for sales promotion effects

Model	Dependent variable	Model	Advantage	Disadvantage	Key studies
			Household-Level Data		
Individual-level purchase behavior models	Brand choice	Multinomial logit model	- Consistent with utility theory	IIA-assumption (can be avoided by using a probit model)	- Guadagni and Little (1983) - Gupta (1988)
	Purchase incidence	Binomial logit model	- Proper model	-	- Gupta (1988) Bucklin et al. (1998)
	Purchase quantity	Poisson model	- Easy to estimate		
	Consumption	Consumption model	- Allows for flexible consumption	Mean-variance equality	Ailawadi and Neslin (1998)
	Store choice	Multinomial logit model	- Consistent with utility theory	IIA-assumption	Bucklin and Lattin (1992)
	Category choice	Multivariate Probit	- Proper model		Manchanda et al. (1998)
	SKU choice	Multinomial logit model	- Parsimonious	IIA-assumption	Fader and Hardie (1996)
	Incidence, choice, and quantity	Dynamic structural model	- Complete, integrated	Difficult to estimate	Erdem et al. (2003), Sun (2005)
			Weekly Store-Level Data		
Baseline model	Brand sales to consumers or to retailers	Time series smoothing procedure to distinguish baseline and promotional sales	- Intuitively appealing - Easy to implement	- Difficult to correct for all confounds - No parameterized model for running policy simulations	- Abraham and Lodish (1987) - Abraham and Lodish (1993)
Regression model	Brand sales at weekly store level	Scan*Pro model: multiplicative regression model	- Fits data well - Tested in many applications	- No dynamic effects - Many independent variables	Wittink et al. (1988)

Table 5.10 (continued)

Model	Dependent variable	Model	Advantage	Disadvantage	Key studies
		Scan*Pro model with lead and lagged effects	- Allows to measure pre- and postpromotion dips	- Many independent variables	Van Heerde et al. (2000)
		System of linear additive models	- Gives decomposition effects	- Linearity assumption - Many independent variables	Van Heerde et al. (2004)
Time series model	Brand sales at market level, or category sales at market level	Vector Autoregressive Model	- Allows for distinction between long- and short-term effects	- Many parameters - Computation of Impulse Response Functions	- Nijs et al. (2001) - Steenkamp et al. (2005)
	Brand sales at market level, or category sales at market level	Vector Error Correction Model	- Separate parameters for long- and short-term effects		- Fok et al. (2006)
Aggregate logit model	Brand sales at store level	Aggregate logit model, derived from aggregating individual logit models	- Consistent with utility theory - Parsimonious	- Hard to implement - No dynamic effects - Identification of heterogeneity - Specification of outside good	-Berry et al. (1995) - Dubé et al. (2002)

Software is increasingly available to estimate the models included in Table 5.10. There is no need to program maximum likelihood estimation for logit models, regression models, or Poisson models, as these are readily available in SPSS, Eviews, Stata, SAS, Limdep and other statistical packages. Stata also provides multinomial probit estimation. For time series models, Eviews, Stata and SAS/ETS are good choices. Some models (such as multivariate probit models, consumption model, dynamic structural models, aggregate logit models) are not (yet) available in the major commercial statistical programs. Custom-made programs are required to estimate these models, which can be accomplished in Gauss, Matlab, Stata, SAS, and the free statistical platform R (see Rossi et al. 2005for several Bayesian models in R). Nevo (2000) provides guidelines how to estimate a heterogeneous aggregate logit model.

5.15 Future Research

We hope this chapter enables researchers to implement models that may lead to more effective and profitable promotions. We also hope this chapter stimulates new research in areas that have not yet obtained sufficient attention. One such area is the effects of sales promotions for non-grocery products. While most of the models discussed in this chapter are for grocery products, it is unclear whether they are applicable to promotion effects for other items such as durables or services. Though some headway has been made (e.g., Van Heerde and Bijmolt (2005) present a promotion model for clothing stores), there is ample room for additional model development. We expect that deceleration effects are stronger in categories that are more expensive (per item) than grocery products. For example, consumers anticipate last-minute holiday deals (which, as a consequence, have become a self-fulfilling prophecy), many consumers postpone purchasing clothes till the sales season starts (Van Heerde and Bijmolt 2005), and the same may apply to car and furniture purchases.

Promotions involve dynamic effects, whose effects are not yet fully captured by current models. For example, we lack optimal retailer models that take into account consumer learning and expectations. One could take the model of Sun, Neslin, and Srinivasan (2003) as a starting point and next optimize profit from the firm perspective. Another gap in the literature are store-level models that disentangle state dependence, reference prices, and purchase timing effects.

The decision models for consumer promotions (Section 5.10) and trade promotions typically (Section 5.11) are based on descriptive models of demand responses to promotions. However, these decision models tend to exclude competitor responses. If competitors respond to a player's "optimal promotion plan", the outcome may become suboptimal for this player. It seems worthwhile to develop decision models that explicitly account for competitive reactions.

While the literature provides many insights into the effects of price promotions, features and displays, relatively little is known about other promotion types. One under-researched promotional vehicle are rebates, which are the durable goods analog of couponing (Blattberg and Neslin 1990, p. 13). While Thompson and Noordewier (1991) study the effects of rebates on sales, to our knowledge there are no studies on rebate effectiveness with household data. It would be highly desirable to develop an optimal rebate model that balances the desire for the rebate to generate a sale with the desire that the rebate is actually not used (since it costs the seller money). The more difficult it is to redeem the rebate, the less likely the rebate is to be redeemed, which increases profits, but makes it less likely that the rebate encourages the sale. A similar trade-off occurs for a refund promotion: a seller would like a refund to increase sales, but hopes that the actual number of refunds remains limited. Furthermore, it is not clear whether promotions that offer more value for the same price (20% extra volume, buy-one-get-one free) are more or less effective than equivalent price promotions (20% lower price, 50% lower price).

Another area worth additional investigation is the effects of promotions in the online world. For example: are the effects of emailed coupons different from the effects of traditional paper coupons? How can we model the click-through conversion process for banner ads and emails? Can we design an optimal contact model for email promotions for frequent shoppers, which maximizes both retailer and manufacturer profit? It seems that the sleeping giant is frequent shopper data. While stores and manufacturers have lots of these data that could be used to tailor promotions, they are reluctant to do this. A possible barrier is the scalability of the models that extract the right information from the data overload. It is up to marketing researchers to develop new models that overcome this barrier.

Appendix: Variable Definition for the Decomposition in Section 5.4.3

Van Heerde et al. (2004) obtain decomposition Equation (5.14) for price index variables with four types of support (with/without feature, with/without display). To achieve this, they transform the original four promotion variables (PI, FEATONLY, DISPONLY, FEAT&DISP) from the Scan*Pro model into seven new variables: price index with feature-support (PF), price index with display-only support (PD), price index with feature and display support (PFD), price index without support (PWO), plus FWO (Feature without price cut), DWO (Display without price cut), and FDWO (Feature&Display without price cut). Regular price is indicated by a price index with value "1". A 20% discount would be indicated by 0.8. The PWO, PF, PD, and PFD variables are defaulted to "1" if there is no price discount, but change depending on whether there is a discount and if so how it is supported. The FWO, DWO, and FDWO variables default to "0" and can equal "1" only if there is a feature, display, or both, without a price cut.

Table A.1 Transforming the four scan*Pro variables into seven new variables

	Scan*Pro variables					Seven new variables (Van Heerde, Leeflang, and Wittink 2000, 2004)						
	Price Index	Feature-only	Display-only	Feature & Display		Price Index without support	Price Index with Feature-only support	Price Index with Display only support	Price Index with Feature and Display support	Feature-only without price cut	Display-only without price cut	Feature and Display without price cut
Case #	PI	FEAT	DISP	FEAT & DISP		PWO	PF	PD	PFD	FWO	DWO	FDWO
1	1	0	0	0		1	1	1	1	0	0	0
2	.8	0	0	0		.8	1	1	1	0	0	0
3	.8	1	0	0		1	.8	1	1	0	0	0
4	.8	0	1	0		1	1	.8	1	0	0	0
5	.8	0	0	1		1	1	1	.8	0	0	0
6	1	1	0	0		1	1	1	1	1	0	0
7	1	0	1	0		1	1	1	1	0	1	0
8	1	0	0	1		1	1	1	1	0	0	1

To illustrate the transformation, Table A.1 contains the four original and seven new variables. In case # 1 there is no promotion, and the original price index (PI) equals 1 while the FEATONLY, DISPONLY, FEAT&DISP are zero, as defined in the Scan*Pro model. Since there is no (supported or unsupported) price discount in case #1, the four new price index variables (PWO, PF, PD, PFD) are all at their nonpromotional value of 1. The FWO, DWO, and FDWO variables are zero since there is no feature or display without a price cut. In case # 2 there is a twenty percent price discount without any support, which shows up in the original variables as a price index of .8 while FEATONLY, DISPONLY, FEAT&DISP remain zero. Since this is a price cut without support, among the new price indices only the price index without support (PWO) variable is decreased to .8. The other three price indices PF, PD, and PFD stay at their nonpromotional level of 1, while the FWO, DWO, and FDWO variables stay at their default value of 0. Case # 3 represents a twenty percent price cut with a feature-only, and hence price index with feature-only support (PF) is lowered to .8 (and again, all other variables are at their nonpromotional levels). Analogously, in cases # 4 and 5 the variables PD and PFD become .8, in turn. In case # 6 there is a feature without a price cut, which can be seen from the original variables since FEATONLY becomes 1 while PI remains 1. Consequently, among the new variables, FWO becomes 1, while DWO and FDWO remain 0, and PWO, PF, PD, and PFD stay 1 since there is no price cut. Cases #7 and 8 show how DWO and FDWO are defined.

Since price cuts tend to be communicated with feature and or display, the four Scan*Pro Variables tend to be highly correlated. The seven new variables, in contrast, describe seven mutually exclusive promotion situations, and they tend to be much less correlated. While the seven new variables are larger in number than the four Scan*Pro variables, a few of them typically do not vary and can therefore be excluded from models (especially the FDWO variable). Researchers who are concerned about multicollinearity in their (store-level) model may consider using the new set of seven variables proposed in this appendix.

References

Abraham, M.M., L.M. Lodish. 1987. Promoter: An Automated Promotion Evaluation System. *Marketing Science* **6**(2) 101–23.

Abraham, M.M., L.M. Lodish. 1993 An Implemented System for Improving Promotion Productivity Using Store Scanner Data. *Marketing Science* **12**(3) 248–69.

Abramson, C., R.L. Andrews, I.S. Currim, M. Jones. 2000. Parameter Bias from Unobserved Effects in the Multinomial Logit Model of Consumer Choice. *Journal of Marketing Research* **37**(4) 410–426.

Ailawadi, K.L., J. Cesar, B. Harlam, D. Trounce. 2007 Quantifying and Improving Promotion Effectiveness at CVS. *Marketing Science* **26**(4) 566–575.

Ailawadi, K.L., K. Gedenk, C. Lutzky, S.A. Neslin. 2007. Decomposition of the Sales Impact of Promotion-Induced Stockpiling. *Journal of Marketing Research* **44**(3) 450–468.

Ailawadi, K.L., K. Gedenk, S.A. Neslin. 1999. Heterogeneity and Purchase Event Feedback in Choice Models: An Empirical Analysis with Implications for Model Building. *International Journal of Research in Marketing* **16**(3) 177–98.

Ailawadi, K.L., S.A. Neslin. 1998. The Effect of Promotion on Consumption: Buying More and Consuming It Faster. *Journal of Marketing Research* **35**(August), 390–98.

Allenby, G.M., N. Arora, J.L. Ginter. 1998. On the Heterogeneity of Demand. *Journal of Marketing Research* **35**(3) 384–389.

Andrews, R.L., A. Ainslie, I.S. Currim. 2002. An Empirical Comparison of Logit Choice Models with Discrete Versus Continuous Representations of Heterogeneity. *Journal of Marketing Research* **39**(November) 479–87.

Andrews, R.L., A. Ansari, I.S. Currim. 2002. Hierarchical Bayes Versus Finite Mixture Conjoint Analysis Models: A Comparison of Fit, Prediction, and Partworth Recovery. *Journal of Marketing Research* **39**(1) 87–98.

Ansari, A., C.F. Mela, S.A. Neslin. 2006. Customer Channel Migration. *Working Paper*. Columbia Business School, New York.

Bell, D.R., J. Chiang, V. Padmanabhan. 1999. The Decomposition of Promotional Response: An Empirical Generalization. *Marketing Science* **18**(4) 504–26.

Bell, D.R., C.A.L. Hilber. 2006. An Empirical Test of the Theory of Sales: Do Household Storage Constraints Affect Consumer and Store Behavior? *Quantitative Marketing and Economics* **4**(2) 87–117.

Bell, D.R., T.-H. Ho, C.S. Tang. 1998. Determining Where to Shop: Fixed and Variable Costs of Shopping. *Journal of Marketing Research* **35**(August) 352–69.

Bell, D.R., J.M. Lattin. 1998. Shopping Behavior and Consumer Preference for Store Price Format: Why "Large Basket" Shoppers Prefer EDLP. *Marketing Science* **17**(1) 66–88.

Bell, D.R., J.M. Lattin. 2000. Looking for Loss Aversion in Scanner Panel Data: The Confounding Effect of Price Response Heterogeneity. *Marketing Science* **19**(2) 185–200.

Ben-Akiva, M., S.R. Lerman. 1991. *Discrete Choice Analysis.* MIT Press, Cambridge, MA.

Berry, S., J. Levinsohn, and A. Pakes. 1995. Automobile Prices in Market Equilibrium. *Econometrica* **63**(4) 841–90.

Besanko, D., J.-P. Dubé, S. Gupta. 2005. Own-Brand and Cross-Brand Retail Pass-Through. *Marketing Science* **24**(1) 123–137.

Besanko, D., S. Gupta, D. Jain. 1998. Logit Demand Estimation Under Competitive Pricing Behavior: An Equilibrium Framework. *Management Science* **44**(11, Part 1 of 2) 1533–1547.

Bijmolt, T.H.A., H.J. Van Heerde, R.G.M. Pieters. 2005. New Empirical Generalizations on the Determinants of Price Elasticity. *Journal of Marketing Research* **42**(May) 141–56.

Blattberg, R.C., R. Briesch, E.J. Fox. 1995. How Promotions Work. *Marketing Science.* **14**(3, Part 2 of 2) g122–g32.

Blattberg, R.C., A. Levin. 1987. Modelling the Effectiveness and Profitability of Trade Promotions. *Marketing Science* **6**(2) 124–146.

Blattberg, R.C., S.A. Neslin. 1990. *Sales Promotion, Concepts, Methods and Strategies.* Prentice Hall, Englewood Cliffs, New Jersey.

Bodapati, A.V., S. Gupta. 2004. The Recoverability of Segmentation Structure from Store-Level Aggregate Data. *Journal of Marketing Research* **41**(August) 351–64.

Bodapati, A.V., V. Srinivasan. 2006. The Impact of Feature Advertising on Customer Store Choice. Working Paper, Stanford Graduate School of Business.

Briesch, R.A., L. Krishnamurthi, T. Mazumdar, S.P. Raj. 1997. A Comparative Analysis of Reference Price Models. *Journal of Consumer Research* **24**(September) 202–214.

Bucklin, R.E., S. Gupta, S. Siddarth. 1998. Determining Segmentation in Sales Response Across Consumer Purchase Behaviors. *Journal of Marketing Research* **35**(May) 189–97.

Bucklin, R.E., J.M. Lattin. 1992. A Model of Product Category Competition Among Grocery Retailers. *Journal of Retailing* **68**(3) 271–93.

Chan, T., C. Narasimhan, Q. Zhang. 2006. Decomposing Purchase Elasticity with a Dynamic Structural Model of Flexible Consumption. *Working Paper*, Olin School of Business, Washington University.

Chang, K., S. Siddarth, C.B. Weinberg. 1999. The Impact of Heterogeneity in Purchase Timing and Price Responsiveness on Estimates of Sticker Shock Effects. *Marketing Science* **18**(2) 178–92.

Chiang, J. 1991. A Simultaneous Approach to the Whether, What and How Much to Buy Questions. *Marketing Science* **10**(4) 297–315.

Chiang, J., S. Chib, C. Narasimhan. 1999. Markov Chain Monte Carlo and Models of Consideration Set and Parameter Heterogeneity. *Journal of Econometrics* **89**(1–2) 223–248.

Chib, S., P.B. Seetharaman, A. Strijnev. 2004. Model of Brand Choice with a No-Purchase Option Calibrated to Scanner-Panel Data. *Journal of Marketing Research* **41**(May) 184–196.

Chintagunta, P.K. 1993. Investigating Purchase Incidence, Brand Choice, and Purchase Quantity Decisions of Households. *Marketing Science* **12**(2) 184–208.

Chintagunta, P.K. 2001. Endogeneity and Heterogeneity in a Probit Demand Model: Estimation Using Aggregate Data. *Marketing Science* **20**(4) 442–56.

Chintagunta, P.K., J.-P. Dubé. 2005. Estimating a Stockkeeping-Unit-Level Brand Choice Model That Combines Household Panel Data and Store Data. *Journal of Marketing Research* **42**(August) 368–379.

Chintagunta, P.K., D.C. Jain, N.J. Vilcassim. 1991. Investigating Heterogeneity in Brand Preferences in Logit Models for Panel Data. *Journal of Marketing Research* **28**(4) 417–428.

Dekimpe, M.G., D.M. Hanssens. 1995. The Persistence of Marketing Effects on Sales. *Marketing Science* **14**(1) 1–21.

Dekimpe, M., D.M. Hanssens. 1999. Sustained Spending and Persistent Response: A New Look at Long-Term Marketing Profitability. *Journal of Marketing Research* **36**(November) 397–412.

Divakar, S., B.T. Ratchford, V. Shankar. 2005. CHAN4CAST: A Multichannel Multiregion Forecasting Model for Consumer Packaged Goods. *Marketing Science* **24**(3) 333–350.

Dodson, J.A., A.M. Tybout, B. Sternthal. 1978. Impact of Deal and Deal Retraction on Brand Switching. *Journal of Marketing Research* **15**(May) 72–81.

Drèze, X., D.R. Bell. 2003. Creating Win-Win Trade Promotions: Theory and Empirical Analysis of Scan-Back Trade Deals. *Marketing Science* **22**(1) 16–39.

Dubé, J.-P., P.K. Chintagunta, A. Petrin, B.J. Bronnenberg, R. Goettler, P.B. Seetharaman, K. Sudhir, R. Thomadsen, Y. Zhao. 2002. Structural Applications of the Discrete Choice Model. *Marketing Letters* **13**(3) 207–20.

Erdem, T., S. Imai, M.P. Keane. 2003. Brand and Quantity Choice Dynamics Under Price Uncertainty. *Quantitative Marketing and Economics* **1**(1) 5–64.

Erdem, T., M.P. Keane. 1996. Decision-Making Under Uncertainty: Capturing Dynamic Brand Choice Processes in Turbulent consumer Goods Markets. *Marketing Science* **15**(1) 1–20.

Erdem, T., G. Mayhew, B. Sun. 2001. Understanding Reference-Price Shoppers: A Within- and Cross-Category Analysis. *Journal of Marketing Research* **38**(November) 445–457.

Erdem, T., B. Sun. 2001. Testing for Choice Dynamics in Panel Data. *Journal of Business and Economic Statistics* **19**(2) 142–152.

Fader, P.S., B.G.S. Hardie. 1996. Modeling Consumer Choice Among SKUs. *Journal of Marketing Research* **33**(November) 442–52.

Fok, D., C. Horváth, R. Paap, P.H. Franses. 2006. A Hierachical Bayes Error Correction Model to Explain Dynamic Effects of Price Changes. *Journal of Marketing Research* **43**(August) 443–461.

Franses, P.H. 1994. Modeling New Product Sales; an Application of Cointegration Analysis. *International Journal of Research in Marketing*. **11**(5) 491 502.

Gedenk, K., S.A. Neslin. 1999. The Role of Retail Promotion in Determining Future Brand Loyalty: Its Effect on Future Purchase Event Feedback *Journal of Retailing* **75**(4) 433–459.

Gönül, F., K. Srinivasan. 1996. Estimating the Impact of Consumer Expectations on Purchase Behavior: A Dynamic Structural Model. *Marketing Science* **15**(3) 262–79.

Guadagni, P.M., J.D.C. Little. 1983. A Logit Model Calibrated on Scanner Data. *Marketing Science* **2**(3) 203–238.

Gupta, S. 1988. Impact of Sales Promotion on When, What and How Much to Buy. *Journal of Marketing Research* **25**(November) 342–55.

Gupta, S., P.K. Chintagunta. 1994. On Using Demographic Variables to Determine Segment Membership in Logit Mixture Models. *Journal of Marketing Research* **31**(1) 128–136.

Ho, T.-H., J.-K. Chong. 2003. A Parsimonious Model of Stockkeeping-Unit Choice. *Journal of Marketing Research* **40**(August) 351–365.

Horsky, D., S. Misra, P. Nelson. 2006. Observed and Unobserved Preference Heterogeneity in Brand-Choice Models. *Marketing Science* **25**(4) 322–335.

Horváth, C., P.H.B.F. Franses. 2003. Deriving Dynamic Marketing Effectiveness From Econometric Time Series Models. in ERIM Report Series Research in Management. Rotterdam: Erasmus Research Institute of Management.

Hsiao, C. 1986. *Analysis of Panel Data*. Econometric Society Monograph 11, University of Cambridge, Cambridge, UK.

Jedidi, K., C.F. Mela, S. Gupta. 1999. Managing Advertising and Promotion for Long-Run Profitability. *Marketing Science* **18**(1) 1–22.

Kahneman, D., A. Tversky. 1979. Prospect Theory: An Analysis of Decision Under Risk. *Econometrica* **47**(March) 263–291.

Kalyanaram, G., R.S. Winer. 1995. Empirical Generalizations from Reference Price Research. *Marketing Science* **14**(3) G161–G169.

Kamakura, W.A., W. Kang. 2007. Chain-Wide and Store-Level Analysis for Cross-Category Management. *Journal of Retailing* **83**(2) 159–170.

Kamakura, W.A., G.J. Russell. 1989. A Probabilistic Choice Model for Market Segmentation and Elasticity Structure. *Journal of Marketing Research* **26**(November) 379–390.

Keane, M.P. 1997a. Modeling Heterogeneity and State Dependence in Consumer Choice Behavior. *Journal of Business and Economic Statistics* **15**(3) 310–327.

Keane, M.P. 1997b. Current Issues in Discrete Choice Modeling. *Marketing Letters* **8**(3) 307–322.

Krishna, A., I.S. Currim, R.W. Shoemaker. 1991. Consumer Perceptions of Promotional Activity. *Journal of Marketing* **55** 4–16.

Krishnamurthi, L., S.P. Raj. 1988. A Model of Brand Choice and Purchase Quantity Price Sensitivities. *Marketing Science* **7**(1) 1–20.

Lam, S.Y., M. Vandenbosch, J. Hulland, M. Pearce. 2001. Evaluating Promotions in Shopping Environments: Decomposing Sales Response into Attraction, Conversion, and Spending Effects. *Marketing Science* **20**(2) 194–215.

Leeflang, P.S.H., D.R. Wittink. 1992. Diagnosing Competitive Reactions Using (Aggregated) Scanner Data. *International Journal of Research in Marketing* **9** 39–57.

Leeflang, P.S.H., D.R. Wittink. 1996. Competitive Reaction Versus Consumer Response: Do Managers Overreact? *International Journal of Research in Marketing* **13**(2) 103–20.

Lodish, L.M. 2007. Another Reason why Academics and Practitioners Should Communicate More. *Journal of Marketing Research* **44**(February) 23–25.

Macé, S., S.A. Neslin. 2004. The Determinants of Pre- and Postpromotion Dips in Sales of Frequently Purchased Goods. *Journal of Marketing Research* **41**(August) 339–50.

Manchanda, P., A. Ansari, S. Gupta. 1999. The "Shopping Basket": A Model for Multicategory Purchase Incidence Decisions. *Marketing Science* **18**(2) 95–114.

McAlister, L. 2007. Cross-Brand Pass-Through: Fact or Artifact?. *Marketing Science* **26**(6) 876–898.

Mela, C.F., S. Gupta, D.R. Lehmann. 1997. The Long-Term Impact of Promotion and Advertising on Consumer Brand Choice. *Journal of Marketing Research* **34**(May) 248–61.

Mela, C.F., K. Jedidi, D. Bowman. 1998. The Long-Term Impact of Promotions on Consumer Stockpiling Behavior. *Journal of Marketing Research.* **35**(May) 250–62.

Moorthy, S. 2005. A General Theory of Pass-Through in Channels with Category Management and Retail Competition. *Marketing Science* **24**(1) 110–122.

Mulhern, F.J., R.P. Leone. 1991. Implicit Price Bundling of Retail Products: A Multiproduct Approach to Maximizing Store Profitability. *Journal of Marketing* **55**(October) 63–76.

Nair, H., J.-P. Dubé, P. Chintagunta. 2005. Accounting for Primary and Secondary Demand Effects with Aggregate Data. *Marketing Science* **24**(3) 444–460.

Narasimhan, C., S.A. Neslin, S.K. Sen. 1996. Promotional Elasticities and Category Characteristics. *Journal of Marketing* **60**(April) 17–30.

Natter, M., A. Mild, T. Reutterer, A. Taudes. 2007. An Assortment-Wide Decision-Support System for Dynamic Pricing and Promotion Planning in DIY Retailing. *Marketing Science* **26**(4) 576–583.

Neslin, S.A. 2002. *Sales Promotion.*Relevant Knowledge Series, Marketing Science Institute, Cambridge, Massachusetts.

Neslin, S.A., S.G. Powell, L.G. Schneider Stone. 1995. The Effects of Retailer and Consumer Response on Optimal Manufacturer Advertising and Trade Promotion Strategies. *Management Science* **41**(5) 749–766.

Nevo, A. 2000. A Practitioner's Guide to Estimation of Random-Coefficient Logit Models of Demand. *Journal of Economics & Management Strategy* **9**(4) 513–548.

Nijs, V., M.G. Dekimpe, J.B. Steenkamp, and D.M. Hanssens. 2001. The Category Demand Effects of Price Promotions. *Marketing Science* **20**(1) 1–22.

Paap, R., P.H. Franses. 2000. A Dynamic Multinomial Probit Model for Brand Choice with Different Long-Run and Short-Run Effects of Marketing-Mix Variables. *Journal of Applied Econometrics* **15**(6) 717–744.

Pauwels, K. 2007. How Retailer and Competitor Decisions Drive the Long-term Effectiveness of Manufacturer Promotions for Fast Moving Consumer Goods. *Journal of Retailing* **83**(3) 297–308.

Pauwels, K., D.M. Hanssens, S. Siddarth. 2002. The Long-Term Effects of Price Promotions on Category Incidence, Brand Choice and Purchase Quantity. *Journal of Marketing Research* **39**(November) 421–39.

Rhee, H., D.R. Bell. 2002. The Inter-Store Mobility of Supermarket Shoppers. *Journal of Retailing* **78**(4) 225–37.

Rossi, P.E., G.M. Allenby, R. McCulloch. 2005. *Bayesian Statistics and Marketing.* John Wiley and Sons, Chichester, West Sussex, England.

Rothschild, M.L., W.C. Gaidis. 1981. Behavioral Learning Theory: Its Relevance to Marketing and Promotions. *Journal of Marketing* **45**(2) 70–78.

Roy, R., P.K. Chintagunta, S. Haldar. 1996. A Framework for Investigating Habits. 'The Hand of the Past,' and Heterogeneity in Dynamic Brand Choice. *Marketing Science* **15**(3) 280–299.

Seetharaman, P.B. 2004. Modeling Multiple Sources of State Dependence in Random Utility Models: A Distributed Lag Approach. *Marketing Science* **23**(2) 263–271.

Seetharaman, P.B., A. Ainslie, P.K. Chintagunta. 1999. Investigating Household State Dependence Effects Across Categories. *Journal of Marketing Research* **36**(4) 488–500.

Sethuraman, R., V. Srinivasan, D. Kim. 1999. Asymmetric and Neighborhood Cross-Price Effects: Some Empirical Generalizations. *Marketing Science* **18**(1) 23–41.

Siddarth, S., R.E. Bucklin, D.G. Morrison. 1995. Making the Cut: Modeling and Analyzing Choice Set Restriction in Scanner Panel Data. *Journal of Marketing Research* **32**(3) 255–266.

Silva-Risso, J.M., R.E. Bucklin, D.G. Morrison. 1999. A Decision Support System for Planning Manufacturers' Sales Promotion Calendars. *Marketing Science* **18**(3) 274–300.

Singh, V., K. Hansen, R. Blattberg. 2006. Market Entry and Consumer Behavior: An Investigation of a Wal-Mart Supercenter. *Marketing Science* **25**(5) 457–476.

Steenkamp, J.B.E.M., V.R. Nijs, D.M. Hanssens, M.G. Dekimpe. 2005. Competitive Reactions to Advertising and Promotion Attacks. *Marketing Science* **24**(1) 35–54.

Sun, B. 2005. Promotion Effects on Endogenous Consumption. *Marketing Science* **24**(3) 430–443.

Sun, B., S.A. Neslin, K. Srinivasan. 2003. Measuring the Impact of Promotions on Brand Switching When Consumers Are Forward Looking. *Journal of Marketing Research* **40**(November) 389–405.

Tellis, G.J., F.S. Zufryden. 1995. Tackling the Retailer Decision Maze: Which Brands to Discount, How Much, When and Why? *Marketing Science* **14**(3, Part 1 of 2) 271–99.

Thompson, P.A., T. Noordewier. 1992. Estimating the Effects of Consumer Incentive Programs on Domestic Automobile Sales. *Journal of Business & Economic Statistics* **10**(4) 409–417.

Trade Promotion. 2005. Spending and Merchandising Study. Wilton, CT: Cannondale Associates.

Train, K. 2003. *Discrete Choice Methods with Simulation.* Cambridge University Press, Cambridge, UK . Also available at http://elsa.berkeley.edu/books/choice2.html.

Tyagi, R.K. 1999. A Characterization of Retailer Response to Manufacturer Trade Deals. *Journal of Marketing Research* **36**(November) 510–516.

Van Heerde, H.J., T.H.A. Bijmolt. 2005. Decomposing the Promotional Revenue Bump for Loyalty Program Members Versus Non-Members. *Journal of Marketing Research* **42**(November) 443–457.

Van Heerde, H.J., S. Gupta. 2006. The Origin of Demand: A System to Classify the Sources of the Sales Promotion Bump. *Working Paper*, University of Waikato.

Van Heerde, H.J., S. Gupta, D.R. Wittink. 2003. Is 75% of the Sales Promotion Bump Due to Brand Switching? No, Only 33% Is. *Journal of Marketing Research* **40**(November) 481–491.

Van Heerde, H.J., P.S.H. Leeflang, D.R. Wittink. 2000. The Estimation of Pre- and Post-promotion Dips with Store-Level Scanner Data. *Journal of Marketing Research* **37**(August) 383–395.

Van Heerde, H.J., P.S.H. Leeflang, D.R. Wittink. 2001. Semiparametric Analysis to Estimate the Deal Effect Curve. *Journal of Marketing Research* **38**(May) 197–215.

Van Heerde, H.J., P.S.H. Leeflang, D.R. Wittink. 2004. Decomposing the Sales Promotion Bump with Store Data. *Marketing Science* **23**(3) 317–34.

Varki, S., P.K. Chintagunta. 2004. The Augmented Latent Class Model: Incorporating Additional Heterogeneity in the Latent Class Model for Panel Data. *Journal of Marketing Research* **41**(2) 226–233.

Villas-Boas, J.M., R.S. Winer. 1998. Endogeneity in Brand Choice Models. *Management Science* **45**(10) 1324–38.

Walters, R.G. 1989. An Empirical Investigation into Retailer Response to Manufacturer Trade Promotions. *Journal of Retailing* **65**(2) 253–272.

Wedel, M., W.A. Kamakura. 1998. *Market Segmentation: Conceptual and Methodological Foundations.* Kluwer Academic Publishers, Boston, MA.

Winer, R.S. 1986. A Reference Price Model of Brand Choice for Frequently Purchased Products. *Journal of Consumer Research* **13**(September) 250–56.

Wittink, D.R., M.J. Addona, W.J. Hawkes, J.C. Porter. 1988. The Estimation, Validation, and Use of Promotional Effects Based on Scanner Data. *Working Paper*, Cornell University.

Zhang, J., L. Krishnamurthi. 2004. Customizing Promotions in Online Stores. *Marketing Science* **24**(4) 561–78.

Chapter 6
Models for Sales Management Decisions

Sönke Albers and Murali Mantrala

6.1 Sales Force as an Instrument of Personal Communication

Personal selling is a critical marketing instrument for acquiring and retaining customers in many industries, e.g., industrial products, financial and business services, medical and health services products, etc. Zoltners et al. (2008) report that by current estimates there are over 20 million full-time salespeople in the US, including over 15 million engaged in direct to consumer selling for companies such as Avon and Amway. Salespeople constitute a channel for two-way communication and social interaction with customers as well as a conduit for collecting market intelligence. Personal selling is the most effective way, especially in business markets, to learn about and assess a customer's needs, inform customers of standard and/or customized solutions, detail and demonstrate complex high-value products, handle objections, close sales and provide long-term continuing service. However, the high impact of sales forces on firms' sales comes at a high cost. Dartnell's *30th Sales Force Compensation Survey: 1998–1999* reports the average company spends 10% and some industries spend as much as 40% of their total sales revenues on sales force costs. In total, the US economy is estimated to spend $800 billion on sales forces, almost three times the amount spent on advertising in 2006 (Zoltners et al. 2008).

A recent meta-analysis of previous empirical studies of personal selling-sales response relationships by Albers et al. (2008) indicates that the mean personal selling-sales elasticity (corrected for methodological biases) is about 0.352, significantly larger than the mean advertising-sales elasticity of 0.22 (0.26) for established (new) products reported by Assmus et al. (1984). Thus, changes in the deployment of personal selling efforts can have large impacts on companies' toplines as well as bottom lines, e.g. profit may be improved by 5–10% through better sales effort allocation and territory design (Zoltners and Sinha 2005). Not surprisingly, models aimed at supporting sales managers' decisions related to

S. Albers
Innovation, New Media and Marketing, Christian-Albrechts-University,
Kiel, Germany
e-mail: albers@bwl.uni-kiel.de

B. Wierenga (ed.), *Handbook of Marketing Decision Models*,
DOI: 10.1007/978-0-387-78213-3_6, © Springer Science+Business Media, LLC 2008

optimizing selling effort allocation have been an important focus of research in marketing (Albers 2000a). Indeed, sales force management was one of the first areas of marketing decision making where models were successfully used. However, considering, that salespeople are human resources as well as marketing instruments, sales force decision models research confronts problems where questions of marketing are intertwined with issues of managing worker motivation and behavior. This convergence of marketing and human resource management issues poses interesting questions as well as challenges for sales force researchers that do not arise in other marketing domains such as advertising or sales promotion. In particular, the necessary data for sales force research such as sales representatives' effort inputs, sales outputs, compensation, personal characteristics etc., are usually difficult to collect from organizations because of their sensitive nature. This appears to be a major reason why the volume of sales force decision models research papers is much smaller than the number of papers devoted to advertising and promotion management over the last 20 years.

Productive selling effort allocation is the cornerstone problem in sales force management. This chapter focuses on a set of related subproblems that have been aptly called issues of either 'direct' or 'indirect' control of selling effort allocation by Zoltners and Gardner (1980). 'Direct' control refers to selling effort allocation decisions that can be directed and/or monitored by sales management, e.g., salespeople's customer call time allocation plans, allocation of selling effort or salespeople available across customer segments or product groups, sales territory design, sales force structuring and sizing, while 'indirect control' refers to the use of compensation plans and incentives to induce salespeople to put in the level and allocation of selling efforts towards various sales activities desired by management. The decidedly more human resource management issues of recruiting, training, development and career management, although very important, fall outside the scope of this chapter (see Albers 2002 for a review). Also, this chapter restricts itself to models for management of field or outside sales forces and does not cover the management of operations of inside sales forces such as retail sales associates, telemarketers or customer service reps.

More specifically, the objectives of this chapter are three-fold: First, we survey the main developments and insights from extant research on direct and indirect control problems with greater emphasis on works that have appeared since the previous reviews by Vandenbosch and Weinberg (1993), Coughlan (1993) and Albers (1996b). Second, we emphasize insights and recommendations useful to practitioners. Third, we identify current and emerging research needs and propose new directions for research in the changing environment of selling. Sales managers today face rapidly changing and increasingly complex selling environments and the need for updated conceptual frameworks, models and tools to address their decision problems is pressing. More specifically, with increasing customer expectations, the personal selling activities and sales cycles in many industries have become more complex, customer relationship-oriented, and team-based, compared to the traditional "lone wolf" model involving single agents engaged in repetitive transactional selling to single buyers (e.g., Weitz and Bradford 1999, Jones et al. 2005, Brown et al. 2005). As we discuss later, such changes in sales settings have been considered only to a limited extent in sales force models research to date and offer interesting and important directions for future research.

The rest of this chapter is organized as follows. Section 6.2 provides an overview of the major selling effort allocation decision areas and their interconnections – what we call the 'selling effort decisions complex' - and evolution of the related modeling literature streams covered in this chapter. The core component of any model for optimal allocation of selling effort across some sales entities or control units such as customers or products is the sales response function, i.e., the relationship representing how the sales output of the relevant sales entity varies with the selling effort applied to it. Section 6.3, therefore, discusses research developments with respect to specification and estimation of sales response functions. Section 6.4 then addresses directly controlled selling effort deployment problems while Section 6.5 addresses problems of indirect control of selling effort. Section 6.6 suggests new questions and directions for further research, and Section 6.7 concludes the chapter.

6.2 Overview of the Selling Effort Decisions Complex

Like other marketing instruments, sales force decisions must be governed by the overarching business strategy of the firm, i.e., the firm's choices with respect to its basic market definition, generic strategy, product offerings, target market segments, and positioning. Within the overarching strategy, the firm must decide its go-to-market strategy i.e., the mix of sales and marketing channels selected to reach target segments, including the choice between employing a company-owned sales force or contracting out (outsourcing) the sales function to independent agents or selling partners. In this chapter, all the decision models we review assume that the firm's business and go-to-market strategy are in place and it employs a direct (company-owned) sales force.

Figure 6.1 displays the 'complex' of selling effort allocation decision areas that we cover in this chapter. It shows the more strategic direct control decision areas with respect to sales force *size* and *structure or organization* at the top and on the upper right-hand side, and the indirect control decision area of sales force compensation strategy, e.g., the *level and form* of the compensation plan, on the upper left-hand side. These are "strategic" decisions in that they are usually based on competitive and business growth strategy considerations and set by top management for several years. They guide lower-level, shorter-term, e.g., annual, operational planning by senior and middle management with respect to *sales territory design*, i.e., the assignment of groups of customers or "sales coverage units" (SCUs) to salespeople, and *specification of the selected*

Fig. 6.1 Selling effort decisions complex

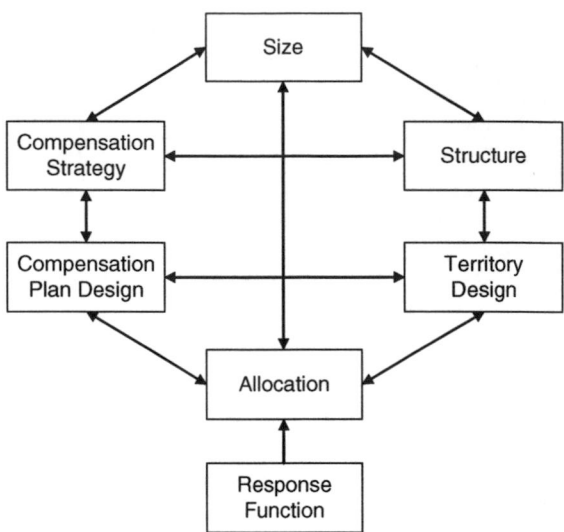

form of compensation plan, e.g., sales commission 'rates' and 'gates' (ranges of sales output to which different commission rates apply). Ultimately, as indicated in Fig. 6.1, these operational decisions will impact tactical selling effort allocation plans and decisions made by middle and front-line management (e.g., district managers) as well as individual sales representatives. Conceptually, these disaggregate effort allocation decisions will be guided by local managers' and/or sales representatives' knowledge of sales response functions of the relevant sales entities figuring in the decision, e.g., products, market segments or individual customers/accounts. Consequently, 'response functions' are shown as the root of Fig. 6.1 because forming assessments of these relationships is a prerequisite for optimizing any of the higher-level decisions.

Figure 6.1 also indicates that all the decision areas are, in principle, interdependent, thereby forming a decisions complex. For example, a fixed sales force size would restrict how the sales force is partitioned (structured), fix the number of sales territories, and determine the total expected compensation payout according to some compensation plan. Conversely, making strategically desirable alterations in the sales force structure and/or compensation plan will impact salespeople's workloads and allocations of efforts, and in turn drive the required overall sales force size. Similarly, the selected sales force structure has implications for the optimal form/s of the compensation plan and sales territory design to be utilized. Further, sales territory design impacts short-term sales goal-setting which in turn would influence sales call targets and the actual allocation of selling effort by an individual representative. Thus, optimization of decisions at each of these levels depends on the assumptions made with respect to lower-level call allocation decision rules and/or call capacity constraints, as well as higher-level policy constraints, e.g., with respect to total sales force size and the form of compensation plan.

These interdependencies considerably complicate the development of models for globally optimizing sales force decisions. Not surprisingly, therefore, sales force research has progressed by (a) separating the treatment of direct control and indirect control (compensation) decision problems and (b) focusing on solving one or a subset (usually two) of direct control decision problems assuming other parts of the selling effort decisions complex are fixed. Examples of such compartmentalized models include Lodish's (1971) CALLPLAN for sales calls allocation across customers subject to a fixed sales force size, structure and territory design; models for sales territory design and effort allocation subject to a fixed sales force size and structure such as those of Lodish (1975), Zoltners and Sinha (1983), Skiera and Albers (1998); models for sales force sizing and allocation subject to a fixed sales force structure such as those proposed by Lodish (1980), Zoltners and Sinha (1980), Lodish et al. (1988) and so on. Very few models, indeed only three to our knowledge, have attempted to integrate and simultaneously solve three or more of the direct control decisions, namely, Beswick and Cravens (1977), Rangaswamy et al. (1990), Drexl and Haase (1999). Among these, only Beswick and Cravens' 'multistage model' suggests a basis for integrating important indirect control decisions like setting sales quotas and evaluating performance. However, as pointed out by Skiera and Albers (2008), such models have had limited success in actual applications because of the differing organizational groups, levels, and time horizons of stakeholders involved in these decisions.

6.2.1 Evolution of Selling Effort Decisions Research

Table 6.1 displays the evolution of research related to direct and indirect control selling effort management problems over the past 4 decades. According to their different foci, we distinguish between the 'classic period' of the years up to 1980; the 'middle period' of 1981–1995, and the 'contemporary period' of 1996 onwards. The classic period research is dominated by an Operations Research (OR)-orientation, e.g., implementable sales resource allocation optimization models utilizing subjectively calibrated sales response modes within a mathematical programming framework, or normative analyses aimed at deriving rules for the optimal design of specific forms of sales compensation plans – rather than establishing the optimal form of the plan under different conditions. In contrast, a transition from an OR orientation to a more Economics orientation is evident in sales management modeling research in the middle period. Thus, there are several papers on econometric sales response estimation using historical data rather than managerial judgments, and the agency-theoretic perspective from theoretical economics became the driver of much of the work done in the sales force compensation research area after the mid-'80s. In the contemporary period, the bulk of the modeling research in the sales management area is now clearly rooted in sophisticated econometrics and theoretical economics paradigms.

Table 6.1 Sales force decisions research literature evolution

	Classic period: up to 1980	Middle period: 1980–1995	Contemporary period: 1996–2007
Sales Response Modeling	Lambert and Kniffin (1970); Lodish (1971) (CALLPLAN); Turner (1971); Darmon (1975)	Hanssens and Levien (1983); LaForge and Cravens (1981/1982); Parsons and Vanden Abeele (1981); Mantrala, Sinha and Zoltners (1992)	Manchanda and Chintagunta (2004); Narayanan, Desiraju and Chintagunta (2004); Manchanda, Rossi and Chintagunta (2004); Mizik and Jacobson (2004); Manchanda et al. (2005): R; Manchanda and Honka (2005): R and MA; Dong et al. (2006); Albers, Mantrala, Sridhar (2008): MA Albers (1996a); Sinha and Zoltners (2001): FAR; Lodish (2001): FAR
Sales Resource Allocation	Lodish (1971) (CALLPLAN); Montgomery, Silk, and Zaragoza (1971) (DETAILER); Lodish (1976); Parasuraman and Day (1977); Fudge and Lodish (1977): (FA) Zoltners, Sinha and Chong (1979); Zoltners & Sinha (1980)	Lodish, Curtis, Ness, Simpson (1988) (Syntex FA); Vandenbosch and Weinberg (1993): R	
Sales Force Sizing	Lodish (1980)	Lodish, Curtis, Ness, Simpson (1988) (Syntex FA); Rao and Turner (1984); Rangaswamy, Sinha and Zoltners (1990)	Horsky and Nelson (1996)
Sales Force Structuring			
Sales Territory Alignment	Hess and Samuels (GEOLINE) (1971); Shanker, Turner and Zoltners (1975); Lodish (1975); Zoltners (1976); Glaze and Weinberg (1979)	Zoltners and Sinha (1983)	Skiera and Albers (1998); Zoltners and Lorimer (2000): FAR; Zoltners and Sinha (2005): FAR

Table 6.1 (continued)

	Classic period: up to 1980	Middle period: 1980–1995	Contemporary period: 1996–2007
Integrative Models	Beswick and Cravens (1977)		Drexl and Haase (1999); Skiera and Albers (2008)
Sales Force Compensation and Incentives	Farley (1964); Berger (1972); Weinberg (1978); Gonik (1978); Darmon (1979)	Srinivasan (1981); Basu, Lal, Srinivasan and Staelin (1985); Lal and Staelin (1986); Darmon (1987); Coughlan and Sen (1989): R Rao (1990); Mantrala and Raman (1990); Basu and Kalyanaram (1990); Lal and Srinivasan (1993); Coughlan (1993): R; Mantrala, Sinha and Zoltners (1994); Raju and Srinivasan (1994); Zhang and Mahajan (1995); Albers (1996b): R	Joseph and Thevaranjan (1998); Kalra and Shi (2001); Godes (2004); Steenburgh (2004); Murthy and Mantrala (2005); Chen (2005); Gopalakrishna, Garrett, Mantrala, Moore (2006)
Price Delegation	Weinberg (1975); Stephenson, Cron, Frazier (1979)	Lal (1986)	Joseph (2001); Bhardwaj (2001); Misra and Prasad (2004, 2005)
Sales - Marketing Mix		Gatignon and Hanssens (1987); Gopalakrishna and Chatterjee (1992); Albers (1996a)	Narayanan, Desiraju and Chintagunta (2004); Murthy and Mantrala (2005); Smith, Gopalakrishna and Chatterjee (2006); Mantrala, Naik, Sridhar, Thorson (2007)

Nomenclature: R = Lit Review; FAR = Field Applications Review; MA = Meta-Analyses

It is evident that much of the foundation for direct control allocation decision models that are popular even today was laid in the classic period starting with the seminal papers of Lodish (1971), Montgomery et al. (1971), and Hess and Samuels (1971) which all appeared in the December 1971 special marketing-management issue of *Management Science*. With the exception of the model for optimal structuring and sizing the sales force organization proposed by Rangaswamy et al. (1990), few really new problems were tackled in the middle period and most of the related published works were focused on refining, extending or integrating the foundation models and solution approaches proposed in the classic period. Since 1996, the flow of new decision models in this area has continued to remain thin. However, there has been more progress in the domain of econometric estimation of sales response functions enabled by the availability of large, disaggregate databases, especially from the pharmaceutical industry, and the development and dissemination of new, more robust and powerful econometric techniques. However, so far they appear to have limited applicability in industries other than pharmaceuticals.

Unlike the direct control literature, the domain of sales force compensation and incentives (including price delegation) research has witnessed fairly active, ongoing research in each of our three time eras. Here, however, there was a paradigmatic shift at the beginning of the middle period. Specifically, the bulk of sales force compensation research in the 1960s and 1970s, beginning with the pioneering work of Farley (1964) and ending with the paper by Srinivasan (1981), adhered to the deterministic, operations research modeling paradigm introduced by Farley (1964) with a few notable exceptions, e.g., Berger (1972). This approach gave way to the agency theoretic perspective with the publication of the paper by Basu et al. (1985). The next ten years witnessed a surge in research based on the agency-theoretic approach. Coughlan and Sen (1989) and Coughlan (1993) have articulated the differences between the Operations Research and agency theoretic perspectives. However, by and large, the research focus in the middle period remained on the optimal design of the basic compensation plan, comprising salary, commissions, quotas and bonuses, for the individual salesperson operating in an independent sales territory. It is only in the contemporary period that research has turned to multi-agent incentives problems such as sales contests and team compensation problems.

In the rest of this chapter, we adopt a bottom-up view of Fig. 6.1 beginning with a review of sales force response function estimation and the cornerstone selling allocation decision models. We then move up the right-side of Fig. 6.1, to review research on sales territory design, sales force structuring and sizing, and integrated decision models in Section 6.4. We then shift to the indirect control models for compensation planning in Section 5 followed by suggestions for future research.

6.3 Estimation of Sales Response Functions

The development of a *sales response function* lies at the heart of all models for optimizing sales management deployment decisions. Below, we survey the different approaches to developing these models that have been utilized in the extant literature, and give recommendations for appropriate approaches.

6.3.1 Sales Response Data and Calibration Principles

In the early years of sales force decision modeling, the lack of appropriate objective data constrained the calibration of sales response functions. Therefore, researchers worked with the information that was available, which in the beginning was largely what resided in experienced managers' minds, i.e., subjective or judgmental data. This *decision calculus* approach rested on the logic that managers and salespeople were already making intuitive decisions based on subjective estimates of sales response behavior. Therefore, it makes sense to explicate and utilize this knowledge to calibrate response functions that could be incorporated in models for optimizing these decisions (Little 1970). Such a model must do better than intuitive allocations because it incorporates the same response function as perceived by the decision-maker, and provides an algorithm for optimization of the relevant objective function which can search over and evaluate many more allocation options than is humanly possible.

The best known example of the decision calculus approach in sales force models research is that utilized in CALLPLAN proposed by Lodish (1971). Subjective estimates about the expected effects on sales of increasing or decreasing selling efforts by 50% from their current ('base case') levels were elicited from knowledgeable sales managers and salespeople. This was complemented by subjective estimates for sales when effort is either reduced to zero (carryover sales) or made very large (saturation sales). The estimation of the response function for the *i*th control unit in the relevant set of units I is based on the functional form (6.1), originally suggested by Little (1970) and called the ADBUDG function, with S_i representing sales, h_i the number of calls, the four parameters, α_i, β_i, γ_i and δ_i, and the subjective input elicitation procedure shown in Fig. 6.2.

$$S_i = \alpha_i + (\beta_i - \alpha_i) \frac{h_i}{\gamma_i + h_i^{\delta_i}} \qquad (i \in I) \qquad (6.1)$$

Two of the elicited inputs directly provide estimates of two parameter values, namely, $\beta_i = S_5$ and $\alpha_i = S_1$. Then, the parameter values for γ_i and δ_i are estimated for the function over the range between zero and the current effort level of h_3 by solving the two equations given by (S_3, h_3) and (S_2, h_2), and again derived for the function over the range of effort greater than or equal to h_3 by

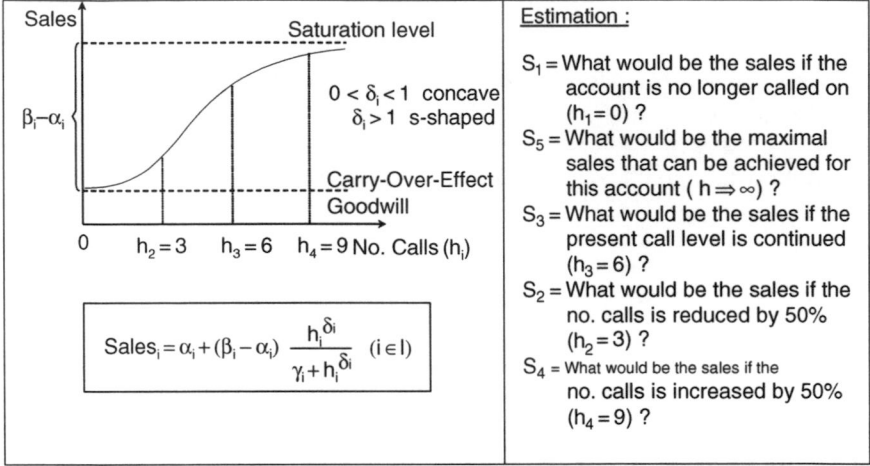

Fig. 6.2 S-shaped ADBUDG function used for subjectively estimated parameter values

solving the equations given by (S_3,h_3 and (S_4,h_4).). This implies that the overall function has different slopes for increasing and decreasing values of calling effort from h_3.

This procedure offers the advantage that the estimated functions exactly run through the current point h_3. This creates the illusion there is no error which leads to a higher acceptance by practitioners. However, the perfect fit obtained by fitting a 4 parameter function with 4 points masks the fact that there is then no way to assess estimation error and/or construct a confidence interval around the parameter estimates. Subsequently, to make room for such assessments, Albers (1996a) presented an application with more subjective estimates than parameters so that a curve could be statistically fitted though the point estimates.

The so-called ADBUDG functional form is flexible in that it can accommodate concave ($\delta \leq 1$) as well as s-shaped relationships ($\delta > 1$). The latter property is intuitively appealing to managers, especially in the pharmaceutical industry, who believe that a threshold number of calls on physicians is required before sales take off but, as effort becomes larger, sales response to increasing effort will eventually plateau. The CALLPLAN approach is also realistic in that it allows for heterogeneity in sales response parameter values across customers and across salespeople.

Lodish and his colleagues validated the CALLPLAN decision calculus approach in a field study at United Airlines (Fudge and Lodish 1977), and reported successful applications at firms such as the Syntex Laboratories (Lodish et al. 1988). Laboratory experiments by McIntyre (1982) have also shown that decision makers are able to reliably estimate differences in individual customer responses to changes in selling effort and, therefore, those inputs are useful for optimizing call budget allocation decisions. However, managers appear to have more difficulty providing reliable estimates of overall sales response to changes in the total budget, raising questions about the usefulness of subjective inputs for investment-level decisions (Chakravarti et al. 1979, 1981, Little and Lodish 1981)

The method of subjective estimation was the dominant method used in reported applications until the end of the 1980s. Since then, the econometric estimation of response functions based on historical data has gained ground primarily because of the increasing availability of objective cross sectional-time series panel data with large numbers of observations at the disaggregate or individual customer level, permitting the derivation of stable estimates and confidence intervals for response model parameters at a detailed level. Many industrial companies with thousands of customers are likely to possess adequate internal data for sales response estimation. However, the bulk of the published econometric applications are coming from the pharmaceutical industry. This is not surprising as this industry relies heavily on large sales forces and has undertaken enormous efforts over the last 3 decades to precisely document the effectiveness of its sales calls, samples and other micro-marketing efforts directed at physicians. However, even this industry is constrained in that any one company cannot directly observe or record all prescription drug sales arising from salespersons' calls on individual physicians. This has led to the emergence in the US of market research companies, e.g., IMS Health and Verispan, that vend data on prescription drug sales by therapeutic category, at the national, physician segment, or individual physician levels collected from pharmacies or drug wholesalers (see, e.g., Manchanda et al. 2005). In Europe, however, the availability of prescription sales data is still restricted to geographically defined sales coverage units comprised of multiple physicians as privacy rules do not allow for tracking of prescriptions by individual physicians. In addition, there are now market research companies (e.g. Cedegim-CAM and Verispan/Scott-Levin) that provide data on expenses of all competitors with respect to detailing, samples, and other advertising related activities. They collect these data from samples of physicians and project competitive activity to the full market.

Aside from data availability, another reason for the ascendancy of the econometric approach is the development of powerful econometric estimation methods and software that can handle many thousands of observations and come up with idiosyncratic estimates per response unit (SCU). These are discussed subsequently.

6.3.2 Functional Form

A couple of key issues about sales response functional form remain unresolved. First, should the sales response function for selling effort be s-shaped or just concave in form? While the ADBUDG function is flexible enough to provide for both cases, the empirically derived parameter values for this function in most documented applications imply s-shaped relationships (Lodish 1971; Fudge and Lodish 1977, Lodish et al. 1988). This could be due to a belief among managers that sales take off only above a threshold level of positive effort and/or the belief that sales respond asymmetrically to decreases as opposed to increases from the base case (current) level of selling effort. That is, the decline in sales due to an x% reduction from the current selling effort is typically perceived to be greater than the increase in sales with the same x% increase in selling effort. Second, we still do not know much about the dynamics of the effectiveness of selling effort over the life cycle of a customer relationship. In the beginning of the relationship, it might take more detailing effort to convince a physician to prescribe a certain drug than later in the relationship when only reminder details to the physician are necessary.

Researchers do agree that sales response functions used in effort allocation decision models must eventually exhibit diminishing returns to increasing effort. While the ADBUDG function fulfills these requirements and its parameter values can be derived analytically, such inherently nonlinear functional forms posed a challenge for econometric estimation in the early years. Thus, until about 15 years ago, econometric applications were limited to the estimation of the parameters of nonlinear sales response functions such as the multiplicative (or Cobb-Douglas) form which can be linearized by taking logarithms of both sides of the function, allowing estimation with linear regression techniques. The coefficient of the logarithm of the independent variable (selling effort) is then its exponent in the multiplicative function and represents the selling effort elasticity. An alternative to this 'double-log' form of the response function estimable by the linear regression method is when sales are related to the logarithm of the independent variable, i.e., the semi-logarithmic function. The double-log and semi-log functions have different implications for optimal allocations. In the former case, the selling effort should be allocated proportional to its elasticity while effort allocation should be proportional to the regression weight in the case of the semi-logarithmic function (see, e.g., Doyle and Saunders 1990, Skiera and Albers 2008). Ultimately, however, the derived optimal effort allocations can be very similar. If selling effort is accompanied by other promotional activities like advertising and samples then the interactions between these variables should be explicitly taken into account by multiplying variables or specifying process functions. Examples of such response models are found in Parsons and Vanden Abeele (1981), Gatignon and Hanssens (1987), Gopalakrishna and Chatterjee (1992), Mizik and Jacobson (2004), and Narayanan et al. (2004).

Today, currently available software for nonlinear regression allows for econometric estimation of inherently nonlinear functions such as the ADBUDG function. However, most applications involving estimation of aggregate sales response functions, e.g., at the level of sales coverage units comprised of several customers, continue to employ simple power or log functions that reflect diminishing returns to increases in effort. This practice is defensible because even if customer-level response functions are s-shaped, aggregate response functions are concave over the operating range of effort assuming that the effort is optimally allocated across the individual customers within SCUs (Mantrala et al. 1992).

For response function estimation at the individual customer level however, the output variable data, e.g., physician-level prescription drug sales y_{it}, is frequently not continuous nor normally distributed as is typically assumed, but is rather count data that are Poisson distributed. Therefore, econometricians have modeled prescriptions in such situations as a probability function with selling effort (or 'detailing') as a covariate. To obtain a function with diminishing returns for which an optimal detailing level can be determined, Manchanda and Chintagunta (2004) model the Poisson distribution parameter λ (the mean prescription rate, see (6.2)) as an exponential function of a quadratic function of selling effort. They also advocate this functional form because it allows for possible supersaturation effects where sales decline if selling effort is increased beyond a certain level. In their study, Manchanda and Chintagunta (2004) report a significant negative parameter value for the quadratic term of detailing implying supersaturation. However, in many instances, the implied levels of effort leading to supersaturation fall beyond the range of data for which the function is estimated, thereby making such levels suspect. Subsequently, Dong et al. (2006) model the impact of selling effort x_{it} with parameters β_{0i} and β_{1i} in (6.3) in such a way that either a concave or convex or s-shaped relationship (but no supersaturation) may evolve:

$$P_i(y_{it}|\lambda_{,it}) = \frac{\lambda_{it}^{y_{it}} \cdot \exp(-\lambda_{it})}{y_{it}!} \qquad (i \in I) \qquad (6.2)$$

$$\lambda_{it} = \exp\left(\beta_{0i} + \frac{\beta_{1i}}{1 + x_{it}}\right) \qquad (i \in I) \qquad (6.3)$$

With regard to the duration of the effect of personal selling, there is agreement that sales effort has substantial carry-over effects (Sinha and Zoltners 2001). This implies that sales effort today will be remembered and thus exert additional influence on sales in the future. These dynamic effects can be taken into account by either lagged dependent variables, leading to the well-known Koyck (1954) model for the case of geometrically decaying memory effects, or by lagged independent or 'stock' variables where the effort is cumulated over time but with a certain depreciation rate per period (Leeflang et al. 2000; Hanssens et al. 2003, Gönül et al. 2001). Given the notion of carry-over, it is plausible to assume that initial calls have an important informational role on reducing uncertainty with respect to product quality while subsequent calls are only made for reminding customers of the product (Narayanan et al. 2005).

Lastly, econometric estimations are implicitly based on extracting the average response of a unit to selling effort. In order to derive allocation recommendations it might be better to base them not on the response on average but on the best practicing salespeople. This can be achieved by applying a stochastic frontier analysis where the regression curve represents the frontier of the cloud of observations. Using this technique, Horsky and Nelson (1996) determine the profit-maximizing sales force size based on optimal allocation of salespeople across districts. However, such response functions rely on the assumption that inefficient districts can be identified and their selling skills can be improved until efficiency is reached.

6.3.3 Dealing with Heterogeneity, Endogeneity, and Hierarchical Influences

6.3.3.1 Heterogeneity

Econometric estimation of sales response models calls for fitting a model to historical observations from several time intervals and/or response units. The simplest model assumes that parameter values are the same over time or across cross-sectional units which is often unrealistic. For example, customers are likely to differ in how they respond to changes in sales effort. In this respect, the early decision calculus approach to calibration had the advantage that it involved estimation of an idiosyncratic sales response function for each customer (or relevant unit of analysis). Thereby, the approach explicitly took into account heterogeneity at the customer level. Early econometric estimation, however, assumed parameter values to be the same across different customers.

The first approach of realizing heterogeneous parameter values for the sales response function is to directly incorporate sources of observed heterogeneity into the model. This requires the researcher to find out why response varies across response units. For instance, this can be due to the differing sales potentials across sales coverage units. If data on sales potentials are available (e.g. number of physicians in a sales coverage unit) then they may be integrated by inserting them as different saturation levels β_i in function (6.1) across units i. Alternatively, selling effort can be decomposed into calls per customer (frequency) multiplied by number of physicians (sales potential) as proposed by Skiera and Albers (2008). Then, the parameter values resulting from the regression coefficients multiplied with the number of physicians can be used as idiosyncratic response parameters for the allocation task.

A second approach to capturing heterogeneity in sales response parameters relies on the estimation of distributions for the parameter values. This is especially appropriate if longitudinal customer panel data are available providing a sufficient number of observations for each customer. Alternatively, instead of estimating the parameter values for each customer from a time series of observations, one could estimate parameter values that follow certain discrete or continuous mixed distributions across the sample of observations. Finite mixture (or latent class) models allow for the estimation of differing response functions across latent classes (segments). By taking into account the probabilities with which each customer or customer group belongs to the uncovered number of latent classes or segments it is even possible to arrive at posterior estimates per customer (see, e.g., Wedel and Kamakura 1999). Such latent class estimates are often a good compromise between taking into account some unobserved heterogeneity and not losing too many degrees of freedom. Another option for capturing heterogeneity in parameter values is to derive distributions of parameter estimates applying either a random coefficients approach (e.g. Narayanan et al. 2004) or a hierarchical Bayes method (e.g. Manchanda and Chintagunta 2004). Both methods provide posterior estimates per customer. Of course, this only leads to stable results if there are enough degrees of freedom. While estimates obtained in this fashion are theoretically superior and avoid estimation biases, so far the conditions under which they are stable enough for making disaggregate level optimal allocation decisions have not been established with the help of simulation studies.

Further, finite mixtures and hierarchical Bayes approaches focus on un-observed heterogeneity, i.e., only help to establish that response is different across response units but do not tell why. This creates a problem when utilizing heterogeneous response parameter estimates in sales force deployment planning or performance evaluation. In our experience, salespeople and sales managers are more willing to accept heterogeneous response parameter estimates that reflect observable differences in response units' characteristics, e.g., their sales potentials. Therefore, in econometric estimation of sales-selling effort response functions, it is sensible to directly incorporate sources of observed heterogeneity into the model as far as possible. An application of this approach incorporating available data on response units' sales potentials (number of customers in a sales coverage unit) which yielded idiosyncratic sales response parameter esti-mates for effort allocation optimization purposes is provided by Skiera and Albers (2008).

6.3.3.2 Endogeneity

An unbiased estimation of the parameter values is only possible when the values of the independent variables are randomly chosen. In practical applications, this is rarely the case. Rather, the chosen levels of selling effort are often based on the subjective knowledge of managers about the sales response and are thus non-random. This is the problem of endogeneity of independent variables. For this situation of nonrandom independent variables, Manchanda et al. (2004) propose that the parameter values be estimated with the help of a maximum likelihood approach fitting sales depending on selling effort as well as selling effort depending on some prior knowledge about the estimated parameter values. More generally, the proponents of such structural approaches advocate inclusion of equations by which the independent variables such as detailing are made dependent on optimality conditions of allocation. However, such a structural approach relies on strong assumptions and it is not clear how mean-ingful are the resulting estimates when salespeople have not optimally allocated their efforts. In addition, this approach offers no room to come up with recommendations for improving the allocation of effort which often is the main reason for undertaking the response function estimation in the first place (Chintagunta et al. 2006, p. 606).

6.3.3.3 Hierarchical Influences

A more recent development is the application of Hierarchical Linear Modeling (HLM), e.g., Raudenbush and Bryk (2002). This is required if one wants to decompose the effects of inputs by sales coverage units, territories and sales regions. In particular, this is helpful for performance evaluation because applying this approach enables attribution of the effects to the various hierarchical levels of a sales force, such as the selling firm versus the salesperson (see, e.g., Palmatier et al. 2006).

6.3.4 Sales Effort Elasticities as Comparable Results of Sales Response Estimation

In the literature many different results about the shape of sales response functions have been reported. Managers very often want to know what the results are so far on average, i.e., they seek generalizations. To provide such information, Albers et al. (2008) have recently carried out a meta-analysis of 46 studies providing selling effort elasticities which are comparable across studies finding an average selling elasticity corrected for methodological bias of about 0.352. Elasticities vary as can be seen from the standard deviation of about 0.12. Approximately 30% of the variation can be explained by environmental and methodological factors. The elasticity reduces by about 0.11 and 0.16 if one takes into account the bias arising from the non-inclusion of promotion and lagged effects. If the elasticities are derived from yearly data, then the elasticity is by 0.15 smaller which confirms results by Tellis and Franses (2006). The results also confirm that elasticities are smaller by 0.21 if the model is based on relative rather than absolute sales.

6.3.5 Implementation Issues of the Specification and Estimation of Sales Response Functions

Comparing the relative merits of objective and subjective data-based sales response calibration we find that historical data are inadequate if not inappropriate when historical sales response relationships have lost their validity as might happen when the sales force structure is redesigned in turbulent markets. On the other hand, in relatively stable situations, the collection of subjective estimates is frequently too time-expensive. Rangaswamy et al. (1990) report, for example, that 15 senior marketing and sales managers spent four days to provide the subjective estimates for a sales force structuring model. In addition, subjective estimates might lead to distorted estimates if strong personal interests of managers are involved. If historical data do not vary appropriately so that effects cannot be estimated statistically one might also collect data from small field experiments that are then used for estimating specific aspects of the response functions (e.g. Hanssens and Levien 1983).

We have pointed out that it is important to estimate idiosyncratic parameter values for each sales response unit. While this was accomplished in the 1970s and 1980s only by subjectively estimating response functions per response unit, nowadays it is possible to do this by applying latent class regressions or Bayesian statistics techniques for estimating distributions of parameter values from which you can derive individual parameter values per response unit. If past data adequately reflect future response then the econometric approach is superior. However, these approaches require sophisticated knowledge not possessed by many analysts at companies. It is possible, however, to develop response functions that incorporate observed heterogeneity by factoring into the response functions the known differences in sales potentials across geographic areas. This together with a fixed effects model (in case of panel data) is much simpler to apply and might be sufficient to get parameter values that are usable for allocation purposes.

6.4 Models for Sales Resource Allocation, Sales Territory Design, Sales Force Structuring and Sizing

6.4.1 Sales Resource Allocation Models

Zoltners and Sinha (1980) review and summarize 24 papers from preceding years focused on the allocation of sales representative call time, number of sales reps or sales calls, and sales effort over various competing sales entities such as channels, customers, products, districts, prospective customers etc.. They also propose a general modeling formulation and solution approach. The models they review differ in terms of their specifications of objective functions and constraints but profit maximization is the dominant motive. Most of these models assume continuous sales response functions, either concave, e.g., the modified exponential or power function, or S-shaped, e.g., the logit or ADBUDG functions. All of these models handle the basic single-period, single-resource, deterministic resource allocation problem assuming separable sales entities.

Only a few deal with more complicated but realistic problems such as those posed by

- *Nonseparable* or interacting sales entities such as when two or more products are to be detailed in the same sales call, or when current and prospective customers must be called upon during the same sales trip (see, e.g., Lodish 1971, Montgomery et al. 1971, Zoltners et al. 1979),

- *Multiple resource-targets*, e.g., a firm's joint allocation of a team of selling and service reps across its key accounts (see, e.g., Layton 1968, Armstrong 1976).

As regards optimization procedures used, they include Lagrange multiplier technique, nonlinear programming, dynamic programming, heuristic procedures, linear programming and integer programming (IP).

A good exemplar of models in this stream of literature is the influential CALLPLAN model of Lodish (1971). We have already referred to this model's basic contributions with respect to specification and estimation of a flexible nonlinear function. However, Lodish's work has had longstanding impact because he addresses and solves a fundamental sales call time deployment problem in sales management which is also reasonably complicated, namely, how should a salesperson's time be allocated between customers and prospects in his/her territory while considering the time required to travel to different sub-areas of the territory? More specifically, the CALLPLAN objective function is to maximize the sum of contributions from all the rep's customers less the associated travel costs. The mathematical formulation of the problem is given below.

Objective function: Maximization of profit contribution

$$\sum_{i \in I} \underbrace{g_i \cdot f_i(h_i)}_{\substack{\text{profit contribution} \\ \text{from sales depending} \\ \text{on the calling time}}} - \sum_i \in J \underbrace{k_j^R \cdot y_j}_{\substack{\text{travel cost} \\ \text{multiplied by the} \\ \text{number of tours} \\ \text{into the subareas}}} \Rightarrow \text{Max!} \qquad (6.4)$$

Available working time is constrained to:

$$\sum_{i \in I} t_i \cdot h_i + \sum_{j \in J} I_j \cdot y_j \leq T \qquad (6.5)$$

Number of tours to subarea j must be higher or equal to the maximum number of calls to customer i:

$$l_j \leq y_j \leq u_j \qquad (j \in J) \qquad (6.6)$$

Lower and upper bound for number of calls:

$$h_i \leq y_j \qquad (i \in IS_j, j \in J) \qquad (6.7)$$

Nonnegativity of number of tours:

$$h_i \geq 0 \qquad (i \in I) \qquad (6.8)$$

In above model, the objective is to find the optimal call vector h* that maximizes the sum of profit contributions from calls to accounts less the total travel costs. The total time constraint (6.2) ensures that salesperson's time is not over allocated. The number of trips constraint (6.3) ensures that calls h_i to a particular account cannot exceed the number of trips made to that account's geographic region. Constraint (6.4) specifies upper and lower bounds on the allocated calls to each account. Lodish solves this problem using a two-stage procedure: In the first stage, calls are optimally allocated among the accounts in each of the J geographic areas independently, as the number of trips to that area is varied between zero and the management-specified maximum number. In the second stage the optimal amount of call time to spend in each geographic area is solved for. The combination of the solutions of the two stages yields the optimal call-frequency schedule. As the s-shaped response functions make the optimization problem to be combinatorial (Freeland and Weinberg 1980) these solutions can only be obtained using an integer programming approach but Lodish recommends a simpler heuristical search procedure in which the sales response function is replaced by its linear concave envelope. This simplification appears to provide solutions sufficiently close to the true optimum for most realistic problems.

Thus, the CALLPLAN model incorporates important constraints which apply to most allocation problems, namely, sales representative's total time available, travel time and cost, and individual differences in productivity. Numerous applications have been reported including the famous field test at United Airlines by Fudge and Lodish (1977) which indicated that salespeople using CALLPLAN achieved a significantly higher level of sales increases than the control group.

Zoltners and Sinha (1980) propose a general modeling approach toward salesperson call-planning system which is conceptually similar to CALLPLAN. Referring to their earlier work (Zoltners et al. 1979) they propose an integer programming (IP) solution procedure. That is, in contrast to Lodish's procedure which assumes a piecewise linear response function, the Zoltners and Sinha (1980) approach utilizes discretized versions of any form of sales response function over a finite set of feasible allocation levels. They claimed the following advantages for the IP procedure over other methods: (1) the assurance of meaningful solutions since only feasible strategies are considered by IP; (2) the existence of efficient optimization algorithms; (3) the elimination of concavity assumptions regarding the shape of the sales response function and (4) an approach which accommodate most of the complicating features of sales resource allocation problems and allows for the incorporation of additional decision variables and constraints. However, a problem with this approach is that often solutions can be stated only in numeric and not in analytic form. Further, much of the advantages of IP claimed in their 1980 article have dissipated over the years with the increasing availability of powerful nonlinear optimization algorithms in standard software such as Microsoft's Excel Solver (Fylstra et al. 1998) which can solve nonlinear problems with any types of constraints and is readily available to all salespeople and managers and thus is more likely to be used (Albers 2000). In light of these developments there appear to be limited reasons to take the IP route today. Indeed as noted by Vandenbosch and Weinberg (1993) even the subsequent work by Zoltners and Sinha has apparently moved away from IP models in favor of response-function models. Integer solutions still matter at the most disaggregate level as sales calls are inherently integer in nature. However for selling effort allocation decisions across more aggregate level SCUs there is no need to ensure integrality of the solution because there is no explicit reference to single customers.

Lastly there have been developments which alter the CALLPLAN model's constraints (6.5) and (6.6) as they relate to travel time. These complicate the solution to the allocation problem. In their algorithm for solving the allocation problem of their COSTA model, Skiera and Albers (1998) are able to replace these by a single total selling time constraint, where selling time equals calling time plus travel time, as they directly incorporate selling time into the SCU-level response functions used in their model. This leads to a much simpler optimization structure that can be solved with standard software such as Microsoft's EXCEL Solver.

Since 1980, very few new sales resource allocation models have been proposed in the marketing literature. One exception is the decision support system CAPPLAN proposed by Albers (1996a) for jointly determining prices and sales call allocations across account groups, a relevant B2B marketing problem when differential pricing across accounts is possible and production costs vary with production (sales) levels that are jointly determined by price and selling effort. Albers (1996a) reports an implementation in which management attributed a 10% increase in the contribution achieved to the use of CAPPLAN. More generally, however, the shortage of work in building new sales resource allocation models over the last two decades is surprising considering that several traditional complications such as interdependent sales entities remain to be satisfactorily treated aside from the new selling environment challenges to be discussed later.

6.4.2 Sales Territory Design

Sales Territory Design deals with the problem of assigning sets of customers to salespersons. While there are some industries where field sales agents can call on any customer they want to, e.g., insurance salespeople, most industries work with salespeople assigned to geographic sales territories. Being assigned his/her own sales territory makes a salesperson feel more responsible and may result in better sales force morale and performance as the salesperson is held accountable for sales in that territory (Zoltners and Sinha 2005). Geographic sales territories are typically formed by combining sales coverage units (SCUs) like zip codes or political areas (counties, states, provinces). Then, the sales territory design problem is to determine the combination of SCUs that form each territory.

Hess and Samuels (1971) were the first to propose a model-based approach for addressing the territory design problem. The goal of their GEOLINE model was to develop balanced territories, i.e., determine sets of contiguous SCUs which are equalized in terms of workload by minimizing a measure of compactness (moment of inertia). They determined the optimal solution with the help of linear programming (LP). As a LP's solution is noninteger, and SCUs can only be assigned in their entirety to one territory or another, GEOLINE had to work with a rounding procedure that leads to differences of activity across territories of up to 15%. Shanker et al. (1975) as well as Zoltners (1976) presented integer programming approaches for the alignment task. Lodish (1975) presented a procedure that attempts to make the marginal profit contribution as equal as possible across territories. Only later Skiera and Albers (1998) showed that the optimal territories can have different marginal profit contribution values, they only have to be equal for SCUs within territories. Zoltners and Sinha (1983) provided a generalization of the models by allowing for any objective function and achieving almost equality for potential or other balancing criteria through the introduction of lower and upper bounds as constraints. However, there remains the question of how to specify the interval between lower and upper bound. As this interval becomes tighter, the objective function itself receives less weight. If one tries to minimize travel time then the scarce resource of time becomes more and more irrelevant until there is only one solution satisfying all constraints. However if one relaxes the constraints then travel time consideration are getting more and more important. Consequently, this model would be more transparent to users if it were set up as a multi-objective criteria problem with explicit weights for all criteria.

The model by Zoltners and Sinha (1983) also offered some other features that they consider to be crucial for implementation. First, territories should not encompass natural boundaries like lakes or mountain ranges that make it nearly impossible to get from one part of the territory to the other one. Zoltners and Sinha could ensure that all parts were easily accessible by taking into account actual travel times via a network of major roads. Second, territories should be contiguous. This is ensured by the additional constraint that all SCUs had at least a road connecting to another SCU over which the base location of the salesperson could be reached. This is to accommodate sales managers who do not want to have territories with SCUs of one salesperson surrounded by SCUs served by other salespersons. While Zoltners and Sinha (1983) take this desire for granted, Skiera and Albers (1998) question this requirement because ultimately it can lead to much more restrictions and the consequence of arriving at less equitable territories. Further investigations are needed to find out whether this requirement really facilitates sales management or whether it is a constraint that has no economic value.

The problem with balancing approaches is that there is only an indirect relationship between profit and territory design. Zoltners and Sinha (2005) claim that equal potential increases the utilization of the salesperson's selling time. However, one might also try to directly maximize profit contribution when aligning sales territories. This can be achieved by the model COSTA (Skiera and Albers 1998) which utilizes a new concept for incorporating travel time effects directly into the sales response function per SCU, depending on the assignment to a certain salesperson (i.e., territory). This formulation of the sales response function allows for a simultaneous solution of the call planning problem (as described in the previous section) and the assignment of SCUs to territories (specified by their base location) to maximize overall profit.

Zoltners and Sinha (2005) argue that the COSTA approach is too complex and managers implement modified solutions anyway so that the optimality from a profit viewpoint is no longer guaranteed. On the other hand, substantial progress has been made in reliably estimating sales response functions. And even if the response functions are misspecified, Skiera and Albers (1998) show that solutions of COSTA are superior on profit-maximizing grounds than those ones derived from balancing approaches. Of course, solutions of both approaches can be modified by managers before implementation but in the case of the profit-maximizing approach the user can calculate the difference in profit implied by any such modification. Furthermore, it should be noted that the alignment is greatly facilitated by mapping software that graphically displays the territories and easily recalculates indicators like profit or sales potential in the case of modifications.

6.4.3 Sales Force Structure Decision Models

The central question of the sales force structure problem is how to divide up the sales activities among different types of salespeople. More specifically, the sales force structure issue involves decisions with respect to sales force roles and specialization that define the types of customers each salesperson will call on, the product or service portfolio that each salesperson will sell, and the activities that each salesperson will perform. Companies' alternatives for sales force specialization include generalist sales forces, product specialists, market or customer specialists, functional specialists, or hybrid specialists who combine two or more of the basic specializations. So the question becomes: Should salespeople be generalists, selling all products and performing all selling tasks for all types of customers? Or should the sales force employ specialists, focusing on a particular product, market and/or selling activity?

One of the early investigations of these questions was done by Rao and Turner (1984). While they did not propose a decision model they did offer a framework for identifying the factors which should influence the nature and degree of sales force specialization most appropriate for different situations. Rao and Turner's basic premise is that selling effectiveness is determined by sales force organization, i.e., the way selling skill and selling effort are allocated to the market, which in turn should depend on two key factors, namely, the need for *product or prospect expertise*, and the *interdependency between products and prospects*. In this framework, non-specialized (specialized) reps are suitable in situations where the product and/or prospect interdependencies are high (low) but selling expertise required is low (high). In situations where both interdependencies and expertise required are high, Rao and Turner suggest the use of staff specialists to supplement the role of the non-specialized field reps. Thus, reps specialized by product (customer type) would be employed in situations with low product (prospect) interdependencies but requiring high levels of product (customer) expertise. However, specialization is not free. The increase in selling effectiveness frequently comes at a higher cost, i.e., sales force travel time costs, coordination costs and account management costs tend to increase with specialization.

In general, there is a paucity of sales force structuring decision models perhaps because this problem involves many more strategic and organizational considerations for a company than simply the operational allocation of selling effort. Indeed Zoltners et al. (2004) say sales force structuring remains more of an art than a science as the associated problems are complex, involving politics as much as economics, and many trade-offs. The only published example of a sales force structuring decision model is that of Rangaswamy et al. (1990), who address two questions of sales force structure in the repetitive buying environment of established prescription drug markets: How many sales forces should the firm have and which products should be assigned to each sales force? As this model also provides recommendations for the optimal size and allocation of selling effort, we discuss it in more depth later under integrated models.

6.4.4 Sales Force Size Decision-Focused Models

In practice, companies often use heuristic or rule-based approaches to setting the size of their sales force, i.e., the number of salespeople they need over a planning horizon, such as 'same as last year" when firm's sales goals are being achieved; or "pay as you go" or earn-your-way strategies that add salespeople as sales grow. Most commonly, sales force sizes are based on a top-down "breakdown" approach under which the total sales force budget (or "costs") is set as a "cost-of-sales" percentage of a sales forecast. This dollar budget divided by the average salesperson salary leads to the selected sales force size. Effectively, therefore, this amounts to a *cost containment* approach. Alternatively, a more data-intensive approach to sales force sizing used by some sales managers is the "bottom-up" *workload buildup* or *activity-based method* (Zoltners et al. 2004). Essentially, these approaches classify customers into segments according to their type and sales potential, e.g., prescriptions volume-based 'deciles' of physicians in the pharmaceutical industry, set norms for the numbers of sales calls per year to be made on customers in each segment – typically these call frequencies are proportional to the average sales potential of customers in each segment - and fix the number of accounts to be covered in each segment (i.e., the reach). The total workload (sales calls or hours) required to cover the customer base is computed based on these assumptions and then divided by the average rep's call capacity to determine the required sales force size.

Both the cost containment and workload buildup approaches are likely to produce sales force sizing errors from a profit-maximizing viewpoint because, first, they do not really focus on profits, and second, they do not fully assess the underlying market sales response functions and impact of resource allocation decisions (see, e.g., Mantrala et al. 1992). More specifically, the breakdown or cost containment approach overlooks that the aggregate sales that are its basis for sales force size selection depend on how the sales force effort is allocated across disaggregate sales entities. Thus, the same aggregate sales can be obtained with different sales force sizes as disaggregate allocation rules are changed. Similarly, the workload buildup approach ignores that many combinations of reach and frequency of detailing yield the same field force size but can result in dramatically different sales and profits when companies allocate effort in various combinations of products and markets.

Recognizing these limitations, a number of normative models for sales force sizing incorporating sales response functions have been proposed. Early sales force sizing decision models focused on utilizing either historical or experimental data to relate aggregate sales levels to territorial potential and workload, estimate the resulting sales response function parameters and then derive normative implications for sizing decisions. Basically, a decision model aimed at determining the profit-maximizing sales force should account for the nonlinear (concave or possibly S-shaped nature of the selling effort-sales relationship) and apply the marginal analysis principle that the optimal size is the level at which the incremental profit from adding one more salesperson is negative. More specifically, based on Dorfman and Steiner's (1954) classic theorem, Albers (2000b) notes that the following formulae work well in practice for determining the optimal sales force size:

$$\frac{\text{Optimal sales force size}}{\text{Profit contribution before sales force cost}} = \text{Sales force effort elasticity} \quad (6.9)$$

$$\frac{\text{Optimal sales force size}}{\text{Revenue}} = \frac{\text{Sales force effort elasticity}}{\text{Price elasticity}} \quad (6.10)$$

Profit contributions (gross margins) are usually known to management. If it can be reasonably assumed that the firm is facing a concave function with constant sales effort elasticity over its operating range of effort, and managers have gauged this elasticity from observing how sales vary with changes in effort, the above formulae directly provide the corresponding optimal sales force size. Conversely, assuming management is operating with the optimum sales force size, the corresponding elasticity being assumed by management can be inferred and its plausibility can be gauged by comparing with known benchmark elasticities for their industry (derived, e.g., from available meta-analyses of estimated sales force effort elasticities in previous studies, e.g., Albers (2000b) and Albers et al. (2008)).

However, the key problem with the above normative approaches is that even they ignore the impact of disaggregate allocation decisions on the shape and behavior of the aggregate model which can lead to sales force sizing errors (Mantrala et al. 1992). To avoid such errors, sales management need to employ integrated models which jointly determine the optimal selling effort level and its allocation utilizing the relevant disaggregate units' response functions. In the next section, we review such models.

6.4.5 Integrated Decision Models

6.4.5.1 Integrated Allocation and Territory Design Models

Several models including some we have already discussed, provide for integrated allocation and territory design solutions. One of the earliest was Lodish (1975) who extended the CALLPLAN model to incorporate the territory-design issue, assuming a fixed sales force size. However, unlike the individual rep-specific customer account response function used by the original CALL-PLAN model, this model extension employs a response function for each account that assumes sales representatives are identical with respect to selling ability. As already noted, Lodish (1975) maximizes profits by equalizing the marginal profit of an additional hour of sales effort across territories. To accomplish this, Lodish (1975) proposes a heuristic solution procedure. First, he solves the problem of allocating selling time across accounts by assuming one super-territory in which the total selling time is equal to the sum of selling times available to all salespersons and applying the CALLPLAN heuristic procedure to determine the optimal number of calls for each account. Then, the decision maker has to reassign accounts step by step intuitively, so that the individual selling-time constraints are met and the marginal profit of selling time has become as equal as possible. However, as already noted, the equal marginal profits of selling time achieved are only optimal for the allocation of selling time across accounts or SCUs per territory, but not across territories. Subsequently, Glaze and Weinberg (1979) present the procedure TAPS, which seeks to maximize sales for a given sales force size while also attempting to achieve equal workload between salespersons and, in addition, minimize total travel time. Their model replaced only parts of Lodish's proposal by a procedure based on the balancing approach, and so they also do not find a profit contribution maximizing territory design solution. Zoltners and Sinha (1983) offer the conceptualization of a "generalized approach" for developing profit-maximizing territories which builds on the ideas of Lodish (1975), Glaze and Weinberg (1979). Specifically, they integrate a model for optimal call time allocation across accounts and prospects comprising each SCU with a model for creating balanced workload territories (where workload associated with each SCU equals the sum of the optimal total call in the SCU plus the estimated travel time and administrative time to service that SCU). Ultimately, however, this approach also does not yield a profit maximizing territory design.

Furthermore, a significant practical difficulty arises with models that use customer accounts as the units of analysis when the application requires calibration of thousands of account-level response functions and produces optimization problems too large to be efficiently solved. A more implementable approach would be to work with aggregated response functions at the level of SCUs. These functions require less data and the corresponding models can be solved with simpler algorithms. Beswick and Cravens (1977) were the first to work with response functions where sales in an SCU depend upon calling time in that SCU. However, they also try to solve the assignment problem through the balancing approach and, therefore, do not maximize profit contribution. We have already noted how the COSTA model of Skiera and Albers (1998) overcomes some of these potential limitations of earlier models for integrated allocation and territory design which have the stated goal of profit-maximization. However, Skiera and Albers' model of course provides direction for optimal allocation of effort across more aggregate SCUs than individual accounts.

6.4.5.2 Integrated Sizing and Allocation Models

An early example of this disaggregated approach is provided by the first stages of Beswick and Cravens (1977) multistage model for sales force management which use sales response functions for small geographic subareas (groups of counties). Subsequently, Lodish (1980) argued that developing sales response functions for numerous geographic subareas would be a formidable undertaking in practice and proposed a decision calculus model for sales force sizing that utilized more aggregate *product-by-market (customer)* segment sales response functions and simultaneously optimized product-by-market segment allocations and total sales force size. The model assumes that all members of a segment will respond similarly on the average. Lodish et al. (1988) applied a version of this model to sales force sizing and allocation across products and customer types (physician specialties) at Syntex Laboratories. Later, Lodish (2001) reported that Syntex credited this model with increasing their profits by over 20%.

Over 2000 successful applications of similar sales force sizing and resource allocation models have also been claimed by Sinha and Zoltners (2001). According to them, typically, the models applied were nonlinear programming models that utilize product-market segment sales-effort response functions and maximize 3–5 year profitability for alternative sales force sizes and product and market allocations. Unfortunately, no more details of these models have been described or published for independent verification and assessment.

6.4.5.3 Integrated allocation, territory design and sizing models

Beswick and Cravens (1977) multistage decision model provides a framework for improving, rather than optimizing, allocation of selling effort and the setting of the sales force size as well as sales territory design. In their approach sales response is estimated at the control-unit level by incorporating both managerial judgment and historical data. Specifically, they model sales as a function of both control-unit variables, e.g., sales potential and allocated selling effort by the salesperson, and territory variables, e.g., assigned salesperson quality and manager's quality. At the allocation stage, using a mathematical programming algorithm, the selling effort level that maximizes each control unit's profit contribution is determined. The sum of these optimal allocations of effort divided by the effort capacity of the average salesperson determines the sales force size. Then a GEOLINE procedure can be applied to design the sales territories. As changes in the territory alignment modify the control unit sales response functions, the next stage of the model is the iterative re-estimation of the optimal allocations of effort to the control units and territory alignment. The iterative procedure is continued until management objectives are met. Beswick and Cravens model provides a useful framework for considering multiple sales management decisions. Its main limitation has already been noted, namely, it may be hard to implement because it calls for the calibration of numerous control unit response functions.

A more recent attempt to solve the four subproblems of sales force sizing, location, alignment and allocation of effort simultaneously is provided by Drexl and Haase (1999). Motivated by the COSTA approach, Drexl and Haase propose a novel nonlinear mixed-integer programming model to solve the four subproblems simultaneously and present fast approximation methods capable of solving large-scale, real-world instances of their model formulation.

6.4.5.4 Integrated Allocation, Structuring, and Sizing Models

It is evident that sales force allocation, structure and size decisions should be considered in an integrated fashion but the only example of such a decision model is that of Rangaswamy et al. (1990). As they note, a sales force utilizing two specialty field forces comprised of 100 people, each deploying their resources optimally, can outperform a single field force of 300 that is deploying the resources inappropriately. At the same time, a single field force of 175 that is optimally deployed may outperform two 100-salesperson field forces that are also optimally deployed. In order to choose between two alternate structures, one has to be assured that both structures will be efficiently sized and deploy their effort optimally.

To solve these interrelated decision problems, Rangaswamy et al. (1990) propose a mathematical programming model which incorporates a product sales response function-based methodology. At the outset, the set of partitions of the firm's product line that correspond to the feasible set of sales force structures is defined. The product sales response functions represent the sales from a particular product j in a market segment k under sales force structure s and allow for product-line interdependencies. The approach to calibrate these functions combines analysis of historical data with a judgmental data estimation procedure. The decision model derives recommendations for optimal number of sales forces, optimal product assignments to sales forces, optimal size of each sales force and optimal effort allocation for the plan period for each product-market-structure combination. However, Rangaswamy et al. (1990) do not explicitly address the tradeoffs that arise between the monetary benefits of specialization and travel times and costs, associated with geographic coverage. Thus a decision model that satisfactorily addresses the effectiveness versus efficiency issues in improving sales force structure remains to be developed.

6.4.6 Empirical Insights, Lessons from Applications

A number of the models described in this section have been applied in practice multiple times mostly by Lodish and his collaborators, and Zoltners, Sinha and their collaborators at the consulting company ZS Associates Inc. Fortunately, both groups have made efforts over the years to document and publish the results of these model applications and associated experiences (e.g., Sinha and Zoltners 2001, Lodish 2001, Zoltners and Lorimer 2000, Zoltners and Sinha 2005). (Many other models proposed by researchers have been applied and reported only once so their impact on practice cannot be fully judged). In general, both groups report that choosing the right model is an art, requiring a good balance between model-complexity and ease of understanding, and sensitivity to corporate management goals. Some more specific insights from their studies and applications are summarized below.

6.4.6.1 Insights with Respect to Sales Force Sizing and Resource Allocation

Based on a sample of sales force sizing studies at 50 companies, Sinha and Zoltners (2001) (see also Zoltners et al. 2006) offer the following insights with respect to optimizing sales force sizes: First, as already mentioned, many companies still use cost containment approaches to sales force sizing. Sinha and Zoltners (2001) report that many companies like to keep the ratio of sales force costs to total sales to be smaller than a preset value. Examining the data from such companies, Sinha and Zoltners observe "Cost-containment sales force sizing is not profit-maximizing" and in fact companies following this approach tend to *undersize* their sales force. This is because this heuristic overlooks the possibility that improvements in sales force productivity may actually support an increase in the sales force size leading to higher profits. Second, assessing sales carryover effects of current selling efforts is important because ignoring these effects leads to suboptimal sales force sizes from a multi-year strategic planning viewpoint. More specifically, on average, the sales force size that maximizes companies' three-year profits is 18% larger than the size that maximizes one-year profits. Third, companies tend to be far from optimality in their selling effort allocation decisions. Based on their assessment of estimated sales response functions for over 400 products promoted by 50 companies, Zoltners and Sinha (2005) report that if these companies were to implement their planned strategies, the ratio of the largest incremental return to the smallest incremental return averaged more than eight (instead of being one as required for optimality)! This is a result of using allocation decision heuristics e.g., equity-based (everyone gets equal share of the resource); sales potential-based; sales volume-based etc., rather than models to make resource allocation decisions. The foregone profits from poor allocation of a given level of selling effort can be significant and in fact much more substantial than foregone profits from nonoptimal sales force sizes. The latter can be very small even for significant deviations from the optimum sales foce size (also called the flat maximum principle in the advertising context, e.g., Tull et al. 1986). On the other hand, a better or worse allocation of effort across products and markets can make a significant difference in profits (Mantrala et al. 1992). Zoltners et al. (2006) report mature companies boosted their margins by 4.5% when they resized their sales forces and allocated resources better. While 29% of those gains came because the companies corrected the size of their sales forces, 71% of the gains were the results of changes in resource utilization.

6.4.6.2 Insights with Respect to Sales Territory Design

Based on 1500 successful implementations of sales territory alignments Zoltners and Sinha (2005) state that an improved alignment may provide a profit increase of 2–7%. For a specific case Zoltners and Lorimer (2000) even report improvement of the growth rate by 100%. Profit improvements of 2–7% are confirmed by the simulation results by Skiera and Albers (1998). This increase is mostly due to better coverage of customers, improved sales force morale from having better territories, and finally an increase of sales (Zoltners and Sinha 2005).

To realize these advantages, it is very valuable to have a graphic tool that is able to display the territories as a map and allow the user to manually alter the assignment of SCUs to territories and obtain rich diagnostics of the effects of these modifications. It is also important to base the territory design on true distances based on powerful routing software. Zoltners and Sinha (2005) attribute much of their success to their provision of such tools and software.

The jury is still out on whether territory design based on response functions is too complex as suggested by Zoltners and Sinha (2005), especially considering recent advances in econometric estimation of response functions. Regardless, future research should investigate whether greater profits result from better salesperson motivation from a balancing approach or profit-maximizing allocations approaches to territory design.

6.4.7 Recommendations for Directly Controlled Selling Effort Allocation Decisions

The main conclusion from our review is that being vaguely right is indeed better than being precisely wrong as Lodish (1974) put it. Given the availability of data and models and computing processing power, the basic concepts put forward in Lodish's CALLPLAN are much more implementable today, and companies can significantly benefit from improving their allocation decisions by developing disaggregate response functions, e.g., customer segment-level function using historical rather than subjective methods. The payoff from this can be substantial relative to the costs of developing these tools. Further the hurdles in the way of applying or disseminating such models to the salesperson level are much lower than in earlier decades. As already noted, many reasonably complex allocation problems can be solved by nonlinear optimization algorithms residing in standard software. Sales force automation has gained ground and most salespeople are now equipped with laptops etc. The use of rules to decide allocation decisions should be much reduced. Companies would have to invest more in analytical training of their sales managers so that things do not remain a black box but the return on such investments would be significant.

6.5 Models for Sales force Compensation Design

Ultimately, a salesperson has control of his/her own work effort. If a firm's managers cannot easily monitor how a representative allocates his/her time in the field then the main mechanism for influencing the level and allocation of the salesperson's selling effort is the compensation plan wherein some proportion of total pay is tied to sales output (Albers 2002). However, compensation planning is a complex task that involves the resolution of several questions (Albers 1996b). First, the company has to make strategic decisions with regard to the level of pay and what percentage of total pay should be variable on average. Second, it has to determine the type of variable compensation. The firm may pay a commission rate on sales or a bonus on the achievement of sales quota or awards for winning sales contests. Advantages and disadvantages of these compensation components are discussed in Albers (2000a). Third, the detailed design or structure of the selected kind of compensation system has to be set. This involves decisions such as the differentiation of commission rates across products or customers. Further, if and when companies delegate pricing authority to the sales force they must decide on the incentive plan that would align the firm and sales representative's interests. These issues are discussed in the subsequent sections.

6.5.1 Determining the Ratio of Variable to Total Pay

Principal-agent theory (or simply *agency theory*) provides direction on how to design contracts between a principal (in this case the company or sales force management) and an agent (in this case the salesperson) that reconcile the conflicting objectives of the two parties. Specifically, it is assumed that the company's objective is to maximize its expected profit, equal to its contribution from sales less the compensation paid out to the salesperson, while the latter's goal is to maximize his/her overall or 'net' utility, given by the utility for (sales output-dependent) income less the disutility associated with the effort required to earn that income. As the relationship between sales and effort is not deterministic and the field salesperson's effort is not observable by management in principle, the company faces a moral hazard problem in implementing the so-called *first best solution* consisting of a contract that simply pays a certain amount of money per unit effort put into selling by the salesperson.

Assuming that the salesperson's utility function for income reflects risk-aversion while the firm is risk-neutral in the face of sales uncertainty, agency theory shows that the (*second best*) solution to the problem is a *risk sharing* contract comprised of a fixed plus output-dependent variable pay. More specifically, Basu et al. (1985) consider a setting where the firm and the salesperson have symmetric information about the uncertain sales response function. They then formulate the firm's problem of compensation plan design as a leader-follower game in which the firm first announces the compensation plan and then, based on the given plan, the salesperson chooses the effort level that maximizes his/her expected net utility. The firm's problem is to determine the optimal plan that maximizes its expected profits subject to (a) the salesperson's expected net utility-maximizing effort decision in response to the plan (known as the *incentive compatability* constraint) and (b) the requirement that for the salesperson to participate, i.e., accept the contract, his/her resultant expected net utility exceed the level obtainable from the best alternative job (known as the *individual rationality* constraint). Based on this model formulation, Basu et al. (1985) show the optimal form of the compensation plan has a nonlinear shape which can be approximated by piecewise linear functions representing a fixed salary plus (sales output dependent) variable pay plan. Evidence from practice indicates that indeed many firms operate with combination compensation plans consisting of a salary plus commissions. Subsequently, considering a setting of asymmetric information with heterogeneous salespeople, where the salespeople are better informed about the uncertain sales response functions of their local areas than the company management, Lal and Staelin (1986) demonstrate that offering a *menu* of compensation plans with different fixed and variable pay parameters is superior to setting a single plan for a heterogeneous sales force.

The above models assume a pure incentives world in which monitoring of salespeople's efforts is infinitely costly. Considering that in reality some monitoring is usually feasible, Joseph and Thevaranjan (1998) revisit the tradeoffs associated with the use of monitoring and incentives in a model wherein the firm chooses the compensation plan parameters as well as the salesperson's risk tolerance (by way of its recruiting decision). They develop a model which compares a pure incentives world with one where partial monitoring of selling effort by the firm is allowed and show that the benefit of monitoring is that it allows the firm to hire a more risk-averse salesperson and lower the weight placed on incentives, which ultimately lowers compensation costs for the firm.

The article by Basu et al. (1985) offers some insights into the advantages of different structures of the compensation depending on certain conditions. For example, the results derived from comparative static investigations suggest that the higher the uncertainty, the higher the fixed component should be, and that the more effective the salesperson the higher the variable component should be. While some of these theoretical results have been supported by empirical studies (e.g., John and Weitz 1989; Coughlan and Narasimhan 1992; Lal et al. 1994: Joseph and Kalwani 1995a; Krafft et al. 2004; Misra et al. 2005) and by experiments (Umanath et al. 1993; Ghosh and John 2000), the key hypothesis of a negative relationship between the proportion of incentive pay and sales uncertainty (i.e., risk faced by the salesperson) has consistently been rejected in cross-sectional studies (Krafft et al. 2004). Further, if one simplifies the Basu et al. (1985) model as in Lal and Srinivasan (1993) and applies plausible numerical values of model parameters then the agency-theoretic solution implies the payment of a *negative salary* to the salesperson as shown by Albers (1996b). An interpretation of this result is that the salesperson must pay some fee or rent to the firm for his territory and then obtains income from his/her commissions on sales (Albers 1996b). However, such plans are rarely observed in practice.

The unrealistic implication of a negative salary derived from the Basu et al. (1985) model as well as the failure to find unequivocal empirical support for its key prescription of lower incentive pay in the face of greater risk suggest that the model formulation is overlooking some important aspect of the sales force compensation problem. Godes (2004) suggests that the problem is that the traditional agency-theoretic framework treats the risk faced by the salesperson as exogenous rather than effort-dependent, i.e., endogenous. Specifically, Godes argues that a sales-person can choose to implement an effort level that corresponds to low risk. With such endogenous risk, the salary portion of the compensation plan can offer no insurance (as it does not influence the selling effort) and the firm can only rely on the commission portion to provide any insurance to the salesperson. The implica-tion is that for the plan to be incentive compatible, the commission must *increase* with the salesperson's risk-aversion. Further, this would explain why compensation plans with higher proportion of incentive pay are observed in environments with higher uncertainty unlike the prediction of the standard agency theory model. Godes' (2004) analysis is thought-provoking but there are still other alternative explanations for why the empirical findings to date are inconsistent with Basu et al. (1985) theoretical results, see, e.g., Krafft et al. (2004). Clearly, more research is needed to resolve these issues as well as develop normative models extensions that produce more plausible, actionable results (Albers 1996b). Next, we discuss the progress made in optimally structuring specific forms of compensation plans.

6.5.2 Determining Optimal Commission Rates

A commission plan ties variable pay directly to the absolute sales level achieved by a salesperson. Typically, companies using a commission scheme set a uniform sales commission rate across their sales force. This presumes that the individual territories are equitable in terms of sales potentials and workloads, otherwise there is bound to be dissatisfaction and loss of sales force morale if varying potentials lead to salespeople realizing very different sales levels in response to the same levels of effort. This issue does not arise in the model by Basu et al. (1985) as they consider only the problem of a firm interacting with a single salesperson, or effectively a homogeneous sales force. In Basu et al.'s (1985) analysis, the optimal commission rate function they derive is either a constant, increasing or decreasing function of realized sales which, in practical applications, is approximated by a piecewise linear function. However, even though the optimal plan is nonlinear, there are reasons for employing simpler linear plans, i.e., fixed salary plus constant commission rate plans. Specifically, linear plans are simple to administer, easy to understand by salespeople and very often not far from optimality (Basu and Kalyanaram 1990). In addition, taking a dynamic perspective, linear plans discourage the costly variation in intertemporal allocation of the salesperson's effort that can be induced over the accounting horizon by a nonlinear plan (Lal and Srinivasan 1993). Larkin (2006) empirically shows a profit reduction of 7% due to such an intertemporal variation of selling effort in the case of an enterprise software vendor.

The sales force compensation models covered so far do not provide a clear answer to the question of what exactly should be the optimal commission rate. If one ignores risk and focuses only on the variable pay component (neglecting the effect of fixed salaries) then Albers (1996b) shows that the optimal commission rate level is given by

$$c_i = g_i \cdot \varepsilon_i / \eta_i \qquad (i \in I), \text{with} \qquad (6.11)$$

c_i: commission rate
g_i: gross margin
ε_i: elasticity of sales with respect to effort
η_i / elasticity of disutility from effort

There is also no conclusive result with regard to how to differentiate commission rates across products or customers with varying gross margins. The seminal paper by Farley (1964) showed that if commission rates were set proportional to gross margins then salespeople will allocate their effort as desired by the firm. Weinberg (1978) confirms this result holds even for non-income maximizing salespeople. Later, however, Srinivasan (1981) pointed out that Farley's (1964) result does not hold if the salesperson's goal is to maximize utility rather than income. In such circumstances, the heuristic rule (6.11) can be applied to set commission rates if product or customer sales-effort elasticities and gross margins are known. Further, almost all the models for setting optimal commissions for a multiple product salesperson following Farley (1964) have assumed away *demand interdependencies* that are likely to be present among products in a salesperson's portfolio. Recognizing this, Zhang and Mahajan

(1995) propose a model for deriving optimal differentiated commission rates for products in a salesperson's portfolio that are complementary or substitutive.

6.5.3 Setting Sales Quota- Bonus Plans

Sales quotas are known to significantly influence salespeople's allocation decisions (e.g., Ross 1991). Accordingly, sales quota-bonus plans in conjunction with fixed salaries are widely observed in practice (Joseph and Kalwani 1995b) and are especially advantageous when the sales force is deployed across sales territories that are heterogeneous with respect to potentials or travel requirements. In such settings, equitable rewards that maintain sales force morale can be ensured by tying incentive pay to actual performance relative to a sales quota rather than to absolute sales volume as in a straight commission plan. This of course presumes that individual rep sales quotas appropriately reflect territorial differences beyond the control of individual salespeople (Rao 1990).

Noting the popularity of sales quota-bonus plans in practice, Raju and Srinivasan (1996) numerically investigate and compare performance under such a plan with that realized with the curvilinear (convex) Basu et al. (1985) solution. In contrast to the Basu et al. plan which is individually tailored to each salesperson/territory, the quota-bonus plan investigated by Raju and Srinivasan is a piecewise linear quota-commission plan wherein sales quotas vary across the heterogeneous sales force but each salesperson receives the same fixed salary and commission rate on his/her dollar sales that exceed the quota. Raju and Srinivasan's numerical experiments show the total nonoptimality is merely about 1% for the parametric scenarios studied. They also note the quota plan is easier to administer than the individually tailored Basu et al. plan. Further, unlike what can occur with the curvilinear Basu et al. plan, Steenburgh (2004) empirically shows that bonuses for quota achievement do not lead to timing games (behaviors that increase incentive payments without providing incremental benefits to the firm) with their sales orders, but actually do motivate salespeople to work harder.

The determination of quotas itself is a rather complicated problem. From the company's viewpoint, setting a sales quota too low does not motivate the salesperson to put in as much effort as possible while setting it too high discourages the salesperson from devoting sufficient effort to selling (Chowdhury 1993). The risk of such quota-setting errors can be mitigated if experienced salespeople share with management the private information they possess about sales prospects in their local territories, taking into account their own selling abilities, as this is likely to be superior to that possessed by remote managers. However, an appropriate incentive plan for eliciting honest and accurate forecasts from salespeople is needed. One such mechanism, originally called the "New Soviet Incentive Scheme," was described by Gonik (1978) and its analytical properties and the responses of both risk-neutral and risk-averse salespeople to it were investigated by Mantrala and Raman (1990). The Gonik scheme is actually an exchange beginning with the communication of management's suggested reference sales quota to a salesperson along with the associated incentive plan. The incentive plan displays the schedule of bonus payouts for actual performance relative to the sales quota ultimately accepted by the salesperson. As shown by Lal and Staelin ((1986), the incentive plan is actually a menu of piecewise linear contracts or schedules – one schedule corresponding to each feasible quota level – from which the salesperson chooses his/her contract by settling the sales quota that he/she would accept. The bonus scheme is structured to induce the expected utility maximizing rep to choose an ambitious sales quota and actually fullfill it. Mantrala and Raman (1990) also provide practical directions for implementing the Gonik plan. More recently, Chen (2005) has demonstrated that a menu of linear contracts as originally proposed by Rao (1990) dominates the Gonik procedure and provides an algorithm for computing the optimal contract parameters.

The Gonik incentive system's aim is to elicit salesepeople's private information about the sales they feel they can and will achieve in their territories for the purposes of setting their sales quotas and motivating their actual fulfillment. Another way for management to learn about the imperfectly known territory sales potentials/abilities of salespeople is by tracking salespeople's performances relative to sales quota-bonus plans set over a multi-period time horizon. Mantrala et al. (1997) provide a model of such a process for optimal quota-setting over time with Bayesian learning of sales response parameters. A third alternative for the design of sales quota-bonus plans proposed by researchers like Darmon (1979, 1987) and Mantrala et al. (1994) is for the firm to measure the salesperson's utility function, reflecting how he/she weighs the utility from income against the disutility of effort associated with earning that income. In making this tradeoff, a salesperson must account for how sales in the territory will respond to variations in his/her effort, i.e., the territory sales response function. This measurement can be done via a conjoint analysis procedure which asks a salesperson to give his/her preference rank-ordering of different sales quota-lump sum bonus combinations. In particular, Mantrala et al. (1994) address a problem of setting a multiproduct sales quota-bonus plan for a heterogeneous sales force by utilizing the following model of the selling time required to achieve a certain specified sales level or quota:

$$S_{ij} = \alpha_{ij} + \left(\beta_{ij} - \alpha_{ij}\right) \cdot \left(1 - e^{-b_{ij}t_{ij}}\right) \qquad (i \in I, j \in J) \qquad (6.12)$$

x_{ij}: i-th product's sales volume achieved by the j-th salesperson,
α_{ij}, β_{ij} : Zero-call or saturation sales volume of the i-th product in the j-th salesperson's territory, respectively,
t_{ij}: working time of the j-th salesperson devoted to selling the i-th product.

Taking the inverse of (6.12), one obtains

$$t_{ij} = \frac{1}{b_{ij}} \cdot \ln\left(\frac{\beta_{ij} - \alpha_{ij}}{\beta_{ij} - S_{ij}}\right) \qquad (i \in I, j \in J) \qquad (6.13)$$

Now, Mantrala et al. (1994) assume the following utility function:

$$w_j = \omega_j \cdot B_j^{\rho_j} - c_j \cdot T_j \qquad (i \in I, j \in J) \qquad (6.14)$$

Replacing the total working time T_j in (6.14) by the sum of the working times t_{ij} from (6.13) over all products i results in:

$$w_j = \omega_j \cdot B_j^{\rho_j} - c_j \sum_{i \in I} \frac{1}{b_{ij}} \cdot \ln\left(\frac{\beta_{ij} - \alpha_{ij}}{\beta_{ij} - S_{ij}}\right) \qquad (i \in I, j \in J) \qquad (6.15)$$

In the next step, the parameter values of the utility function (6.14) for bonuses B_j and working-times t_{ij} is estimated from preference judgments for different combinations of quotas per product and the corresponding bonuses for their achievement. Based on such parameter values, Mantrala et al. (1994) describe applications in two pharmaceutical companies with two and four products, respectively. However, the individual quotas have been specified at a certain percentage of maximum sales which is questionable with respect to equity. This model represents the most comprehensive and applicable approach for sales force compensation at the moment.

6.5.4 Sales Contests

In addition to the regular compensation plan, many companies use *sales contests* in which sale representatives can win prizes, e.g., cash, merchandise, or travel awards, for surpassing a specified own sales goal or other salespeople's performances in some special short-term sales campaign (see Murphy and Dacin 1998 for a review of research related to the use of sales contests in sales management). Sales contest formats are typically either "*closed–ended*" contests, in which salespeople compete with each other for the available prizes, or *open-ended* contests i.e., events in which salespeople must exceed a given sales target to win a prize or special bonus. Open-ended contests are like short-term sales quota-bonus schemes which we have already dealt with in the previous section. Therefore, here, we focus on closed-ended contests where relative performance, e.g., rank-order of performances, determines prize-winners, and a pre-specified number of top performer/s out of all the participants in the event receive prizes of known values.

Economic "tournament" theorists (e.g., Lazear and Rosen 1981, Green and Stokey 1983) have shown that if common uncertainty (random environmental disturbances affecting all agents equally) is relatively large and dominant in the selling environment then closed-ended contests offer advantages over individualistic absolute output-based commission plans incentives. Specifically, relative comparisons of performance difference out or eliminate the effects of a common disturbance from the individual reward structure. Consequently, the total uncertainty associated with each rep's output-effort relationship gets reduced and the firm has to pay a lower risk premium to risk-averse salespeople rewarded under a relative performance contest format than by an individualistic commission scheme. From the perspective of the risk-averse reps, a closed-ended contest is more motivating than an individualistic scheme because it insulates them from common risk. The more risky the common disturbance, the better is the closed-ended contest. Such contests also are more efficient than piece rate or commission schemes when the sales force size is large (since it is generally cheaper to observe relative position or order of performances than it is to monitor absolute performance levels required by a commission scheme, and these economies increase as sales force size increases) and incentive budgets are tight (because the total payout under a contest is fixed in advance), see. e.g., Mantrala et al. (1999). On the other hand, closed-ended sales contests, if not properly designed and timed, can be problematic for a variety of reasons including wide variation in contestants' abilities, collusion, sabotage etc., misallocation of effort and possible timing games (Gopalakrishna et al. 2006). Because contests foster internal rivalry, Gaba and Kalra (1999) show with the help of experiments that salespeople may engage in high-risk (low-risk) behavior if only few (many) salespeople can become winners. Thus, it is still not clear what the best format for a sales contest is.

The optimal design of contests (particularly with regard to the prize structure) has received some attention in the marketing science literature resulting in some useful prescriptions, e.g., Kalra and Shi (2001), Murthy and Mantrala (2005). However, so far empirical evidence related to sales response dynamics, their effectiveness, and ROI has been limited (Wotruba and Schoel 1983; Wildt et al. 1987). In a recent paper, Gopalakrishna et al. (2006) establish three life insurance sales contests have positive ROI once both pre-contest and post-contest sales responses are taken into account and provide insights with respect to the optimal length of a contest in relation to the product sales cycle length. More such research is needed.

6.5.5 Delegating Pricing Decisions

Weinberg (1975) proved in a theoretical paper that delegating pricing authority to salespeople is not a problem as long as the commission is based on realized gross margins and not on sales. This finding has been questioned by Stephenson et al. (1979) who showed in their empirical analysis that companies applying no or limited pricing delegation realize higher growth and profits. This has led to a variety of agency-theoretic models that investigate under various assumptions whether centralized pricing is superior to decentralized pricing or vice versa. In the case of information asymmetry, meaning that the salesperson better knows the price elasticity of the customers, Lal (1986) showed that delegating pricing authority is better than centralized pricing. Joseph (2001) added the possible substitution of selling effort by price discounting and arrives at the conclusion that pricing delegation is not always optimal. While these approaches assume monopolistic markets Bhardwaj (2001) reinvestigates this issue under competition. He finds that firms should delegate the pricing decisions when price competition is intense. Reanalyzing the model by Lal (1986), Misra and Prasad (2004) show that centralized pricing performs at least as well as price delegation when the salesperson's private information can be revealed to the firm through contracting. This model is extended by the same authors (Misra and Prasad 2005) to the case of competition. Under asymmetric information, they find that there always exists an equilibrium where all firms use centralized pricing that is either unique or payoff equivalent to equilibria that have a combination of contract types. Given these mixed results future research should investigate more what firms have in mind when delegating pricing authority and then should model these aspects in order to arrive at meaningful results that can be implemented in practice.

6.6 Special Topics and Directions for Future Research

It is evident from our survey so far of directly and indirectly controlled selling effort deployment decisions research literature that there have been really few new and significant publications in this area since about the mid-80s aside from several falling in the domain of sales force compensation and incentives planning. Even in this domain, the agency-theoretic models developed so far seem to require modification in order to arrive at more relevant solutions while the jury is still out on the theory's applicability to the actual design of compensation plans in practice even though it does help to provide one framework to guide the practical design of plans. Overall, however, research on sales force resource allocation models seems to have slowed to a trickle, with only a few active proponents, after the deluge in the 1970s. However, this can hardly be attributed to a lack of interesting or important new problems awaiting more attention in the sales force management area. In this section, we briefly discuss four broad areas of outstanding issues and directions for research related to selling effort decision problems that we see in sales management.

6.6.1 Classic Problems

As already noted, among the fundamental decision areas that we depict in Fig. 6.1, the problem of optimizing the *sales force structure* in different selling situations remains the most under-researched perhaps due to the complex tradeoffs, ranging from the economic to the political involved. Currently, according to Zoltners et al. (2004), the "best practices" comprehensive approach to sales force structuring appears to be a multi-step process rather than mathematical model, involving careful assessments of the *salesperson bandwidth*, i.e., the amount of information that can be carried through a communication channel which has three components: the *product bandwidth* (length and complexity of the product line), *activity bandwidth* (range and complexity of selling functions), and *customer bandwidth* (number and diversity in customers' buying processes). When a sales job exceeds a salesperson bandwidth it is time for specialization. For example, if the activity and product bandwidths involved in serving a customer become overly extended then the company should consider creating either product specialists or perhaps sales account teams with different functional specialists. However, the increased selling effectiveness from doing so have to be weighed against the associated costs. Zoltners et al. (2004) do not propose a decision model but clearly their ideas could be the basis for one which would be an important contribution given the dependence of optimal sales force sizing and allocation decisions on the form of the sales force structure.

6.6.2 New Industry Contexts

Sales force research so far is dominated by pharmaceutical industry applications – just like sales promotion research has concentrated on grocery retailing. However, there are other industry contexts than pharma that face varying selling effort deployment management challenges that demand attention. For example, Mantrala et al. (2007) investigate optimal ad space selling effort investments in the daily newspaper industry which operates in an interrelated 'dual revenues' (newspaper subscriptions and advertising revenues) or 'two-sided' market which is a problem setting that has not been addressed in the previous sales management literature even though it is a common situation for most media industries that use sales forces to sell advertising space.

6.6.3 New Selling Environment and Marketing Strategy Contexts

Many of the classic as well as recent improvements in sales force decision modeling continue to be grounded in a "transactional sales" setting where selling effort directly and immediately affects sales. However, sales production in many industries today is a consultative, relationship-oriented process requiring multiple calls on a customer represented by multiple decision-makers by multiple salespeople or teams (see, Table 6.2 for a summary of the key differences between the traditional and new selling environments). In this sort of strategic selling environment that is gaining ground, even previously successful sales force decision models are largely unsuitable. In our view, while some very basic principles such as those of marginal analysis will still apply, there is a pressing need for new, more dynamic decision models for optimal allocation of sales resources over extended sales cycles and buying centers.

Table 6.2 Classic versus Contemporary Selling Environments, Source: Brown et al. (2005)

	Traditional Selling Environment	New Selling Environment
Metrics	Individualistic	Multiple agent (team)
	Transaction-specific	Customer relationship-oriented
	Product-focused outcomes or behaviors (activities)	outcomes or behaviors
		Customer-focused, such as customer
	Individualistic sales outputs	satisfaction or
	Sales function-oriented	Team production outputs
		Cross-functional team-oriented
Goals	Individualistic	Multiple agent/team goals
	Product sales quotas	Customer profitability; cost-to-serve
	Product selling activity quotas	Customer satisfaction; value-building and engagement goals
Controls	Individual sales outcome-based or behavior-based	Hybrid (outcome and behavior) controls
	Sales function-oriented	Cross-functional team-oriented
	Formal controls emphasized	Informal controls emphasized
Compensation	Individualistic plans	Multiple agent (team) plans
	Individualistic sales output-based	Team output-based (e.g., corporate profits)
	Absolute output-based	Relative performance-based
	Product sales-based plans	Customer satisfaction-based
		Customer profitability and equity-based

In particular, while modeling research on Customer Equity and Relationship Management has taken off (see, e.g., the October 2005 Special issue of the *Journal of Marketing*), focused research on the optimal deployment and motivation of a key instrument for CRM – the sales force – is sparse. Brown et al. (2005), for example, provide a detailed assessment of how sales force motivation and compensation research needs to be adapted to address the new environment where personal selling effort is the key to the "3 Rs" of the New Marketing, namely, retention of customers, related products sales (cross-selling) to and referrals generation from existing customers. For example, more research on the pros and cons of shifting from short-term sales-based incentives to customer satisfaction-based incentives for sales forces and the optimal design of the latter is needed (e.g., Hauser et al. 1994, Sharma 1997).

6.6.4 New Integrated Marketing Communications Contexts

There is great interest today in the question of how to improve integration of the marketing-sales interface (e.g., Kotler et al. 2006) in general, and in Integrated Marketing Communications (IMC) in particular which exploit the interactions or synergistic effects between various marketing instruments, e.g., Naik and Raman (2003). Despite these trends, there are still few new decision models for jointly optimizing the mix of personal selling and impersonal marketing communications efforts following the works of Gatignon and Hanssens (1987), Gopalakrishna and Chatterjee (1992) which investigated the interaction between sales force effort and advertising in models for determining the optimal ratio of sales force to advertising expenditures (see e.g., Mantrala 2002). In a recent paper, Smith et al. (2004) assess the complementary effect of trade shows on sales force performance and suggest normative implications for optimizing sales force allocations based on previous communications exposure. Most recently, Smith et al. (2006) have examined the effects of timing of exposure to sequential communications and implications for effective resource deployment by a home improvement marketer. In their innovative model, the sales process is specified as a sequence of three stages marked by concrete outcomes – *lead generation* by impersonal marketing communication, e.g., radio and newspaper advertising, and direct mail; *appointment conversion* i.e., the conversion of leads into sales appointments followed by a sales call (after a time lag or delay), *and sales closure*, i.e., the conversion of appointments into sales. The delay between customer inquiry and a sales call adversely affects the purchase likelihood because consumer decisions to invest in home improvement tend to be transient, competing with alternative uses of the available funds. Significant delays in the sales visit, associated with high lead volume, warrant careful analysis of the allocation/timing of lead-generating communications that best complement follow up sales effort. Smith et al. (2006) formulate, estimate and validate a linked decision model to solve this problem and provide a computer-based decision tool to help managers assess the impact of different media expenditures on outcomes.

Very often, routine selling activities can be directed to an Internet communication thus freeing sales people for their real task of communicating face-to-face with customers (Johnson and Bharadwaj 2005). This asks for a subtle coordination of the various forms of communication. In addition, the Internet may be used as a distribution channel which may take away sales opportunities from the salespersons which requires explicit compensation solutions for solving this channel conflict.

6.7 Conclusions

Models for sales management to date have addressed and even quite successfully resolved some of the traditional strategic, operational and tactical selling effort decision problems, the "low-hanging fruit" as it were, e.g., sales resource allocation, sales territory design, sales force sizing, regular sales force compensation plan design, in fairly stable environments involving one or multiple independent sales entities, and individual sales reps operating independently of others. Some refinements and extensions in solutions in these problem areas are needed but the core ideas are in place. Unfortunately, the selling environment is rapidly evolving and many new albeit difficult sales management problems are crying for attention offering significant opportunities for new models-based research. However, there may not be any "quick hits" among these and the need is for a fresh and sustained onslaught on these problems by many more academic researchers than appear to be active in this area at present. We hope this chapter plays a role in stimulating such research.

References

Albers, S. 1996a. CAPPLAN: A Decision Support System for Planning the Pricing and Sales Effort Policy of a Salesforce. *European Journal of Marketing* **30**(7) 68–82.

Albers, S. 1996b. Optimization Models for Salesforce Compensation. *European Journal of Operational Research* **89** 1–17.

Albers, S. 2000a. Sales-force Management. K. Blois, *The Oxford Textbook of Marketing.* Oxford University Press, 292–317.

Albers, S. 2000b. Impact of Types of Functional Relationships, Decisions, and Solutions on the Applicability of Marketing Models. *International Journal of Research in Marketing*, **17** 169–175.

Albers, S. 2002. Salesforce Management – Compensation, Motivation, Selection and Training. B.A. Weitz, R. Wensley, *Handbook of Marketing*, Sage: London, Thousand Oaks and New Delhi, 248–266.

Albers, S., M.K. Mantrala, S. Sridhar. 2008. A Meta-Analysis of Personal Selling Elasticities. *Working Paper*, Marketing Science Institute, Cambridge MA.

Armstrong, G.M. 1976. The SCHEDULE Model and the Salesman's Effort Allocation. *California Management Review* **18**(4) 43–51.

Assmus, G., J.U. Farley, D.R. Lehmann. 1984. How Advertising Affects Sales: A Meta Analysis of Econometric Results. *Journal of Marketing Research* **21**(1) 65–74.

Basu, A.K., G. Kalyanaram. 1990. On the Relative Performance of Linear Versus Nonlinear Compensation Plans. *International Journal of Research in Marketing* **7** 171–178.

Basu, A.K., R. Lal, V. Srinivasan, R. Staelin. 1985. Salesforce Compensation Plans: An Agency Theoretic Perspective. *Marketing Science* **4** 267–291.

Berger, P.D. 1972. On Setting Optimal Sales Commissions. *Operations Research Quarterly* **23** 213–215.

Beswick, C.A., D.W. Cravens. 1977. A Multistage Decision Model for Salesforce Management. *Journal of Marketing Research* **14** 135–144.

Bhardwaj, P. 2001. Delegating Pricing Decisions. *Marketing Science* **20** 143–169.

Brown, S.P., K.R. Evans, M. Mantrala, G. Challagalla. 2005. Adapting Motivation, Control, and Compensation Research to a New Environment. *Journal of Personal Selling & Sales Management* **25**(2) 155–167.

Chakravarti, D., A. Mitchell, R. Staelin. 1979. Judgment Based Marketing Decision Models: An Experimental Investigation of the Decision Calculus Approach. *Management Science* **25** 251–263.

Chakravarti, D., A. Mitchell, R. Staelin. 1981. Judgment Based Marketing Decision Models: Problems and Possible Solutions. *Journal of Marketing* **45**(Fall), 13–23.

Chen, F. 2005. Salesforce Incentives, Market Information, and Production/Inventory Planning. *Management Science* **51** 60–75.

Chintagunta, P.K., T. Erdem, P.E. Rossi, M. Wedel. 2006. Structural Modeling in Marketing: Review and Assessment. *Marketing Science* **25** 604–616.

Chowdhury, J. 1993. The Motivational Impact of Sales Quotas on Effort. *Journal of Marketing Research* **30** 28–41.

Coughlan A.T. 1993. Salesforce Compensation: A Review of MS/OR Advances J. Eliashberg, G.L. Lilien, *Marketing, Handbooks in Operations Research and Management Science 5,* North-Holland, Amsterdam, 611–651.

Coughlan, A.T., C. Narasimhan. 1992. An Empirical Analysis of Sales-Force Compensation Plans. *Journal of Business* **65** 93–121.

Coughlan, A.T., S.K. Sen. 1989. Salesforce Compensation: Theory and Managerial Implications. *Marketing Science* **8** 324–342.

Darmon, R.Y. 1975. Scheduling Sales Calls with a Communication Response Model. E.M. Mazze, *1975 Combined Proceedings*, Chicago, 530–533.

Darmon, R.Y. 1979. Setting Sales Quotas with Conjoint Analysis. *Journal of Marketing Research* **16** 133–140.

Darmon, R.Y. 1987. QUOPLAN: A System for Optimizing Sales Quota-Bonus Plans. *Journal of the Operational Research Society* **38** 1121–1132.

Dong, X., P. Manchanda, P.K. Chintagunta. 2006. Quantifying the Benefits of Individual Level Targeting under the Presence of Firm Strategic Behavior. *Working Paper*. University of Chicago, June.

Dorfman, R., P.O. Steiner. 1954. Optimal Advertising and Optimal Quality. *American Economic Review* **44** 826–836.

Doyle, P., J. Saunders. 1990. Multiproduct Advertising Budgeting. *Marketing Science* **9** 97–113.

Drexl, A., K. Haase. 1999. Fast Approximation Methods for Sales Force Deployment. *Management Science* **45**(10) 1307–1323.

Farley, J.U. 1964. An Optimal Plan for Salesmen's Compensation. *Journal of Marketing Research* **1**(2) 39–43.

Freeland, J.R., C.B. Weinberg. 1980. S-shaped Response Functions: Implications for Decision Models. *Journal of the Operational Research Society* **31** 1001–1007.

Fudge, W.K., L.M. Lodish. 1977. Evaluation of the Effectiveness of a Model Based Salesman's Planning System by Field Experimentation. *Interfaces*. **8/1**/Part 2, 97–106.

Fylstra, D., L. Lasdon, J. Watson, A. Waren. 1998. Design and Use of the Microsoft Excel Solver. *Interfaces* **28**(5) 29–55.

Gaba, A., K. Ajay. 1999. Risk Behavior in Response to Quotas and Contests. *Marketing Science* **18** 417–434.

Gatignon, H., D.M. Hanssens. 1987. Modeling Marketing Interactions with Application to Salesforce Effectiveness. *Journal of Marketing Research*. **24** 247–257.

Ghosh, M., G. John. 2000. Experimental Evidence for Agency Models of Salesforce Compensation. *Marketing Science* **19** 348–365.

Glaze, T.A., C.B. Weinberg. 1979. A Sales Territory Alignment Model and Account Planning System (TAPS). R.P. Bagozzi, *Sales Management: New Developments from Behavioral and Decision Model Research*. Mass. MSI, Cambridge 325–342.

Godes, D. 2004. Contracting Under Endogenous Risk. *Quantitative Marketing and Economics* **2** 321–345.

Gonik, J. 1978. Tie Salesmens' Bonuses to Their Forecasts. *Harvard Business Review* **56**(3), 116–123.

Gönül, F.F., F. Carter, E. Petrova, K. Srinivasan. 2001. Promotion of Prescription Drugs and Its Impact on Physicians' Choice Behavior. *Journal of Marketing* **65**(July) 79–90.

Gopalakrishna, S., R. Chatterjee. 1992. A Communications Response Model for a Mature Industrial Product: Application and Implications. *Journal of Marketing Research* **29** 189–200.

Gopalakrishna, S., J. Garrett, M.K. Mantrala, J.. Moore. 2006. Determining the Effectiveness of Sales Contests. *Working Paper*. University of Missouri.

Green, J.R., N.L. Stokey. 1983. A Comparison of Tournaments and Contracts. *Journal of Political Economy* **91**(3), 349–364.

Hanssens, D.M., H.A. Levien. 1983. An Econometric Study of Recruitment Marketing in the U.S. Navy. *Management Science* **29** 1167–1184.

Hanssens, D.M., L.J. Parsons, R.L. Schultz. 2003. *Market Response Models: Econometric and Time Series Analysis.* 2 nd ed., Kluwer, Boston.

Hauser, J.R., D.I. Simester, B. Wernerfelt. 1994. Customer Satisfaction Incentives. *Marketing Science* 13, 327–350.

Hess, S.W., S.A. Samuels. 1971. Experiences with a Sales Districting Model: Criteria and Implementation. *Management Science* 18 P41–P54.

Horsky, D., P. Nelson. 1996. Evaluation of Salesforce Size and Productivity through Efficient Frontier Benchmarking. *Marketing Science* 15 301–320.

John, G., B. Weitz. 1989. Salesforce Compensation: An Empirical Investigation of Factors Related to Use of Salary Versus Incentive Compensation. *Journal of Marketing Research.* 26, 1–14.

Johnson, D.S., S. Bharadwaj. 2005. Digitization of Selling Activity and Sales Force Performance: An Empirical Investigation. *Journal of the Academy of Marketing Science* 33(1) 3–18.

Jones, E., S.P. Brown, A.A. Zoltners, B.A. Weitz. 2005. The Changing Environment of Selling and Sales Management. *Journal of Personal Selling & Sales Management* 25(2) 105–111.

Joseph, K. 2001. On the Optimality of Delegating Pricing Authority to the Sales Force. *Journal of Marketing* 65(January) 62–70.

Joseph, K., M.U. Kalwani. 1995a. The Impact of Environmental Uncertainty on the Design of Salesforce Compensation Plans. *Marketing Letters* 6 183–197.

Joseph, K., M.U. Kalwani. 1995b. The Role of Bonus Pay in Salesforce Compensation Plans. *Industrial Marketing Management* 27 147–159.

Joseph, K., A. Thevaranjan. 1998. Monitoring and Incentives in Sales Organizations: An Agency-Theoretic Perspective. *Marketing Science* 17 107–123.

Kalra, A., M. Shi. 2001. Designing Optimal Sales Contests: A Theoretical Perspective. *Marketing Science* 20 170–193.

Kotler, P., N. Rackham, S. Krishnaswamy. 2006. Ending the War between Sales & Marketing. *Harvard Business Review* 84(July–August) 68–78.

Koyck, L.M. 1954. *Distributed Lags and Investment Analysis.* North Holland, Amsterdam.

Krafft, M., S. Albers, R. Lal. 2004. Relative Explanatory Power of Agency Theory and Transaction Cost Analysis in German Salesforces,.*International Journal of Research in Marketing* 21 265–283.

LaForge, R.W., D.W. Cravens. 1981/1982. A Market Response Model for Sales Management Decision Making. *Journal of Personal Selling and Sales Management* 2(1) 10–16.

Lal, R. 1986. Delegating Pricing Responsibility to the Salesforce. *Marketing Science* 5 159–168.

Lal, R., D. Outland, R. Staelin. 1994. Salesforce Compensation Plans: An Individual-Level Analysis. *Marketing Letters.* 5 117–130.

Lal, R., V. Srinivasan. 1993. Compensation Plans for Single- and Multi-product Salesforces: An Application of the Holmstrom-Milgrom Model. *Management Science* 39. 777–793.

Lal, R., R. Staelin. 1986. Salesforce Compensation Plans in Environments with Asymmetric Information. *Marketing Science* 5 179–198.

Lambert, Z.V., F.W. Kniffin. 1970. Response Functions and Their Application in Sales Force Management. *Southern Journal of Business.* 5 1–11.

Larkin, I. 2006. *The Cost of High-Powered Incentives: Employee Gaming in Enterprise Software Sales. Working Paper.* UC Berkeley.

Layton, R.A. 1968. Controlling Risk and Return in the Management of a Sales Team. *Journal of Marketing Research* 5 277–282.

Lazear, E.P., S. Rosen. 1981. Rank-Order Tournaments as Optimum Labor Contracts. *Journal of Political Economy* 89 841–864.

Leeflang, P.S.H., D. Wittink, M. Wedel, P. Naert. 2000. *Building Models for Marketing Decisions.* Kluwer: Boston.

Little, J.D.C. 1970. Models and Managers: The Concept of a Decision Calculus. *Management Science* **16** B466–B485.

Little, J.D.C., Boston.L.M. Lodish. 1981. Commentary on "Judgment Based Marketing Decision Models". *Journal of Marketing* **45**(Fall), 24–29.

Lodish, L.M. 1971. CALLPLAN: An Interactive Salesman's Call Planning System. *Management Science*. **18**. P25–P40.

Lodish, L.M. 1974. 'Vaguely Right' Approach to Sales Force Allocations. *Harvard Business Review* **52**(Jan–Feb) 119–124.

Lodish, L.M. 1975. Sales Territory Alignment to Maximize Profit. *Journal of Marketing Research* **12** 30–36.

Lodish, L.M. 1976. Assigning Salesmen to Accounts to Maximize Profits. *Journal of Marketing Research* **13** 440–444.

Lodish, L.M. 1980. A User Oriented Model for Sales Force Size, Product and Market Allocation Decisions. *Journal of Marketing* **44**(Summer) 70–78.

Lodish, L.M. 2001. Building Marketing Models that Make Money. *Interfaces* **31**(3) 45–55.

Lodish, L.M., E. Curtis, M. Ness, M.K. Simpson. 1988. Sales Force Sizing and Deployment Using a Decision Calculus Model at Syntex Laboratories. *Interfaces*. **18**(1) 5–20.

Manchanda, P., P.K. Chintagunta. 2004. Responsiveness of Physician Prescription Behavior to Salesforce Effort: An Individual Level Analysis. *Marketing Letters* **15**(2–3) 129–145.

Manchanda, P., E. Honka. 2005. The Effects and Role of Direct-to-Physician Marketing in the Pharmaceutical Industry: An Integrative Review. *Yale Journal of Health Policy, Law and Economics* **5** 785–822.

Manchanda, P., P.E. Rossi, P.K. Chintagunta. 2004. Response Modeling with Nonrandom Marketing-Mix Variables. *Journal of Marketing Research* **61** 467–478.

Manchanda, P., D.R. Wittink, A. Ching, P. Cleanthous, M. Ding, X.J. Dong, P.S.H. Leeflang, S. Misra, N. Mizik, S. Narayanan, T. Steenburgh, J.E. Wieringa, M. Wosinska, Y. Xie. 2005. Understanding Firm, Physician and Consumer Choice Behavior in the Pharmaceutical Industry. *Marketing Letters* **16**(3–4) 293–308.

Mantrala, M.K. 2002. Allocating Marketing Resources, B.A. Weitz, R. Wensley, *Handbook of Marketing*, Sage: London, Thousand Oaks and New Delhi, 409–435.

Mantrala, M.K., P.A. Naik, S. Sridhar, E. Thorson. 2007. Uphill or Downhill?: Locating Your Firm on a Profit Function. *Journal of Marketing* (April) **71**(2) 26–44.

Mantrala, M.K., K. Raman. 1990. Analysis of a Salesforce-Incentive Plan for Accurate Sales Forecasting And Performance. *International Journal of Research in Marketing* **7** 189–202.

Mantrala, M.K., K. Raman, R. Desiraju. 1997. Sales Quota Plans: Mechanisms for Adaptive Learning. *Marketing Letters* **8** 393–405.

Mantrala, M.K., M. Krafft, B.A. Weitz. 1999. An Empirical Examination of Economic Rationales for Companies' Use of Sales Contests, German Economic Association of Business Administration, Discussion Paper No. 00-07. Available at SSRN: http://ssrn.com/abstract=310063

Mantrala, M.K., P. Sinha, A.A. Zoltners. 1992. Impact of Resource Allocation Rules on Marketing Investment-Level Decisions and Profitability. *Journal of Marketing Research*. **29** 162–175.

Mantrala, M.K., P. Sinha, A.A. Zoltners. 1994. Structuring a Multiproduct Sales Quota-Bonus Plan for a Heterogeneous Salesforce: A Practical Approach. *Marketing Science* **13** 121–144.

McIntyre, S.H. 1982. An Experimental Study of the Impact of Judgment-Based Marketing Models. *Management Science* **28** 17–33.

Misra, B.K., A. Prasad. 2004. Centralized Pricing versus Delegating Pricing to the Salesforce under Information Asymmetry. *Marketing Science* **23** 21–28.

Misra, B.K., A. Prasad. 2005. Delegating Pricing Decisions in Competitive Markets with Symmetric and Asymmetric Information. *Marketing Science* **24** 490–497.

Misra, S., A.T. Coughlan, C. Narasimhan. 2005. Salesforce Compensation: An Analytical and Empirical Examination of the Agency Theoretic Approach. *Quantitative Marketing and Economics* **3** 5–39.

Mizik, N., R. Jacobson. 2004. Are Physicians 'Easy Marks'? Quantifying the Effects of Detailing and Sampling on New Prescriptions. *Management Science* **50** 1704–1715.

Montgomery, D.B., A.J. Silk, C.E. Zaragoza. 1971. A Multiple-Product Sales Force Allocation Model. *Management Science* **18** P3–P24.

Murphy, W.H., P.A. Dacin. 1998. Sales Contests: A Research Agenda. *Journal of Personal Selling & Sales Management* **18**(Winter) 1–16.

Murthy, P., M.K. Mantrala. 2005. Allocating a Promotion Budget between Advertising and Sales Contest Prizes: An Integrated Marketing Communications Perspective. *Marketing Letters* **16**(1) 19–35.

Naik, P.A., K. Raman. 2003. Understanding the Impact of Synergy in Multimedia Communications. *Journal of Marketing Research* **40**(4) 375–388.

Narayanan, S., R. Desiraju, P.K. Chintagunta. 2004. Return on Investment Implications for Pharmaceutical Promotional Expenditures: The Role of Marketing-Mix Interactions. *Journal of Marketing* **68**(4) 90–105.

Narayanan, S., P. Manchanda, P.K. Chintagunta. 2005. Temporal Differences in the Role of Marketing Communication in New Product Categories. *Journal of Marketing* **42**(3) 278–290.

Palmatier, R.W, S. Gopalakrishna, M.B. Houston. 2006. Returns on Business-to-Business Relationship Marketing Investments: Strategies for Leveraging Profits. *Marketing Science* **25**(5), 477–493.

Parasuraman, A., R.L. Day. 1977. A Management-Oriented Model for Allocating Selling Effort. *Journal of Marketing Research* **14** 22–33.

Parsons, L.J., P. Vanden Abeele. 1981. Analysis of Sales Call Effectiveness. *Journal of Marketing Research* **18** 107–113.

Raju, J.S., V. Srinivasan. 1996. Quota-based Compensation Plans for Multiterritory Heterogeneous Salesforces. *Management Science* **42** 1454–1462.

Rangaswamy, A, P. Sinha, A. Zoltners. 1990. An Integrated Model-Based Approach for Sales Force Structuring. *Marketing Science* **9** 279–298.

Rao, R.C. 1990. Compensating Heterogeneous Salesforces: Some Explicit Solutions. *Marketing Science*. **10** 319–341.

Rao, R.C., R.E. Turner. 1984. Organization and Effectiveness of the Multiple-Product Salesforce. *Journal of Personal Selling & Sales Management* **4**(May) 24–30.

Raudenbush, S.W., A.S. Bryk. 2002. *Hierarchical Linear Models: Applications and Data Analysis Methods* (2nd ed.). Sage, Thousand Oaks, CA.

Ross Jr., W.T. 1991. Performance Against Quota and the Call Selection Decision. *Journal of Marketing Research* **28** 296–306.

Shanker, R.J., R.E. Turner, A.A. Zoltners. 1975. Sales Territory Design: An Integrated Approach. *Management Science*. **22** 309–320.

Sharma, A. 1997. Customer Satisfaction-Based Incentive Systems: Some Managerial and Salesperson Considerations. *Journal of Personal Selling & Sales Management* **17**(2) 61–70.

Sinha, P., A.A. Zoltners. 2001. Sales-Force Decision Models: Insights from 25 Years of Implementation. *Interfaces* **31**(3), Part 2 of 2, S8–S44.

Skiera, B., S. Albers. 1998. COSTA: Contribution Optimizing Sales Territory Alignment. *Marketing Science* **18** 196–213.

Skiera, B., S. Albers. 2008. Prioritizing Sales Force Decision Areas for Productivity Improvements Using a Core Sales Response Function. *Journal of Personal Selling and Sales Management*, **XXVIII**(2) 145–154.

Smith, T.M., S. Gopalakrishna, R. Chatterjee. 2006. A Three-Stage Model of Integrated Marketing Communications at the Marketing-Sales Interface. *Journal of Marketing*

Research, Special Section on Academic and Practitioner Collaborative Research **43**(November) 564–579.

Smith, T.M., S. Gopalakrishna, P.M. Smith 2004. The Complementary Effect of Trade Shows on Personal Selling. *International Journal of Research in Marketing* **21**(1) 1–76.

Srinivasan, V. 1981. An Investigation of the Equal Commission Rate Policy for a Multiproduct Salesforce. *Management Science*. **27** 731–756.

Steenburgh, T. 2004. *Effort or Timing: The Effect of Lump-Sum Bonuses. Working Paper 05-051.* Harvard Business School, Boston.

Stephenson, P.R., W.L. Cron, G.L. Frazier. 1979. Delegating Pricing Authority to the Sales Force: The Effects on Sales and Profit Performance. *Journal of Marketing* **43**(2) 21–28.

Tellis, G.J., P.H. Franses. 2006. Optimal Data Interval for Estimating Advertising Response. *Marketing Science* **25** 217–229.

Turner, R.E. 1971. Market Measures from Salesmen: A Multidimensional Scaling Approach. *Journal of Marketing Research* **8** 165–172.

Tull, D.S., V.R. Wood, D. Duhan, T. Gillpatrick, K. R. Robertson, J.G. Helgeson. 1986. Leveraged Decision Making in Advertising: The Flat Maximum Principle and Its Implications. *Journal of Marketing Research* **23** 25–32.

Umanath, N.S., M.R. Ray, T.L. Campbell. 1993. The Impact of Perceived Environmental Uncertainty and Perceived Agent Effectiveness on the Composition of Compensation Contracts. *Management Science* **39** 32–45.

Vandenbosch, M.B., C.B. Weinberg. 1993. Salesforce Operations. J. Eliashberg, G.L. Lilien, *Marketing, Handbooks in Operations Research and Management Science 5,* North-Holland, Amsterdam, 653–694.

Wedel, M., W.A. Kamakura. 1999. *Market Segmentation. Conceptual and Methodological Foundations,* Kluwer: Boston

Weinberg, C.B. 1975. An Optimal Commission Plan for Salesmen's Control Over Price. *Management Science* **21** 937–943.

Weinberg, C.B. 1978. Jointly Optimal Sales Commissions for Nonincome Maximizing Sales Forces. *Management Science*, 24, 1252–1258.

Weitz, B.A., K. Bradford. 1999. Personal Selling and Sales Management: A Relationship Marketing Perspective. *Journal of the Academy of Marketing Science* **27**(2) 241–254

Wildt, A.R., J.D Parker, C.E. Harris jr. 1987. Assessing the Impact of Sales-Force Contests: An Application. *Journal of Business Research* **15** 145–155.

Wotruba, T.R., D.J. Schoel. 1983. Evaluation of Salesforce Contest Performance. *Journal of Personal Selling & Sales Management.* **3**(1) 1–10.

Zhang, C., V. Mahajan. 1995. Development of Optimal Salesforce Compensation Plans for Independent, Complementary and Substitutable Products. *International Journal of Research in Marketing* **12** 355–362.

Zoltners, A.A. 1976. Integer Programming Models for Sales Territory Alignment to Maximize Profit. *Journal of Marketing Research* **13** 426–430.

Zoltners, A.A., K.S. Gardner, 1980. *A Review of Sales Force Decision Models. Working Paper.* Northwestern University, Evanston, IL.

Zoltners, A.A., S.E. Lorimer. 2000. Sales Territory Alignment: An Overlooked Productivity Tool. *Journal of Personal Selling and Sales Management* **20**(3) 139–150.

Zoltners, A.A., P. Sinha. 1980. Integer Programming Models for Sales Resource Allocation, *Management Science* **26** 242–60.

Zoltners, A.A., P. Sinha. 1983. Sales Territory Alignment: A Review and Model, *Management Science* **29** 1237–1256.

Zoltners, A.A., P. Sinha. 2005. Sales Territory Design: Thirty Years of Modeling and Implementation. *Marketing Science* **24** 313–331.

Zoltners, A.A., P. Sinha, P.S.C. Chong. 1979. An Optimal Algorithm for Sales Representative Time Management. *Management Science* **29** 1237–1256.

Zoltners, A.A., P. Sinha, S.E. Lorimer. 2004. *Sales Force Design for Strategic Advantage*, Palgrave Macmillan, Houndmills.

Zoltners, A.A., P. Sinha, S.E. Lorimer. 2006. Match Your Sales Force Structure to Your Business Cycle. *Harvard Business Review* **84**(July–August) 81–89.

Zoltners, A.A., P. Sinha, S.E. Lorimer. 2008. Sales Force Effectiveness: A Framework for Researchers and Practitioners. *Journal of Personal Selling and Sales Management*, Special Issue on Enhancing Sales Force Productivity, (forthcoming).

Chapter 7
Modeling Competitive Responsiveness

Peter S.H. Leeflang[*]

7.1 Competitive Responsiveness

The study of competition and competitive responsiveness has a long tradition, involving a variety of models developed and applied in many different situations. We give a brief survey of specific applications and methodologies used to model competitive responsiveness and summarize findings about competitive reaction effects and factors that may explain competitive reactions. In addition, we attend to the use of competitive response models for normative decision making. For all these purposes, we use an evolutionary model building scheme that demonstrates the unique development of different models and methods.

A brand's or firm's success depends on the degree to which its managers' decisions satisfy selected consumers' needs and preferences better than competing brands/firms do (Day and Reibstein, 1997). Thus, firms' actions *and* reactions to competitive actions strongly influence their performance. In modern marketing, much attention has been devoted to competition. The intensity of competition may increase when markets show minimal growth. New product introductions and the reactions to these new entries may both result from and contribute to more intense competition. Recent research also demonstrates the importance of so-called cross-brand effects (substitution between brands); for example, Van Heerde et al. (2003) and Van Heerde et al. (2004) find that cross-brand effects contribute an average of one-third to sales bumps due to price promotions.

---

[*] The author benefited from insightful comments and valuable suggestions from David Reibstein, Harald Van Heerde, and Berend Wierenga.

P.S.H. Leeflang
Department of Economics, University of Groningen, Groningen,
The Netherlands
e-mail: p.s.h.leeflang@rug.nl

However, other recent research findings (Montgomery et al. 2005) demonstrate that though managers consider competitors in their decision making, competitive considerations focus primarily on competitors' past or current behavior rather than on their *anticipated reactions*. The low incidence of strategic competitor reasoning stems from managerial perceptions of the low returns they can derive from anticipating competitor reactions compared with the high cost of doing so. Therefore, research efforts are needed to convince managers that models and methods can be applied fruitfully to predict competitive reactions and define firms' future actions.

Although competitive responsiveness represents only part of a comprehensive competitive marketing strategy, it remains a vital part (Shugan, 2002). The plethora of different aspects and dimensions of competitive responsiveness means that no one issue of a journal (Shugan, 2005) or chapter in a monograph can consider each one.

In this chapter, we instead discuss several models used to study competitive responsiveness. We choose the perspective of a company that must design and execute its marketing policies and wants to take into account the effects of the marketing policies of its competitor(s). These policies may refer to autonomous actions, as well as reactions to the initial actions of the focal company.

More specifically, we consider the following questions:

- How can we model competitive behavior and its effect on relevant variables of the focal company, such as sales, market share, and profit?
- What do we know from existing research about the factors that drive competitive behavior and the effects of this behavior?
- How can companies use this existing information to devise their strategies with regard to competitors?

We start by discussing specification and estimation of competitive response models (Section 7.2). In Section 7.3, we detail the main findings of existing research into competition. Next, we provide a discussion of how companies might use this knowledge and current approaches to devise strategies to deal with competition in Section 7.4. Finally, we offer a brief overview of possible avenues for further research.

7.2 Modeling Competitive Responsiveness: Specification and Estimation

In this section, we briefly sketch some opportunities for modeling competitive behavior. Many developed models and methods attempt to diagnose and predict competitive behavior. The modeling of competitive responsiveness functions as an evolutionary process, as we depict in Fig. 7.1, in which we consider the different steps involved and 12 sets of models.

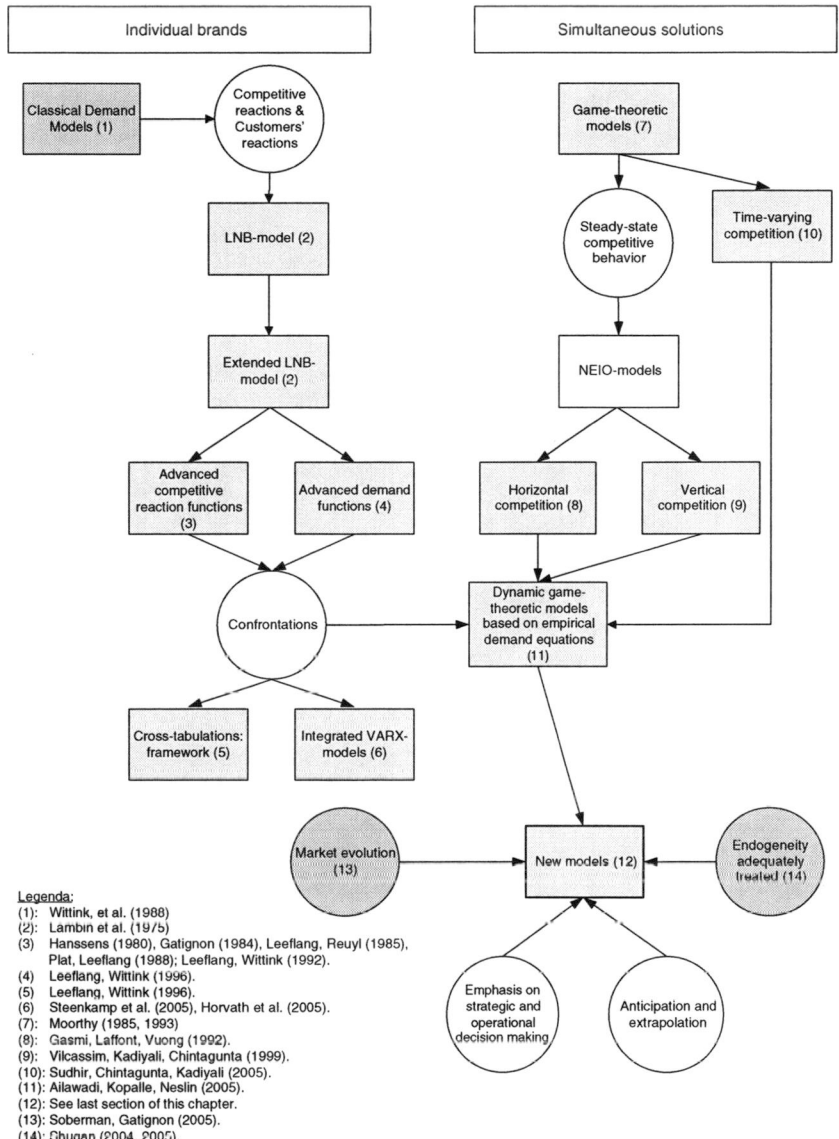

Fig. 7.1 Evolutionary model building in competitive responsiveness

The first step consists of building relatively simple models,[1] which subsequently may be expanded to incorporate additional elements and become more complex. Day and Wensley (1988) dichotomize competitive response models

---

[1] Cf. Urban and Karash (1971) and Van Heerde et al. (2002).

into competitor-centered methods and customer-focused approaches. *Competitor-centered assessments* employ direct management comparisons between the firm and a few target competitors and often include determinations of the relative strengths and weaknesses of each firm and the extent to which competitors quickly match marketing activities initiated by another firm. *Customer-focused assessments* start with detailed analyses of customer benefits within end-user segments and work backward from the customer to the company to identify the necessary actions that will improve performance.

Customer-focused assessments become possible by calibrating *demand models*[2] that include competitive marketing variables. Classical micro-economic theory (1 in Fig. 7.1) considers the impact of competitive actions on demand on the basis of cross-price-elasticities. However, more specific marketing models also include marketing mix instruments other than price and use brand sales as the demand measure.

In addition, demand equations may be supplemented by competitive reaction functions (Telser, 1962). For example, Lambin et al. (1975) calibrate competitive reaction functions (2 in Fig. 7.1) using data about a low-priced consumer durable in West Germany. Extensions to their classical 'LNB model' include more advanced competitive reaction functions (3) and demand functions (4). Using a framework based on cross-tabulations, researchers also have studied reaction and demand functions simultaneously (5). Furthermore, VARX models provide a means to estimate advanced demand and competitive reaction functions simultaneously (6).

These models (1–6) can determine the optimal marketing mix for one brand, assuming particular reaction patterns by competitors. That is, they do not offer a simultaneous optimum for all brands in a product class. *Game-theoretic approaches* address this issue, though most early game-theoretic models were theoretical and without empirical applications[3] (7 in Fig. 7.1). Since the early 1980s, powerful advances in game theory have taken place, particularly in the area of dynamic games. As a result, the theory has become far more applicable to modeling real-world competitive strategies. Even more recently, marketers have embraced the new empirical industrial organization (NEIO)-based approach to infer the competitive behavior of firms[4] in terms of both horizontal (8) and vertical (9) competition. Horizontal competition occurs between brands or organizations (retailers) that compete to match the preferences of the customers, whereas vertical competition exists within the same (distribution) channel between different partners that have, at least in principle, different groups of customers. Therefore, vertical competition deals with the allocation of total profits in the distribution channel among manufacturers, wholesalers, and

---

[2] The numbers refer to the 12 sets of models that we distinguish in Fig. 7.1.

[3] Examples are Friedman (1958), Mills (1961), Shakun (1966), Baligh and Richartz (1967), Gupta and Krishnan (1967a, b), and Krishnan and Gupta (1967).

[4] See Kadiyali et al. (2001) for a review.

retailers. In structural models such as these, price levels in the market depend on demand and cost conditions, as well as the nature of interfirm interactions in the market.[5] By estimating both demand and supply functions, this approach decomposes price levels into the unique effects of demand, cost, and competitive behavior (note that these models typically assume 'steady-state' competitive behavior). In models that study time-varying competition (10), the direct effects of demand and cost changes on prices and the indirect effects on *competitive intensity* all come in to play.[6]

One of the most advanced models used to study competitive response (11) [7]

- considers vertical *and* horizontal competition;
- is based on advanced demand and competitive reaction functions; and
- is dynamic.

Finally, new models of competitive response (12) should satisfy various criteria and deal with many different issues. We discuss these issues in more detail in Section 7.4.

7.2.1 *Classical Demand Models*

Incorporating competitive marketing instruments into a demand model offers opportunities to determine the effects of competitive actions in a relatively simple way. As an example, we specify the following model:

$$\hat{q} = \hat{\alpha} + \hat{\beta}_p p + \hat{\beta}_{pc} p_c + \hat{\beta}_a a + \hat{\beta}_{ac} a_c, \qquad (7.1)$$

where

$\hat{q} =$ (estimated) demand of a brand (say, brand j) in units (brand sales);
$p, p_c =$ price of a brand j and the competitive price, respectively; and
$a, a_c =$ advertising expenditures of brand j and a competitor, respectively.

We do not use the indices j (brand) or t (time) for q, p, and a to restrict the number of indices. We also assume that the parameters $\hat{\alpha}$ and $\hat{\beta}_p, \ldots, \hat{\beta}_{ac}$ have been estimated through time-series data. The effects of competitive actions on $\hat{q}$ are represented through $\hat{\beta}_{pc}$ and $\hat{\beta}_{ac}$, and the effects of competitive actions on sales can be predicted by substituting the expected future values of p_c and a_c in the estimated relationship.[8]

This classical, simple model does not account for how brand j may react to competitive actions or how brand j's competitor reacts to brand j's actions, nor

[5] We closely follow Sudhir et al. (2005, p. 99).
[6] For example, see models developed by Ellison (1994) and Sudhir et al. (2005).
[7] The model of Ailawadi et al. (2005) fits these features.
[8] See, for example, Alsem et al. (1989).

does it address how these reactions ultimately modify consumer demand. The LNB-model explicitly considers these competitive actions.

7.2.2 LNB-Models

Consider the following functions for Q, product class sales, and m, a brand's market share:

$$Q = QT(p, a, k, pc, ac, kc, ev), \text{ and} \qquad (7.2)$$

$$m = m_j(p, a, k, pc, ac, kc),$$

where

QT, m_j = functional forms for *Total Quantity* and brand *j*'s *m*arketshare, respectively;

p, p_c = price of a brand (say, brand *j*) and an index of competitors' prices, respectively;

k, k_c = quality measure for brand *j* and an index of competitors' quality measures, respectively;

a, a_c = advertising expenditures of brand *j* and an index of competitors' advertising expenditures, respectively; and

ev = a vector of environmental variables.

These functions also provide examples of equations that represent consumers' reactions to competitive actions (p_c, a_c, k_c). Brand *j*'s sales elasticity with respect to its advertising ($\eta_{q,a}$) equals the total product class elasticity ($\eta_{Q,a}$) plus the total market share elasticity with respect to brand *j* 's advertising ($\eta_{m,a}$):

$$\eta_{q,a} = \eta_{Q,a} + \eta_{m,a}, \qquad (7.3)$$

where the expression for the total product and market share elasticities are as given in Equations (7.6) and (7.7), respectively.

These elasticity measures capture the effect of advertising by one brand on consumer demand, but to capture total, actual impact, we must consider how competitors react to brand advertising changes and how this reaction modifies consumer demand. The competitive reactions belong to the set of competitor-centered approaches. Specifically, we distinguish *direct* and *indirect partial effects* of brand *j*'s advertising on product class sales and on brand *j*'s own market share. An indirect partial effect captures the following scenario: If brand *j* changes its advertising expenditure level (Δa), competitors may react by similarly adapting their spending level (Δa_c), and a_c in turn influences Q and/ or m. According to this explanation, as is usually assumed in oligopoly theory, competitors react with the same marketing instrument as that which caused their reactions. Thus, competitors react to a change in price for *j* by changing their prices, to a change in advertising by an advertising response, and so forth. This type of reaction reflects the *simple competitive reaction* case. A more realistic approach, consistent with the *concept of the marketing mix*, accommodates *multiple competitive reactions*, such that a competitor may react to a price change by not just changing its price but also changing its advertising and other such marketing instruments.

With a general case of multiple competitive reactions, we can write $\delta Q/\delta a$ and $\delta m/\delta a$ as follows:[9]

$$\frac{\delta Q}{\delta a} = \frac{\delta Q_T}{\delta a} + \frac{\delta Q_T}{\delta p_c}\frac{\delta p_c}{\delta a} + \frac{\delta Q_T}{\delta a_c}\frac{\delta a_c}{\delta a} + \frac{\delta Q_T}{\delta k_c}\frac{\delta k_c}{\delta a}, \tag{7.4}$$

and

$$\frac{\delta m}{\delta a} = \frac{\delta m_j}{\delta a} + \frac{\delta m_j}{\delta p_c}\frac{\delta p_c}{\delta a} + \frac{\delta m_j}{\delta a_c}\frac{\delta a_c}{\delta a} + \frac{\delta m_j}{\delta k_c}\frac{\delta k_c}{\delta a}. \tag{7.5}$$

Multiplying both sides of Equation (7.4) by a/Q, we obtain the product class elasticity, $\eta_{Q,a}$:

$$\eta_{Q,a} = \eta_{Q_T,a} + (\rho_{p_c,a})(\eta_{Q_T,p_c}) + (\rho_{a_c,a})(\eta_{Q_T,a_c}) + (\rho_{k_c,a})(\eta_{Q_T,k_c}), \tag{7.6}$$

where

η_{Q_T}, a = direct product class sales elasticity with respect to brand j's advertising,

η_{Q_T}, uc = product class sales elasticity with respect to competitors' marketing instrument u_c ($= pc, ac,$ or k_c), and

ρ_{u_c}, a = reaction elasticity of competitors' instrument u_c ($= p_c, a_c,$ or k_c) with respect to brand j's advertising expenditures.

Similarly, $\eta_{m,a}$ can be decomposed as:

$$\eta_{m,a} = \eta_{mj,a} + (\rho_{p_c,a})(\eta_{mj,p_c}) + (\rho_{a_c,a})(\eta_{mj,a_c}) + (\rho_{k_c,a})(\eta_{mj,k_c}). \tag{7.7}$$

In Equation (7.3), total brand sales elasticity $\eta_{q,a}$ is the sum of the components on the right-hand sides of Equations (7.6) and (7.7):

$$\begin{aligned} \eta_{q,a} &= \eta_{Q_T,a} + (\rho_{p_c,a})(\eta_{Q_T,p_c}) + (\rho_{a_c,a})(\eta_{Q_T,a_c}) + (\rho_{k_c,a})(\eta_{Q_T,k_c}) \\ &+ \eta_{mj,a} + (\rho_{p_c,a})(\eta_{mj,p_c}) + (\rho_{a_c,a})(\eta_{mj,a_c}) + (\rho_{k_c,a})(\eta_{mj,k_c}). \end{aligned} \tag{7.8}$$

---

[9] In Equations (7.4) and (7.5), $\delta Q_T/\delta a$ and $\delta m_j/\delta a$ are the *direct* effects, and $\delta Q/\delta a$ and $\delta m/\delta a$ are the *total* effects.

Furthermore, Lambin, Naert, and Bultez (LNB, 1975) apply the concept of multiple competitive reactions to the market for a low-priced consumer durable in West Germany. Specifically, they use a multiplicative market share function:[10]

$$m_j = \alpha m_{j-1}^{\lambda} (p^r)^{\beta_p} (a^r)^{\beta_a} (k^r)^{\beta_x},$$ (7.9)

where $u^r = u/u_c$; $u = p, a, k$; and $m_{j-1} = m_{j,t-1}$, and the exponents in the multiplicative relations represent elasticities. Because $u^r = u/u_c$, it follows that

$$\eta_{m_j,u^r} = \eta_{m_j,u} = -\eta_{m_j,u_c}.$$ (7.10)

If industry sales are insensitive to changes in marketing activities, $\eta_{Q_T,u} = 0$. By using Equation (7.10), we can simplify Equation (7.8) as

$$\eta_{q,a} = (1 - \rho_{a_c,a})(\eta_{m_j,a^r}) - (\rho_{p_c,a})(\eta_{m_j,p^r}) - (\rho_{k_c,a})(\eta_{m_j,k^r}).$$ (7.11)

Estimation of Equation (7.9) by Lambin et al. yields,

$$\eta_{m_j,a^r} = 0.147, \; \eta_{m_j,p^r} = -3.726, \text{and } \eta_{m_j,k^r} = 0.583.$$

Next, using three multiplicative *reaction functions*, they estimate the reaction elasticities,

$$u_c = \alpha_u p^{\rho_{u,p}} a^{\rho_{u,a}} k^{\rho_{u,k}},$$ (7.12)

where $u_c = p_c, a_c,$ and k_c for the three equations, respectively. The estimates of the reaction elasticities to advertising for brand j are $\hat{\rho}_{a_c,a} = 0.273, \hat{\rho}_{p_c,a} = 0.008,$ and $\hat{\rho}_{k_c,a} = 0.023$.

Brand j's sales elasticity (i.e., total market share elasticity, because $\eta_{Q_T,u} = 0$) can be assessed by substituting the estimated market share and reaction elasticities into Equation (7.11):

$$\hat{\eta}_{q,a} = (1 - 0.273)(0.147) - (0.008)(-3.726) - (0.023)(0.583) = 0.124,$$

such that the total brand sales elasticity $\hat{\eta}_{q,a}$ is 0.124, comparable to a direct (market share) elasticity of 0.147. Thus the net or total effect of advertising for brand j is smaller than the direct effect.

The LNB model can be fruitfully applied if a company

- is not particularly interested in the effects of individual competitors but rather in the effects of the aggregate of other brands/firms,
- does not face vertical competition, and
- specifies its marketing mix independently from retailers.

Extended LNB models relax on one or more of these conditions.

---

[10] We omit time for convenience. Some variables in the reaction functions are specified with a one-period lag.

7.2.3 *Extended LNB Models with Advanced Competitive Reaction Functions*

In our discussion of these models, we relax the following assumptions:

1. All brands are represented by an aggregate brand.
2. Marketing mix decisions are specified independently from retailers.

The LNB model assumes that the market consists of a leader that uses marketing instruments p, a, and k and a follower, defined as the aggregate of other firms in the market. For example, $p_c = \sum_{r=2}^{n} p_r/(n-1)$, $p = p_1$, $a_c = \sum_{r=2}^{n} a_r$, $a = a_1$, and so forth, where n = total number of brands and '1' indicates the leading brand.

In extended LNB models, modelers make no distinction between leaders and followers but rather consider all brands separately in what amounts to a decomposition of competitive interactions.

An example of an extended LNB model is Hanssens's (1980) approach: [11]

$$x_{\ell jt} = h(x_{\ell' rt} - x_{\ell jt}), \ \ell, \ell' = 1, \ldots, L, j, r = 1, .., n, j \neq r, t = 1, .., T, \quad (7.13)$$

where $x_{\ell jt}$ is the value of the ℓth marketing instrument of brand j in period t.

Equation (7.13) allows for joint decision making when $j = r$, which summarizes the possibility that changes in one variable result in changes in one or more alternative variables for a given brand. These relations between different variables for the same brand are known as *intrafirm* activities.

In Equation (7.13), the number of equations to be estimated is Ln, and the many predictor variables can make its estimation difficult. For example, each equation may have $(Ln - 1)$ predictors, even if we do not consider time lags.

The data used to calibrate the reaction functions in these studies generally involve manufacturers' actions and reactions. In the past, researchers used monthly, bimonthly, or quarterly data, but scanner data offer new and ample opportunities to study competitive reactions. However, calibrating competitive reaction functions with weekly scanner data collected at the *retail level* involves its own problems, because changes in marketing activities may reflect the actions and reactions of retailers as well as manufacturers. For example, ultimately, price decisions about a brand are made by retailers (Kim and Staelin, 1999). Temporary price cuts, displays, refunds, and bonuses introduced at the retail level depend on the degree to which retailers accept (pass-through rates) promotional programs. Thus, especially with scanner data, researchers who

---

[11] In Equation (7.13), the "subtraction" of $x_{\ell jt}$ means that instrument ℓ for brand j in period t is *not* a predictor variable.

estimate competitive reaction functions should create models that reflect the roles of both manufacturers and retailers.

Leeflang and Wittink (1992) distinguish, in this respect, four categories of reactions: parallel movements, short- and long-run retailer-dominated reactions, and manufacturer-dominated reactions. Using these categories, they find that competition among the seven largest brands in the detergent market in the Netherlands is dominated by price and promotional programs.

Parallel movements involve price or promotion fluctuations of brand j, $j = 1$, ..., n, that parallel the price fluctuations or promotional expenditures of other brands, $r = 1, ..., n$, when $j \neq r$, and occur in the same time period t or with a delay of one time period (e.g., one week). Such parallel movements may occur because of planned programs (e.g., promotion calendars). For example, some retail chains offer a price promotion for brand j when other chains do so for brand r.

Retailer-dominated reactions: short-run. If promotional activities in a product category are frequent, a retailer may run a short-run (e.g., one-week) promotional activity for a brand, followed by activity for another brand in the next week. As a result, the price for brand j decreases as the price for brand $r(r \neq j)$ increases. These short-run retailer-dominated reactions generally occur either simultaneously or with a maximum lag of one period (e.g., one week).

Retailer-dominated reactions: long-run. In the longer run, such as within two to four weeks, retailers may make price or promotion changes for brand j in reaction to changes in similar variables for the same or competing brands offered by competing retailers. If retailers take these initiatives, retailers' competition exists, but if the activities are motivated by manufacturers' trade promotions, their nature and frequency may reflect competitive reactions by manufacturers.

Manufacturer-dominated reactions. Finally, to measure manufacturers' reactions, which can involve temporary price changes and other promotional variables, scanner data (which indicate retail sales and retailers' promotional activities) reveal these reactions only if retailers cooperate with manufacturers. This cooperation often results from adaptive annual planning procedures, which generally takes five to ten weeks.

Leeflang and Wittink (1992) study the following marketing instruments: price (p), sampling (sa), refunds (rf), bonus offers (bo), and featuring (ft) (retailer advertising). For each brand, they estimate competitive reaction functions for each marketing instrument and express the criterion variables in the competitive reaction functions as changes. For example, the logarithm of the ratio of prices in two successive periods represents price, because price changes for brands with different regular price levels are more comparable on a percentage rather than an absolute basis.

Other promotional activities are specified in terms of simple differences, because zero values may occur in these cases. To illustrate the price of brand j (p_{jt}), the following competitive reaction function may be specified:

$$\ln(p_{jt}/p_{j,t-1}) = \alpha_j + \sum_{r=1,r\neq j}^{n} \sum_{t^*=1}^{T^*+1} \beta_{jrt^*} \ln(p_{r,t-t^*+1}/p_{r,t-t^*})$$

$$+ \sum_{t^*=2}^{T^*+1} \beta_{jjt^*} \ln(p_{j,t-t^*+1}/p_{j,t-t^*}) \qquad (7.14)$$

$$+ \sum_{r=1}^{n} \sum_{t^*=1}^{T^*+1} \sum_{x=1}^{4} \tau_{xjrt^*}(x_{r,t-t^*+1} - x_{r,t-t^*}) + \varepsilon_{jt},$$

$$\text{for } j = 1,\ldots,n \text{ and } t = T^* + 2,\ldots,T,$$

where

$x = 1 = sa,$
$\quad = 2 = rf,$
$\quad = 3 = bo,$
$\quad = 4 = ft;$
$T^* = $ the maximum number of time lags ($T^* = 10$);
$T = $ the number of observations available;
$n = $ the number of brands; and
$\varepsilon_{jt} = $ a disturbance term.

Equation (7.14) also includes lagged endogenous variables to account for the phenomenon that periods with heavy promotions frequently are followed by periods with relatively low promotional efforts.

Further inspection of Equation (7.14) makes it clear that the number of predictor variables is so large that they easily exceed the number of observations.[12] Leeflang and Wittink (1992) therefore use bivariate causality tests to select potentially relevant predictor variables.[13][14]

7.2.4 Extended LNB Models with Advanced Demand Functions

In this section, we relax the assumptions that (1) a limited number of marketing instruments of (2) one competitive brand affects the demand function.

A customer-focused approach relies on information about consumers' sensitivity to changes in marketing instruments; that is, it considers estimated market response functions. We discuss an example in which demand gets

---

[12] For example, suppose that $n = 7$ (brands), each with five instruments, $T^* = 10$ (lagged periods), and $T = 76$. Then, we have 76 observations to estimate 391 parameters, under the assumption that all manufacturers use all marketing instruments.

[13] See also Bult et al. (1997)

[14] For a discussion of other models that calibrate competitive reaction functions, see Kadiyali et al. (1999) and Vilcassim et al. (1999). In all cases, the reaction functions attempt to capture the use of marketing instruments to react to changes in other instruments without regard to consumer responses.

specified at the market share level and we assume competitive behavior is asymmetric.

The structure of the model (developed by Leeflang and Wittink, 1996) is similar to that used for the competitive reactions (Equation (7.14)). The criterion variable is the natural logarithm of the ratio of market shares in successive periods for brand $j = 1, \ldots, n$, $\ln(m_{jt}/m_{j,t-1})$, which in turn is a function of the natural logarithm of the ratio of prices in successive periods and the first differences of the four promotional variables introduced before of all brands $r = 1, \ldots, n$:

$$
\ln(m_{jt}/m_{j,t-1}) = \lambda_j + \sum_{r=1}^{n} \sum_{t^*=1}^{T^*+1} \gamma_{jrt^*} \ln(p_{r,t-t^*+1}/p_{r,t-t^*})
$$
$$
+ \sum_{r=1}^{n} \sum_{t^*=1}^{T^*+1} \sum_{x=1}^{4} \xi_{xjrt^*} (x_{r,t-t^*+1} - x_{r,t-t^*}) + u_{jt},
$$
(7.15)

where u_{jt} is a disturbance term and all other variables are as defined previously.

As an illustration, we provide the predictor variables with statistically significant effects for each brand's market share equation in Table 7.1. This sample study has obtained 13 own-brand effects (i.e., 13 cases in which $j = r$), and the marketing instrument of brand j has a statistically significant effect in the expected direction on the brand's own market share. Because not every brand uses all marketing instruments, the maximum possible number of own-brand effects varies among brands (maxima appear in the last row). Across brands, the maximum number of own-brand effects is 28.

Table 7.1 Statistically significant effects in market share response functions

Criterion variable	Relevant predictors for each brand						
Market share[a]	1	2	3	4	5	6	7
$\tilde{m}_1$	p, ft	ft		sa		sa	
$\tilde{m}_2$		p, bo, ft	ft	ft	p	p^b	
$\tilde{m}_3$			p		ft		
$\tilde{m}_4$		ft	ft^b	bo, ft			sa
$\tilde{m}_5$	p			bo^b	p, ft	sa, ft	
$\tilde{m}_6$	p	p, bo	sa			rf, sa	
$\tilde{m}_7$	ft	p				p^b	p
Maximum possible number of effects per cell	2	4	3	5	4	5	5

Notes: Abbreviations refer to predictor variables that have statistically significant effects in the multiple regression; namely, p = price, sa = sampling, rf = refund, bo = bonus, and ft = feature, as defined in Equation (7.14). Own-brand effects appear in cells on the diagonal; cross-brand effects are in the off-diagonal cells.
[a]Market share: $\tilde{m}_j = \ln m_{jt}/m_{j,t-1}$.
[b]The sign of the coefficient for the predictor in the multiple regression is contrary to expectations.
Source: Leeflang and Wittink (1996, p. 114).

In addition, the table indicates 18 significant cross-brand effects with the expected signs, which appear as the off-diagonal entries. The maximum number of cross-brand effects equals 168, so the proportion of significant cross-brand effects (18/168 or 11%) is much lower than the proportion of significant own-brand effects (13/28 or 46%). From Table 7.1, we also can draw some conclusions about competition on the basis of consumers' response function estimates. For example, brand 3's market share is affected only by feature advertising for brand 5, whereas brand 7 only affects brand 4's market share through sampling.

7.2.5 Frameworks and Cross-Tabulations

The *framework* approach can enhance the congruence between competitor-oriented and customer-focused decision making, because the framework itself relates consumer response and competitive reaction effects and thus provides a basis for categorizing over- and underreactions by managers.

We consider three kinds of elasticities: reaction elasticity, cross-elasticity, and own elasticity. For simplification, we restrict the framework to the absence/presence of effects, such that the elasticities are either 0 or not, which results in eight possible combinations, as we show in Fig. 7.2. We consider two brands: the defender brand i and the attacker brand j. Brand i uses marketing instrument ℓ to react to an attack of brand j (with instrument h).

In cell A of Fig. 7.2, all three effects are non-zero, which implies intense competition, so brand i uses marketing instrument ℓ to restore its market share, influenced by brand j's use of variable h. In the presence of a cross-brand market share effect, brand j cannot recover its loss of market share if:

- the own-brand market share effect is 0, as in cell B;
- there is no competitive reaction effect, as in cell C; or

	Cross-Brand Market Share Effect			
	YES		NO	
Own-Brand	Competitive Reaction Effect		Competitive Reaction Effect	
Market Share Effect	YES	NO	YES	NO
YES	A Intense competition	C Underreaction: Lost opportunity for defender[a]	E Defender's game	G Defender's game
NO	B Spoiled arms for defender[a]	D Ineffective arms	F Overreaction: Spoiled arms for defender[a]	H No competition

[a] Note that the defender brand may lack information about its own-brand market share effects.

Fig. 7.2 A framework of cross-market share, competitive reaction, and own-market share effects
Source: Leeflang and Wittink (1996, p. 106)

- there is neither a competitive reaction effect nor an own-brand market share effect, as in cell D.

In other words, Cell B indicates the use of an ineffective instrument ('spoiled arms') chosen by i to react to j. Cell C represents *underreactions*, such that brand i should defend its market share but does not react, even though instrument ℓ would be effective. We define this case as a lost opportunity for defender i. If there are no reaction effects and the own-brand market share elasticities equal 0, we recognize ineffective arms (cell D).

In case of no cross-brand market share effect, competitive reaction effects should not occur if the firm's objective is simply to preserve its market share. In the third column of Fig. 7.2, we identify some associated *overreactions*. In cell E (defender's game), the reactions include an instrument that has an own-brand effect, even though no cross-brand market share effect exists. Cell F involves (unnecessary) reactions with an ineffective instrument, which we call spoiled arms for the defender. Finally, cells G and H reflect no competition because of the absence of both a cross-brand market share effect and a competitive reaction effect.

This framework suggests that knowledge about *cross-*and *own-brand* market share effects enables managers to prepare themselves better for competitors' activities in terms of whether and which reactions are desirable. Thus, a consumer-focused approach that captures consumer responses to marketing helps management diagnose competition.

Although the estimation of reaction matrices captures the nature of competitive reactions, it falls short of explaining reaction patterns. In other words, it fails to provide sufficient insight into the underlying reasons for observed reactions (Ramaswamy et al., 1994; Kadiyali et al., 2001). In response, researchers developed the VARX models, as well as the NEIO models that we discuss subsequently, to provide such insights. Another drawback of competitive reaction models involves the understanding who is the defender and who is the attacker, i.e. the one who initiates a move.

7.2.6 VARX Models

Modern time-series analysis (TSA) offers the opportunity to use demand and reaction functions simultaneously to diagnose and predict competition. Vector AutoRegressive models with eXogenous variables (VARX) may be applied in cases in which the marketer wants to:

- account for the dynamic effects of marketing instruments on the sales of individual brands in a market, or
- distinguish among immediate (instantaneous), gross, and net effects.

The direct effects again refer to the unaltered influence of marketing actions on a performance measure; indirect effects capture their impact on performance through competitive (or other) reactions. Among the direct effects, we may distinguish between immediate effects and gross effects, or the sum of the direct effects over a specified time horizon. In addition, the net effects reflect the sum of the direct and indirect effects measured during the same time horizon and therefore account for competitive reactions, whereas gross effects do not. To estimate immediate, gross, and net effects, we employ an impulse response analysis (IRA).

We illustrate the use of a VARX model by discussing a model specified and calibrated by Horváth et al. (2005), which simultaneously considers market response and competitive reaction functions and relies on pooled store data for each of three brands of tuna fish for calibration.[15]

7.2.6.1 Response Functions

We use an adaptation of ACNielsen's SCAN*PRO model (see Christen et al., 1997), in which the variables of interest are the logarithms of the unit sales and price indices (ratio of actual to regular price) for brands at the store level. The SCAN*PRO model includes several own- and cross-brand promotional variables: price index, feature only, display only, and feature and display. We extend this model by including dynamic price promotion effects (delayed responses) and purchase reinforcement effects (through lagged sales), though we do not include separate lagged non-price instruments to reduce concerns about the degrees of freedom. However, we allow for additional dynamic effects through lagged endogenous variables.

We define two types of price promotion variables: (1) own- and other-brand temporary discounts without support and (2) own- and other-brand temporary discounts with feature and/or display support. Van Heerde et al. (2000; 2001; 2004) use four different price promotion variables so that the discount effects depend on four support conditions. By definition, such promotion variables are minimally correlated. Therefore, we employ the same idea but use only two variables, also in an effort to reduce degrees of freedom problems.

All parameters are brand specific, and all lagged variables have unique parameters. Therefore, we specify the market response function as:

$$\ln S_{qi,t} = \alpha_{qi} + \sum_{k=1}^{2} \sum_{j=1}^{n} \sum_{t^*=0}^{P_{ijk}^{SP}} \beta_{PIijk,t^*} \ln PI_{qjk,t-t^*} + \sum_{j=1}^{n} \sum_{t^*=1}^{P_{ij}^{SS}} \varphi_{ij,t^*} \ln S_{qj,t-t^*}$$

$$+ \sum_{j=1}^{n} \beta_{Fij} F_{qj,t} + \sum_{j=1}^{n} \beta_{Dij} D_{qj,t} + \sum_{j=1}^{n} \beta_{FDij} FD_{qj,t} + \varepsilon_{qi,t}, \tag{7.16}$$

$$q = 1, \ldots, Q; i = 1, \ldots, I; \text{ and } t = 1, \ldots, T,$$

---

[15] We closely follow Horváth et al. (2005) and pool the data over stores. For a thorough discussion of VARX models, see also Dekimpe et al. (2008).

where

$\ln S_{qi,t}$ = natural logarithm of sales of brand i in store q in week t,

$\ln PI_{qik,t}$ = log price index (actual to regular price) of brand i in store q in week t ($k = 1$ denotes the feature-/display-supported price cuts, and $k = 2$ denotes price cuts that are not supported),

$F_{qj,t}$ = feature-only dummy variable for *non-price*promotions of brand j in store q at time t,

$D_{qj,t}$ = display-only dummy variable for *non-price* promotions of brand j in store q at time t,

$FD_{qj,t}$ = combined use of feature and display supports of *non-price* promotions of brand j in store q at time t,[16]

α_{qi} = store-specific intercept for brand i and store q,

$\beta_{PIijk,t*}$ = (pooled) elasticity of brand i's sales with respect to brand j's price index,

$\varphi_{ij,t*}$ = (pooled) substitution elasticity of brand i's sales with respect to competitive (j) sales in week t ($i \neq j$),

$\beta_{Fij}, \beta_{Dij}, \beta_{FDij}$ = effects of feature-only (F), display-only (D), and feature and display (FD),

PI_{ijk}^{SP} = number of lags for price index variable k of brand i included in the equation for brand j,

P_{ij}^{SP} = number of lags of the sales variable of brand i included in the equation for brand j,

n = number of brands in the product category,

Q = number of stores, and

$\varepsilon_{qi,t}$ = disturbances.

We test for the equality of slopes across stores and fail to reject this null hypothesis; therefore, the specification of the demand model does not allow for slope heterogeneity. This specification captures purchase reinforcement ($\varphi_{ii,t*}$), immediate sales response ($\beta_{PIijk,t*}$ for $t^* = 0$), and delayed response ($\beta_{PIijk,t*}$ for $t^* > 0$).

7.2.6.2 Reaction Functions

In the preceding text, we defined competitive reactions as the reactions of brand managers to the marketing activities of other brands, but this reaction is not the only possible type, nor is it necessarily the most efficient. For example, managers often track market share or sales, and a drop in either measure may prompt them to react with a marketing instrument. Similarly, they track other brands' performance and may interpret an increase as a competitive threat.

---

[16] The variables F, D, and FD only deviate from zero if a feature/display exists but *no* price discount does.

Therefore, we incorporate these ideas as feedback effects in the reaction functions. We also account for inertia in decision making and coordination between own-brand instruments (internal decisions):

$$\ln PI_{qi\ell,t} = \delta_{qi\ell} + \sum_{t^*=1}^{P_{ii\ell\ell}^{PP}} \gamma_{i\ell,t^*} \ln PI_{qi\ell,t-t^*} + \sum_{t^*=1,k\neq\ell}^{P_{ii\ell k}^{PP}} \gamma_{ik,t^*} \ln PI_{qik,t-t^*}$$

$$+ \sum_{k=1}^{2} \sum_{j=1,j\neq i}^{n} \sum_{t^*=1}^{P_{ij\ell k}^{PP}} \gamma_{i\ell jk,t^*} \ln PI_{qjk,t-t^*} + \sum_{j=1}^{n} \sum_{t^*=1}^{P_{ij\ell}^{PS}} \eta_{ij,t^*} \ln S_{qj,t-t^*} + \upsilon_{qi\ell,t} \tag{7.17}$$

$$q = 1,\ldots,Q; i = 1,\ldots,n(\ell = 1,2); \text{and } t = 1,\ldots,T,$$

where the variables are defined as in Equation (7.16). The super- and subindices of P indicate that the number of included lags may vary per equation and per variable. Equation (7.17) thus captures internal decisions (inertia in decision making: $\gamma_{i\ell,t^*}$, intrafirm effects: γ_{ik,t^*}, $k \neq \ell$), competitive reactions ($\gamma_{i\ell jk,t^*}$, $j \neq i$), and own-brand (η_{ii,t^*}) and cross-brand ($\eta_{ij,t^*} j \neq i$) feedback effects, which refer to reactions to the consequence of an action. If marketing managers who track their own-brand market share or sales perceive a decrease in either measure, they may react by changing their marketing activities. In the same way, they may track and react to other brands' performance (cross-feedback effects). The functions of internal decisions that reflect inertia and intrafirm effects relate closely to these effects. Unlike Equation (7.16), in which price variables have immediate effects on performance variables, we assume that prices are not immediately influenced by sales in Equation (7.17) because feedback effects require time. For the same reason, we posit that competitive reactions cannot occur in the same period.

Using 104 weeks of store-level data from 24 stores and three brands of tuna fish, we can estimate this system of relations. Because we have one demand equation and two reaction equations for each brand–store combination, the simultaneous system includes $3 \times 3 \times 24 = 216$ equations.

The reduced form of the VARX model may be estimated using feasible generalized least squares with dummy variables (FGLSDV). In reduced form, the values of the endogenous variables are expressed as functions of predetermined variables (lagged endogenous and exogenous variables). We list the immediate effects (short-term price elasticities) in Table 7.2, from which we may conclude that the immediate own-brand elasticities are substantial and, as expected, higher for supported prices than for non-supported prices (averages of –5.30 and –3.31, respectively). Van Heerde et al. (2000; 2001; 2004) report analogous findings.

In addition, we find that the supported cross-brand elasticities tend to be greater than the corresponding non-supported elasticities (0.65 and 0.40, respectively), and brands with higher own-brand elasticities tend to have higher cross-brand elasticities. These brands also are generally more sensitive to the effects of prices of other brands than are brands with lower own-brand elasticities.

Table 7.2 Price elasticities based on the (pooled) fixed effects model: Tuna data
Own- and Cross-Brand Price Elasticities

Variable	Brand 1	Brand 2	Brand 3
Supported price brand 1	−6.00*	0.35*	1.08*
Non-supported price brand 1	−3.92*	0.04	0.74*
Supported price brand 2	0.50*	−3.14*	0.88*
Non-supported price brand 2	0.38	−1.65*	0.62*
Supported price brand 3	0.81*	0.27*	−6.77*
Non-supported price brand 3	0.45*	0.17	−4.36*

*$p < 0.05$.
Source: Horváth et al. (2005, p. 421).

The own-brand price elasticities tend to be much greater (in absolute value) than the sum of the relevant cross-brand price elasticities, partly because the own-brand effects reflect cross-period (stockpiling) and category expansion effects, which together tend to account for the majority of own-brand unit sales increases that result from temporary price cuts (see also Van Heerde et al., 2004).

Before we continue our discussion about the possibilities of modeling competitive behavior, we believe a wrap-up discussion is appropriate. Thus far, we have detailed six different approaches; we summarize their characteristics in Table 7.3.

The models we have discussed so far all assume that each manager treats the competitors' strategies as a given and computes his or her own best response. In the models that we discuss next, managers may achieve simultaneous solutions for, at least in principle, all relevant brands in the marketplace. Such simultaneous solutions call for game-theoretic approaches.

7.2.7 Game-Theoretic Models

The preceding discussions make clear that in the marketplace, managers consider not only their perceptions of consumer responses but also their

Table 7.3 Characteristics of methods to model competitive response for individual brands

Method	Characteristics
(1) Classical demand models	Simple, no interactions among actions, reactions, and responses.
(2) Classical LNB model	Interactions, aggregation of competitive brands, horizontal competition, no effects of retailers' decisions.
(3–5) Extended LNB models	Interactions, actions and reactions of/on individual brands, horizontal competition, accounting for the effects of retailers' decisions, no simultaneous equation system (framework instead), no explanations of reactions.
(6) VARX models	Interactions, individual brands, horizontal competition, accounting for retailers' decisions, simultaneous equation system with emphasis on dynamic effects, some explanation of competitive moves.

expectations of competitor reactions to a potential marketing initiative. These complexities make the choice of an action in a competitive situation seem intractable, because the optimal choice for one brand depends on what other brands may do, which in turn depends on what the focal brand does, and so on (Moorthy, 1985). Game theory offers a means to study these inter-dependencies.[17]

Game theory may be distinguished into cooperative and non-cooperative categories. Cooperative game theory examines the behavior of colluding firms by maximizing a weighted average of all firms' profits. If two firms earn profits π_1 and π_2, then

$$\max_{x_{\ell j}} \pi = \lambda \pi_1 + (1 - \lambda)\pi_2, \tag{7.18}$$

where

λ = the weight for firm 1 and
$x_{\ell j}$ = the marketing instrument ℓ of firm j, j = 1,2, ℓ = 1,..., L.

In empirical studies, the weight λ is determined by the data.

In the modern world, competition takes place among a few competitors with interdependent interests, such that each competitor's actions affect the others. This situation is characterized by strategic competition, which requires non-cooperative game theory. The Nash (1950) equilibrium represents the central concept of non-cooperative game theory and involves a set of strategies, one for each competitor, defined such that no competitor wants unilaterally to change its strategy. In a Nash equilibrium, each strategy is a competitor's best option, given the best strategies of its rivals, where the meaning of 'best' depends on specified objectives. If the objective is profit, Nash equilibriums are obtained for all ℓ and j:

$$\frac{\delta \pi_j}{\delta x_{\ell j}} = 0, j = 1, \ldots, n, \ell = 1, \ldots, L, \tag{7.19}$$

where

$$\pi_j = f(x_{\ell j}).$$

Models that use game-theoretic principles date back to Cournot (1838), who argued that *quantity* (*q*) should be the choice variable, and Bertrand (1883), who posited *price* (*p*) as the choice variable. In Cournot's model, competitors

---

[17] More complete treatments of game theory in a marketing context can be found in Hanssens et al. (2001, pp. 367–74), Erickson (1991), and Moorthy (1985; 1993). A managerial treatment of game theoretic principles appears in Brandenburger and Nalebuff (1996). For a general introduction to modern game theory, see Fudenberg and Tirole (1991) and Mass-Callell et al. (1995).

conjecture the quantities supplied by other firms and assume that other firms will act as necessary to sell those quantities, leading to a 'Cournot equilibrium.' In the Bertrand model, price is the decision variable and creates a 'Bertrand equilibrium' For single-firm decision making under certainty, the choice of either price or quantity as a decision variable is moot, but when solving for an equilibrium, each firm's conjecture about the other firm's strategy variable must be correct. Therefore, modelers must evaluate and specify different alternatives. For example, with two firms and quantity and prices serving as decision variables, four kinds of equilibriums may emerge: (price, price), (price, quantity), (quantity, price), and (quantity, quantity). Specifically, the (price, quantity) equilibrium results if firm 1 chooses price and conjectures that firm 2 sets quantity, while firm 2 sets quantity and conjectures that firm 1 sets price.

The so-called conjectural variation (CV) approach, pioneered by Iwata (1974), estimates CVs from the data. Different equilibriums imply different CV estimates for the structural equation system of demand and supply equations, as we discuss in more detail in Section 7.2.8.

Non-cooperative game theory also provides a natural vehicle for models of oligopolistic competition (Moorthy, 1985, p. 268). In a Stackelberg leader–follower game, one competitor's actions occur independent of the other's, but the other firm considers these actions during its decision making.

Most early game-theoretic models were theoretical and lacked empirical applications, but powerful advances in game theory, particularly in the area of dynamic games, have emerged since the early 1980s. As a result, game theory is more applicable to modeling real-world competitive strategies.[18]

7.2.8 New Empirical Industrial Organization (NEIO)-Based Approach: Horizontal Competition

The move from theoretical, static game-theoretic models to empirical, dynamic models has shifted attention from normative models to *descriptive game theory*, which applies game-theoretic models to test whether marketplace data are consistent with model specifications. A rich tradition of empirical research in marketing strategy examines the impact of cost and competitive characteristics of a market on the profitability of a firm and generally follows the (market) structure → conduct (marketing mix, entry of new products, R&D expenditures) → performance (profitability) → paradigm (SCP) of empirical industrial organization (EIO) theory. Empirical studies use cross-sectional data across industries to find empirical regularities.

Research that applies advanced game theory also has led to the insights that conduct and performance are not merely functions of structural market

---

[18] We closely follow Kadiyali et al. (2001).

characteristics, such as concentration, growth, barriers to entry, and product differentiation, as used in SCP studies. These insights provide the basis for new empirical industrial organization (NEIO) literature, which focuses on developing and estimating structural econometric models of strategic, competitive behavior by firms, in which context

- 'structural' means that the firm's decisions are based on some kind of optimizing behavior, and
- 'econometric models' reflect simultaneous equations of demand and supply of all relevant competitors.

Usually, an NEIO model contains the following ingredients:

- demand functions,
- cost functions,
- specifications for competitive interactions, and
- an objective function (usually profit).

Furthermore, the typical steps required to specify and estimate empirical game theory models are as follows:

1. Specify demand functions (including competitive marketing instruments).
2. Specify cost functions.
3. Specify objective functions (usually profit functions).
4. Specify the game.
5. Derive first-order conditions for optimal marketing instruments.
6. Add observed variables to identify the system.
7. Estimate the models.

Simultaneous equation models usually rely on a simultaneous equation instrumental variable approach for estimation, such as the three-stage least squares (3SLS), full information maximum likelihood (FIML), and generalized method of moments (GMM) approaches. Dubé et al. (2005) discuss various other computational and methodological issues, and Chintagunta et al. (2006) offer a review of structural modeling in marketing.

To serve as an example, we discuss a study by Gasmi et al. (1992), who investigate the behavior of Coca-Cola and Pepsi using quarterly data from the United States about quantity sold, price, and advertising. They estimate various model specifications to allow for the possible existence of both cooperative and non-cooperative strategic behavior in this industry ('the game'). Their work proceeds by specifying an objective function for each firm (profit function), as well as demand and cost functions. Using these specifications, they obtain a system of simultaneous equations based on assumptions about the firms' behavior. Throughout their work, they also assume a one-to-one relation between firm j and brand j and therefore use those terms interchangeably. Gasmi et al. (1992) propose the following demand function for brand j:

$$q_j = \gamma_{j0} + \alpha_{jj}\, p_j + \alpha_{jr}\, p_r + \gamma_{jj}\, \alpha_j^{1/2} + \gamma_{jr}\, \alpha_r^{1/2},\ j \neq r, j, r = 1, 2, \quad (7.20)$$

where

q_j = quantity demanded from brand j,
p_j = price per unit for brand j, and
a_j = advertising expenditure for brand j.

We omit an error term and a subscript t for time periods from Equation (7.20) for convenience. To illustrate the use of this model, we assume the cost function is:

$$C_j(q_j) = c_j q_j, \quad (7.21)$$

where

c_j = the constant variable cost per unit of brand j.

The profit function therefore can be written as:

$$\pi_j = p_j\, q_j - C_j(q_j) - a_j$$
$$= (p_j - c_j)(\gamma_{j0} + \alpha_{jj}p_j + \alpha_{jr}p_r + \gamma_{jj}a_j^{1/2} + \gamma_{jr}a_r^{1/2}) - a_j. \quad (7.22)$$

In addition, Gasmi et al. (1992) consider six games:

1. Firms set prices and advertising expenditures simultaneously (naive static Nash behavior in price and advertising).
2. Firm $j = 1$ is the leader in both price and advertising, and firm $r = 2$ is the follower.
3. Firm $j = 1$ is the leader in price but the two firms 'behave Nash' in advertising.
4. Total collusion exists, which maximizes Equation (7.18), a weighted average of both firms' profits.
5. Firms first collude on advertising and later compete on prices.
6. Firms collude on price, knowing that they will compete later on advertising expenditures.

The first three games are based on non-cooperative behavior, whereas the last three games consider tacit collusion.

To illustrate the specification of a system of simultaneous equations, we consider the first game. The first-order conditions corresponding to a unique Nash equilibrium of the (one-stage) game are (expressed in terms of optimal reaction functions):

$$p_1^* = \frac{\alpha_{11}c_1 - \gamma_{10} - \alpha_{12}p_2^* - \gamma_{11}(a_1^*)^{1/2} - \gamma_{12}(a_2^*)^{1/2}}{2\alpha_{11}}$$

$$p_2^* = \frac{\alpha_{22}c_2 - \gamma_{20} - \alpha_{21}p_1^* - \gamma_{21}(a_1^*)^{1/2} - \gamma_{22}(a_2^*)^{1/2}}{2\alpha_{22}} \qquad (7.25)$$

$$a_1^* = \{\gamma_{11}(p_1^* - c_1)/2\}^2$$

$$a_2^* = \{\gamma_{22}(p_2^* - c_2)/2\}^2.$$

If total collusion occurs, as in the fourth game, a specific form of Equation (7.18) is maximized:

$$\max_{p_1,p_2,a_1,a_2} \pi = \lambda\pi_1(p_1,p_2,a_1,a_2) + (1-\lambda)\pi_2(p_1,p_2,a_1,a_2). \qquad (7.24)$$

The first-order conditions of this maximization are:

$$\frac{\delta\pi}{\delta p_1} = \lambda\left[(p_1 - c_1)\alpha_{11} + \gamma_{10} + \alpha_{11}p_1 + \alpha_{12}p_2 + \gamma_{11}a_1^{1/2} + \gamma_{12}a_2^{1/2}\right]$$

$$+ (1-\lambda)(p_2 - c_2)\alpha_{21} = 0$$

$$\frac{\delta\pi}{\delta p_2} - \lambda(p_1 - c_1)\alpha_{12} + (1-\lambda)[(p_2 - c_2)\alpha_{22} + \gamma_{20} + \alpha_{22}p_2 + \alpha_{21}p_1$$

$$+ \gamma_{22}a_2^{1/2} + \gamma_{21}a_1^{1/2}] = 0 \qquad (7.25)$$

$$\frac{\delta\pi}{\delta a_1} = \lambda\left[(p_1 - c_1)\frac{1}{2}\gamma_{11}a_1^{-1/2} - 1\right] + (1-\lambda)\left[(p_2 - c_2)\frac{1}{2}\gamma_{21}a_1^{-1/2}\right] = 0$$

$$\frac{\delta\pi}{\delta a_2} = \lambda\left[(p_1 - c_1)\frac{1}{2}\gamma_{12}a_2^{-1/2}\right] + (1-\lambda)\left[(p_2 - c_2)\frac{1}{2}\gamma_{22}a_2^{-1/2} - 1\right] = 0.$$

This system of four linear equations uniquely defines the four endogenous variables p_1, p_2, a_1, and a_2. The Hessian matrix of second-order conditions must be negative semi-definite, which imposes certain restrictions on the parameters.

Gasmi et al. (1992) include additional exogenous variables and specify functions for the demand intercepts (γ_{j0}) and marginal costs (c_j), which makes the system identifiable. These functions together with the demand functions in Equation (7.20) can be estimated as a system of simultaneous equations. Gasmi et al. (1992) thus derive a general model specification, which they use to test the six games. The empirical results suggest that, for the period covered by the sample (1968–1986), tacit collusive behavior prevailed in advertising between Coca-Cola and Pepsi in the market for cola drinks, though collusion on prices is not as well supported by the data. Thus, the results favor the specification for game 5.

Their study deals with horizontal competition and collusion, but their model also can be extended to consider *vertical competition*/collusion between competitors/partners in the marketing system (Jeuland and Shugan, 1983).

The structure of the demand Equation (7.20) also appears in other game-theoretic models, such as studies by Kadiyali (1996) and Putsis and Dhar (1999). For other well-known demand equations, we refer to Vidale and Wolfe (1957).[19] Furthermore, in the past decade, aggregate logit models have become the prevalent demand functions.[20]

7.2.9 NEIO-Based Approach: Vertical Competition

The eight sets of models that we have discussed thus far deal primarily with horizontal competition and therefore cannot be applied if the focal company confronts vertical competition, which, in modern Western markets, almost always refers to competition between manufacturers and retailers. Historically, retailers have been local, fragmented, and technically primitive, so powerful multinational manufacturers, such as Coca-Cola and Procter & Gamble, behaved like branded bulldozers, pushing their products and promotion plans onto retailers, who were expected to accept them subserviently. Within the span of two or three decades, this situation has become history. The largest retailers (Carrefour, METRO, Tesco, Wal-Mart) enjoy global footprints that have shifted power structures, and their global purchasing practices have brought enormous price pressures to bear even on leading consumer packaged good companies, which has increased vertical competition in channels.

Many game-theoretic models deal with vertical competition, especially pass-through in channels. Models that consider vertical competition must optimize the objective functions of at least two partners simultaneously. Therefore, game theoretic approaches determine joint, simultaneous solutions. As an example, we discuss the (general) structure of a pass-through model developed by Moorthy (2005), who considers two retailers (1 and 2), each with two brands, 1 and 2, such that brand 1 is common to both retailers and brand 2 is a private label. If D_{ij}, $i = 1, 2, j = 1, 2$, denotes brand j's demand function at retailer i, the demand functions become the functions of all four retail prices: p_{11}, p_{21}, p_{12}, and p_{22}. Then, retailer i's ($i = 1, 2$) category profit function is given by:

$$\pi_i(\tilde{p}) = (p_{i1} - w_1 - c_{i1} - c_i - c)D_{i1}(\tilde{p}) + (p_{i2} - c_{i2} - c_i - c)D_{i2}(\tilde{p}),$$
$$i = 1, 2, \tag{7.26}$$

---

[19] Also see Kimball (1957), and for examples, see Chintagunta and Vilcassim (1994), Erickson (1991), and Naik et al. (2005).

[20] See, for example, Chintagunta and Rao (1996), Sudhir (2001), and Sudhir et al. (2005).

where

$\tilde{p} = (p_{11}, p_{21}, p_{12}, p_{22})$;

$w_1 =$ wholesale price of the national brand, usually assumed to be common to both retailers;

$c_{i1}, c_{i2} =$ retailers i's nonbrand-specific marginal operating costs; and

$c =$ nonretailer-specific, nonbrand-specific marginal operating costs.

Because brand 2 is a private label, the model provides no specific wholesale price for it. If the vector of marginal costs (w_1, c_{i1}, c_i, c) is taken as given, the optimal retail prices for both brands of both retailers may be determined, assuming the demand functions are available. Solving the system of four first-order conditions leads to optimal price determinations, at least in principle.[21]

In this field, interesting efforts work to detect how the equilibrium changes when marginal costs change, the effects on the equilibriums under different assumptions about the demand interdependencies of the two brands, and so forth.[22]

7.2.10 Time-Varying Competition

Normative models typically suggest that prices rise when demand and cost are higher, but in many markets, prices fall when demand or costs rise. This inconsistency occurs because normative models assume that competitive intensity is constant over time. In contrast, time-varying competition models explicitly consider the so-called *indirect effects* of demand and cost changes on competition, which complement the *direct effects* of demand and cost on prices.

The idea to integrate competitive intensity in a game-theoretic model can be illustrated as follows: Consider a profit function (π_{jt}) of brand j at t,

$$\max_{(p_{jt})} \pi_{jt} = M_t(p_{jt} - c_{jt})m_{jt},$$

$$(7.27)$$

where

$M_t =$ potential size of the market at time t,

$p_{jt} =$ price per unit at time t,

$c_{jt} =$ cost per unit at time t, and

$m_{jt} =$ market share of brand j at t where $m_{jt} = (p_{jt})$.

---

[21] The system of equations should have a negative-definite Hessian matrix.

[22] For a similar model, see Villas-Boas and Zhao (2005).

Solving the first-order conditions for profit maximization under the assumption of a Nash-Bertrand equilibrium, we find

$$p_{jt} = c_{jt} - \frac{m_{jt}}{\frac{\delta m_{jt}}{\delta p_{jt}}}. \qquad (7.28)$$

The so-called Bertrand margin therefore is

$$margin_{jt}^{Bertr.} = -\frac{m_{jt}}{\frac{\delta m_{jt}}{\delta p_{jt}}}. \qquad (7.29)$$

In addition, the indirect effect of changes in competitive intensity on price may be captured by introducing a multiplier w_{jt} on the Bertrand margin. The pricing equation then is specified as:

$$p_{jt} = c_{jt} + w_{jt} \; margin_{jt}^{Bertr.}. \qquad (7.30)$$

The multiplier w_{jt} is a function of the predictor variables that affect competitive behavior. Sudhir et al. (2005) use quarterly dummy variables, which measure consumer confidence, costs of material and labor, and so forth, as predictor variables and thereby explicitly model the indirect effects of demand and cost changes on competition.

   The last link in the evolutionary chain of building models of competitive response consists of dynamic, empirical game-theoretic models.

7.2.11 Dynamic, Empirical Game-Theoretic Models

The model developed by Ailawadi et al. (2005) encompasses the following equations:

- Demand equations for all brands in a product category.
- The objective function of a retailer.
- The objective function of the brand manufacturer(s).

The demand equations include *temporal* response phenomena and capture, for example, stockpiling and promotion wear-out effects. Ailawadi et al. (2005) model the channel structure as a dynamic series of manufacturer–retailer Stackelberg games solved by forward-looking players, which enables them to formulate the optimization as a dynamic programming problem in discrete time.

   Therefore, this model can predict competitive response to a major policy change. In the context of responses to Procter & Gamble's 'value-pricing' strategy, in which P&G made major promotional cuts and instead provided lower everyday prices to retailers and consumers, Ailawadi et al. (2005) generate predictions of competitor and retailer responses and test their accuracy. Specifically, they compare the predictive ability of their model with the reaction function approach (Leeflang and Wittink, 1992; 1996) and a dynamic model that assumes the retailer is nonstrategic. The dynamic, empirical game-theoretic model offers better predictive ability than either benchmark model; thus, such models provide the means to account for important changes in competitive strategy (see also Shugan, 2005) and are more consistent with strategic competitive reasoning than with the extrapolation of past reactions to the future.

7.3 Findings

The study of competition and competitive response has a long tradition in micro-economic theory, starting with the work of Cournot (1838) and Bertrand (1883), and resulting in the development of multiple models of competitive responsiveness in the past 30 years. These studies on competitive responsiveness can be classified according to different (overlapping) criteria, such as[23]

1. Area of application.
2. Type of competition.
3. Type of competitive strategies.
4. Type of analyses.

We discuss several examples of studies that employ criteria 1–3 to expand on our summary of different types of analyses in Section 7.2. After this brief but not exhaustive survey, we explicate the most important findings of these studies.

7.3.1 Area of Application

Most studies on competitive responsiveness refer to *frequently purchased consumer goods* (FPCG) and consider manufacturers' actions and reactions. The most prominent examples in this respect are studies by Nijs et al. (2001) and Steenkamp et al. (2005), who study 1200 brands of 442 FPCG categories.

Several studies also that analyze competition in *durable goods* markets. For example, Lambin et al. (1975) investigate competition among manufacturers of electronic razors in the West German market, Sudhir (2001) studies car markets, and Kadiyali (1996) and Sudhir et al. (2005) address the competitive responsiveness of two major players in the U.S. photographic film industry market (i.e., Fuji and Kodak).

In another arena, Jain et al. (1999) and Roberts et al. (2005) examine competition in the telephone industry by specifically considering *service competition*.

More recently, rapid and overwhelming developments in information technology, especially the diffusion of the *Internet,*have enhanced the focus on competition among retailers, wholesalers, and manufacturers, who now offer products through various *channels*. A nonempirical study by Balasubramanian

---

[23] See also Horváth (2003), which is based on Leeflang (2001).

(1998) analyses the entry of direct book marketers into a retail market, whereas Bakos and Brynjolfssen (2000) study the Internet's development as an infrastructure for distributing digital information goods. They conclude that the Internet has dramatically influenced competitive marketing and selling strategies based on large-scale bundling of information goods. Additional empirical studies that consider the competition between Internet and conventional channels include Lynch and Ariely (2000) in the wine market; Clay et al. (2001) and Goolsbee and Chevalier (2002) for books; and Sorensen (2000) in the prescription drug industry.

Recent articles also explore competitive responses in the context of *retailing*; several examples include Desai and Purohit (2004), Shankar and Bolton (2004), Wang (2004), and Padmanabhan and Png (2004).

Examples of models of competitive responsiveness in *business-to-business markets* are more difficult to find. Lilien and Yoon (1990) investigate entry timing for new industrial products. Ramaswamy et al. (1994) consider competitive marketing behavior in industrial markets and explicitly distinguish between retaliatory behavior (e.g., both firms cut prices or increase marketing expenditures) and cooperative behavior (e.g., both increase prices or decrease marketing expenditures). They find that market concentration has the greatest impact on retaliatory behavior, though market growth and standardization also have sizable influences, and that market growth has the greatest impact on cooperative behavior.

Chintagunta and Desiraju (2005) assess pricing and retailing behavior in the pharmaceutical industry for a specific class of prescription drugs across five countries. Therefore, their model accommodates market responses within markets and interfirm strategic interactions both within and across markets. They find considerable heterogeneity in preferences and market response across markets, which favors a regional strategic approach. Other studies on competitive responses in an *international marketing* context deal with the speed of international market rollouts and suggest that brands typically follow two types of strategies: a sprinkler strategy in which the brand enters several countries at the same time (fast rollout) or a waterfall strategy in which the brand enters several markets sequentially over time (slow rollout) (Kalish et al., 1995). Other studies in this field include those by Dekimpe et al. (2000), Tellis et al. (2003), and Gielens and Steenkamp (2004).

7.3.2 Type of Competition

The type of competition may be characterized by the marketing mix instruments that dominate competition. For example, many competitive response models consider flexible price and non-price *promotions* and *advertising* (Leeflang and Wittink, 1992; 1996; 2001; Dubé and Manchanda, 2005; Horváth et al., 2005, Steenkamp et al., 2005). Such instruments usually display significant variation over time, unlike quality and distribution instruments.

A topic that has received a great deal of attention in recent literature on competitive responsiveness is retail pass-through (Van Heerde and Neslin, 2008), which refers to the cost savings a retailer passes on to customers (Moorthy, 2005). The general problem of retail pass-through pertains to the question of how a retailer changes its prices when its costs change as a result of trade promotions or when manufacturers change their regular wholesale prices. Retailers' reactions to changes in costs appear in many studies, such as Neslin et al. (1995), Kim and Staelin (1999), Tyagi (1999), Kumar et al. (2001), Besanko et al. (2005), and Moorthy (2005). For example, Besanko et al. (2005) investigate the pass-through behavior of a major U.S. supermarket chain for 78 products across 11 categories. They find positive and negative *cross-brand* pass-through effects, which indicates that retailers adjust the prices of competing products upward or downward in response to changes in the wholesale price of any particular product.

The oldest form of competition, *price* competition, continues to play a crucial role in many competitive response models, especially game-theoretic models, as exemplified by Dockner and Jørgensen (1988), Gasmi et al. (1992), Rao and Bass (1985), Chintagunta and Rao (1996), Fruchter and Kalish (1997), Vilcassim et al. (1999), Hildebrandt and Klapper (2001), and Chintagunta and Desiraju (2005).

Moreover, modern research suggests a growing interest in calibrating competitive response models that deal with *quality* competition, as reflected in Lilien and Yoon (1990), Berndt et al. (1995), Dutta et al. (1995), Aoki and Prusa (1997), Lehmann-Grube (1997), Liu et al. (2004), and Chambers et al. (2006). In another developing field, Cohen and Klepper (1996), Sutton (1998), and Ofek and Sarvary (2003) examine *research and development* competition.

Pauwels and Srinivasan (2004) also demonstrate that store brand *entry* strengthens a retailer's bargaining position with regard to national brand manufacturers, though reactions to *new entries* have been studied in many other articles as well. A detailed description of the methodologies used in this context would require at least another chapter in this handbook, so we suffice to mention a few of the most important studies in this arena: Robinson (1988), Gatignon et al. (1989), Gatignon et al. (1997), Shankar (1997, 1999), Kalra et al. (1998), Narasimhan and Zang (2000), Waarts and Wierenga (2000), Deleersnijder et al. (2001), Debruyne and Reibstein (2005), Roberts et al. (2005), and Kornelis et al. (2008).

7.3.3 Type of Competitive Strategies

Most models that consider competitive responsiveness assume that competitive reactions are based on past observations, but models that rely on historical data, no matter how successful in the short run, generally cannot predict the impact of any future changes in competitive strategy.[24] Implementing entirely new (i.e., dynamic) strategies inescapably changes past behavior, and common marketing activities, such as new product development, repositioning, altering ancillary services, or major pricing policy changes (Ailawadi et al. 2005), alter the nature of competition among incumbents and thereby invalidate any relationships based on past observations. In turn, models must account for dynamic *strategies*, perhaps according to principle of strategic foresight, a notion that requires managers to look forward and anticipate competing brands' likely future decisions. Managers may then reason backward to deduce their own optimal decisions in response to the best decisions to be made by all other brands (Naik et al., 2005). Day and Reibstein (1997) and Montgomery et al. (2005) both confirm the need to develop dynamic strategic models; specifically, Day and Reibstein identify two strategic errors:

- The failure to anticipate competitors' moves (likely actions).
- The failure to recognize potential interactions over time (reactions).

More recent models, such as those proposed by Rao et al. (1995), Chintagunta and Rao (1996), Vilcassim et al. (1999), Ailawadi et al. (2005), Dubé and Manchanda (2005), and Sudhir et al. (2005), also account for dynamic strategic decision making.

Another aspect that determines the type of competitive strategies is whether the focus is *competition* between firms/brands, that is, *retaliatory behavior*, or collusion, *collusive/cooperative behavior*. Gasmi et al. (1992) provide an empirical methodology for studying various forms of implicit and explicit collusive behavior in terms of price and advertising with their investigation of Pepsi and Coca-Cola.

7.3.4 Outcomes

The models of competitive response that we have introduced have generated outcomes of great value for policy decisions in actual practice.

7.3.4.1 Under- and overreactions

Leeflang and Wittink (1996) find that marketing managers of a Dutch detergent brand tend to overreact, even though no reaction represents the dominant competitive response mode. In a replication study, Brodie et al. (1996) confirm their finding with New Zealand data.

Steenkamp et al. (2005) study simple and multiple reactions to both price promotions and advertising, including both short- and long-run effects. They also examine the moderating impact of *brand-* and *category*-related

---

[24] We closely follow Shugan (2005, p. 4).

characteristics on competitive reaction elasticities. In contrast to Leeflang and Wittink (1992; 1996), Steenkamp et al. (2005) distinguish two types of reactions: accommodations (i.e., reductions in marketing support after a competitive attack) and retaliations. On the basis of this differentiation, they find that

- The most common form of competitive reaction is a passive lack of *reaction*.
- When reactions occur, they are more often in response to *price promotions* than advertising.
- Retaliation with a price promotion against price promotion attacks is more prevalent than any other action–reaction combination.
- Simple competitive reactions are generally retaliatory, whereas multiple reactions are either retaliatory or accommodating.
- All forms of competitive reactions generally are restricted to short-run changes in brands' marketing spending that do not prompt permanent changes in spending behavior.

Because the most common form of competitive reaction is *no reaction* to an attack (cells $C + D + G + H$ in Fig. 7.2), we must question whether this decision is managerially sound, in the sense that sales protection appears unnecessary. Steenkamp et al. (2005) find that responses to promotional attacks fall into cells $G + H$ 82% of the time. Of these cases, no effects emerge for 78%, whereas in 22%, positive cross-sales effects occur. In the 18% of all cases that suffer negative cross-sales effects $(C + D)$, retaliation would have been ineffective 30% of the time—that is, in $30\% \times 18\% \approx 5\%$ of *all* cases (cell D). This finding suggests that underreactions (cell C) occur in about 13% of all cases, but they rarely occur in response to advertising attacks. Steenkamp et al. also find a substantial number of overreactions (cells $E + F$); across all cases and situations, 45% of defenders respond with a promotion to a promotion attack, even when the initial promotion has no effect on them $(E + F/E + F + A + B)$.

7.3.4.2 Explaining Competitive Reactions

Dolan (1981) studies several industries and identifies specific variables that determine the nature of competition:[25]
1. High fixed costs promote competitive reactions (to gain market share).
2. Low storage costs reduce competitive reactions.
3. Growing primary demand reduces competitive reactions.
4. Large firms avoid price competition.

Clark and Montgomery (1998) also propose and test a framework built around credibility and deterrence. The empirical results they obtain from MBA students making *Markstrat2* decisions and providing survey responses show that

---

[25] We closely follow Leeflang and Wittink (2001) here.

- A credible reputation deters an attack if the potential attacker considers the target firm a minor competitor (whereas a major competitor is very likely to be attacked, independent of the target's credibility).
- The more successful a firm is, the more likely it is perceived as a credible defender.
- Consistently high levels of marketing activity relative to competitors' activities help a firm gain a reputation as a credible defender.

These results are intriguing. It seems reasonable, for example, that managers would attack major competitors because large firms have more demand share to lose. Yet in the real world, such attacks depend on the defender's credibility, even if there is no evidence for such dependence in a Markstrat setting.

Chen et al. (1992) use a formal empirical approach to identify the characteristics of actions that lead to competitive reactions and test the hypothesized relationships with a sample of competitive moves among U.S. airlines. On the basis of their findings, they propose the following characteristics to explain competitive reactions.

- *The competitive impact*, which they define as the pervasiveness of an action's effect on competitors, measured by the number of competitors actually affected by an action (i.e., the number of airlines that served at least one of the airports affected by the action of the initiator).
- *The attack intensity*, or the extent to which an action affects each competitor's key markets, measured as the proportion of passengers served by the airline who potentially are affected by the action.
- *The implementation requirement*, which refers to the degree of effort a firm requires to execute an action and reflects the amount of time between the announcement of an action and the date the action occurs (delay).
- *Type of action,* in terms of its strategic versus tactical nature, such that a strategic action includes a significant investment in fixed assets and/or people and structures, whereas tactical actions do not involve such commitments.

They further operationalize the *competitive reaction variables* as follows.

- *Number of responses,* the total number of competitors who reacted to an action (number of counteractions).
- *The response lag,* the length of time a competitor took to react to an initiator's action.

Chen et al. (1992) find that the number of competitive reactions relates positively to the competitive impact and attack intensity. Actions with greater implementation requirements and strategic (versus tactical) actions provoke fewer counteractions, and strategic actions and actions that require a substantial amount of time generate slower reactions.

Leeflang and Wittink (2001) use more formal approaches to explain competitive reaction effects. If brand j ($u_{\ell j}$) uses only one marketing instrument (ℓ) in reaction to a change in a marketing instrument h for brand i (u_{hi}), then to preserve market share, the reaction elasticity (RE) must equal:

$$RE = \rho_{u_{\ell j}, u_{hi}} = \frac{\eta_{m_j, u_{hi}}}{\eta_{m_j, u_{\ell j}}}, \tag{7.31}$$

where

$\eta_{m_j, u_{hi}}$ = cross-elasticity for brand j with respect to i's instruments, and
$\eta_{m_j, u_{\ell j}}$ = own elasticity for brand j with respect to j's instrument ℓ.

It follows from Equation (7.31) that the reaction elasticity (RE) relates positively to the (absolute) cross-brand market share elasticity and negatively to the own-brand market share elasticity.

In their empirical analysis, Leeflang and Wittink (2001) also find support for the idea that competitive reaction elasticities are

- a positive function of cross-brand market share elasticities, and
- a negative function of own-brand market share elasticities.

In their large-scale empirical study of short- and long-run reactions to promotions and advertising shocks, Steenkamp et al. (2005) uncover several factors that affect the intensity of competitive reactions. Specifically, for *simple* reactions to *price promotions and advertising*, the reactions are stronger when:

- The attacker is more powerful,
- The relative power structure in the dyad favors the defenders,
- The category is less concentrated, and
- The interpurchase time is higher.

Price promotion reactivity is *stronger* in categories that involve more impulse buying.

Finally, a*dvertising* reactivity is *lower*:

- in growing categories;
- for storable products; and
- in categories with lower advertising intensity.

In Section 7.2, we discussed the application of a VARX model to determine the simultaneous effects of actions and reactions on sales over time. In a similar vein, to estimate gross and net sales, Horváth et al. (2005) add forecasted sales effects over the dust-settling period and attempt to determine the impact on the sales effect of a firm's own (1) competitive reactions, (2) reactions to the consequences of own actions or competitive actions (own-feedback effects and cross-feedback effects, respectively), and (3) internal decisions (see also Equation (7.17)). The internal decisions represent intrafirm effects (relationships between different variables of the same brand) and inertia (lagged endogenous variables). Their research indicates that cross-brand feedback effects (in terms of sales) are more relevant than competitive reaction effects, which suggests managers are more sensitive to competitors' sales than to competitors' actions. Thus, models must accommodate cross-brand sales feedback effects in addition to competitive reaction effects. The same holds true for internal decisions; inertia and intrafirm decisions represent crucial determinants for specifying sales promotion decisions. These findings fall in line with several recent studies that report an aggressive competitive reaction does not constitute an important factor in market behavior (e.g., Pauwels, 2004; Steenkamp et al., 2005).

7.4 Taking Stock: Implementation

From our discussions in Sections 7.2 and 7.3, we recognize that models used to determine competitive responsiveness have a long history and that recent developments provide opportunities to integrate different research streams, as we illustrate in Fig. 7.1. We do not expect that one type of model will dominate others, because those that predict strategic competitive moves differ from models that support operational decisions. The latter models usually provide extrapolations of prior reactions into the future, whereas models that include more dynamic aspects are particularly appropriate to predict reactions in case of major policy changes.

In this final section, we distinguish among models designed to support operational decisions and models that can be used to support strategic decisions. Specifically, models 1–6 can, at least in principle, *predict short-term (operational) reactions*. By substituting appropriate values of the marketing instruments into equations such as Equation (7.14), marketers may determine competitive reactions. Because these reactions lead to new reactions, the system of equations represented by Equations (7.16) and (7.17) may be more appropriate for determining the effects on competitive reactions and sales on the long(er) term. Such effects can be determined only with appropriate assumptions about the expected values of the competitive marketing instruments. We recommend simulations that can determine the sensitivity of competitive reactions to different assumptions about competitive actions.

However, simple demand functions, such as those summarized in Equations (7.1), (7.9), and (7.15), offer the most value to attempts to determine whether to react to competitive actions. In general, only a limited number of competitors, which possess a limited number of marketing instruments, can actually affect own sales, as we illustrate in Table 7.1. Therefore, any estimation of demand models that includes competitive marketing instruments provides a basis for *normative decision making*. Demand equations also offer the basis to decide whether to react and thus may reduce over- and underreactions.

Normative decision-making in marketing that accounts for competitive actions and reactions also may benefit from the findings and generalizations discussed in the preceding section, such as that

- Competitive reactions are stronger when the cross-brand elasticities are higher.
- Competitive reactions are weaker then the own-brand elasticities are higher.

Game-theoretic models assist normative decision making by determining the conditions for equilibriums between brands in the same product category (horizontal competition) and among agents (retailers, wholesalers, manufacturers) in the same channel (vertical competition). Specifically, game-theoretic models based on empirical demand and reaction functions are quite useful in this respect. The structure of such models appears in Equations (7.20)–(7.25) (horizontal competition) and Equation (7.26) (vertical competition).

However, the question remains regarding whether competitive response models are adequate tools to predict *strategic changes*. Ailawadi et al. (2005) demonstrate that game-theoretic models that consider vertical and horizontal competition and that are based on empirical demand equations are superior to reaction-based models (e.g., models 2–6) for predicting actual competitor and retailer responses to a major policy change. Thus, though it is based on a simplified the reality, the model that Ailawadi et al. (2005) develop is quite complicated.

In turn, the remaining challenges for this research area require

1. More adequate methods and approaches for predicting *strategic* response (Montgomery et al., 2005).
2. Tailored models to fit unique situations.[26]

Furthermore, optimal decisions based on normative models can be obtained analytically only when the number of horizontal and vertical competitors is limited; when the number increases, substantive analytical solutions are difficult to obtain. We therefore suggest simulations of these more complicated demand and supply systems, which may provide a means to derive the optimal solutions.

Following Shugan (2004, 2005), we believe that endogenizing competitive responses, that is, adding more variables to the models, is beneficial. In this respect, it will be useful to explore the ideas articulated by Soberman and Gatignon (2005), suggesting a link between competitive dynamics and market evolution. The potential link between these two areas offers many opportunities to enrich the theory of model evolution, as well as the theory and practice surrounding competitive responsiveness.

---

[26] An example of the latter models is a prelaunch diffusion model for evaluating market defense strategies in the telecom sector developed by Roberts et al. (2005).

The models presented in this chapter have been applied in a wide array of areas, but in other areas, they have barely been applied, nor will they be because the data required by these models are unavailable in areas such as business-to-business markets or services (e.g., banking, insurance, industrial), which have intensive competitive battles that the traditional scanner data–based models presented herein do not model.

Most models consider price-, non-price, and advertising competition, but competition through and *between* retailers has not been fully exploited.

References

Ailawadi, K.L., P.K. Kopalle, S.A. Neslin. 2005. Predicting Competitive Response to a Major Policy Change: Combining Game-Theoretic and Empirical Analyses. *Marketing Science* **24** 12–24.

Alsem, K.J., P.S.H. Leeflang, J.C. Reuyl. 1989. The Forecasting Accuracy of Market Share Models Using Predicted Values of Competitive Marketing Behavior. *International Journal of Research in Marketing* **6** 183–198.

Aoki, R., T.J. Prusa. 1997. Sequential versus Simultaneous Choice with Endogenous Quality. *International Journal of Industrial Organization* **15** 103–121.

Bakos, Y., E. Brynjolfsson. 2000. Bundling and Competition on the Internet. *Marketing Science* **19** 63–82.

Balasubramanian, S. 1998. Mail versus Mall: A Strategic Analysis of Competition between Direct Marketers and Conventional Retailers. *Marketing Science* **17** 181–195.

Baligh, H.H., L.E. Richartz. 1967. Variable-Sum Game Models of Marketing Problems. *Journal of Marketing Research* **4** 173–183.

Berndt, E.R., L. Bui, D.R. Reiley, G.L. Urban. 1995. Information, Marketing, and Pricing in the U.S. Antiulcer Drug Market. *American Economic Review* **85** 100–105.

Bertrand, J. 1883. Théorie Mathématique de la Richesse Sociale. *Journal de Savants* 499–508.

Besanko, D., J.P. Dubé, S. Gupta. 2005. Own-Brand and Cross-Brand Pass-Through *Marketing Science* **24** 123–137.

Brandenburger, A.M., B.J. Nalebuff. 1996. *Co-opetition*, Double-Day, New York.

Brodie, R.J., A. Bonfrer, J. Cutler. 1996. Do Managers Overreact To Each Others' Promotional Activity? Further Empirical Evidence. *International Journal of Research in Marketing* **13** 379–387.

Bult, J.R., P.S.H. Leeflang, D.R. Wittink. 1997. The Relative Performance of Bivariate Causality Tests in Small Samples. *European Journal of Operational Research* **97** 450–464.

Chambers, C., P. Kouvelis, J. Semple. 2006. Quality-Based Competition, Profitability, and Variable Costs. *Management Science* **52** 1884–1895.

Chen, M.J., K.G. Smith, C.M. Grimm. 1992. Action Characteristics as Predictors of Competitive Response. *Management Science* **38** 439–455.

Chintagunta, P.K., R. Desiraju. 2005. Strategic Pricing and Detailing Behavior in International Markets. *Marketing Science* **24** 67–80.

Chintagunta, P.K., T. Erdem, P. Rossie, M. Wedel. 2006. Structural Modeling in Marketing: Review and Assessment. *Marketing Science* **25** 1–13.

Chintagunta, P.K., V.R. Rao. 1996. Pricing Strategies in a Dynamic Duopoly: A Differential Game Model. *Management Science* **42** 1501–1514.

Chintagunta, P.K., N.J. Vilcassim. 1994. Marketing Investment Decisions in a Dynamic Duopoly: A Model and Empirical Analysis. *International Journal of Research in Marketing* **11** 287–306.

Christen, M., S. Gupta, J.C. Porter, R. Staelin and D.R. Wittink. 1997. Using Market-Level Data to Understand Promotion Effects in a Nonlinear Model. *Journal of Marketing Research* **34** 322–334.

Clark, B.H., D.B. Montgomery. 1998. Deterrence, Reputations, and Competitive Cognition. *Management Science* **44** 62–82.

Clay, K., R. Krishnan, E. Wolff. 2001. Price and Price Dispersion on the Web: Evidence from the Online Book Industry. *Journal of Industrial Economics* **49** 521–539.

Cohen, W.M., S. Klepper. 1996. Firm Size and the Nature of Innovation within Industries: The Case of Process and R&D. *Review of Economics and Statistics* **78** 232–243.

Cournot, A. 1838. *Recherches sur les Principes Mathématiques de la Théorie des Richesses*, Paris.

Day, G.S., D.J. Reibstein. 1997. *Wharton on Dynamic Competitive Strategy*, Wiley, New York.

Day, G.S., R. Wensley. 1988. Assessing Advantage: A Framework for Diagnosing Competitive Strategy. *Journal of Marketing* **52**(Spring) 1–20.

Debruyne, M., D.J. Reibstein. 2005. Competitor See, Competitor Do: Incumbent Entry in New Market Niches. *Marketing Science* **24** 55–66.

Dekimpe, M.G., P.H. Franses, D.M. Hanssens, P.A. Naik. 2008. Time-Series Models in Marketing. Wierenga, B. *Handbook of Marketing Decision Models* , Springer Science + Business Media, New York.

Dekimpe, M.G., P.M. Parker, M. Sasvary. 2000. Global Diffusion of Technological Innovations: A Coupled Hazard Approach. *Journal of Marketing Research* **37** 47–59.

Deleersnijder, B., I. Geyskens, K. Gielens, M.G. Dekimpe. 2001. How Cannibalistic is the Internet Channel? A Study of the Newspaper Industry in the United Kingdom and The Netherlands. *International Journal of Research in Marketing* **19** 337–348.

Desai, P.S., D. Purohit. 2004. Let Me Talk to my Manager: Haggling in a Competitive Environment. *Marketing Science* **23** 219–233.

Dockner, E., S. Jørgenson. 1988. Optimal Pricing Strategies for New Products in Dynamic Oligopolies. *Marketing Science* **7** 315–334.

Dolan, R.J. 1981. Models of Competition: A Review of Theory and Empirical Evidence. Enis B., K. Roering, *Review of Marketing* , American Marketing Association, Chicago 224–234.

Dubé, J.P., P. Manchanda. 2005. Differences in Dynamic Brand Competition across Markets: An Emprirical Analysis. *Marketing Science* **24** 81–95.

Dubé, J.P., K. Sudhir, A. Ching, G.S. Crawford, M. Draganska, J.T. Fox, W. Hartmann, G.J. Hitsch, V.B. Viard, M. Villas-Boas, N. Vilcassim. 2005. Recent Advances in Structural Economic Modeling: Dynamics, Product Positioning and Entry. *Marketing Letters* **16** 209–224.

Dutta, P.K., S. Lach, A. Rustichini. 1995. Better Late than Early: Vertical Differentiation in the Adoption of New Technology. *Journal of Economics and Management Strategy* **4** 563–589.

Ellison, G. 1994. Cooperation in the Prisoner's Dilemma with Anonymous Random Matching. *Review of Economic Studies* **61** 567–588.

Erickson, G.M. 1991. *Dynamic Models of Advertising Competition* . Kluwer Academic Publishers, Boston.

Friedman, L. 1958. Game Theory Models in the Allocation of Advertising Expenditures. *Operations Research* **6** 699–709.

Fruchter, G.E., S. Kalish. 1997. Closed-Loop Advertising Strategies in a Duopoly. *Management Science* **43** 54–63.

Fudenberg, D., J. Tirole. 1991. *Game Theory* . The MIT Press, Cambridge, Mass.

Gasmi, F., J.J. Laffont, Q. Vuong. 1992. Econometric Analysis of Collusive Behavior in a Soft-Drink Market. *Journal of Economics and Management Strategy* **1** 277–311.

Gatignon, H. 1984. Competition as a Moderator of the Effect of Advertising on Sales. *Journal of Marketing Research* **21** 387–398.

Gatignon, H., E. Anderson, K. Helsen. 1989. Competitive Reactions to Market Entry: Explaining Interfirm Differences. *Journal of Marketing Research* **26** 44–45.

Gatignon, H., T.S. Robertson, A.J. Fein. 1997. Incumbent Defense Strategies against New Product Entry. *International Journal of Research in Marketing* **14** 163–176.

Gielens, K., J.B.E.M Steenkamp. 2004. What Drives New Product Success?: An Investigation Across Products and Countries. *MSI Working Paper*. 04–108.

Goolsbee, A., J. Chevalier. 2002. Measuring Prices and Price Competition Online: Amazon and Barnes and Noble. *NBER Working Paper*, no. 9085.

Gupta, S.K., K.S. Krishnan. 1967a. Differential Equation Approach to Marketing. *Operations Research* **15** 1030–1039.

Gupta, S.K., K.S. Krishnan. 1967b. Mathematical Models in Marketing. *Operations Research* **15** 1040–1050.

Hanssens, D.M. 1980. Market Response, Competitive Behavior and Time Series Analysis. *Journal of Marketing Research* **17** 470–485.

Hanssens, D.M., L.J. Parsons, R.L. Schultz. 2001. *Market Response Models: Econometric and Time-Series Analysis* . Kluwer Academic Publishers, Boston.

Hildebrandt, L., D. Klapper. 2001. The Analysis of Price Competition Between Corporate Brands. *International Journal of Research in Marketing* **18** 139–159.

Horváth, C. 2003. Dynamic Analysis of Marketing Systems *Dissertation*. University of Groningen.

Horvàth, C., P.S.H. Leeflang, J.E. Wieringa, D.R. Wittink. 2005. Competitive Reaction- and Feedback Effects Based on VARX Models of Pooled Store Data. *International Journal of Research in Marketing*. **22**(4). 415–426.

Iwata, G. 1974. Measurement of Conjectural Variations in Oligopoly. *Econometrica* **42** 947–966.

Jain, D.C., E. Muller, N.J. Vilcassim. 1999. Pricing Patterns of Cellular Phones and Phone-calls: A Segment-Level Analysis. *Management Science* **45** 131–141.

Jeuland, A.P., S.M. Shugan. 1983. Managing Channel Profits. *Marketing Science* **2** 239–272.

Kadiyali, V. 1996. Entry, its Deterrence, and its Accommodation: A Study of the U.S. Photographic Film Industry. *Rand Journal of Economics* **27** 452–478.

Kadiyali, V., K. Sudhir, V.R. Rao. 2001. Structural Analysis of Competitive Behavior: New Empirical Industrial Organization Methods in Marketing. *International Journal of Research in Marketing* **18** 161–186.

Kadiyali, V., N.J. Vilcassim, P.K. Chintagunta. 1999. Product Line Extensions and Competitive Market Interactions: An Empirical Analysis. *Journal of Econometrics* **89** 339–363.

Kalish, S., V. Mahajan, E. Muller. 1995. Waterfall and Sprinkler New Product Strategies in Competitive Global Markets. *International Journal of Research in Marketing* **12** 105–119.

Kalra, A., S. Rajiv, K. Srinivasan. 1998. Response to Competitive Entry: A Rationale for Delayed Defensive Reaction. *Marketing Science* **17** 380–405.

Kim, S.Y., R. Staelin. 1999. Manufacturer Allowances and Retailer Pass-Through Rates in a Competitive Environment. *Marketing Science* **18** 59.76.

Kimball, G.E. 1957. Some Industrial Applications of Military Operations Research Methods. *Operations Research* **5** 201–204.

Kornelis, M., M.G. Dekimpe, P.S.H. Leeflang. 2008. Does Competitive Entry Structurally Change Key Marketing Metrics? *International Journal of Research in Marketing* **25**, forthcoming.

Krishnan, K.S., S.K. Gupta. 1967. Mathematical Models for a Duopolistic Market. *Management Science* **13** 568–583.

Kumar, N., S. Rajiv, A. Jeuland. 2001. Effectiveness of Trade Promotions: Analyzing the Determinants of Retail Pass Through. *Marketing Science* **20** 382–404.

Lambin, J.J., P.A. Naert, A. Bultez. 1975. Optimal Marketing Behavior in Oligopoly *European Economic Review* **6** 105–128.

Leeflang, P.S.H. 2001. Lectures for PhD's Competitive Responsiveness. *Research Seminars NOBEM*. The Netherlands.

Leeflang, P.S.H., J.C. Reuyl. 1985. Competitive Analysis Using Market Response Functions. Lusch, R.F. et al. *Educators' Proceedings, American Marketing Association*, Chicago 388–395.

Leeflang, P.S.H., D.R. Wittink. 1992. Diagnosing Competitive Reactions Using. (Aggregated) Scanner Data. *International Journal of Research in Marketing* **9** 39–57.

Leeflang, P.S.H., D.R. Wittink. 1996. Competitive Reaction Versus Consumer Response: Do Managers Overreact? *International Journal of Research in Marketing* **13** 103–119.

Leeflang, P.S.H., D.R. Wittink. 2001. Explaining Competitive Reaction Effects. *International Journal of Research in Marketing* **18** 119–137.

Lehmann-Grube, U. 1997. Strategic Choice of Quality when Quality is Costly: The Persistence of the High-Quality Advantage. *RAND Journal of Economics* **28** 372–384.

Lilien, G.L., E. Yoon. 1990. The Timing of Competitive Market Entry: An Exploratory Study of New Industrial Products. *Management Science* **36** 568–585.

Liu, Y, D.S. Putler, C.B. Weinberg. 2004. Is Having More Channels Really Better? A Model of Competition Among Commercial Television Broadcasters. *Marketing Science* **23** 120–133.

Lynch Jr., J.G., D. Ariely. 2000. Wine Online: Search Costs Affect Competition on Price, Quality and Distribution. *Marketing Science* **19** 83–103.

Mass-Callell, A., Whinston, M., J.R. Green. 1995. *Microeconomic Theory*, Oxford University Press, Oxford, UK.

Mills, H.D. 1961. A Study of Promotional Competition. Bass, F.M., R.D. Buzzell, *Mathematical Models and Methods in Marketing*, Richard D. Irwin, Homewood, Ill. 271–288.

Montgomery, D.B., M. C. Moore, J.E. Urbany. 2005. Reasoning About Competitive Reactions: Evidence from Executives. *Marketing Science* **24** 1. 138–149.

Moorthy, K.S. 1985. Using Game Theory to Model Competition. *Journal of Marketing Research* **12** 262–282.

Moorthy, K.S. 1993. Competitive Marketing Strategies: Game-Theoretic Models. Eliashberg, J., G.L. Lilien, *Handbooks in Operations Research and Management Science 5, Marketing*, North-Holland, Amsterdam 143–192.

Moorthy, S. 2005. A General Theory of Pass-Through in Channels with Category Management and Retail Competition. *Marketing Science* **24** 110–122.

Naik, P.A., K. Raman, R.S. Winer. 2005. Planning Marketing-Mix Strategies in the Presence of Interaction Effects. *Marketing Science* **24** 25–34.

Narasimhan, C., Z.J. Zang. 2000. Market Entry Strategy under Firm Heterogeneity and Asymmetric Payoffs. *Marketing Science* **19** 313–327.

Nash, J. 1950. Equilibrium Points in n-person Games. *Proceedings of the National Academy of Sciences* **36** 48–49.

Neslin, S.A., S.G. Powell, L.G. Schneider Stone. 1995. The Effects of Retailer and Consumer Response on Optimal Manufacturer Advertising and Trade Promotion Strategies. *Management Science* **41** 749–766.

Nijs, V.R., M.G. Dekimpe, J.B.E.M. Steenkamp, D.M. Hanssens. 2001. The Category-Demand Effects of Price Promotions. *Marketing Science* **20** 1–22.

Ofek, E., M. Sarvary. 2003. R&D, Marketing, and the Success of Next-Generation Products. *Marketing Science* **22** 355–370.

Padmanabhan, V., I.P.L. Png. 2004. Reply to "Do Returns Policies Intensify Retail Competition?" *Marketing Science* **23** 614–618.

Pauwels, K. 2004. How Dynamic Consumer Response, Competitor Response, Company Support and Company Inertia Shape Long-Term Marketing Effectiveness. *Marketing Science* **23** 596–610.

Pauwels, K., S. Srinivasan. 2004. Who Benefits from Store Brand Entry? *Marketing Science* **23** 364–390.

Plat, F.W., P.S.H. Leeflang. 1988. Decomposing Sales Elasticities on Segmented Markets. *International Journal of Research in Marketing* **5** 303–315.

Putsis, W.P., R. Dhar. 1999. Category Expenditure, Promotion and Competitive Market Interactions: Can Promotions Really Expand the Pie? Paper London Business School/ Yale School of Management, London.

Ramaswamy, V., H. Gatignon, D.J. Reibstein. 1994. Competitive Marketing Behavior in Industrial Markets. *Journal of Marketing* **58** 45–55.

Rao, R.C., R.V. Arjunji, B.P.S. Murthi. 1995. Game Theory and Empirical Generalizations Concerning Competitive Promotions. *Marketing Science* **14** G89-G100.

Rao, R. C., F.M. Bass. 1985. Competition, Strategy, and Price Dynamics: A Theoretical and Empirical Investigation. *Journal of Marketing Research* **22** 3. 283–296.

Roberts, J.H., C.J. Nelson, P.D. Morrison. 2005. A Prelaunch Diffusion Model for Evaluating Market Defense Strategies. *Marketing Science* **24** 150–164.

Robinson, W.T. 1988. Marketing Mix Reactions to Entry. *Marketing Science* **7** 368–385.

Shakun, M.F. 1966. A Dynamic Model for Competitive Marketing in Coupled Markets. *Management Science* **12** 525–530.

Shankar, V. 1997. Pioneers' Marketing Mix Reactions to Entry in Different Competitive Game Structures: Theoretical Analysis and Empirical Illustration. *Marketing Science* **16** 271–293.

Shankar, V. 1999. New Product Introduction and Incumbent Response Strategies: Their Inter-Relationship and the Role of Multimarket Contact. *Journal of Marketing Research* **36** 327–344.

Shankar, V., R.N. Bolton. 2004. An Empirical Analysis of Determinants of Retailer Pricing Strategy. *Marketing Science* **23** 28–49.

Shugan, S.M. 2002. Editorial: Marketing Science, Models, Monopoly Models, and Why We Need Them. *Marketing Science* **21** 223–228.

Shugan, S.M. 2004. Endogeneity in Marketing Decision Models. *Marketing Science* **23** 1–3.

Shugan, S.M. 2005. Comments on Competitive Responsiveness. *Marketing Science* **24** 3–7.

Soberman D., H. Gatignon. 2005. Research Issues at the Boundary of Competitive Dynamics and Market Evolution. *Marketing Science* **24** 165–174.

Sorensen, C.A. 2000. Equilibrium Price Dispersion in Retail Markets for Prescription Drugs. *Journal of Political Economy* **108** ,833–850.

Steenkamp, J.B.E.M., V.R. Nijs, D.M. Hanssens, M.G. Dekimpe. 2005. Competitive Reactions to Advertising and Promotion Attacks. *Marketing Science* **24** 35–54.

Sudhir, K. 2001. Competitive Pricing Behavior in the Auto Market: A Structural Analysis. *Marketing Science* **20** 42–60.

Sudhir, K., P.K. Chintagunta, V. Kadiyali. 2005. Time-Varying Competition. *Marketing Science* **24** 96–109.

Sutton, J. 1998. *Technology and Market Structure: Theory and History* . MIT Press, Cambridge, MA.

Tellis, G.J., S. Stremersch, E. Yin. 2003. The International Takeoff of New Products: The Role of Economics, Culture and Country Innovativeness. *Marketing Science* **22** 188–208.

Telser, L.G. 1962. The Demand for Branded Goods as Estimated from Consumer Panel Data. *Review of Economics and Statistics* **44** 300–324.

Tyagi, R.K. 1999., 'A Characterization of Retailer Response to Manufacturer Trade Deals. *Journal of Marketing Research* **36** 510–516.

Urban, G.L., R. Karash. 1971. Evolutionary Model Building. *Journal of Marketing Research* **8** 62–66.

Van Heerde, H.J., S. Gupta, D.R. Wittink. 2003. Is 75% of the Sales Promotion Bump Due to Brand Switching? No, Only 33% Is. *Journal of Marketing Research* **40** 481–491.

Van Heerde, H.J., P.S.H. Leeflang, D.R. Wittink. 2000. The Estimation of Pre- and Post-promotion Dips with Store-Level Scanner Data. *Journal of Marketing Research* **37** 383–395.

Van Heerde, H.J., P.S.H. Leeflang, D.R. Wittink. 2001. Semiparametric Analysis to Estimate the Deal Effect Curve. *Journal of Marketing Research* **38** 197–215.

Van Heerde, H.J., P.S.H. Leeflang, D.R. Wittink. 2002. How Promotions Work: SCAN*PRO-Based Evolutionary Model Building. *Schmalenbach Business Review* **54** 198–220.

Van Heerde, H.J., P.S.H. Leeflang, D.R. Wittink. 2004. Decomposing the Sales Promotion Bump with Store Data. *Marketing Science* **23** 317–334.

Van Heerde, H.J., S.A. Neslin. 2008. Sales Promotion Models. Wierenga, B. *Handbook of Marketing Decision Models*, Springer Science + Business Media, Berlin.

Vidale, H.L., H.B. Wolfe. 1957. An Operations-Research Study of Sales Response to Advertising. *Operations Research* **5** 370–381.

Vilcassim, N.J., V. Kadiyali, P.K. Chintagunta. 1999. Investigating Dynamic Multifirm Market Interactions in Price and Advertising. *Management Science* **45** 499–418.

Villas-Boas, J.M., Y. Zhao. 2005. Retailers, Manufacturers, and Individual Consumers: Modelling the Supply Side in the Ketchup Marketplace. *Journal of Marketing Research* **42** 83–95.

Waarts, E., B. Wierenga. 2000. Explaining Competitor's Reactions to New Product Introductions: The Role of Event Characteristics, Managerial Interpretation, and Competitive Context. *Marketing Letters* **11** 67–80.

Wang H. 2004. Do Returns Policies Intensify Retail Competition? *Marketing Science* **23** 611–613.

Wittink, D.R., M.J. Addona, W.J. Hawkes, J.C. Porter. 1988. SCAN*PRO: The Estimation, Validation and Use of Promotional Effects Based on Scanner Data. *Internal Paper*, Cornell University, New York.

Part IV

Customer-Centric Marketing Models

Chapter 8
Models of Customer Value

Sunil Gupta and Donald R. Lehmann

8.1 The Importance of Customer Lifetime Value

Customers are critical assets of any company: without customers a firm has no revenues, no profits and no market value. Yet, when a firm faces resource constraints, marketing dollars are typically among the first to be cut. Moreover, of all the senior managers, Chief Marketing Officers have the shortest average tenure. Part of this is due to the inability to show a return on marketing spending. For example, Marketing managers find it hard to quantify how much a company needs to spend to increase customer satisfaction from, say, 4.2 to 4.3 on a 5-point scale as well as what such an increase is worth.

Improving marketing metrics such as brand awareness, attitudes or even sales and share does not guarantee a return on marketing investment. In fact, marketing actions that improve sales or share may actually harm the long run profitability of a brand. This led many researchers to examine the long run impact of marketing actions on sales (e.g., Mela et al. 1997) and profitability (e.g., Jedidi et al. 1999).

Recently, the concept of customer lifetime value (CLV) has become more salient among both academics and practitioners. Companies such as Harrah's have had tremendous success in managing their business based on CLV and database techniques. Academics have written scores of articles and books on this topic (Rust et al. 2000; Blattberg et al. 2001; Gupta and Lehmann 2005; Kumar and Reinartz 2006).

The growing interest in this concept is due to multiple reasons. Importantly, focusing on CLV leads to a customer orientation (as opposed to the company/product orientation of traditional P&L statements and organizational structures), something many firms are trying to develop. Second, it places emphasis on future (vs current) profitability instead of share or sales. Third, CLV helps a firm assess the value of individual customers and target them more efficiently

S. Gupta
Edward W. Carter Professor of Business Administration at the Harvard Business
School, Harvard University, Boston, USA
e-mail: sgupta@hbs.edu

B. Wierenga (ed.), *Handbook of Marketing Decision Models*,
DOI: 10.1007/978-0-387-78213-3_8, © Springer Science+Business Media, LLC 2008

through customized offerings. Fourth, improvements in information technology and the easy availability of transaction data now permit companies to perform individual level analysis instead of relying on aggregate survey-based measures such as satisfaction.

Customer lifetime value is the present value of future profits generated from a customer over his/her life of business with the firm. It provides a common focus and language that bridges marketing and finance.

Why do we need CLV in additional to profits, cash flow and other traditional financial metrics? In many businesses CLV provides greater insight than traditional financial metrics for several reasons. First, the drivers of CLV (e.g., customer retenton) provide important diagnostics about the future health of a business which may not be obvious from traditional financial metrics. For example, in subscriber-based businesses such as telecommunication, magazines, cable, financial services etc., customer retention is a critical driver of future profitability and its trend provides a forward-looking indicator of future growth. Second, CLV allows us to assess profitability of individual customers. The profit reported in financial statements is an average that masks differences in customer profitability. In most businesses, a large proportion of customers are unprofitable which is not clear from aggregate financial metrics. In addition, it is hard to use traditional financial methods (e.g., discounted cash flow or P/E ratio) to assess the value of high growth companies that currently have negative cash flow and/or negative earnings. CLV allows us to value these firms when standard financial methods fail. Finally, if nothing else, it provides a structured approach to forecasting future cash flows that can be better than using a simple extrapolation approach (e.g., average compound annual growth based on the last 5 years) as is commonly used in finance.

The plan for this chapter is as follows. We start in Section 8.2 with a simple conceptual framework and highlight the links that will be the focus of this chapter. In Section 8.3, we lay out CLV models, starting with the simplest models. This is followed by a detailed discussion of the behavioral (e.g., retention) and perceptual (e.g., satisfaction) factors that affect (drive) CLV. Next we examine the link between CLV and shareholder value as well as between customer mind-set (e.g., satisfaction) with both CLV and shareholder value. This is followed by a discussion of practical and implementation issues. We then discuss areas of future research and make some concluding remarks.

8.2 Conceptual Framework

We posit the value chain in Fig. 8.1 as the basic system model relating customer lifetime value (CLV) to its antecedents and consequences. This flowchart initially links market actions to customer thoughts or mind set (e.g., attitude) and then to customer behavior (e.g., purchase or repurchase). Customer behavior, in aggregate, drives overall product-market results (e.g., share, revenue, profits). These product market results drive financial metrics such as ROI and

Fig. 8.1 The value chain

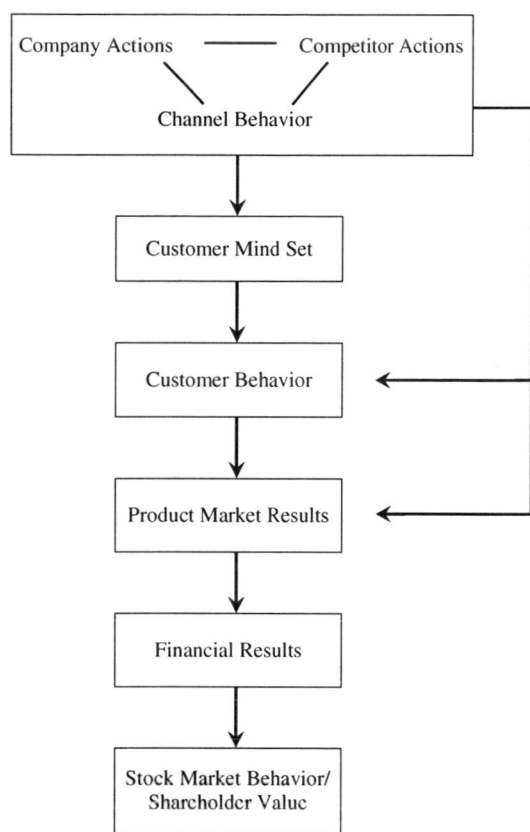

discounted cash flow which in turn are key determinants of shareholder value and the P/E ratio. Not shown in the figure are two key elements: feedback loops (e.g. from product market or financial results to company actions) and the repetitive nature of the process over time (i.e. carryover effects).

In terms of components of CLV, we consider the "standard" three determinants of acquisition, retention/defection, and expansion levels/rates as well as their costs. It is useful to recognize that the three basic components of CLV are closely related to RFM (recency, frequency, monetary value), the traditional metrics of direct marketing. For example a non-linear S-shaped link has been established between recency of purchase and CLV (Fader et al. 2005) for CDNOW customers.

What influences these components of CLV? Several studies have examined the direct impact of marketing actions on the components of CLV (e.g., the impact of price on acquisition and retention). Obviously knowing the impact of the actions of the company, competitors, and channels is critical for optimizing marketing spending. Such studies are the focus of Chapter 10 by Reinartz and Venkatesan.

Other studies have examined the impact of perceptual or mindset constructs (e.g., satisfaction) on components of CLV. In this chapter, we discuss this link. To capture customer mindset, we utilize the categories described by Keller and Lehmann (2003) for assessing brand equity. Specifically, we consider five aspects of the customer mind set which form a logical hierarchy:

1. Awareness
2. Associations (image, attribute associations)
3. Attitude (overall liking plus measures like satisfaction)
4. Attachment (loyalty including intention measures)
5. Advocacy (essentially WOM including measures such as Reichheld's net promoter score)

In general, variables later in the hierarchy (e.g., attachment and advocacy) are more closely related to CLV than variables early in the hierarchy (e.g., awareness and associations).

In the aggregate CLV is the key product market outcome, net discounted revenue from the operating business. In turn, this drives shareholder value:

$$CLV + Value\ of\ Assets + Option\ Value = Shareholder\ Value$$

Assets include fixed and financial assets not related to the production of operating income and option value represents the potential for a new business model to change the firm's operating revenue (i.e., CLV). To an extent, the link from CLV to shareholder value should be algebraic, i.e. an identity, if the financial market is efficient. Nonetheless, we examine evidence as to the strength of the links in this model.

To summarize, we concentrate on three main links:

1. Customer Mind Set to CLV or its indicators
2. Customer Mind Set directly to Shareholder Value
3. CLV and its indicators to Shareholder Value

Before examining these links, however, we first discuss models for measuring CLV.

8.3 Fundamentals of CLV

CLV is the present value of future profits obtained from a customer over his/her life of relationship with a firm. CLV is computed via the discounted cash flow approach used in finance, with two key differences. First, CLV is typically defined and estimated at an individual customer or segment level. This allows us to identify customers who are more profitable than others and target them appropriately. Further, unlike finance, CLV explicitly incorporates the possibility that a customer may defect to competitors in the future.

The CLV for a customer is (Gupta et al. 2004; Reinartz and Kumar 2003), [1]

$$CLV = \sum_{t=0}^{T} \frac{(p_t - c_t)r_t}{(1 + i)^t} - AC \qquad (8.1)$$

where,

p_t = price paid by a consumer at time t,
c_t = direct cost of servicing the customer at time t,
i = discount rate or cost of capital for the firm,
r_t = probability of customer repeat buying or being "alive" at time t,
AC = acquisition cost,
T = time horizon for estimating CLV.

Researchers and practitioners have used different approaches for modeling and estimating CLV. For example, it is common in the industry to use a finite, and somewhat arbitrary, time horizon for estimating CLV. This time horizon is typically based on what the company considers a reasonable planning horizon (e.g., 3 years) or is driven by the forecasting capabilities (e.g., some firms feel uncomfortable projecting demand beyond 5 years). CLV can then be calculated using a simple spreadsheet (or a similar computer program). Table 8.1 shows an illustration of this approach. In this table, the CLV of 100 customers is calculated over a 10 year period. For this cohort of 100 customers, costs and retention rates are estimated over the time horizon (how these are estimated is discussed later). In this example, the firm acquires 100 customers with an acquisition cost per customer of $40. Therefore, in year 0, it spends $4,000. Some of these customers defect each year. The present value of the profits from this cohort of customers over 10 years is $13,286.51. The net CLV (after deducting acquisition costs) is $9,286.51 or $928.65 per customer.

To avoid using an arbitrary time horizon for calculating CLV, several researchers have used an infinite time horizon (e.g., Gupta et al. 2004; Fader et al. 2005). Conceptually, this formulation is true to the spirit of customer *lifetime* value. Practically, this creates a challenge in projecting margins and retention over a very long (infinite) time horizon. Gupta and Lehmann (2003, 2005) show that if margins (m = p-c) and retention rates are constant over time and we use an infinite time horizon, then CLV (ignoring AC) simplifies to the following:

$$CLV = \sum_{t=0}^{\infty} \frac{mr^t}{(1 + i)^t} = m \frac{r}{(1 + i - r)} \qquad (8.2)$$

In other words, CLV simply becomes margin (m) times a *margin multiple* (r/1+i−r).

---

[1] We typically include acquisition cost (AC) for yet-to-be-acquired customers. To estimate the CLV for an already acquired customer, this cost is sunk and is not included in the CLV calculations.

Table 8.1 A Hypothetical example to illustrate CLV calculations

	Year 0	Year 1	Year 2	Year 3	Year 4	Year 5	Year 6	Year 7	Year 8	Year 9	Year 10
Number of Customers	100	90	80	72	60	48	34	23	12	6	2
Revenue per Customer		100	110	120	125	130	135	140	142	143	145
Variable cost per customer		70	72	75	76	78	79	80	81	82	83
Margin per customer		30	38	45	49	52	56	60	61	61	62
Acquisition Cost per customer	40										
Total Cost or Profit	−4000	2700	3040	3240	2940	2496	1904	1380	732	366	124
Present Value	−4000	2454.55	2512.40	2434.26	2008.06	1549.82	1074.76	708.16	341.48	155.22	47.81

Table 8.2 Margin multiple

$$\frac{r}{1 + i - r}$$

Retention Rate	Discount Rate			
	10%	12%	14%	16%
60%	1.20	1.5	1.11	1.07
70%	1.75	1.67	1.59	1.52
80%	2.67	2.50	2.35	2.22
90%	4.50	4.09	3.75	3.46

Table 8.2 shows the margin multiple for various combinations of r and i. This table shows a simple way to estimate CLV of a customer. For example, when retention rate is 90% and discount rate is 12%, the margin multiple is about four. Therefore, the CLV of a customer in this scenario is simply their annual margin multiplied by four. Clearly these estimates become more complex if retention rates are not constant over time.

As mentioned before, in finance the tradition is to value an investment over a fixed life (e.g. 8 years) and assume at that point it has a salvage value (which can be 0). In principle Equation (8.2) allows for an infinite life (a pleasant but unrealistic prospect). However, in practice the contribution of distant periods to CLV is essentially zero. For example, the expected margin from a customer ten years out, discounted to the present, is $mr^{10}/(1+i)^{10}$. Even assuming a high retention rate (e.g., 90%) and a low cost of capital (e.g., 10%), by year 10 the effective discount factor is $r^{10}/(1+i)^{10} = 0.13$. The reason for this is that the value of the expected future margin from a customer is effectively doubly discounted: to reflect the traditional cost of capital (time value of money) *and* to reflect the likelihood (risk) the customer will defect. Thus while the value of a perpetuity for 10% cost of capital is $1/i = 1/0.1 = 10$, the value of a customer that has a 10% chance of defection each year is $r/(1+i-r)$ or 4.5, i.e. less than half that of a perpetuity.

Equation (8.2) assumes margins to be constant over time. Is this a reasonable assumption? There is significant debate and conflicting evidence over how margins change over time. Reichheld (1996) suggests that the longer customers stay with a firm, the higher the profits generated from them. In contrast, Gupta and Lehmann (2005) show the data of several companies where there is no significant change in margins over time. It is possible that while long lasting customers spend more money with the firm, over time competition drives prices down. The net effect of these two opposing forces can keep margins constant.

Gupta and Lehmann (2005) also show how Equation (8.2) can be modified when margins grow at a constant rate (g). In this case, CLV of a customer is given by[2]

---

[2] This expression holds only if $(1+i) > r(1+g)$.

Table 8.3 Margin multiple with margin growth (g)

$$\frac{r}{1 + i - r(1 + g)}$$

Retention Rate	Margin Growth Rate (g)				
	0%	2%	4%	6%	8%
60%	1.15	1.18	1.21	1.24	1.27
70%	1.67	1.72	1.79	1.85	1.92
80%	2.50	2.63	2.78	2.94	3.13
90%	4.09	4.46	4.89	5.42	6.08

Assumes discount rate (i) = 12%

$$CLV = m \frac{r}{1 + i - r(1 + g)} \tag{8.3}$$

To estimate CLV for a given customer, all that is needed is are current margin (m) and discount rate (i) and estimates of retention (r) and margin growth (g). Table 8.3 provides the ratio of CLV to current period margin (the margin multiple) for a variety of cases given a 12% discount rate. Note that even when the margins grow every year at 8% forever (an optimistic scenario), the margin multiple for 90% retention increases only from about 4 for no growth case to about 6.

Many researchers have used the use *expected* customer lifetime as the time horizon for estimating CLV (Reinartz and Kumar 2000; Thomas 2001). This is also a common practice in the industry. Reichheld (1996) suggests a simple way to estimate the expected lifetime based on retention rate. Specifically, he argues that if retention rate is r, then the expected life of a customer is:

$$E(T) = \frac{1}{(1 - r)} \tag{8.4}$$

Therefore, for a cohort of customers with 80% annual retention rate, the expected life is 5 years. However, it should be noted that this is true only if we assume a constant retention (or hazard) rate for customers (as in Equations (8.2) and (8.3)). Consider the case where the hazard of defection is distributed exponential with rate $\lambda = 1\text{-}r$, where r is the retention rate. The exponential distribution is memoryless and its hazard is constant over time. The expected time for this distribution is $1/\lambda$ or $1/(1-r)$. In the discrete case, the geometric distribution is the counterpart of the exponential distribution which also has a constant hazard rate. If r is the retention rate, then the probability that a customer leaves at time t is equal to the probability that he survived until time t–1 times the probability that he left at time t, i.e.,

$$P(t) = r^{t-1}.(1 - r) \tag{8.5}$$

Therefore, the mean time for survival is (assuming constant retention rate over time)

$$E(T) = \sum_{0}^{\infty} t.P(t) \quad = \quad \sum_{0}^{\infty} t.r^{t-1}(1-r) \quad = \quad \frac{1}{1-r} \qquad (8.6)$$

Gupta and Lehmann (2005) show that using the expected lifetime can lead to serious over-estimation of CLV. To illustrate this, consider the case of Netflix, a company that provides an online entertainment subscription service in the United States. As of December 2005, it had the average revenue per subscriber of about $18 per month. Its gross margin was 47.1% and other variable costs (e.g., fulfillment etc.) were 13.9%, giving it a margin of about 33.2%. In other words, the margin per subscriber was about $6 per month or about $72 per year. Netflix also reported a monthly churn rate of about 4.2%, making the annual retention rate equal to $(1-0.042)^{12}$, about 60%. Using Equation (8.4), the expected lifetime of a customer is $1/0.042$ or about 24 months. Using a 12% annual discount rate, this translates into CLV of $121.68. In contrast, using Equation (8.2), the CLV estimate is $83.08. In other words, using an expected lifetime method over-estimates CLV by over 46%.

Figure 8.2 shows the reasons for this discrepancy. Netflix is losing 4% customers every month. This implies that the true CLV of its customers is area A in Fig. 8.2. However, the expected lifetime method assumes that a Netflix customer stays with a firm with *certainty* for 24 months. Therefore, this method estimates CLV as area B in Fig. 8.2. Note this approach over-estimates the profits in early time periods and under-estimates profits after 24 months. Since the over-estimation in early periods is discounted less than the under-estimation in later periods, the result is an over-estimation of CLV.

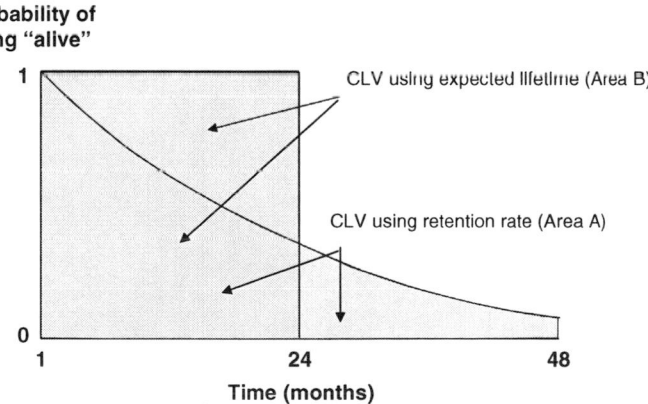

Fig. 8.2 Customer lifetime value using expected lifetime versus retention rate

This discussion applies to companies who deal with intermediate (retailer) customers as well. For example, **P&G** views Walmart, etc. as its customers, franchisers can do the same with their franchises, and retailers with their stores. The analogy is direct, i.e., acquisition is new stores opened or stocking the product and expansion is increase in same store sales. For sake of simplicity, however, here we focus on the discussion of the CLV of final customers.

8.4 Components of CLV

As is clear from Equation (8.2), three factors are critical components of CLV – customer acquisition, retention and expansion (margin or cross-selling). We briefly discuss models for each of these three components.

8.4.1 Customer Acquisition

Customer acquisition refers to the first time purchase by new or lapsed customers. Customer acquisition is a necessary condition for positive CLV, i.e. without a C, there is no LV. Traditionally marketing has placed a strong emphasis on customers in terms of market share. Ceteris paribus, greater share translates into more purchases and profits. In fact share was a key variable in the classic work on the PIMS data (see Farris and Moore 2004). In effect, share was a forerunner of CLV as a key marketing metric.

Research in this area focuses on forecasting the number of customers acquired in a time period as well as the factors that influence buying decisions of these new customers. Broadly speaking, these models can be categorized into three groups.

8.4.1.1 Logit or Probit Models

A commonly used model for customer acquisition is a logit or a probit (Thomas 2001; Thomas et al. 2004; Reinartz et al. 2005). Specifically, customer j is acquired at time t (i.e., $Z_{jt} = 1$) as follows,

$$Z*_{jt} = \alpha_j X_{jt} + \varepsilon_{jt}$$
$$Z_{jt} = 1 \quad \text{if } Z*_{jt} > 0 \tag{8.7}$$
$$Z_{jt} = 0 \quad \text{if } Z*_{jt} \leq 0$$

where X_{jt} are the covariates and α_j are consumer-specific response parameters. Depending on the assumption of the error term, one can obtain a logit or a probit model (Thomas 2001; Lewis 2005).

Researchers have also linked acquisition and retention in a single model. Using data for airline pilots' union membership, Thomas (2001) showed the importance of linking acquisition and retention decisions. She found that ignoring this link can lead to CLV estimates that are 6–52% different from her model. Thomas et al. (2004) found that while low price increased the probability of acquisition, it reduced the relationship duration. Therefore, customers who may be inclined to restart a relationship based on a promotion may not be the best customers in terms of retention.

8.4.1.2 Vector-Autoregressive (VAR) Models

VAR models have been developed recently in the time series literature. These models treat different components (e.g., acquisition, retention or CLV) as part of a dynamic system and examine how a movement in one variable affects other system variables. It then projects the long-run or equilibrium behavior of a variable or a group of variables of interest.

Villanueva et al. (2006) show how a VAR approach can be used for modeling customer acquisition. Their model is as follows:

$$
\begin{pmatrix} AM_t \\ AW_t \\ V_t \end{pmatrix} = \begin{pmatrix} a_{10} \\ a_{20} \\ a_{30} \end{pmatrix} + \sum_{l=1}^{p} \begin{pmatrix} a_{11}^l & a_{12}^l & a_{13}^l \\ a_{21}^l & a_{22}^l & a_{23}^l \\ a_{31}^l & a_{32}^l & a_{33}^l \end{pmatrix} \begin{pmatrix} AM_{t-l} \\ AW_{t-l} \\ V_{t-l} \end{pmatrix} + \begin{pmatrix} e_{1t} \\ e_{2t} \\ e_{3t} \end{pmatrix} \tag{8.8}
$$

where AM is the number of customers acquired through the firm's marketing actions, AW is the number of customers acquired from word-of-mouth, and V is the firm's performance. The subscript t stands for time, and p is the lag order of the model. In this VAR model, (e_{1t}, e_{2t}, e_{3t}) are white-noise disturbances distributed as N (O, Σ). The direct effects of acquisition on firm performance are captured by a_{31}, a_{32}. The cross effects among acquisition methods are estimated by a_{12}, a_{21}, performance feedback effects by a_{13}, a_{23} and finally, reinforcement (carryover) effects by a_{11}, a_{22}, a_{33}. As with all VAR models, instantaneous effects are reflected in the variance-covariance matrix of the residuals (Σ).

This approach has three main steps (details are in Dekimpe and Hanssens 2004). First, you examine the evolution of each variable to distinguish between temporary and permanent movements. This involves a series of unit-root tests and results in VAR model specifications in levels (temporary movements only) or changes (permanent movements). If there is evidence in favor of a long-run equilibrium between evolving variables (based on a *cointegration test*), then the resulting system's model will be of the vector-error correction type, which combines movements in levels and changes. Second, you estimate the VAR model, as given in Equation (8.8). This is typically done using least-square methods. Third, you derive impulse response functions that provide the short and long-run impact of a single shock in one of the system variables. Using this approach, Villanueva et al. (2006) found that marketing-induced customer acquisitions are more profitable in the short run, whereas word-of-mouth acquisitions generate performance more slowly but eventually become twice as valuable to the firm.

8.4.1.3 Diffusion Models

New customer acquisition is critical especially for new companies (or companies with really new products). In effect becoming a customer is equivalent to adopting a new product (i.e., adopting a new company to do business with). Consequently it can be modeled using standard diffusion models which allow for both independent adoption and contagion effects.

As an example, consider the well-known Bass (1969) model. This model can be used directly to monitor acquisitions of customers new to the category. In its discrete version, the model assumes the probability (hazard) of a non-customer becoming a customer is (p+qN/M). Here p is a coefficient of innovation, i.e. the tendency to adopt on their own, possibly influenced by company advertising, etc., q is a probability of imitation, i.e. response to the adoption by others, N is the total number who have adopted by the beginning of the time period, and M is the number who eventually will adopt (become customers), i.e. market potential. The number who adopt during period t is then

$$n_t = \left(p + q\frac{N}{M} \right)(M - N) \tag{8.9}$$

where $(M{-}N)$ is the number of potential customers who have not yet adopted. Rewriting this produces:

$$n_t = pM + (q - p)N - \frac{q}{M}N^2 \tag{8.10}$$

Forecasts can be made based on assumptions about p, q, and M, ideally based on close analogies or meta analyses (e.g. Sultan et al. 1990). As data becomes available, direct estimation of Equation (8.10) can be used by ordinary least squares or non-linear least squares (Srinavasan and Mason 1986). It is also possible to include marketing mix variables in this model as suggested in the diffusion literature (Bass et al. 1994).

Kim et al. (1995), Gupta et al. (2004) and Libai et al. (2006) follow this general approach. For example, Gupta et al. (2004) suggested that the cumulative number of customer N_t at any time t be modeled as

$$N_t = \frac{\alpha}{1 + \exp(-\beta - \gamma\,t)} \tag{8.11}$$

This S-shaped function asymptotes to α as time goes to infinity. The parameter γ captures the slope of the curve. The number of new customers acquired at any time is,

$$n_t = \frac{dN_t}{dt} = \frac{\alpha\,\gamma\,\exp(-\beta - \gamma\,t)}{[1 + \exp(-\beta - \gamma\,t)]^2} \tag{8.12}$$

This model, called the Technological Substitution Model, has been used by several researchers to model innovations and project the number of customers (e.g., Fisher and Pry 1971; Kim et al. 1995).

8.4.2 Customer Retention

Customer retention is the probability of a customer being "alive" or repeat buying from a firm. In contractual settings (e.g., cellular phones), customers inform the firm when they terminate their relationship. However, in non-contractual settings (e.g., Amazon), a firm has to infer whether a customer is still active. Most companies define a customer as active based on simple rules-of-thumb. For example, eBay defines a customer to be active if s/he has bid, bought or listed on its site during the last 12 months. In contrast, researchers generally rely on statistical models to assess the probability of retention.

As indicated in Tables 8.2 and 8.3, retention has a strong impact on CLV. Reichheld and Sasser (1990) found that a 5% increase in customer retention could increase firm profitability from 25 to 85%. Reichheld (1996) also emphasized the importance of customer retention. Gupta et al. (2004) also found that 1% improvement in customer retention may increase firm value by about 5%. The importance of retention has led researchers to spend a large amount of time and energy in modeling this component of CLV. Broadly speaking, these models can be classified into five categories.

8.4.2.1 Logit or Probit Models

In contractual settings where customer defection is observed, it is easy to develop a logit or a probit model of customer defection. This model takes the familiar logit (or probit) form as follows:

$$P(Churn) = \frac{1}{1 + \exp(\beta X)} \tag{8.13}$$

where X are the covariates. For example, the churn in a wireless phone industry can be modeled as a function of overage (spending above the monthly amount) or underage (leaving unused minutes) and other related factors (Iyengar 2006). Neslin et al. (2006) describe several models which were submitted by academics and practitioners as part of a "churn tournament." Due to its simplicity and ease of estimation, this approach is commonly used in the industry.

8.4.2.2 Hazard Models

One can also model the inter-purchase time using a hazard model. indeed, logit or probit models are a form of discrete time hazard models. Hazard models fall into two broad groups – accelerated failure time (AFT) or proportional hazard (PH) models. The AFT models have the following form (Kalbfleisch and Prentice 1980):

$$\ln(t_j) = \beta_j X_j + \sigma \mu_j \tag{8.14}$$

where t is the purchase duration for customer j and X are the covariates. If $\sigma = 1$ and μ has an extreme value distribution then we get an exponential duration model with constant hazard rate. Different specifications of σ and μ lead to different models such as Weibull or generalized gamma. Allenby et al. (1999), Lewis (2003) and Venkatesan and Kumar (2004) used a generalized gamma for modeling relationship duration. The kth interpurchase time for customer j can be represented as.

$$f(t_{jk}) = \frac{\gamma}{\Gamma(\alpha)\lambda_j^{\alpha\gamma}} t_{jk}^{\alpha\gamma-1} e^{-(t_{jj}/\lambda_j)^\gamma} \tag{8.15}$$

where α and γ are the shape parameters of the distribution and λ_j is the scale parameter for customer j. Customer heterogeneity is incorporated by allowing λ_j to vary across consumers according to an inverse generalized gamma distribution.

Proportional hazard models are another group of commonly used duration models. These models specify the hazard rate (λ) as a function of baseline hazard rate (λ_0) and covariates (X),

$$\lambda(t; X) = \lambda_0(t) \exp(\beta X) \tag{8.16}$$

Different specifications for the baseline hazard rate provide different duration models such as exponential, Weibull or Gompertz. This approach was used by Gonul et al. (2000), Knott et al. (2002) and Reinartz and Kumar (2003).

8.4.2.3 Probability Models

A special class of retention hazard models, also sometimes called probability or stochastic models, was first proposed for Schmittlein et al. (1987). These models use the recency and frequency of purchases to predict probability of a customer being alive in a specified future time period and are based on five assumptions. First, the number of transactions made by a customer is given by a Poisson process. Second, heterogeneity in transaction rate across customers is captured by a gamma distribution. Third, each customer's unobserved lifetime is exponentially distributed. Fourth, heterogeneity in dropout rates across customers also follows a gamma distribution. Finally, transaction and dropout rates are independent. Using these five assumptions, Schmittlein and Peterson (1994) derive a Pareto/NBD model. This model gives the probability of a customer being "alive" as (for $\alpha > \beta$):

$$P(alive|r, \alpha, s, \beta, X = x, t, T) = \left[1 + \frac{s}{r + x + s} \left\{ \left(\frac{\alpha + T}{\alpha + t} \right)^{r+x} \left(\frac{\beta + T}{\alpha + t} \right)^{s} \right. \right.$$
$$\left. \left. F(a_1, b_1; c_1, z_1(t)) - \left(\frac{\beta + T}{\alpha + T} \right)^{s} F(a_1, b_1; c_1; z_1(T)) \right\} \right]^{-1} \quad (8.17)$$

where r and α are the parameters of the gamma distribution that account for consumer heterogeneity in transactions; s and β are the parameters of the gamma distribution that capture consumer heterogeneity in dropout rates; x is the number of transactions (or frequency) of this customer in the past, t is time since trial at which the most recent transaction occurred, T is the time since trial and $F(\bullet)$ is the Gauss hypergeometric function.

This model and variations on it have been used by Colombo and Jiang (1999), Reinartz and Kumar (2000, 2003) and Fader et al. (2005). Note that this model implicitly assumes a constant retention rate (exponential dropout rate). Further, this model does not typically incorporate marketing covariates. Therefore its focus is to simply predict the probability of a customer being alive rather than identify which factors influence retention. Third, this model assumes Poisson transaction rates which are not suited for situations where customers have a non-random or periodic purchase behavior (e.g., grocery shopping every week). Nonetheless, it provides a good benchmark.

8.4.2.4 Markov Models

While most previous models implictly assume that a customer who defects is "lost for ever," in Markov models customers are allowed to switch among competitors and therefore considered as having "always a share". These models estimate the transition probabilities of a customer in a certain state moving to other states. Using these transition probabilities, CLV can be estimated as follows (Pfeifer and Carraway 2000),

$$\mathbf{V'} = \sum_{t=0}^{T} [(1 + i)^{-1} \mathbf{P}]^t \mathbf{R} \quad (8.18)$$

where $\mathbf{V'}$ is the vector of expected present value or CLV over the various transition states, $\mathbf{P}$ is the transition probability matrix which is assumed to be constant over time, and $\mathbf{R}$ is the margin vector which is also assumed to be constant over time. Bitran and Mondschein (1996) defined transition states based on RFM measures. Pfeifer and Carraway (2000) defined them based on customers' recency of purchases as well as an additional state for new or former customers. Rust et al. (2004) defined **P** as brand switching probabilities that vary over time as per a logit model. Further, they broke **R** into two components – the customer's expected purchase volume of a brand and his probability of buying a brand at time t.

Rust et al. (2004) argue that "lost for good" approach understates CLV since it does not allow a defected customer to return. Others have argued that this is not a serious problem since customers can be treated as renewable resource (Dreze and Bonfrer 2005) and lapsed customers can be re-acquired (Thomas et al. 2004). It is possible that the choice of the modeling approach depends on the context. For example, in many industries (e.g., cellular phone, cable and banks) customers are usually monogamous and maintain their relationship with only one company. In other contexts (e.g., consumer goods, airlines, and business-to-business relationship), customers simultaneously conduct business with multiple companies and the "always a share" approach may be more suitable.

8.4.2.5 Computer Science Models

The marketing literature has typically favored structured parametric models, such as logit, probit or hazard models. These models are based on utility theory and easy to interpret. In contrast, the vast computer science literature in data mining, machine learning and non-parametric statistics has generated many approaches that emphasize predictive ability. These include projection-pursuit models, neural network models (Hruschka 2006), decision tree models, spline-based models such as Generalized Additive Models (GAM) and Multivariate Adaptive Regression Splines (MARS), and support vector machines.

Many of these approaches may be more suitable to the study of customer churn where we typically have a very large number of variables, commonly referred to as the "curse of dimensionality". The sparseness of data in these situations inflates the variance of the estimates making traditional parametric and nonparametric models less useful. To overcome these difficulties, Hastie and Tibshirani (1990) proposed generalized additive models where the mean of the dependent variable depends on an additive predictor through a nonlinear link function. Another approach to overcome the curse of dimensionality is Multivariate Adaptive Regression Splines or MARS. This is a nonparametric regression procedure which operates as multiple piecewise linear regression with breakpoints that are estimated from data (Friedman 1991).

More recently, we have seen the use of support vector machines (SVM) for classification purposes. Instead of assuming that a linear line or plane can separate the two (or more) classes, this approach can handle situations where a curvilinear line or hyperplane is needed for better classification. Effectively the method transforms the raw data into a "featured space" using a mathematical kernel such that this space can classify objects using linear planes

(Vapnik 1998; Kecman 2001; Friedman 2003). In a recent study, Cui and Curry (2005) conducted extensive Monte Carlo simulations to compare predictions based on multinomial logit model and SVM. In all cases, SVM out predicted the logit model. In their simulation, the overall mean prediction rate of the logit was 72.7%, while the hit rate for SVM was 85.9%. Similarly, Giuffrida et al. (2000) report that a multivariate decision tree induction algorithm outperformed a logit model in identifying the best customer targets for cross-selling purposes.

Predictions can also be improved by combining models. The machine learning literature on bagging, the econometric literature on the combination of forecasts, and the statistical literature on model averaging suggest that weighting the predictions from many different models can yield improvements in predictive ability. Neslin et al. (2006) describe the approaches submitted by various academics and practitioners for a "churn tournament." The winning entry combined several trees, each typically having no more than two to eight terminal nodes, to improve prediction of customer churn through a gradient tree boosting procedure (Friedman 2003).

Recently, Lemmens and Croux (2006) used bagging and boosting techniques to predict churn for a US wireless customer database. Bagging (*B*ootstrap *AGG*regat*ING*) consists of sequentially estimating a binary choice model, called the base classifier in machine learning, from resampled versions of a calibration sample. The obtained classifiers form a group from which a final choice model is derived by aggregation (Breiman 1996). In boosting the sampling scheme is different from bagging. Boosting essentially consists of sequentially estimating a classifier to adaptively reweighted versions of the initial calibration sample. The weighting scheme gives misclassified customers an increased weight in the next iteration. This forces the classification method to concentrate on hard-to-classify customers. Lemmens and Croux (2006) compare the results from these methods with the binary logit model and find a relative gain in prediction of more than 16% for the gini coefficient and 26% for the top-decile lift. Using reasonable assumptions, they show that these differences can be worth over $3 million to the company. This is consistent with the results of Neslin et al. (2006) who also find that the prediction methods matter and can change profit by $100,000's.

8.4.3 Customer Expansion

The third component of CLV is the margin generated by a customer in each time period t. This margin depends on a customer's past purchase behavior as well as a firm's efforts in cross-selling and up-selling products to the customer. There are two broad approaches used in the literature to capture margin, one which models margin directly while the other explicitly models cross-selling. We briefly discuss both approaches.

8.4.3.1 Regression-Based Models of Margin

Several authors have made the assumption that margins for a customer remain constant. Reinartz and Kumar (2003) used average contribution margin of a customer based on his/her prior purchase behavior to project CLV as did Gupta et al. (2004). Importantly, Gupta and Lehmann (2005) show that this may be a reasonable assumption.

Venkatesan and Kumar (2004) found a simple regression model captured changes in contribution margin over time. Specifically, they modeled the change in contribution margin for customer j at time t as

$$\Delta CM_{jt} = \beta X_{jt} + e_{jt} \tag{8.19}$$

Covariates (X_{jt}) for their B2B application included lagged contribution margin, lagged quantity purchased, lagged firm size, lagged marketing efforts and industry category. Their model had an R^2 of 0.68 with several significant variables.

8.4.3.2 Logit or Probit Models

Verhoef et al. (2001) used an ordered probit to model consumers' cross-buying. Kumar et al. (2006) used a choice model to predict who will buy, what and when. Knott et al. (2002) used logit, discriminant analysis and neural networks models to predict which product a customer would buy next and found that all models performed roughly the same (predictive accuracy of 40–45%) and significantly better than random guessing (accuracy of 11–15%). In a field test, they further established that decisions based on their model had an ROI of 530% compared to the negative ROI from the heuristic used by the bank which provided the data. Knott et al. (2002). complemented their logit model which addressed which product a customer is likely to buy next with a hazard model which addressed when customers are likely to buy this product. They found that adding the hazard model leads to decisions which improved profits by 25%.

8.4.3.3 Multivariate Probit Model

In some product categories, such as financial services, customers acquire products in a natural sequence. For example, a customer may start his relationship with a bank with a checking and/or savings account and over time buy more complex products such as mortgage and brokerage services. Kamakura et al. (1991) argued that customers are likely to buy products when they reach a "financial maturity" commensurate with the complexity of the product. Recently, Li et al. (2005) used a similar conceptualization for cross-selling sequentially ordered financial products. Specifically, they used a multivariate probit model where consumer i makes binary purchase decision (buy or not buy) on each of the j products. The utility for consumer i for product j at time t is given as:

$$U_{ijt} = \beta_i |O_j - DM_{it-1}| + \gamma_{ij} X_{it} + \varepsilon_{ijt} \tag{8.20}$$

where O_j is the position of product j on the same continuum as demand maturity DM_{it-1} of consumer i and X includes other covariates that influence consumer's utility to buy a product. They further model demand or latent financial maturity as a function of cumulative ownership, monthly balances and the holding time of all available J accounts (covariates Z), weighted by the importance of each product (parameters λ):

$$DM_{it-1} = \sum_{j=1}^{J} [O_j D_{ijt-1} (\lambda_k Z_{ijk-1})] \tag{8.21}$$

8.4.3.4 Probability Models

Fader et al. (2005) use a probability model to estimate margins. The basic intuition of their model is that the margin estimates for a customer who, on average, has bought significantly more than the population mean should be brought down (i.e., regression to the mean) and vice versus. Fader et al. assume that the transactions of a customer are i.i.d. gamma distributed with parameters (p,v). They account for consumer heterogeneity by assuming that v is distributed gamma (q, γ) across customers. Under these assumptions, the expected average transaction value for a customer with an average spend of m_x across x transactions is given as:

$$E(M|p, q, \gamma, m_x, x) = \frac{(\gamma + m_x x)p}{px + q - 1} \tag{8.22}$$

Equation (8.22) is a weighted average of the population mean and the observed average transaction value of a customer.

8.4.4 Costs

Costs are integral part of estimating CLV. These costs can be grouped into three categories – variable costs (e.g., cost of goods sold), customer acquisition costs and customer retention costs. Apart from the challenges of cost allocation (e.g., how do you allocate advertising cost to acquisition vs. retention), there are also unanswered questions about projecting these costs in the future.

Traditionally variable costs have been described by monotonically decreasing curves (e.g. the experience curve, Moore's Law). For example the experience curve assumes variable cost decreases exponentially as cumulative production increases.

Similarly Moore's Law posited a doubling of transistors on a chip every two years. In the customer area, however, evidence suggests that acquisition costs may increase over time as the "low hanging fruit" is captured first and it becomes increasingly expensive to acquire subsequent (and more marginal, i.e. with lower reservation prices) customers. On the other hand, Gupta and Lehmann (2004) found that over a three (3) year period, acquisition costs for five (5) firms showed no discernable pattern, i.e. were essentially constant.

Modeling of acquisition costs, therefore, requires a flexible (non-linear) function. There is also a question of whether acquisition costs depend on time or the number of customers acquired by either the firm or the industry. Absent theory, a quadratic or cubic function may be the appropriate exploratory modeling form.

As in the case of acquisition costs, the pattern of retention costs over time is unclear. While learning and economics of scale should drive these down, intensified competition for customers as industries mature will drive them up.

One simple way to capture non-linear patterns in acquisition, retention, and expansion is through a polynomial. While based on no behavioral theory, small order polynomials (e.g. a quadratic) can parsimoniously approximate a variety of patterns. In addition, there is some theoretical support for such models. For example, in the context of brand choice, Bawa (1990) used Berlyene's theory to develop a repeat purchase probability that was quadratic and captured increasing, decreasing, and u-shaped repurchase probabilities based on the number of consecutive previous purchases as well as its squared value. This also suggests that the large literature on brand choice and variety seeking may provides useful analogues for considering customer choice of companies (brands) to do business with, i.e. what, when, and how much to buy (Gupta 1988).

8.5 CLV and Firm Value

At a conceptual level, a link between customer lifetime value and financial performance of a firm is guaranteed almost by definition. CLV focuses on the long-term profit rather than the short-term profit or market share. Therefore maximizing CLV is effectively maximizing the long-run profitability and financial health of a company. While not using the CLV per se, Kim et al. (1995) use a customer-based method to evaluate cellular communications companies. They show a strong relationship between both the net present value of cash flows and the growth in the number of customers and stock prices.

Gupta et al. (2004) explicitly built a link between CLV and firm value. They argued that since the value of a firm's customer base is the sum of the lifetime value of its current and future customers (also called *customer equity*) it should provide a good proxy for a firm's market value. They captured this by first building a model for the lifetime value for each cohort of customers and then aggregating across current and future cohorts. We briefly describe their approach for valuing customers.

We start with a simple scenario where a customer generates margin (m) for each period t, the discount rate is i and retention rate r is constant. The lifetime value of this customer is simply the present value of future income stream, or

$$CLV = \sum_{t=0}^{\infty} m_t \frac{r^t}{(1+i)^t} \tag{8.23}$$

To estimate the lifetime value of the entire customer based, recognize that the firm acquires new customers in each time period and that each cohort of customers goes through the defection and profit pattern shown in Table 8.4. Here the firm acquires n_0 customers at time 0 at an acquisition cost of c_0 per customer. Over time, customers defect such that the firm is left with $n_0 r$ customers at the end of period 1, $n_0 r^2$ customers at the end of period 2, and so on. Therefore the lifetime value of cohort 0 at current time 0 is given by

$$CLV_0 = n_0 \sum_{t=0}^{\infty} m_t \frac{r^t}{(1+i)^t} - n_0 c_0 \tag{8.24}$$

Cohort 1 follows a pattern similar to cohort 0 except that it is shifted in time by one period. Therefore, the lifetime value of cohort 1 at time 1 is given by

$$CLV_1 = n_1 \sum_{t=1}^{\infty} m_{t-1} \frac{r^{t-1}}{(1+i)^{t-1}} - n_1 c_1 \tag{8.25}$$

Table 8.4 Number of customers and margins for each cohort

Time	Cohort 0 Customers	Margin	Cohort 1 Customers	Margin	Cohort 2 Customers	Margin
0	n_0	m_0				
1	$n_0 r$	m_1	n_1	m_0		
2	$n_0 r^2$	m_2	$n_1 r$	m_1	n_2	m_0
3	$n_0 r^3$	m_3	$n_1 r^2$	m_2	$n_2 r$	m_1
.	.	.	$n_1 r^2$	m_3	$n_2 r^2$	m_2
.	.	.	.	.	$n_2 r^3$	m_3
.	.	.	.	.	.	.

where n_1 represents the customers acquired at time 1 at an acquisition cost of c_1 per customer In present value, this becomes:

$$CLV_1 = \frac{n_1}{1+i} \sum_{t=1}^{\infty} m_{t-1} \frac{r^{t-1}}{(1+i)^{t-1}} - \frac{n_1 c_1}{1+i} \qquad (8.26)$$

In general, the lifetime value for the k-th cohort at current time 0 is given by

$$CLV_k = \frac{n_k}{(1+i)^k} \sum_{t=k}^{\infty} m_{t-k} \frac{r^{t-k}}{(1+i)^{t-k}} - \frac{n_k c_k}{(1+i)^k} \qquad (8.27)$$

The value of the firm's customer base is then the sum of the lifetime value of all cohorts.

$$Value = \sum_{k=0}^{\infty} \frac{n_k}{(1+i)^k} \sum_{t=k}^{\infty} m_{t-k} \frac{r^{t-k}}{(1+i)^{t-k}} - \sum_{k=0}^{\infty} \frac{n_k c_k}{(1+i)^k} \qquad (8.28)$$

Equation (8.28) provides customer value before any tax considerations. The next step is to estimate the five key inputs to this model: the number of customers and their growth (if any), margin per customer, customer retention rate, customer acquisition cost, and discount rate for the firm. Historical data along with statistical models can be used to forecast the value of these input variables. For example, Gupta et al. (2004) used Equation (8.12) to estimate the number of customers in the future. Similar models can be created for other variables.

8.5.1 Application of Customer-Based Valuation

The premise of this valuation approach is simple—if we forecast the growth in number of customers, margin per customer, etc., then it is easy to value the current and future customer base of a company. To the extent that this customer base forms a large part of a company's overall value, it provides a useful proxy for firm value.

While the customer-based valuation approach benefits tremendously from detailed customer-level information contained in the database of many companies, Gupta et al. based their analysis on published information such as annual reports and other financial statements. This makes their approach valuable for external constituencies such as investors, financial analysts, and acquiring companies who may not have access to detailed internal data of a company.

They applied this model to five companies. These companies were chosen because: (a) all the firms are primarily based on customer-driven business; (b) they publicly reported customer data each quarter; and (c) many of them were difficult to evaluate using traditional financial methods. The basic data for the five companies is given in Table 8.5.

Table 8.5 Customer data for companies in the analysis

Company	Data Period From	To	No. of Customers	Quarterly Margin	Acquisition Cost	Retention Rate
Amazon	Mar 1997	Mar 2002	33,800,000	$3.87	$7.70	70%
Ameritrade	Sep 1997	Mar 2002	1,877,000	$50.39	$203.44	95%
Capital One	Dec 1996	Mar 2002	46,600,000	$13.71	$75.49	85%
eBay	Dec 1996	Mar 2002	46,100,000	$4.31	$11.26	80%
E*Trade	Dec 1997	Mar 2002	4,117,370	$43.02	$391.00	95%

Number of customers is at the end of March 2002.
Quarterly margin is per customer based on the average of the last four quarters.
Acquisition cost is per customer based on the average of the last four quarters.
Source: Sunil Gupta, Donald R. Lehmann, and Jennifer Stuart, "Valuing Customers," Journal of Marketing Research (February 2004), pp. 7–18; and company reports. Reprinted by permission from the American Marketing Association.

Almost all the data were gathered through the companies' financial statements. The growth in number of customers over time was S-shaped as is shown in Figs. 8.3, 8.4, 8.5, 8.6 and 8.7. All five companies exhibit an S-shaped growth pattern which made it fairly easy to predict the future growth in customers and hence the future source of revenues and profits. Figure 8.8 shows the results and compares estimates of aggregate customer value (post-tax) with the reported market value of the firms as of March 2002. The customer-value-based estimates are reasonably close to the market values for E*Trade, Ameritrade, and to some extent Capital One, but are significantly lower for Amazon and eBay.

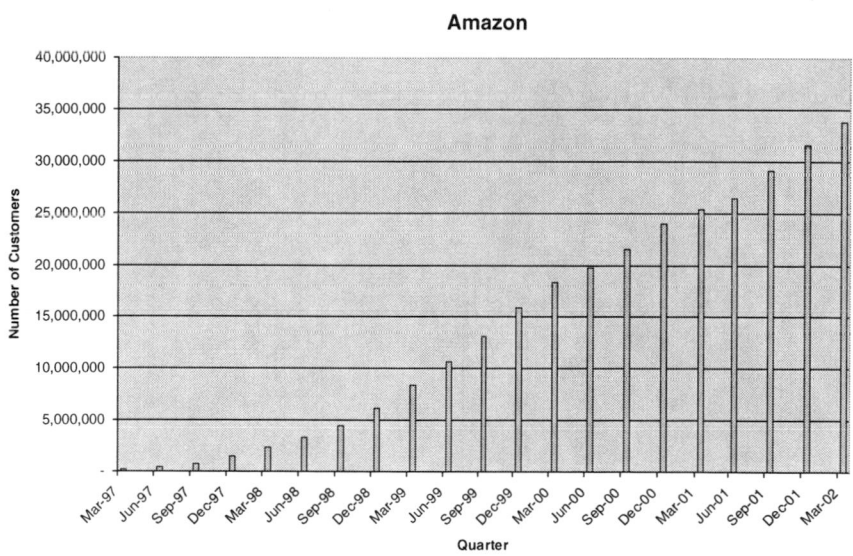

Fig. 8.3 Customer growth for Amazon

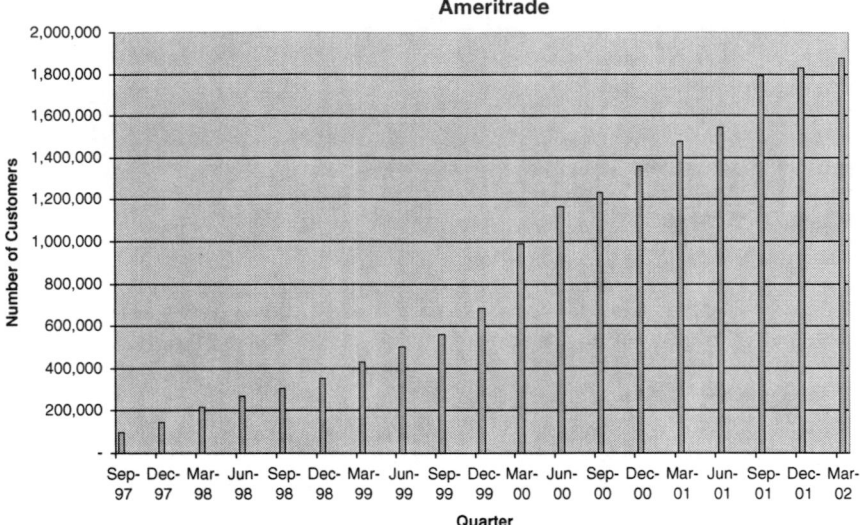

Fig. 8.4 Customer growth for Ameritrade

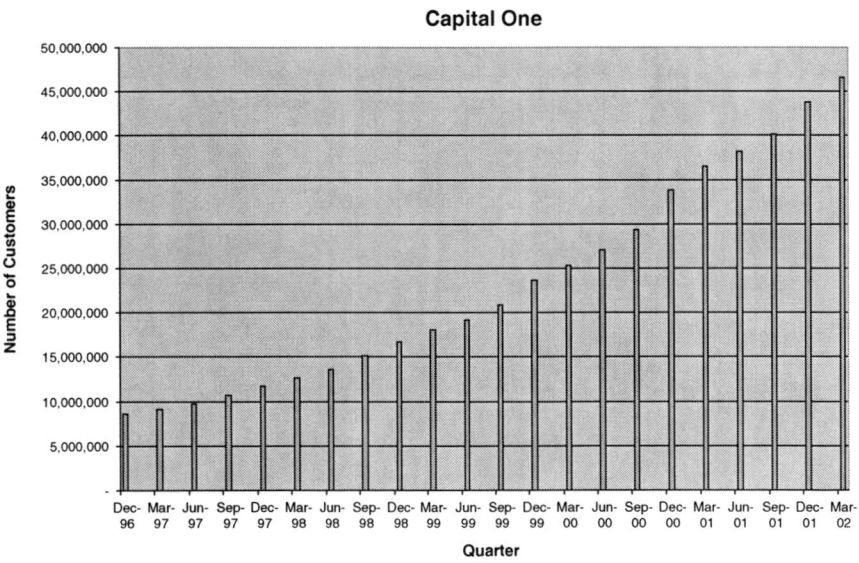

Fig. 8.5 Customer growth for capital one

While it is possible that these two firms may achieve a much higher growth rate in customers or margins than estimated or that they have some other very large "option value" that is not captured here, this analysis raises questions about the market value of these firms.

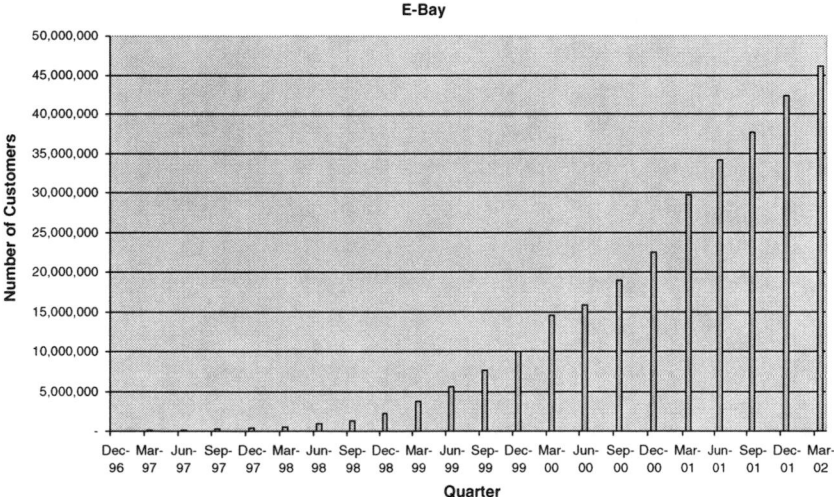

Fig. 8.6 Customer growth for eBay

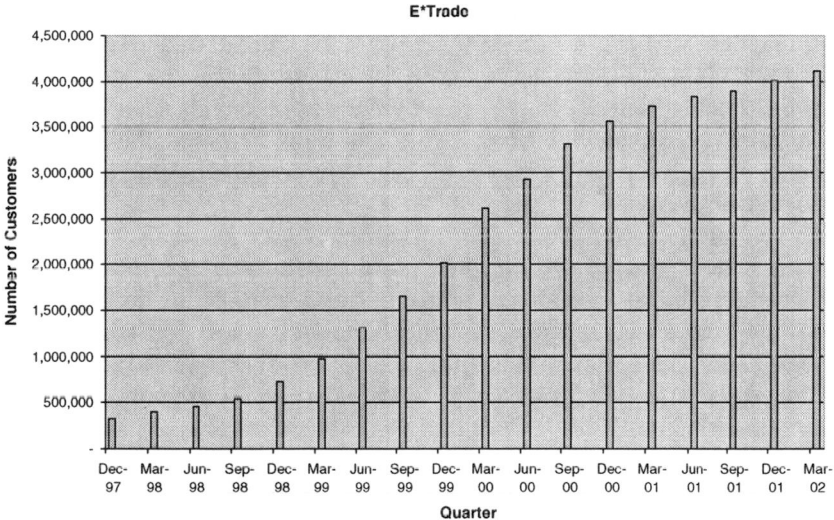

Fig. 8.7 Customer growth for E*Trade

8.5.2 Additional Studies

Following Gupta et al. (2004), other studies also attempted to establish the link between CLV and firm value. Wiesel and Skiera (2005) demonstrated the algebraic link between CLV and shareholder value. They then analyzed the

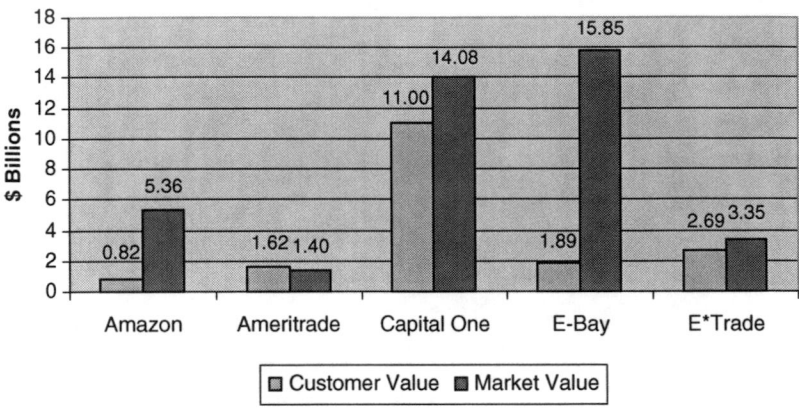

Fig. 8.8 Customer and firm value

shareholder value of two internet firms (T-online and Freenet) and found that their measure of consumer equity (aggregate CLV) closely approximated the value of the two firms. Recently, Libai et al. (2006) used a Bass diffusion model with customer defection and replicated the customer valuation for the same five firms examined by Gupta et al. (2004). Rust et al. (2004) used a survey of 100 customers for airlines to estimate CLV for American Airlines. Using this estimate and the total number of airline passengers, they estimated the overall customer value of American Airlines in 1999 as $7.3 billion. Considering that this estimate did not include international traffic and other non flight sources of revenue, it was reasonably close to the $9.7 billion market value of American Airlines at that time.

Gupta and Lehmann (2005, 2006) discussed how customer-based valuation approaches sometimes do better when traditional financial methods (e.g., DCF or P/E ratio) fail. They also noted that after the bursting of the dot com bubble many financial analysts became skeptical about customer metrics. However, this skepticism is misplaced if one deals with CLV rather than simply observing the number of page views, stickiness or number of customers (without considering their profitability).

8.6 Link Between Customer Mind-Set and CLV

While CLV impacts the financial performance of a firm, CLV itself is a consequence of marketing actions. As suggested by Fig. 8.1, marketing actions influence customers' attitudes, satisfaction and other mind-set metrics which then impact product-market results which in turn drive financial performance. For example, Berger et al. (2002) develop a framework to assess the impact of marketing actions on customer lifetime value. In this framework CLV influences the allocation of marketing resources but is also influenced by marketing actions. CLV, which captures customer level behavior, depends on acquisition, retention and expansion. While many studies have followed this general approach of modeling the direct impact of marketing actions on acquisition, retention or CLV, others have captured their influence through perceptual metrics such as customer satisfaction (Gupta and Zeithaml 2006). In this section we focus on the latter link (Chapter 10 of this book discusses the other link in more detail).

Hallowell (1996) used a regression-based model to study customers of a retail bank and found that satisfaction was positively related to retention. Using a logistic regression on retail bank customers, Rust and Zahorik (1993) found that increasing customer satisfaction from 4.2 to 4.7 on a 5-point scale is likely to increase retention from 95.9 to 96.5%. Notice, this type of empirical result makes marketing investment accountable. While it is difficult to say how much a company should spend in increasing customer satisfaction from 4.2 to 4.7, knowing its link with retention and thus CLV makes it possible to assess the return on marketing investment.

Ittner and Larcker (1998) also used a regression-based model and found that a 10-point increase in the satisfaction (0-100 scale) of telecommunication customers increased their retention by 2% and revenues by $195. Using business unit data from 73 retail bank branches, they also demonstrated that satisfaction was positively related to revenues and number of customers (retention). Bolton (1998) used a hazard model to examine the duration of relationship of cellular phone customers by tracking their actual behavior over a 22 month period. Using two waves of surveys to get information on satisfaction, she found that satisfaction was positively related to the duration of relationship but explained only 8% of the variance.

Using retail bank data and a regression-based model, Loveman (1998) showed that satisfaction was positively related to customer retention, number of services used by a customer (cross-sell), and customer share of wallet. He further found that customer satisfaction had its biggest impact on cross-selling. In contrast, Verhoef et al. (2001) used data from insurance customers over two time periods and concluded that there was no main effect of satisfaction on cross-buying. Consistent with Bolton (1998), however, they found that as relationship length increases, the effect of satisfaction on cross-buying increases.

Verhoef et al. (2001) also tested the impact of trust, commitment, and satisfaction on customer referrals and number of services purchased (cross-selling). While trust, affective commitment, and satisfaction were positively related to customer referrals, only affective commitment had a positive impact on the number of services purchased. Bolton et al. (2000) showed that loyalty rewards programs have a positive effect on customer evaluations, behavior, and repeat purchase intentions.

Logically, greater satisfaction should lead to a higher repurchase (retention) rate. Importantly, customers who feel an attachment to the company do have higher retention rates (Gustafson et al., 2005). Indeed satisfaction is generally positively related to intention to purchase. However, in survey research some of the correlation may be due to method or halo effects, i.e. respondents answering both questions on the basis of response style or overall attitude (Chandon et al., 2005). While higher intentions are better ceteris paribus, they do not always translate into behavior (Juster, 1966; Kalwani and Silk 1982; Jamierson and Bass 1989; Bolton 1998; Kamakura et al. 2002; Mittal and Kamakura 2001). For example, Mazursky and Geva (1989) found that satisfaction and intentions were highly correlated when measured in the same survey (time t_1) but that the same subjects' satisfaction at t_1 had no correlation with their intentions after a 2-week interval (t_2). A number of factors (e.g. purchase convenience) influence the relation of satisfaction to behavior at the individual level (Morwitz and Schmittlein 1992).

Several studies have also shown that the relationship between satisfaction and retention is nonlinear. Jones and Sasser (1995) argued that there is a major difference between satisfied and very satisfied customers. While the latter are loyal, the former may defect. Mittal and Kamakura (2001) confirmed that the relationship between satisfaction and actual behavior exhibited increasing returns (i.e., is a convex function). They found that a linear model under-estimated the impact of a change in satisfaction score from 4 to 5 by 64%, causing managers to incorrectly pull back resources from "completely" satisfying customers. In contrast, the difference between "somewhat" and "very dissatisfied" customers is not as large as a linear model suggests. Ittner and Larcker (1998) also found that the relationship between satisfaction and retention was characterized by several satisfaction thresholds that must be reached before retention increases. In contrast to Jones and Sasser (1995) and Mittal and Kamakura (2001), they found that at very high level of satisfaction, retention shows diminishing, rather than increasing returns. In an interesting study, Mittal and Kamakura (2001) show that while the satisfaction-intention link shows decreasing returns, the satisfaction-behavior link shows increasing returns.

8.7 Link Between Customer Mind-Set and Firm Value

Another important link in the value chain (Fig. 8.1) is the link between customer mind-set and financial performance. A large number of studies have focused on establishing a link between customer satisfaction and firm's financial performance. Researchers have used different metrics to assess financial performance: profit, stock price, Tobin's q (the ratio of the market value of a firm to the replacement cost of its tangible assets), return on assets (ROA), return on investment (ROI), abnormal earnings, and cash flows (Rust et al. 2004). Most studies have used a regression-based model (linear, log or log-log). Most of these studies have been cross-sectional in nature and therefore examined the differences in firms' financial performance as a function of customer satisfaction and other firm or industry-level variables.

Most of these studies have shown a strong link between customer satisfaction and firm profitability. For example, Anderson et al. (1994) showed that a 1-point increase in satisfaction (on a 100-point scale) each year over five years would have generated over a 10% increase in ROA for Swedish firms. When Anderson et al. (1997) compared the impact of satisfaction for goods and services, they found that both customer satisfaction and productivity were positively associated with ROI for goods and services. However, the interaction between satisfaction and productivity was positive for goods and negative for services. Hallowell (1996) found a positive link between customer satisfaction and profitability using data on retail banking customers.

Some studies demonstrate the link between customer satisfaction at the aggregate level and measures of shareholder value. Ittner and Larcker (1998) found that firm-level satisfaction measures impacted the stock market. Bernhardt et al. (2000) showed that an increase in customer satisfaction has a positive impact on profits. Anderson et al. (2004) also found a positive association between customer satisfaction (satisfaction scores based on ACSI) and shareholder value. Further, Fornell et al. (2006) have shown that satisfied customers produce both higher returns and less risk and that firms with high satisfaction ratings out perform the market.

By contrast, relatively little is known about the direct impact of most other mind-set measures such as awareness, associations, attitude, attachment, and advocacy on CLV or firm value. It is logical to assume that changes in customer awareness, attitude and attachment towards a firm would influence the shareholder value of the firm. However, most marketing studies have focused their attention on establishing a link between marketing actions like advertising and sales promotions and customer mind-set variables. For these perceptual measures to be managerially meaningful and financially accountable, a link between them and CLV needs to be established.

8.8 Future Research

In the last decade, there have been significant methodological improvements as well as substantive applications of the CLV concept. However, much remains to be done. Here we briefly highlight some fruitful areas for future research.

8.8.1 Network Effects

Most of the research on CLV has implicitly assumed that the value of a customer is independent of other customers. However, in many situations customer network effects can be strong and ignoring them may lead to underestimating CLV. Hogan et al. (2003) showed that word of mouth or direct network effects can be substantial for online banking. Villanueva et al. (2006) found that word-of-mouth driven customer acquisitions are twice as valuable to the firm as acquisitions generated via traditional marketing instruments. As word-of-mouth and buzz marketing become more and more important, we need to have better understanding of how WOM contributes to the value of a customer over and beyond his/her purchases.

In many situations there are also strong indirect network effects. For example, firms such as Ebay and Monster.com have two related populations (buyers and seller, or job seekers and employers). The growth in one population affects the growth of the other populations and vice versa. However, only one population actually generates direct profit for the firm (e.g., sellers for ebay and employers for Monster). How much should a firm pay to acquire the non-paying buyers or job-seekers? Gupta et al. (2006) is one of the first studies to examine this issue and more work is needed in this important area.

With the increasing popularity of network communities such as myspace or facebook, it is clear that such networks are important and more complex than simply two populations of buyers and sellers. Significant research has been done in social science, physics and computer science to study complex networks and the interactions of various agents (e.g., Watts 2003; Newman 2003; Wasserman and Faust 2005). Gupta et al. (2006) have used this framework to examine the tangible (through direct purchases or CLV) as well as intangible (through network) value of a customer. Their results show that a large proportion of customers with low CLV may have significant intangible value, i.e. may be very valuable to a firm even if they do not provide any direct revenues or CLV. Once again, this is a relatively new area where more work is needed.

8.8.2 Competition

Most studies of CLV use companies' internal customer data. These databases are generally large – many track every transaction of millions of customers over several years. In spite of this rich data, firms lack information about competition. In other words they have no information about customers' wallet share. Even if a customer spends a small amount of money with a firm, he may have a large potential if he spends a large amount of money with a competitor. Interestingly, the majority of marketing models have been built in the last two decades using scanner data where we have information about a firm as well as its competitors. This information is missing in most CLV models.

A few studies have found innovative ways to overcome this problem. For example, Kamakura et al. (2003) supplemented a bank's internal customer database with a survey of a few thousand customers. Since it is impossible to survey millions of bank customers, they used the data from the survey sample to impute the missing information (e.g., wallet share) for the remaining customers in the database. We need more studies that either uses such innovative methods to account for competition or that show the potential bias from ignoring this information.

8.8.3 Brand and Customer Equity

Two streams of marketing literature, brand equity and customer equity, have developed almost in parallel without any link between the two. As indicated earlier, there are several studies that establish a link between CLV or customer equity and firm value. Similarly, several studies have established a link between brand equity and firm's financial performance (e.g., Aaker and Jacobson 1994, 2001). However, there are virtually no studies that connect these two parallel streams.

8.8.4 Costs

Marketing has typically focused on building models of sales or share. Consequently we have paid very little attention to costs. Most studies either assume a percentage margin or assume stable costs. Yet, costs are an important component that determines margin and hence the CLV. As briefly discussed earlier, cost allocation also creates some challenges. For example, it is not clear how to allocate many marketing activities (e.g., advertising) into acquisition versus retention costs. We also have not developed models to forecast these costs. Without such forecasts, we cannot appropriately estimate future margins and future CLV. Overall, then, we need to better bridge the gap between marketing and accounting to understand and model costs.

8.9 Conclusion

Customer lifetime value is an important construct. It provides specific guidelines on customer selection, campaign management, and retention programs as well as resource allocation between acquisition and retention. By moving beyond satisfaction, share or sales, it also makes marketing more accountable. Since CLV is inherently a long term customer construct, it encourages managers to be customer oriented and long-term focused. Finally, by establishing a link between CLV and firm value, it bridges the gap between marketing and finance. This means some marketing metrics (e.g., retention) are important enough for senior managers to track, since they drive future stock prices The sooner people in both marketing and finance "get it", the better.

References

Aaker, D., R. Jacobson. 1994. The Financial Information Content of Perceived Quality. *Journal of Marketing Research* **31**(2) 191–201.

——, ——. 2001. The Value Relevance of Brand Attitude in High-Technology Markets. *Journal of Marketing Research.* **38**(November) 485–493.

Allenby, G., R. Leone, L. Jen. 1999. A Dynamic Model of Purchase Timing with Application to Direct Marketing. *Journal of the American Statistical Association* **94** 365–374.

Anderson, E.W., C. Fornell, D.R. Lehmann. 1994. Customer Satisfaction, Market Share, and Profitability: Findings from Sweden. *Journal of Marketing* **58** 53–66.

Anderson, E.W., C. Fornell, R. Rust. 1997. Customer Satisfaction, Productivity, and Profitability: Differences Between Good and Services. *Marketing Science* **16**(2) 129–145.

Anderson, E.W., C. Fornell, S.K. Mazvancheryl. 2004. Customer Satisfaction and Shareholder Value. *Journal of Marketing* **68**(October) 172–185.

Bass, F.M. 1969. A New Product Growth Model for Consumer Durables. *Management Science* **69**(15), (January) 215–227.

Berger, P.D., N.L. Nasr. 1998. Customer Lifetime Value: Marketing Models and Applications. *Journal of Interactive Marketing* **12**(1) 17–30.

Berger, P., R. Bolton, D. Bowman, E. Briggs, V. Kumar, A. Parasuraman, C. Terry. 2002. Marketing Actions and the Value of Customer Assets: A Framework for Customer Asset Management. *Journal of Service Research* **5**(1) 39–54.

Bernhardt, K., N. Donthu, P. Kennett. 2000. A Longitudinal Analysis of Satisfaction and Profitability. *Journal of Business Research* **5**(1) 39–54.

Bitran, G., S. Mondschein. 1996. Mailing Decisions in the Catalog Sales Industry. *Management Science* **42**(9).

Blattberg, R.C., G. Getz, J.S. Thomas. 2001. Customer Equity: Building and Managing Relationships as Valuable Assets. Harvard Business School, Boston.

Bolton, R.N. 1998. A Dynamic Model of the Duration of the Customer's Relationship with a Continuous Service Provider: The Role of Satisfaction. *Marketing Science* **17**(1) 45–65.

Bolton, R., P.K. Kannan, M.D. Bramlett. 2000. Implications of Loyalty Program Membership and Service Experience for Customer Retention and Value. *Journal of the Academy of Marketing Science.* Winter 95–108.

Breiman, L. 1996. Bagging Predictors. *Machine Learning* **24**(2) 123–140.

Chandon, P., V.G. Morwitz, W.J. Reinartz. 2005. Do Intentions Really Predict Behavior: Self-Generated Validity Effects in Survey Research. *Journal of Marketing* **69**(April) 1–14.

Colombo, R., W. Jiang. 1999. A Stochastic RFM Model. *Journal of Interactive Marketing* **13**(Summer) 2–12.

Cui, D., D. Curry. 2005. Prediction in Marketing Using the Support Vector Machine. *Marketing Science* **24**(Fall) 595–615.

Dekimpe, M., D.M. Hanssens. 2004. Persistence Modeling for Assessing Marketing Strategy Performance, in *Assessing Marketing Strategy Performance*, C. Moorman and D. Lehmann, eds. Marketing Science Institute, Cambridge, MA.

Doyle, P. 2000. Value-Based Marketing – Marketing Strategies for Corporate Growth and Shareholder Value. John Wiley & Sons, New York.

Dréze, X., A. Bonfrer. 2005. Moving From Customer Lifetime Value to Customer Equity. *Working Paper*, University of Pennsylvania.

Fader, P., B. Hardie, Ka Lee. 2005. RFM and CLV: Using Iso-Value Curves for Customer Base Analysis. *Journal of Marketing Research.* **42**(4) 415–430.

Farris, Paul W., M.J. Moore. 2004. The Profit Impact of Marketing Strategy Project. Cambridge University Press, Cambridge, U.K.

Fornell, C., S. Mithas, F. Morgeson, M.S. Krishnan. 2006. Customer Satisfaction and Stock Prices: High Risk, Low Return. *Journal of Marketing*. January 3–14.

Friedman, J.H. 1991. Multivariate Adaptive Regression Splines. (with discussion). *Annals of Statistics* **19** 1.

Friedman, J.H. 2003. Recent Advances in Predictive (Machine) Learning. *Working Paper,* Department of Statistics, Stanford University, CA.

Giuffrida, G., W. Chu, D. Hanssens. 2000. Mining Classification Rules from Datasets with Large Number of Many-Valued Attributes. in *Lecture Notes in Computer Science, 1777.* Springer Verlag.

Gonul, F., B.-Do Kim, M. Shi. 2000. Mailing Smarter to Catalog Customers. *Journal of Interactive Marketing*. **14**(2) 2–16.

Gruca, T.S., L.L. Lego. 2003. Customer Satisfaction, Cash Flow, and Shareholder Value. *Working Paper (03-106)*. *Marketing Science Institute.*

Gruca, T.S., L.L. Lego. 2005. Customer Satisfaction, Cash Flow, and Shareholder Value. *Journal of Marketing*. **69**(July) 115–130.

Gupta, S., D.R. Lehmann. 2003. Customers as Assets. *Journal of Interactive Marketing*. **17**(1) 9–24.

Gupta, S., D.R. Lehmann. 2005. *Managing Customers as Investments*. Wharton School Publishing.

Gupta, S., D.R. Lehmann. 2006. Customer Lifetime Value and Firm Valuation. *Journal of Relationship Marketing*. **5**(2/3), 87–110.

Gupta, S., V. Zeithaml. 2006. Customer Metrics and Their Impact on Financial Performance. *Working Paper*. Columbia University.

Gupta, S., D.R. Lehmann, J.A. Stuart. 2004. Valuing Customers. *Journal of Marketing Research*. **41**(1) 7–18.

Gupta, S., C. Mela, J.M. Vidal-Sanz. 2006. The Value of a 'Free' Customer. *Working Paper*. Harvard Business School.

Gupta, S., S. Han, R. Iyengar. 2006. The Tangible and Intangible Value of Customers. *Working Paper*. Columbia University.

Gustafsson, A., M.D. Johnson, I. Roos. 2005. The Effects of Customer Satisfaction, Relationship Commitment Dimensions, and Triggers on Customer Retention. *Journal of Marketing*. **69**(4) 210–218.

Hallowell, R. 1996. The Relationships of Customer Satisfaction, Customer Loyalty, and Profitability: An Empirical Study. *International Journal of Service Industry Management*. **7**(4) 27–42.

Hastie, T.J., R.J. Tibshirani. 1990. *Generalized Additive Models*. Chapman and Hall, NY.

Hogan, J.E., K.N. Lemon, B. Libai. 2003. What is the True Value of a Lost Customer? *Journal of Service Research* **5**(3) (February) 196–208.

Hogan, J.E., D.R. Lehmann, M. Merino, R.K. Srivastava, J.S. Thomas, P.C. Verhoef. 2002. Linking Customer Assets to Financial Performance. *Journal of Service Research*. **5**(1) (August) 26–38.

Hruschka, H. 2006. Neural Nets and Genetic Algorithms in Marketing," in *Handbook of Marketing Decision Models*, editor, Berend Wierenga, Rotterdam.

Ittner, C., D. Larcker. 1998. Are Non-Financial Measures Leading Indicators of Financial Performance? An Analysis of Customer Satisfaction. *Journal of Accounting Research*. **36**(Supplement) 1–35.

Iyengar, R. 2006. A Demand Analysis of Wireless Services Under Nonlinear Pricing Schemes. *Working Paper,* Wharton School, University of Pennsylvania.

Jain, D., S. Singh. 2002. Customer Lifetime Value Research in Marketing: A Review and Future Directions. *Journal of Interactive Marketing*. **16**(2).

Jamieson, L., F. Bass. 1989. Adjusting Stated Intention Measures to Predict Trial Purchase of New Products: A Comparison of Models and Methods. *Journal of Marketing Research*. **26**(August) 336–345.

Jedidi, K., C. Mela, S. Gupta. 1999. Managing Advertising and Promotion for Long-Run Profitability. *Marketing Science*. **18**(1) 1–22.

Jones, T., E. Sasser. 1995. Why Satisfied Customers Defect. *Harvard Business Review*. **73**(November-December) 88–99.

Juster, T. 1966. Consumer Buying Intentions and Purchase Probability: An Experiment in Survey Design. *Journal of the American Statistical Association*. **61**(September) 658–697.

Kalbfleisch, J., R. Prentice. 1980. *Statistical Analysis of Failure Time Data*. John Wiley and Sons, New York.

Kalwani, M., A. Silk. 1982. On the Reliability and Predictive Validity of Purchase Intention Measures. *Marketing Science*. 1(Summer) 243–286.

Kamakura, W., S. Ramaswami, R. Srivastava. 1991. Applying Latent Trait Analysis in the Evaluation of Prospects for Cross-Selling of Financial Services. *International Journal of Research in Marketing*. **8** 329–349.

Kamakura, W., V. Mittal, F. de Rosa, Jose Afonso Mazzon 2002. Assessing the Service-Profit Chain. *Marketing Science*. **21**(3) 294–317.

Kamakura, W.A., M. Wedel, F. de Rosa, Jose Afonso Mazzon 2003. Cross-Selling Through Database Marketing: Mixed Data Factor Analyzer for Data Augmentation and Prediction. *International Journal of Research in Marketing*. **20**(1), (March) 45–65.

Kamakura, W.A., B. Kossar, M. Wedel 2004. Identifying Innovators for the Cross-Selling of New Products. *Management Science*. **50**(8) 1120–1133.

Kecman, V. 2001. *Learning and Soft Computing: Support Vector Machines, Neural Networks and Fuzzy Logic Models*. The MIT Press, Cambridge, MA.

Keller, K.L., D.R. Lehmann. 2003. How Do Brands Create Value?. *Marketing Management*. **12**(3), (May/June) 26–31.

Kim, N., V. Mahajan, R.K. Srivastava. 1995. Determining the Going Market Value of a Business in an Emerging Information Technology Industry: The Case of the Cellular Communications Industry. *Technological Forecasting and Social Change*. **49** 257–279.

Knott Aaron, A. Hayes, S. Neslin. 2002. Next-Product-to-Buy Models for Cross-Selling Applications. *Journal of Interactive Marketing*. **16**(3).

Kumar, V., W. Reinartz. 2006. *Customer Relationship Management: A Database Approach*. John Wiley and Sons, NY.

Kumar, V., R. Venkatesan, W. Reinartz. 2006. Knowing What to Sell, When to Whom. *Harvard Business Review*. March 131–137.

Lemmens, A., C. Croux. 2006. Bagging and Boosting Classification Trees to Predict Churn. *Journal of Marketing Research*. **43**(2), 276–286.

Lewis, M. 2003. Customer Acquisition Promotions and Customer Asset Value. *Working Paper*. University of Florida.

Lewis, M. 2005a. A Dynamic Programming Approach to Customer Relationship Pricing. *Management Science*. **51**(6)986–994.

Li, S., B. Sun, R. Wilcox. 2005. Cross-Selling Sequentially Ordered Products: An Application to Consumer Banking Services. *Journal of Marketing Research*. **42**(2) 233–239.

Libai, B., E. Muller, R. Peres. 2006. The Diffusion of Services. *Working Paper*. Tel Aviv University.

Loveman, G.W. 1998. Employee Satisfaction, Customer Loyalty, and Financial Performance: An Empirical Examination of the Service Profit Chain in Retail Banking. *Journal of Service Research*. **1**(1) 18–31.

Malthouse, E.C., R.C. Blattberg. 2005. Can We Predict Customer Lifetime Value? *Journal of Interactive Marketing*. **19**(1) 2–16.

Mazursky David, A. Geva. 1989. Temporal Decay in Satisfaction-Intention Relationship. *Psychology and Marketing*. **6**(3) 211–227.

Mela, C., S. Gupta, D.R. Lehmann. 1997. The Long Term Impact of Promotion and Advertising on Consumer brand Choice. *Journal of Marketing Research.* **34**(May) 248–61.

Mittal, V., W. Kamakura. 2001. Satisfaction, Repurchase Intent, and Repurchase Behavior: Investigating the Moderating Effect of Customer Characteristics. *Journal of Marketing Research.* **38**(1) 131–142.

Morwitz, V.G., D. C. Schmittlein. 1992. Using Segmentation to Improve Sales Forecasts Based on Purchase Intent: Which 'Intenders' Actually Buy? *Journal of Marketing Research* **29**(November) 391–405.

Neslin, S., S. Gupta, W. Kamakura, J. Lu, C. Mason 2006. Defection Detection: Measuring and Understanding the Predictive Accuracy of Customer Churn Models. *Journal of Marketing Research.* **43**(2), 204–211.

Newman, M.E.J. 2003. The Structure and Function of Complex Networks. SIAM Review. **45**(2) 167–256.

Pfeifer, P.E., R.L. Carraway. 2000. Modeling Customer Relationships as Markov Chains. *Journal of Interactive Marketing.* **14**(2) 43–55.

Pfeifer, P. E., P.W. Farris. 2004. The Elasticity of Customer Value to Retention: The Duration of a Customer Relationship. *Journal of Interactive Marketing.* **18**(2) 20–31.

Reichheld, F.F. 1996. *The Loyalty Effect.* Harvard Business School Press.

Reichheld, F. F., W. Earl Sasser Jr. 1990. "Zero Defections: Quality Comes to Services. *Harvard Business Review.* (September-October) 105–111.

Reichheld, F. F. 2003. The One Number You Need. *Harvard Business Review.* (December) 46–54.

Reinartz, W.J., V. Kumar. 2000. On the Profitability of Long-Life Customers in a Noncontractual Setting: An Empirical Investigation and Implications for Marketing. *Journal of Marketing.* **64**(October) 17–35.

——. 2003. The Impact of Customer Relationship Characteristics on Profitable Lifetime Duration. *Journal of Marketing.* **64**(January) 77–99.

Reinartz, W.J., J. Thomas, V. Kumar. 2005. Balancing Acquisition and Retention Resources to Maximize Customer Profitability. *Journal of Marketing.* **69**(1), (January) 63–79.

Rust, R.T., A. Zahorik. 1993. Customer Satisfaction, Customer Retention, and Market Share. *Journal of Retailing.* **69**(2) 193–215.

Rust, R., K. Lemon, V. Zeithaml. 2004. Return on Marketing: Using Customer Equity to Focus Marketing Strategy. *Journal of Marketing.* **68**(1), January 109–126.

Rust, R.T., T. Ambler, G. Carpenter, V. Kumar, R. Srivastava. 2004. Measuring Marketing Productivity: Current Knowledge and Future Directions. *Journal of Marketing.* **68**(October) 76–89.

Rust, R. T., V. A. Zeithaml, K.N. Lemon. 2000. Driving Customer Equity: Focusing Strategic Decisions for Long-term Profitability. The Free Press, New York.

Schmittlein, D., R. Peterson. 1994. Customer Base Analysis: An Industrial Purchase Process Application. *Marketing Science.* **13**(1) 41–68.

Schmittlein, D., D. Morrison, R. Columbo. 1987. Counting Your Customers: Who Are They and What Will They Do Next? *Management Science.* **33**(1) 1–24.

Srinivasan, V., C. Mason. 1986. Nonlinear Least Squares Estimation of New Product Diffusion Models. *Marketing Science* **5**(2), Spring 169–178.

Sultan, F., J.U. Farley, D.R. Lehmann. 1990. A Meta-Analysis of Applications of Diffusion Models. *Journal of Marketing Research.* **27**(1), (February) 70–77.

Thomas, J. 2001. A Methodology for Linking Customer Acquisition to Customer retention. *Journal of Marketing Research.* **38**(2), May 262–268.

Thomas, J.S., R.C. Blattberg, E. Fox. 2004. Recapturing Lost Customers. *Journal of Marketing Research.* **16**(February) 31–45.

Vapnik, V. 1998. *Statistical Learning Theory.* John Wiley and Sons, New York.

Venkatesan, R., V. Kumar. 2004. A Customer Lifetime Value Framework for Customer Selection and Resource Allocation Strategy. *Journal of Marketing*. **68**(October) 106–125.

Verhoef, P., P. Franses, J. Hoekstra. 2001. The Impact of Satisfaction and Payment Equity on Cross-Buying: A Dynamic Model for a Multi-Service Provider. *Journal of Retailing*. **77**(3) 359–378.

Villanueva, J., S. Yoo, D.M. Hanssens. 2006. The Impact of Marketing-Induced vs. Word-of-Mouth Customer Acquisition on Customer Equity. *Working Paper*. UCLA Anderson School of Management.

Wasserman, S., K. Faust. 2005. *Social Network Analysis*. Cambridge University Press.

Watts, D. 2003. *Six Degrees: The Science of a Connected Age*. Norton, NY.

Wiesel, T., B. Skiera. 2005. Linking Customer Metrics to Shareholder Value. *Working Paper*. Johann Wolfgang Goethe University.

Chapter 9
Decision Models for Customer Relationship Management (CRM)

Werner J. Reinartz and Rajkumar Venkatesan

9.1 Introduction

The conceptual shift from a product-centric to a customer-centric organization has been a topic for discussion for more than a decade (Webster 1992; Day 1999). Despite the rhetoric and its conceptual appeal, the change to customer-centric organizations has, in reality, been slow (Webster et al. 2005). Yet in recent years, significant activities, in both managerial practice and academia, have emerged around the concept of customer relationship management (CRM) (Boulding et al. 2005), representing a step closer to creating a stronger customer orientation. In managerial practice, these activities seem to revolve around IT-related questions and practices, whereas in academia, the discussion focuses on issues such as customer satisfaction, retention, and profitability.

The purpose of this chapter is to describe and summarize existing academic models and approaches that have found CRM applications. As such, we attempt to provide an integrated, structured overview of some key issues prevalent in academic CRM thinking. Within the scope of this chapter, we also identify some aspects of CRM that require new models or extensions.

According to Reinartz et al. (2004), existing literature suggests four distinct characteristics should be reflected in a CRM conceptualization: (1) building and managing ongoing customer relationships delivers the essence of the marketing concept (Webster 1992; Morgan and Hunt 1994), (2) relationships evolve with distinct phases (Dwyer et al. 1987), (3) firms interact with customers and manage relationships at each stage (Srivastava et al. 1998), and (4) the distribution of relationship value to the firm is not homogenous (Mulhern 1999; Niraj et al. 2001). In recognition of these factors, the heart of CRM activities is differential, systematic resource allocations to *customers* (not products, geographies, or so forth) with different economic values for the organization.

Fundamental to this conceptualization is the notion of customers' economic value to a business. Managers should attempt to maximize the value that

W.J. Reinartz
University of Cologne, Germany
e-mail: reinartz@wiso.uni-koeln.de

B. Wierenga (ed.), *Handbook of Marketing Decision Models*,
DOI: 10.1007/978-0-387-78213-3_9, © Springer Science + Business Media, LLC 2008

customers embody, particularly in a longitudinal sense. This notion of longer-term economic value gives rise to the metric of customer lifetime value (CLV), the net present value of discounted cash flows over time. Conceptually, the most appealing form of a CLV metric is oriented toward the future, and the concept of CLV is essential for most CRM-related research.

More specifically, the net present value of a firm's future profits from current customers (i.e., customer equity) can be represented as the sum of individual CLV s of the firm's current customers. For the purpose of illustration, a simplified measure of a firm's net present value of future profits at time period t = 0 can be represented as follows:

$$Customer\ Equity = \sum_{i=1}^{n} CLV_i, \text{ and} \tag{9.1}$$

$$CLV_i = \sum_{t=1}^{T} \frac{\sum_{p=1}^{P} M_{tp}{}^{*}Q_{itp} - \sum_{j=1}^{J} CS_{itj}}{(1+r)^t} - AC_i, \tag{9.2}$$

where

    Customer equity = net present value of future profits for the firm across current customers,

    CLV = net present value of future profits for the firm for a single customer,

    M_{tp} = gross margin (i.e., net of cost of goods sold) for product p in time period t,

    Q_{itp} = quantity purchased of product p by customer i in time period t,

    CS_{jit} = cost to serve customer i in time period t through channel J,

    AC_i = acquisition cost for customer i,

    r = discount rate, and

    n = number of customers of the firm at time t = 0.

For this formulation, the firm is assumed to have information about a customer's *activity* status – that is why information on customer retention is not part of this specification. In some cases, firms can treat acquisition costs as sunk costs and not include them in CLV calculations. Inclusion of acquisition costs is critical in scenarios where a customer transitions from being unprofitable to profitable over time (e.g., insurance and telecommunications industries). The metrics of customer equity and CLV provide the basic objective function for our discussion because the ultimate objective of CRM models is to maximize the value of the customer base. For example, customer selection frameworks attempt to determine the number of customers (n) a firm should target in its marketing communications, and cross-buying models function to increase the number of products (p) purchased by a customer.

Related to the formal measurement of customer equity and CLV and linked to the conceptualization of CRM, the dynamics of the customer relationship must be considered *over time*. A prospect must first be acquired to become a customer, who can then proceed to make repeat purchases (i.e., be retained) or cease making purchases (i.e., exit). Repeat purchases can expand (or decrease) the products purchased and therefore generate growth (or decline). Subsequent to customer exit, a firm can decide to win back (or reacquire) a customer or the customer could return to purchase from the firm. Firm actions (which lead to marketing costs) based on CRM decision models thus can influence one or more aspects of a customer relationship with the firm. From conceptual and managerial decision perspectives, the different aspects of that relationship—namely, (1) acquisition, (2) growth (or decline), (3) retention (or exit), and (4) win back—should be reflected in any overview of existing models.

In this chapter, we use the conceptual model of the customer–firm relationship in Fig. 9.1 and the notions of customer equity and CLV (Equations (9.1) and (9.2)) to structure our discussion of various CRM decision models. In addition, we follow the traditional assumption that the firm has an individual-level interaction with each customer, which enables it to allocate its various resources differentially to different customers.

The structure of our chapter is such that we investigate a set of typical questions and decisions that managers face when operating in a CRM context. Specifically, if customer interactions occur during each stage—acquisition, retention, growth, and win back—then managers face two key issues:

I. Which customer to select? (i.e., apply a decision or action), and
II. How to manage selected customers? (i.e., apply desired action).

More specifically, typical managerial questions are as follows:

I. Which Customer to Select?

1. Which customers should we acquire? (or Which customers should we win back?)

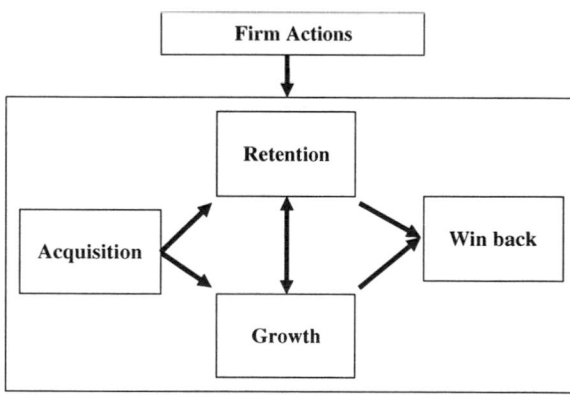

Fig. 9.1 Conceptual model of customer-firm relationships

2. Which customers should we retain? (or When is a customer alive? and Which customers should we select for relationship termination?)
3. Which customers should we focus on growing?

II. How to Manage Selected Customers?

1. How do we acquire customers?
2. How should we allocate resources to retain customers?
3. How should we allocate resources to grow customers?

9.2 Which Customer to Select?

9.2.1 Which Customers Should We Acquire?

Successful customer management begins with the right customers. As obvious and noncontroversial as this statement may sound, it does not reflect the reality of many businesses. Most businesses indiscriminately apply a hunting mentality and seem to believe that every new customer is a good customer. For example, the focus on "head-count" marketing campaign success as the de facto acquisition success metric and the inattentiveness to longer-term repurchase and costs to serve are characteristic of traditional acquisition models. In that sense, customer acquisition traditionally has been a tactical topic with few strategic implications. Although this indiscriminate acquisition approach might contain some truth, especially in growing markets, in highly mature and saturated markets, it clearly is suboptimal. Today's businesses must become much more strategic in their acquisition approaches; as more and more businesses have found, more customers are not necessarily better, but more of the *right* customers are (Reinartz et al. 2005). Thus, we expect that in a world driven by a CRM go-to-market approach, the strategic acquisition of the right customers plays a significant role. In this section, we review the evolution, practices, and implications of CRM-related customer acquisition approaches.

Customer acquisition has been very much an empirical question (David Shepard Associates 1999) and not much addressed in academic research (Steenburgh et al. 2003). The direct marketers, who by definition worked with a set of addressable customers, pioneered systematic, individual-level customer acquisition activities. The notions of list buying and list management are tightly linked with such activity. For more than 80 years, businesses have been buying and trading lists that form the core of the direct marketing industry (Burnett 1988). These lists of potential targets that satisfy certain demographic or behavioral conditions supposedly generate "new blood" in direct marketers' existing customer databases because the names on the lists provide promising targets for marketing campaigns. Moreover, among the many potential decision variables, the focus traditionally has been on the quality of the prospect (as opposed to the quality or timing of the offer). Conventional wisdom in the direct marketing field suggests that a mailing package of mediocre quality sent to the best prospects from an excellent list will generally prove more profitable than a high-quality package sent to mediocre prospects (Oldstein 1989). Direct mail practitioners generally agree that, of all the decision variables, the target plays the most important role.

In the field of direct marketing, we can observe an evolution in the practice of acquisition activities however. Over time, this evolution has infiltrated the related domain of CRM. At the heart of this evolution process is an objective function used to discriminate among prospects in the target pool (Fig. 9.2). This objective function may be, at one extreme, a simple response likelihood for a specific campaign. The next step then involves an objective function that relies on longitudinal past information on customer-level revenues or purchase behavior (e.g., purchase frequency). Subsequently, an objective function accounts for the cost of goods sold and ideally for the cost to serve, that is, a gross profit or contribution margin-based approach. Finally, the objective function might become a forward-looking assessment of the prospect's potential long-term value to the business, in terms of either revenue or profit metrics. As Fig. 9.2 shows, objective functions differ in terms of their longitudinal scope (short-term vs. long term), as well as their past versus future orientation.

The most generic form of an acquisition process can be described as follows: The decision maker aims to direct a discrete action at a small set of prospects in a given pool. First, the decision maker selects an objective function to pursue, such as maximum response likelihood or maximum revenue for the next purchase. Second, the decision maker profiles existing customers classified as attractive according to the chosen objective function. Naturally, profiling variables must be available for the prospects, such as information on prior purchase behavior. Frequently used variables include demographic variables, psychographic factors, or certain behaviors (e.g., mail order propensity). Instead of using existing customers, the marketer can also

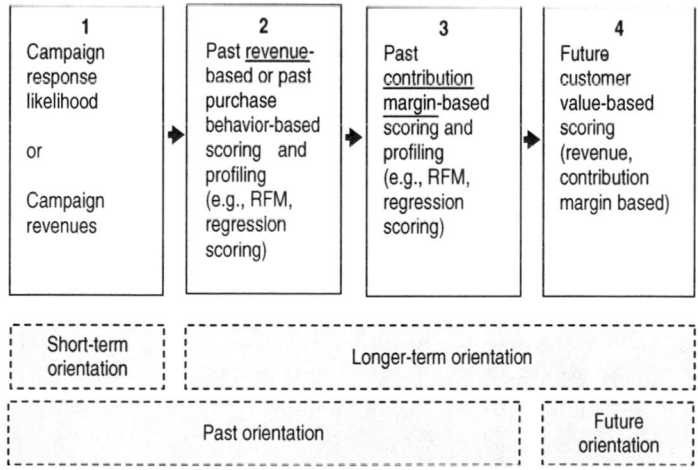

Fig. 9.2 Evolution of customer acquisition objective functions over time

run a test campaign for profiling purposes. Third, the ideal customer profile gets extracted and generated for all persons in the prospect pool. The data for this exercise typically are purchased from external data providers. Fourth, those prospects that match the desired profile, subject to some threshold criterion, are selected for the acquisition campaign. Such approaches are known as "prospect scoring models" (Bodapati and Gupta 2004) or "clone marketing" (Steenburgh et al. 2003).

Given this general process template, variation and sophistication emerges through (1) the specific objective function used and (2) the profiling process and input.

In a CRM context, the principle of profile- and scoring-based acquisition does not change, except that the decision maker uses an objective function that falls in line with a CRM go-to-market strategy.

9.2.1.1 Objective Function for Customer Acquisition in a CRM Context

According to the CRM principles, maximizing economic customer value for the business is the key objective. This economic customer value has been operationalized in various ways, such as past and current revenues, past and current profitability, and future value (both revenue and profits).

Past and current revenues: The key assumption underlying this class of models is that the future best customers should look a lot like prior best customers. Historically, the most frequently used selection technique has been the receny, frequency, and monetary value (RFM) model (Bult and Wansbeek 1995). Alternatives to and extensions of the basic RFM framework include automatic interaction detection models (David Shepard Associates 1999) and regression scoring models (Bauer 1988; Malthouse 2001). Although the RFM model remains a workhorse of the direct mail industry, it has several known shortcomings: It omits sources of heterogeneity other than RFM and does not take full advantage of the customer's longitudinal purchase history. In addition, unless the RFM variables are all mutually independent (which is unlikely), the model cannot account for redundancy. However, a recent article by Fader et al. (2005b) highlights the analogies between the rather ad-hoc RFM approach and the behaviorally based negative binomial distribution (NBD)/Pareto model. Specifically, their Iso-Value approach uses well-established stochastic models of buying behavior (Schmittlein et al. 1987) to make not only a next-period forecast but also predictions for periods beyond that. Assuming that monetary value is independent of the underlying transaction process, Fader, Hardie, and Lee show that the future value of customers can be represented by information on recency and frequency alone. The Iso-Value approach does a much better job uncovering the interactions among input parameters than traditional regression. For example, for customers who made a relatively large number of transactions in the past, recency plays a disproportionate role in determining their CLV. In addition, their model can capture the "increasing frequency" paradox, as depicted in Fig. 9.3.

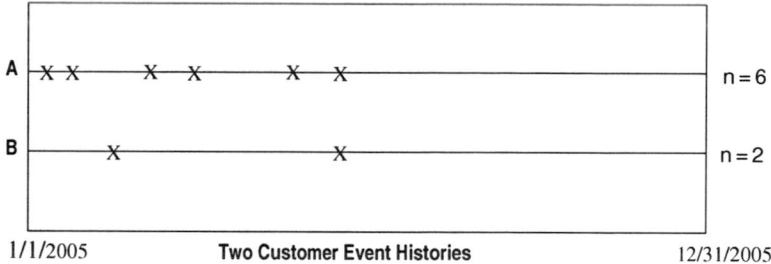

Fig. 9.3 The "increasing frequency" paradox

If we assume customers A and B were active on December 31, 2005, we would expect customer A to have greater value, given his or her higher number of prior purchases, but the pattern strongly suggests customer A is no longer active. Conversely, customer B has a lower underlying purchase rate, so the future value of customer B is much higher on December 31 than is that of customer A. Whereas a regression-based scoring model would likely miss this pattern and lead to faulty inferences for a large portion of the recency/frequency space, the behaviorally based Iso-Value model captures these effects properly. In a similar spirit, Gönül et al. (2000) find that monotonic measures, as implied by RFM model (e.g., the more recent the better), may err if they eliminate customers with relatively high recency rates; specifically, they find that people may start to buy again after prolonged periods.

Past and current profitability: The key difference between profit- and revenue-based objective functions is that the former take into account the cost of goods sold and, even more important, the customer-level cost to serve. In general, this step has represented an important evolution in customer and prospect classification models, in that marketers realize that revenues rarely translate linearly into contribution margins, an idea that has been taken for granted for too long. Several studies show that because the cost-to-serve component (customer-level expenses for sales, marketing, advertising, logistics, returns, risk, terms and conditions, financing, and so forth) varies widely (Reinartz and Kumar 2000; Niraj et al. 2001), managers absolutely must look beyond revenue-based metrics.

Several models use a profitability-based, long-term assessment of customer value (panel 3 in Fig. 9.2) that can generate attractive profiles for the acquisition process (Krafft and Peters 2005). However, no publications exist that focus on past CLV assessments and how they might inform acquisition decisions about *new* customers, despite the many applications of information about long-term past profitability or contribution margins to resource allocation decisions about those same customers (Thomas et al. 2004; Reinartz et al. 2005). In principal, these approaches could generate attractive profiles and indicate which prospects to target.

An additional idea for further research would incorporate dual objective functions in the pursuit of new customers by focusing not only on the profile of high-value customers, as derived from the profile of prior high-value customers, but also subsegment further and include response likelihoods. In other words, the targeting should focus on prospects with the highest *expected* value, taking into account the response likelihood. We discuss this idea of skimming the best prospects from the target pool in the next section.

Future value: Regardless of what a customer or prospect has done in the past, in an ideal world, a manager wants to invest disproportionately in those consumers or businesses that hold the most future potential. The most encompassing future value metric is future lifetime or long-term value, but a great disconnect seems to exist between wishlist status and actual forecasting capability. Most decision makers express a need for such metric, but academic marketing has little to offer. If it is difficult to make a reliable forecast about future long-term economic value, it is even harder to identify and profile acquisition targets.

In the context of forecasting future long-term value, the disconnect between the conceptual simplicity of the CLV discounted cash flow approach and the actual empirical estimation difficulties becomes evident. Malthouse and Blattberg (2005) show across four different empirical contexts, using three different scoring methods, that predictions of long-term future value are not at all straightforward. In particular, they note the level of Type I and II errors (Fig. 9.4) across different conditions.

Malthouse and Blattberg (2005) arrive at some generalizations across the different conditions, which they call the "20-55 rule" and the "80-15 rule." The 20-55 rule says that of the future top 20% CLV customers, 55% will be misclassified as low-value customers (= Type I error); according to the 80-15

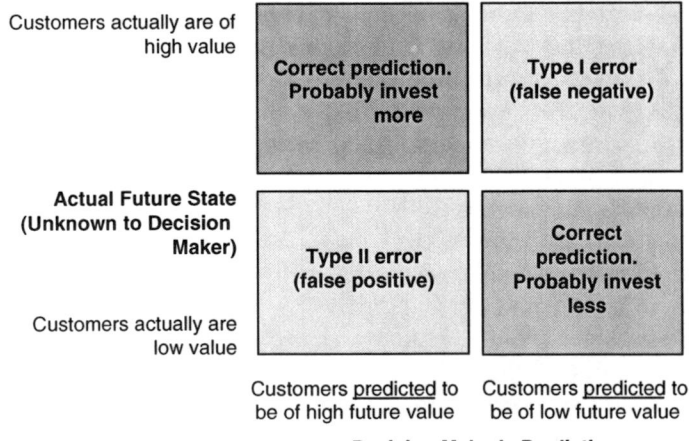

Fig. 9.4 Type I and Type II errors

rule, of the future bottom 80% CLV customers, 15% will be misclassified as high value (= Type II error). Thus, their study offers a sobering view of our ability to predict future long-term value—at least with established statistical approaches. Generally, they argue that the success of CLV prediction depends on (1) the misclassification probability, (2) the misclassification cost, (3) additional revenues generated as a result of a correct decision, and (4) the cost of special treatment for high-value customers.

Generally speaking, two complications make the prediction task difficult: difficulty in individual level prediction and endogeneity . First, there is the need to make a decision (e.g., invest or not) at the individual customer/prospect level. Because the stochastic component of individual-level behavior is high (cf. Lilien et al. 1992, pp. 31–42), marketers might have to resort to probabilistic models that can account for the uncertainty in individual-level customer relationships (Schmittlein and Peterson 1994; Pfeiffer and Carraway 2000). Unlike simplistic algebraic CLV formulae that employ the retention rates of cohorts and average profits from segments, these models incorporate probability estimates and expected value and therefore are better suited to model relationships with individual customers.

The second problem that is creating significant problems is one of endogeneity of customer and firm behavior. To the extent that customers have been targeted with different marketing incentives on the basis of their prior behavior, endogeneity bias becomes an issue (Shugan 2004). This issue will be dealt with in more detail in a later section

Another model in the domain of future customer value models is the split hazard model of Thomas et al. (2004). In the context of a contractual relationship (e.g., newspaper subscription), they model the relationship duration of a reacquired customer until the customer terminates that relationship. Conceptually, this approach is similar to a CLV model, except that it includes more information on each customer because of the previous relationship. Its objective is to determine drivers of "second lifetime value" and forecast it. Not only do they find that they can predict second lifetime value well, they also find sufficient CLV heterogeneity and sensitivity with respect to the offer strategy. Particularly, in a simulation, the most profitable reacquisitions stem from a low-priced reacquisition offer and subsequent price increases after the second relationship has been established.

Generally, from an empirical perspective, customer classification based on an understanding of customer's future long-term value is not easy, in particular with respect to methodological issues. Yet, great managerial interest remains focused on those studies that are able to advance our understanding in this arena.

9.2.1.2 Profiling Issues

After identifying an ideal target segment on the basis of a specific objective function, the manager needs to profile that segment so that it can identified and matched to a larger prospect pool. By definition, behavior information is generally not available for noncustomers, so marketers use variables that can be obtained. The first type of information is some form of aggregated information, such as geodemographic information (e.g., block group, zip code) pertaining to household income, property ownership, or education. Naturally, this type of data, though widely available, is less effective than the next type of data: individual-level information on demographic or psychographic factors. If reliable individual-level information is available to assign scores to prospects and match them with an ideal profile, there should be little performance decrease with respect to customer scoring. However, in many situations, individual-level prospect information does not exist, so marketers must resort to area-level data matching. Direct marketers usually ignore the aggregated nature of these data and treat them as if they were individual-level data (Steenburgh et al. 2003). Steenburgh et al. (2003) suggest a hierarchical Bayes variance components model that uses zip code–level, rather than individual-level, information. Such a model improves predictive power, and the model parameters enable marketers to better understand their target market, which assists them with segmentation issues.

To summarize, there is a general shift with respect to the objective function used to target prospects that has moved from short- to longer-term orientations to measure customer value and from past to future orientations. However, considerable issues still must be addressed with respect to the reliability of future CLV estimates and to solve the issues of marketing action endogeneity. Situations where (a) a customer finds a firm (i.e., no acquisition cost) and (b) where a firm is required to serve a customer by law, have important customer valuation and management implications, and there is almost no research in this topic.

9.2.2 Which Customers Should We Retain? (or When is a Customer Alive? Which Customers Should We Select for Relationship Termination?)

The issues involved in evaluating and scoring high-value existing customers are identical to many of those described in the previous section, so we do not repeat them here. With respect to the question of which customers to retain, we highlight some additional concerns that appear in existing CRM research, specifically, determining customers' activity levels and accommodating potential selection biases.

9.2.2.1 Determining Customers' Activity Levels

Dwyer (1989) discusses the distinction between "always-a-share" (noncontractual) relationships and "lost-for-good" (contractual) scenarios. In the contractual case, the business knows whether a customer is active (e.g., magazine or Internet subscription), whereas in the noncontractual case, it is nontrivial to determine whether a customer is still "around" (e.g., direct mail, store shopping). For the noncontractual context, marketers have devised and used a plethora of proxies to determine a customer's activity status and determine their optimal resource allocations. These proxies might include the time since the last purchase, some type of RFM or regression scoring, or similar heuristics. Yet, they are mostly empirically derived without a clear theoretical rational supporting them.

However, a few theoretically motivated stochastic models offer much stronger justifications for customer-level decisions. Two of the key models are the NBD/Pareto model by Schmittlein et al. (1987) and the purchase timing model by Allenby et al. (1999).

The NBD/Pareto model describes the purchase process when customers' "drop-outs" are unobserved. It assumes that customers buy at a steady, stochastic rate and then become inactive. More specifically, it models time to dropout using the Pareto (exponential-gamma mixture) timing model and repeat buying behavior but employs the NBD (Poisson-gamma mixture) counting model to represent activity. The data points entered into the model are quite simple and usually exist in many organizations: time since first purchase, time from first purchase until most recent purchase, total number of transactions. On the basis of these inputs, the NBD/Pareto model predicts the likelihood that a customer is still active at some time t. Thus, decision makers have a potentially powerful model to drive theoretically based customer-level decisions. Yet, despite its great potential, only a small set of studies have applied the model (Schmittlein and Peterson 1994; Reinartz and Kumar 2000, 2003; Fader et al. 2005b), possibly because of its difficult parameter estimation. Maximum likelihood (ML) and method-of-moment estimations are feasible, though the former imposes a heavy computational burden. Even the more straightforward method-of-moment estimation is not entirely easy to implement. In addition, the method-of-moment estimation lacks the desirable statistical properties that ML estimation yields. Fader et al. (2005a) have developed a beta geometric/NBD model, which requires only a slight variation in the behavioral assumptions but is much easier to implement—its results can be obtained easily with spreadsheet software, whereas the NBD/Pareto model requires software such as Mathematica or Matlab. The outcome of the NBD/Pareto model is a continuous measure (probability) of a customer being active at time t, from which marketers can determine a discrete duration during which the customer is assumed to be alive by generating a threshold above which the customer is assumed to be active (Fig. 9.5).

Researchers have used both a fixed threshold of 0.5 (Reinartz and Kumar 2000) and a threshold that varies on the basis of the expected profits to be gained from a customer (Reinartz and Kumar 2003). Expected future profits are driven by the customer's probability of being active and the expected contribution margin. A comparatively high customer contribution margin justifies keeping that customer for a longer span, even if he or she has a lower probability of being active (and vice versa). Additional research should attempt

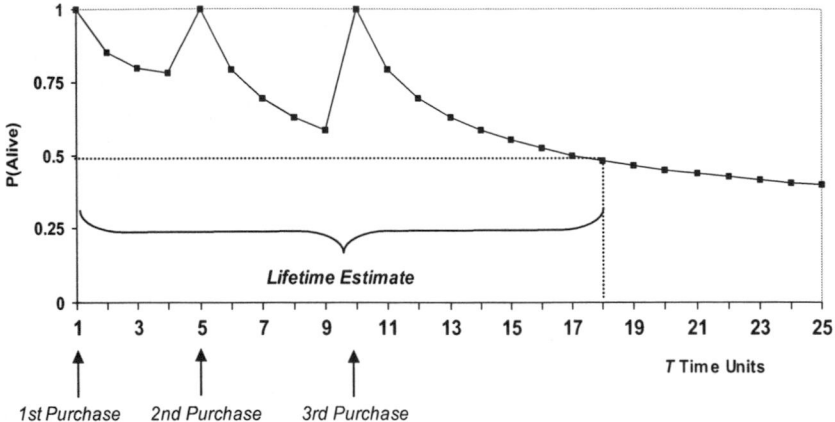

Fig. 9.5 Illustrative lifetime determination of individual customer

to overcome the two-step process of calculating a discrete customer activity period and then assessing potential drivers of this period. Generally, given the simplifications of the estimation process that Fader, Hardie, and Lee offer, the NBD/Pareto and beta geometric/NBD models should be used more in the future, but research also must verify the conditions in which these models apply and ensure they do not provide panaceas.

Another type of model that has been used to classify customers' activity status is the interpurchase timing model by Allenby et al. (1999). It assumes that changes (increases) in customer's interpurchase times signal a potential threat of leaving the relationship and therefore require managerial intervention. Interpurchase times also are assumed to follow a generalized gamma distribution, and the model allows for both cross-sectional and temporal heterogeneity. In the context of investment decisions, Allenby et al. (1999) find three segments that vary according to their activity status: superactive accounts, active accounts, and inactive accounts. In practice, firms would use the model to identify customers who are likely to move from an active to a less active state by recalculating their probability estimates periodically and monitoring individual customers. More recently, Venkatesan and Kumar (2004) have used the model to predict future purchases, which then feed into a prediction of future customer profitability.

Neslin et al. (2006) provide an interesting meta-analysis of how customer defection might be predicted across methodological approaches. In the context of a churn modeling tournament, they identify how specific methodological and process factors contribute to correctly identifying customers who will leave. In terms of estimation technique, logit and tree analyses outperform discriminant, explanatory, and novice approaches. In addition, from a practical standpoint, the predictive ability of their model does not diminish during three months. Moreover, the differences among the more than 40 entries in the tournament yield significant differences in terms of incremental profits for the organization. That is, model quality and predictive accuracy matter.

9.2.2.2 Accommodating for Potential Selection Biases

An important development in CRM models that deal with customer acquisition and customer retention/growth is the accommodation in more recent models of the conceptual linkage between customer acquisition and retention. Whereas early work by Blattberg and Deighton (1996) treated acquisition and retention activities as independent, more recent work acknowledges the dependency between the two stages. For example, a customer with a higher acquisition likelihood probably also has a higher retention likelihood because he or she draws a higher utility from the firm's offering. A competing argument could be that a customer who has a high promotional affinity (i.e., is easy to acquire) has also a higher likelihood to leave, because such a customer will be attracted by competitive promotional offerings. In other words, the subsample of existing customers probably is not drawn randomly from the population of prospects, and a proper model structure must accommodate for this potential selection bias. Recent work that has considered such a link includes Thomas et al. (2004), Reinartz et al. (2005) and Du et al. (2005).

The typical procedure of these approaches is first to specify an acquisition equation that describes how prospects enter the customer pool. In the subsequent stage, the behavior of all customers is modeled, *conditional* on their self-selection into the firm's customer pool. Methodologically, a covariance correction term introduces its conditional nature and enters the specification of the second stage.

For example, Reinartz et al. (2005) provide two equations in the second stage, one for lifetime duration and one for customer profitability:

(Cumulative profitability equation)
$$y_{Li} = \beta'_{Ls}x_{Li} + \gamma'_s y_{Di} + \varepsilon_{Lis} \quad \text{if} \quad z_i = 1$$
$$= 0 \text{ otherwise} \tag{9.3}$$

(Duration equation)
$$y_{Di} = \beta'_{Ds}x_{Di} + \varepsilon_{Dis} \quad \text{if} \quad z_i = 1$$
$$= 0 \text{ otherwise} \tag{9.4}$$

(Acquisition equation)
$$z^*_i = \alpha'_s v_i + \mu_{is}$$
$$z_i = 1 \quad \text{if } z^*_i > 0 \tag{9.5}$$
$$z_i = 0 \quad \text{if} z^*_i \leq 0$$

where:

y_{Li} = the cumulative profitability of customer i,
x_{Li} = a vector of covariates impacting customer i's CLV,

y_{Di} = the duration of customer i's relationship with the firm,

x_{Di} = a vector of covariates impacting the duration of customer i's relationship with the firm,

z^*_i = a latent variable indicating customer i's utility of engaging in a relationship with the firm,

z_i = an indicator variable showing whether customer i is acquired ($z_i = 1$) or not ($z_i = 0$),

v_i = a vector of covariates that affect the acquisition of customer i,

$\alpha_s, \beta_{Ls}, \beta_{Ds}$ = segment-specific parameters,

ε = error term, and

μ = error term.

These authors specify a recursive simultaneous equation model in which a probit model determines the selection or acquisition process and two distinct regression equations characterize duration and long-term customer profitability. Logically, duration and customer profitability are observed only if the customer is acquired. Thus, the duration and profitability equations are conditional regressions determined partly by the acquisition likelihood of a customer. The linkages among the three equations are captured in the error structure of the model. Specifically, this model assumes that the error terms (ε_{Lis}, ε_{Dis}, μ_{is}) are multivariate normal.

The first step involves simply estimating a probit model for all the data (i.e., acquired and nonacquired prospects). Using the estimated parameters from the probit, a selectivity variable, *lambda* (λ_{is}) (also commonly known as the inverse mills ratio) is constructed for the acquired customers and included as an independent variable in the duration and cumulative profitability equations. Mathematically, the selectivity variable is an artifact of the correlation between the error term in the acquisition equation (Equation (9.5)) and each of the errors in the conditional regression equations (Equations (9.3) and (9.4)). Therefore, unbiased parameter estimates can be obtained only by taking conditional expectations of the error terms. Although this method for estimation and bias correction in selection models has its basis in econometrics (Heckman 1976, 1979), similar bias correction approaches have been applied in marketing contexts (Winer 1983; Krishnamurthi and Raj 1988).

The second step of the process requires the estimation of the duration model with regressors, including the estimated lambda and the relevant covariates that affect duration. Estimation in step two distinguishes between noncensored and right-censored observations and uses a standard right-censored Tobit model. On the basis of the estimated parameters and data about the acquired sample, a forecast can be made about the expected relationship duration for each individual customer; that forecast becomes a covariate in step three.

In step three, customer profitability is estimated according to regressors such as a vector of exogenous variables that affect the long-term profitability of a customer, the forecasted relationship duration from step two, and the estimated lambda from Equation (9.5). The cumulative profitability model specified in Equation (9.1) is also estimated with a standard right-censored Tobit model.

Generally speaking, we expect to see more of this type of modeling in the future, because it is much better suited to capture the intrinsic dependencies of the customer management process. From a methodological perspective, these models are not difficult to implement; software packages such as LimDep (2002) offer such functionality. Probably the most difficult aspect of these models is information availability (or lack thereof) for prospects who have not been acquired. Most organizations do not routinely keep this information, which makes it impossible to estimate the acquisition equation.

Finally, to the extent that customers have been targeted with different marketing incentives on the basis of their prior behavior, endogeneity bias becomes an issue in any CLV model (Shugan 2004). For example, CLV and therefore the customer equity of a firm are influenced by customer-level behavior, which itself is influenced by actions taken by the company and competitors, as well as market and channel behavior. The company's actions or customer-specific strategies to improve CLV are in turn based on the CLV of the customers and competitive behavior, which leads to simultaneity/endogeneity issues that current CLV models do not address sufficiently. In the CRM domain, few studies expressly account for endogeneity, so structural models that explicitly accommodate these conditions in their estimation of model parameters would be particularly useful (such as, Manchanda et al. 2004). Current research does not provide clear evidence on the extent to which managerial decisions change when model models that account for endogeneity are used.

9.2.3 Which Customers Should We Focus on Growing?

Traditionally, much thought has been given to how to retain customers and drive down customer attrition. Increasingly, however, organizations have begun thinking about how to expand and grow their relationships in terms of both revenue and profits. Because many organizations increasingly collect large amounts of data on the individual customer level, it is a natural next step to use some of that information to target customers with pertinent cross- and up-selling offers. Before a customer is targeted, the organization must identify those customers who represent appropriate targets, specifically, those who either have new needs according to their lifecycle evolution or spend a sizable share of their wallet with competitors.

The notion of cross- and up-selling in response to changing customer needs derives from the longstanding observation that purchases follow a natural evolution over time (Paroush 1965). In certain product categories, such as consumer durables (Hebden and Pickering 1974) or financial services (Kamakura et al. 1991), product acquisition over time has been subject to early inquiry. This line of research has tried to explain systematic acquisition patterns mostly as a function of time. More recently, interest has centered on targeting customers who do not own the product or product line even though the company offers it and they may have a need for it. In either case, the underlying objective is to capture more of the customers' share of wallet.

Recent advances for identifying potential cross-selling prospects include the data factor analyzer by Kamakura et al. (2003) and a model for targeting innovators for cross-sales of new products (Kamakura et al. 2004). Kamakura et al.'s (2003) model follows the notion of a latent-trait model, which makes a probabilistic prediction that consumers use particular products on the basis of their ownership of other products and the characteristics of the new one. However, to use this approach, the firm needs to know the customer's total ownership structure, including patronage of competitors, which is highly unlikely. The advantage of the data factor analyzer is that it accommodates missing and nonnormal variables, such as zero-one or count variables. The model attempts to achieve a low-dimensional representation of the data and identify products likely to be owned simultaneously. Moreover, it enables managers to target services to customers who currently use those of competitors or have a high probability of usage but have not yet acquired the service.

When it comes to identifying customers who are the best potential targets for new products, Kamakura et al. (2004) suggest a hazard-model approach. Data from previous new product introductions calibrate the model, which then identifies customers who are more likely to adopt a new offer early. The model is based on a split-hazard formulation (i.e., it allows for the possibility that a customer never will adopt the new product), which can be extended to the multivariate case because it is calibrated across several previously introduced products. The outcome is an expected hazard rate for the new product for each potential target in the population.

Another type of model employs actual individual-level data for the focal firm and actual or imputed data about competitors. Du and Kamakura (2005) first distinguished between consumer lifetime value, which refers to customer's buying behavior across firms, and simple CLV, which refers to the customer's buying behavior from the focal firm and thereby offers only a partial view of the customer. Du et al. (2005) use a latent variable approach to model three types of customer decisions: ownership (whether to own a category), total (total category requirements of a customer who decides to own the category), and share (share of customer requirements served by the focal firm). These three decisions, which are linked across categories, are a function of observed and unobserved characteristics. Applied to a financial services context, the link between share of wallet and relationship length is not strong, similar to the findings of Reinartz and Kumar (2000). Using simulations, they find that customer targeting can be improved substantially through estimated total wallet and share of wallet. For example, 13% of customers in their holdout sample are identified as high-potential customers because their estimated total wallet is high but their estimated share of wallet with the focal firm is below average.

9.3 How to Manage Selected Customers?

Once the decision regarding which customer to select has occurred, the next question that arises is how to manage the resource allocation process to enhance customer behavior according to the lifetime dynamics depicted in Fig. 9.1: acquisition, retention, growth, and win back. In the following sections, we discuss in detail models and findings related to the management of marketing resources to improve customer profitability.

9.3.1 How Should We Acquire Customers?

We focus on studies that investigate whether the long-term profitability of customers differs on the basis of how they were acquired, that is, the long-term consequence of acquisition campaigns. The basic premise in these studies is that the design of an acquisition campaign (irrespective of whether an acquisition campaign targeted a certain segment of customers) influences the type of customers a firm attracts. These acquired customers in turn become part of the customer base and therefore affect the success of retention campaigns and the value of the firm's customer assets. Clarifying differences in the long-term consequences of acquisition campaigns thus offers guidance to managers about how they should acquire customers to maximize the long-term profitability of customers to the firm.

Acquisition campaigns differ according to the communication channel through which a prospect is acquired and the message used to attract that prospect. At the top level, prospects are attracted either directly through marketing campaigns or indirectly through referrals from the prospect's social network (i.e., word of mouth). A firm has a greater control (and higher expenses) over marketing campaigns and lesser control (and lesser expenses) over word of mouth (WOM) acquisitions. For example, a firm can control the message and the targeted prospect list for a direct mail campaign but not a referral program that provides incentives to current customers for referring new customers. At the same time, the cost of a direct mail campaign is greater than the cost of a referral program. Finally, a marketing campaign could be either a brand-building message that describes the benefits that a firm's product (i.e., build primary demand), or highlight the services provided to a customer or inform about a monetary incentive.

Research on this aspect of CRM has been scant relative to other aspects, probably because of the lack of data availability. Studies primarily focus on the long-term differences in the profitability of customers acquired through the various acquisition channels, such as direct mail, television or radio advertising, Web sites, e-mail, and WOM, as well as whether a monetary incentive was offered.

9.3.1.1 Impact of Acquisition Channel

Acquisitions channels can be classified as follows: (1) mass media (TV/ radio, print), (2) direct marketing (direct mail, outbound telephone or telesales), (3) Internet (e-mail, Web sites), (4) personal selling (door-to-door, networks), (5) intermediaries (agents, dealers, retail chains), and (6) WOM (Verhoef and Donkers 2005). Firms often use direct response commercials to acquire customers through mass media, and the customers frequently take the initiative to contact firms through Web sites.

For a Dutch financial services firm, retention and cross-buying vary significantly according to the type of acquisition channel (Verhoef and Donkers 2005), including mass media, direct marketing, Web site, and coinsurance. This last channel refers to those customers acquired through the financial services firm's offer of special discounts to employers and large interest groups that can be passed on to employees or members of the interest groups.

However, in the study, the effects of acquisition channels were weaker on cross-buying than on retention, possibly because cross-buying requires a second step in the customer relationship, which probably is influenced by the firm's subsequent marketing interventions. Customers acquired through mass media, direct mail, the Web site, and WOM had lower retention probabilities than those acquired through coinsurance, and customers acquired through direct mail were less likely to cross-buy than were those acquired through coinsurance. None of the acquisition channels had a significantly higher influence than the coinsurance channel on either retention or cross-buying, and the mass media and direct mail channels attracted customers with the lowest overall values (i.e., product of retention and cross-buying probabilities).

Coinsurance thus appears to be the most effective acquisition channel because of the attractive product offers associated with it and the resultant higher switching costs for these customers. In other words, the influence of the coinsurance acquisition channel occurs throughout the customer's lifetime, whereas the other acquisition channels do not affect the customer after the first purchase occasion. In contrast, the direct mail channel seems to attract a large number of unprofitable customers, i.e., it suffers from an adverse selection problem.

In addition to their direct effect on customer behavior, acquisition channels also can have cross-effects on acquisition through other channels, reinforcement, and feedback effects on firm and customer performance (Villanueva et al. 2006). Cross-effects measure how two types of customer acquisition channels affect each other, such as how marketing-induced customer acquisition (e.g., direct mail) influences future acquisitions generated through WOM. Feedback effects represent how a firm's current performance may affect the future number of customers acquired, such that firms that develop stronger reputations through better performance could increase their future customer acquisitions. Both performance and customer acquisitions may have future effects on themselves, or reinforcement effects. Using a vector autoregression (VAR) model, these authors study the direct, cross, feedback, and reinforcement effects of acquisition channels, and the impulse response functions they obtain from the VAR model estimates enable them to disentangle immediate and long-term effects of acquisition channels.

With regard to direct effects, they find that customers acquired through marketing contribute more to the firm's performance in the short term than do those acquired through WOM. The effect of marketing-induced acquisition settles down after only three weeks, whereas the WOM effect lasts for approximately 6 weeks. Regarding the WOM effects, customers acquired through WOM are better at future WOM generation than are those acquired by marketing-induced channels. For example, each customer acquired through marketing brings in approximately 1.59 new customers throughout his or her lifetime; a customer acquired through WOM attracts 3.23. Overall, the focal Internet firm could increase its short-run revenue more using marketing-induced customer acquisition than WOM, but in the long run, the latter has a greater financial impact than the former.

9.3.1.2 Impact of Incentives

Uncertainty about the utility of a product or service can entice consumers to try products provided on discount. Several psychological theories about the negative consequences of promotional price discounts (e.g., coupons) are applicable for understanding the consequences of monetary incentives for customer acquisition on long-term profitability (e.g., Lewis 2006). For example, adaptation-level theory implies that a deeply discounted initial price leads to the formation of reference prices far below the regular price. When the price of a product or service increases beyond the initial promotional discount, customers may decrease their spending levels or stop purchasing altogether, which negatively affects the profitability of the firm's customer portfolio.

Lewis (2006) analyses the impact of price discounts used to acquire customers on the prices paid by those customers in future time periods in the context of newspaper subscribers and a cohort of customers acquired during the second quarter of an Internet retailer's operation. He uses a logistic regression to study the influence of price discounts on the customer's propensity to repeat purchase; to calculate customer asset value, he uses a survival analysis for the newspaper subscribers and a Tobit model for the online retailer. For newspaper data, customer asset value represents the product of expected lifetime length and prices charged over that time.

For both firms, acquisition discount depth negatively relates to repeat buying rates and customer asset value. For instance, a 35% acquisition discount for newspaper customers results in customers with approximately half the long-term value of those not acquired through promotion. Similarly, for the Internet retailer, promotionally acquired customers are worth about half the value of non-promotionally acquired customers. When discounts are rare and precisely targeted, we might expect the CLV of repeat buyers to be independent of the acquisition discount. In contrast, when discounts are periodically offered, the acquisition discount may explain differences in CLV even among the repeat-buying segment. These results are similar to the findings in the scanner panel literature that in the long run promotions negatively impact the brand equity of a firm and increase the price sensitivity of customers. One can expect these effects to decrease the profitability of a firm's customers.

In summary, acquisition channels used to attract prospects have an important influence on the long-term profitability of the firm. Direct mail, compared with other channels, tends to attract customers who have lower profitability (i.e., adverse selection problem). Prospects acquired through indirect social networks, instead of direct communications from the firm, entail higher profitability, possibly because customers realize that the main goal of direct marketing communications is to influence their beliefs and/or attitudes about the firm, and in response, they work to cope with these attempts. Among the indirect acquisition channels, programs that provide customers with benefits tied to the acquisition channel (e.g., coinsurance) seem to perform better than simple customer referral programs.

Evaluating how the acquisition techniques affect the long-term profitability of a firm seems like a ripe area for further research. Investigating the interaction of acquisition message and acquisition channel has the potential to contribute to the literature. As has been speculated, direct mail may attract less profitable customers because its focus is on price (Verhoef and Donkers 2005). If so, we need to evaluate whether the acquisition channel affects customer profitability after we control for the acquisition message. For example, would the direct mail acquisition channel attract profitable customers if the direct mail message focused on product/brand attributes rather than price?

The response rate and ratio of profitable to unprofitable customers provided by an acquisition channel can also determine the level of resources managers should invest in each acquisition channel. Therefore, another area for additional research is the optimal trade-off between the level of price discount messages and product attribute/brand-building messages that can maximize overall firm profits. Yet another issue for further research is the efficacy of customer acquisition in different channel contexts.

9.3.2 How Should We Allocate Resources to Retain Customers?

Customer retention can be viewed as the means of ensuring positive gross margins (M_{tp} in Equation (9.2)) in the foreseeable future or the planning horizon. Marketing contacts represent a significant marketing instrument available to managers in this context. The common intuition in academic studies links investments in marketing activities to customers' future activity status (or profitability) and investigates any nonlinearity, such as threshold effects or diminishing returns, in the link. We note that most studies in this section do not make an explicit distinction between customer retention and customer growth but study the impact of marketing investments on customer profitability directly. However, as we mentioned previously (and as is evident from Equation (9.2)), customer profitability must be determined by both retention and growth. To the extent that customer retention is necessary for customer growth, we assume here that any evidence regarding the link between marketing investments and customer profitability is applicable to customer retention, though the level of investment required to maximize customer retention may differ from that required to maximize customer profitability (Reinartz et al. 2005).

Role of Marketing Contacts. Emerging empirical evidence indicates that marketing contacts through different channels (e.g., direct mail, telesales, salespeople) are critical for influencing customer retention. The approaches for linking marketing investment to customer retention differ along the same dimensions as models that attempt to determine which customers to retain. Reinartz and Kumar (2003) use a two-step approach to link marketing activities to customer profitability: a NBD/Pareto model to determine a customer's profitable lifetime duration, and a proportional hazard framework to uncover the positive relationship between the number of catalogs sent to a customer and his or her profitable lifetime duration.

However, many marketing communications can be dysfunctional to a relationship (Fournier et al. 1998). In other words, though we do not question the utility of marketing contacts, too much contact can overload customers and lead to negative consequences, such as termination. In the business-to-business (B2B) context, Venkatesan and Kumar (2004) find that marketing contacts through rich (salesperson contacts) and standardized (direct mail, telesales) modes indirectly influence customer retention. In a purchase frequency model with a concomitant mixture framework, Venkatesan and Kumar (2004), show that the frequency of marketing contacts has a significant influence on whether a customer belongs to an active (i.e., high retention probability) or inactive (i.e., low retention probability) segment. However, the influence of marketing contacts is nonlinear, which means an optimal level of marketing contacts exists and can ensure customer retention, but beyond that threshold, marketing contacts lead a customer to inactivity. This nonlinear influence of marketing also is evident when customer retention is modeled directly (Reinartz et al. 2005). The nonlinear influence of marketing contacts provides a demand- (or customer-) side justification for the differential allocation of marketing resources in CRM. Optimal investment levels that ensure customer retention therefore should match both a firm's profitability maximization objective and the threshold at which customers positively respond to marketing contacts.

In summary, marketing interventions through contacts seem to have a positive influence on customer retention. Understanding the customer decision-making process in response to marketing programs is essential for designing resource allocation strategies that effectively improve retention. Loyalty programs also serve as important instruments for retaining customers. We do not discuss the link between loyalty programs and customer retention because the literature offers no clear conclusions regarding the influence of loyalty programs (e.g., Reinartz 2005; Lewis 2004; Sharp and Sharp 1997), nor does it address the issue of customizing loyalty programs according to customer value, which is the focus of this chapter.

9.3.3 How Should We Allocate Resources to Grow Customers?

The systematic and differential allocation of resources to individual customers to grow the profits related to them sits at the heart of CRM activities. Even within the CRM realm, the initial intuitive thinking asserted that customers who were loyal provided more profits to the firm and that customer profits increased over the span of a customer's relationship (Reichheld and Teal 1996). These results were based on average profits for all the customers in a cohort or in contractual situations for financial services. However, the correlation between customer loyalty (or customer tenure) and customer profitability becomes much weaker when customer heterogeneity is taken into consideration and in noncontractual setting such as catalogs, B2B firms, and retailing (Reinartz and Kumar 2002). Therefore, the objective of customer resource allocation should to be to maximize lifetime customer profits directly rather than any proxy of customer profitability, such as customer tenure. To this end, customer resource allocation models adopt long-term customer profitability (customer equity, customer CLV) rather than one-time transactional sales or profits as the criterion for resource allocation (Blattberg and Deighton 1996; Berger and Nasr-Bechwati 2001). Most models in this literature use growth in customer profits between two time periods as the dependent variable. The effect of marketing on growing customer profits can be much clearer if growth in customer profitability is adjusted for a baseline or natural growth (e.g., due to changes in lifecycle stages) in customer profits. As an example, Rust (2007), include growth in GDP as a control variable when investigating the impact of marketing on changes in customer profitability.

Different approaches for managing profits earned from individual customers vary according to the aspect of customer profits (for a representation of customer profits, see Equation (9.1)) they manipulate. Research thus far has focused on growing or maintaining customer profits by (Fig. 9.6) (1) effectively managing the costs allocated to the customers, (2) increasing the number of products purchased by a customer (i.e., cross-selling), or (3) managing the

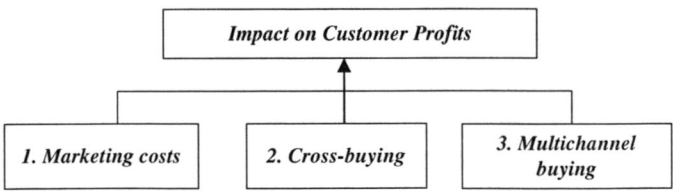

Fig. 9.6 How to grow customer profits

number of channels through which a customer transacts with a firm (i.e., multichannel marketing). We discuss each of these avenues for managing customer profits in detail.

9.3.3.1 Allocating Marketing Costs

If we assume that the revenue provided by a customer does not increase over time, the customer contribution margin (equal to revenue minus cost of goods sold and cost to serve) can be improved by managing the costs allocated to the customer. Various marketing costs that are customizable and have been studied thus far include price promotions, direct mail (including catalogs), e-mail, and salesperson and telesales contacts. All models rely on the basic notions of estimating future customer revenue and restricting the level of marketing resources allocated to the customer so that they are lower than the estimated gross margin.

This strategy originated in the catalog industry, in which marketing decision criteria essentially entail the number of catalogs needed to mail a customer before the customer makes a purchase. Catalog mailing decisions are based primarily on the customer's propensity to make a purchase and the expected revenue from that customer, given a purchase. The proliferation of information about all aspects of customer–firm interactions through CRM systems has led to the adoption of this approach even in industries whose primary method of interacting with customers is not restricted to direct mail. The move toward managing resources to enhance firm profitability is further substantiated by evidence in business markets that a supplier firm's marketing (or customer management) efforts have a significant influence on the customer's perception of the performance attributes of the products, satisfaction with the products, share of category requirements, and, ultimately, the profitability of the customer (Bowman and Narayandas 2004). A focus on individual customers is imperative in this case, because resource allocations at the market or segment level may lead to suboptimal strategies and additional marketing efforts directed toward a customer create diminishing returns. At least in business markets, accounting for competition also is necessary to explain customer profitability satisfactorily (Bowman and Narayandas 2004).

Two methods have been adopted widely to determine resource allocations to customers: decision calculus[1] and econometric methods. The first one, the decision calculus approach is suitable for determining the optimal level of marketing resources for an entire population or segments of customers, as well as the optimal balance of resources between activities, such as acquisition and retention (Blattberg and Deighton 1996). It is fairly straightforward, easy

---

[1] The approach of calibrating quantitative models by examining subjective (managerial) judgments about outcomes of the investigated process (e.g., market share or sales of a firm) under a variety of hypothetical scenarios (e.g., advertising spending level, promotion expenditures). Once the model linking process outcomes to marketing decision variables has been calibrated, it is possible to derive an optimal marketing recommendation.

to implement approach that can be implemented when little reliable data exist. The second one, the econometric approach, is used when sufficient reliable data exist. It is also quite flexible and has been used to determine resource allocation levels for both an entire population of customers and individual customers. Its basic approach proceeds through the following steps:

Step 1: Specify the objective function for resource allocation. For example, Venkatesan and Kumar (2004) specify the objective function as each customer's CLV, measured as:

$$CLV_i = \sum_{y=1}^{T_i} \frac{CM_{i,y}}{(1+r)^{y/\text{frequency}_i}} - \sum_{l=1}^{n} \frac{\sum_m c_{i,m,l}{}^* x_{i,m,l}}{(1+r)^{l-1}} \tag{9.6}$$

Where

CLV_i = lifetime value of customer i;

$CM_{i,y}$ = predicted contribution margin from customer i (computed from a contribution margin model) in purchase occasion y; measured in dollars;

r = discount rate for money (15% annual rate in the study);

$c_{i,m,l}$ = unit marketing cost for customer i in channel m in year l (the formula- tion of CLV does not change if l is used to represent time periods other than a year);

$x_{i,m,l}$ = number of contacts to customer i in channel m in year l;

frequency$_i$ = predicted purchase frequency for customer i;

n = number of years to forecast; and

T_i = predicted number of purchases made by customer i before the end of the planning period

Step 2: Specify a model that predicts various aspects of customer behavior required to determine the objective function. For example, in Equation (9.6), the specified models predict purchase frequency and contribution margin, and models for predicting customer behavior are specified as a function of marketing decision variables ($x_{i,d}$), covariates ($x_{i,cov}$), and unknown response parameters (βs). The marketing decision variables in Venkatesan and Kumar (2004) include the number of contacts through salesperson, direct, and telesales channels.

Step 3: Use calibration data to estimate the unknown response parameters, given observed customer behavior, marketing decision variables, and covariates.

Step 4: Given the response parameters estimated in Step 3 and the model specified in Step 2, predict customer behavior for the planning period. The predicted customer behaviors then measure the objective function. The marketing decision variables ($X_{i,d}$) and covariates ($X_{i,cov}$) also can be predicted or assumed at the most recent values.

Step 5: Vary the marketing decision variables to determine the maximization level for the objective function. Venkatesan and Kumar (2004) vary the number of contacts through salesperson, direct, and telesales channels to determine the level of contacts through each channel that maximizes each customer's CLV.

The preceding framework can be adapted to customize resource allocation decisions for each customer, a segment of customers, or the entire population, based on the level at which the response parameters (βs) are specified and estimated in Steps 2 and 3. For example, if managers want to customize resource allocations for each customer, the response parameters should be estimated at the individual customer level (i.e., β_is).

Venkatesan and Kumar (2004) apply this methodology to a B2B high-technology firm to link its marketing expenditures to CLV (Equation (9.6)) and evaluate the level of marketing resources for each customer that would maximize his or her CLV. They specify the marketing decision variables (contacts through the various channels) and covariates to influence both customer purchase frequency and contribution margin. The response parameters in the model are specified for each individual customer, which enables customized marketing resource allocations. After they have estimated the models and calculated the CLV for each customer, Venkatesan and Kumar use a genetic algorithm to determine the optimal level of marketing contacts that would maximize a customer's CLV.

Venkatesan and Kumar (2004) also highlight the importance of considering each customer's responsiveness to marketing communication, along with the costs involved across the various channels of communication, when making resource allocation decisions. They suggest potentially substantial improvements in CLV through the appropriate design of marketing contacts across various channels. Moreover, they find that the influence of marketing communications on customer interpurchase time is nonlinear, such that too much communication can have dysfunctional consequences and, in some cases, lead to a reduction in CLV. Customer profits increase when marketers incorporate the differences in individual customer responsiveness to various channels of communication and determine the optimal level of marketing communications to maximize each customer's CLV (given its nonlinear influence). The resource allocation strategy thus can act as a basis for evaluating the potential benefits of CRM implementations in organizations and provides accountability for strategies geared toward managing customer assets.

The econometric approach for resource allocation also has been adopted to determine the optimal balance between acquisition and retention investments to maximize customer profitability (Reinartz et al. 2005) rather than the optimal distribution of a particular type of resource, such as retention expenses, across customers. The procedure used to link customer acquisition, relationship duration, and profitability is explained in the section on "accommodating selection bias." The level of marketing contacts undertaken before the customer is acquired can predict the acquisition model; the level during the relationship serves the retention and profitability models.

The level of investment that optimizes the acquisition rate for a firm differs from the investment levels required to optimize retention rates and customer profitability (Reinartz et al. 2005). Underspending is more detrimental and results in smaller returns on investment (ROI) than does overspending, and a suboptimal allocation of retention expenditures has a greater impact on long-term customer profitability than do suboptimal acquisition expenditures. Both Venkatesan and Kumar (2004) and Reinartz et al. (2005) find that the relative effectiveness of highly interpersonal salesperson contacts is greater than that of less interpersonal or standardized modes of communication.

Elsner et al. (2004) apply the econometric approach to resource allocation in the direct mail catalog industry and employ a dynamic multilevel modeling (DMLM) approach to determine the optimal (1) segmentation of customers on the basis of customer–firm interaction covariates, (2) number of customer segments to receive each direct mail campaign (i.e., size of a campaign), and (3) number of direct marketing campaigns to maximize customer response and order size given customer response. The DMLM approach consists of three levels. In the first, the order size and response elasticity for an additional promotion is calculated through a regression analysis. In the second level, the size of each segment (i.e., number of catalogs to send for each campaign) and minimum order size threshold necessary for a profitable campaign is calculated through analytical derivations of the objective function. In the third level, the covariates related to the customer–firm interactions available in the firm's database are used to segment the firm's customers and determine which segments should receive each campaign. The DMLM approach gets repeated over a rolling window of one year after responses to the current campaign have been integrated into the customer database.

Elsner et al. (2004) also provide empirical evidence of the benefits obtained from implementing this approach for resource allocation. With its status quo strategy, the study company, Rhenania, sent catalogs to only customers whose expected revenue exceeded the total cost of the merchandising, order fulfillment, and mailing. Implementing the DMLM approach resulted in a 43% improvement in sales for Rhenania, even though market growth during the same period was only 15%. As a consequence, Rhenania was able to acquire two major competitors. Subsequent to these acquisitions, Rhenania extended its DMLM approach to a multivariate setting, such that a single firm handled three separate catalogs selling different brands. The DMLM approach developed after the acquisitions explicitly accommodated global customer response to the number of catalogs obtained from Rhenania and the number of catalogs from each separate brand.

9.3.3.2 Cross-Selling

One means to grow customer profits is by increasing the number of products a customer purchases from the firm, or cross-selling. Whereas cross-selling is a firm-side action employed to broaden customer relationships, its counterpart on the demand side, cross-buying, refers to a customer's propensity to make cross-category purchases. Cross-selling yields both immediate profit and the potential to deepen an existing relationship, thereby increasing the switching costs associated with purchasing from another vendor.

Early cross-selling literature focused on aggregate outcomes of cross-selling activities, such as firm-level sales or store choice (Drèze and Hoch 1998; Chen et al. 1999). The importance of measuring individual customer outcomes in organizations, however, has shifted the focus to the effect of cross-selling on the individual level. Within this research realm, the order of product acquisition over time has been a key subject of inquiry. Two observations motivate researchers to predict product acquisition patterns. First, to implement a cross-selling strategy efficiently, managers need to know about the purchase patterns of each individual customer across various product categories. In other words, knowledge about cross-buying behavior should influence cross-selling strategies. Second, customers have predictable lifecycles and, as a result, purchase certain items before others (Li et al. 2005). This predictable phenomenon provides the opportunity for firms to cross-sell additional products or services. Markets that are especially prone to this behavioral regularity include those in which consumers' wants or needs evolve after some preliminary consumption, consumers face some uncertainty about the quality of the product or service offering, or consumer learning is required to receive the full benefit of the product.

The general approach to modeling product acquisition patterns involves ordering multiple products and customers' demand for these products along a common continuum that reflects the development of customer demand maturity. Formally, the latent utility (U) of a given household i choosing product j on occasion t is as follows:

$$U_{ijt} = \beta_i |O_j - DM_{it-1}| + \gamma_{ij}^*(\text{Covariates}) + \varepsilon_{ijt}, \qquad (9.7)$$

where O_j defines the position of product j ranked along the same continuum as demand maturity. DM_{it-1} denotes the demand maturity of consumer i at the end of time $t - 1$, and various other covariates such as satisfaction are included. β and γ denote the respective regression parameters and ϵ is the error term. In the financial service context, demand maturity captures the lifecycle stages of a customer. As a customer grows or matures, their demand for different types of financial services also broadens. For example, a customer may first have a need for a basic checking account, and over time (or as they mature), they may have needs for savings accounts, home loans and a mutual fund account.

The latent product utilities are mapped to observed product purchase decisions through a multivariate framework. At the next level of the hierarchy, demand maturity is modeled as a function of a customer's cumulative number of transactions, spending, and tenure in the product category. Customer demographics, such as education, gender, age, and income, are modeled to discern their impact on customer responsiveness to demand maturity and other covariates.

Li et al. (2005) find that bank customers usually invest more aggressively in financial instruments that promise stable returns (e.g., CDs, money market) after they obtain basic financial services (e.g., checking, savings, debit, credit, loan) and invest in high-risk, high-return brokerage accounts last. However, the movement of households on the demand maturity continuum varies according to customer demographics. Finally, the impact of customer satisfaction is greatest for advanced financial products (e.g., brokerage).

From the firm's perspective, it is natural to focus on determining the product or category with the highest purchase likelihood for each customer, and this element recently attracted attention in the context of CRM strategies (Verhoef et al. 2001; Knott et al. 2002). Knott et al. (2002) attempt to uncover the benefits (measured in profits) derived from a targeted cross-selling strategy with a field experiment and propose a next product to buy (NPTB) model, in which they use a series of independent logistic regressions (one logistic regression for each product category j) to model a customer's propensity to purchase a particular product that he or she has not previously purchased, given current product ownership and demographic characteristics. They illustrate the effectiveness of the NPTB approach with field test for a loan offer in a retail bank. Customers were assigned to one of three groups: heuristic, NPTB, or prospect. Customers in the heuristic test group owned homes valued as greater than $100,000 or were unknown (i.e., a simple, customer demographic–based rule of thumb). Those in the NPTB group were predicted by the NPTB to purchase the loan product. The prospect group consisted of the bank's prospects obtained from a list source. Customers in each group then were randomly assigned to a test or control sample; those in the test sample received a promotional mailing for a loan offer. The results show that customers in the NPTB test group provided more profits than the customers in the heuristic test group and that profits were incrementally better than sales that would have occurred through other channels (i.e., the test group customers provided more revenue than the control group customers). Also, the heuristic and NPTB test group customers provided more revenues than the prospect group, which indicates that targeting retained customers is more profitable than targeting prospects.

On the downside, attempting to sell additional products or product lines can have detrimental impacts on a customer–firm relationship. First, frequent and mistargeted selling attempts are likely to increase customer resentment, which, in the worst case, results in relationship termination by the customer. Second, unsuccessful attempts to increase the range of products with the customer are synonymous with resource misallocation. It is therefore critical to know not only what customers are most likely to buy next but also when they will buy the product of highest affinity (Kumar et al. 2006). Knott et al. (2002) suggest a strong potential for improvement in models that integrate a customer's purchase time and category choice decisions.

Adapting the dynamic McFadden model for brand choice and purchase time, Kumar et al. (2006) test the impact of a cross-selling model that predicts a customer's purchase time and product category choice on the efficiency and effectiveness of sales calls. The joint probability of purchase timing and category choice $P_i(t, j)$ is the product of the marginal probability of purchase timing $P_i(t)$ and the conditional probability of category choice given purchase timing $P_i(J \mid t)$, or

$$P_i(t, j) = P_i(t)^* P_i(j|t). \tag{9.8}$$

The marginal probability of purchase timing is modeled with an accelerated failure time framework, and the conditional probability of product category choice given purchase timing is modeled as a multivariate probit model. The predicted purchase time for a customer serves as one of the covariates in the multivariate probit model and thereby accommodates the dependence between purchase timing and product category choice.

The authors evaluate the benefits of targeting customers with a joint model of purchase timing and product category choice through a field experiment conducted in a B2B firm. Customers assigned to a test group were contacted through the strategy recommended by the timing and category choice model, whereas those in the control group were contacted through the supplier's status quo strategy, which entailed dedicated salespeople who proactively pitched only products in their own product categories during their sales calls to the customers. For each product category, the company typically used a binomial logit model to predict a customer's propensity for the next year. The sales force for each product category used these propensity scores to prioritize customers for sales calls in the next year. The timing of sales calls within the year typically occurred at the discretion of the sales force, and in general, customers with higher propensity scores were contacted before customers with lower propensity scores.

Across all the product categories, in the year the field experiment was conducted, there was a significant increase in customer profitability and ROI compared with the pre-experimental period for the test group but no significant difference in profits among the control group. Also, customers in the test group provided significantly higher profits and ROI than did customers in the control group. The field experiment shows that recommendations from a cross-selling model that predicts both purchase timing and category choice can lead to more effective and efficient sales campaigns that result in higher profits and ROI.

While effective cross-selling is expected to increase customer profitability, it is also theoretically possible that selling additional products to a customer increases the chances that one of products may not satisfy a customer needs. Dissatisfaction with one of the products could also potentially lead to customer defection. Research on the conditions when cross-selling may not be effective for improving customer profits would provide a valuable contribution to the literature.

9.3.3.3 Multichannel Marketing

A dramatic trend in the shopping environment in the past decade has been the proliferation of channels through which customers can transact with firms. The

Internet, kiosks, ATMs, call centers, direct marketing, home shopping net-works, and catalogs, as well as bricks-and-mortar stores, are now common-place. Many firms consider maintaining multiple transaction channels with a customer essential for their sustained growth in the modern competitive envir-onment (Wind and Mahajan 2002). Consequently, CRM activities have grown increasingly complex as firms maintain and expand their customer relationships across multiple transaction channels (Thomas and Sullivan 2005). This trend also has created a challenge for firms that want to manage their environment effectively, as well as opportunities for academics who want to produce insights that can help address these challenges.

A "channel" in this literature stream is defined as a customer contact point or medium through which the firm and the customer interact (Neslin et al. 2006). The emphasis on the term "interact" reflects that one-way communications, such as television advertising, are not included, with the exception of home shopping television networks and direct response advertising in mass media. Furthermore, multichannel marketing is the design, deployment, coordination, and evaluation of marketing activities across multiple channels to enhance customer value. A multichannel customer is one who has used more than one channel to transact with the firm. The emphasis on multichannel marketing among firms partially results from several practitioner studies that indicated multichannel customers have a higher annual purchase volume than do single channel customers (e.g., DoubleClick 2004). Congruent with these practitioner studies, academic research finds that multichannel shoppers provide signifi-cantly higher lifetime profits than do single channel shoppers (Kumar and Venkatesan 2005; Thomas and Sullivan 2005).

In this context, two broad issues are relevant for the success of multichannel marketing:

1. Does customer profitability increase when customers shop in multiple channels?
2. Can marketing communication influence customers to shop in multiple channels and, if so, how?

Although the answers to these questions remain unanswered, we present findings from some recent studies that offer encouraging results. Although there are various aspects of multichannel customer management, such as cus-tomer channel choices for shopping and browsing and multichannel competi-tion among retailers, we focus on the preceding two questions because they are directly relevant to growing customer profits, the focus of this section.

Does customer profitability increase when customers shop in multiple channels? Initial studies have answered this question by comparing the lifetime profits, lifetime revenues, lifetime duration, and purchase frequency of multi-channel and single channel customers. In a B2B environment, Kumar and Venkatesan (2005) find that multichannel customers have longer lifetime dura-tions and provide higher revenues and profits than do single channel shoppers.

Investigating the customer database of a multichannel retailer[2] with a bricks-and-mortar store, a catalog, and an online store, Thomas and Sullivan (2005) find that multichannel customers provide more revenues than do single channel shoppers but that, among multichannel shoppers, customers who shop across all three channels are not necessarily different from those who shop in only two channels in their revenues and purchase frequency.

Correlational evidence that multichannel customers are more profitable than single channel shoppers only implies that managers should provide a synchronized experience across multiple channels because profitable customers tend to shop in multiple channels. A cross-sectional analysis precludes researchers from understanding whether profitable customers in general tend to shop in multiple channels (i.e., self-selection) or if shopping in multiple channels causally leads to higher customer profits. If shopping in multiple channels increases customer profits, managers should grab this opportunity and encourage customers to shop in multiple channels.

Venkatesan et al. (2007) use longitudinal information about customer transactions with an apparel retailer to explore whether shopping in multiple channels increases customer profits. Their intuition regarding the impact of multichannel shopping on changes in customer profits leads them to track customer profits during each quarter and explore whether profits are higher when a customer engages in multichannel shopping, after they account for any general time trends and customer-specific variations in profits due to omitted variables. Using partial regression analyses, they find a significant influence of multichannel shopping on customer profitability, over and beyond any general time trends, possibly because customers allocate greater shares of their wallet or are more satisfied with the firm's offerings (Neslin et al. 2006). These results substantiate customer management strategies that encourage customers to shop in multiple channels. Of course, further research and analysis is needed to explore why customer profits are higher when the customer shops in multiple channels. In particular, an issue that needs consideration is the reinforcing impact of multichannel shopping and purchase frequency (or volume) on each other and on customer profitability. For example, customers with higher purchase frequency are more likely to shop in multiple channels, which can influence their perceptions of the firm's products and in turn affect purchase frequency, which can further improve a customer's propensity to shop in multiple channels, and so forth. Disentangling the pure multichannel effect from the purchase volume effects is important for the effective management of customers in multichannel environments. It is also possible that multichannel customers are simply more interested in the firm's products. Even under this alternative argument, a firm with multiple channels would need to focus their marketing efforts on multichannel shopping because they are likely to have better (or positive)

---

[2] Research studies in this stream have focused on customer data from retailers that own their own brick and mortar stores and therefore have direct contact with customers in this channel.

attitudes about the firm's products. Overall, providing a multichannel experience to customers seems to offer the potential for customer as well as firm growth.

Can marketing communication influence customers to shop in multiple channels and, if so, how? If transacting in multiple channels leads to higher customer profits, the natural next strategic question is how marketing can influence customers to shop in multiple channels. This question represents perhaps the most heavily researched area in multichannel customer management.

The emerging consensus on this topic suggests that marketing communications are critical in influencing customer channel choices (Thomas and Sullivan 2005), and communications though different channels (i.e., direct mail, telesales, salesperson) have a positive, synergistic influence on multichannel shopping (Kumar and Venkatesan 2005). In other words, customers who are contacted through a variety of channels are more likely to shop in a variety of channels. Ansari et al. (2005) find that marketing communications to a multichannel-/Internet-loyal group provide a potential explanation for the sales levels of multichannel customers, who also received more marketing than the catalog-loyal group and tended to respond to it more strongly in terms of their purchase incidence.

Similar to the relationship between customer value and marketing communications, the impact of marketing communications on multichannel shopping is nonlinear in both customer's channel choices at each purchase instance (Thomas and Sullivan 2005) and the time a customer takes to start shopping in an additional channel (Venkatesan et al. 2007). Thomas and Sullivan (2005) suggest a six-step process for designing multichannel marketing communications: (1) estimate a segment-level channel choice model, (2) assign existing customers to the segments identified in step 1 and profile the segments, (3) predict customer's channel choice probability over time, (4) develop a segment-specific communications strategy, (5) classify first-time customers into existing segments, and (6) update segment affiliation over time as more customer interaction data are accumulated. For an office supplies retailer that sells through a catalog, the Internet, and a bricks-and-mortar store, Thomas and Sullivan (2005) identify a nonlinear influence of marketing communications on channel choice. Increasing marketing communications up to a certain threshold motivates customers to purchase from the catalog or the bricks-and-mortar store, depending on the segment to which they belong.

Predicting the time a customer takes to adopt an additional channel would provide a better forward-looking allocation of marketing resources to individual customers. On the basis of customer transactions with an apparel retailer that sells through a full-price bricks-and-mortar store, a discount bricks-and-mortar store, and the Internet, Venkatesan et al. (2007) find that customer–firm interaction characteristics pertaining to purchase occasions, the frequency of interactions, and channel characteristics are associated with varied channel adoption durations. Marketing communication is critical in influencing customer channel choices, but the influence is nonlinear; therefore, managers must be aware of the optimal frequency of communication for each customer because overcommunicating to customers can have dysfunctional consequences, such as longer channel adoption duration.

In summary, managers have the potential to grow customer profits through multichannel marketing. Given the importance of marketing for influencing customer channel choice and the variability in profits among multichannel customers, resource allocation is essential for maximizing customer profitability. Investigating the reasons multichannel customers provide higher profits also is necessary to design effective multichannel marketing strategies. Several propositions, including increased loyalty, expansion of customer category requirements, self-selection, and pure marketing effect, have been forwarded that require empirical verification (Neslin et al. 2006).

9.4 Conclusion

This review of the literature on CRM decision models reveals that customer-level marketing actions change when a firm's strategic focus shifts from maximizing short-term customer responses to maximizing long-term customer value. The concentration on the economic value of a customer has implications for all aspects of a customer relationship—acquisition, retention, growth, and win back. The accurate measurement of customer CLV and a rigorous estimation of the link between marketing actions and CLV are critical for designing effective CRM strategies. However, customer retention and growth issues have attracted more attention than customer acquisition issues, largely due to the challenge posed by the lack of detailed transaction information on prospects.

The major challenges facing academicians and practitioners with regard to CRM decision models include (1) long-term value prediction, (2) addressing the endogeneity and simultaneity issue in CLV models that include marketing actions, (3) developing methods that accommodate missing data pertaining to both prospects and customers, (4) understanding the impact of channel resources on customer acquisition and growth, (5) assessing how customer attitudes affect their CLV, and (6) evaluating whether the level of returns provided by the more complete models of customer behavior to justify the firm investments in collecting customer level information required for these models. Finally, issues such as addressability, purchase frequency, purchase involvement, cost-to-serve, and the importance of loyalty vary widely across organizations and industries. Therefore, in the future, contingency-based CRM decisions models will be called for.

References

Allenby, G.M., R.P. Leone, L. Jen. 1999. A Dynamic Model of Purchase Timing with Application to Direct Marketing. *Journal of American Statistical Association* **94**(June) 365–374.

Ansari, A., C. Mela, S. Neslin. 2005. Customer Channel Migration. Working Paper, Dartmouth University.

Bauer, C.L. (1988). A Direct Mail Customer Purchase Model. *Journal of Direct Marketing* **2**(3) 16–24.

Berger, P.D., N. Nasr-Bechwati. 2001. The Allocation of Promotion Budget to Maximize Customer Equity. *The International Journal of Management Science* **29**(1) 49–61.

Blattberg, R., J. Deighton. 1996. Manage Marketing by the Customer Equity Test. *Harvard Business Review* July–August, 136–144.

Bodapati, A., S. Gupta. 2004. A Direct Approach to Predicting Discretized Response in Target Marketing. *Journal of Marketing Research* **41**(February) 73–85.

Boulding, W., R. Staelin, M. Ehret, W.J. Johnston. 2005. A Customer Relationship Management Roadmap: What Is Known, Potential Pitfalls, and Where to Go. *Journal of Marketing* **69**(October) 155-166.

Bowman, D., D. Narayandas. 2004. Linking Customer Management Effort to Customer Profitability in Business Markets. *Journal of Marketing Research* **41**(4) 433–447.

Bult, J.R., T. Wansbeek. 1995. Optimal Selection for Direct Mail. *Marketing Science* **14**(4) 378–94.

Burnett, Ed. 1988. *The Complete Direct Mail List Handbook*. Prentice Hall, New York.

Chen, Y., J.D. Hess, R. Wilcox, Z.J. Zhang. 1999. Accounting Profits Versus Marketing Profits: A Relevant Metric for Category Management. *Marketing Science* **18**(3) 208–29.

David Shepard Associates. (1999). *The New Direct Marketing*, 3d ed. Irwin Professional Publishing, New York.

Day, G. 1999. *The Market Driven Organization.*The Free Press, New York.

Doubleclick 2004. Retail Details: Best Practices in Multi-Channel Integration (March), DoubleClick, Inc.. New York.

Drèze, X., S. Hoch. 1998. Exploiting the Installed Base Using Cross-merchandising and Category Destination Programs. *International Journal of Research in Marketing* **15**(December) 459–471.

Du, R., W. Kamakura. 2005. Household Lifecycles and Lifestyles in the United States. *Journal of Marketing Research* **43**(February) 121–132.

———, ———, C. Mela. 2005. Size and Share of Customer Wallet. Working Paper, Teradata Center, Duke University.

Dwyer, R. 1989. Customer Lifetime Valuation to Support Marketing Decision Making. *Journal of Direct Marketing* **3**(4) 8–15.

Dwyer, R. R., P.H. Schurr, S. Oh. 1987. Developing Buyer-Seller Relations. *Journal of Marketing* **51**(April) 11–28.

Elsner, R., M. Krafft, A. Huchzermeier. 2004. Optimizing Rhenania's Direct Marketing Business Through Dynamic Multilevel Modeling (DMLM) in a Multicatalog-Brand Environment. *Marketing Science* **23**(2) 192–206.

Fader, P.S., B.G.S. Hardie, Ka.L. Lee. 2005a. Counting Your Customers the Easy Way: An Alternative to the Pareto/NBD Model. *Marketing Science* **24**(Spring) 275–284.

———, ———, ———. 2005b. RFM and CLV: Using Iso-value Curves for Customer Base Analysis. *Journal of Marketing Research* **42**(November) 415–430.

Fournier, S., S. Dobscha, D.G. Mick. 1998. Preventing the Premature Death of Relationship Marketing. *Harvard Business Review* (January–February) 42–51.

Gönül, F.F., B. Kim, M. Shi. 2000. Mailing Smarter to Catalog Customers. *Journal of Interactive Marketing* **14**(2) 2–16.

Hebden J.J., J.F. Pickering. 1974. Patterns of Acquisition of Consumer Durables. *Bulletin of Economics and Statistics* **36** 67–94.

Heckman, J. 1976. The Common Structure of Statistical Models of Truncation, Sample Selection and Limited Dependent Variables, and a Simple Estimator for Such Models. *Annals of Economic and Social Measurement* **5** 475–492.

——— 1979. Sample Selection Bias as a Specification Error. *Econometrica* **47**(January) 153–61.

Kamakura, W.A., B. Kossar, M. Wedel. 2004. Identifying Innovators for the Cross-Selling of New Products. *Management Science* **50**(August) 1120–1133.

———, S.N. Ramaswami, R.K. Srivastava. 1991. Applying Latent Trait Analysis in the Evaluation of Prospects for Cross-Selling of Financial Services. *International Journal of Research in Marketing* **8**(4) 329–350.

———, ———, F. de Rosa, J.A. Mazzon. 2003. Cross-Selling through Database Marketing: A Mixed Data Factor Analyzer for Data Augmentation and Prediction. *International Journal of Research in Marketing* **20**(1) 45–65.

Knott, A., A.F. Hayes, S. Neslin. 2002. Next-product-to-buy Models for Cross-Selling Applications. *Journal of Interactive Marketing* **16**(3) 59–75.

Krafft, M., K. Peters. 2005. Empirical Findings and Recent Trends of Direct Mailing Optimization. *Marketing – Journal of Research and Managment* **27**(2) 26–40.

Krishnamurthi, L., S.P. Raj. 1988. A Model of Brand Choice and Purchase Quantity Price Sensitivities. *Marketing Science* **7**(1) 1–20.

Kumar, V., R. Venkatesan. 2005. Who Are the Multichannel Shoppers and How do they Perform? Correlates of Multichannel Shopping Behavior. *Journal of Interactive Marketing* **19**(2) 44–62.

Kumar, V., R. Venkatesan, W. Reinartz. 2006. Does Marketing Improve Efficiency and Effectiveness of Sales Campaigns: Experimental Evidence Working Paper, University of Connecticut.

Lewis, M. 2004. The Influence of Loyalty Programs and Short Term Promotions on Customer Retention. *Journal of Marketing Research* **41**(3) 281–292.

——— 2006. Customer Acquisition Promotions and Customer Asset Value. *Journal of Marketing Research* **43** (2) 195–203.

Li, S., B. sun, R.T. Wilcox. 2005. Cross Selling Sequentially Ordered Products: An Application to Consumer Banking. *Journal of Marketing Research* **42**(May) 233–239.

Lilien, G.L., P. Kotler, K.S. Moorthy. 1992. *Marketing Models* Prentice Hall.

LimDep 2002. Econometric Software Inc., Plainview, NY

Malthouse, E. 2001. Assessing the Performance of Direct Marketing Scoring Models. *Journal of Interactive Marketing* **15**(1) 49–62.

———, R. Blattberg 2005. Is it Possible to Predict Customer Long-Term Value? *Journal of Interactive Marketing* **19**(1) 2–16.

Manchanda, P., P.E. Rossi, P.K. Chintagunta. 2004. Response Modeling with Nonrandom Marketing-Mix Variables. *Journal of Marketing Research.* **41**(4) 467

Morgan, R.M., S.D. Hunt. 1994. The Commitment-Trust Theory of Relationship Marketing. *Journal of Marketing* **58**(July) 20–38.

Mulhern, F. 1999. Customer Profitability Analysis: Measurement, Concentration, and Research Directions. *Journal of Interactive Marketing* **13**(Winter) 25–40.

Neslin, S., S. Gupta, W. Kamakura, J. Lu, C. Mason. 2006. Defection Detection: Measuring and Understanding the Predictive Accuracy of Customer Churn Models. *Journal of Marketing Research* **43**(2) 204–211.

Niraj, R., M. Gupta, C. Narasimhan. 2001. Customer Profitability in a Supply Chain. *Journal of Marketing* **65**(July) 1 16.

Oldstein, J. 1989. Working Effectively with a List Brokerage Firm. *Direct Marketing Manual.* The Direct Marketing Association, Inc., New York.

Paroush, J. 1965. The Order of Acquisition of Consumer Durables. *Econometrica* **33**(1) 225–35.

Pfeiffer, P., R. Carraway. 2000. Modelling Customer Relationships as Markov Chains. *Journal of Interactive Marketing* **14**(2) 43–55.

Reichheld, F., T. Teal. 1996. *The Loyalty Effect.* Harvard Business School Press, Boston, MA.

Reinartz, W. 2005. Understanding Customer Loyalty Programs. *Retailing in the 21st Century. Current and Future Trends*, Mantrala M., M. Krafft, Eds. Springer Verlag.

Reinartz, W., M. Krafft, W. Hoyer. 2004. The CRM Process: Its Measurement and Impact on Performance. *Journal of Marketing Research* **41**(August) 293–305.

———, V. Kumar. 2000. On the Profitability of Long-Life Customers in a Non-Contractual Setting: An Empirical Investigation and Implications for Marketing. *Journal of Marketing* **64**(October), 17–35.

———, ——— 2002. The Mismanagement of Customer Loyalty. *Harvard Business Review.* **80**(July) 86–94.

———, ——— 2003. The Impact of Customer Relationship Characteristics on Profitable Lifetime Duration. *Journal of Marketing* **67**(January) 77–99.

———, J. S. Thomas, V. Kumar. 2005. Balancing Acquisition and Retention Resources to Maximize Customer Profitability *Journal of Marketing* **69**(1) 63–79.

Rust, Roland, T. 2007. Seeking Higher Roi? Base Strategy on Customer Equity. Advertising Age **78**(36) 26–27.

Schmittlein, D., D. G. Morrison, R. Colombo. 1987. Counting Your Customers: Who Are They and What Will They do Next?. *Management Science* **33**(January) 1–24.

———, R. A. Peterson. 1994. Customer Base Analysis: An Industrial Purchase Process Application. *Marketing Science* **13** 41–67.

Sharp, B., A. Sharp. 1997. Loyalty Programs and Their Impact on Repeat-Purchase Loyalty Patterns. *International Journal of Research in Marketing* **14**(5) 473–86.

Shugan, S. 2004. Endogeneity in Marketing Decision Models *Marketing Science* **23**(1) 1–3.

Srivastava, R., T. Shervani, L. Fahey. 1998. Marketing-Based Assets and Shareholder Value: A Framework for Analysis. *Journal of Marketing,* **62**(January) 2–18.

Steenburgh, T., A. Ainslie, P.H. Engebretson. 2003. Revealing the Information in Zipcodes: Bayesian Massively Categorical Variables and Aggregated Data in Direct Marketing. *Marketing Science* **22**(Winter) 40–57.

Thomas, J.S., R.C. Blattberg, E.J. Fox. 2004. Recapturing Lost Customers. *Journal of Marketing Research* **41**(February) 31–45.

———, U. Sullivan. 2005 Managing Marketing Communications with Multichannel Customers. *Journal of Marketing* **69** 239–251.

Venkatesan, R., V. Kumar. 2004. A Customer Lifetime Value Framework for Customer Selection and Resource Allocation Strategy. *Journal of Marketing* **68**(October) 106–25.

Venkatesan, R., V. Kumar, N. Ravishanker. 2007. The Impact of Customer-Firm Interaction Characteristics on Channel Adoption Duration. *Journal of Marketing* forthcoming.

Verhoef, P.C., B. Donkers. 2005. The effect of acquisition channels on customer loyalty and cross-buying. *Journal of Interactive Marketing* **19**(2) 31–43.

Verhoef, P.C., P.H. Franses, J.C. Hoekstra. 2001. The Impact of Satisfaction and Payment Equity on Cross-Buying: A Dynamic Model for Multi-Service Provider. *Journal of Retailing* **77**(Fall) 359–378.

Villanueva, J., S. Yoo, D. Hanssens. 2006. The Impact of Marketing-Induces vs. Word-of-Mouth Customer Acquisition on Customer Equity. Working Paper, IESE Business School, University of Navarra, No. 516.

Webster, F., Jr. 1992. The Changing Role of Marketing in the Corporation. *Journal of Marketing* **56**(October) 1–17.

———, A. Malter, S. Ganesan. 2005. Understanding the Changing Role of Marketing Management. *MIT Sloan Management Review* **46**(4) 35–43.

Wind, Y., V. Mahajan. 2002. *Convergence Marketing: Strategies for Reaching the New Hybrid Customer*. Prentice Hall, Inc., Upper Saddle River, NJ.

Winer, R.S. 1983. Attrition Bias in Econometric Models Estimated with Panel Data. *Journal of Marketing Research* **20**(May) 177–86.

Chapter 10
Marketing Models for Electronic Commerce

Randolph E. Bucklin

10.1 Introduction

The Internet continues to grow dramatically as a vehicle for facilitating commerce. For example, online sales transactions in the U.S. consumer sector will pass $200 billion in calendar year 2007, growing at a rate of 17 percent per year (comScore 2007). Omitting travel (the largest single category for Internet commerce), online retail sales account for about five percent of the total retail sales in the United States. The success and continued rapid growth of e-commerce (in both consumer and business-to-business sectors), makes it likely that marketing managers working to improve decision making will increasingly seek out modeling approaches suitable for use in this domain. The objective of this chapter is provide an overview of some of the key developments and advances in the application of marketing models to electronic commerce. Given that e-commerce began in earnest little more than a decade ago, all of these advances are quite recent. Indeed, almost all have been published since the year 2000.

Many academic fields share a keen interest in studying the Internet and e-commerce. Economists, for example, are interested in the implications of the Internet for search, price dispersion, and competition. Computer scientists and experts in information systems develop new algorithms for optimizing web site operations and analyzing the data collected from Internet usage and transactions. Sociologists are interested in the impact of the Internet on social networks, among other topics. Even within marketing, research on the Internet and aspects of e-commerce is quite diverse; theoretically oriented researchers (e.g., those pursuing game theory types of approaches) have investigated numerous aspects of the Internet (e.g., Lal and Sarvary 1999) while researchers in consumer psychology have published a wide array of experimentally-based studies bearing on shopping behavior in the Internet environment (e.g., Zauberman 2003). The focus of this chapter will be on the *modeling* contributions which have appeared in the marketing literature.

R.E. Bucklin
UCLA Anderson School, Los Angeles, CA, USA
e-mail: randy.bucklin@anderson.ucla.edu

B. Wierenga (ed.), *Handbook of Marketing Decision Models*,
DOI: 10.1007/978-0-387-78213-3_10, © Springer Science+Business Media, LLC 2008

Researchers studying the Internet and e-commerce have already begun to address a broad array of modeling problems. Many of these problems parallel the issues which occupied researchers studying so-called "bricks-and-mortar" or conventional retailing: traffic generation, assortment, pricing, promotions, customer service, purchase behavior, and repeat patronage or loyalty. Firms operating in electronic commerce also worry about attracting potential customers (or visitors) to their sites, need to understand the drivers of purchase behavior, and are concerned with sustaining the patronage of their customers. Though there are many parallels, one difference between e-commerce and conventional retailing is in the role of physical location. Conventional retailers often rely upon location to generate store traffic, whereas web-based retailers cannot. This further heightens the importance of how to best attract potential customers to the e-commerce web site.

10.1.1 Clickstream Data

With a few exceptions, most of the models discussed in this chapter have been applied to data pertaining to one or more e-commerce web sites. Data are commonly drawn from the so-called "clickstream," which provides detailed records of the online activities of visitors to the web sites (e.g., pages visited, time of visit, duration of visit, etc.). Clickstream data can also be classified as user-centric or site-centric (e.g., Bucklin et al. 2002). User-centric clickstream data records activities for a panel of users across multiple (potentially competing) web sites. It must be collected using panel-based methods and is generally available only from syndicated suppliers such as comScore, Inc. and Nielsen Net Ratings. It is analogous to UPC scanner-panel data in conventional retailing. On the other hand, site-centric clickstream data provides records of activities for visitors at a given web site and is collected and processed by the operators of that site. While providing detailed records of what visitors do when they come to a site, it lacks information regarding the activities of those users on other web sites as well as the profile information available from panel-data (e.g., demographics). In this sense, site centric data are analogous to store register receipt data in conventional retailing.

Though user-centric data might initially appear to be the better source of information for modeling purposes, it can suffer from two limitations. First, despite the very large number of panelists (e.g., more than one million) maintained by syndicated data suppliers in user-centric data, sampling issues can arise if there is a need to focus on the detailed activities of a single e-commerce web site. This may be especially true when the site attracts low traffic volumes or has a very low visit-to-purchase conversion rate (thereby reducing the number of purchase observations available for modeling purposes). Second, depending upon the level of detail captured from the clickstream, it can be difficult to match information recorded in the user-centric panel records to specific activities on a given web site. These limitations of user-centric data must be balanced against the need to incorporate users' cross-site activities into the model.

10.1.2 Organization of the Chapter

Despite the short time span marketing researchers have been developing models relevant to e-commerce, there already have been a large number of promising advances. Taking the perspective of the Internet shopper, the discussion of these advances will follow the logic of "before, during, and after." E-commerce operators must determine how to attract customers to the site, diagnose what customers do while at the site, endeavor to improve the site to enhance conversion rates (the likelihood of completing a transaction given a site visit) or order sizes, and monitor the performance of the site in relation to alternatives both outside and inside the firm (e.g., multi-channel retailers). Following the above, the modeling advances discussed in this chapter are organized into three broad categories:

- attracting visitors to the site,
- understanding site usage behavior, predicting purchase, and managing the site, and
- assessing activity across multiple sites and multiple channels.

In some cases, a given modeling application may provide insight across more than one of the above categories. Nevertheless, instances of such models remain uncommon in the marketing literature – perhaps owing to the complexity of covering one topic, let alone two or more. In what follows, Section 10.2 takes up models relevant to attracting visitors, Section 10.3 considers models for site usage, purchase prediction, and site management, and Section 10.4 deals with models that consider multiple sites or multiple channels (e.g., alternate channels such as catalogs and stores in addition to e-commerce).

10.2 Attracting Visitors to the Site

Because web sites do not occupy a physical space, managers must rely entirely upon marketing communications to develop awareness and to bring visitors to the site. The challenge of acquiring site traffic at affordable costs is a critical concern among e-commerce managers. In order to manage this process, firms need to understand the response that potential visitors are likely to have to investments in various forms of marketing communications. Modeling advances in this area typically measure the effect that various communication vehicles have on the propensity of a user to come to the web site being promoted. Models developed to date have dealt specifically with offline advertising, online advertising (e.g., banner ads), referral sites such as shop-bots, outbound email, and word-of-mouth. In these models, the dependent variable will often, but not always, take the form of a so-called "click-through"– and action which carries the user from where he/she is on the web to a landing on the desired site. Table 10.1 provides a summary of the key models covered in this section.

Table 10.1 Summary of Models for Attracting Visitors to a Web Site

Article	Modeling objective	Type of model and dependent variable(s)	Data	Key finding(s)
Ilfeld and Winer (2002)	Determine effects of advertising on web site awareness and visits	Regression; awareness and site visits	Clickstream panel, online and offline advertising	Elasticity of site visits with respect to online advertising estimated at 0.14
Chatterjee et al. (2003)	Understand banner ad clickthrough	Binary logit; clickthrough	Site-centric clickstream	Extensive heterogeneity in baseline clickthrough rate and response
Manchanda et al. (2006)	Estimate effects of banner ad exposure on web purchasing	Hazard function; purchase timing	Internal company data on banner ad exposure and web site transactions	Concave response to banner ad exposure; elasticity of purchase with respect to banner ad exposure is 0.02
Smith and Brynjolfsson (2001)	Understand user clickthrough choices at a shopbot	Multinomial logit; choice of link at the shopbot	Internal company data on shopbot links and choices	Shoppers prefer branded sites; links in top rank positions more likely to be clicked
Ansari and Mela (2003)	Customize links in outbound email to maximize clickthrough to site	Binary probit with an optimization module; link clickthrough	Site-centric clickstream with outbound email data	Rank of link position in the email and link content both affect clickthrough; customization raises clickthrough rate by 50–60 percent

10.2.1 Acquiring Traffic Through Advertising

Internet companies invest in both traditional media as well as online advertising. Online advertising consists of several different formats, including display related, search, classifieds, lead generation, and email. The two major categories are display type advertisements (so-called "banner" ads) and paid search advertising. (In paid search listings, companies bid to have their text ads placed in desirable positions on search engines such as Google and Yahoo in response to user search queries on key words.) In 2006, companies spent close to $17 billion on Internet advertising in the U.S., of which 40 percent went to paid search and 32 percent went to display (Internet Advertising Bureau 2007).

In one of the first modeling efforts to link advertising by Internet companies to site visitation, Ilfeld and Winer (2002) proposed a three-equation regression model of awareness, site visits, and brand equity. Their best-fitting formulation of the model was specified as follows:

$$AWARENESS = \alpha_0 + \alpha_1 ONLINE + \alpha_2 OFFLINE + \alpha_3 PRBUZZ$$
$$+ \alpha_4 WOM + \alpha_5 BRICKS + \varepsilon$$
$$VISITS = \beta_0 + \beta_1 ONLINE + \beta_2 OFFLINE + \beta_3 AWARENESS$$
$$+ \beta_4 LINKS + \varepsilon \tag{10.1}$$
$$BRANDEQ = \delta_0 + \delta_1 ONLINE + \delta_2 OFFLINE + \delta_3 VISITS$$
$$+ \delta_4 QUALITY + \delta_5 PGVIEW + \delta_6 PUBLIC + \varepsilon$$

Information from a variety of sources was combined to estimate the model on data for 88 Internet companies. For example, panel data from Media Metrix (now part of comScore) provided web site visits (VISITS), past web site visits (used as a proxy for WOM, word-of-mouth), and page views (PGVIEW). Advertising (ONLINE and OFFLINE) was measured by tabulating the spending for each company on both online and offline media (radio, television, cable, outdoor, newspapers and magazines). The number of links from other web sites (LINKS) to the focal site was determined from the Internet search engine, Google.

Estimating their model using three-stage least squares, Ilfeld and Winer found that site visits were positively related to online advertising spending with an elasticity of 0.14 (an effect size in the normal range for advertising elasticities per Hanssens et al. 2001). Though offline advertising was negatively related to web site visits in the VISITS equation, this variable was positively related to the AWARENESS and BRANDEQ dependent variables (measures both compiled by Landor Associates). Because AWARENESS was found to be strongly and positively predictive of VISITS, this provided an indirect path for offline advertising to positively influence web site visitation. LINKS also was found to have a strong positive effect on VISITS. The authors concluded that online advertising was effective in generating traffic, offline advertising was effective in generating awareness which further aids traffic, and links (which may be from partnerships and paid sponsorships) were also effective.

The Ilfeld and Winer modeling approach is potentially useful at a strategic level of media planning for generating web site traffic. It is notable for illustrating how multiple advertising vehicles can influence site traffic and how web-related data from different sources (e.g., some clickstream-based, some survey-based, etc.) can be combined together to effectively predict web site visitation. A potential limitation of the model for applied use is its data requirements. Information across many different web sites is needed to provide an adequate number of observations for estimation purposes. Data also must be gathered systematically from different sources and carefully aligned.

10.2.2 Modeling Response to Banner Ads

Banner advertisements can bring potential customers directly to an e-commerce web site when Internet users, browsing elsewhere online, click on banner ads sponsored by the site.[1] Though so-called "click through" rates can be quite low for banner advertisements, those users who do click can be excellent prospects when their site visits convert to purchase transactions at a high rate. Click-stream data enables firms to track exposure to banner ads and capture the visitor's decision to click on the ad or not. This setting is a natural fit for the use of discrete choice models which can be fitted to the recorded actions in indivi-dual-level clickstream data. The results from such models can be used to under-stand the factors driving higher or lower rates of banner ad click through and to calibrate the productivity of those ads as a vehicle to attract visitors to an e-commerce web site.

Chatterjee et al. (2003) develop a model of banner ad click through behavior based on a binary logit formulation. The model predicts the probability of an individual clicking on a banner ad exposure, given that the ad has not yet been clicked on by that user during the current web site session. Following the authors' notation,[2] this conditional click/no-click probability is given by the binary logit model:

$$\pi_{iso} = Logit(a_i + \theta' X_{iso} + \beta' Y_{is} + \lambda' Z_i + \varepsilon_{iso}) \tag{10.2}$$

where

π_{iso} = the probability that individual i clicks at exposure occasion o during session s,

a_i = an individual-specific constant for the clicking propensity of individual i,

X_{iso} = vector of variables for banner exposure occasion o for session s of individual i,

Y_{is} = vector of session-specific variables for session s and individual i,

---

[1] Banner ads are typically 480×60 pixels large, occupying about 10 percent of an average web page. Ads usually have both graphic and text content and contain a link to the advertiser's web site which is activated by clicking on the ad.

[2] Equation 10.2 follows the authors' notation from their article. Note that the binary logit model can also be written as $\pi_{iso} = \exp(U)/(1 + \exp(U))$ where U is given by $a_i + \theta' X_{iso} + \beta' Y_{is} + \lambda' Z_i$.

Z_i = vector of individual-specific variables, constant across
      sessions, and

$\theta', \beta', \lambda'$ = vectors of coefficients to be estimated.

The above set-up allows the model to capture factors that are changing (1) within a session, (2) across sessions, and (3) across individuals. Using random-effects specifications for the coefficients also allows the model to capture differences in response parameters across individuals. The authors estimated their model on enhanced clickstream data from a sponsored content web site (a so-called "e-zine") spanning eight months in 1995. Banner advertisements from two sponsors (both high-tech firms) were studied.

Looking at factors changing within a session (the X_{iso} vector), the authors included the following variables: the number of times individual i had been exposed to the banner ad in the session so far, $Banner_{iso}$, a quadratic term for the same variable, $Banner_{iso}^2$, the number of pages already browsed during the session, $Pages_{iso}$, and a dummy variable to account for differences across the two ad sponsors, $Advertiser_{iso}$. Results showed that exposure to more banner ads within the same session was negatively related to click through probability but at a decreasing rate (the linear term was negative while the quadratic term was positive). Thus, given that a user has not yet clicked on an ad in a session, the chances of doing so decline with further exposure to banner ads. This rate of decline, however, slows to zero after 11 exposures and, due the impact of the quadratic term in the model, actually becomes positive thereafter. The mean of the coefficient for the number of pages already browsed was not significantly different from zero. However, in the random effects specification the variance estimated for this coefficient was large. This suggests positive effects for some users and negative effects for others, resulting in a mean near zero. Sponsor identity was not a significant predictor of banner ad click through in this case.

The model also included a series of variables capturing session-specific effects in the Y_{is} vector (i.e., factors that did not change across exposures within a session). These included the time since last click in prior sessions, $TLClick_{iso}$, intersession time, IST_{is}, number of times the individual has visited the site, $Session_{is}$, and cumulative banner exposures in prior sessions, $TBanner_{is}$. The estimation results showed that time since last click, intersession time, and the cumulative number of banner exposures were all positively related to ad click through. On the other hand, the number of sessions at the site was negatively related to click probability, perhaps due to experience and learning effects among users. The authors note that, as a rule, new visitors and less frequent visitors are more likely to click on ads than regular visitors.

Lastly, the modeling results also revealed considerable differences across individuals in click proneness. The estimated intercept term for clicking propensity gives a baseline click probability of 0.039 when all other explanatory variables are set equal to zero. But because a very large variance was estimated in the random effects specification for the intercept, substantial dispersion in this baseline click rate existed across individuals. This heterogeneity, together with the heterogeneity found in response to many of the other explanatory factors, clearly demonstrates the potential for vastly different responses to Internet banner advertising across users. Individual-level clickstream data may enable marketing modelers to extend the framework proposed by Chatterjee et al. to identify targeting opportunities for banner ads, thereby enhancing the productivity of efforts to bring new visitors to the site.

The data used in the Chatterjee et al. study was from 1995. Since then, industry reports have documented a steep decline in click-through rates, questioning the effectiveness of banner ads. In an experimental study, Drèze and Hussherr (2003) investigated why Internet users do not click on banner ads. Using an eye-tracking method, they found that about half of the users actually deliberately avoided looking at banner ads. But they also found, in a large-scale survey study, that banner ads were effective in boosting recall, recognition, and awareness. Drèze and Hussherr concluded that banner ads do indeed remain effective but that a broader set of measures – in addition to click-through rates – will be needed to gauge banner ad response.

One such broader measure may be to look directly at the effects that banner ads have on the actual purchases made at an e-commerce site. This is the approach proposed by Manchanda et al. (2006). In their article, they do not explicitly model the traffic acquisition function of banner ads, but connect banner ad exposure directly to purchase behavior. The authors studied the online purchases made by customers of a web site selling health care items, beauty products, and nonprescription drugs directly to consumers. The study period covered 13 weeks of activity in the year 2000. Data were available at the individual level and included complete records of the exposure of users to banner ads sponsored by the site along with their purchase transactions on the site.

To capture the impact of banner advertising on purchase, Manchanda et al. proposed a piecewise exponential hazard model where a purchase is treated as a "failure" in the hazard model. The probability of purchase in any of the j time intervals (weeks) for a customer i is specified as

$$\Pr_{ij}(purchase) = 1 - \exp[-\exp(u_{ij})] \qquad (10.3)$$

where

$$u_{ij} = \sum_{j=1}^{J}(\lambda_j \times I_j) + \sum_{p=1}^{P}(x_{pij} \times \beta_{pi}).$$

In the model, λ_j is a vector of failure rate parameters estimated for each week j, I_j is a vector of indicator variables for weeks j, x_{pij} is a vector of p covariates (described below) for customer i at week j, and β_{pi} is a vector of p response parameters for customer i. Individual-level heterogeneity in the response parameters is modeled using a hierarchical Bayesian approach and parameter estimates are obtained via Bayesian simulation methods.

In equation (10.3), the authors specify four covariates in the x-vector. Two of these capture banner ad exposure and two control for differences across users. For banner ad exposure, VIEWNUM is the total number of banner ad exposures (for the sponsoring site) in each week for each customer and ADNUM is the number of different creative executions for the banner ads that the customer was exposed to each week. To capture diminishing marginal returns to advertising exposure, VIEWNUM enters the model in log form (i.e., as LVIEWNUM = log(1+VIEWNUM)). For the control variables, the authors specify SITENUM as the total number of unique web sites on which the customer was exposed to the banner advertising each week and PAGENUM as the number of unique web pages where the customer was exposed to ads from the sponsoring site.

Estimating the model, the authors find that the log of the number of banner ad exposures, LVIEWNUM, was positively related to the probability of making a purchase on the web site. This finding establishes an individual-level connection between exposure to banner ads and e-commerce site transactions, regardless of the rate of click-through. The diversity of advertising exposure, ADNUM, was found to be negatively related to purchase probability. Thus, exposure to different ad executions lowers e-commerce transactions, a result which may be due to clutter and the lack of a consistent message or creative execution. The two control covariates, SITENUM and PAGENUM, were found to be positively related to purchase. This indicates that ad exposure at more locations (both sites and pages) raises the likelihood of a purchase transaction by that customer. In light of the findings, the authors suggest that Internet banner ad campaigns be designed so that customers see fewer (and more consistent) creatives appearing on many web sites and web pages.

In addition to these campaign implications, the modeling results were also extended to elasticity and targeting. Using the model, the authors gauge the mean elasticity of purchase with respect to banner advertising exposure to be 0.02. (Though significantly positive, it is relatively small for an advertising elasticity.) Second, the authors also report that they found considerable heterogeneity across customers in their response parameters (a result consistent with Chatterjee et al. 2003). While average response may be low, the heterogeneity implies that response to banner ads is higher for some customers. If these customers can be identified, it may be possible to improve the returns to banner advertising through targeting, as the authors discuss in an example. Though the modeling work on banner ads remains limited to date, it has clearly demonstrated the potential for models to improve decision making going forward. The ability to track and model response to banner ads at the individual level should enable researchers and practitioners to better understand how these ads work, predict their effects, and improve their productivity.

10.2.3 Paid Search Advertising

Besides banner or display-type ads, the second major form of Internet advertising is related to search. In paid search, companies bid with search engines such as Google and Yahoo to have small text ads placed into the search results presented to Internet users. When users click on these ads, they are taken to a landing page on the sponsor's web site and the sponsor is billed for their bid amount per click. For example, a user who enters a query into Google for "Las Vegas hotels" will be presented with a listing of both so-called "organic" and paid search results pertaining to Las Vegas hotels and travel. The organic search results are presented and ordered based on the search engine's algorithms and there is no charge when users click on those links. The position order of the paid search results depends, in part, on how much each sponsor is willing to pay per click. If the user clicks on the paid search (or sponsored) text ad for, say, the Las Vegas Hilton, Hilton's account (or its agency's account) would be debited for the cost of the click. Advertisers are not billed for impressions (i.e., ads that are served and presented but not clicked). While most of the funds spent on search engine marketing are for paid search, it is worth noting that firms also engage in activities, often subcontracted, to optimize their placement in the organic search listings.

Despite the meteoric growth of paid search and the success of firms such as Google and Yahoo, no published academic research in marketing has yet modeled paid search as of this writing. Economists have become interested in the properties of the online auctions for text ad placement for search terms (or so-called key words) where sponsors bid against each other to obtain higher positions in the display of search results to the user (Edelman et al. 2007). There is also an extensive practitioner literature on search engine marketing, consisting primarily of shorter "white papers" written by advertising agencies or consulting firms describing their capabilities to assist companies in managing search engine marketing campaigns. (The interested reader is referred to www.sempo.org for more information and examples.)

Marketing modelers are likely to find many aspects of paid search and search engine marketing especially fertile for research. Thus, the current dearth of published work is likely to prove short lived. One example of early academic work in this area is a study by Rutz and Bucklin (2007). Using data on paid search activity in the lodging industry in the U.S., the authors investigate the role of branded versus generic search terms. A branded search term includes a company brand name (e.g., "Hilton Las Vegas"), whereas a generic search term does not (e.g., "Las Vegas Hotels"). The cost per click pertaining to generic search terms runs substantially higher than for branded terms yet generic terms are associated with a much lower rate of user conversion from click to purchase (in this case, a lodging reservation) than branded terms. This raises the question why firms are willing to continue to spend far more on generic terms versus branded terms.

In their working paper, Rutz and Bucklin develop a model of advertising dynamics in which the effects of generic search are allowed to "spill over" into effects on subsequent branded search. Using search data from the Google and Yahoo search engines, the study finds that the spill over effect is large enough to justify the premium placed on generic search terms. Thus, when deciding which generic terms to bid for – and how much to bid for them – advertisers need to factor in the extent of the spillover that a generic term might provide. Failing to do so means that managers would be relying on inappropriate metrics for evaluating the productivity of paid search key words. More generally, modeling work in paid search will need to address more aspects of how users respond to these ads, understand the productivity of spending on paid search, and the potential opportunities for targeted campaigns.

10.2.4 Shopbots

Another method for attracting traffic to an e-commerce web site is through so-called shopbots (short for shopping robot). Internet shopbots provide consumers with one-stop access to information on price, shipping costs, and availability from Internet retailers competing to sell the same product or similar type of product. Users who click on an offering from one of the retailers are then linked to the retailer's web site where they may place an order. Thus, retailers who can provide product offerings which compare favorably to the competition may find that working with shopbots is a good way to generate traffic. This raises the question what makes for an attractive offering on the listing provided to the user by a shopbot. If shopbot users are more price sensitive on average than all users, one might anticipate that price would be a key attribute.

Smith and Brynjolfsson (2001) develop a choice modeling approach to investigate the drivers of consumer decision-making at shopbots. In their model, the choice made by the consumer is not a purchase but a click-through on one of the competing offerings. The probability of selecting a given retailer's offering is modeled using the multinomial logit model (and, in an extension also discussed in the paper, a nested logit model). In the logit model, this probability is a function of the attractiveness of each of the alternatives presented to the user by the shopbot. This attractiveness, or latent utility for the consumer, is a linear function of the attributes of each competing offering and an error term. This is given by

$$U_{it} = \mathbf{x}'_{it}\beta + \varepsilon_{it} \tag{10.4}$$

where U_{it} is the latent utility index for offer t in session i,$\mathbf{x}'_{it}$ is a vector of the product's attributes, and β is a coefficient vector of salience weights or preferences for the attributes. For the proposed shopbot model, the attributes in the latent utility include price, shipping charge, sales tax, delivery time, retailer brand name, and offer position. Offer position is captured by dummy variables for first on the list and presence on the first screen.

The authors apply their model to data on book shopping at EvenBetter.com, a prominent Internet shopbot in the late 1990's. The data set consists of shopbot decisions and listings for about two months during late 1999. Users identified a specific book, the shopbot returned listings of offerings from competing Internet book retailers (e.g., Amazon, Barnes and Noble, and Borders), and the resulting click-throughs were recorded.

Estimation of the logit model on the book shopping data revealed that consumers, as expected, are very sensitive to item price, shipping charges, and taxes. They were also found to be sensitive to delivery time estimates. Consumers also were more likely to select offerings if they were listed first or were listed on the first screen. Finally, shoppers also had a strong preference for selecting offerings from the three major brands of Internet booksellers (Amazon, Barnes and Noble, Borders). Even though the item offered is identical across retailers (in this case, a book), there was a strong role for the retailer's brand in the consumer decision-making process. Some of this may be due to consumer uncertainty regarding shipping time, return policies, or other factors. Using the choice modeling results, the authors quantified the premium that could be commanded by the three major Internet retailer brands to be $1.72 over generic retailers. Amazon, when analyzed by itself, held a $2.49 price premium advantage over generic retailers and a $1.30 advantage over Barnes and Noble and Borders.

The ability to quantify the trade-offs in consumer decision-making at a shopbot could provide valuable input to e-commerce retailers. This can be used to gauge the extent to which shopbots are likely to forward significant numbers of well-qualified customer prospects and to assess how this might vary with changes in prices or shipping policies. Though the clicks at the shopbot are not purchases, the insights provided about decision-making could also help managers seeking to optimize pricing and shipping policies for products in the retailer's assortment.

Taking the perspective of the shopbot itself, Montgomery et al. (2004a) build upon the utility framework developed by Smith and Brynjolfsson (2001) to address the problem of how the shopbot should determine which retail listings to display to the user. Conceptually, a shopbot which provides a faster and better set of alternatives to the user will receive more click-throughs and therefore become more profitable as its referral fees increase from affiliated retailers. The Montgomery et al. modeling approach augments the consumer's utility function to include the disutility from waiting for the shopbot to respond and from the cognitive effort needed on behalf of consumers to process a larger number of alternatives. The key idea is that from the consumer's perspective, more listings are not necessarily better, especially if the shopbot's response time is slowed by the need to query a large number of retailers for updated information on prices and shipping terms. Thus, the shopbot must decide how many retailers to query and which offers to present to the user. To do this it can use previous information on customer trade-offs (calibrated from analyzing prior data on consumer decisions) as well as the expected attractiveness of offerings from different retailers.

Though the Montgomery et al. model provides an optimization approach for the shopbot, as opposed to an e-commerce site, it highlights the factors that are likely to be important in determining how shopbots work in practice. The authors provide an example of how the optimization algorithm would function in a simulated environment. This illustrates the trade-offs between providing shoppers with more offers and the disutility from evaluating that additional information. The interested reader may wish to consult the discussion on decision aids provided by Murray and Häubl (2008) in Chapter 3 of this Handbook.

10.2.5 Email

Another method for bringing traffic to a web site is to send emails to registered users (or simply to potential customers for whom an email address is available). These outbound communications may contain text, editorial content, and graphics designed to promote the site and attract users to visit the site. Typically a link or set of links is contained within the email, enabling the user to move directly to the site by clicking on one. Though emails are inexpensive to send on a variable cost basis, the wrong content can make email ineffective and, worse, lead to its classification by the user as coming from a "junk email" address. Given the differences across users in potential interests, an important question is whether or not customizing outbound emails might be effective in increasing click-through rates.

This question is comprehensively addressed in the model proposed by Ansari and Mela (2003). They develop a two-phase approach to customizing email communications. The first phase models click-through probability as a function of the content and design features of the email. The model incorporates heterogeneity in response parameters, giving an individual-specific response function for an email. The second phase uses the parameter estimates as input into an optimization module which recommends an email configuration customized for the recipient and time.

For the first phase, Ansari and Mela propose a binary probit model to represent the click-through probability for a given link contained in an email sent to a registered user. The probability of click-through for user i depends upon his or her latent utility for link k of email j. This is specified as

$$u_{ijk} = \mathbf{x}'_{ijk}\mu + \mathbf{z}'_{jk}\lambda_i + \mathbf{w}'_{ik}\theta_j + \gamma_k + e_{ijk} \qquad (10.5)$$

where the vector $\mathbf{x}'_{ijk}$ contains observed user-level, email-level, and link-level variables. The email-level variables pertain to design aspects of the email while link-level variables pertain to the content associated with a given link within the email. The coefficients in the vector μ are the population-level impacts of the covariates. The next two terms capture different sources of heterogeneity: $\mathbf{z}'_{jk}\lambda_i$ accommodates heterogeneity in individual-level response for user i to elements of the email and the links within it; $\mathbf{w}'_{ik}\theta_j$ handles heterogeneity in the impact of a given email j on the latent utility for clicking. Unobserved content heterogeneity pertaining to link k is accommodated in the γ_k term.

The authors applied their response model to clickstream data from a major content-oriented web site which derives most of its revenue from the sale of advertising space. The data set included records of outbound emails sent to registered users for a three-month period in 1999 along with corresponding records for whether or not the user clicked on one of the links embedded in the email. The number of links per email averaged 5.6 and ranged from 2 to 8 and the average click-through rate was approximately 7 percent.

In specifying the latent utility model, the authors included covariates for the nature of the editorial content for each link (broken into 12 categories), the position of each link within the email, the number of links contained within the email, and whether or not the email was sent in text or html format. The model also included a covariate for the number of days since the time of the user's last click. After fitting the response model to the data, the authors found that the nature of the content (e.g., specific topic associated with the link) was predictive of click-through for a given link. The position of the link was, as expected, negatively related to click-through along with the time since last click.[3] Neither the number of items contained in the email nor whether or not the email was text or html were significantly related to click-through (as far as population-level results were concerned). The heterogeneity in individual-level response parameters, however, indicates that these covariates were explanatory factors for at least some of the users.

The second phase uses the estimated parameters from the click response model to forecast user reactions to changes in email content and configuration. A combinatorial optimization approach then can be used to find the best customization for each email and user. If the objective function is to maximize the expected number of click-throughs, the specification is as follows:

$$\text{Maximize} \sum_{i=1}^{n} \sum_{j=1}^{k} p_{ij|k} x_{ij}$$

$$\text{Subject to} \sum_{j=1}^{k} x_{ij} \leq 1 \text{ for } i = 1, 2, \ldots, n, \text{ and} \tag{10.6}$$

$$\sum_{i=1}^{n} x_{ij} = 1 \text{ for } j = 1, 2, \ldots, k.$$

Here, n is the total number of possible content links that can be included in an email. The quantity $p_{ij|k}$ is the probability that the user clicks on link i if it is placed in position j, when the total number of links included in the email is equal to k. (This is obtained from the forecast provided by the probit click-response model.) The quantity x_{ij} is an indicator variable equal to 1 when content link i is placed in position j ($j = 1$ for the first position and k for the lowest position) in the email and 0 otherwise. The authors propose detail an approach to solving the optimization problem.

---

[3] Note that position takes a higher numeric value as the link appears farther down the list; this makes higher position associated with lower click-through.

How much does customizing an email potentially improve response? To answer this, Ansari and Mela conduct a validation study of their approach. They find that it produces a 62 percent improvement in the expected number of clicks versus the original configuration of the emails used by the web site. If the objective function is specified as maximizing the probability of at least one click, the improvement was found to be 56 percent.

The Ansari and Mela modeling approach is notable for bringing together a state-of-the-art response model, estimated on individual-level clickstream data, with an optimization module. Because it also included an optimization component, the study demonstrated the potential value of the response modeling. While the authors applied their model to email customization, the potential applications for this approach are much broader. Other problems involving customization of online content (e.g., web sites themselves) might be addressed with the modeling approach developed in this article.

One aspect of email management not directly addressed by Ansari and Mela (2003) is the frequency with which the firm should send them out. The very low marginal costs of email communication need to be balanced against the potential for wear-out – or opting out – from receiving additional emails from the site. While no published paper has yet addressed this problem specifically, work by Drèze and Bonfrer (2006) provides a first look at capturing the issues in this trade-off.

10.2.6 Word-of-Mouth

Yet another form of marketing communication which could drive traffic to an e-commerce web site is word-of-mouth (WOM). WOM usually refers to communications originated from customers or users towards others in which the firm does not directly control the content, timing, or nature of the message. Sometimes firms may specifically seek to generate WOM through viral marketing campaigns (i.e., by stimulating a chain of communications among customers). At present, there are no modeling studies that explicitly link WOM communications to site traffic generation. Chevalier and Mayzlin (2006), however, do link online reviews (a form of electronic WOM) to changes in sales rankings at e-commerce sites; this article is discussed in detail in Section 10.3.3 below.

Godes and Mayzlin (2004) link online measures of WOM frequency and dispersion for television shows to the Nielsen ratings for those programs. Though the dependent variable is not an e-commerce outcome, the article shows how to collect data on WOM from the Internet and how to develop metrics which may be useful in future research. Researchers and managers also may wish to consider the implications from a theoretical paper by Mayzlin (2006). This article discusses the use of so-called "promotional chat" by firms to promote products or entertainment artists. Promotional chat is disguised WOM activity undertaken by the firm on the web without explicit identification of the firm as its source (i.e., other users or consumers are unsure where the "chat" is coming from). The implications from Mayzlin's work are that firms (a) do have an incentive to engage in promotional chat on the Internet and (b) such an incentive is higher for low quality product offerings than high quality offerings. The second result differs from the usual findings in the advertising signaling literature which hold that firms with better offerings advertise more than others. Mayzlin shows analytically that the reversal is due to the anonymous nature of the promotional chat. This results helps highlight the potential differences between so-called "electronic WOM" or eWOM and traditional WOM. In Section 10.3.3, several articles related to eWOM will be discussed as they relate to what users do on the site or to purchase outcomes.

10.3 Models for Site Usage Behavior, Purchase Conversion, and Site Management

Given that a potential customer has been attracted to the site and commences a visit, the next set of issues centers on what transpires while the visitor is there. This section discusses modeling advances focused on (1) developing an under-standing of how customers use the site (and/or change their usage of the site over time), (2) predicting conversion from visit to purchase, and (3) improving site features, ease of use and likelihood of purchase. Table 10.2 provides a summary of the key models covered. As in the previous section on traffic generation, most of the modeling work has used individual-level clickstream data, either site centric or user-centric.

10.3.1 Site Usage Behavior

Perhaps the most commonly tracked (and reported) metrics on Internet site usage are number of visits and visit durations. Visit duration is defined as the amount of time a user is on a web site and has sometimes been referred to as "stickiness." With these basic measures (and how they may change over time), managers can tell a great deal about the attractiveness of their sites and their ability to hold visitor attention. Indeed, at the height of the Internet stock "bubble," in 1999 and 2000, data on site visit duration could be statistically linked to stock returns (Demers and Lev 2001). As several researchers have cautioned, however, it can be potentially misleading to assess web site perfor-mance based on simple aggregate measures of site visits and visit durations (e.g., Bucklin and Sismeiro 2003, Moe and Fader 2004a). Fortunately, the use of individual-level clickstream data can avoid these difficulties. For example, Moe and Fader (2004a) develop a stochastic model of evolving visit behavior fitted to

Table 10.2 Summary of Models for Site Usage Behavior, Purchase Conversion, and Site Management

Article	Modeling objective	Type of model and dependent variable(s)	Data	Key finding(s)
Site Usage Behavior				
Johnson et al. (2003)	Investigate user learning in web site usage via the power law of practice	Regression (log-log); site visit durations	User-centric clickstream panel with usage for 30 web sites	Power law holds for most web sites; doubling visits cuts duration time by an average of 19 percent
Bucklin and Sismeiro (2003)	Study web-site browsing behavior by page view and page-view duration	Type-II Tobit (binary probit for page request and regression for page view duration)	Site-centric clickstream for an automotive web site	Page view durations increase as more pages are viewed; repeat visits have fewer page views, but same page-view durations
Danaher et al. (2006)	Explain variation in site visit duration	Regression; log of visit duration	User-centric clickstream panel for 50 sites in New Zealand	Visit-occasion is primary source of duration variance, not user demographics or site features
Moe (2003)	Study patterns of web site usage and shopping behavior	Cluster analysis of individual-level site usage metrics	Site-centric clickstream for nutrition products site	Four clusters describe site usage behavior: search/ deliberation, directed buying, hedonic browsing, and knowledge building
Purchase Conversion				
Moe and Fader (2004b)	Model effects of previous site visits on future purchase conversion	Stochastic model: purchase given visit	User-centric clickstream panel focusing on Amazon.com	Prior visits increase purchase conversion probabilities, but at a decreasing rate

Table 10.2 (continued)

Article	Modeling objective	Type of model and dependent variable(s)	Data	Key finding(s)
Sismeiro and Bucklin (2004)	Model web site purchase behavior using a multi-stage approach with sequential task completion	Series of conditional binary logit models; task completions	Site-centric clickstream for an automotive web site	Multi-stage model predicts web-site purchase better than single-stage; factors influencing completion of different tasks can be identified
Montgomery et al. (2004b)	Model effects of the user's prior browsing path on site usage and purchase conversion	Dynamic multinomial probit models embedded in a hidden Markov; page-type choice	User-centric clickstream panel with focus on Barnes and Noble web site	User browsing paths predict page-type choice and purchase conversion; users may switch between browsing and deliberation during a visit
Site Management				
Ansari et al. (2000)	Improve Internet recommendation systems	Bayesian regression; product ratings	Movie ratings from an Internet site and user demographics	Incorporating user heterogeneity in the system improves recommendation quality
Chevalier and Mayzlin (2006)	Effects of on online book reviews on book sales rankings	Regression; log sales rank	Rankings and reviews collected from Amazon and bn.com web sites	Sales rank increases with more reviews and higher ratings from reviewers; negative reviews have more impact
Lewis et al. (2006)	Effect of shipping fees on order-size and incidence	Ordered logit; order-size categories	Orders and shipping fees for an online retailer of grocery and drugstore items	Increases in shipping fees lead to smaller and fewer orders

clickstream data for site visits to CDNow and Amazon that was collected by Media Metrix in 1998. (Media Metrix was subsequently acquired by comScore Networks.) Their modeling results showed that changing patterns of site visitation at the disaggregate level would be masked at the aggregate level, potentially resulting in misleading implications for site performance.

The foregoing raises the question how managers might think more strategically about measures of site visitation and visit duration. Would decreasing visit duration for a segment of users potentially indicate a problem with the site? For example, like the bricks-and-mortar shopper who becomes more efficient at finding his or her way around the store, do Internet users become more adept at navigating a site as they gain more experience with it?

10.3.1.1 Learning

The idea that web users may learn how to use a given site more efficiently over time was explored in detail by Johnson et al. (2003). They applied the power law of practice, an empirical generalization about learning developed by cognitive psychologists, to clickstream data on web site usage. The power law of practice is given by the following formula:

$$T = \beta N^{\alpha} \tag{10.7}$$

where T is the time required to complete the task and N is the number of trials. β is the baseline, representing the performance time on the first trial (where $N = 1$) and the rate of improvement is given by α, the slope of the learning curve. A negative sign is expected for α. The power law also can be expressed in log-log form as

$$\log(T) = \log(B) + \alpha \log(N) \tag{10.8}$$

which makes the model easily estimable by regression methods, given data on time and number of trials. Johnson et al. mapped the model into the Internet domain by considering an individual's site visit count as trials and visit durations as task completion times. If Internet users learn how to navigate sites more efficiently (e.g., find information more quickly, complete purchase transactions faster), the average visit duration should decline with additional visits to the site (but at a decreasing rate, given the power law expression for learning).

The authors fit the power law model to Media Metrix panel data for a large sample of Internet users during 1997–1999. The study focused on retail web sites in the travel, book and music categories. Some 30 travel sites (e.g., Expedia.com, Priceline.com), two book sites (Amazon.com, BarnesandNoble.com), and four music sites (e.g., CDNow.com, MusicBoulevard.com) were included the empirical analysis. The power law model coefficients were estimated using individual-linear regressions for each site. This yielded a set of coefficients specific to each user and site. Most sites (28 of 36) had significantly more negative than positive individual-level estimates for the learning rate coefficient, α. The overall average learning rate was equal to –0.19. This rate implies that each doubling in the number of site visits by a user corresponds to a 19 percent drop in visit duration. The authors also validated these results using a random effects model in which a mean coefficient for α and β were estimated along with individual-level heterogeneity.

In addition to the visit duration analysis, the Johnson et al. study examined a subset of the sites where the occurrence of a purchase transaction could be discerned in the clickstream data. The authors hypothesized that users who learned how to navigate a site fastest would be more likely, other things being equal, to make a purchase from the site. For the three categories of sites (book, music, and travel), they found that users with higher learning rates for the site were indeed more likely to buy. The Johnson et al. article provides a simple, but highly useful framework for thinking about patterns of site usage behavior over time (especially for relatively new sites or for users new to the site). It also highlights the potential importance of site design and ease of navigation as a learning facilitator. As the findings suggest, sites that are easier for customers to learn how to use may enjoy higher rates of purchase conversion. Besides ease of use, other elements of site design, such as visual primes, have been shown in laboratory experiments to influence product choice on the web (Mandel and Johnson 2002).

10.3.1.2 Page Views

A web site user's visit duration can be broken down into a sequence of page-views from the site and the duration of each page view. This means that web site visits of the same duration could look quite different in terms of how the user browses the site. A site visit lasting 10 minutes could consist of two page-views or 10 page-views. In the former case, the user spends five minutes per page while in the latter case the user spends one minute per page. This raises the question whether additional insight into web site usage behavior can be obtained by decomposing visit durations into the number of page-views and page-view duration.

Bucklin and Sismeiro (2003) develop a type II tobit model of user page-request and page-view duration and apply it to site-centric clickstream (server log file) data from an Internet automotive retailer collected in October 1999. The modeling approach permits investigators to examine the factors influencing a user's decision to view additional pages on the site versus a user's decision to spend more time viewing a given page. For example, different covariates can be incorporated in the page-request versus page-view duration aspects of the model and/or the same covariates may have different effects on the two user decisions.

The first component of the type II tobit is a page-request model in which the user's decision to request an additional page from the site (i.e., continue browsing) or exit the site is a binary probit choice model. This choice is modeled for each page-view occasion, given that the user has initiated a visit to the web site, up until site exit. Following the notation in the article, the latent utility of requesting an additional page within the site for visitor i at page-view occasion j is given by

$$y_{1ij} = \mathbf{x}_{1ij}\,\beta_{1i} + u_{1ij} \tag{10.9}$$

where y_{1ij} is the latent utility associated with the request of an additional page, $\mathbf{x}_{1ij}$ is a vector of individual- and page-specific covariates that includes an intercept, β_{1i} is a vector of visitor-specific parameters, and u_{1ij} is a normally distributed error term.

The second component is a page-view duration model where the user's time spent viewing a given page is modeled for each recorded page view up until site exit. (The authors use the time stamp information recorded in the clickstream data to measure the dependent variable; in site-centric data, the duration for the last page view is not known because there is no record of what the user did after leaving the web site.) Bucklin and Sismeiro model the page-view durations for individual i as

$$y_{2ij} = \mathbf{x}_{2ij}\,\beta_{2i} + u_{2ij} \tag{10.10}$$

where y_{2ij} is the log of the page-view duration at page occasion j, $\mathbf{x}_{2ij}$ is a vector of covariates which includes an intercept term, β_{2i} is a vector of visitor-specific parameters, and u_{2ij} is a normally distributed error term. In both the page-view request and duration components of the model, heterogeneity in the visitor parameter vectors is modeled with random coefficients estimated with Bayesian methods.

The authors developed a series of covariates, measured at the individual user and page level (i.e., the variables change dynamically as the user moves from page to page and across sessions at the site). CPAGE, the cumulative number of page views prior to arriving on the current page, captured the effect of visit depth. CSESSION, the cumulative number of site visits made by the visitor as of the current page view, captured the effect of repeat visitation. These measures are useful for assessing the "stickiness" of the site, both within and across visits, as well as the potential for learning effects. Additional covariates controlled for the nature of the content on each page, previous actions undertaken by the visitor on the site (such as specifying a vehicle configuration), and the technical performance of the site (e.g., lack of errors, fast server response times, etc.).

Estimation results showed that as visit depth increased, the probability of requesting another page view declined but at a decreasing rate (as CPAGE entered the best-fitting model in log form). On the other hand, visit depth (CSESSION) was associated with longer page-view duration. This means that page viewing times went up as visitors browsed the site more extensively. The authors also found that, on average, users with more repeat visits to the site had fewer page views but no change in page-view duration. Going back to the power law results, the new finding from this study is that lower session duration times are coming from fewer page views, not from reduced viewing times per page.

10.3.1.3 Visit Duration Across Sites

Danaher et al. (2006) further investigate the modeling of web site visit duration. They propose a decompositional modeling approach to identifying the factors affecting visit duration across a variety of web sites. In particular, they study duration behavior across the top 50 web sites of panelists in a user-centric NetRatings data set from New Zealand. Like the two previous models, the Dahaner et al. model also looks at the logarithm of duration as the natural dependent variable for this problem (due to skewing to the right). Indeed, they point out that the log of visit duration times in their data is almost exactly normally distributed.

The proposed basic model for log visit duration is

$$y_{ijk} = \beta_j^X X_i + \beta_i^Z Z_j + \beta_{ij}^M M_k + \varepsilon_{ijk} \tag{10.11}$$

where y_{ijk} is the log visit duration for person i on web site j for the kth visit. X_i is a vector of person i's demographic characteristics, Z_i is a vector of web site j's characteristics, and M_k is a vector of the characteristics of the kth observed visit, such as the day of the week or the number of previous visits to the site. Parameter vectors corresponding to each set of covariates are allowed to vary across web sites, individuals, and both individuals and web sites, respectively. The model can also be written in variance decomposition form where the random effects for the three components each follow a normal distribution whose variance is a function of the three classes of covariates. The multiple components of the model permit the authors to decompose the sources of variation in web site duration across users, sites, and visit-occasions.

In terms of substantive results, the authors find that two demographic variables, gender (coded female = 1, male = 0) and age, are significant factors in explaining duration variance – both positively signed in the model. Somewhat surprisingly, education and occupation are not significant predictors. Web site characteristics including text content, graphics, and advertising content, as well as functionality are all significantly related to visit duration. Notably, advertising content is negatively related to visit duration (sites with more ads have shorter visits), but a negative interaction with age was found, indicating that older users spend more time on sites with high ad content. The variance decomposition of the heterogeneity indicated that individual-level, site-specific, and visit-occasion heterogeneity accounted for 7, 12, and 81% of the total, respectively. Thus, the principal source of heterogeneity is the visit-occasion, suggesting that most of the variability in visit duration is driven by the situation, not by the traits of the individual or fundamental aspects of the web site itself.

10.3.1.4 Patterns of Site Usage Behavior

The site usage models so far discussed in this section share a focus on the time-related dimensions of web site usage. Clickstream data from online retailers can also be analyzed to examine different patterns of behavior on the site. Analogous to offline retailing, in some cases shoppers come to the store ready to buy while others, more oriented to information search, have purchase horizons in the future. Moe (2003) investigates whether different patterns of web site shopping or usage behavior can be found in clickstream data and, if so, whether they might be related to purchase. Using site-centric data from an e-commerce site that sells nutrition products, she hypothesizes that visitors can be clustered into one of four shopping strategies:

1. *Directed buying*. Visitors exhibit goal-directed search behavior, have a specific product in mind when entering the site and are likely to exit the store having made a purchase.
2. *Search/deliberation*. These visitors also exhibit goal-directed search behavior, but have only a general product category in mind. They may need multiple visits to gather more information before making a purchase.
3. *Hedonic browsers*. Users in this category tend to enter the site without a product or category in mind. Purchases that may occur are therefore likely to be impulse buys.
4. *Knowledge-building*. This group has no intention of buying and is simply visiting the online store to gather information.

Moe proposed a series of measures, computed from the clickstream data, to characterize the site usage behavior for a sample of 5,730 visitors to the site in May–June 2000. These measures included general session usage (number of pages viewed and average time spent per page), session focus (e.g., usage of pages describing the category, product, or brand), session variety (e.g., the extent to which the category, brand or product pages viewed were unique), and the maximum level of repeat viewing of a product page. Moe conducted a k-means cluster analysis of the entire set of measures and selected a five cluster solution as the best representation of the data. The fifth segment consisted almost entirely of visitors with very few page views at the site; though numerous (5,185), these very shallow visits had too little information to identify the shopping strategy, if any, which may have been associated with the visit. The remaining four clusters corresponded well with those hypothesized in the conceptual framework.

In Table 10.3, some of the findings from Moe's cluster analysis study are highlighted.[4] Entries in the table are cluster means, with the exception of the number of site visits. Note that in Moe's analysis, the occurrence of a purchase was not included among the variables used to form the clusters. Thus, the

---

[4] The interested reader is referred to the original article, Moe (2003), for the complete set of empirical results.

Table 10.3 Selected results from a cluster analysis of web site shopping visits (reported in Moe (2003))

Session measure	Knowledge building	Hedonic browsing	Directed buying	Search/ deliberation
Number of page views	3.95	5.84	18.76	26.24
Average time per page (Seconds)	1698	69	117	87
Category pages unique (Percent)	7.7	72.9	30.7	22.7
Product pages unique (Percent)	3.8	62.7	61.2	93.0
Brand pages unique (Percent)	9.8	12.1	10.2	9.7
Products unique per category	0.04	0.62	1.51	2.83
Maximum product page repeat views	0	0	1.62	0.34
Purchase conversion rate	0.00	0.02	0.13	0.08
Number of site visits in the cluster	78	1083	255	237

reported conversion rate for each cluster serves as further validation of the framework as visits classified as directed buying or search/deliberation had a much higher likelihood of purchase conversion than those classified as knowledge building or hedonic browsing. The analysis also showed how directed buying differs from search/deliberation as the former type of visit is characterized by fewer total page views on average, more time spent per page, and a significantly greater tendency to repeat view product pages.

Moe's article also presents a stepwise discriminant analysis which assesses the extent to which the various visit measures are predictive of cluster membership. The measures for category pages unique and maximum product page repeat viewing were found to be the two most significant. Using Moe's approach and detailed clickstream data, an online retailer could improve its understanding of site usage behavior and purchase propensity across visitors.

10.3.2 Predicting Conversion from Visit to Purchase

The articles discussed above shed a great deal of light on e-commerce site usage. However, they stop short of providing managers with models designed to *predict* whether or not a given site visit will include a purchase transaction. This a focus of the several models discussed in this section. Two general approaches have been proposed for modeling the probability of purchase, given a site visit. In the first approach, illustrated by the work of Moe and Fader (2004b), the focus of the model is to dynamically predict visit-to-purchase conversion as site visits occur over time. The second approach takes a within-visit focus, modeling the likelihood of purchase – and how it might vary– as the visitor navigates the site. Examples of this approach include Sismeiro and Bucklin (2004) and Montgomery et al. (2004b). Lastly, this latter approach can also be extended to model consideration sets (Wu and Rangaswamy 2003) and product viewing (Moe 2006), in addition to product purchase.

10.3.2.1 Stochastic Modeling Approach

Moe and Fader (2004b) propose a stochastic model of purchase conversion which can be estimated on clickstream records of historical visits and purchases. They estimate their model on user-centric data collected by Media Metrix for site visits and purchases at Amazon.com in 1998. The model can also be estimated with site-centric data, provided that past visits and purchases are tracked at the user level (e.g., through registration, cookies, or IP address identification). In their model, Moe and Fader capture several factors influencing purchase conversion. These include baseline purchase propensity, the effect of cumulating past visits, and the effect of a purchasing threshold. Each of these effects is allowed to vary across visitors and the effects of past visits and threshold are also allowed to evolve over time.

For customers who have purchased in the past, Moe and Fader specify the probability of buying as

$$f(p_{ij}|x_{ij}>0) = \frac{V_{ij} + x_{ij}}{V_{ij} + \tau_{ij} + n_{ij}} \qquad (10.12)$$

where p_{ij} is the probability of buying for customer i at visit j, x_{ij} is the number of prior purchases, V_{ij} is the net visit effect up to the time of visit j, τ_{ij} is the purchasing threshold, and n_{ij} is the number of prior visits. The net visit effect term, V_{ij}, includes effects for baseline propensity as well as cumulating past visits and is modeled to follow a gamma distribution across visitors. The purchasing threshold, τ_{ij}, is also modeled to follow a gamma distribution and is allowed to evolve over time as the customer accumulates purchase experience. The quantities x_{ij} and n_{ij} are unique to each visitor and update the ratio. Thus, the estimated purchase probabilities for customers with more recorded activity in site visitation and purchase will be based more on the empirical ratio of purchases to visits for the individual rather than the distributions estimated across visitors.

For site visitors who have yet to make a purchase, equation (10.12) is modified to allow for the possibility of so-called "hard core never buyers." These are buyers who never convert from visit to purchase. Site visitors who have yet to make a purchase are modeled to have the following buying probability:

$$f(p_{ij}|x_{ij} = 0) = (1 - \pi) + \pi \frac{V_{ij}}{V_{ij} + \tau_{ij} + n_{ij}} \qquad (10.13)$$

where $(1 - \pi)$ is the fraction of the population that is hard-core never buyer (i.e., π is the fraction that may buy). The flexibility built into this equation allows the model to accommodate site users pursuing knowledge building or hedonic browsing as well as visitors whose site navigation is so brief or limited that purchase is not possible.

Estimating their full model on the visit and purchase records for Amazon, the authors find that prior visits do increase the future probability of purchase conversion (over and above a baseline), but the effect is not constant. In particular, subsequent visits have a diminishing positive impact on purchase probabilities. Purchasing thresholds are found to increase with purchase experience. Though a somewhat unexpected result, it might be attributed to a decrease in the novelty of buying online for their sample of users at that time. The size of the hard-core never buyer group was estimated to be about 21 percent of the sample. The authors also compared their full model against four benchmark models. The full model performed better than three of the four benchmarks and about as well as a nested model without threshold dynamics. From a statistical perspective, this indicates that the dynamics in the purchasing threshold simply may not be a significant factor for these data.

The flexible model developed and tested by Moe and Fader (2004b) is well-suited to studying the purchase problem when the focus is on the rate of conversion from visit to purchase and should be generally applicable to a broad class of e-commerce sites. As the authors note, their model does not examine the activities (e.g., page views) visitors undertake while navigating the site or the potential relationship of those activities to completing a purchase. These factors are taken up in the modeling approaches proposed by Sismeiro and Bucklin (2004) and Montgomery et al. (2004b).

10.3.2.2 Predicting Purchase Using Within-Site Activity

The model proposed by Sismeiro and Bucklin (2004) decomposes the probability of purchase conversion (given a visit to the site) into a series of conditional probabilities corresponding to the tasks which users must complete. Thus, the probability of purchase is modeled as the product of the probabilities corresponding to completing the series of "nominal user tasks" (NUTs) required for an e-commerce transaction on the site. By breaking purchase conversion down into a series of steps and then modeling those steps individually, the approach is designed to avoid the modeling problem of needing to predict the statistically uncommon event of an online purchase given a site visit. It also can provide additional insight into the factors facilitating or impeding online purchase by identifying the stage at which potential buyers fail to advance and the factors associated with those failures.

In their article, Sismeiro and Bucklin present an application of their model to site-centric data (i.e., data from company server files) from an Internet car retailer. The authors modeled three user tasks: (1) completion of product configuration, (2) input of personal information, given (1), and (3) order confirmation with credit card provision, given (1) and (2). In their data, about two percent of site visitors completed an order transaction. This decomposed as follows across the tasks: 30 percent of visitors to the site completed task (1), 20 percent of those then went on to complete task (2), and 34 percent of those completing tasks (1) and (2) went on to complete task (3). In this case the probabilities being modeled at each task are no longer tiny, but instead average between 20 and 35 percent. More generally, these steps follow the familiar sequence of e-commerce tasks of placing an item in the "shopping cart," entering shipping information, and placing the order with a credit card. While the application presented is to the online ordering of a consumer durable, the modeling framework should be broadly applicable to a wide array of consumer-oriented e-commerce sites. Note that in this framework so-called "shopping cart abandonment" occurs after the user has completed task (1) but prior to completing task (3). Thus, the model has the potential to aid managers in diagnosing why site visitors who go to the effort to select and specify a product (an effortful task) fail to complete a purchase.

Mathematically, the general form of Sismeiro and Bucklin's task completion model is given by

$$l_{is}(C_{is}^1, C_{is}^2, \ldots, C_{is}^M) = P(C_{is}^1)P(C_{is}^2 \mid C_{is}^1)P(C_{is}^3 \mid C_{is}^1, C_{is}^2) \ldots$$
$$P(C_{is}^M \mid C_{is}^1, C_{is}^2, \ldots, C_{is}^{M-1})$$

(10.14)

The left-hand side of (10.14) gives the likelihood that visitor i from region s completes all tasks from 1 to M, thereby completing a purchase. C_{is}^M indicates the completion of task M by visitor i from region s, where the last task, M, is taken to be the last nominal task required to complete a purchase. The right-hand side decomposes the purchase likelihood into a series of M probabilities, where tasks from 2 to M are modeled to be conditional upon the completion of the previous tasks. For the application to new car buying reported in the article, M is equal to 3.

The probability of task completion task is modeled with a binary probit where the utility of completing each task depends upon covariates that capture what visitors are exposed to on the site and what they have done. In the Sismeiro and Bucklin application, the covariates were developed from the data in company server files and included measures of browsing behavior (time spend and page views), repeat visitation, use of decision aids, input effort and information gathering, and exposure to site design and structure (designed to capture the visitor's individual experience on the site). The full set of covariates was tested in the probit model for each task (with heterogeneity in the response parameters incorporated at the local level via Bayesian estimation). The authors found most proposed covariates to significantly explain task completion for the first and second tasks, while a more limited set was significant in explaining completion of the third task.

One of the interesting empirical findings was a set of significant sign reversals for many of the covariate parameters from one task to another. For example, exiting and returning to the site was not predictive of task one completion (product configuration), but it was positively related to task two (personal information) and negatively related to task three (order and payment). The results also showed that the number of site visits, per se, was not predictive of purchase. This finding differs from the Moe and Fader (2004b) result for their Amazon data, where they document that more site visits lead to greater purchase likelihood. The discrepancy may be due to the differences in shopping behavior for books versus new automobiles. In particular, knowledge building and hedonic browsing may be higher for new cars than books, leading many users to accumulate a large number of site visits without ever purchasing.

Montgomery et al. (2004b) also develop a detailed model of site visit behavior and purchase using clickstream data. Unlike the Sismeiro and Bucklin (2004) model, which predicts the completion of sequential user tasks, the Montgomery et al. model predicts the browsing path followed by each user as defined by the sequence of page-type choices. From this model, purchase conversion can be predicted by dynamically estimating the probability that a given visitor will end up selecting the page which completes an order. The authors apply their model to user-centric data provided by comScore Media Metrix but focus their analysis on the site visits panelists made to the Barnes and Noble bookseller. As the authors point out, their modeling approach is also suitable for use on site-centric data from company servers. (Likewise, Sismeiro and Bucklin's approach, estimated on site-centric data, also can be applied to user-centric data.)

The Montgomery et al. approach first classifies e-commerce site pages into several types (i.e., home page, account, category, product, information, shopping cart, and order). The model is set up to predict the sequence of page-type choices that each visitor makes as he or she navigates the site. (One can also think of this as a transition matrix across page categories.) The model uses the path followed by a given visitor up to that point to predict what type of page will be selected next. If the page selected is the "order" page, that signifies that the user has made a purchase.

Mathematically, the choices made by visitors are represented by the indicator variable Y_{iqtc} which is equal to one if user i in session q at time t chooses page category c and 0 otherwise. This yields a multinomial choice model, for which the authors use a dynamic probit formulation coupled with a Bayesian estimation procedure. The utility associated with each page-type choice, U_{iqtc}, is specified to be a function of covariates observable to the visitor at time $t-1$ (i.e., up to and including the previous page view), lagged utility, and an error term. Restrictions can be added to ensure consistency with the page-type alternatives available to the visitor at any given juncture in the browsing path. For example, in the Barnes and Noble clickstream, the only path restriction necessary was that the order page had to be accessed via the shopping cart page.

Given this foundation, the authors then add dynamic changes in navigational state as users progress from page to page. This flexibility allows visitors to transition from, say, a browsing oriented state to a deliberation oriented state (and vice versa) as they navigate the site. Adding dynamic latent states is an important extension to the Moe (2003) article in which visitors were clustered by browsing orientation, but transitions *during a site visit* were not analyzed.

After estimating and validating the model, the authors show how it can be used to dynamically predict visit-to-purchase conversion. This prediction is obtained by using the model to provide forecasts of the page-type choices for users as they navigate the site. For the Barnes and Noble data, the mean purchase rate was 7 percent. After one page view, for example, the model begins to discriminate between session visits that will include a purchase (13.3% correctly classified) versus those which will not (6.1%). After three page views the discriminating power grows to 23.4% for buyers versus 5.9% for non-buyers. After six page views, the predictions are 41.5% and 5.7%, respectively. These results suggest that models of the within-site browsing path and purchase process could become powerful decision aids to e-commerce managers in areas such as site design and targeting.

10.3.2.3 Consideration Sets and Product Viewing

While the studies discussed above focused on predicting purchase conversion, the detailed clickstream records of user activity they are based upon can also permit researchers to obtain substantive insights into the consumer search and consideration process. Using offline data from surveys and scanner panels, marketing researchers have extended choice models to incorporate a consideration stage and a final choice stage (e.g., Roberts and Lattin 1991, Bronnenberg and Vanhonacker 1996). An analogous approach can be taken to clickstream data. Generally speaking, the approach calls for the first stage to predict the alternatives considered while the second stage predicts the alternative that is ultimately selected, given consideration. Two articles have applied this type of two-stage model to e-commerce web sites. Wu and Rangaswamy (2003) model consideration and choice for liquid detergent at the online grocer, Peapod. Moe (2006) models product viewing and choice using clickstream data for two product categories (weight loss aids and meal replacements) at an online retailer of nutritional products.

In the data analyzed by Wu and Rangaswamy (2003), shopper use of two online decision aids (a personal list and a sorting capability) were available along with data on prices, promotions, and product characteristics. Using a fuzzy set modeling approach to the consideration set problem, the authors studied the impact of the use of the list and sorting tools. First, the proposed model was compared to one which did not include information on these activities; the authors showed that incorporating the decision aid variables added substantially to the predictive power of the choice model. Extending their analysis to multiple latent segments, the authors found that the shoppers in their data formed consideration sets in different ways. In a two-segment analysis, they labeled the first group "seekers" (because they actively used online search tools) and the second group "non-seekers" (because they relied more heavily on personal lists).

Like many existing models of consideration, the Wu and Rangaswamy approach infers the consideration set by harnessing the structure of the two-stage model. Detailed clickstream data also provide the ability to track the products that are viewed by the shopper. Modeling the product view decision – along with the purchase decision – is the focus of the article by Moe (2006). In her approach, the first stage model predicts product viewing while the second stage model predicts purchase, given that the product has been viewed. Product viewing *per se* need not indicate consideration (i.e., some products may be viewed but not enter the shopper's mental consideration set). On the other hand, product viewing is accurately captured by clickstream data and, argu-ably, the decision to view a product is likely to share many of the aspects of consideration. From an e-commerce perspective, the product viewing decision is also of interest for better understanding how shoppers proceed from visit to purchase.

Moe's approach to modeling the product view decision follows the cost-benefit trade-off developed in the early consideration set literature (e.g., Roberts and Lattin). The idea is that the shopper will add items to his or her consideration set so long as the utility of expanding the set exceeds the costs of doing so. In Moe's model, the probability of viewing a given product option in the category is modeled as a function of the utility of search for the products available and a search cost. The shopper's purchase decision is modeled in a second stage, where the probability of buying a given item, given that it had been viewed, is a function of purchase utilities. In both model components, the utility is a function of price and product-specific attributes (e.g., size, brand-name, specific ingredients).

Comparing the proposed two-stage model with a purchase-only benchmark model, Moe reports better predictive validity; in particular, out-of-sample hit rates are higher when the product view decision is incorporated. Moe's model is also useful for examining the role of different product attributes in the viewing or screening phase versus the purchase phase. For example, she finds that fewer attributes are used in the first stage than in the final stage. In particular, price and size tend to be used in only a single phase while attributes for product ingredients tend to be given weight by shoppers in both phases. Thus, findings from applying the model could prove useful for site design and targeting of online interventions such as promotions or product displays.

10.3.3 Models for Site Management

The models discussed in Section 10.3.2 predict e-commerce choice outcomes as a function data contained in the clickstream. In many instances, these models also yield insights about shopping behavior in the e-commerce setting which could be useful to managers in improving purchase conversion (e.g., through changes in site design or via targeted interventions). In contrast, another group of models focuses specifically on particular aspects of the site. These models have examined decision aids (e.g., recommendation systems or product reviews) as well as promotional pricing and shipping terms. This section discusses a number of the modeling advances in this area.

10.3.3.1 Decision Aids and eWOM

A wide variety of decision aids have become commonplace on e-commerce websites. Some of the aids which have been studied in the e-commerce marketing literature include side-by-side product comparison tools, recommendation agents, and product reviews. Much of this research has been conducted by controlled experiment. For example, Häubl and Trifts (2000) find that use of recommendation agents and comparison matrices improves several aspects of the e-commerce shopping experience. Senecal and Nantel (2004) report that subjects who consulted product recommendations were twice as likely to buy the recommended products than subjects who did not.

From a modeling perspective, several articles are relevant to the study of decision aids in e-commerce. Sismeiro and Bucklin (2004), previously discussed in Section 10.3.2 above, assess the performance of a comparison matrix. Ansari et al (2000) discuss models for recommendation systems and Chevalier and Mayzlin (2006) model the effect of product reviews on web site sales. These last two papers illustrate how site managers can embed the views of other users, i.e.., electronic word-of-mouth (eWOM), in their sites so as to potentially influence purchase.

In their model of purchase based on task completion, Sismeiro and Bucklin (2004) examine the role played by a comparison matrix in the task completion and purchase decisions of site visitors, as captured in clickstream data. In contrast to previous experimental work, they report that use of the comparison matrix by site visitors was negatively associated with progressing through the tasks on the e-commerce site they studied (new car buying). This suggests that site managers should be wary of the possibility that their decision aids could hinder e-commerce objectives, perhaps due to information overload or difficulty in use. The differing results reported so far could be due to the product category and/or the quality with which the comparison matrix was implemented on the site or in the experiment. Thus, such a modeling approach (or the one used by Montgomery et al. 2004b), estimated with clickstream data, can provide managers with an early warning about the performance of their decision aids.

Ansari et al. (2000) propose a regression-based system for recommendations which incorporates heterogeneity via Bayesian estimation. In their modeling application to movies, the ratings given by users are modeled as follows:

$$r_{ij} = Genre_j + Demographics_i + ExpertEvaluations_j + Interactions_{ij} +$$
$$CustomerHeterogeneity_{ij} + MovieHeterogeneity_{ij} + e_{ij} \qquad (10.15)$$

where r_{ij} is customer i's scale rating for movie j. The Bayesian regression approach allows the model to easily incorporate heterogeneity at the customer and movie level, alongside information describing the film (genre and expert evaluation) and the customer (demographics). The authors discuss the potential advantages of this system versus other types of recommendation systems (e.g., collaborative filtering) and provide a series of assessments in holdout samples. From an e-commerce management perspective, the article is quite helpful for understanding the dimensions of recommendation systems and the alternatives available for use. Because the modeling work focuses on the recommendation system per se, it does not assess whether or not implementation of different systems would have an effect on site usage or purchase conversion.

Many e-commerce sites now include product reviews provided by users. While such reviews do not "recommend" a product to a shopper, they serve as an organized form of eWOM for the product and can conceivably have large impacts on sales. Such reviews were visibly pioneered by Amazon, among other large sites. More recently, developing and implementing these product review systems has become a key focus area for many e-commerce site managers (e.g., Mangalindan 2007). Chevalier and Maylin (2006) examine the effect of online book reviews at Amazon.com and BarnesandNoble.com (bn.com). They collected data on reported sales rankings, prices, number of reviews, and the star-rating (e.g., one to five, with five being the highest) of the reviews for approximately 2000 books during May 2003, August 2003, and May 2004. Though the authors did not have actual book sales data, the publicly reported sales rankings serve as good proxies for the relative sales of books on the sites. This correspondence enables the authors to examine the effect that online reviews have on sales, without requiring access to proprietary data from either company.

Chevalier and Mayzlin model the natural logarithm of book sales rank as a function of a book-site fixed effect, a book fixed effect, prices, characteristics of the online review or word-of-mouth, and promised shipping times. For the Amazon.com data, their model is

$$\ln(rank_i^A) = \mu_i^A + v_i + \alpha^A \ln(P_i^A) + \gamma^A \ln(P_i^B) + X\Gamma^A + S\Pi^A + \varepsilon_i^A \ (10.16)$$

where $rank_i^A$ is the reported sales rank for book i at Amazon, P_i^A is the price of book i at Amazon, P_i^B is the price of book i at bn.com, X is a vector of product review variables, and S is a vector of indicator variables for shipping times. Parameters to be estimated are the book-site fixed effect μ_i^A, the book fixed effect v_i, and coefficients α^A, γ^A, Γ^A, and Π^A. An analogous equation is specified for the bn.com data as well as a model for relative sales rank, obtained by taking the difference across the two sites.

Turning to their data, Chevalier and Mayzlin report that reviews at both sites are generally quite positive on average, with about 60 percent of reviews rating books as "five stars" and only about 5 percent of reviews rating books as "one star." Though the reviews are similar in terms of average rating, Amazon.com has many more reviews per book than bn.com. Variables tested in the book review vector, X, included log number of reviews, average star rating, fraction of five-star reviews, fraction of one-star reviews, and average review length. The authors find that relative sales rank is improved (i.e., relative book sales increase) when there are a greater number of reviews for the book, the star rating is higher, the fraction of five-star reviews is greater, and the fraction of one-star reviews is lower. In particular, the results show a relatively large impact for the negative, one-star reviews. Interestingly, the authors also find that longer average reviews are associated with lower relative sales ranks for the book.

The Chevalier and Mayzlin study shows how regression models can be used to assess the effects of word-of-mouth marketing. E-commerce managers, with access to their own proprietary data, should be able to adjust the model to handle actual sales and product review data (versus the publicly available information used by the authors). Given such data, an interesting area for future research would be to investigate whether the product reviews also have an effect on overall site sales. As the authors note, it is possible that the book reviews are just moving sales from one book to another within each site. In addition to further analysis of produce reviews, also of interest in the eWOM area would be studies on weblogs and viral marketing on the Internet.

10.3.3.2 Promotions and Shipping Fees

Besides decision aids, e-commerce managers are also concerned with numerous other aspects of the site which might impact purchase conversion. Two areas with recent modeling advances include price promotions for products on the site and determining shipping fees. Zhang and Krishnamurthi (2004) develop and illustrate a model to customize the timing of price promotions at an online grocery retailer. Lewis et al. (2006) examine the effect of shipping fee policies on order incidence and order size.

Zhang and Krishnamurthi (2004) study the problem of how to determine individual-level targeted promotions in e-commerce. In developing their model, they draw upon well established choice models for consumer packaged goods (e.g., Chintagunta 1993, Tellis and Zufryden 1995, Silva-Risso et al. 1999). Their proposed approach extends and adapts this modeling tradition to handle the challenge of timing the targeted promotions at the level of the individual site visit. The authors specify a demand model for purchase incidence, brand choice, and quantity, incorporating variety seeking and heterogeneity. An optimization module then derives the optimal price discount for each household, at the shopping trip or visit level. The demand model is estimated on data from the butter and laundry detergent categories from an online grocery retailer in the Midwest from 1997 to 1999. An extensive validation of the promotion optimization algorithm is presented for the butter data, in which the profitability of recommended promotions is assessed in a holdout time period. As the authors note, the model is best suited for repeat-purchase consumer goods in established product categories.

Since e-commerce firms incur shipping costs to bring product to their customers, the question of how to incorporate those incremental costs into pricing policy is an important one. Since these costs are typically non-linear in order size, if shipping fees follow costs, the site runs the risk of discouraging small orders because the fees end up constituting a large fraction of the shopper's total spending on the site. Lewis et al. (2006) develop a model to investigate the impact of shipping fee policies on order size and incidence. The setting for their empirical study is an online retailer specializing in nonperishable grocery and drugstore items. The retailer had experimented with a variety of shipping fee structures which provided an excellent setting to assess the impact of different fee policies on shopper behavior.

The modeling approach proposed by Lewis et al. is based on the ordered logit. They conceptualize the problem as one of predicting several classes of basket size, including a no purchase option, where the classes match up with the breakpoints in the site's shipping fee policy. Mathematically, the model predicts the probability that a given shopper's result will fall into one of the order-size categories. The relative attractiveness of the groupings depends upon the shipping fee for the order-size and a series of control variables including demographics and prior shopper-specific behavior. Thus, as shipping fees vary, it may become more or less attractive for the shopper to place an order or to increase its size, thereby shifting the result from one order-size category to another. The model is designed to capture this effect.

For the retailer under study, the order-size categories are small baskets (0–$50), medium baskets ($50–$75), and large baskets (over $75). The authors test the proposed model on a sample of roughly 2,000 customers with an average order size of $57 and 8.5 items. Empirical results show that shipping fees have a significant impact on order incidence and size and work in the intuitively expected directions. For example, higher shipping fees for a small orders increase the likelihood of observing the no-buy option. As the cost to ship a medium-sized order rises, there is an increase in small orders, and so on. These results can then be used in a profit contribution analysis to optimize policy.

The authors also estimate their model with latent segment heterogeneity, selecting a four-segment solution as the best fitting. The results show substantial differences in how responsive shoppers are to shipping fees. For example, a free-shipping promotion increases order incidence by 10 percent or more across all shoppers, but raises it by 35 percent in the most responsive segment. The segmentation results show that e-commerce retailers may have promising opportunities to tailor shipping fee policies at the customer level. By estimating the model on historical data and grouping customers by responsiveness, managers can further refine their attempts at shipping fee optimization by adding customization.

10.4 Models for Multiple Sites and Multiple Channels

The discussion in the previous sections has focused primarily on models which examine activities at or related to a single web site at a time — i.e., bringing visitors to the site and converting those visits to e-commerce transactions. Of course, e-commerce web sites do not exist in a competitive vacuum. They vie for business with other sites as well as from alternate channel formats (usually bricks-and-mortar stores and catalogs), which in some cases may be operated by the same firm (e.g., Barnes and Noble stores versus bn.com). This creates the need for models to shed light on the use of the site in both competitive and multi-channel settings.

Though this is clearly a vital topic for managers, there are still only a relative handful of modeling advances in this area. This may be due, in part, to the difficulty in obtaining and working with the necessary data. Studying shopping behavior across multiple, competing e-commerce sites requires user-centric panel data. Modeling multi-channel problems requires performance data for the web site as well as the alternate channels. Thus, researchers working on these topics need very high levels of company cooperation and access to sensitive proprietary data.

10.4.1 Models for Multiple Web Sites

Some of the models discussed earlier were applied to user-centric data across multiple web sites. One of these was the power law model of Johnson et al. (2003). While this study did not look at cross site behavior *per se*, the power law model suggests that users become better at navigating (and buying) from a given website when they use it more often. The nature of this site-specific consumer learning sets up the basis for cognitive lock-in and a potentially higher level of site loyalty than one might initially expect to observe on the Internet. This finding has important implications for studying cross-site behavior. The notion of cognitive lock-in on the Internet has also been supported in the experimental literature. Zauberman (2003), for example, found that experimental subjects exhibited substantial lock-in to a given site when executing tasks that would benefit substantially from additional cross-site search.

Given the foregoing, it is of interest to model the cross-site search, usage, and purchase behavior for Internet shoppers. Two published articles and one working paper have addressed this. Johnson et al. (2004) examined and modeled the extent to which Media Metrix (now comScore) panelists searched across multiple web sites in a given e-commerce category. Park and Fader (2004) modeled the cross-site visitation dynamic for two sets of two competing web sites each, again using Media Metrix data. Lastly, Trusov and Bucklin (2006) studied the effects of prior Internet search on site usage behavior observed at focal web site in the automotive industry.

Johnson et al. (2004) study Media Metrix data for a panel of 10,000 house-holds from July 1997 to July 1998. They examine the behavior of the panelists across competing web sites in three product categories: CDs (16 sites), books (13 sites), and air travel (22 sites). Looking at panelist behavior at the monthly level, they report strikingly low overall levels of cross-site search. For example, in the first month of the data, the average number of sites searched per panelist was 1.2 for CD's, 1.1 for books, and 1.8 for travel. Some 70 percent of the CD shoppers, 70 percent of the book shoppers, and 42 percent of the travel shoppers were loyal to just one site throughout the data.

The authors also explore the extent to which cross-site search might depend upon experience and panelist search activity (i.e., some panelists are more active shoppers in the category than others). To do this, Johnson et al. propose the following model based on the logarithmic distribution for the probabilities of searching different numbers of sites:

$$\Pr[X_{ij} = x_{ij}] = \frac{a_{ij}\theta_{ij}^{x_{ij}}}{x_{ij}}. \tag{10.17}$$

In (10.17), x_{ij} is the number of sites searched by panelist i in month j, θ_{ij} is an individual-level search propensity (which must lie between 0 and 1) and $a_{ij} = -1/(\ln(1 - \theta_{ij}))$. To model experience and panelist search activity, θ becomes a function of time, in months, and a user-specific shopping activity measure. Estimating the model on the three categories, the authors find that users' category-level search activity is positively related to the number of sites searched in a given month (i.e., more active shoppers visit more sites) in all three cases. On the other hand, experience had no effect of cross-site search levels for books or CDs and a negative effect on travel (i.e., the model suggested that cross-site search was actually dropping over time). In addition to providing these types of findings, the authors note that their model could serve as a tool for e-commerce managers to track the dynamics in their customer base over time.

Though Johnson et al. (2004) study found that cross-site search was low overall, it did reveal that more extensive search across multiple sites is taking place among more active shoppers. Since these are likely to be the more valuable customers in e-commerce, modelers may still need to take into account cross-site visitation behavior. Park and Fader (2004) examine the visitation behavior of user-centric data panelists across competing web sites. They propose an elaborate stochastic model to improve the prediction of future visit behavior at a given site by harnessing the information in visit behavior at competing sites, in addition to the given site. Their modeling approach is designed to capture the potential dependence between the visitation patterns across sites. In so doing, this should improve forecasting and also provide insight into the behavior of the "zero class" – Internet users active in the product class but who have not yet visited a given site.

The authors study visit behavior of a large sample of Media Metrix panelists from 1997 to 1998 in two product categories, books, and CDs. In each category, they focus on two online retailers, Amazon.com and bn.com for books and CDNOW.com and Musicboulevard.com for music CDs. Results show that incorporating correlations in visit behavior across competing sites adds significantly to the predictive power of the models in both the books and music categories. The authors also illustrate how their model helps to understand the behavior of the zero class and show how panelists in that group may be targeted for acquisition efforts. Because it focuses on the visit behavior of panelists, a limitation of the modeling approach (as the authors note) is that it does not examine the effects of marketing activity or detailed measures of within-site browsing activity on future visit behavior.

As researchers improve their ability to tease out detailed activities from user-centric clickstreams, it is likely that future modeling advances in multiple-site research will be able to go beyond the focus on visit occurrence alone. For example, a working paper by Trusov and Bucklin (2006) uses comScore panel data to examine the impact of prior search behavior on what users do while visiting an e-commerce site. Looking at data for the automotive category, the authors show that the nature of prior exposure (visitation and time spent) to different types of web sites (informational, transactional, or manufacturer) is significantly related to the likelihood that visitors complete a product configuration task during their first visit to a given e-commerce site. The results reflect the existence of cross-site effects (i.e., what users do at previous sites affects what they will do at another site). Nevertheless, the authors also report that the relative magnitude of these effects (versus other factors influencing behavior) is small. Should the findings generalize, it suggests that results from site-centric models (i.e., models focused on within-site behavior alone) need not suffer from undue omitted variable bias or loss in predictive accuracy.

10.4.2 Models for Multiple Channels (Online and Offline)

While there continue to be e-commerce sites which lack alternate channels such as stores or catalogs (e.g., Amazon.com), it is now uncommon to find a major retailer without an online presence. The reality of retailing via the Internet alongside traditional channels raises a series of important questions for managers, some of which are beginning to be addressed by recent modeling advances. The extent to which an Internet sales channel cannibalizes sales from the firm's traditional channel was modeled by Biyalogorsky and Naik (2003) for music sales at Tower Records. The question of which customers prefer to shop across multiple channels and why was investigated by Kumar and Venkatesan (2005), looking at business-to-business sales at a computer hardware and software company. Verhoef et al. (2007) studied the tendency of consumer to use the Internet for research versus shopping, modeling survey

data of Dutch Internet customers. Lastly, Ansari et al. (2008) modeled
the migration of customers from the catalog channel to the Internet using
individual-level records of sales and marketing activity for a U.S. retailer of
consumer durables and apparel. Collectively, these advances have succeeded in
launching a promising set of modeling approaches in this critical area.

In the modeling set-up developed by Biyalogorsky and Naik (2003), the
firm's sells through retail stores and a relatively new online store. The objective
of the model is to determine the extent to which online activity cannibalizes
offline sales. To do this, the authors propose a dynamic model of five simultaneous equations. The model is set up for estimation on weekly data for retail
sales, on-line orders, and site visits and is specified as follows:

$$S_t = \lambda_1 \alpha_t + \gamma LS_t + \varepsilon_{1t} \tag{10.18a}$$

$$W_t = \lambda_2 \alpha_t + \varepsilon_{2t} \tag{10.18b}$$

$$O_t = \alpha_t + \varepsilon_{3t} \tag{10.18c}$$

$$\alpha_t = \beta_1 X_t + \beta_2 \mu_{t-1} X_t + \varepsilon_{4t} \tag{10.18d}$$

$$\mu_t = \delta \mu_{t-1} + \beta_3 X_t + \varepsilon_{5t} \tag{10.18e}$$

In (10.18a–e), S_t, LS_t, W_t and O_t are weekly variables for offline sales, prior
year offline sales (to control for seasonality), online sales, and the number of
online orders placed, respectively. Two unobservable constructs, α_t and μ_t,
capture online purchase behavior and online equity, also on a weekly basis.
The parameter λ_1 represents the estimated extent to which online purchase
behavior contemporaneously cannibalizes offline sales. The remaining terms
are additional parameters and errors.

Using Kalman filter methods, the authors estimate their model on weekly
data provided by Tower Records (a leading music retailer in the U.S. at the
time) for the period August 1998–July 1999. The cannibalization parameter, λ_1,
was estimated to be –0.888. Though the negative sign indicates the presence of
same-week cannibalization, it was not significantly different from zero. The
authors reported that the magnitude of the cannibalization effect was about
$0.89 on an average order size of $32.06, or a negligible 2.8 percent. The results
suggest that cannibalization of offline sales due to the Internet may be modest.
While more empirical findings are certainly needed, in the meantime, the model
provides a useful approach to the cannibalization question using data which
should be readily available to company managers.

Biyalogorsky and Naik's study used in-house company data on aggregate
sales. Many companies may also track sales data at the individual level (e.g.., in
CRM systems or data warehouses). Kumar and Venkatesan (2005) show how
such data can be used to understand the nature of multichannel shopping in a

business-to-business setting (their data is from a large, multinational computer hardware and software company for 1998–2001). In their article, the authors propose that a series of customer characteristics (e.g., cross-buying, returns, tenure, purchase frequency) and supplier factors (e.g.., contact rates by salesperson, telephone, direct mail, etc.) are related to the extent of multichannel shopping. Customer demographics (company size, annual sales), and industry category are also included as control variables. Customers could purchase from the company in four different channels: salespersons, direct mail, telephone sales, and online.

To assess the relationship between the hypothesized factors and the extent of multichannel shopping, the authors estimate an ordered logit model where the dependent variable takes the values of 1, 2, 3, and 4 (i.e., the number of channels observed to be used by the customer). Cross-buying (the number of different product categories that the customer had bought from the firm), customer-initiated contacts, web-based contacts, tenure, and purchase frequency were all positively associated with the use of more channels.

While Kumar and Venkatesan looked at the extent of multichannel shopping, Ansari et al. (2008) studied the choices that shoppers at one firm made between buying from its traditional channel (catalog) versus its online channel. Using four years (1998–2001) of individual customer data for a catalog and online retailer of consumer durables and apparel, the authors investigated the factors influencing this channel choice decision over time. Ansari et al. proposed a simultaneous individual-level model of order incidence, order size, and channel choice. The order incidence and size component was set up as a type II tobit model and the channel choice component was set up as a probit model. In the model, the three decisions are influenced by four sets of effects: customer demographics (e.g., age and income), previous ordering experience with the catalog and web site (captured by several time varying measures), marketing activity (catalogs and emails sent to the customer), and time (trend and seasonality).

During the course of the study period, much of the firm's business migrated from the catalog channel to the online channel. In a fascinating set of results, the authors show that this development was not necessarily a positive one for the firm. In contrast to popular expectations, customers who migrated to the web actually tended to patronize the firm less as time went by. The authors note that this could be due to lower switching costs on the web and to the decrease in contact with the firm's phone sales representatives. Results from the channel choice model revealed that the firm can influence channel choice through marketing effort. In particular, catalog mailings tend to result in use of the catalog channel while emails tend to increase the selection of the online channel.

The Ansari et al. model illustrates some of the insights which can come from careful analysis of individual-level marketing and purchase data. One limitation of such data is that it does not contain information on search or other pre-purchase activity. Addressing this may require modelers to be able to match user-centric panel data with multichannel purchase records. In the absence of such data, researchers can turn to survey methods for insight into the search versus purchase use of different channels. The work of Verhoef et al. (2007) provides a nice demonstration of what can be accomplished with the creative modeling of survey data. Surveying a large sample of Dutch consumers who use the Internet, they sought to investigate the role of search versus purchase in a multichannel setting (stores, internet, and catalog) across six categories (loans, vacations, books, computers, clothing, and electronic appliances). In particular, they focused on the problem of the "research shopper" – a customer who uses a channel for search but buys in an alternate channel.

Their survey results strongly supported the contention of many in e-commerce that the Internet is often more of a search channel than a purchase channel. The model based on the survey findings showed that, unlike stores and catalogs, consumers who used the Internet for search did not feel disposed to use it for purchase (i.e., there was little "lock-in" from search to purchase or vice versa). For companies without stores or catalogs, the ability to convert search to purchase is a major strategic concern. In addition to the survey-based results, Verhoef et al. go on to examine different approaches that firms might take to manage the research shopper problem. For example, two factors which hurt the Internet as a purchase channel are lower ratings for service and privacy when compared to stores. Taking steps to mitigate these concerns in the minds of site visitors could produce sharp increases in online purchase propensity.

10.5 Conclusion

The purpose of this chapter has been to provide researchers and practitioners with an organized review of state-of-the-art modeling approaches to marketing decision problems in e-commerce. Modeling advances were classified into three broad categories: (1) models for attracting customers to the site, (2) models for understanding site usage, predicting purchase conversion, and improving site management, and (3) models for multiple sites and multiple channels. While all of the e-commerce models discussed here are quite recent, having appeared only since the year 2000, it is quite encouraging for both academics and managers that the field has already produced such an impressive set of advances.

With much work ongoing (some of which has been touched on here), many of the gaps and limitations that exist in the scope of currently available models are likely to be filled or addressed in the near future. Nevertheless, several suggestions for needed future work might be noted.

Turning first to the models for attracting customers to the site, more work is needed on the management of online advertising and its relative effectiveness versus traditional media. For example models for display-type ads may be further developed to examine the impact of different executional formats, the effect of placement alongside site content, and placement within the structure of the referring web site (e.g., home page versus subsequent pages). Research on the rapidly growing category of paid search advertising is also needed, with models needed which can aid managers in evaluating the return on their investments in this area. As a logical extension to that, advertising and marketing mix models need to be extended to incorporate online media alongside offline spending.

With respect to the second category, considering usage within the site, purchase conversion, and site management, there is also a long list of modeling advances which would be worthwhile. For example, purchase conversion models, which have so far been based on relatively coarse measures of site structure and content, need to be extended to take into account more aspects of site design, page appearance, and page-level content. In the area of site management, further work is needed to build models which will guide managers in setting prices in an online environment. Given that e-commerce managers are online retailers, it is a striking omission that there are no models for online merchandising or assortment planning. In a very interesting article, Brynjolfsson et al. (2003) discuss the social value created by the larger assortments online, but do not deal with the managerial problem of what to carry and how to present it online.

In the last category, models for multiple sites and multiple channels, more work is needed to understand the effects of competition between sites. New modeling frameworks might be developed to capture the idiosyncratic nature of online retail competition (e.g., how can "distance" or location be modeled when competition occurs online versus offline?). Similarly, critical questions in multi-channel management need to be addressed with new models. Part of the challenge here is likely to be access to the proprietary (and comprehensive) data needed to capture the key elements of the environment. In sum, while much encouraging progress has been made in all three areas, there is a great deal of important – and exciting – work which lies ahead.

References

Ansari, A., S. Essegaier, R. Kohli. 2000. Internet Recommendation Systems. *Journal of Marketing Research* **37**(August) 363–375.

Ansari, A., C.F. Mela. 2003. E-Customization. *Journal of Marketing Research* **40** (May) 131–145.

Ansari, A., C.F. Mela, S.A. Neslin. 2008. Customer Channel Migration. *Journal of Marketing Research*, **45**(February) 60–76.

Biyalogorsky, E., P. Naik. 2003. Clicks and Mortar: The Effect of On-line Activities on Off-line Sales. *Marketing Letters* **14**(1) 21–32.

Bronnenberg, B.J., W. Vanhonacker. 1996. Limited Choice Sets, Local Price Response, and Implied Measures of Price Competition. *Journal of Marketing Research* **33**(May) 163–173.

Brynjolfsson, Erik, Yu (Jeffrey) Hu, M,D. Smith. 2003. Consumer Surplus in the Digital Economy: Estimating the Value of Increased Product Variety at Online Booksellers. *Management Science* **49**(11) 1580–1596.

Bucklin, R.E., J.M. Lattin, A. Ansari, S. Gupta, D. Bell, E. Coupey, J.D.C. Little, C. Mela, A. Montgomery, J. Steckel. 2002. Choice and the Internet: From Clickstream to Research Stream. *Marketing Letters* **13**(3) 245–258.

Bucklin, R.E., C. Sismeiro. 2003. A Model of Web Site Browsing Behavior Estimated on Clickstream Data. *Journal of Marketing Research* **40**(August) 249–267.

Chatterjee, P., D.L. Hoffman, T.P. Novak. 2003. Modeling the Clickstream: Implications for Web-Based Advertising Efforts. *Marketing Science* **22**(4) 520–541.

Chevalier, J.A., D. Mayzlin. 2006. The Effect of Word of Mouth on Sales: Online Book Reviews. *Journal of Marketing Research* **43**(August) 345–354.

Chintagunta, P.K. 1993. Investigating Purchase Incidence, Brand Choice and Purchase Quantity Decisions of Households. *Marketing Science* **12**(2) 184–208.

comScore Networks. 2007. Retail E-Commerce Climbs 23 Percent in Q2 Versus Year Ago. www.comscore.com/press/release.asp?press = 1545, accessed August 27, 2007.

Danaher, P.J., G.M. Mullarkey, S. Essegaier. 2006. Factors Affecting Web Site Visit Duration: A Cross-Domain Analysis. *Journal of Marketing Research* **43**(May) 182–194.

Demers, E., B. Lev. 2001. A Rude Awakening: Internet Shakeout in 2000. *Review of Accounting Studies* **6**(August) 331–359.

Drèze, X., A. Bonfrer. 2006. An Empirical Investigation of the Impact of Communication Timing on Customer Equity. working paper, Wharton School, University of Pennsylvania.

Drèze, X., F.-X. Hussherr. 2003. Internet Advertising: Is Anybody Watching? *Journal of Interactive Marketing* **17**(4) 8–23.

Edelman, B., M. Ostrovsky, M. Schwarz. 2007. Internet Advertising and the Generalized Second Price Auction: Selling Billions of Dollars' Worth of Keywords. *American Economic Review* **97**(1) 242–259.

Godes, D., D. Mayzlin. 2004. Using Online Conversations to Study Word-of-Mouth Communication. *Marketing Science* **23**(4) 545–560.

Hanssens, D.M., L.J. Parsons, R.L. Schultz. 2001. *Market Response Models: Econometric and Time Series Analysis*, 2 nd edition, Kluwer Academic Publishers, Boston.

Häubl, G., V. Trifts. 2000. Consumer Decision-Making in Online Shopping Environments: The Effects of Interactive Decision Aids. *Marketing Science* **19**(1) 4–21.

Ilfeld, J. S., R.S. Winer. 2002. Generating Website Traffic. *Journal of Advertising Research* (September–October) 49–61.

Internet Advertising Bureau. 2007. Internet Advertising Revenues Grow in '06 . www.iab.net/news/pr_2007_05_23.asp, accessed August 27, 2007.

Johnson, E.J., S. Bellman, G.L. Lohse. 2003. Cognitive Lock-In and the Power Law of Practice. *Journal of Marketing* **67**(April) 62–75.

Johnson, E.J., W.W. Moe, P.S. Fader, S. Bellman, J. Lohse. 2004. On the Depth and Dynamics of Online Search Behavior. *Management Science* **50**(3) 299–308.

Kumar, V., R. Venkatesan. 2005. Who are the Multichannel Shoppers and How Do They Perform?: Correlates of Multichannel Shopping Behavior. *Journal of Interactive Marketing* **19**(2) 44–62.

Lal, R., M. Sarvary. 1999. When and How is the Internet Likely to Decrease Price Competition?" *Marketing Science* **18**(4) 485–503.

Lewis, M., V. Singh, S. Fay. 2006. An Empirical Study of the Impact of Nonlinear Shipping and Handling Fees on Purchase Incidence and Expenditure Decisions. *Marketing Science* **25**(1) 51–64.

Manchanda, P., J.-P. Dubé, K. Yong Goh, P.K. Chintagunta. 2006. The Effect of Banner Advertising on Internet Purchasing. *Journal of Marketing Research* **43**(February) 98–108.

Mandel, N., E.J. Johnson. 2002. When Web Pages Influence Choice: Effects of Visual Primes on Experts and Novices. *Journal of Consumer Research* **29**(September) 235–245.

Mangalindan, M.. 2007. Web Stores Tap Product Reviews. *Wall Street Journal* (September 11), B3.

Mayzlin, D. 2006. Promotional Chat on the Internet. *Marketing Science* **25**(2) 155–163.

Moe, W.W. 2003. Buying, Searching, or Browsing: Differentiating Between Online Shoppers Using In-Store Navigational Clickstream. *Journal of Consumer Psychology* **13**(1&2) 29–39.

Moe, W.W. 2006. An Empirical Two-Stage Choice model with Varying Decision Rules Applied to Internet Clickstream Data. *Journal of Marketing Research* **38**(November) 680–692.

Moe, W.W., P.S. Fader. 2004a. Capturing Evolving Visit Behavior in Clickstream Data. *Journal of Interactive Marketing* **18**(1) 5–19.

Moe, W.W., P.S. Fader. 2004b. Dynamic Conversion Behavior at e-Commerce Sites. *Management Science* **50**(3) 326–335.

Montgomery, A.L., K. Hosanagar, R. Krishnan,, K.B. Clay. 2004a. Designing a Better Shopbot. *Management Science* **50**(2) 189–206.

Montgomery, A.L., S. Li, K. Srinivasan, John C. Liechty. 2004b. Modeling Online Browsing and Path Analysis Using Clickstream Data. *Marketing Science* **23**(4) 579–595.

Murray, K., G. Häubl. 2008. Interactive Consumer Decision Aids. in *Handbook of Marketing Decision Models,* Berend Wierenga, ed., Springer Science + Business Media this volume, chapter 3, p 55–77.

Park, Y.-H., P.S. Fader. 2004. Modeling Browsing Behavior at Multiple Websites. *Marketing Science* **23**(3) 280–303.

Roberts, J.H., J.M. Lattin. 1991. Development and Testing of a Model of Consideration Set Composition. *Journal of Marketing Research* **28**(November) 429–440.

Rutz, O.J., R.E. Bucklin. 2007. From Generic to Branded: A Model of Spillover Dynamics in Paid Search Advertising. working paper, School of Management, Yale University.

Senecal, S., J. Nantel. 2004. The Influence of Online Product Recommendations on Consumers' Online Choices. *Journal of Retailing* **80** 159–169.

Silva-Risso, J.M., R.E. Bucklin, D.G. Morrison. 1999. A Decision Support System for Planning Manufacturers' Sales Promotion Calendars. *Marketing Science* **18**(3) 274–300.

Sismeiro, C., R.E. Bucklin. 2004. Modeling Purchase Behavior at an E-Commerce Web Site: A Task-Completion Approach. *Journal of Marketing Research* **41**(August) 306–323.

Smith, M.D., E. Brynjolfsson. 2001. Consumer Decision-Making at an Internet Shopbot: Brand Still Matters. *Journal of Industrial Economics* **99**(4) 541–558.

Tellis, G.J., F.S. Zufryden. 1995. Tackling the Retailer Decision Maze: Which Brands to Discount, How Much, When and Why? *Marketing Science* **14**(3) 271–299.

Trusov, M., R.E. Bucklin. 2006. Should We Hope You Shopped Around? Effects of Prior Internet Search on E-Commerce Site Activity. working paper, Robert H. Smith School of Business, University of Maryland.

Verhoef, P.C., S.A. Neslin, B. Vroomen. 2007. Multichannel Customer Management: Understanding the Research-Shopper Phenomenon. *International Journal of Research in Marketing* **24**(2) 129–148.

Wu, J., A. Rangaswamy. 2003. A Fuzzy Set Model of Search and Consideration with an Application to an Online Market. *Marketing Science* **22**(3) 411–434.

Zauberman, G. 2003. The Intertemporal Dynamics of Consumer Lock-In. *Journal of Consumer Research* **30**(December) 405–419.

Zhang, J., L. Krishnamurthi. 2004. Customizing Promotions in Online Stores. *Marketing Science* **23**(4) 561–578.

Part V

Special Model Approaches

Chapter 11
Time-Series Models in Marketing

Marnik G. Dekimpe, Philip Hans Franses, Dominique M. Hanssens, and Prasad A. Naik

11.1 Introduction

Marketing data appear in a variety of forms. A frequently occurring form is time-series data, for example, sales per week, market shares per month, the price evolution over the last few years, or historically-observed advertising-spending patterns. The main feature of time-series data is that the observations are ordered over time, and hence that it is likely that earlier observations have predictive content for future observations. Indeed, if relative prices are, say, 1.50 today, they most likely will be around 1.50 tomorrow too, or in any case, not a value of 120.

Time series can refer to a single variable, such as sales or advertising, but can also cover a vector of variables, for example sales, prices and advertising, jointly. In some instances, marketing modelers may want to build a univariate model for a time series, and analyze the series strictly as a function of its own past. This is, for example, the case when one has to forecast (or extrapolate) exogenous variables, or when the number of variables to be analyzed (e.g. the number of items in a broad assortment) is so large that building multivariate models for each of them is too unwieldy (Hanssens, Parsons and Schultz 2001). However, univariate time-series models do not handle the cause-and-effect situations that are central to marketing planning. To specify the lag structure in response models, one extends the techniques of univariate extrapolation to the case of multiple time series.

Time-series data can be summarized in time-series models. However, not all models built on time-series data are referred to as time-series models. Unlike most econometric approaches to dynamic model specification, time-series

M.G. Dekimpe
Tilburg University, Tilburg, The Netherlands and Catholic University Leuven,
Leuven, Belgium
e-mail: M.G.Dekimpe@uvt.nl

The authors are indebted to Scott Neslin, Vincent Nijs and the editor, Berend Wierenga, for useful comments on an earlier version of the chapter.

modelers take a more data-driven approach. Specifically, one looks at histori-cally-observed patterns in the data to help in model specification, rather than imposing a priori a certain structure derived from marketing or economic theory on the data. As put by Nobel Laureate Sir Clive Granger (1981, p. 121):

> It is well known that time-series analysts have a rather different approach to the analysis of economic data than does the remainder of the econometric profession. One aspect of this difference is that we admit more readily to looking at the data before finally specifying the model; in fact, we greatly encourage looking at the data. Although econometricians trained in a more traditional manner are still very much inhibited in the use of summary statistics derived from the data to help model selection, or identification, it could be to their advantage to change some of these attitudes.

This feature of looking at the data to help in model specification can be illustrated as follows. Given a hypothesized model for a time series, one can derive the properties of empirical data in case that model would truly describe the data. For example, a simple model that says that y_t only depends on y_{t-1} using the scheme $y_t = \rho\, y_{t-1} + e_t$ would imply that y_t shows a correlation with y_{t-1} of size ρ, with y_{t-2} of size ρ^2, and so on. If such a correlation structure were to be found in empirical data, one would have a first guess at what the best descriptive model could look like. If $|\rho| < 1$, the impact of past events becomes smaller and smaller, which is not the case when $\rho = 1$ (the so-called unit-root scenario, discussed in more detail in Section 11.2). A competing model with structure $y_t = e_t - \theta\, e_{t-1}$ would show a non-zero correlation between y_t and y_{t-1}, and a zero correlation between y_t and, respectively, $y_{t-2}, y_{t-3}, \ldots$ By compar-ing the empirically-observed correlation patterns (referred to as the empirical autocorrelation function) with the one associated theoretically with a given model structure, a model is selected that is likely to have generated the data. Other summary statistics that are useful in this respect are the partial auto-correlation function and (in case of multiple variables) the cross-correlation function (see e.g. Hanssens et al. 2001 for a review). While time-series mode-lers highly stimulate this "looking at the data", critics refer to this practice as data-mining, arguing that time-series models "lack foundations in marketing theory" (Leeflang et al. 2000, p. 458).

This criticism is one of the reasons why, historically, time-series models were not used that often in the marketing literature. Other reasons, described in detail in Dekimpe and Hanssens (2000), were (i) marketing scientists' tradi-tional lack of training in time-series methods, (ii) the lack of access to user-friendly software, (iii) the absence of good-quality time-series data, and (iv) the absence of a substantive marketing area where time-series modeling was adopted as primary research tool. However, over the last few years, these inhibiting factors have begun to disappear. Several marketing-modeling text-books now contain chapters outlining the use of time-series models (see e.g Hanssens et al. 2001; Leeflang et al. 2000), while others include an overview chapter on time-series applications in marketing (see e.g. the current volume, or Moorman and Lehmann 2004). In terms of software, several user-friendly PC-based packages have become available (e.g. Eviews), while new data sources (e.g. long series of scanner data) have considerably alleviated the data concern. In terms of the substantive marketing area, several time-series techniques have been specifically designed to disentangle short- from long-run relationships. This fits well with one of marketing's main fields of interest: to quantify the long-run impact of marketing's tactical and strategic decisions. In terms of the critique on the a-theoretic character of time-series modeling, we observe three recent developments. First, the choice of which endogenous and exogenous variables to include in the VARX (*Vector-AutoRegressive* models with *eXogenous* variables) models is increasingly theory-driven. Second, some time-series techniques (e.g. cointegration testing for theoretically-expected equilibria) have a more confirmatory potential. Finally, following a 1995 special issue of *Marketing Science*, there is growing recognition of the value of Empirical Generalizations obtained through the repeated application of data-driven techniques on multiple data sets. We refer to Dekimpe and Hanssens (2000) for an in-depth discussion on these issues. Because of these developments, time-series models have become increasingly accepted in the marketing literature. Moreover, we see an increasing convergence between regression approaches (which often focused on obtaining unbiased estimates of marketing-mix effectiveness, but did not rely much on summary statistics derived from the data at hand to help in model specification), time-series techniques (which were used primarily to derive good forecasts or extrapolations), and structural models (which start from economic fundamentals but ignored dynamics until recently).

Time-series modelers make use of a wide array of techniques, which are discussed in detail in textbooks such as Hamilton (1994) or Franses (1998), among others. In this chapter, we will not attempt to review all of these techniques. Instead, we will focus on two domains that have recently received considerable attention in the marketing literature: (i) the use of persistence modeling to make long-run inferences (Section 11.2), and (ii) the use of state-space models and their integration with normative decision making (Section 11.3). Finally, we will discuss a number of opportunities and challenges for time-series modelers in marketing (Section 11.4).

11.2 Persistence Modeling

Long-run market response is a central concern of any marketing strategy that tries to create a sustainable competitive advantage. However, this is easier said than done, as only short-run results of marketing actions are readily available. Persistence modeling addresses the problem of long-run market-response identification by combining into one metric the net long-run impact of a chain reaction of consumer response, firm feedback, and competitor response that emerges following an initial marketing action. This marketing action could be an unexpected increase in advertising support (e.g. Dekimpe and Hanssens 1995a), a price promotion (e.g. Pauwels, Hanssens, and Siddarth 2002), or a competitive activity (e.g. Steenkamp et al. 2005), and the performance metric

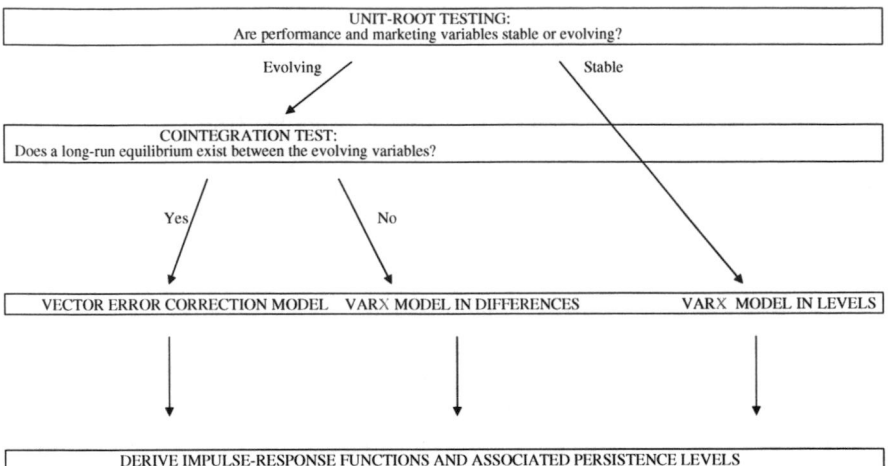

Fig. 11.1 Overview of persistence modeling procedure

could be primary (Nijs et al. 2001) or secondary (Dekimpe and Hanssens 1995a) demand, profitability (Dekimpe and Hanssens 1999), or stock prices (Pauwels, Silva-Risso, Srinivasan and Hanssens 2004), among others.

Persistence modeling is a multi-step process, as depicted in Fig. 11.1 (taken from Dekimpe and Hanssens 2004). In a first step, one applies unit-root tests to the different performance and marketing-support variables of interest to determine whether they are stable (mean or trend-stationary) or evolving. In the latter case, the series have a stochastic trend, and one has to test whether a long-run equilibrium exists between them. This is done through cointegration testing. Depending on the outcome of these preliminary (unit-root and cointegration) tests, one specifies a VARX model in the levels, a VARX model in the differences, or a Vector Error Correction Model. From these VARX models, one can derive impulse-response functions (IRFs), which trace the incremental effect of a one-unit (or one-standard-deviation) shock in one of the variables on the future values of the other endogenous variables.

Without going into mathematical details,[1] we can graphically illustrate the key concepts of the approach in Fig. 11.2 (taken from Nijs et al. 2001):

In this Figure, we depict the *incremental* primary demand that can be attributed to an initial price promotion. In the stable detergent market of Panel A, one observes an immediate sales increase, followed by a post-promotional dip. After some fluctuations, which can be attributed to factors such as purchase reinforcement, feedback rules, and competitive reactions, we observe that the incremental sales converge to zero. This does not imply that no more detergents are sold in this market, but rather that in the long run no additional sales can be attributed to

---

[1] We refer to Enders (1995) or Franses (1998) for excellent technical discussions on the various tests involved. Dekimpe and Hanssens (2004) review key decisions to be made in this respect.

A: Impulse response function for a stationary market

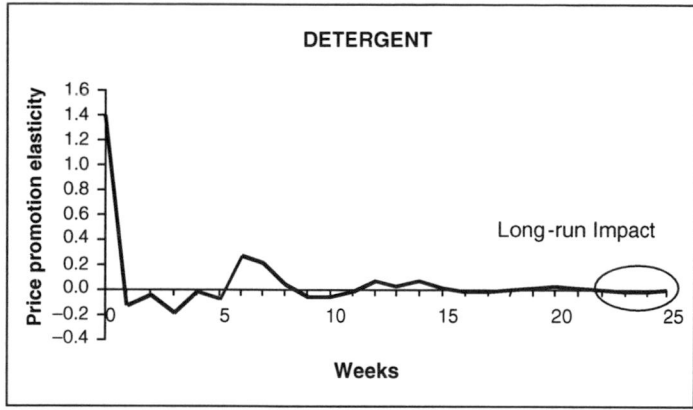

B: Impulse response function for an evolving market

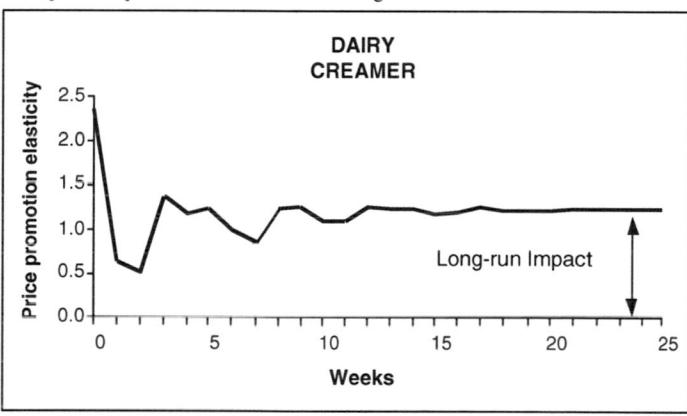

Fig. 11.2 Impulse response functions

the initial promotion. In contrast, in the evolving dairy-creamer market depicted in the bottom panel of Fig. 11.2, we see that this incremental effect stabilizes at a non-zero, or persistent, level. In that case, a long-run effect has been identified, as the initial promotion keeps on generating extra sales. This could be due to new customers who have been attracted to the category by the initial promotion and now make repeat purchases. Alternatively, existing customers may have increased their product-usage rates. From these impulse-response functions, one can derive various summary statistics, such as:

(i) the immediate performance impact of the price promotion;
(ii) the long-run or permanent (persistent) impact, i.e., the value to which the impulse-response function converges; and
(iii) the combined cumulative effect over the dust-settling period. This period is defined as the time it takes before the convergence level is obtained. For the

Figure in panel A, for example, the total effect over the dust-settling period (also referred to as the short-run effect) amounts to the area under the curve (specifically, the sum of the IRF estimates that have not yet converged to zero).

Persistence modeling offers two distinct advantages. First, it offers a clear and quantifiable distinction between short- and long-run promotional effectiveness, based on the difference between temporary and permanent movements in the data. Second, it uses a system's approach to market response, in that it combines the forces of customer response, competitive reaction, and firm decision rules. Indeed, the chain reaction of all these forces is reflected in the impulse-response functions, which are themselves derived from the multi-equation vector-autoregressive model. By incorporating such a chain reaction over time, the impulse-response function expands upon the more conventional direct & instantaneous elasticity estimates.[2]

Persistence modeling has been used extensively in the recent marketing literature, and has resulted in several strategic insights. We summarize these insights in Table 11.1, which updates Dekimpe and Hanssens (2004).

Many of these insights have been derived in a two-step modeling approach. In a first step, the procedure described in Fig. 11.1 is applied to multiple brands and/or product categories (see e.g. Nijs et al. 2001; Srinivasan et al. 2004; Steenkamp et al. 2005). In a second step, one explains the observed variability across brands or product categories in the aforementioned summary statistics (i.e. the immediate effect, the long-run effect and the dust-settling effect) through a variety of marketing-theory-based covariates.[3] These could include, for example, the advertising intensity or concentration rate in the category, or the strength and nature (private label or national brand) of the brand. However, this approach was recently criticized in Fok et al. (2006) for not appropriately accounting for the uncertainty in the first-stage parameter estimates when estimating the second-stage model. They therefore proposed a single-step Hierarchical Bayes Error Correction Model. As an added benefit, their approach offers direct estimates of a marketing instrument's short- and long-run effects. This is more parsimonious than through the aforementioned summary statistics, which are a function of many VARX parameters. A similar Error Correction Model was used in van Heerde, Helsen, and Dekimpe (2007), who investigated how short- and long-run price and advertising elasticities changed following a product-harm crisis. Both studies used a single-equation approach, however, treating all marketing-mix variables as exogenous. VARX models, in contrast, allow many of these variables to be endogenous.

---

[2] From these impulse-response functions, one can also derive a Forecast Error Variance Decomposition (FEVD) to calculate what percentage of the variation in an endogenous variable (e.g. retail price) can be attributed to contemporaneous and past changes in each of the endogenous variables (e.g. competing prices) in the system. We refer to Hanssens (1998) or Nijs et al. (2006) for an in-depth discussion on FEVD.

[3] This again helps to alleviate the criticism of being a-theoretical.

Table 11.1 Strategic insights from persistence modeling

Study	Contribution
Baghestani (1991)	Advertising has a long run impact on sales if both variables are (a) evolving and (b) in long-run equilibrium (cointegrated).
Bronnenberg, Mahajan, and Vanhonacker (2000)	Distribution coverage drives long-run market shares, especially the coverage evolution early in the life cycle.
Cavaliere and Tassinari (2001)	Advertising is not a long-run driver of aggregate whisky consumption in Italy.
Chowdhury (1994)	No long run equilibrium (cointegration) relationship is found between UK aggregate advertising spending and a variety of macro-economic variables.
Dekimpe and Hanssens (1995a)	Persistence measures quantify marketing's long-run effectiveness. Image-oriented and price-oriented advertising messages have a differential short- and long-run effect.
Dekimpe and Hanssens (1995b)	Sales series are mostly evolving, while a majority of market-share series is stationary.
Dekimpe and Hanssens (1999)	Different strategic scenarios (business as usual, escalation, hysteresis and evolving business practice) have different long-run profitability implications.
Dekimpe, Hanssens, and Silva-Risso (1999)	Little evidence of long-run promotional effects is found in FPCG markets.
Dekimpe et al. (1997)	New product introductions may cause structural breaks in otherwise stationary loyalty patterns.
Franses (1994)	Gompertz growth models with non-constant market potential can be written in error-correction format.
Franses, Kloek, and Lucas (1999)	Outlier-robust unit-root and cointegration tests are called for in promotion-intensive scanner environments.
Franses, Srinivasan, and Boswijk (2001)	Unit root and cointegration tests which account for the logical consistency of market shares.
Hanssens (1998)	Factory orders and sales are in a long-run equilibrium, but shocks to either have different long-run consequences.
Hanssens and Ouyang (2002)	Derivation of advertising allocation rules (in terms of triggering versus maintenance spending) under hysteresis conditions.
Horváth et al. (2005)	The inclusion/exclusion of competitive reaction and feedback effects affects the net unit sales effects of price reductions, as do intrafirm effects.
Horváth, Leeflang, and Otter (2002)	Structural relationships between (lagged) consumer response and (lagged) marketing instruments can be inferred through canonical correlation analysis and Wiener-Granger causality testing.
Johnson et al. (1992)	The long-run consumption of alcoholic beverages is not price sensitive.
Joshi and Hanssens (2006)	Advertising has a long-run positive effect on firm valuation.
Jung and Seldon (1995)	Aggregate US advertising spending is in long-run equilibrium with aggregate personal consumption expenditures.

Table 11.1 (continued)

Study	Contribution
Lim, Currim, and Andrews (2005)	Consumer segmentation matters in persistence modeling for price-promotion effectiveness.
McCullough and Waldon (1998)	Network and national spot advertising are substitutes.
Nijs et al. (2001)	Limited long-run category expansion effects of price promotions. The impact differs in terms of the marketing intensity, competitive structure, and competitive conduct in the industry.
Nijs, Srinivasan, and Pauwels (2006)	Retail prices are driven by pricing history, competitive retailer prices, brand demand, wholesale prices, and retailer category management considerations.
Pauwels (2004)	Restricted policy simulations allow to distinguish four dynamic forces that drive long-term marketing effectiveness: consumer response, competitor response, company inertia and company support.
Pauwels and Srinivasan (2004)	Permanent performance effects are observed from store brand entry, but these effects differ between manufacturers and retailers, and between premium-price and second-tier national brands.
Pauwels and Hanssens (2007)	Brands in mature markets go through different performance regimes, which are influenced by their marketing policies.
Pauwels et al. (2002)	The decomposition of the promotional sales spike in category-incidence, brand-switching and purchase-quantity effects differs depending on the time frame considered (short versus long run).
Pauwels et al. (2004)	Investor markets reward product innovation but punish promotional initiatives by automobile manufacturers.
Srinivasan and Bass (2000)	Stable market shares are consistent with evolving sales if brand and category sales are cointegrated.
Srinivasan, Popkowski Leszczyc, and Bass (2000)	Temporary, gradual and structural price changes have a different impact on market shares.
Srinivasan et al. (2004)	Price promotions have a differential performance impact for retailers versus manufacturers.
Steenkamp et al.(2005)	Competitive reactions to promotion and advertising attacks are often passive. This rarely involves a missed sales opportunity. If reaction occurs, it often involves spoiled arms.
Villanueva, Yoo, and Hanssens (2006)	Customers acquired through different channels have different lifetime values.
Zanias (1994)	Feedback effects occur between sales and advertising. The importance of cointegration analysis is demonstrated with respect to Granger causality testing and multi-step forecasting.

As indicated before, persistence and error-correction models have resulted in several empirical generalizations on the presence/absence of long-run marketing effects. However, these insights have remained largely descriptive. While some studies (see e.g. Pauwels 2004; van Heerde et al. 2007) have used these models for policy simulations,[4] their use for normative decision-making has remained the exception rather than the rule, and remains an important challenge for time-series modelers. The linkage with normative decision making has been made explicitly in recent applications of state-space modeling, which we review in Section 11.3. We offer somewhat more technical detail on these methods, as their usefulness for marketing has, to the best of our knowledge, not yet been covered in a review chapter.

11.3 State-Space Models, the Kalman Filter, and Normative Decision Making[5]

State-space models offer many advantages, of which we list ten at the end of Section 11.3.1. In what follows we first explain what a state-space model is; then its estimation and inference; its applications in marketing; and, finally, its role in normative analysis.

11.3.1 State Space Models

Linear state-space models are expressed by two sets of equations:

$$Y_t = Z_t\alpha_t + c_t + \varepsilon_t, \text{ and} \tag{11.1}$$

$$\alpha_t = T_t\alpha_{t-1} + d_t + v_t, \tag{11.2}$$

---

[4] Most applications of persistence modeling consider the impact of marketing decisions (e.g. an unexpected advertising increase, an additional promotion) that do not alter the nature of the data-generating process (see e.g. Dekimpe et al. 1999 or Srinivasan et al. 2004). As such, the implications of more drastic regime changes (e.g. a switch from EDLP to HiLo pricing strategy) tends to fall outside the scope of these studies. Still, restricted policy simulations where the data-generating process is altered were considered in Pauwels (2004), and offered many managerially useful insights. We refer to Franses (2005) or van Heerde, Dekimpe, and Putsis (2005) for an in-depth discussion on the use of time-series modeling for policy simulation, and their resulting sensitivity to the Lucas critique.

[5] A gentle introduction may be found in Meinhold and Singpurwalla (1983), who explain the Kalman filter using the language of Bayesian updating. The following recommended references are arranged in increasing level of sophistication: Harvey (1994) offers econometric applications; Shumway and Stoffer (2006) describe applied time-series models; Harrison and West (1997) provide a Bayesian perspective; Durbin and Koopman (2001) present a unifying perspective underlying Bayesian and frequentist views; Lewis (1986) explains both the normative (i.e., optimal actions) and estimation (i.e., model identification) issues; finally, Jazwinski (1970), the *pioneering* book on this topic, reveals the provenance of Kalman filters in Mathematics and Control Engineering (predating their use in statistical and social sciences).

where $\varepsilon_t \sim N(0, H_t)$, $v_t \sim N(0, Q_t)$, Y is a random vector (m×1) and α is random vector (n×1), where m could be greater than, less than or equal to n. The vector $Y_t = (y_{1t}, y_{2t}, \ldots y_{mt})'$ contains observed time-series such as sales of brand A, sales of brand B, and so on observed over several time periods t = 1, ..., R. Similarly, $\alpha_t = (\alpha_{1t}, \alpha_{2t}, \ldots \alpha_{nt})'$ includes multiple state-variables. A state variable α_t can play diverse roles, for example, a time-varying parameter like copy wearout in Naik, Mantrala and Sawyer (1998) or Bass et al. (2007); a construct such as goodwill or brand equity as in Sriram and Kalwani (2007); a set of variables such as market shares as in Naik, Raman and Winer (2005); a reading of a performance barometer as in Pauwels & Hanssens (2007); a random variable to capture non-stationarity and heterogeneity as in van Heerde, Mela and Manchanda (2004), or to impute missing values via the cubic spline as in Biyalogorsky and Naik (2003). A discrete-valued α_t opens up new class of models such as "Hidden Markov Models" as in Smith, Naik and Tsai (2006) or Netzer, Latting and Srinivasan (2008).

The dimensions of other matrices and vectors in the dynamic system conform to those of (Y, α). Specifically, the link matrix Z is an m x n matrix; T is an n x n transition matrix; the drift vectors (c, d) are m × 1 and n × 1, respectively; the covariance matrices H and Q have dimensions m x m and n x n, respectively. For example, in Naik and Raman (2003) integrated marketing communications (IMC) model $S_t = \lambda S_{t-1} + \sum_{i=1}^{2} \beta_i x_i + \kappa x_1 x_2 + v_t$, we note that the scalar state variable $\alpha = S$, the 1×1 transition matrix $T = \lambda$, the 1×1 drift vector $d = \Sigma \beta_i x_i + \kappa x_1 x_2$, the transition noise $Q = \sigma_v^2$, $Y = S + \varepsilon$, so $Z = 1, c = 0$ and the observation noise $H = \sigma_\varepsilon^2$. In this manner, several well-known marketing models may be expressed as special cases of the state-space form (see Table 11.4).

Equation (11.2) is called the transition (or plant) equation, which captures the dynamics of the physical system explicitly. It is linked to the observed (i.e., measured) variables via equation (11.1), which is therefore called the measurement or observation equation. The vector Y is the observation vector; α is the state vector. The drift vectors (c, d) represent the effects of exogenous variables (e.g., $c_t = X_t'\beta$, $d_t = W_t'\gamma$, where X and W contain multiple variables, and (β,γ) are conformable parameter vectors). The subscript t denotes that the given quantity can change over time, indicating that it is potentially time-varying and therefore implicitly dynamic (besides the state vector, which is explicitly dynamic). Table 11.2 summarizes the names and dimensions of vector-matrices in the state-space form.

The state-space form, given by (11.1) and (11.2), is very general. For example, standard time-series models like VAR, VMA, ARIMAX are special cases (see, e.g., Durbin and Koopman 2001, Harvey 1994). In addition, structural models that capture dynamic marketing phenomena such as Brandaid, the Nerlove-Arrow model, the Vidale-Wolfe model, Tracker, Litmus, the Bass diffusion model and the IMC model have a state-space representation (see Tables 11.3 and 11.4 for details). When the state-space form is nonlinear, we express equation (11.2) more generally as $\alpha_t = T(\alpha_{t-1}) + d_t + v_t$, where $T(\alpha)$ denotes a transition function (see, e.g., the Bass diffusion model in Tables 11.3 and 11.4).

Table 11.2 Names and notation for vectors and matrices in state space models

Notation	Vector or Matrix	Name	Dimension
Y	Vector	Observation Vector	$m \times 1$
α	Vector	State Vector	$n \times 1$
T	Matrix	Transition Matrix	$n \times n$
$T(\alpha)$	Vector-valued function	Transition function	$n \times 1$ outputs; $n \times 1$ arguments
C	Vector	Drift vector (in observation)	$n \times 1$
D	Vector	Drift vector (in transition)	$m \times 1$
Z	Matrix	Link Matrix (from state to observation)	$m \times n$
ε	Vector	Observation errors	$m \times 1$
v	Vector	Transition errors	$n \times 1$
H	Matrix	Observation noise matrix	$m \times m$
Q	Matrix	Transition noise matrix	$n \times n$

The Kalman filter is a method for determining the moments (e.g., mean and covariance) of the dynamic state vector α_t, at each instant t, given the observations in Y_t. It is called a "filter" because it extracts the signal from noisy observations in Y_t via two steps. The first step, known as the *time-update*, predicts the moments of α as the system in (11.2) moves from the previous instant t-1 to the current instant t. In this time-update step, before any new observations become available, changes in the moments of α are solely due to the motion of the system in (11.2). In the second step, which is called *measurement-update*, the moments of α are updated based on the information made available in the observation vector Y, which could be noisy or incomplete (i.e., missing data) or redundant (i.e., multiple measurements on a given state variable). The exact formulae for time- and measurement- updates are given in equation (11.17) of the Appendix. Specifically, the prior mean and covariance is due to time-updating; the posterior mean and covariance is due to a measurement update. In between the prior and posterior moments in (11.17), there appears a weighting factor, known as the Kalman gain, which optimally balances (i.e., in the sense of minimizing mean squared errors) the accuracy of the dynamic model relative to the precision of actual observations. Intuitively, when observations are noisy, the filter discounts the observed data by placing a small weight; on the other hand, when model forecasts are inaccurate, the filter discounts these forecasts by relying more on the actual observed data. Thus the Kalman filter via the recursive equations in (11.17) optimally combines information from both the dynamic model and the actual observations to determine the current state of the system (i.e., the distribution of α).

Last but not least, there are many practical advantages for casting ARIMAX or any other structural dynamic model in the above state-space form:

Table 11.3 Description of dynamic marketing models

Model	The Mathematical Model	Model Description
Vidale and Wolfe (1957)	$\frac{dA}{dt} = \beta(1-A)u - \delta A$ *Discrete Version* $A_t = (1 - \beta u_t - \delta)A_{t-1} + \beta u_t$	Over a small period of time, increase in brand awareness (A) is due to the brand's advertising effort (u), which influences the unaware segment of the market, while attrition of the aware segment occurs due to forgetting of the advertised brand.
Nerlove and Arrow (1962)	$\frac{dA}{dt} = \beta u - \delta A$ *Discrete Version* $A_t = (1 - \delta)A_{t-1} + \beta u_t$	The growth in awareness depends linearly on the advertising effort, while awareness decays due to forgetting of the advertised brand.
Brandaid (Little 1975)	$A_t = \lambda A_{t-1} + (1-\lambda)g(u_t)$ $g(u) = \dfrac{u^\beta}{\phi + u^\beta}$	Brand awareness in the current period depends partly on the last period brand awareness and partly on the response to advertising effort; the response to advertising effort can be linear, concave, or S-shaped.
Tracker (Blattberg and Golanty 1978)	$A_t - A_{t-1} = (1 - e^{\alpha - \beta u_t})(1 - A_{t-1})$	The incremental awareness depends on the advertising effort, which influences the unaware segment of the market.
Litmus (Blackburn and Clancy 1982)	$A_t = (1 - e^{-\beta u_t})A^* + e^{-\beta u_t}A_{t-1}$	The current period awareness is a weighted average of the steady-state ("maximum") awareness and the last period awareness. The weights are determined by the advertising effort in period t.
Bass Model (1969)	$S_t = S_{t-1} + p(M - S_{t-1})$ $+ q\dfrac{S_{t-1}}{M}(M - S_{t-1})$	Sales grow due to both the untapped market and contagion effects.
IMC Model (Naik and Raman 2003)	$S_t = \alpha + \beta_1 u_{1t} + \beta_2 u_{2t} + \kappa u_{1t}u_{2t}$ $+ \lambda S_{t-1}$	Sales grow due to not only direct effects of advertising (β_i), but also indirect effects of synergy (κ) between advertising.

   i. the *exact* likelihood function can be computed to obtain parameter estimates, infer statistical significance, and select among model specifications;

  ii. a *common* algorithm, based on Kalman filter recursions, can be used to analyze and estimate diverse model specifications;

 iii. *multivariate* outcomes are handled as easily as univariate time-series;

 iv. inter-equation *coupling* and correlations across equations can be estimated;

  v. *missing values* do not require special algorithms to impute or delete data;

Table 11.4 System matrices for comparison of models

System Matrices	Vidale-Wolfe	Nerlove-Arrow	Brandaid	Tracker	Litmus	Bass model	IMC model
State Vector, α_t	$[A_t]$	$[A_t]$	$[A_t]$	$[A_t]$	$[A_t]$	$[S_t]$	$[S_t]$
Observation Vector, z	[1]	[1]	[1]	[1]	[1]	[1]	[1]
Transition Matrix, T_t	$[1-g(u_t)$ $-\delta]$	$[1-\delta]$	$[\lambda]$	$[1-g(u_t)]$	$[1-g(u_t)]$		$[\lambda]$
Transition function, T(S)						$(1-p+q)S$ $-qS^2/M$	
Drift Vector, d_t	$[g(u_t)]$	$[g(u_t)]$	$[(1-\lambda)g(u_t)]$	$[g(u_t)]$	$[A^*g(u_t)]$	pM	g(u)
Observation Noise, H	σ_ε^2	σ_ε^2	σ_ε^2	σ_ε^2	σ_ε^2	σ_ε^2	σ_ε^2
Transition Noise, Q	σ_v^2	σ_v^2	σ_v^2	σ_v^2	σ_v^2	σ_v^2	σ_v^2
Response Function, g(x)	βx	βx	$x^\gamma/(\phi+x^\gamma)$	$1-e^{\alpha-\beta x}$	$1-e^{-\beta x}$	–	$\alpha+\Sigma\beta_i x_i$ $+\kappa x_1 x_2$

vi. *unequally spaced* time-series observations pose no additional challenges;
vii. *unobserved* variables such as goodwill or brand equity, can be incorporated;
viii. *time-varying coefficients* and *non-stationarity* can be specified;
ix. *heterogeneity* via random coefficients can be introduced seamlessly;
x. *normative decision-making* can be integrated with econometric analyses.

Below, we briefly describe the maximum-likelihood estimation of state-space models, which are widely available in standard software packages (e.g., Eviews, SAS, GaussX, Matlab).

11.3.2 Parameter Estimation, Inference, Selection

Suppose we observe the sequence of multivariate time series $Y = \{Y_t\}$ and $X = \{X_t\}$ for $t = 1, \ldots, R$. Then, given the model equations (11.1) and (11.2), the probability of observing the entire trajectory $(Y_1, Y_2, \ldots, Y_R)$ is given by the likelihood function,

$$
\begin{aligned}
L(\Theta; X; Y) &= p(Y_1, Y_2, \cdots, Y_R) \\
&= p(Y_1)p(Y_2|Y_1)p(Y_3|(Y_1, Y_2))\cdots p(Y_R|(Y_1, \cdots, Y_{R-1})) \\
&= p(Y_1|\Im_0)p(Y_2|\Im_1)p(Y_3|\Im_2)\cdots p(Y_R|\Im_{R-1}) \quad (11.3) \\
&= \prod_{t=1}^{R} p(Y_t|\Im_{t-1}).
\end{aligned}
$$

In equation (11.3), $p(Y_1, Y_2,\ldots, Y_R)$ denotes the joint density function, and $p(Y_t|(Y_1,\ldots;, Y_{t-1})) = p(Y_t|\mathfrak{S}_{t-t})$ represents the conditional density. The Appendix provides the moments of the random variable $Y_t|\mathfrak{S}_{t-1}$ via Kalman filter recursions. In addition, the information set $\mathfrak{S}_{t-1} = Y_1, Y_2, \ldots, Y_{t-1}$ contains the history generated by market activity up to time t-1.

Next, we obtain the parameter estimates by maximizing the log-likelihood function with respect to Θ:

$$\hat{\Theta} = \underset{\Theta}{\text{ArgMax}}\, \text{Ln}(L(\Theta)), \tag{11.4}$$

which is asymptotically unbiased and possesses minimum variance.

To conduct statistical inference, we obtain the standard errors by taking the square-root of the diagonal elements of the covariance matrix:

$$\text{Var}(\hat{\Theta}) = \left[-\frac{\partial^2 \text{Ln}(L(\Theta))}{\partial\Theta\partial\Theta'} \right]^{-1}_{\Theta=\hat{\Theta}}, \tag{11.5}$$

where the right-hand side of (11.5) is the negative inverse of the Hessian matrix evaluated at the maximum-likelihood estimates (resulting from (11.4)).

Finally, for model selection, we compute the expected Kullback-Leibler (K-L) information metric and select the model that attains the smallest value on this K-L metric (see Burnham and Anderson 2002 for details). An approximation of the K-L metric is given by Akaike's information criterion, $\text{AIC} = -2L^* + 2p$, where $L^* = \max \text{Ln}(L(\Theta))$ and p is the number of variables in X_t. As model complexity increases, both L^* and p increase; thus, the AIC balances the tradeoff between goodness-of-fit and parsimony. However, the AIC ignores both the sample size and the number of variables in Y_t. Hurvich and Tsai (1993) provide the bias-corrected information criterion for finite samples:

$$AIC_C = -2L^* + \frac{R(Rm + pm^2)}{R - pm - m - 1}, \tag{11.6}$$

where R is the sample size, p and m are the number of variables in X and Y, respectively. To select a specific model, we compute (11.6) for different model specifications and retain the one that yields the smallest value.

11.3.3 Marketing Applications

In marketing, Xie et al. (1997) and Naik et al. (1998) pioneered the Kalman filter estimation of dynamic models. Specifically, Xie et al. (1997) studied the nonlinear but univariate dynamics of the Bass model, while Naik et al. (1998)

estimated the multivariate but linear dynamics of the modified Nerlove-Arrow model. To determine the half-life of an advertising campaign, Naik (1999) formulates an advertising model with time-varying, non-stationary effects of advertising effectiveness and then applies the Kalman filter to estimate copy and repetition wear out. His empirical results suggest that the half-life of Docker's "Nice Pants" advertising execution was about 3 months. Neelamegham and Chintagunta (1999) incorporated non-normality via a Poisson distribution to forecast box-office sales for movies. To control for the biasing effects of measurement errors in dynamic models, Naik and Tsai (2000) propose a modified Kalman filter and show its satisfactory performance on both statistical measures (e.g., means square error) and managerial metrics (e.g., budget, profit). In the context of multimedia communications, Naik and Raman (2003) design a Kalman filter to establish the existence of synergy between multiple media advertising. Biyalogorsky and Naik (2003) develop an unbalanced filter with m = 3 dependent variables and n = 2 unobserved state variables to investigate the effects of customers' online behavior on retailers' offline sales and find negligible cannibalization effects (contrary to managers' fears). They also show how to impute missing values by fitting a cubic spline smoothing via a state-space representation. To investigate the effects of product innovation, van Heerde, Mela and Manchanda (2004) deploy state space models to incorporate non-stationarity, changes in parameters over time, missing data, and cross-sectional heterogeneity, while Osinga, Leeflang and Wieringa (2007) employ state-space models to capture multivariate persistence effects.

To understand how to integrate normative decision-making with empirical state-space models, see Naik and Raman (2003) for multimedia allocation in the presence of synergy and Naik et al. (2005) for marketing-mix allocation in the presence of competition. In the context of multiple themes of advertising, Bass et al. (2006) generalize an advertising wearout model for a single ad copy developed by Naik et al. (1998). Their results indicate that copy wearout for a price-offer theme is faster than that for reassurance ads, furnishing new market-based evidence to support the notion that "hard sell" ads (e.g., informative) wear out faster than "soft sell" ads (e.g., emotional appeals). Comparing the optimal versus actual allocation of the total GRPs across the five different themes, they investigate the policy implications for re-allocating the same level of total budget. Optimal re-allocation suggests that the company increases spending on reconnect and reassurance ads at the expense of the other three themes. This re-allocation would generate an additional 35.82 million hours of calling time, which represents about 2% increase in demand.

An important question is whether or not it is possible to discover the synergy between different communication activities with traditional methods. This issue was investigated in Monte-Carlo studies by Naik, Schultz and Srinivasan (2008), who check whether regression analysis accurately estimates the true impact of marketing activities. They report the eye-opening result that *regression analysis yields substantially biased parameter estimates because market data contain measurement noise.* This result holds even when a *dependent* variable in dynamic advertising models is noisy. More specifically, in their simulation studies, the bias in ad effectiveness estimates range from 34 to 41%, whereas both carryover effects and cross-media synergy display downward bias of 13.6 and 27.5%, respectively. Naik and Tsai (2000) also offer similar evidence suggesting that measurement noise causes parameter biases in dynamic models. Empirical analysis based on actual market data also comport with these simulation-based findings. For example, the analyses of Toyota Corolla's multimedia campaign reveal that the estimated effects of magazine and rebate effectiveness are more than twice as large as they should be.

Given the perils of regression analysis, are there alternative approaches that managers can adopt to estimate the effects of marketing activities and synergies? Fortunately, the answer is affirmative—the Kalman filter approach described above yields unbiased estimates even in the presence of measurement noise. Naik, Schultz, and Srinivasan (2008) compare the performance of Kalman filter estimation with regression analysis under identical conditions, and they show that the Kalman filter approach yields improved estimates that are much closer to the true effects of multimedia campaign than the corresponding regression estimates.

11.3.4 Normative Decision-Making

One of the advantages of state-space modeling, as noted earlier, is that we can integrate econometric analyses with normative decision-making problems faced by managers. Below we set up such a marketing problem and illustrate how to solve it.

11.3.4.1 Managerial Decision Problem

Consider a company spending resources on two marketing activities, say television and print advertising. A brand manager faces the decision problem of determining the total budget and its allocation to these activities over time. Suppose she decides to spend effort over time as follows: $\{u_1, u_2, \ldots, u_t, \ldots\}$ and $\{v_1, v_2, \ldots, v_t, \ldots\}$. For example, "effort" can be defined specific to a context, for example, GRPs in advertising management or the number of sales calls in salesforce management. Given this specific plan $\{(u_t, v_t) : t \in (1, 2, \ldots)\}$, she generates the sales sequence $\{S_1, S_2, \ldots, S_t, \ldots\}$ and earns an associated stream of profits $\{\pi_1, \pi_2, \ldots, \pi_t, \ldots\}$. Discounting the future profits at the rate ρ, she computes the net present value $J = \sum_{t=1}^{\infty} e^{-\rho t} \pi_t(S_t, u_t, v_t)$. In other words, a media plan $(u, v) = \{(u_t, v_t) : t = 1, 2, \ldots\}$ induces a sequence of sales that yields a stream of profits whose net present value is $J(u, v)$.

Formally, the budgeting problem is to find the *optimal* plan (u^*, v^*)—one that attains the maximum value J^*. To this end, the brand manager needs to determine $u^*(t)$ and $v^*(t)$ by maximizing

$$J(u, v) = \int_0^\infty e^{-\rho t} \Pi(S(t), u(t), v(t)) dt, \tag{11.7}$$

where ρ denotes the discount rate, $\Pi(S, u, v) = mS - c(u, v)$ is the profit function with margin m and cost function $c(\cdot)$, and $J(u, v)$ is the performance index for any *arbitrary* multimedia policies $(u(t), v(t))$. To capture diminishing return of incremental effort, we further assume a quadratic cost function $c(u, v) = u^2 + v^2$. Below we illustrate how to derive the optimal plan using the IMC model proposed by Naik and Raman (2003).

11.3.4.2 Solution via Optimal Control Theory

In their IMC model, the sales dynamics is $S_t = \beta_1 u_t + \beta_2 v_t + \kappa u_t v_t + \lambda S_{t-1}$, where S_t is brand sales at time t, (β_1, β_2) are the effectiveness of marketing activities 1 and 2, (u_1, u_2) are dollars spent on those two activities, κ captures the synergy between them, and λ is the carryover effect. For other marketing problems, the essential dynamics would arise from the transition equation (11.2). If we have multiple transition equations in (11.2), the following approach generalizes (as we explain below). We re-express this dynamics in continuous-time as follows:

$$\frac{dS}{dt} = \beta_1 u(t) + \beta_2 v(t) + \kappa u(t) v(t) - (1 - \lambda) S(t), \tag{11.8}$$

where dS/dt means instantaneous sales growth.

Then, to maximize our objective function in (11.7) subject to the dynamics specified in (11.8), we define the Hamiltonian function:

$$H(u, v, \mu) = \Pi(S, u, v) + \mu(\beta_1 u + \beta_2 v + \kappa uv - (1 - \lambda)S), \tag{11.9}$$

where $\Pi(S, u, v) = mS - u^2 - v^2$ and μ is the co-state variable. We note two points; first, it is convenient to maximize $H(.)$ in (11.9) rather than $J(.)$ in (11.7), although the resulting solutions satisfy both these functions. Second, if we have an $n \times 1$ vector transition equation in the state space model (11.2), we would extend $H(.)$ in (11.9) by adding additional co-state variables because each state equation has an associated co-state variable $\mu_j, j = 1, \ldots, n$.

At optimality, the necessary conditions are as follows:

$$\frac{\partial H}{\partial u} = 0, \quad \frac{\partial H}{\partial v} = 0, \quad \frac{d\mu}{dt} = \rho\mu - \frac{\partial H}{\partial S}. \tag{11.10}$$

Furthermore, these conditions are also sufficient because $H(\cdot)$ is concave in u and v. Applying the optimality conditions, we differentiate (9) with respect to u and v to get

$$\frac{\partial H}{\partial u} = 0 \quad \Rightarrow -2u + \beta_1\mu + \kappa\mu v = 0$$

$$\frac{\partial H}{\partial v} = 0 \quad \Rightarrow -2v + \beta_2\mu + \kappa\mu u = 0$$

Solving these algebraic equations simultaneously, we express the solutions in terms of the co-state variable:

$$u^* = \frac{\mu(2\beta_1 + \mu\beta_2\kappa)}{4 - \mu^2\kappa^2} \quad \text{and} \quad v^* = \frac{\mu(2\beta_2 + \mu\beta_1\kappa)}{4 - \mu^2\kappa^2}. \tag{11.11}$$

The remaining step is to eliminate the co-state variable $\mu(t)$ by expressing it in terms of model parameters. To this end, we use the third optimality condition in (11.10):

$$\frac{d\mu}{dt} = \rho\mu - \frac{\partial H}{\partial S} \quad \Rightarrow \frac{d\mu}{dt} = -m + \mu(1 - \lambda) + \rho\mu.$$

To solve this differential equation, we note that transversality conditions for an autonomous system with infinite horizon are obtained from the steady-state for state and co-state variables (Kamien and Schwartz 1991, p. 160), which are given by $\partial S/\partial t = 0$ and $\partial \mu/\partial t = 0$, respectively. Consequently, $\mu(t) = \frac{m}{(1-\lambda+\rho)}$, which we substitute in (11.11) to obtain the optimal spending plans:

$$u^* = \frac{m(\beta_2\kappa m + 2\beta_1(1 + \rho - \lambda))}{4(1 + \rho - \lambda)^2 - \kappa^2 m^2} \quad \text{and} \quad v^* = \frac{m(\beta_1\kappa m + 2\beta_2(1 + \rho - \lambda))}{4(1 + \rho - \lambda)^2 - \kappa^2 m^2}. \tag{11.12}$$

From (11.12), we finally obtain the total budget $B = u^* + v^*$ as

$$B = \frac{(\beta_1 + \beta_2)m}{2(1 + \rho - \lambda) - \kappa m}, \tag{11.13}$$

and the optimal media mix $\Lambda = u^*/v^*$ as

$$\Lambda = \frac{2\beta_1(1 + \rho - \lambda) + m\beta_2\kappa}{2\beta_2(1 + \rho - \lambda) + m\beta_1\kappa}. \tag{11.14}$$

11.3.4.3 Normative Insights

Although we can generate several propositions by analyzing comparative statics via (11.13) and (11.14), we present three main insights and implications (see Naik and Raman 2003 for their proofs and intuition).

Proposition 1 *As synergy (κ) increases, the firm should increase the media budget.*

This result sheds light on the issue of overspending in advertising. The marketing literature (see Hanssens et al. 2001, p. 260) suggests that advertisers *overspend*, i.e., the actual expenditure exceeds the optimal budget implied by normative models. However, the claim that "advertisers overspend" is likely to be exaggerated in an IMC context because the optimal budget itself is *understated* when models ignore the impact of synergy. To see this clearly, we first compute the optimal budget from (13) with synergy ($\kappa \neq 0$) and without it ($\kappa = 0$). Then, we find that the optimal budget required for managing multimedia activities in the presence of synergy is always larger than that required in its absence. Hence, in practice, if advertisers' budgets reflect their plans for integrating multimedia communications, then overspending is likely to be smaller.

Proposition 2 *As synergy increases, the firm should decrease (increase) the proportion of media budget allocated to the more (less) effective communications activity. If the various activities are equally effective (i e , $\beta_1 = \beta_2$), then the firm should allocate the media budget equally amongst them, regardless of the magnitude of synergy.*

The counter-intuitive nature of this result is its striking feature. To understand the gist of this result, suppose that two activities have unequal effectiveness (say, $\beta_1 > \beta_2$). Then, in the absence of synergy ($\kappa = 0$), the optimal spending on an activity depends only on its own effectiveness; hence, a larger amount is allocated to the more effective activity (see Proposition 1). However, in the presence of synergy ($\kappa \neq 0$), optimal spending depends not only on its own effectiveness, but also on the spending level for the *other* activity. Consequently, as synergy increases, marginal spending on an activity increases at a rate proportional to the spending level for the other activity. Hence, even though the optimal spending levels are endogenous actions, they also affect each other due to synergy. Optimal spending on the more effective activity increases slowly, relative to the increase in the optimal spending on the less effective activity. Thus, the proportion of budget allocated to the *more* effective activity *decreases* as synergy increases.

If the two activities are equally effective, then the optimal spending levels on both of them are equal. Furthermore, as synergy increases, marginal spending on each of them increases at the *same* rate. Hence, the optimal allocation ratio remains constant at fifty percent, regardless of the increase or decrease in synergy.

To clarify this result, we present a numerical example. Consider two communications activities: TV and print advertising. Let TV ads be twice as effective as print ads; specifically, $\beta_1 = 2$ and $\beta_2 = 1$. For this illustration, we assume that $\kappa = 1$, $\rho = m = (1 - \lambda) = 0.1$. Then, substituting these values in Equations (11.13) and (11.14), we compute the optimal budget $B = 1$ and the optimal allocation Λ is 60:40. Now suppose that synergy increases from $\kappa = 1$ to $\kappa = 2$. Then, the total budget increases from B $= 1$ to B $= 1.5$, but the allocation ratio Λ becomes 55:45. In other words, the budget allocated to the more effective TV advertising decreases from 60 to 55%, and that for the less effective print advertising increases from 40 to 45%.

This finding has implications for emerging media, for example, Internet advertising. Companies should not think of Internet advertising and offline advertising (TV, Print) as *competing* alternatives. Rather, these activities possess different effectiveness levels and may benefit from integrative efforts to generate cross-media synergies. If so, the total media budget as well as its allocation to Internet advertising would grow.

Proposition 3 *In the presence of synergy, the firm should allocate a non-zero budget to an activity even if its direct effectiveness is zero.*

This result clearly demonstrates that companies must *act differently* in the context of IMC. According to extant models of advertising that ignore synergy, an advertiser should allocate a zero budget to an ineffective activity (i.e., $v^* = 0$ if $\beta_2 = 0$). In contrast, in the presence of synergy, the company benefits not only from the direct effect of an activity but also from its joint effects with *other* activities. Hence, they should *not* eliminate spending on an ineffective activity because it can enhance the effectiveness of other activities by its synergistic presence. We call this phenomenon the *catalytic influence* of an activity.

In marketing, many activities exert a catalytic influence on one another. For example, business-to-business advertising may not directly influence purchase managers to buy a company's products, but it may enhance sales call effectiveness. Another example comes from the pharmaceutical industry; product samples or collateral materials may not directly increase sales of prescription medicines, but it may enhance the effectiveness of detailing efforts (Parsons and Vanden Abeele 1981). Indeed, marketing communications using billboards, publicity, corporate advertising, event marketing, in-transit ads, merchandising, and product placement in movies arguably may not have measurable impacts on sales. Yet, advertisers spend millions of dollars on these activities. Why? The IMC framework implies that these activities, by their mere presence in the communications mix, act like catalysts, and enhance the effectiveness of other activities such as broadcast advertising or salesforce effort.

The above discussion clearly illustrated how time-series models can be linked to normative decision making. More research is needed along these lines, however, especially on how models that distinguish between short- and long-run marketing effectiveness (as described in Section 11.2) can be used to derive optimal pricing and spending policies, reflecting management's short- and long-run objectives.

11.4 Conclusion

In this paper, we reviewed two time-series approaches that have received considerable attention in the recent marketing literature: (i) persistence modeling, and (ii) state-space modeling. However, this by no means offered an exhaustive discussion of all time-series applications in marketing. Because of space limitations, we did not review the use of "more traditional" time-series techniques in marketing, such as univariate ARIMA modeling, multivariate transfer-function modeling, or Granger-causality testing. A review of these applications is given in Table 11.1 of Dekimpe and Hanssens (2000). Similarly, we did not discuss the frequency-domain approach to time-series modeling (see e.g. Bronnenberg, Mela and Boulding 2006 for a recent application on the periodicity of pricing), nor did we review recent applications of band-pass filters to isolate business-cycle fluctuations in marketing time series (see e.g. Deleersnyder et al. 2004 or Lamey et al. (2007), or the use of smooth-transition regression models to capture different elasticity regimes (see e.g. Pauwels, Srinivasan and Franses 2007). Indeed, the use of time-series techniques in marketing is expanding rapidly, covering too many techniques and applications to be fully covered in detail in a single chapter.

Referring to the expanding size of marketing data sets, the accelerating rate of change in the market environment, the opportunity to study the marketing-finance relationship, and the emergence of internet data sources, Dekimpe and Hanssens argued in 2000 that "for time-series modelers in marketing, the best is yet to come." (p. 192). In a recent *Marketing Letters* article, Pauwels et al. (2004) identified a number of remaining challenges, including ways to (i) capture asymmetries in market response, (ii) allow for different levels of temporal aggregation between the different variables in a model, (iii) cope with the Lucas Critique, (iv) handle the short time series often encountered when working at the SKU level, and (v) incorporate Bayesian inference procedures in time-series modeling. In each of these areas, we have already seen important developments. For example, Lamey et al. (2007) developed an asymmetric growth model to capture the differential impact of economic expansions and recessions on private-label growth, and Ghysels, Pauwels and Wolfson 2006 introduced Mixed Data Sampling (MIDAS) regression models in marketing to dynamically relate hourly advertising to daily sales; see also Tellis and Franses (2006) who derive for some basic models what could be the optimal level of aggregation. Tests for the Lucas critique are becoming more widely accepted in marketing (see e.g. Franses 2005, van Heerde et al. 2005, 2007). Krider et al. (2005) developed graphical procedures to test for Granger causality between short time series, and Bayesian procedures are increasingly used to estimate error-correction specifications (see e.g Fok et al. 2006, van Heerde et al. 2007).

In sum, the diffusion of time-series applications in marketing has started. We hope the current chapter will contribute to this process.

Appendix: Moments of the Conditional Density $p(Y_t|\vartheta_{t-1})$

This appendix provides the moments of the conditional density $p(Y_t|\vartheta_{t-1})$. We recall that the observation equation is $Y_t = Z_t\alpha_t + c_t + \varepsilon_t$, the transition equation is $\alpha_t = T_t\alpha_{t-1} + d_t + v_t$, and error terms are distributed as $\varepsilon_t \sim N(0, H_t)$ and $v_t \sim N(0,Q_t)$. Since the error terms are distributed normally and both the transition and observation equations are linear in the state variables α_t, the random variable $(Y_t|\vartheta_{t-1})$ is normally distributed (because the sum of normal random variables is normal.)

Let $\hat{Y}_t$ denote the mean and f_t be the variance of the normal random variable $(Y_t|\vartheta_{t-1})$. By taking the expectation of observation equation, we obtain

$$
\begin{aligned}
\hat{Y}_t &= E[Y_t|\vartheta_{t-1}] \\
&= E[Z_t\alpha_t + c_t + \varepsilon_t|\vartheta_{t-1}] \\
&= Z_t E[\alpha_t|\vartheta_{t-1}] + c_t + 0 \\
&= Z_t a_{t|t-1} + c_t,
\end{aligned}
\tag{11.15}
$$

where $a_{t|t-1}$ is the mean of the state variable $\alpha_t|\vartheta_{t-1}$ Similarly, the variance of $(Y_t|\vartheta_{t-1})$ is

$$
\begin{aligned}
f_t &= \mathrm{Var}[Y_t|\vartheta_{t-1}] \\
&= \mathrm{Var}[Z_t\alpha_t + \varepsilon_t|\vartheta_{t-1}] \\
&= Z_t \mathrm{Var}[\alpha_t|\vartheta_{t-1}]Z_t' + \mathrm{Var}[\varepsilon_t|\vartheta_{t-1}] \\
&= Z_t P_{t|t-1} Z_t' + H_t,
\end{aligned}
\tag{11.16}
$$

where $P_{t|t-1}$ is the covariance matrix of state variable $\alpha_t|\vartheta_{t-1}$.

Next, we obtain the evolution of mean vector and covariance matrix of α_t via the celebrated Kalman recursions (see, e.g., Harvey 1994 for details):

Prior mean :	$a_{t|t-1} = T_t a_{t-1} + d_t$	
Prior covariance :	$P_{t|t-1} = T_t P_{t-1} T_{t-1}' + Q_t$	
Kalman Gain Factor :	$K_t = P_{t|t-1} Z_t' f_t^{-1}$	(11.17)
Posterior mean :	$a_{t|t} = a_{t|t-1} + K_t(Y_t - \hat{Y}_t)$	
Posterior covariance :	$P_{t|t} = P_{t|t-1} - K_t Z_t P_{t|t-1}.$	

Finally, we apply recursions in (11.17) for each t, t = 1, . . .,R to obtain $a_{t|t-1}$ and $P_{t|t-1}$, starting with a diffused initial prior on $\alpha_0 \sim N(a_0, P_0)$. For example, given (a_0, P_0), we get $(a_{1|0}, P_{1|0})$ and thus $(a_{1|1}, P_{1|1})$; now given $(a_{1|1}, P_{1|1})$, we get $(a_{2|1}, P_{2|1})$ and thus $(a_{2|2}, P_{2|2})$; and so on. Knowing $a_{t|t-1}$ and $P_{t|t-1}$ for each t, we determine the moments of $(Y_t|\vartheta_{t-1})$ via equations (11.15) and (11.16). The initial mean vector, a_0, is estimated by treating it as hyper-parameters in the likelihood function.

References

Baghestani, H. 1991. Cointegration Analysis of the Advertising-Sales Relationship. *Journal of Industrial Economics* **34** 671–681.

Bass, F., N. Bruce, S. Majumdar, B.P.S. Murthi. 2007. A Dynamic Bayesian Model of Advertising Copy Effectiveness in the Telecommunications Sector. *Marketing Science* **26**(March–April) 179–195.

Biyalogorsky, E., P.A. Naik. 2003. Clicks and Mortar: The Effect of Online Activities on Offline Sales. *Marketing Letters* **14**(1) 21–32.

Blackburn, J.D., K.J. Clancy. 1982. LITMUS: A New Product Planning Model. A.A. Zoltners, *Marketing Planning Models*, North-Holland Publishing Company, New York, NY, 43–62.

Blattberg, R., J. Golanty. 1978. TRACKER: An Early Test Market Forecasting and Diagnostic Model for New Product Planning. *Journal of Marketing Research* **15**(May) 192–202.

Bronnenberg, B.J., V. Mahajan, W.R. Vanhonacker. 2000. The Emergence of Market Structure in New Repeat-Purchase Categories: The Interplay of Market Share and Retailer Distribution. *Journal of Marketing Research* **37**(1) 16–31.

Bronnenberg, B.J., C. Mela, W. Boulding. 2006. The Periodicitiy of Pricing. *Journal of Marketing Research* **43** 477–493.

Burnham, K. P., D.R. Anderson. 2002. *Model selection and Multimodel Inference: A Practical Information-Theoretic Approach.* 2 nd Edition, Springer-Verlag, New York, USA.

Cavaliere, G., G. Tassinari. 2001. Advertising Effect on Primary Demand: A Cointegration Approach. *International Journal of Advertising* **20** 319–339.

Chowdhury, A.R. 1994. Advertising Expenditures and the Macro-Economy: Some New Evidence. *International Journal of Advertising* **13** 1–14.

Dekimpe, M.G., D.M. Hanssens. 1995a. The Persistence of Marketing Effects on Sales. *Marketing Science* **14**(1) 1–21.

Dekimpe, M.G., D.M. Hanssens. 1995b. Empirical Generalizations about Market Evolution and Stationarity. *Marketing Science* **14**(3,2) G109-G121.

Dekimpe, M.G., D.M. Hanssens. 1999. Sustained Spending and Persistent Response: A New Look at Long-Term Marketing Profitability. *Journal of Marketing Research* **36**(4) 397–412.

Dekimpe, M.G., D.M. Hanssens . 2000. Time-series Models in Marketing: Past, Present and Future. *International Journal of Research in Marketing* **17**(2–3) 183–193.

Dekimpe, M.G., D. M. Hanssens. 2004. Persistence Modeling for Assessing Marketing Strategy Performance. in Moorman, C., D.R. Lehmann, *Assessing Marketing Strategy Performance.* Marketing Science Isntitute, Cambridge MA, 69–93.

Dekimpe, M.G., D.M. Hanssens, J.M. Silva-Risso. 1999. Long-Run Effects of Price Promotions in Scanner Markets. *Journal of Econometrics* **89**(1/2) 269–291.

Dekimpe, M.G., J.-B.E.M. Steenkamp, M. Mellens, P.Vanden Abeele. 1997. Decline and Variability in Brand Loyalty. *International Journal of Research in Marketing* **14**(5) 405–420.

Deleersnyder, B., M.G. Dekimpe, M. Sarvary, P.M. Parker. 2004. Weathering Tight Economic Times: The Sales Evolution of Consumer Durables over the Business Cycle.*Quantitative Marketing and Economics* **2**(4) 347–383.

Durbin, J., S.J. Koopman 2001. *Time Series Analysis by State Space Methods.* Oxford University Press: London, UK.

Enders, W. 1995. *Applied Econometric Time Series.*John Wiley, New York, N.Y.

Fok, D., C. Horváth, R. Paap, P.H. Franses 2006. A Hierarchical Bayes Error Correction Model to Explain Dynamic Effects of Price Changes. *Journal of Marketing Research* **43** 443–461.

Franses, P.H. 1994. Modeling New Product Sales; An Application of Cointegration Analysis. *International Journal of Research in Marketing* **11** 491–502.

Franses, P.H. 1998. *Time Series Models for Business and Economic Forecasting.* Cambridge University Press, Cambridge.

Franses, P.H. 2005. On the Use of Econometric Models for Policy Simulations in Marketing. *Journal of Marketing Research* **42**(1) 4–14.

Franses, P.H., T. Kloek, A. Lucas. 1999. Outlier Robust Analysis of Long-Run Marketing Effects for Weekly Scanner Data. *Journal of Econometrics.* **89**(1/2) 293–315.

Franses, P.H., S. Srinivasan, H. Peter Boswijk. 2001. Testing for Unit Roots in Market Shares. *Marketing Letters* **12**(4) 351–364.

Ghysels, E., K.H. Pauwels, P.J. Wolfson. 2006. The MIDAS touch: Linking Marketing to Performance at Different Frequencies.*Working Paper.*

Granger, C.W.J. 1981. Some Properties of Time Series Data and their Use in Econometric Model Specification. *Journal of Econometrics* **16**(1) 121–130.

Hamilton, J.D. 1994 *Time Series Analysis.*Princeton University Press, Princeton, N.J.

Hanssens, D.M. 1998. Order Forecasts, Retail Sales, and the Marketing Mix for Consumer Durables. *Journal of Forecasting* **17**(3) 327–346.

Hanssens, D.M., M. Ouyang. 2002. Hysteresis in Market Response: When is Marketing Spending an Investment? *Review of Marketing Science* 419

Hanssens, D.M., L.J. Parsons, R.L. Schultz. 2001. *Market Response Models: Econometric and Time Series Analysis.*Kluwer Academic Publishers, Boston, MA.

Harrison, J., M. West. 1997. *Bayesian Forecasting and Dynamic Models.* 2 nd edition, Springer: New York, NY.

Harvey, A.C. 1994. *Forecasting, Structural Time Series Models and the Kalman Filter.* Cambridge University Press: New York

Horváth, C., P.S.H. Leeflang, J. Wieringa, D.R. Wittink. 2005. Competitive Reaction- and Feedback Effects Based on VARX Models of Pooled Store Data. *International Journal of Research in Marketing* **22**(4) 415–426.

Horváth, C., P.S.H. Leeflang, P.W. Otter. 2002. Canonical Correlation Analysis and Wiener-Granger Causality Tests: Useful Tools for the Specification of VAR Models. *Marketing Letters,* **13**(91) 53–66.

Hurvich, C., C.-L. Tsai. 1993. A Corrected Akaike Information Criterion for Vector Autoregressive Model Selection. *Journal of Time Series Analysis* **14**(3) 271–279.

Jazwinski, A.H. 1970. *Stochastic Process and Filtering Theory.* Academic Press: New York, NY.

Johnson, J.A., E.H. Oksanen, M.R. Veal, D. Frets. 1992. Short-run and Long-run Elasticities for Canadian Consumption of Alcoholic Beverages: An Error-Correction Mechanism/ Cointegration Approach. *The Review of Economics and Statistics* **74**, 64–74.

Joshi, A., D.M. Hanssens. 2006. Advertising Spending and Market Capitalization. *Working Paper.* UCLA Anderson Graduate School of Management.

Jung, C., B.J. Seldon. 1995. The Macroeconomic Relationship between Advertising and Consumption. *Southern Economic Journal* **61**(3) 577–588.

Kamien, M.I., N. Schwartz. 1991. *Dynamic Optimization: The Calculus of Variations and Optimal Control in Economics and Management.* 2 nd edition, North Holland, Amsterdam..

Krider, R.E., T. Li, Y. Liu, C. B. Weinberg. 2005. The Lead-Lag Puzzle of Demand and Distribution: A Graphical Method Applied to Movies. *Marketing Science* **24**(4) 635–645.

Lamey, L., B. Deleersnyder, M.G. Dekimpe, J-B.E.M. Steenkamp. 2007. How Business Cycles Contribute to Private-Label Success: Evidence from the U.S. and Europe. *Journal of Marketing* **71**(January) 1–15.

Leeflang, P.S.H., D.R. Wittink, M. Wedel, P.A. Naert. 2000. *Building Models of Marketing Decisions.* Kluwer Academic Publishers, Boston, MA.

Lewis, F.. 1986. *Optimal Estimation: With Introduction to Stochastic Control Theory.* John Wiley & Sons, New York, NY.

Lim, J., I. Currim, R.L. Andrews. 2005. Consumer Heterogeneity in the Longer-term Effects of Price Promotions. *International Journal of Research in Marketing* **22**(4) 441–457.

Little, J.D.C. 1975. Brandaid: A Marketing Mix Model, Part 1-Structure. *Operations Research* **23** 628–655.

McCullough, B.D., T. Waldon. 1998. The Substitutability of Network and National Spot Television Advertising. *Quarterly Journal of Business and Economics* **37**(2) 3–15.

Meinhold, R.J., N.D. Singpurwalla. 1983. Understanding the Kalman Filter. *The American Statistician* **37**(2) 123–127.

Moorman, C., D.R. Lehmann. 2004. *Assessing Marketing Strategy*.Marketing Science Institute, Cambridge MA.

Naik, P.A. 1999. Estimating the Half-life of Advertisements. *Marketing Letters* **10**(3) 351–362.

Naik, P.A., K. Raman. 2003. Understanding the Impact of Synergy in Multimedia Communications. *Journal of Marketing Research* **40**(3) 375–388.

Naik, P.A., C.-L. Tsai. 2000. Controlling Measurement Errors in Models of Advertising Competition. *Journal of Marketing Research* **37**(1) 113–124.

Naik, P.A., M.K. Mantrala, A. Sawyer. 1998. Planning Pulsing Media Schedules in the Presence of Dynamic Advertising Quality. *Marketing Science* **17**(3) 214–235.

Naik, P., K. Raman, R. Winer. 2005. Planning Marketing-Mix Strategies in the Presence of Interactions. *Marketing Science* **24**(1) 25–34.

Naik, P.A., D.E. Schultz and S. Srinivasan. 2007. Perils of Using OLS to Estimate Multimedia Communications Effects. *Journal of Advertising Research* 257–269.

Neelamegham, R., P. Chintagunta. 1999. A Bayesian Model to Forecast New Product Performance in Domestic and International Markets, *Marketing Science* **18**(2) 115–136.

Nerlove, M., K. Arrow. 1962. Optimal Advertising Policy Under Dynamic Conditions. *Econometrica* **29**(May) 129–42.

Netzer, O., J. Lattin, V. Srinivasan. 2008. A Hidden Markov Model of Customer Relationship Dynamics. *Marketing Science* **27**(March–April) 185–204.

Nijs, V.R., M.G. Dekimpe, J.-B.E.M. Steenkamp, D.M. Hanssens. 2001. The Category Demand Effects of Price Promotions. *Marketing Science* **20**(1) 1–22.

Nijs, V., S. Srinivasan, K. Pauwels. 2006. Retail-Price Drivers and Retailer Profits. *Marketing Science* forthcoming.

Osinga, E.C., P.S.H. Leeflang, J. Wieringa. 2007. The Persistence of Marketing Effects over the Brand's Life Cycle. *Working Paper*. University of Groningen.

Parsons, L.J., P.V. Abeele. 1981. Analysis of Sales Call Effectiveness. *Journal of Marketing Research* **18**(1) 107–113.

Pauwels, K. 2004. How Dynamic Consumer Response, Dynamic Competitor Response and Expanded Company Action Shape Long-Term Marketing Effectiveness. *Marketing Science* **23**(4) 596–610.

Pauwels, K., I. Currim, M.G. Dekimpe, E. Ghysels, D.M. Hanssens, N. Mizik, P. Naik. 2004. Modeling Marketing Dynamics by Time Series Econometrics. *Marketing Letters* **15**(4) 167–183.

Pauwels, K., and D.M. Hanssens. 2007. Performance Regimes and Marketing Policy Shifts in Mature Markets. *Marketing Science*, **26**(May–June) 293–311.

Pauwels, K., D.M. Hanssens, S. Siddarth. 2002. The Long-Term Effect of Price Promotions on Category Incidence, Brand Choice and Purchase Quality. *Journal of Marketing Research* **39**(4) 421–439.

Pauwels, K., J. Silva Risso, S. Srinivasan, D.M. Hanssens. 2004. The Long-Term Impact of New-Product Introductions and Promotions On Financial Performance and Firm Value. *Journal of Marketing* **68**(4) 142–156.

Pauwels, K., S. Srinivasan. 2004. Who Benefits from Store Brand Entry? *Marketing Science* **23**(3) 364–390.

Pauwels, K., S. Srinivasan, P.H. Franses. 2007. When Do Price Thresholds Matter in Retail Categories", *Marketing Science* **26**(1) 83–100.

Shumway, R.H., D.S. Stoffer. 2006. *Time Seies Analysis and Its Applications*. Springer: New York, NY.

Smith, A., P. Naik, C.-L. Tsai. 2006. Markov-switching Model Selection Using Kullback-Leibler Divergence. *Journal of Econometrics* **134**(2) 553–577.

Srinivasan, S., F.M. Bass. 2000. Cointegration Analysis of Brand and Category Sales: Stationarity and Long-run Equilibrium in Market Shares. *Applied Stochastic Models in Business and Industry* **16** 159–177.

Srinivasan, S., P.T.L. Popkowski Leszczyc, F.M. Bass. 2000. Market Share Response and Competitive Interaction: The Impact of Temporary, Permanent and Structural Changes in Prices. *International Journal of Research in Marketing* **17**(4) 281–305.

Srinivasan, S., K. Pauwels, D.M. Hanssens, M.G. Dekimpe. 2004. Do promotions increase profitability and for whom. *Management Science* **50**(5) 617–629.

Sriram, S., M. Kalwani. 2007. Optimal Advertising and Promotion Budgets in Dynamic Markets with Brand Equity as a Mediating Variable. *Management Science* **53**(1) 46–60.

Steenkamp, J.-B.E.M., V.R. Nijs, D.M. Hanssens, M.G. Dekimpe. 2005. Competitive Reactions to Advertising and Promotion Attacks. *Marketing Science* **24**(1) 35–54.

Tellis, G.J., P.H. Franses. 2006. Optimal Data Interval for Estimating Advertising Response. *Marketing Science* **25** 217–229.

Van Heerde, H.J., M.G. Dekimpe, W.P. Putsis, Jr. 2005. Marketing Models and the Lucas Critique. *Journal of Marketing Research* **42**(1) 15–21.

Van Heerde, H.J., K. Helsen, M.G. Dekimpe. 2007. The Impact of a Product-Harm Crisis on Marketing Effectiveness. *Marketing Science* **26**(2) 230–245.

Van Heerde, H.J., C.F. Mela, P. Manchanda. 2004. The Dynamic Effect of Innovation on Market Structure, *Journal of Marketing Research* **41**(2) 166–183.

Vidale, M.L., H.B. Wolfe. 1957. An Operations-Research Study of Sales Response to Advertising. *Operations Research* **5**(June) 370–381.

Villanueva, J., S. Yoo, D.M. Hanssens. 2006. Customer Acquisition Channels and Customer Equity: A Long-Run View. *Working Paper*. UCLA Anderson Graduate School of Management.

Xie, J., M. Song, M. Sirbu, Q. Wang. 1997. Kalman Filter Estimation of New Product Diffusion Models. *Journal of Marketing Research* **34**(3) 378–393.

Zanias, G.P. 1994. The Long Run, Causality, and Forecasting in the Advertising-Sales Relationship. *Journal of Forecasting* **13** 601–610.

Chapter 12
Neural Nets and Genetic Algorithms in Marketing

Harald Hruschka

12.1 Introduction

First publications on marketing applications of neural nets (NNs) and genetic algorithms (GAs) appeared in the early and mid 1990s, respectively. NNs mainly serve to estimate market response functions or compress data. Most of the relevant studies use GAs to solve optimization problems, although some of them apply GAs to estimate or select market response models.

Rational marketing decision making requires information on effects of marketing instruments, which as a rule are derived from market response functions. That is why I only discuss NNs which have been used to estimate market response functions. NNs for data compression are not treated (examples of marketing applications can be found in Hruschka and Natter 1999; Reutterer and Natter 2000; Mazanec, 2001).

Section 12.2 gives an overview on multilayer perceptrons (MLPs), which are the kind of NNs the overwhelming majority of studies determining market response considers. This section deals with specification, estimation, model evaluation, pruning and interpretation of MLPs. Section 12.3 introduces GAs and especially focuses on variants of genetic operators which have been applied in marketing studies. Sections 12.4 and 12.5 describe marketing applications of MLPs and GAs, respectively. Section 12.6 summarizes results of relevant studies, formulates expectations on future research avenues and presents a few selected software tools.

12.2 Multilayer Perceptrons

12.2.1 Specifications

The MLP with one layer of hidden units appears to be the most popular NN type in other scientific domains, too. Originally the MLP was inspired by

H. Hruschka
University of Regensburg, Germany
e-mail: harald.hruschka@wiwi.uni-regensburg.de

B. Wierenga (ed.), *Handbook of Marketing Decision Models*,
DOI: 10.1007/978-0-387-78213-3_12, © Springer Science+Business Media, LLC 2008

conceptions on the functioning of the human brain. But nowadays most researchers prefer to see it as flexible nonlinear regression or nonlinear classification model relating a set of predictors to one or several response variables (Cheng and Titterington 1994; Hastie and Tibshirani 1994).

MLPs with one layer of hidden units can be represented as networks which consist of input units, hidden units and output units. Computations run in one direction, starting with input units, continuing with hidden units and ending with output units. Input units simply obtain values of predictors. Output units compute values of dependent variables. Hidden units perform a nonlinear transformation of predictors. Contrary to input and output units values of hidden units are not directly observed.

The NN literature calls functions which provide values of output units or hidden units 'activation functions'. Activation functions of output units receive as argument a linear combination of values of hidden units. Activation functions of hidden units in their turn work on a linear combination of values of predictors. These linear combinations are labeled 'potentials' by the NN literature.

The MLP for K dependent variables $y_{ki}, k = 1, K$ with one layer of H hidden units can be written as follows ($i = 1, I$ is the observation index):

$$y_{ki} = \begin{cases} f^{(2)}(a_{ki}^{(2)}) \\ f^{(2)}(a_{ki}^{(2)}, a_{1i}^{(2)}) \\ f^{(2)}(a_{ki}^{(2)}, a_{-ki}^{(2)}) \end{cases} \qquad (12.1)$$

$$a_{ki}^{(2)} = w_{0k}^{(2)} + \sum_{h=1}^{H} w_{hk}^{(2)} z_{hi} \qquad (12.2)$$

$$z_{hi} = f^{(1)}(a_{hi}^{(1)}) \qquad \text{for } h = 1, H \qquad (12.3)$$

$$a_{hi}^{(1)} = w_{0h}^{(1)} + \sum_{p=1}^{p} w_{ph}^{(1)} x_{pi} \quad \text{for } h = 1, H \qquad (12.4)$$

Activation function $f^{(2)}$ in the output layer transforms alternatively one potential $a_{ki}^{(2)}$, two potentials a_{ki}, a_{1i} or K potentials $a_{ki}^{(2)}, a_{-ki}^{(2)}$ into the value of the respective response variable ($a_{-ki}^{(2)}$ denotes the vector of K-1 potentials obtained by removing potential $a_{ki}^{(2)}$). Potentials $a_{ki}^{(2)}$ are linear functions of hidden units with weights $w_{hk}^{(2)}$ and $w_{0k}^{(2)}$ symbolizing H coefficients of hidden units z_{hi} and a constant term, respectively.

Activation function $f^{(1)}$ in the hidden layer transforms potential $a_{hi}^{(1)}$ into the value of the respective hidden unit z_{hi}. Potentials $a_{hi}^{(1)}$ are linear functions of predictors with weights $w_{ph}^{(1)}$ linking predictors $p = 1, P$ to hidden unit h and weight $w_{0h}^{(1)}$ as constant term.

Given a sufficient number of hidden units with S-shaped activation functions MLPs approximate any continuous multivariate function and its derivatives to the desired level of precision (Cybenko 1989; Hornik et al. 1989; Ripley 1993). MLPs are capable to identify interactions, threshold effects or concave relationships of predictors. Mathematical proofs show that MLPs possess better approximation properties than other flexible models based on polynomial expansions, splines or kernels (Hornik et al. 1989; Barron 1993).

As activation function of hidden units most studies in marketing use the binomial logit or logistic function, a few also try the hyperbolic tangent. These functions are both S-shaped (sigmoid). The binomial logit model (BNL) with output values in $[0, 1]$ is:

$$BNL(a) = 1/(1 + \exp(-a)) \tag{12.5}$$

Equations 12.1–12.4 combine two transformations of the original values of predictors, a nonlinear projection from the original input space followed by another transformation, which may be linear or nonlinear depending on the type of activation function $f^{(2)}$.

For regression problems with metric response variables the identity function $ID(a) = a$ often serves as activation function $f(a_{ki}^{(2)})$ in the output layer. In this case each response variable is simply set equal to its potential. For obvious reasons such MLPs are said to have linear output units. Sometimes metric response variables are transformed into a smaller interval, e.g. $[0.1, 0.9]$, to enable the use of the binomial logit as output activation function (this transformation is shown for predictors by 14).

MLPs with linear output units or binomial logit output may also be applied to market share modeling. Both approaches do not guarantee that the sum of estimated market shares equals one. Using linear output units estimated market shares even may lie outside the unit interval. To overcome these problems attraction models have been developed for market share analysis (Cooper and Nakanishi 1988).

Attraction models postulate that market share ms_{li} of brand 1 equals the ratio of its attraction A_{li} to the sum of attractions across all brands $A_{ki}, k = 1, K$ of a product category in period i given that attractions are greater than zero:

$$ms_{li} = A_{li}/(\sum_{k=1}^{K} A_{ki}) \tag{12.6}$$

Estimation of attraction models can be simplified by applying the log ratio transformation (McGuire et al. 1977) to market shares with one of the brands as reference (in the following brand 1):

$$y_{li} \equiv \log(ms_{li}/ms_{1i}) = \log(A_{li}) - \log(A_{1i}) \tag{12.7}$$

A MLP extension of the attraction model, called ANNAM (Artificial Neural Net Attraction Model), results from equating logs of attractions to potentials of output units (Hruschka 2001):

$$y_{ki} = a_{ki}^{(2)} - a_{1i}^{(2)} \tag{12.8}$$

Sometimes MLPs with linear output units are used to model categorical response. For binary response MLPs based on this approach comprise either one or two binary response variables. MLPs for $K > 2$ categories usually have response variables coded as K binary dummies which assume the value one for the category observed.

If weights of these MLPs are determined by minimizing the sum of squared errors (see Section 12.2.2) they generalize linear discriminant analysis. Their weights depend on the total covariance matrix and the between class covariance matrix of hidden units. In the two category case the between class covariance matrix is equivalent to Fisher's discriminant criterion times a multiplicative constant. What really distinguishes such a MLP from linear discriminant analysis is the use of nonlinear transformations to compute values of hidden units (further details can be found in Bishop 1995).

Dummy variable coding of categorical response variable has the drawback that outputs may not lie in the $[0, 1]$ interval. A better approach consists in specifying activation function(s) of output units as binomial or multinomial logit function. In the case of binary response (i.e. $K = 1$) such a MLP has one response variable with the binomial logit giving the probability of a positive binary response y_{1i} of person i:

$$y_{1i} = f^{(2)}(a_{1i}^{(2)}) = BNL(-a_{1i}^{(2)}) \tag{12.9}$$

If purchase incidence is analyzed by such a MLP, potential $a_{1i}^{(2)}$ can be interpreted as deterministic utility of a purchase of person i. A MLP defined by Equations 12.9, 12.5 and (12.1–12.4) constitutes an extension of the conventional loglinear binomial logit model, as its potentials (deterministic utilities) are nonlinear w.r.t. weightss.

For the MNL model the conditional probability y_{li} that person i chooses alternative l or belongs to category l leads to the following well-known closed form expression, which in the NN literature is known as softmax activation function (Bishop 1995):

$$y_{li} = f^{(2)}(a_{li}^{(2)}, a_{-li}^{(2)}) = MNL(a_{li}^{(2)}, a_{-li}^{(2)}) = \exp(a_{li}^{(2)})/(\sum_{k} \exp(a_{ki}^{(2)})) \tag{12.10}$$

In choice applications each potential $a_{ki}^{(2)}$ can be interpreted as deterministic utility of person i for alternative k.

Expressions 10 and 1–4 define the neural net multinomial logit model (NN-MNL). In accordance with most brand choice models its weights are equal across brands except for alternative-specific constants. The NN-MNL model specifies deterministic utilities as flexible functions of predictors and therefore extends the conventional MNL model for which deterministic utilities are linear in coefficients (Hruschka et al. 2004).

Sometimes a linear combination of predictors $\sum_{p=1}^{p} w_{pk}^{(L)} x_{pi}$, whose weights $w_{pk}^{(L)}$ the NN literature calls skip layer connections, is included in the equations for potentials of output units $a_{ki}^{(2)}$ giving:

$$a_{ki}^{(2)} = w_{0k}^{(2)} + \sum_{h=1}^{H} w_{hk}^{(2)} z_{hi} + \sum_{p=1}^{p} w_{pk}^{(L)} x_{pi} \qquad (12.11)$$

Hidden units of a MLP with skip layer connections serve to reproduce nonlinear effects which are at work in addition to a linear relationship. Moreover, such a MLP nests conventional linear regression, BNL and MNL models, if its output activation functions are the identity, BNL and MNL functions, respectively.

Market response models for heterogeneous units (e.g. stores, households) based on estimation of the posterior distribution of unit-level coefficients constitute an important stream of research in the last ten years (Rossi et al. 2005). Heterogeneous MLPs generalize some of these recently developed models. In contrast to homogeneous MLPs defined by 1, 11, 3 and 4 potentials of output and hidden units of heterogeneous MLPs have weights varying across units:

$$a_{ki}^{(2)} = w_{0ki}^{(2)} + \sum_{h=1}^{H} w_{hki}^{(2)} z_{hi} + \sum_{p=1}^{p} w_{pki}^{(L)} x_{pi} \qquad (12.12)$$

$$a_{hi}^{(1)} = w_{0hi}^{(1)} + \sum_{p=1}^{p} w_{phi}^{(1)} x_{pi} \qquad (12.13)$$

12.2.2 Estimation

Before estimation values of predictors are usually z-transformed or transformed into into a smaller value range $[\tilde{x}^{min}, \tilde{x}^{max}]$, e.g. $[0.1, 0.9]$, to avoid numerical problems:

$$\tilde{x}_{pi} = \begin{cases} (x_{pi} - \bar{x}_p)/s_p \\ \tilde{x}^{min} + (\tilde{x}^{max} - \tilde{x}^{min})(x_{pi} - x_p^{min})/(x_p^{max} - x_p^{min}) \end{cases} \qquad (12.14)$$

$\bar{x}_p, s_p$ denote arithmetic mean and standard deviation, x_p^{max}, x_p^{min} maximum and minimum observed value of predictor p.

Weights of MLPs are determined by minimizing an error function, of which sum of squared errors (SSE) and negative log likelihood (-LL) are most widespread (minimizing negative log-likelihood is, of course, equivalent to maximizing log likelihood).

SSE can be defined as:

$$SSE = \sum_i \sum_k (y_{ki} - t_{ki})^2 \qquad (12.15)$$

t_{ki} symbolizes the observed or target value of response variable k, y_{ki} its value estimated by the MLP.

The negative log-likelihood can be written for responses with two categories and more than two categories, respectively, as:

$$-LL = \begin{cases} \sum_i -[t_{1i} \ln y_{1i} + (1 - t_{1i}) \ln(1 - y_{1i})] \\ \sum_i -[\sum_k t_{ki} \ln y_{ki}] \end{cases} \qquad (12.16)$$

Here t_{ki} is a binary indicator equal to one, if person i chooses alternative k (belongs to category k), y_{ki} is the corresponding conditional probability estimated by a MLP.

Determination of weights by minimizing a differentiable error function like SSE or -LL can be divided into two steps. In the first step, gradients, i.e. derivatives of the error function w.r.t. weights, are computed. In the second step, weights are adjusted based on these derivatives. Backpropagation in a narrow sense is an effective computational technique for the first step. It propagates errors (more precisely: error terms) backwards through the network. It starts with weights linking hidden units to output units and continues with weights linking input units to hidden units.

But most authors see backpropagation as combination of the technique just described and gradient descent. That is why we will adhere to this somewhat sloppy terminology in the following. In stochastic or online backpropagation observations are presented in random order and weights are updated after each observation. This approach reduces the risk of getting trapped in a local minimum. In contrast offline backpropagation updates weights based on gradients for all observations of the estimation sample (for an excellent description of backpropagation and related estimation techniques see Bishop 1995).

Slow gradient descent can be replaced by faster nonlinear optimization techniques like scaled conjugate gradients (Møller 1993), BFGS (Saito and Nakano 1997) and Levenberg-Marquardt (Bishop 1995). Experience shows that these techniques often provide solutions which are local minima. This weakness can be alleviated by multiple random restarts or by hybrid algorithms. The latter use as first step a stochastic method (e.g. stochastic backpropagation or a GA, see Section 12.3) to explore weight space and a fast optimization techniques as second step (e.g. Hruschka 2001).

A MLP whose complexity is too high fits estimation data very well, but its performance deteriorates if it is applied to new data. There are several ways to limit complexity. One of these consists in restricting connections, e.g. by linking each predictor to only one of several hidden units (Hruschka and Natter 1993a and 1993b; Kumar et al. 1995). Another way allows only monotone relationships between predictors and responses by restricting weights. Such an approach is appropriate if well-founded by theoretical or empirical knowledge (Hruschka 2006).

A more technical way to deal with complexity is offered by regularization methods, which add explicit or implicit penalties to obtain smoother MLPs. Among regularization methods one can distinguish weight decay, early stopping, jittering and soft weight sharing. Weight decay (weights go exponentially to zero with the number of iterations) starts from an enlarged error function F, which often is obtained by adding the sum of squared errors of weights E_w to the error function E:

$$F = E + \alpha E_w \text{ with } E_w = \frac{1}{2}\sum_i w_i^2 \qquad (12.17)$$

This form of weight decay is equivalent to ridge regression well-known from statistics. Minimizing F leads to smaller weights which cause MLPs to become smoother. As explained below the decay parameter α may be determined by a Bayesian approach.

For early stopping estimation data are split into two sets, a training and a validation set. Weights are optimized based on the training set, but optimization stops if the error function deteriorates for the validation set.

Jittering adds noise to values of the predictors during training to prevent that the MLP fits the data too closely.

In soft weight sharing (groups of) weights assume similar values. This is achieved by introducing a distribution on weights (Bishop 1995). In a quite similar way, the hierarchical Bayesian approach explained below results in soft similarities across unit-level weights.

Among Bayesian methods to estimate weights of MLPs both the evidence framework and Monte Carlo Markov Chain (MCMC) methods have been applied in marketing studies. The evidence framework of MacKay (1992a, 1992b) is a Gaussian approximation of the posterior distribution of weights. It starts from a regularised objective function F with weight decay. Maximizing the posterior probability of weights is equivalent to minimizing F and can therefore by solved by standard optimization techniques. For problems with categorical response variables the evidence framework introduces one hyperparameter, the decay parameter α with a Gaussian prior having mean 0 and variance $1/\alpha$, which is periodically updated after several iterations of the standard optimization.

More recently, MCMC techniques which sample from the posterior of weights of MLPs have been introduced (Neal 1996; Müller and Insua 1998;

Lee 2000; Lampinen and Vehtari 2001; Ghosh et al. 2004). These estimation methods are limited to homogeneous MLPs whose weights do not vary across units and to the best of my knowledge these techniques have not been applied in a marketing context.

Hruschka (2006) developed a MCMC technique for heterogeneous MLPs with a metric response variable. Unit-level coefficients are on one hand allowed to differ across units, but are on the other hand restricted to be broadly similar across units by introducing a multivariate normal prior. The posterior of unit-level coefficients combines information from the individual units with information from all units. Therefore estimates differ from those obtained by separate unit-specific models and are closer to estimates of a pooled model (Lindley and Smith 1972). Weights are expected to be less noisy and unstable compared to estimates of separate unit-specific MLPs.

Methods discussed so far dealt with estimation of one MLP. Ensemble methods (like model averaging, stacking, bagging, boosting) estimate several MLPs usually by one of the methods introduced above and aggregate their results (Hastie et al. 2002). In model averaging aggregation corresponds to simple or weighted averages of results. A Bayesian approach takes as weights posterior model probabilities, which can be approximated by BIC (see expression 19) or estimated by MCMC methods.

There are many variants of stacking all working with hierarchies of MLPs. One variant, which has been used in a marketing study, consists of two levels. Level zero MLPs are based on observed predictors. Predicted response variables of level zero models then serve as predictors of a level one MLP. This form of stacking can be seen as generalization of model averaging with the level one MLPs performing aggregation.

In bagging (shortly for bootstrap aggregating) L bootstrap samples are generated by nonparametric bootstrap, i.e. L times I observations are sampled with replacement. Then a MLP is estimated for each of these L samples. Outputs of the L MLPs are aggregated by averaging or majority voting. For the SSE error function bagging with averaging reduces the danger of overfitting without deteriorating model fit.

Boosting combines several MLPs by a weighted majority vote. Weights of each MLP are computed by a boosting algorithm which iterates over MLPs giving more weight to accurate MLPs. Moreover, the boosting algorithm determines weights for observations. It increases (decreases) weights of misclassfied (correctly classified) observations by the MLP of the previous iteration. Therefore each MLP focuses on observations misclassified by its predecessor.

12.2.3 Evaluating and Pruning

The performance of MLPs can be evaluated by measures based on squared errors or absolute errors. The latter are less sensitive w.r.t. large errors. The first group includes sum of squared errors (SSE), mean squared error ($MSE = SSE/I$), root mean squared error ($RMSE = \sqrt{MSE}$). To the second group belong mean absolute error ($MAE = \sum_i |y_{ki} - t_{ki}|$) and mean absolute percentage error ($MAPE = 100/I \sum_i |y_{ki} - t_{ki}|/t_{ki}$). For MLPs with categorical response variables log likelihood value and hit rate (i.e. the proportion of correctly classified observations usually assigned to the category with maximum posterior probability) are more appropriate performance measures.

Specialised approaches to measure performance are available for binary response. A disadvantage of hit rates is dependence on the cut off value (mostly set to 0.5) the posterior probability of an observation must exceed to be classified as positive (e.g. as purchase or defection). The receiver operating characteristic curve (ROC) makes this dependence explicit. It plots for decreasing cut off values the true-positive rate (TPR), i.e. the percentage of correctly classified positives, versus the false-positive rate (FPR), i.e. the percentage of incorrectly classified negatives (e.g. non-purchases, non-defections).

Each ROC connects points (0,0) and (1,1). The highest cut off value for which all persons are classified as negatives corresponds to point (0,0), the lowest cut off value for which all persons are classified as positives is presented by the point (1,1). A model whose ROC lies above that of another model dominates because it attains a higher TPR for all cutoff values. If ROCs of different models intersect, the size of the area under the receiver operating characteristic curve (AUC) can be used as performance measure (Hastie et al. 2002; Baesens et al. 2002). It should be kept in mind that seemingly small improvements of measures like TPR or AUC can lead to remarkable profit increases in direct marketing applications (Baesens et al. 2002).

Very similar to the ROC is the gains chart (also called lift curve) which is well-known in direct marketing. It plots for decreasing cut off values TPR vs. proportion of persons exceeding the cut of value. A model dominates if its lift curve lies above that of a competing model.

Each of the performance measures mentioned so far leads to an overly optimistic evaluation if they are determined for the same data which were used for estimation. This problem usually aggravates with higher complexity of a model. Better estimates of performance measures are obtained by randomly dividing the whole data set into two parts, using one part for the estimation and the other part, a holdout sample, to compute performance measures. This procedure has the drawback that error measures are biased upwards (Ripley 1996).

An alternative method, K-fold cross-validation, randomly splits the whole data set into K exhaustive and disjoint subsets. For each subset weights estimated from data of the remaining $K - 1$ subsets are used to compute a performance measure. The arithmetic mean of performance measures across subsets serves to evaluate a model. The literature recommends $5 \le K \le 10$ (Bishop 1995; Ripley 1996). For small data sets one can use leaving-one-out instead, which consists in predicting the response of each observation by a model which is estimated using the other I-1 observations (Bishop 1995).

Table 12.1 Information criteria

based on -LL	based on SSE
$AIC = -2LL + 2df$,	$AIC = 2\log(MSE) + 2df/I$
$BIC = -2LL + df \log(I)$,	$BIC = 2\log(MSE) + df \log(I)/I$
	$PC = MSE(1 + df/I)$

Information criteria offer another way to both consider a model's fit and its complexity, the latter measured by degrees of freedom (df). Given the same fit a less complex model is prefered. Table 12.1 contains information criteria often used to evaluate MLPs (Akaike 1974; Schwartz 1979; Amemiya 1980).

As a rule, researchers have set degrees of freedom of a MLP equal to the number of its weights. Recently, by drawing on projection theory of linear models Ingrassia and Morlini (2005) show that degrees of freedom correspond to the number of hidden neurons plus one for a MLP with one hidden layer if a constant term is used (if skip layer connections exist one has to add their number). This result means that practically all researchers working with MLPs may have overestimated their complexity and could explain why cross-validation often recommends a higher number of hidden units than information criteria.

Posterior model probabilities which also penalize models for complexity can be used to evaluate models. Assuming equal a priori model probabilities the posterior probability of a model m' can be computed from marginal model densities $p(y|m)$:

$$p(y|m') = p(y|m')/(\sum_m p(y|m)) \tag{12.18}$$

Using MCMC draws marginal model densities may be determined by the harmonic mean estimator of Gelfand and Dey (1994).

An approximate way to compute posterior model probabilities starts from BIC values of models BIC_m:

$$p(y|m') \approx \exp(-\frac{1}{2}BIC_{m'})/((\sum_m \exp(-\frac{1}{2}BIC_m)) \tag{12.19}$$

Complexity of a MLP can be reduced by pruning (i.e. eliminating) less salient weights or hidden units whose elimination deteriorates cross-validated performance measures or information criteria only slightly. Salient weights (hidden units) can be determined by estimating different MLPs which either include or exlude them.

A less time consuming way to decide on pruning tries to identify weights which lead to a small increase of the error function. Assuming that estimation has converged to a minimum and neglecting third-order terms this increase is approximately w_i / H_{ii}^{-1} with H_{ii}^{-1} as appropriate diagonal element of the inverse of the hessian of the error function (Bishop 1995).

Under regularity conditions the (asymptotic) covariance matrix of weights for -LL corresponds to the inverse of the Hessian, for SSE to the the inverse of the Hessian multipled by two times the residual variance (Greene 2003). But regularity conditions do not hold, because weights linking the $h + 1$ hidden unit to response variables lie on the boundary of the space if the null hypothesis of h hidden units holds. Therefore likelihood ratio tests or t-tests for individual weights are not appropriate and are advisable only if the number of hidden units is fixed beforehand.

A Bayesian method not limited by regularity conditions looks at credible intervals of individual weights which can be computed for MLPs estimated by MCMC methods (Carlin and Louis 1996). Weights whose credible intervals encompass negative as well as positive reals are candidates for pruning.

Automatic relevance determination (ARD) offers a Bayesian soft approach to select predictors (MacKay 1992a). ARD introduces p + 3 weight decay parameters α_c (one for each of p predictors, for all constant terms linked to output units, for all constant terms linked to hidden units, for all all weights linking hidden units to output units). Decay parameters have Gaussian priors with mean 0 and variance $1/\alpha_c$. After estimation less relevant predictors have higher weight decay values, which are equivalent to higher variances of weights.

12.2.4 Interpretation

MLPs are often critized for their black box character (e.g. Rangaswamy 1993). For a fully connected MLP which is not subject to monotonicity restrictions the sign of a single weight as a rule does not indicate whether the effect of a predictor is positive or negative, i.e. whether a response variable increases or decreases with higher values of the predictor. This property distinguishes MLPs from (generalized) linear models.

I will only look at MLPs with linear output units and no skip layer connections. Extensions to MLPs with different output activation function are straightforward. Moreover, it is assumed that all hidden units have the binomial logit as activation function. The marginal effect of predictor p on response variable k is:

$$\frac{\partial y_{ki}}{\partial x_{pi}} = \sum_{h=1}^{H} w_{hk}^{(2)} z_{hi}(1 - z_{hi}) w_{ph}^{(1)} \tag{12.20}$$

This expression includes the first derivative of the binary logit $z_{hi}(1 - z_{hi})$, which is always positive. For a MLP with only one hidden unit ($H = 1$), the marginal effect of predictor p is positive, if the signs of two weights $w_{1k}^{(2)}, w_{ph}^{(1)}$ which connect predictor p to the hidden unit and the hidden unit to the response variable are equal, otherwise the marginal effect is negative. Signs of marginal effects can be seen easily for this simple type of MLP and are valid over the whole value range of a predictor.

Of course, things become more complicated for MLPs with more hidden units for which partial dependence plots may serve to gain insight into non-linearities and interactions of predictors. Frequently the response variable or its potential estimated by the MLP are plotted versus the value range of a predictor for one or several fixed constellations of remaining predictors (e.g. Hruschka 2001; Vroomen et al. 2004; Hruschka et al. 2004).

Marginal partial dependence plots show marginal averages of a response variable, its potential or its elasticity. They are determined by averaging across observations and therefore illustrate the effect of a predictor across its value range after accounting for the average effects of the other predictors (Hastie et al. 2002, for a marketing application see Hruschka 2006).

Elasticities divide the relative change of a dependent variable by the relative change of the respective predictor. Two equivalent definitions of the point elasticity of a predictor x_{pi} w.r.t. response variable k are:

$$el(x_{pi}) \equiv \frac{\partial y_{ki}}{\partial x_{pi}} \frac{x_{pi}}{y_{ki}} \equiv \frac{\partial \log(y_{ki})}{\partial \log(x_{pi})} \tag{12.21}$$

Table 12.2 contains expressions of point elasticities for different types of MLPs, which represent generalizations of well-known expressions for conventional models. They consist of coefficient $w_{pk}^{(L)}$ of the linear component and a nonlinear term Z_{pi} which is a weighted sum of marginal effects of the (usually transformed) predictor on hidden units.

Usually MLPs have transformed predictors as inputs and one has to multiply by the first derivative of the transformed w.r.t. the original predictor $\frac{\partial \tilde{x}_{pi}}{\partial x_{pi}}$ to obtain the elasticity (e.g. by $1/s_p$ and $(\tilde{x}^{max} - \tilde{x}^{max})/(x_p^{max} - x_p^{min})$ for the two transformations 14).

Table 12.2 Point elasticity for different MLPs

MLP Type	$el(x_{ip})$
Linear output	$\frac{x_{pi}}{y_{ki}}(w_{pk}^{(L)} + Z_{pi})\frac{\partial \tilde{x}_{pi}}{\partial x_{pi}}$
Linear output, response variable and predictors log transformed	$(w_{pk}^{(L)} + Z_{pi})\frac{\partial \tilde{x}_{pi}}{\partial x_{pi}}$
ANNAM	$(1 - ms_{ki})(w_{pk}^{(L)} + Z_{pi})\frac{\partial \tilde{x}_{pi}}{\partial x_{pi}}$
Binomial or multinomial logit output	$(1 - y_{ki})(w_{pk}^{(L)} + Z_{pi})\frac{\partial \tilde{x}_{pi}}{\partial x_{pi}}$

$$Z_{pi} = \sum_{h=1}^{H} w_{hk}^{(2)} z_{hi}(1 - z_{hi})w_{ph}^{(1)}$$

12.3 Genetic Algorithms

Applying the principle of natural selection of organisms to difficult optimization problems, which are characterized by large search spaces, complex objective functions or multiple local optima can be seen as the fundamental idea of
GAs (Goldberg 1989; Michalewicz 1996; Mitchell, 1995). GAs search a solution
x which maximizes objective function $f(x)$:

$$max_x \, f(x) \tag{12.22}$$

In each iteration GAs construct a generation, i.e. a set of G solutions
$X_k = \{x_1, \cdots, x_G\}$ by applying genetic operators to the previous generation
X_{k-1} (as a rule, $30 \le G \le 100$). Usually the first generation X_1 is determined
at random. The objective function $f(x)$ is evaluated for each solution of a
generation. $f(x)$ or a monotone transformation $T(f(x))$ measures the fitness of
a solution. GAs stop after a maximum number of iterations is reached or no
improvement is found for a certain number of iterations.

Each solution is represented by a n-dimensional string $x_g = (x_{g,1}, \cdots, x_{g,n})$.
Depending on the application this string contains values of decision variables or
parameters of estimation problems. Often binary strings are used, sometimes
strings consist of integer values. Substrings may be associated with a certain
decision variable.

Most GAs apply variants of three genetic operators, namely selection (repro-
duction), crossover (mating) and mutation. Selection operators prefer solutions
with higher fitness values. Selected solutions are copied and enter the so-called
mating pool Y_k.

Widespread variants of selection are roulette wheel selection , fitness ranking
and tournament selection. Roulette wheel selection forms the mating pool Y_k
by drawing from X_k according to selection probabilities p_g defined as:

$$p_g = \frac{T(f(x_g))}{\sum_{x \in X_k} T(f(x))} \tag{12.23}$$

Fitness ranking puts the fittest s (e.g. $s = G/2$) solutions into the mating pool
Y_k. Tournament selection draws h solutions from X_k with replacement and
selects the fittest of these solutions until Y_k contains G solutions (for $h = 2$ it is
called binary tournament selection).

Crossover draws without replacement two solutions (parents) from the
mating pool Y_k with crossover rate (probability), which is usually set to values
≥ 0.6. Let us assume that the following two solutions y_1 and y_2 have been drawn
as parents:

$$
\begin{aligned}
(y_{1,1}, \cdots, y_{i,1}, y_{i+1,1}, \cdots, y_{1,j}, y_{1,j+1}, \cdots, y_{1,n}) \\
(y_{2,1}, \cdots, y_{2,i}, y_{2,i+1}, \cdots, y_{2,j}, y_{1,j+1}, \cdots, y_{2,n})
\end{aligned} \tag{12.24}
$$

Crossover operators generate new solutions (offsprings). Frequently used operators are one point, two point and uniform crossover. One point crossover creates new solutions by swapping the substrings starting after a randomly choosen integer cut point i with $1 \leq i \leq n - 1$. This way it creates the following two offsprings:

$$(y_{1,1}, \cdots, y_{1,i}, y_{2,i+1}, \cdots, y_{2,n})$$
$$(y_{2,1}, \cdots, y_{2,i}, y_{1,i+1}, \cdots, y_{1,n}) \qquad (12.25)$$

Two point crossover chooses two cut points $j > i$ randomly and exchanges substrings lying between these two cut points. This way the following offsprings are obtained:

$$(y_{1,1}, \cdots, y_{2,i}, \cdots, y_{2,j}, y_{1,j+1} \cdots, y_{1,n})$$
$$(y_{1,1}, \cdots, y_{1,i}, \cdots, y_{1,j}, y_{2,j+1} \cdots, y_{2,n}) \qquad (12.26)$$

Uniform crossover exchanges each substring between two parents with probability 0.5 to form new offsprings.

A single product design example serves to illustrate the working of crossover operators starting from a randomly selected pair of product configurations (Table 12.3). In this example a product configuration consists of five attributes whose values are represented by integers between one and four. One point crossover uses the third attribute as cut point, two point crossover uses the second and fourth attributes, uniform crossover uses the first and fifth attributes.

Mutation selects a solution from the mating pool with a given probability (mutation rate) and randomly changes one of the substrings (e.g. one of the product attributes in the product design example).

For most GAs the new generation consists of offsprings only. But if a GA follows an elitist strategy, the new generation consists of the G fittest configurations both from the old generation and the offsprings recently produced.

Table 12.3 Product design example for different crossover operators

	parents				
	4	2	1	3	1
	3	1	2	4	3
	offsprings				
one point crossover	4	2	1	4	3
(3rd attribute)	3	1	2	3	1
two point crossover	4	1	2	4	1
(2nd and 4th attributes)	3	2	1	3	3
uniform crossover	3	2	1	3	3
(1st and 5th attributes)	4	1	2	4	1

Special GAs have beeen developed to deal with multiobjective optimization problems. For such problems fitness ranking may be modified to assign higher ranks to efficient solutions (Goldberg 1989). Moreover, techniques of niche formation are recommended to guarantee that solutions vary. Goldberg and Richardson (1987) suggest to divide the raw fitness of each solution by the sum of its similarities with all solutions of a generation. Fitness values transformed this way decrease with the number of similar solutions, therefore dissimilar solutions get a greater chance of being selected.

Most search methods used in marketing (e.g. quasi-Newton methods used to maximize log likelihoods) are local. A main benefit of GAs is the fact that they are global search methods and may escape from local optima. Simulated annealing (SA) represents another group of global search algorithms, which also have been used to solve marketing problems. SA works sequentially in contrast to GAs which consider a set of solutions. In each iteration SA generates one candidate solution from one actual solution by means of a transition rule. SA may escape from local optima, because it also accepts a candidate solution which is worse than the actual solution with a certain probability. This acceptance probability descends slowly towards zero as the number of iterations increases (Romeijn and Smith 1994). Marketing applications of SA deal with data analysis (e.g. DeSarbo et al. 1989; Brusco et al. 2002) or the determination of optimum or equilibrium values of marketing instruments (e.g. Natter and Hruschka 1998a; Silva-Russo et al. 1999). This chapter considers GAs only because in marketing they have been used more often than SA.

12.4 Market Response Modeling with Multilayer Perceptrons

Tables 12.4–12.7 refer to studies on aggregate, binary and multicategorical market response. These tables inform response variables, predictors, nature and number of observations, specification of MLPs (activation function of output untis, number of hidden units) and estimation (error function, estimation method).

The following studies use MLPs to model aggregate market response, i.e. sales or market share (Table 12.4). Hruschka (1993) compares MLPs to a linear econometric model estimated by GLS. The MLP with only one hidden unit reduces MSE and MAD for the estimation set by 49% and 43%, respectively. These measures are reduced by 85% and 64% compared to the econometric model by the MLP with four hidden units.

van Wezel and Baets (1995) estimate linear and multiplicative models by OLS. They examine four different model specifications per brand (absolute and relative predictors, logs of absolute or relative predictors). They evaluate models by RMSE for a holdout set of 25 observations. RMSE of the best MLP is lower than RMSE of the best regression model by 12%.

Table 12.4 MLPs modeling aggregate market response

Study	Response variables: predictors	Observations	Output unit, number of hidden units	Error function, estimation method
Hruschka (1993)	sales: price, (lagged) advertising	1 brand 60 months	BNL 1–4	SSE sbp
van Wezel and Baets (1995)	market share: price, advertising share, distribution	5 brands 51 bi-months	bl 5	SSE + wd bp
Wierenga and Kluytmans (1996)	market share: relative price, advertising share, distribution, trend	5 brands 51 bi-months	tanh 6	SSE sbp
Natter and Hruschka (1997, 1998b)	market share: price, lagged market share, trend	7 brands 21 outlets 73 weeks	BNL 2 or 7	SSE sbp
Gruca et al. (1998)	market share: price, feature and display or lagged market share	7 and 4 brands 58 and 156 weeks	BNL 7 or 4	SSE bp
Hruschka (2001)	market share: price, feature	4 brands 104 weeks	ANNAM 1–4	SSE sbp + BFGS
Pantelidaki and Bunn (2005)	sales: price (reduction), feature, display, weighted number of SKUs, lagged sales	7 brands 104 weeks	linear 3–4	SSE bp, early stopping
Lim and Kirikoshi (2005)	prescriptions, sales: number, duration, costs of sales calls, advertising, product samples	1 pharma-ceutical brand 21 months	linear 5	SSE sbp, jittering
Hruschka (2006)	log(sales): log(prices)	9 brands 81 stores 61–88 weeks	linear 1–3	posterior probability MCMC

The empirical part of the paper of Wierenga and Kluytmans (1996) reports that the MLP reduces RMSE by 36% and 32% compared to a linear and a multiplicative model for a holdout set of 8 observations. The MLP provides better prediction in about 78% of the holdout observations. The MLP implies much higher price effects than the two econometric models. In the simulation part of their paper, Wierenga and Kluytmans demonstrate that MLPs predict significantly better for high levels of noise and multicollinearity.

Table 12.5 MLPs modeling binary market response

Study	Response variables: predictors	Observations	Output unit, number of hidden units	Error function, estimation method
Dasgupta et al. (1994)	purchase: demographics	ca. 800	BNL	SSE sbp
Kumar et al. (1995)	product acceptance by retail chain: financial, competition, strategic etc. attributes	ca. 1,000	BNL 5	SSE sbp
Desmet (1996)	donation: past donation behavior	20,000	BNL 5	SSE bp
West et al. (1997)	patronage of retailers: perceived store attributes	ca. 900	BNL with dvc	SSE sbp, early stopping
Zahavi and Levin (1997)	purchase: past purchase behavior	10,000	tanh 2 hidden layers	SSE bp
Heimel et al. (1998), Hruschka et al. (1998)	brand choice: demographics, (lagged) prices, promotion, choice history	ca. 4,000	BNL 1 or 3	SSE sbp
Hu et al. (1999)	product choice: demographics, situational variables	ca. 1,500	BNL 1	SSE growing algorithm (OLS + NLS)
Hu and Tsoukalas (2003)	product choice: demographics, situational variables	3,800	BNL 1–5	SSE bp, early stopping
Baesens et al. (2002)	repeat purchase: past purchase behavior	100,000	BNL 2–15	-LL evidence framework
Racine (2002)	purchase: past purchase behavior	6,000	BNL 3	SSE NLS
Buckinx and van den Poel (2005)	partial defection: demographics past purchase behavior	32,000	BNL	-LL ARD framework
Ha et al. (2005)	purchase: past purchase behavior	ca. 7,000	BNL 7–17, 14	SSE NLS
Kim et al. (2005)	purchase: demographics past purchase behavior psychographics	ca. 6,000	1 or 3	

Table 12.6 MLPs modeling multicategorical market response (1)

Study	Response variables: predictors	Observations	Output unit, number of hidden units	Error function, estimation method
Hruschka and Natter (1993a, 1993b)	patronage of 5 brands: demographics psychographics	ca. 200	BNL with dvc 5	SSE sbp
Heilman et al. (2003), Kaefer et al. (2005)	loyalty segments: demographics, relative price, loyalty	ca. 270	BNL	SSE sbp
Agrawal and Schorling (1996)	brand choice: price, feature, display	> 2,301	BNL with dvc 5	SSE sbp
Bentz and Merunka (1996, 2000)	brand choice: price (reduction) brand and size loyalties	ca. 5,000	MNL 4	-LL
Fish et al. (2004)	brand choice: price (reduction) promotion, lagged promotional purchases, loyalty	ca. 3,300	11 or 4	SSE bp or GA
Hruschka et al. (2002)	brand choice: reference price, feature, display, brand loyalty	> 11,000	MNL 3, 7, 10	-LL sbp + BFGS
Hruschka et al. (2004)	brand choice: reference price, feature, display, brand loyalty	> 11,000	MNL 4 or 5	-LL sbp + BFGS

Natter and Hruschka (1997, 1998b) compare two variants of MLPs to several econometric models which differ according to functional form (linear, exponential, logistic and asymmetric logistic), reference price mechanism and (a)symmetry of effects of reference prices (Winer 1988). MLP models comprise (competitive) reference prices as hidden units with autoregressive connections (Elman 1991). The first MLP variant has two hidden units (one for the respective and one for its competing brands), the second seven hidden units (one for each brand). MLP models with two hidden units do not perform better than the best econometric models. MLP models with 7 hidden units reduce average PC by 3.7%.

Gruca et al. (1998) apply a MLP to market share prediction for two product categories. They compare the MLP to a differential effects MCI attraction model in a category with 58 weekly observations, to a MCI model with all cross effects in a category with 156 weekly observations. Performance is evaluated by MAPE for a holdout sample of 9 and 10 weeks, respectively. Whereas the MLP performs better for the smaller data set, so did the MCI model with all cross effect in the other category.

Table 12.7 MLPs modeling multicategorical market response (2)

Study	Response variables: predictors	Observations	Output unit, number of hidden units	Error function, estimation method
Vroomen et al. (2004)	brand choice: price, feature, display, household attributes	ca. 2,000	MNL 6	-LL bp, early stopping
Potharst et al. (2005)	brand choice: price, feature, display, household attributes	ca. 2,000	MNL 6	-LL bp, early stopping
Knott et al. (2002)	product choice past purchase behaviour, demographics	ca. 21,000		

Hruschka (2001) introduces ANNAM, a MLP extension of the MNL differential effects attraction model (see Section 12.2.2). A rather simple ANNAM variant with one hidden unit for each of two brands and no hidden unit for the other two brands clearly dominates both the conventional MNL attraction model and 45 other ANNAM variants differing by the numbers of brand-specific hidden units. This ANNAM variant attains a posterior model probability close to 1.0 approximated on the basis of BIC values. Compared to the conventional MNL attraction model partial dependence plots indicate weaker price effects for two brands over most of the observed price range. Accordingly ANNAMs imply lower absolute values for price elasticities and based on these models higher optimal prices result.

In addition to a MLP Pantelidaki and Bunn (2005) estimate five parametric models by OLS and WLS (linear, multiplicative, exponential, log reciprocal and a multifunctional model with different nonlinear transformations for each predictor). For three out of seven brands the MLP performs best in terms of MAPE in the holdout sample of the last 26 observations. The MLP reduces MAPE by 36%, 31% and 5% compared to the best parametric model.

Having two response variables Lim and Kirikoshi (2005) compare two MLPs to two multiple linear regression models. Regression models reproduce 21% and 8% of the variance, MLPs 91% and 96%. For the whole data set regression models lead to a MAPE of 8.4 and 14.3, MLPs to 2.1 and 2.4. Presumably MLP scope better with multicollinearity than the regression models which both have no statistically significant coefficient except for the constant.

Based on a preliminary study which showed that the multiplicative model outperformed other heterogeneous parametric models (i.e. linear, exponential.

semi-log, logistic, asymmetric logistic), Hruschka (2006) compares the hetero-geneous MLP to a heterogeneous multiplicative model. MLPs dominate multi-plicative models as they attain posterior model probabilities close to the best value of 1.00. These results indicate the superiority of a more flexible model even if heterogeneity is considered. Marginal dependence plots of sales vs. price for three different price levels of competitors serve to interpret these models. For 7 out of 9 brands these plots show large differences between the MLP and the multiplicative model, especially at high prices of competitors. As a rule the MLP implies higher sales. Marginal dependence plots of absolute price elasti-cities give a (sometimes incomplete) bell-shape w.r.t. price. Quite contrary, for the multiplicative model absolute price elasties are slowly decreasing with price.

The following studies (Table 12.5) use MLPs to model binary market response (mostly purchase). Note that only two papers consider the -LL as error function, all the others still stick to the theoretical less appealing SSE. In Dasgupta et al. (1994) the MLP performs better than the BNL model and discriminant analysis for a holdout sample of about 25% of the whole data set, but its hit rates are not significantly higher.

The MLP estimated by Kumar et al. (1995) has restricted connectivity. Each hidden unit is linked to only one group of predictors (e.g. financial variables). Both a BNL model with all first-order interactions of predictors and the MLP are evaluated for a 1/3 holdout sample. The MLP performs better, especially w.r.t. the hit rate for non-buyers which is higher by about 6%. Moreover, estimation of the BNL model suffered from convergence problems.

Desmet (1996) compares a MLP to several conventional methods (OLS regression, BNL, probit and AID). Whereas for the estimation sample the MLP achieves the lowest SSE, for the holdout sample of 50% of the total data methods did not differ much.

West et al. (1997) compute a binary response variable, product acceptance. for two or four randomly generated attributes by means of three decision rules, two of which are noncompensatory. Both w.r.t. estimation and holdout samples the MLP outperforms linear discriminant analysis and a BNL model for non-compensatory decision rules and is not significantly worse for the compensa-tory decision rule.

In the empirical part of their paper West et al. analyse consumer patronage towards retailers. They estimate separate MLPs and BNL models for each of three retailers. MLPs achieve much much higher hit rates than BNL models in a 20% holdout sample (e.g. 84% vs. 73% for one of the retailers). BNL models consistently perform better than linear discriminant analysis.

In contrast to the other marketing studies Zahavi and Levin (1997) estimate MLPs with two hidden layers (10 hidden units in the first, 10 or 20 hidden units in the second hidden layer). One might suspect that the complexity of this MLP is too high. The authors did not use a holdout sample, but compared performance of this MLP and a BNL model for a rollout sample of 40,000 already-targeted prospects. In terms of hit rates for the rollout sample the MLP performs less well, though differences to the logit model are very small.

Heimel et al. 1998 (a shorter english version can be found in Hruschka et al. 1998) study choices of four brands of a category. Brand choices are treated as binary, as the household panel data used do not provide price and promotion variables of brands which a household does not choose at a given purchase. For one of the brands the most simple MLP with one hidden unit performs best with respect to forecasting market share in the holdout sample of 6 consecutive weeks. For the remaining three brands MLPs with three hidden units achieve the best forecasting performance. Compared to the BNL model these MLPs reduce average absolute forecast error of each brand by at least 48%.

Hu et al. (1999) estimate MLPs by means of a growing algorithm (Bishop 1995) which begins with an OLS regression for skip-layer connections and then adds one hidden unit after another with weights being determined by a non-linear least squares method keeping weights estimated so far fixed. Backwards elimination based on SSE in a validation sample shows that one hidden unit is sufficient and suggests 4 and 7 predictors for the MLP and the BNL model, respectively. The MLP increases the hit rate for the holdout sample of 20% of the data by 3% compared to the BNL model.

Hu and Tsoukalas (2003) combine MLPs by stacked generalization with level 0 and level 1 models having the same number of hidden units. Level 1 models use predictions made by the five best level 0 models as inputs. For a holdout data set of 400 observations stacked generalization reduces MSE by 73%, a single MLP by 72% compared to a BNL model.

Baesens et al. (2002) compare MLP to a BNL model, linear and quadratic discriminant analysis. Evaluation refers to averages across 10 bootstrap samples each of which is split into an estimation and a validation set of 50%. MLPs perform significantly better than the other models. Compared to the BNL model, MLPs increase TPR and AUC for the holdout subsets by 1.2% and 1.3%, respectively. Only two hidden units turn out to be sufficient. MLPs pruned by ARD do not lead to significantly higher values of the two performance criteria than MLPs without pruning.

Racine (2002) evaluates forecasting performance of various approaches for a holdout sample consisting of 25% of the total data set. TPR values demonstrate superiority of more flexible compared to parametric models. TPR values amount to 3% for the probit model, 8% for the BNL model, 34% for the semiparametric maximum score model, 36% both for the semiparametric index model and the MLP, 38% for a nonparameteric model with kernels.

Buckinx and van den Poel (2005) want to predict which loyal customers defect partially, i.e. become less loyal. Loyal customers are defined by high frequency of purchase and low variation of interpurchase time. The authors estimate BNL models, MLP and random forests. The latter consist of 5,000 randomly generated trees (Breiman 2001). All methods are evaluated by hit rates and AUC. For a one half holdout sample the BNL model is slightly worse, but there are no great differences between the other methods w.r.t. hit rate and AUC.

Ha et al. (2005) estimate a BNL model, single MLPs and bagged MLPs (24 bootstrap samples, majority voting). They use 40% of the data as holdout sample. Based on hit rates in the holdout sample 9 hidden units are chosen for single MLPs. For bagged MLPs the number of hidden units is set to 14. The BNL model has problems with predicting non-purchase. It leads to a high FPR of 62%, whereas bagged MLPs have a FPR of only 18%. ROCs and gains charts show that one of 20 estimated single MLPs performs best. But averaged across 20 repetitions bagged MLPs are preferable.

Kim et al. (2005) select predictors out of a total of 83 by means of a stripped down GA which applies only the mutation operator to binary strings, whose lengths correspond to the total number of predictors (see Table 12.9). The GA considers two objectives, accuracy (depending on the area under the lift curve) and complexity (depending on the number of selected predictors) and stores only efficient solutions. Selection of strings is based on relative fitness compared to that of other strings with similar fitness values. Strings are removed if relative fitness is lower than a threshold value.

For each selected string a MLP is trained on 2/3 and validated on 1/3 of the data. Actually, the authors look at two MLP configurations. One is more complex and has three hidden units (MLP-3), the other is a MLP with only one hidden unit (MLP-1). The best candidate solutions determined by GA undergo 10-fold cross-validation which is repeated five times. Finally, the solution with the highest expected hit rate comprising less than 10% of predictors is chosen. This procedure results in 7 and 6 predictors for MLP-3 and MLP-1, respectively.

Both MLP models are estimated using all training data and compared to a logit model with 22 principal components as predictors (PCA-logit). For the holdout set, PCA-logit, MLP-1 and MLP-3 attain hit rates of 13.6%, 14.4% and 15.0% respectively. For mailings adressing the top 20% prospects, MLP-3 leads to the highest TPR. On the other hand PCA-logit is best w.r.t. the area under the lift curve.

The following studies use MLPs to model multicategorical market response (Tables 12.6 and 12.7). About half of these studies minimize -LL and have a MNL function for outputs. But in spite of theoretical reservations even many of the more recent studies minimize SSE and have BNL output functions.

The MLP in Hruschka and Natter (1993a, 1993b) has restricted connectivity. Each hidden unit is linked to exactly one category of predictors (e.g. indicators of product-related attitudes). Therefore the number of hidden units is fixed beforehand. The authors consider as response variable brand patronage (i.e. the brand which a consumer prefers the most out of a set of 5 brands). Several specifications of both the MLP and the MNL model with different predictors are estimated. MLPs and MNL models attain hit rates determined by leaving-one-out of about 34% and 20%, respectively. Note that hit rates of the MNL models are not higher as what can be expected from a purely random classification.

Heilman et al. (2003) assign each household of their sample to one of eight segments which differ by the percentage of purchases the household allocates to triples, pairs and each of three brands. As predictors of segment membership Heilman et al. use besides household demographics brand loyalties computed from the 1–20 purchases from the beginning of its purchase history in the product category. 10-fold cross-validation serves to compare MLPs to MNL models. The MLP improves average hit rates by 44%, if loyalties are ignored and by 34%, if loyalties based on the first three purchases are considered as predictors.

Kaefer et al. (2005) use the same data set and validation procedure as Heilman et al. (2003), but analyze a less fine grained classification of three segments. Results of the comparison of MLP and MNL models are similar to those obtained by Heilman et al. (2003).

Agrawal and Schorling (1996) compare MLPs to MNL models based on brand choice data for three product categories.Models are estimated for all households and a priori clusters of households which are formed by the number of different brands they purchase. The authors evaluate model performance by MAE of weekly market shares which are compared to average predicted choice probabilities for holdout periods of various lengths. MLPs turn out to have significantly lower MAE in two categories and about equal MAE in the remaining third category.

Bentz and Merunka (1996, 2000) introduce the NN-MNL model (see Section 12.2.2). In the simulation part of their paper they generate brand choice data from MNL models with an interaction term of two predictors. For these artificial data a MLP with six hidden units outperforms a MNL model with linear utility in terms of log likelihood. In the empirical part they compare a MLP with four hidden units to a MNL model with linear utility. Both for the estimation and the 10% holdout sample the MLP is slightly better. The MLP implies weak non-linearities (i.e. threshold effects for price reductions and an interaction of loyalty and price reductions).

Fish et al. (2004) study two different specifications of MLP models. The first specification has brand-specific weights and 11 hidden units, the second equal coefficients across brands and four hidden units. They estimate the first configuration by backpropagation. The second kind of MLP is alternatively estimated by backpropagation and a GA. This GA works on 20 strings containing possible weights of this MLP and uses inverse SSE as fitness value (see Table 12.9).

In a 50% holdout sample hit rates for the first specification of MLP are lower than those for the linear utility MNL model. Compared to the MNL model hit rates for the holdout sample increase by 1% and 2%, if the second specification is estimated by backpropagation and by the GA. This MLP also predicts brand shares better than the MNL model for a 30% holdout period of 72 weeks. If estimated by backpropagation and the GA the MLP reduces MAE by 9% and 21%, respectively.

Using choice data of two categories Hruschka et al. (2002) compare the NN-MNL model to the linear utility MNL and its latent class extension developed by Kamakura and Russel (1989). Both the latent class and the neural net approaches clearly outperform the homogeneous linear utility MNL model. The latent class extension of the MNL model leads to higher log likelihood values on estimation data. But for 10-fold cross-validation the NN-MNL models achieve much better average log likelihood values than their latent class rivals. Elasticities differ significantly between the latent class and the NN-MNL models. Partial dependence plots for deterministic utilities for the MLP indicate interaction effects for loyalty and sales promotion, threshold effects and saturation effects for loyalty and an inverse S-shape for reference price on deterministic utility.

In another study of the NN-MNL model Hruschka et al. (2004) consider two alternative nonlinear versions of the MNL model, the generalized additive (GAM-MNL) model of Abe (1999) and a MNL model with Taylor series approximation of deterministic utility. The latter model turns out to be clearly worse than the conventional linear utility MNL model. Differences of BIC values between models show that approximate posterior probabilities of NN-MNL models approach the maximum value of 1.0 both with regard to the linear utility MNL and the GAM-MNL models. The NN-MNL model also attains the best position of all models considered in terms of average log likelihood for 10-fold cross-validation.

In their MLP model Vroomen et al. (2004) set the number of hidden units equal to the number of brands. Inputs of each hidden unit are household attributes and the respective brand's marketing variables. That way the MLP has restricted connectivity and the output of the BNL activation function of each hidden unit can be interpreted as probability that the corresponding brand belongs to the consideration set of a household. This MLP model consists of brand-specific weights contrary to the NN-MNL model. The authors compare it to a fully connected MLP model with BNL output units, to the conventional linear utility MNL model and the consideration set model (CSM) of Bronnenberg and Vanhonacker (1996). Model performances in a 25% holdout sample differ according to the measure used. The MLP model of Vroomen et al. (2004) has slightly better hit rates than the CSM model, both models are superior to a fully connected MLP and the conventional MNL model. In terms of log likelihood the CSM model clearly turns out to be best.

Potharst et al. (2005) apply boosting and stacking to the model of Vroomen et al. (2004). In their case stacking changes the model weights determined by boosting according to hit rates in a validation set. For a 25% holdout set boosting and stacking have average hit rates of 78.6% and 79.1% compared to 75.9% of the single Vroomen et al. model.

Knott et. al. (2002) want to predict the next two of 13 product categories that a customer will buy. They compare hit rates of different methods for a holdout sample of ca. 11,000 customers. The MLP performs slightly, but not significantly better than a MNL model. Linear discriminant analysis performs significantly worse than the other two methods.

12.5 Marketing Applications of Genetic Algorithms

Tables 12.8 and 12.9 refer to studies in which GA serve to determine optimum or equilibrium solutions and to estimate and select models, respectively. These tables inform about the problem dealt with (response variables and predictors, nature and number of observations) and characterize the applied GAs (population size, selection and crossover methods, mutation rate).

Balakrishnan and Jacob (1996) look at the problem of single product design with the objective to maximize market share. Solutions are represented by

Table 12.8 Determination of optimum and equilibrium solutions by GAs

Study	Problem	Population size	Selection	Crossover	Mutation rate
Balakrishnan and Jacob (1996)	single product design	50,100, 200	elitist, fitness ranking	uniform rate 0.756	0.001 * length of string
Hurley et al. (1997)	network of outlets	50	roulette wheel		0.015
Naik et al. (1998)	media schedule				
Steiner and Hruschka (2000, 2002)	product line design	130–250	binary tournament	one point rate ≥ 0.9	0.05 or 0.01
Alexouda and Paparrizos (2001)	product line design	150	fitness ranking	uniform rate 0.4	0.2
Balakrishnan et al. (2004, 2006)	product line design	400	fitness ranking	uniform	0.04
Nichols et al. (2005)	product line selection and pricing	100 or 300	fitness ranking	one point rate 0.75	0.05
Gruca and Klemz (2003)	new brand positioning		roulette wheel	rate 0.90	0.01
Nair and Tarasewich (2003)	design of mailings	200	fitness ranking	uniform 0.8	
Venkatesan and Kumar (2004)	customer contact levels	200			0.25
Jonker et al. (2004)	segmentation and mailings	200	roulette wheel	one point	0.1
Midgley et al. (1997)	pricing strategies	25		uniform	0.0001
Rhin and Cooper (2005)	discovery of stable sets			two point	

Table 12.9 Model estimation and selection by GAs

Study	Problem	Population size	Selection	Crossover	Mutation rate
Klemz (1999)	pricing rules	50	roulette wheel	one point rate 0.90	0.01
Venkatesan and Kumar (2002)	Bass diffusion model				
Venkatesan et al. (2004)	Bass diffusion model			one point	
Fish et al. (2004)	MLP	20	roulette wheel	one point	0.1
Li et al. (2005)	dynamic choice model	50	roulette wheel	one point	0.01
Kim et al. (2005)	MLP				1.0 (mutation only)

(K + 1) substrings for $K + 1$ product attributes. The fitness criterion equals the number of persons preferring a product design and depends on part worths obtained by individual-level conjoint analysis. For 192 artificial data sets the GA attains an average approximation degree of 99.13%, compared to 97.67% of the dynamic programmming (DP) heuristic of Kohli and Krishnamurthi (1987). This amounts to an improvement of 3%. The GA (DP heuristic) finds the optimal solution in 64% (26%) of the cases analyzed. Approximation by the GA improves with population size, harder stopping criteria and use of crossover. The mutation rate has little effect.

Hurley et al. (1997) try to determine the sales maximizing network of retail outlets. Solutions are represented by binary strings. Sales depend on travel times, outlets of the respective firm and its competitors and are computed by summing across different household segments based on MNL attraction models. Hurley et al. compare the GA to the 1-opt heuristic, which basically consists of adding or dropping an outlet from the network if this way sales are increased until no further improvement is found. Across 10 random restarts the GA turns out to be better by 3.5–4.6% than 1-opt for larger problems (6 segments, 50 zones, between 70 and 100 existing outlets) generated by simulation.

Naik et al. (1998) search for the media schedule, which maximizes total awareness plus terminal value. They allocate a total advertising budget (measured in GRPs) across weeks in such a way that the same amount is spent in weeks with advertising. For 52 weeks this problem has $2^{52} - 1 \approx 4.5 \times 10^{15}$ possible solutions. Response to advertising is measured by a Nerlove-Arrow model extended by wearout effects. The GA increases total awareness by 55% and 80% relative to the actual practice for two product categories over planning horizons of 75 and 91 weeks, respectively.

Steiner and Hruschka (2000) study the profit-maximizing product line design problem. Sales of a product are obtained by summing sales volume times choice probabilities across segments. Choice probabilities are derived from segment-level MNL models which comprise as alternatives all products of the firm and of the firm's competitors. Deterministic utility of a product is a linear additive function of attribute levels including price. Variable costs and fixed costs are specified as linear-additive functions of attribute levels. Solutions are represented by R (K + 1) substrings for R products to be selected by the firm and K + 1 product attributes. Each substring has L_k bits for the levels of attribute k. Only one bit (for the attribute level chosen) is set to one, the other bits are set to zero. For 276 artificial data sets the GA has an average approximation degree of 99.87% of the true maximal profit and finds the optimum in 85% of the cases

Steiner and Hruschka (2002) compare the GA just described to the greedy heuristic of Green and Krieger (1985). For 324 artificial data sets the GA performs better than the heuristic in 25% of the cases, the heuristic beats the GA in 11% of the cases. Both methods find the same solution in 64% of the cases. Compared to the respective other method the worst solutions of the GA are lower by 3%, of the greedy heuristic by 9%. The highest improvement of the GA amounts to 1.7%.

Alexouda and Paparrizos (2001) also deal with profit-maximizing product line design. Response to products is measured by individual level partworths determined by conjoint analysis. They compare the GA to Beam Search (BS) developed by Nair et al. (1995). For smaller (larger) problems GA performs better than BS in 54% (93%) of the cases. For larger problems GA improves BS on average by 8%.

Similarly Balakrishnan et al. (2004) consider product line design, process individual level partworths and compare to BS, but their objective is to maximize sales of the new products introduced by the firm. In a hybrid variant of GA the attribute selected for mutation is set to its value determined by BS with probability of 0.5. In 83% of 800 artificial data sets GAs outperform BS and on average the objective value they achieve is higher by 2.6% (for the basic GA algorithm even by 3.4%).

In a related study Balakrishnan et al. (2006) compare several GAs to the DP approach of Kohli and Krishnamurthi (1987). All GAs outperform the DP approach, the GA with elitist selection performs best. The worst performing GA is better than DP by 2.5%, the best performing GA by 6.7%.

Nichols et al. (2005) examine the product line selection and pricing problem with the objective to maximize profit. They start from the model of Dobson and Kalish (1988), which requires a set of reference products described by consumer specific utilities, variable costs and fixed costs. The product line is formed by selection from these reference products. Nichols et al. apply three different solution methods, a pure GA, a branch and bound algorithm that solves product line problems given different price vectors generated by a GA (GR1) and a shortest path algorith solving the pricing problem for different product lines generated by a GA (GR2). For uniformly distributed utilities GR1 and GR2 perform comparable. GR1 and GR2 increase profits for medium problems (80 products) and large problems (100 products) compared to a basic GA by 11% and 24%, respectively. If utilities are not uniformly distributed, GR1 increases profit compared to the next best solution method by at least 36%.

Gruca and Klemz (2003) determine the market share maximizing position of a new brand from MDS-based maps of perceptions and preferences. Market share depends on sales potentials of ideal points and inverse Euclidean distances of products to ideal points. They compare the GA to PRODSRCH of Sudharsan et al. (1987). For the GA each dimension of the MDS map is represented by a 32 bit coding scheme which allows $2^{32} \approx 4.295 10^9$ different positions. A simulation study shows that the GA consistently leads to higher market shares. In an empirical application based on household scanner data the market share obtained by the GA is higher by 31%.

Nair and Tarasewich (2003) optimize the design of mailings to holders of a retailer credit card with attributes like gift retail value, immediate benefit, yearly benefit etc. As objective function they use the agreement of the utility of a design as perceived by a retailer's analysts and customers over a horizon of T periods subject to restrictions on the repeated use of certain sales promotion instruments. Utilities are obtained from conjoint analysis. The four period problem the authors solve has approximately $4.7 10^{19}$ solutions.

Based on a stochastic model for purchase frequencies with two segments and a regression model for predicting purchase frequencies and contribution margins Venkatesan and Kumar (2004) allocate contacts across two distribution channels to individual customers. The objective of this allocation problem is maximum customer lifetime value (CLV). As the two segment model may cause multiple local optima, Venkatesan and Kumar use a GA. Compared to contact levels of the previous year the best solution found by the GA increases CLV over a three years horizon by 83% based on communication costs which are higher by 48%.

Contrary to Venkatesan and Kumar (2004) who start from a fixed two segment model Jonker et al. (2004) use a GA to generate and evaluate different segmentations of customers. Each solution of this GA consists of breakpoints for several RFM (recency, frequency, monetary value) variables which together define a segmentation. The fitness of a solution is set equal to the maximal discounted net revenue which is computed by a dynamic optimization algorithm for a time horizon of one year. The number of mails received by each segment in each period constitute the decision variables of the dynamic optimization.

Midgley et al. (1997) use a GA to determine competitive pricing strategies which assign a price level to one of several states (the latter are price levels of the previous period). As the authors distinguish four price levels (actions) and three brands, they deal with $4^3 = 64$ states. Strategies are evaluated by profit of a brand across 52 weeks. Sales are computed based on a MNL attraction model and a sales volume model. The GA co-evolves populations of strategies of each brand against all its competitors. The unconstrained problem results in low prices for all brands. Results more varied across brands are obtained if sales volume is constrained to fall back to the historical average after seven weeks with higher volume. Most of the 25 best strategies determined by the GA are shown to be markedly better than human managers.

Rhin and Cooper (2005) develop a two-stage game theoretic model for new product positioning (first stage) and pricing (second stage). Product positions are defined by discrete attributes. The search space for pure Nash equilibria can be narrowed by so-called stable sets which indicate how many products (if any) can occupy positions. Rhin and Cooper use a GA to discover stable sets. Fitness comprises two weighted objectives, viability (average closeness to the maximum number of products that positions can accomodate) and survival (average number of firms across solutions divided by the number of firms of a respective solution). Solutions are represented by strings with integer values (number of products filling any slot). Population size varies as the age of a solution increases with its fitness relative to average fitness up to a maximum lifetime. A probabilistic add and drop heuristic generates the initial population. The GA applies two special crossover operators (geographical crossover, which selects a position randomly and exchanges all positions within a randomly determined distance, and projection crossover, which mimics a drop heuristic by mating with a zero vector).

Klemz (1999) uses a GA to determine rules which associate price comparisons of two brands for the same or previous periods to market share of one of the brands. Price comparisons are ordinal with values equal, higher, lower. Average market share increases in a 8 week holdout period of a total of 58 weeks serves as fitness criterion. The search space of the empirical applications consists of 2^{12} possible rules. In contrast to private brands the best rules for national brands only refer to price changes of the same brand and did not include prices of competitive brands.

Because of multiple local optima Li et al. (2005) estimate the log-likelihood of a dynamic binary choice problem (purchase incidence) by a GA. Customers are assumed to maximize long term utility over an infinite time horizon. Each customer's current utility depends on advertising, price, recency and frequency. For the GA parameter values are transformed into binary codes. In each iteration a stochastic dynamic programming problem is solved conditional on the set of parameter values.

Venkatasan and Kumar (2002) estimate the Bass diffusion model by a GA minimizing SSE. A simulation study demonstrates that results of the GA are similar to NLS and OLS estimation if complete time series are used. If these artificial time series are censored before the inflection point, estimates produced by the GA are less biased than those of the other estimation methods. For real diffusion data of seven countries the model estimated by the GA predicts future sales, peak sales period and peak sales clearly better. In a related study Venkatasan et al. (2004) obtain similar results for simulated time series. For 11 real time series Bass models estimated by GA have a clearly better predictive performance w.r.t. future sales, peak sales period and peak sales in comparison to models estimated by grid search and augmented Kalman-Filter (Xie et al. 1997) as well.

12.6 Conclusions

Studies in the marketing domain demonstrate as a rule that MLPs perform at least quite as good as conventional statistical methods and often lead to much better results. To specify a MLP so that it nests the related conventional model seems to be a fruitful approach which is followed by many researchers. More research effort could be devoted to Bayesian estimation methods which already have turned out to be successful for more conventional models.

Interpretability of MLPs can be increased by restricting connections or weights. Moreover, fully connected MLPs can be interpreted by partial dependence plots for response variables, potentials (utilities) or elasticities.

Evaluation of MLPs should not consider either interpretability (low model complexity) or goodness of fit, but both aspects. A more complex model (e.g. a MLP with many hidden units) should be preferred if it fits much better than a less complex model (e.g. a conventional model or a MLP with fewer hidden units). Accordingly many studies presented above have looked at information criteria, cross-validated performance measures and posterior model probabilities.

Many marketing decision problems are characterized by large search spaces, complex objective functions or multiple local optima. These properties apply to allocation problems with dimensions such as products, customers, time periods, media vehicles, distribution channels, geographic zones. Given these circumstances the number of GA applications so far appears to be rather limited. Therefore one could expect more publications which use GAs either to solve such difficult problems directly or indirectly to evaluate known or newly developed heuristics.

Available software tools could promote the diffusion of MLPs and GAs. Table 12.10 contains a selection of software tools which all are integrated within software platforms many marketing researchers are already acquainted with.

Table 12.10 MLP and GA software examples

Basic software platform	MLP software	GA software
Excel Add-Ins	NeuralSolutions: backpropagation and nonlinear optimization	Evolver
R or S-Plus Packages	nnet: mimization of SSE or -LL by BFGS	genalg
GAUSS	GAUSSX: nonlinear optimization	GENO
MATLAB Toolboxes	Neural Network TB: various estimation methods incl. evidence framework	Genetic Algorithm TB

References

Abe, M. 1999. A Generalized Additive Model for Discrete Choice Data. *Journal of Business and Economics.* **17** 271–284.

Agrawal, D., C. Schorling. 1996. Market Share Forecasting: An Empirical Comparison of Artificial Neural Networks and Multinomial Logit Model. *Journal of Retailing* **72** 383–407.

Akaike, H. 1974. A New Look at Statistical Model Identification. *IEEE Transactions on Automatic Contribution* **19** 716–727.

Alexouda, G., K. Paparrizos. 2001. A Genetic Algorithm Approach to the Product Line Design Problem Using the Seller's Return Criterion: An Extensive Comparative Computational Study. *European Journal of Operational Research* **134** 165–178.

Amemiya, T. 1980. Selection of Regressors. *International Economic Review* **21** 331–354.

Baesens, B., S. Viaene, D. van den Poel, J. Vanthienen, G. Dedene. 2002. Bayesian Neural Network Learning for Repeat Purchase Modelling in Direct Marketing. *European Journal of Operational Research* **134** 191–211.

Balakrishnan, P.V., R. Gupta, V.S. Jacob. 2004. Development of Hybrid Genetic Algorithms for Product Line Designs. *IEEE Transactions on Systems, Man and Cybernetics – Part B* **33** 468–483.

Balakrishnan, P.V., R. Gupta, V.S. Jacob. 2006. An Investigation of Mating and Population Maintenance Strategies in Hybrid Genetic Heuristics for Product Line Design. *Computers and Operational Research* **33** 639–659.

Balakrishnan, P.V., V.S. Jacob. 1996. Genetic Algorithm for Product Design. *Management Science* **42** 1105–1117.

Barron, A.R. 1993. Universal Approximation Bounds for Superpositions of a Sigmoidal Function. *IEEE Transactions on Information Theory* **39** 930–945.

Bentz, Y., D. Merunka. 1996. La modélisation du choix des marques par le modéle multinomial logit et les réseaux de neurones artificiels: proposition d'une approche hybride. *Recherche et Applications en Marketing* **11** 43–61.

Bentz, Y., D. Merunka. 2000. Neural Networks and the Multinomial Logit for Brand Choice Modelling: A Hybrid Approach. *Journal of Forecasting* **19** 177–200.

Bishop, C.M. 1995. *Neural Networks for Pattern Recognition*, Clarendon Press, Oxford, UK.

Breiman, L. 2001. Random Forests. *Machine Learning* **45**(1) 5–32.

Bronnenberg, B.J., W.R. Vanhonacker. 1996. Limited Choice Sets, Local Price Response and Implied Measures of Price Competition. *Journal of Marketing Research* **33** 163–173.

Brusco, M.J, J.D. Cradit, S. Stahl. 2002. A Simulated Annealing Heuristic for a Bicriterion Partitioning Problem in Market Segmentation. *Journal of Marketing Research* **39** 99–109.

Buckinx, W., D. van den Poel. 2005. Customer Base Analysis: Partial Defection of Behaviourally Loyal Clients in a Non-contractual FMCG Retail Setting. *European Journal of Operational Research* **164** 252–268.

Carlin, B.P., T.A. Louis. 1996. *Bayes and Empirical Bayes Methods for Data Analysis*. Chapman and Hall, London.

Cheng, B., D.M. Titterington. 1994. Neural Networks. A review from a Statistical Perspective. *Statistics Science* **9** 2–54.

Cooper, L.G., M. Nakanishi. 1988. *Market-Share Analysis*. Kluwer, Boston.

Cybenko, G. 1989. Continuous Value Neural Networks with Two Hidden Layers are Sufficient. *Mathematics of Control, Signal and Systems* **2** 303–314.

Dasgupta, C.G., G.S. Dispensa, S. Ghose. 1994. Comparing the Predictive Performance of a Neural Network Model with Some Traditional Market Response Models. *International Journal of Forecasting* **10** 235–244.

DeSarbo, W.S., R.L. Oliver, A. Rangaswamy. 1989. A Simulated Annealing Methodology for Clusterwise Linear Regression. *Psychometrika* **4** 707–736.

Desmet, P. 1996. Comparaison de la prédictivité d'un réseau de neurones à rétropropagation avec celle des méthodes de régression linéaire, logistique et AID, pour le calcul des scores en marketing direct. *Recherche et Applications en Marketing* **11** 17–27.

Dobson, G., S. Kalish. 1988. Positioning and Pricing of a Product Line: Formulation and Heuristics. *Marketing Science* **7** 107–125.

Elman, J.L. 1991. Distributed Representations, Simple Recurrent Networks, and Grammatical Structure. *Machine Learning* **7** 195–225.

Fish, K.E., J.D. Johnson, R.E. Dorsey, J.G. Blodgett. 2004. Using an Artificial Neural Network Trained with a Genetic Algorithm to Model Brand Share. *Journal of Business Research* **57** 79–85.

Gelfand, A.E., D.K. Dey. 1994. Bayesian model choice: asymptotics and exact calculations. *Journal of the Royal Statistical Society Series B* **56** 501–514.

Ghosh, M., T. Maiti, D. Kim, S. Chakraborty, A. Tewari. 2004. Hierarchical Bayesian Neural Networks: An Application to a Prostate Cancer Study. *Journal of the American Statistical Association* **99** 601–608.

Goldberg, D.E. 1989. *Genetic Algorithm in Search, Optimization, and Machine Learning* Addison Wesley, Reading, MA.

Goldberg, D.E., J. Richardson. 1987. Genetic Algorithm with Sharing for Multimodal Function Optimization. Second Conference on Genetic Algorithms, 41–49.

Greene, W.H. 2003. *Econometric Analysis*, 5th edition, Prentice Hall, Upper Saddle River, NJ.

Green, P.E., A.M. Krieger. 1985. Models and Heuristics for Product Line Selection. *Marketing Science* **4** 1–19.

Gruca, T.S., B.R. Klemz. 2003. Optimal New Product Positioning: A Genetic Algorithm Approach. *European Journal of Operational Research* **146** 621–633.

Gruca, T.S., B.R. Klemz, E.A. Petersen. 1998. Mining Sales Data Using a Neural Network Model of Market Response. *SIGKDD Explorations* **1**(1) 39–43.

Ha, K., S. Cho, D. MacLachlan. 2005. Response Models Based on Bagging Neural Networks. *Journal of Interactive Marketing* **19**(1) 17–30.

Hastie, T.J., R. Tibshirani. 1994. Nonparametric Regression and Classification. Part I – Nonparametric Regression. Cherkassky, V., J.H. Friedman, H. Wechsler, Eds. *From Statistics to Neural Networks*. Springer, Berlin, 62–69.

Hastie, T., R. Tibshirani, J. Friedman. 2002. *The Elements of Statistical Learning*. Springer, New York.

Heilman, C.M., F. Kaefer, S.D. Ramenofsky. 2003. Determining the Appropriate Amount of Data for Classifying Consumer for Direct Marketing Purposes. *Journal of Interactive Marketing* **17**(3) 5–28.

Heimel, J.P., H. Hruschka, M. Natter, A. Taudes. 1998. Konnexionistische Kaufakt- und Markenwahlmodelle. *Zeitschrift für betriebswirtschaftliche Forschung* **50** 596–613.

Hornik, K., M. Stinchcombe, H. White. 1989. Multilayer Feedforward Networks are Universal Approximators. *Neural Networks* **3** 359–366.

Hruschka, H. 1993. Determining Market Response Functions by Neural Network Modeling. A Comparison to Econometric Techniques. *European Journal of Operational Research* **66** 27–35.

Hruschka, H. 2001. An Artificial Neural Net Attraction Model (ANNAM) to Analyze Market Share Effects of Marketing Instruments. *Schmalenbach Business Review-zfbf* **53** 27–40.

Hruschka, H. 2006. Relevance of Functional Flexibility for Heterogeneous Sales Response Models: A Comparison of Parametric and Seminonparametric Models. *European Journal of Operational Research* **174** 1009-1020.

Hruschka, H., W. Fettes, M. Probst. 2004. An Empirical Comparison of the Validity of a Neural Net Based Multinomial Logit Choice Model to Alternative Model Specifications. *European Journal of Operational Research* **159** 166–180.

Hruschka, H., W. Fettes, M. Probst, C. Mies. 2002. A Flexible Brand Choice Model Based on Neural Net Methodology. A Comparison to the Linear Utility Multinomial Logit Model and its Latent Class Extension. *OR Spectrum* **24** 127–143.

Hruschka, H., J.P. Heimel, M. Natter, A. Taudes. 1998. Connectionist and Logit Models of Brand Choice. Arnott, D. et al., Eds. *Marketing: Progress, Prospects, Perspectives*, Proceedings of the Annual Conference of the European Marketing Academy (EMAC), Warwick Business School, UK, 1772–1778.

Hruschka, H., M. Natter.1993a. Analyse von Marktsegmenten mit Hilfe konnexionistischer Modelle. *Zeitschrift für* Betriebswirtschaft **63** 425–442.

Hruschka, H., M. Natter. 1993b. A-Posteriori Segmentation in Marketing by Neural Network Models. Janssens, J., C.H. Skiadas, Eds. *Applied Stochastic Models and Data Analysis*, Vol. I, World Scientific Singapore, 375–387.

Hruschka, H., M. Natter 1999. Comparing Performance of Feedforward Neural Nets and K-Means for Cluster-Based Market Segmentation. *European Journal of Operational Research* **114** 346–353.

Hu, M.Y., M. Shanker, M.S. Hung. 1999. Estimation of Posterior Probabilities of Consumer Situational Choices with Neural Network Classifiers. *International Journal of Research in Marketing* **16** 307–317.

Hu, M.Y., C. Tsoukalas. 2003. Explaining Consumer Choice Through Neural Networks: The Stacked Generalization Approach. *European Journal of Operational Research* **146** 650–660.

Hurley, S., L. Moutinho, S.F. Witt. 1997. Genetic Algorithms for Tourism Marketing. *Annals of Tourism Research* **25** 498–514.

Ingrassia, S., I. Morlini. 2005. Neural Network Modeling for Small Datasets. *Technometrics* **47** 297–311.

Jonker, J.-J., N. Piersma, D. van den Poel. 2004. Joint Optimization of Customer Segmentation and Marketing Policy to Maximize Long-Term Profitability. *Expert Systems with Applications* **27** 159–168.

Kaefer, F., C.M. Heilman, S.D. Ramenofsky. 2005. A Neural Network Application to Consumer Classification to Improve the Timing of Direkt Marketing Activities. *Computers and Operational Research* **32** 2505–2615.

Kamakura, W.A., G.J. Russel. 1989. A Probabilistic Choice Model for Market Segmentation and Elasticity Structure. *Journal of Marketing Research* **26** 379–390.

Kim, Y., W.N. Street, G.J. Russell, F. Menczer. 2005. Customer Targeting: A Neural Network Approach by Genetic Algorithms. *Management Science* **51** 264–276.

Klemz, B. 1999. Using Genetic Algorithms to Assess the Impact of Pricing Activity Timing. *Omega* **27** 363–372.

Knott, A., A. Hayes, S.A. Neslin. 2002. Next-Product-to-Buy Models for Cross-selling Applications. *Journal of Interactive Marketing* **16**(3) 59–75.

Kohli, R., R. Krishnamurthi 1987. A Heuristic Approach to Product Design. *Management Science* **33** 1523–1533.

Kumar, A., V.R. Rao, H. Soni. 1995. An Empirical Comparison of Neural Networks and Logistic Regression Models. *Marketing Letters* **6** 251–263.

Lampinen, J., A. Vehtari. 2001. Bayesian Approach for Neural Networks – Review and Case Studies. *Neural Networks* **14** 257–274.

Lee, H.K.H. 2000. A Noninformative Prior for Neural Networks. Working Paper, ISDS, Duke University, Durham NC.

Li, C., Y. Xu, H. Li. 2005. An Empirical Study of Dynamic Customer Relationship Management. *Journal of Retailing and Consumer Services* **12** 431–441.

Lim, C.W., T. Kirikoshi. 2005. Predicting the Effects of Physician-Directed Promotion on Prescription Yield and Sales Uptake Using Neural Networks. *Journal of Targeting, Measurement and Analysis for Marketing* **13** 156–167.

Lindley, D.V., A.F.M. Smith. 1972. Bayes Estimates for the Linear Model. *Journal of the Royal Statistical Society B* **34** 1–14.

MacKay, D.J.C. 1992a. A Practical Bayesian Framework for Backpropagation Networks. *Neural Computation* **4** 448–472.

MacKay, D.J.C. 1992b. Bayesian Interpolation. *Neural Computation* **4** 415–447.

Mazanec, J.A. 2001. Neural Market Structure Analysis: Novel Topology-Sensitive Methodology. *European Journal of Marketing* **35** 894–914.

McGuire, T.W., D.L. Weiss, F.S. Houston. 1977. Consistent Multiplicative Market Share Models. Greenwood, B.A., D.N. Bellinger, Eds. *Contemporary Marketing Thought*, AMA, Chicago, 129–134.

Michalewicz, Z. 1996. *Genetic Algorithms + Data Structures = Evolutionary Programs*, 3rd edition, Springer, Berlin.

Midgley, D.F., R.E. Marks, L.G. Cooper. 1997. Breeding Competitive Strategies. *Management Science* **43** 257–275.

Mild, A., T. Reutterer. 2003. An Improved Collaborative Filtering Approach for Predicting Cross-Category Purchases Based on Binary Market Basket Data. *Journal of Retailing and Consumer Services* **10** 123–133.

Mitchell, M. 1995. *An Introduction to Genetic Algorithms* MIT Press, Cambridge, MA.

Møller, M. 1993. A Scaled Conjugated Gradient Algorithm for Fast Supervised Learning. *Neural Networks* **6** 525–533.

Müller, P., D.R. Insua. 1998. Issues in Bayesian Analysis of Neural Network Models. *Neural Computation* **10** 571–592.

Naik, P.A., M.K. Mantrala, A.G. Sawyer. 1998. Planing Media Schedules in the Presence of Dynamic Advertising Quality. *Marketing Science* **17** 214–235.

Nair, S.K., P. Tarasewich. 2003. A Model and a Solution Method for Multi-Period Sales Promotion Design. *European Journal of Operational Research* **150** 672–687.

Nair, S.K., L. Thakur, K.-W. Wen. 1995. Near Optimal Solutions for Product Line Design and Selection: Beam Search Heuristics. *Management Science* **41** 767–785.

Natter, M., H. Hruschka. 1997. Ankerpreise als Erwartungen oder dynamische latente Variablen in Marktreaktionsmodellen. *Zeitschrift für betriebswirtschaftliche Forschung* **49** 747–764.

Natter, M., H. Hruschka. 1998a. Evaluation of Aggressive Competitive Pricing Strategies. *Marketing Letters* **9** 337–347.

Natter, M., H. Hruschka. 1998b. Using Artificial Neural Nets to Specify and Estimate Aggregate Reference Price Models. Aurifeille, J.-M., C. Deissenberg, Eds. *Bio-Mimetic Approaches in Management Science*. Kluwer, Dordrecht, Netherlands, 101–118.

Neal, R.M. 1996. *Bayesian Learning for Neural Networks*. Springer, New York.

Nichols, K.B., M.A. Venkataramanan, K.W. Ernstberger. 2005. Product Line Selection and Pricing Analysis: Impact of Genetic Relaxations. Mathematical and Computer Modelling **42**, 1397–1410.

Pantelidaki, S., D. Bunn. 2005. Development of a Multifunctional Sales Response Model with the Diagnostic Aid of Artifical Neural Networks. *Journal of Forecasting* **24** 505–521.

Potharst, R., M. van Rijthoven, M. van Wezel. 2005. Modeling Brand Choice Using Boosted and Stacked Neural Networks. Voges K. E. et.al., Eds. *Business Applications and Computational Intelligence*. Idea Group Inc.

Racine, J.S. 2002. 'New and Improved' Direct Marketing: A Non-parametric Approach. Fraanses, P.H., A.L. Montgomery, Eds. *Econometric Models in Marketing*. JAI Amsterdam, 141–164.

Rangaswamy, A. 1993. Marketing Decision Models: From Linear Programs to Knowledge-Based Systems. Eliashberg, J., G.L. Lilien, Eds. *Marketing*, North-Holland. Amsterdam, 733–771.

Reutterer, T., M. Natter. 2000. Segmentation Based Competitive Analysis with MULTICLUS and Topology Representing Networks. *Computers and Operational Research* **27** 1227–1247.

Rhin, H., L.G. Cooper. 2005. Assessing Potential Threats to Incumbent Brands: New Product Positioning Under Price Competition in a Multisegmented Market. *International Journal of Research in Marketing* 22 159–182.

Ripley, B.D. 1993. Statistical Aspects of Neural Networks. Barndorff-Nielsen, O.E., J.L. Jensen, W.S. Kendall, Eds. *Networks and Chaos – Statistical and Probabilistic Aspects.* Chapman & Hall, London, 40–123.

Ripley, B. 1996. Pattern Recognition and Neural Networks, Cambridge Univeristy Press, Cambridge, UK.

Romeijn, H.E., R. Smith. 1994. Simulated Annealing for Constrained Global Optimization. *Journal of Global Optimization* 5, 101–126.

Rossi, P.E., G.M. Allenby, R. McCulloch 2005. *Bayesian Statistics and Marketing.* Wiley John, Chichester.

Saito, K., R. Nakano. 1997. Partial BFGS Update and Efficient Step-Length Calculation for Three-Layer Neural Networks. *Neural Computation* 9 123–141.

Schwarz, G. 1979. Estimating the Dimension of a Model. *Annals of Statistics* 6 461–464.

Silva-Russo, J.M., R.E. Bucklin, D.G. Morrison. 1999. A Decision Support System for Planning Manufacturers' Sales Promotion Calendars. *Marketing Science* 18 274–300.

Steiner, W., H. Hruschka. 2000. A Probabilistic One-Step Approach to the Optimal Product Line Design Problem Using Conjoint and Cost Data. *Review of Marketing Science 441.*

Steiner, W., H. Hruschka. 2002. Produktliniengestaltung mit Genetischen Algorithmen. *Zeitschrift für betriebswirtschaftliche Forschung* 54 575–601.

Sudharsan, D., J.H. May, A.D. Shocker. 1987. A Simulation Comparison of Methods for New Product Location. *Marketing Science* 6 182–201.

Venkatesan, R., V. Kumar. 2002. A Genetic Algorithms Approach to Forecasting of Wireless Subscribers. *International Journal of Forecasting* 18(4) 625–646.

Venkatesan, R., V. Kumar. 2004. A Customer Lifetime Value Framework for Customer Selection and Resource Allocation Strategy. *Journal of Marketing* 68(October) 106–125.

Venkatesan, R., T.V. Krishnan, V. Kumar. 2004. Evolutionary Estimation of Macro-Level Diffusion Models Using Genetic Algorithms: An Alternative to Non Linear Least Squares. *Marketing Science* 23 451–464.

Vroomen, B., P.H. Franses, E. van Nierop. 2004. Modeling Considerations Sets and Brand Choice Using Artificial Neural Networks. *European Journal of Operational Research* 154 206–217.

West, P.M., P.L. Brocket, L. Golden. 1997. A Comparative Analysis of Neural Networks and Statistical Methods for Predicting Consumer Choice. *Marketing Science* 16 370–391.

van Wezel, M.C., W.R.J., Baets. 1995. Predicting Market Responses with a Neural Network: The Case of fast moving consumer goods. *Marketing Intelligence & Planning* 13(7) 23–30.

Wierenga, B., J. Kluytmans. (1996). Prediction with Neural Nets in Marketing Time Series Data. *Management Report Series no. 258.* Erasmus Universiteit Rotterdam.

Winer, R.S. 1988. Behavioral Perspective on Pricing: Buyers' Subjective Perceptions of Price Revisited. Devinney T.M., Ed. *Issues in Pricing.* Lexington Books, Lexington, MA, 35–57.

Xie, J., X.M. Song, M. Sirbu, Q. Wang. 1997. Kalman Filter Estimation of New Product Diffusion Models. *Journal of Marketing Research* 34 378–393.

Zahavi, J., N. Levin. 1997. Applying Neural Computing to Target Marketing. *Journal of Direct Marketing* 11(1) 5–22.

Part VI

Industry-Specific Models

Chapter 13
Decision Models for the Movie Industry

Jehoshua Eliashberg, Charles B. Weinberg, and Sam K. Hui

13.1 Introduction

The movie industry represents a challenging domain for scholarly research in general and for modelers in particular. The industry is characterized by a product (content) with multiple distribution outlets, each having a relatively short window of opportunity (see Fig. 13.1). Distribution outlets for movies include domestic and foreign theatres, home video, cable TV, and network TV. In each of these windows, many different parties and decision makers are involved. While some emphasize the creative and artistic aspects of the product, others focus on the business issues. Some industry pundits claim that the artistic nature of the product and its uncertain quality make the movie industry inherently different from others; hence, any formal methods or models employed in other industries to improve operational and commercial performance are irrelevant. Furthermore, unlike other industries where trends and consumer tastes are tracked continuously, studios see themselves more as trend setters than as trend followers. Views of industry experts are divided when it comes to reasons for recent box office declines: some blame it on deteriorating product qualities, others on changes in consumer behavior. Our experiences and perspectives are different from those who argue that movie is a form of art that cannot be understood with formal quantitative methods. Rather, we think that there is a creative tension between art and science that, if balanced properly, can lead to improvement in both the business and the artistic spheres of the industry.

Decision-making style varies across the different parties involved in the production and distribution of movies. Film makers, coming from artistic backgrounds, tend to believe in more intuitive styles. In contrast, executives in the home video sector, who interact more closely with retailers and consumers, generally see more value in formal decision models. The rise of a new breed of business-educated executives, who are starting to fill high

J. Eliashberg
The Wharton School, University of Pennsylvania,
e-mail: eliashberg@wharton.upenn.edu

B. Wierenga (ed.), *Handbook of Marketing Decision Models*,
DOI: 10.1007/978-0-387-78213-3_13, © Springer Science+Business Media, LLC 2008

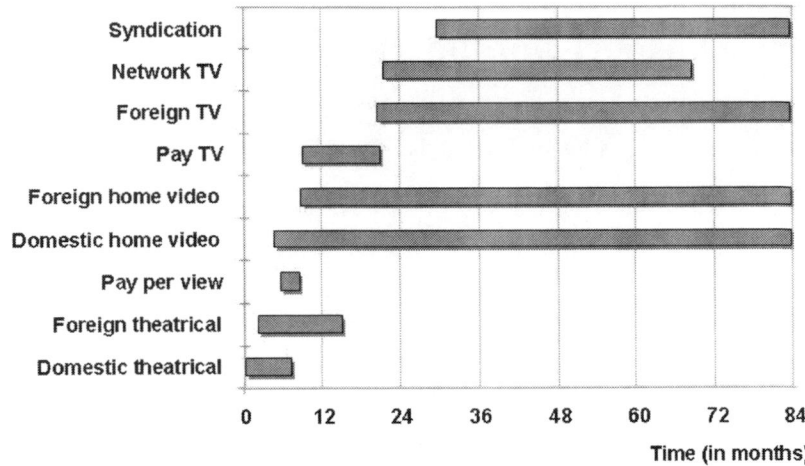

Fig. 13.1 Distribution outlets for movies (Vogel 2001)

level positions in the supply chain, also encourages the development and application of new models, specifically addressing the unique need of the movie industry. This is the focus of this chapter.

There already exist a number of published reviews of research in the movie industry; e.g., Moul (2005), and Eliashberg et al. (2006). Unlike these reviews, our focus in this chapter is on models which have been implemented or which, we believe, have the potential for implementation. By implementation we specifically mean employed by the industry. While this review is by no means exhaustive, we survey and comment on various (published) models that have been developed to address the idiosyncratic characteristics of the movie industry. The models chosen for discussion in this chapter take the perspectives of different audiences, including academics, movie distributors, movie exhibitors, and public policy decision makers. We describe the various models in terms of the model's (potential) users, the problem(s) it addresses, its key features, input and data requirements, and its output and main implications.

The remainder of this chapter is organized as follows. In Section 13.2, we review decision models for theatrical distribution of movies, for exhibition, and for the home video market. Section 13.3 discusses our experience in implementing marketing decision models in the movie industry and provides some insights on the implementation process. Section 13.4 provides our views on what the opportunities are for further modeling efforts.

13.2 What Has Been Done to Date: Review

13.2.1 Theatrical Distribution Models

This section reviews models that have implications for the distributor's decision making. In 2007, 590 movies were released in the U.S. market (http://www.mpaa.org). The movie distributors design the distribution strategy and make decisions regarding the marketing campaign, the production and distribution of copies of the movies ("prints") to the exhibitors, and the release timing of each movie. The average cost of producing a movie is $70.8 million, while the average marketing campaign and the cost of the prints for MPAA movies amounted to $35.9 million. In light of such high (and escalating) costs, two key challenges the distributor faces are (i) forecasting the box office performance of a movie after its production but prior to its theatrical release, and (ii) deciding on a strategy of a movie's release timing. Models reviewed in this section are listed in Table 13.1.

13.2.1.1 Forecasting Theatrical Performance

Early Regression Models

One way of approaching the distributor's forecasting problem is through a simple regression model with the box office performance taken as the dependent variable and various factors (e.g., production budget, number of screens) as independent variables. Although more recent work typically uses more complex modeling approaches, it is worthwhile to look at some of the early approaches to this problem as they have set the stage for later work. Examples of models that used this approach include Litman and Ahn (1998) and Ravid (1999). The regression results reported in Ravid (1999) are shown in Table 13.2.

In both of these studies, (log-) cumulative domestic gross box office receipts was chosen as the dependent variable.[1] As shown in Table 13.2, Ravid (1999) considered independent variables such as production budget, stars, reviews, number of screens, academy awards, genres, seasonality, whether the movie is a sequel, and MPAA ratings. Both studies reported moderate R-square value (0.46 by Litman and Ahn 1998; 0.61 by Ravid 1999). Ravid (1999) found that the following factors are significant and positively correlated with higher box office performance: higher budget, PG rating, the number of reviews, and the movie being a sequel.

In a more recent study, Ainslie et al. (2005) modeled the weekly market share of each movie using a "sliding window" logit model, with a gamma diffusion pattern that captures the buildup/decay of a movie over time. They define an

---

[1] In a separate regression equation, Ravid (1999) also considered "return-to-investment" as the dependent variable. The R-square value is low (0.25), and MPAA ratings (G, PG) are the only significant predictors.

Table 13.1 A summary of a representative sample of papers with theatrical revenue models

	Research Issue	Dependent Variable	Predictors	Data	Approach
Jones and Ritz (1991)	Forecasting box office receipts using interdependence between tickets and screens	Weekly box office revenue	Weekly number of screens	94 movies released between 1983 and 1984	Coupled differential equations
Sawhney and Eliashberg (1996)	Forecasting box office receipts	Weekly box office revenue	None (can also be used with covariates)	111 movies released between 1990 and 1991	Behavior-based model
Zufryden (1996)	Forecasting box office receipts and advertising effectiveness	Weekly box office ticket sales	Weekly advertising expenditure, number of theatres, genre	63 movies released between Jan to June 1993. Consumer awareness, intention to see films.	Behavior-based model
Krider and Weinberg (1998)	Modeling movie release timing	Weekly box office revenue	Competition	102 movies released between 1990 and 1992	Regression of delay of release week on weekend box office and half-life
Litman and Ahn (1998)	Forecasting box office receipts	Cumulative box office	Budget, reviews, screens, star, award, competition, distributor, seasonality, MPAA rating	Top 100 box office gross movies released between 1993 and 1995	Multiple linear regression
Ravid (1999)	Forecasting box office receipts/ROI	Cumulative box office	Budget, reviews, stars, award, seasonality, MPAA rating, sequel	200 movies released between late 1991 and early 1993	Multiple linear regression

Table 13.1 (continued)

	Research Issue	Dependent Variable	Predictors	Data	Approach
Eliashberg et al. (2000)	Forecasting box office receipts	Cumulative box office revenue	Word-of-mouth impact, advertising exposure, theme acceptability	Experimental data collected from "consumer clinic"	Flow model calibrated using a "consumer clinic"
Elberse and Eliashberg (2003)	Forecasting box office receipts	Weekly box office revenue and number of screens	Budget, reviews, star, distributor, seasonality, competition, director, advertising	164 movies released between 1999 to 2000	Dynamic simultaneous-equations model
Ainslie et al. (2005)	Modeling weekly market share of movies	Weekly market share of movies	Media expenditure, screens, critic rating, star, director, sequel, genre, distributor	825 movies release between 1995 to 1998	Sliding-window logit model
Hennig-Thurau et al. (2006)	Modeling movie's commercial success based on marketing actions	Cumulative box office revenue	Reviews, seasonality, quality, advertising, sequel, seasonality	331 movies released between 1999 to 2001	Latent class regression model
Einav (2007)	Explaining seasonality in movie box office	Weekly market share of movies	Movie "quality" as a fixed effect	1956 movies release from 1985 to 1999	Individual-level modeling using logit formulation

Table 13.2 Regression result in Ravid (1999). Dependent variable: log domestic gross. Independent variables include log production budget (LNBUDGET), whether participants had received Academy Awards (AWARD), whether cast members could not be found in standard film references (UNKNOWN), whether a cast member had participated in a top-grossing film (B.O. STAR), MPAA ratings (G, PG, PG13, R), percentage of non-negative reviews (% NON-NEGATIVE REVIEWS), number of reviews (NO. OF REVIEWS), a seasonality variable (RELEASE), and a dummy variable indicating sequel (SEQUEL)

	Coefficient	S.E.	t	pvalue	Sig. (*** p < 0.05)
Intercept	−3.81	0.80	−4.73	0.0000	***
LNBUDGET	1.35	0.17	7.98	0.0000	***
AWARD	−0.27	0.39	−0.69	0.4920	
UNKNOWN	0.54	0.36	1.48	0.1405	
B.O. STAR	−0.04	0.45	−0.10	0.9236	
G	1.34	0.84	1.58	0.1150	
PG	1.35	0.52	2.60	0.0101	***
PG13	0.47	0.48	0.98	0.3272	
R	0.35	0.44	0.81	0.4179	
% NON-NEGATIVE REVIEWS	0.07	0.60	0.12	0.9067	
NO. OF REVIEWS	0.07	0.02	3.76	0.0002	***
RELEASE	0.06	0.78	0.07	0.9404	
SEQUEL	1.14	0.51	2.24	0.0267	***

indicator variable , which takes value 1 if movie i is available at week t, and 0 otherwise. Then, they model the deterministic utility of a movie in each week using a gamma distribution (with modified parametrization), and the stochastic component using an extreme value distribution, as follows:

$$U_{it} = V_{it} + \varepsilon_{it}$$
$$V_{it} = \ln(\eta_i w_{it}^{\gamma_i/\beta_i} e^{(1-w_{it})/\beta_i})$$

(13.1)

where w_{it} represents the number of weeks since movie i has been released. The movie-specific parameters $\eta_i, \gamma_i, \beta_i$ captures the attractiveness of a movie, the time when peak attractiveness occur, and the speed in which attractiveness evolves, respectively.

By including an hypothetical "outside goods" in their model to capture the underlying weekly seasonality, Ainslie et al. (2005) derived their final model from standard random utility theory:

$$M_{it} = \frac{\eta_i w_{it}^{\gamma_i/\beta_i} e^{(1-w_{it})/\beta_i} I_{it}}{e^{V_{0t}} + \sum_j \eta_j w_{jt}^{\gamma_j/\beta_j} e^{(1-w_{jt})/\beta_{jt}} I_{jt}}$$

(13.2)

where M_{it} denotes the expected market share of movie i in week t, and V_{0t} denotes the deterministic component of the utility of the outside goods, which implicitly takes into account seasonality in the box office receipts. The model in Equation (13.2) was then linked to movie characteristics and estimated using a Hierarchical Bayes framework. They found that incorporating the impact of competition generally improves model fit and yield interesting substantive insights. Specifically, the results from the model suggested that competition from movies of the same genre and/or MPAA ratings will adversely affect a movie's box-office revenue.

Behavioral-Based Models

The relationship between box office gross and its drivers are likely to be more complex than the linear relationship assumed in the aforementioned regression models. Other researchers recognized this complexity and developed more realistic models, based on reasonable behavioral assumptions, that relate box offices to its predictors. For instance, Zufryden (1996) captured the relationship through an awareness/intention/behavior model. His modeling approach is described graphically in Fig. 13.2. In his model, advertising increases the proportion of consumers who are aware of the movie. Awareness, together with other movie characteristics such as its genre, determines consumers' intention to watch the movie. Finally, box office receipts are linked to intentions based on a log-linear formulation. Using awareness and intention "tracking" data to calibrate his model, Zufryden (1996) reported that the proposed model provided an excellent fit to the box office data for the 63 movies in his sample.

In a similar vein, another behavioral-based model was developed by Sawhney and Eliashberg (1996). Its behavioral premise is that the average consumer goes through two stages in executing his/her decision to attend a movie in the theater. The two stages give rise to two time periods—time to decide to attend the movie, denoted as T, and the time to act upon the decision, denoted as τ. The sum of these two time periods, denoted as t, is the overall time that it takes for the consumer to enter the theatre and watch the movie. T and τ are both assumed to be independent and exponentially distributed with rate parameter λ and γ respectively. Then, it can be shown (see Sawhney and Eliashberg 1996) that t follows a Generalized Gamma distribution. Let X, Y, and Z be the cumulative distribution function for T, τ, and t respectively. Formally,

Model Framework

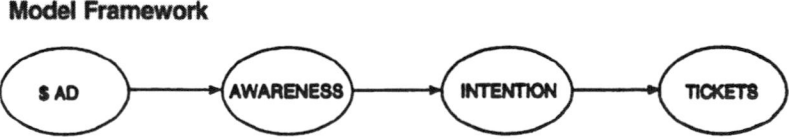

Fig. 13.2 A graphical summary of Zufryden (1996)'s awareness/intention/behavior model

$$X(T) = 1 - e^{-\lambda T} ; \quad Y(\gamma) = 1 - e^{-\tau T} \tag{13.3}$$

$$Z(t) = \frac{1}{\lambda - \gamma}\left[(\lambda - \gamma) + \gamma e^{-\lambda t} - \lambda e^{-\gamma t}\right] \tag{13.4}$$

Finally, the cumulative number of adopters by time t, $N(t)$, is modeled as:

$$N(t) \sim Binomial(N, Z(t)) \tag{13.5}$$

where N denotes the market potential of the movie. From Equation (13.5), the expected number of adopters by time t, E(N(t)), is given by a three-parameter equation.

$$E(N(t)) = \frac{N}{\lambda - \gamma}\left[(\lambda - \gamma) + \gamma e^{-\lambda t} - \lambda e^{-\gamma t}\right] \tag{13.6}$$

The three parameters, i.e., the average time to decide (λ), average time to act (γ), and the size of the market potential (N) can be estimated for each movie separately, from its previous-weeks' box office revenues. These parameter estimates can be of potential relevance to distributors, who may then allocate their resources accordingly to influence the parameter values. The authors also showed that their model can be estimated not only on time series data that are available after a movie is released, but also on information on movie characteristics that is available before release. To predict box office performance before the release, a database containing the parameter values of other movies, along with their features (e.g., genre, sequel, sexual content, special effects, MPAA rating, stars), is prepared. Then, the distributor can forecast the gross box office performance of the new movie by "benchmarking" it against the other movies in the database (e.g., Lilien and Rangaswamy 2005) based on the characteristics of the new movie.

Models that Jointly Consider Demand and Supply

While behavioral-based models offer improved predictive performance and a richer behavioral story over simpler regression models, a key aspect that determines a movie's performance, namely the interdependency between demand (box office receipts) and supply (number of screens), is not explicitly modeled. Empirically, the number of screens on which the movie is played and the movie's commercial success are highly interdependent over time and across markets. This suggests that single equation-based, regression-type models may be limited in the insights that they provide, and consequently, in their predictive performance.

Jones and Ritz (1991) first tackled that problem by modeling the relationship between the number of screens and box office receipts via two coupled differential equations, as shown in Equations (13.7) and (13.8) below:

$$\frac{dS}{dt} = [c + b(S - S_0)][\bar{S} - S] \qquad (13.7)$$

$$\frac{dR}{dt} = a[pS(t) - R] \qquad (13.8)$$

where $S(t)$ denotes the number of screens showing the movie at time t, S_0 denotes the initial number of screens, $\bar{S}$ denotes the maximum number of screens, and $R(t)$ denotes the box office receipts at time t. Equation (13.8) explicitly captures the interdependency between supply and demand by specifying that the size of the consumers' potential market at time t is determined by the size of the supply at that time(i.e., number of screens). The authors calibrated their model with actual box office and screens data, and found that their model outperformed other benchmark models including the simple linear model, the Bass model (Bass 1969), and the NUI (non-uniform influence) model (Easingwood et al. 1983).

A key limitation of Jones and Ritz (1991)'s model is that the number of screens is allowed to affect box office receipts but not vice versa. It does not allow for the possibility that the number of screen may be endogenous, i.e., a distributor may change the number of screens based on the observed box office performance of a movie. Elberse and Eliashberg (2003) recognized this limitation and developed a dynamic simultaneous-equations model that explicitly captures this interrelationship. More specifically, their model consists of two equations capturing the weekly box-office revenues (opening and beyond the opening week) and two similar equations representing the dynamics of screens allocation. The box office revenues are modeled as a function of the number of screens, time-varying covariates (e.g., word of mouth and competition for the attention of the audience), as well as time-invariant covariates (e.g., star and director), as shown in Equations (13.9) and (13.10):

$$LN(REVENUE_{it}) = \alpha_0 + \alpha_1 LN(SCREEN_{it}) + \alpha_2 LN(X_{Rit})$$
$$+ \alpha_3 LN(Z_{Ri}) + \varepsilon_{Rit} \qquad \text{for } t = 1 \qquad (13.9)$$

$$LN(REVENUE_{it}) = \alpha_0 + \alpha_1 LN(SCREEN_{it}) + \alpha_2 LN(X_{Rit})$$
$$+ \alpha_3 D_{Rit} + \varepsilon_{Rit} \qquad \text{for } t \geq 2 \qquad (13.10)$$

where X_{Rit} is a vector of time-varying (e.g., word of mouth), and Z_{Ri} denotes time-invariant covariates (e.g., star and director) which is assumed to affect only the opening week box office. D_{Rit} denotes (t-1) time dummies used for estimation.

Similarly, the dynamics of the screens are also modeled as functions of time-varying and time-invariant covariates that includes *expected* opening box office revenues, actual previous week box office revenues, competition on screens from new and ongoing movies, advertising and production expenditures, stars, and directors, as shown in Equations (13.11) and (13.12) below:

$$LN(SCREEN_{it}) = \beta_0 + \beta_1 LN(REVENUE_{it}^{**}) + \beta_2 LN(X_{Sit}) + \beta_3 LN(Z_{Si})$$
$$+ \beta_4 D_{Si} + \varepsilon_{Sit} \qquad (13.11)$$
$$\text{for } t = 1$$

$$LN(SCREEN_{it}) = \beta_0 + \beta_1 LN(REVENUE_{it}^{**}) + \beta_2 LN(X_{Sit}) + \beta_3 D_{Si} + \varepsilon_{Sit}$$
$$\text{for } t \geq 2 \qquad (13.12)$$

Elberse and Eliashberg (2003) estimated their model using a three-stage least-square (3SLS) procedure. Their results indicated high level of R-squared values (0.8 and above). While most of their results are consistent with the previous literature, they found that contrary to previous results, variables such as movie attributes and advertising expenditures do not influence audiences directly. Instead, those factors generally affect box office indirectly through their impact on the exhibitors' screens allocations.[2]

Note that some researchers have empirically studied the effect of marketing actions (e.g., promotion activities, release schedules) on a movie's commercial success. For instance, Hennig-Thurau et al. (2006) used a structural equations model to study the extent to which marketing actions and movie quality affect a movie's box office performance, both for the opening week and thereafter. Their conceptual framework is depicted in Fig. 13.3. Their results suggested that (i) both the studio's action and movie quality have a positive impact on the box office, both for the opening-week and for the "long-term," and (ii) the studio's action have a stronger impact than movie quality on the opening week, and a weaker impact on the long term box office.

Pre-test Market Approaches

The models discussed above rely on "hard" data, that is, box office ticket sales. However, prior to distributing the movie in theaters, the distributor has the option of playing the new movie to a sample of moviegoers, and surveying them for their reactions. This is in line with pre-test market approaches that have been used extensively in consumer goods context (Silk and Urban 1978). Testing the movie under a simulated test market environment can provide the distributor with a box office forecast as well as with diagnostic information

---

[2] In a related study, Krider et al. (2005) used a graphical approach to model the lead-lag relationship between distribution and demand for motion pictures. They found that, after the first week, the number of theatres a movie is shown is influenced by its performance in the previous week.

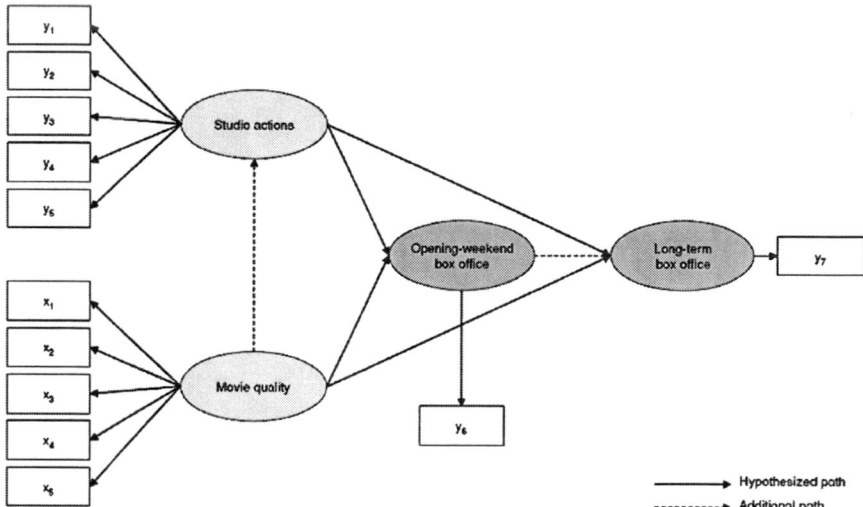

Fig. 13.3 Conceptual framework by Hennig-Thurau et al. (2006). x_1: average critics' rating; x_2: opening weekend ratings from Cinemascore.com; x_3: IMDB.com ratings; x_4: rating in Martin and Porter movie guide; x_5: rating by Maltin movie guide. y_1: stars and director; y_2: sequel/remake; y_3: advertising expenditure; y_4: number of screens; y_5: production budget; y_6: opening weekend box office revenues; y_7: total box office revenues (excluding opening week)

concerning the effectiveness of the contemplated distribution strategy. This is the key objective of Eliashberg et al. (2000) who developed the MOVIEMOD decision support system. The approach taken by the authors is that of a flow model where the target audience is broken down into sub-groups (e.g., unaware consumers, aware but waiting for the opportunity to attend the theater, and positive/negative spreaders of word of mouth) and probabilistic flows that move consumers across the different sub-groups, as shown graphically in Fig. 13.4.

Some of these flows are influenced directly by the distributor's strategic decisions (e.g., advertising, number of prints). The inputs required to implement the model are: consumer responses (e.g., tendency to talk about movies, degree of liking the tested movies), collected via simulated test market and under a contemplated "base" marketing strategy. The output provided by the model indicates that expected box office grosses under the base strategy, as well as the incremental increases/decreases that are likely to occur as a result of deviations from the base strategy. An implementation of the model in The Netherlands led to a change in the distributor's base strategy and predicted the resulting box office performance with a reasonable degree of accuracy.

The major movie studios have access to weekly surveys conducted by private research firms. While these studies are influential in theatrical distribution decision making, as far as we can determine, there are no published studies of formal models that incorporate such data into forecasting structures. While the published models surveyed here have reported good forecasting performance,

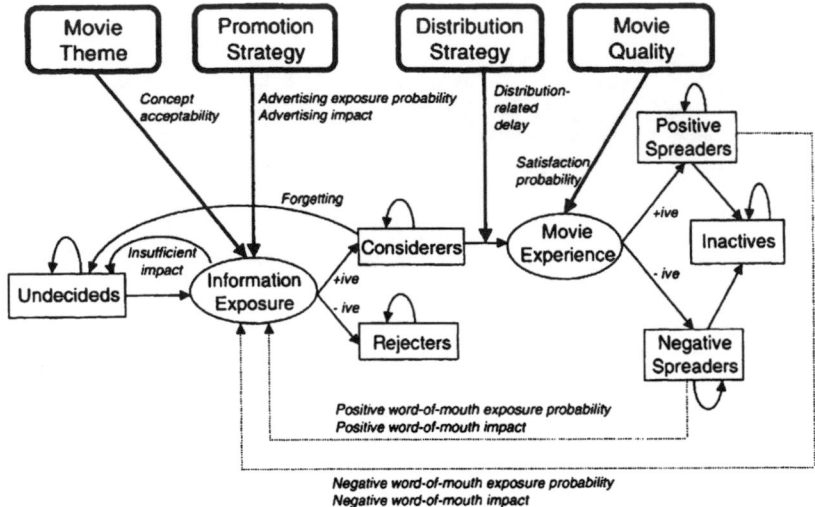

Fig. 13.4 The MOVIEMOD decision support system (Eliashberg et al. 2000)

systems incorporating both hard and soft data are likely to improve results, and hence encourage managerial usage.

Having reviewed the different forecasting approaches proposed in the literature, we conclude this section with an intriguing question: how early in the production/distribution process of a movie can researchers make prediction of its success? Not only is this issue of academic interest, but it is also of huge economic importance for major distributors, who are often also participate in the production of movies. To answer this question, Eliashberg et al. (2007) forecasted the theatrical performance at the very early stage of the production process, when movie makers are reviewing and selecting scripts for possible production. Combining domain knowledge in scriptwriting with techniques from natural language processing and machine learning, Eliashberg et al. (2007) extracted textual and content information from the storyline of a script and used it to predict the return-on-investment of a motion picture. In the future, we expect to see more models that enable forecasting earlier in the production process.

13.2.1.2 Theatrical Release Timing

The aforementioned models do not explicitly recognize the strategic nature of the distributor's release timing. However, a movie's box office performance in a certain week depends not only on the demand side (i.e., consumers' leisure time and willingness to see the movie), but also on the supply of movies that is available in that week. The latter is the aggregate result of the competing distributors' release strategies. Taken together, those two factors determine the seasonality observed in the data. Einav (2007) attempted to separate out the extent of the two effects using a panel of weekly box office grosses that contains 1956 movies from 1985 to 1999. He started by assuming that a consumer's utility to see a movie is a function of the (unobserved) quality of the movie and its "age." More specifically, the utility that consumer i receive from going to movie j on week t is given by

$$u_{ijt} = \theta_j - \lambda(t - r_j) + \xi_{jt} + \zeta_{it} + (1 - \sigma)\varepsilon_{ijt} \tag{13.13}$$

where θ_j denotes the (unobserved) quality of the movie j. $t - r_j$ is the number of weeks that have elapsed since the movie's release. ξ_{jt} is a movie-week random effect, while $\zeta_{it} + (1 - \sigma)\varepsilon_{ijt}$ is an individual error term. The utility of the corresponding "outside option", i.e., not watching any movies, is given by

$$u_{i0t} = -\tau_t + \zeta'_{it} + (1 - \sigma)\varepsilon_{i0t} \tag{13.14}$$

where τ_t is a week fixed effect that captures the underlying seasonality of the demand.

Combining Equations (13.13) and (13.14) yield a logit formulation for the share of each movie in each week. After some algebraic manipulations, the author showed that the share for movie j in week t, denoted by s_{jt}, can be written as

$$\log(s_{jt}) = \log(s_{0t}) + \theta_j + \tau_t - \lambda(t - r_j) + \sigma \log\left(\frac{s_{jt}}{1 - s_{0t}}\right) + \xi_{jt} \tag{13.15}$$

The estimated seasonality and the observed seasonality are shown in the top and bottom panel of Fig. 13.5, respectively. By comparing the two panels in the figure, one can see that the underlying seasonality observed in the movie market is amplified by the release decisions of movie studios. Apparently, the best movies are scheduled in the most favorable seasons, which magnifies the seasonality observed in the data. In particular, if the fixed effect terms that represent movie quality are omitted from the model, the standard deviation of the estimated week dummy variable τ_i increases from 0.236 to 0.356. Based on this result, the author claimed that the endogeneity of movie quality amplifies seasonality by about 50%.

Krider and Weinberg (1998) utilized a game-theoretical approach to model the strategic competition between two distributors. Under their model, each movie is characterized by its "marketability" parameter (α) and "playability" parameter (β). The revenue generated by each movie is then captured using a share-attraction model. The attraction of movie i at time t is assumed to follow an exponential model, given by

$$A_i(t) = e^{\alpha_i - \beta_i(t - t_{0i})} \quad , \quad t_{0i} \ (= 0 \text{ otherwise}) \tag{13.16}$$

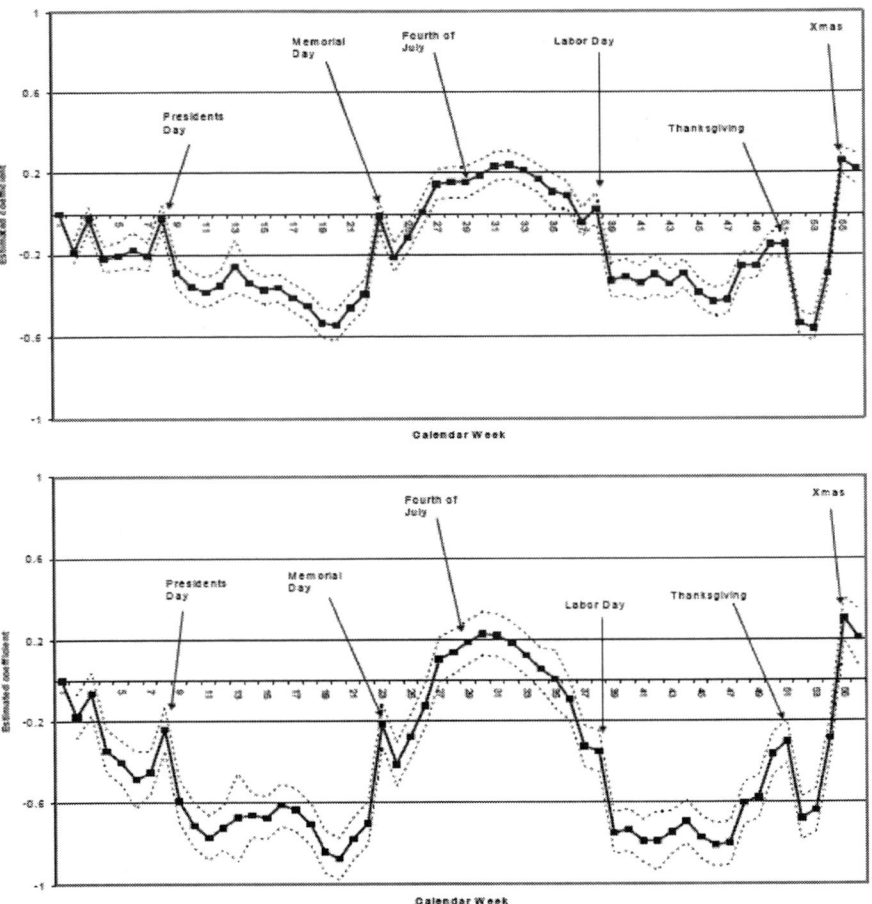

Fig. 13.5 Top panel: Estimated seasonality; bottom panel: observed seasonality of movies (Einav 2007). As can be seen, the observed seasonality is amplified compared to the estimated seasonality

where t_{0i} denotes the release time for the movie i. While the empirical analysis in the paper considered all movies available in a week, the release timing game was based on two (major) movies that might be released in the same week. Thus, i may take value 1 or 2 only. In the 2-movie model, the total revenue for picture i can be written as:

$$R_i = \int_{t_{0i}}^{t_f} \frac{A_i(t)}{A_1(t) + A_2(t) + 1} dt \qquad (13.17)$$

where t_f is the planning horizon under consideration. With this model set-up, Nash equilibrium strategies were identified; the precise solution was found using numerical techniques, since no closed form solutions are available. Three different equilibrium strategies emerged: (1) a single equilibrium strategy with both movies opening simultaneously at the beginning of the season, (2) a single equilibrium with one movie opening at the beginning of the season and one delaying, and (3) dual equilibria, with either movie delaying opening. In particular, the model predicted that stronger movies, i.e., movies that have high opening strength (α) and/or longer legs (β), will open earlier in the peak summer season. This prediction is confirmed by an empirical analysis of the actual release pattern of movies for one summer season. In addition, the authors found that most movie studios appeared to place, appropriately, a great deal of emphasis on the opening strength of a movie, but underestimated the importance of the decay rate in deciding when to release their movies.

13.2.2 Exhibition Models

In this section, we focus on models whose potential users are the exhibitors. Two key decisions that a movie exhibitor has to make are theatre location and movie schedule; we review works that study each of these issues below.

13.2.2.1 Facility Location

From 1990 to 2000, the number of movie theater screens in the U.S. grew from 23,814 to 36,280, an increase of 50%, while the box office revenues increased only by 16% from $6.6 to $7.6 billion (Davis 2006). Such asymmetrical expansion proved to be unhealthy. In the early 2000s, a number of theater chains went bankrupt; by 2004, the exhibition industry had undergone a period of consolidation, and at the end five major chains controlled more than 50% of the U.S. movie screens (*Variety* 2004). While we could identify no published papers which directly looked at what we believe is a very important decision—how many theaters and screens to have in an area and where they should be located—a number of researchers have looked at the effects of location on revenues obtained by theaters. These papers are primarily useful for public policy decision makers who are typically concerned about the competitive effects of horizontal and vertical mergers.

Davis (2006) is a representative study. In this paper, the author modeled the revenue received at a particular theatre as a function of the number of local competitors (i.e., the other theatres owned by the same or other chains). The estimation equation proposed is as follows[3]:

---

[3] In the paper, the author also estimated other specifications that are similar (and some slightly more general) than Equation (13.18). Interested readers are encouraged to see Davis (2006) for more details.

$$R_{hmt} = \alpha_h + \tau_t - \sum_{d=1}^{D} \theta_d^{own} \tilde{W}_{hmt}^{d,own} - \sum_{d=1}^{D} \theta_d^{rival} \tilde{W}_{hmt}^{d,rival} + \xi_{hmt} \qquad (13.18)$$

where R_{hmt} denotes the revenue for theater h, in market m, and at time t. α_h is a theater fixed effect, τ_t is a time fixed effect, and ξ_{hmt} is a normally distributed error term. $\tilde{W}_{hmt}^{d,own}$ represents the number of screens, owned by the same chain, that is within distance d of the focal theater. $\tilde{W}_{hmt}^{d,rival}$ represents the number of screen owned by a different chain within distance d of the focal theater. Thus, the third and fourth term of Equation (13.18) represents the degree of "cannibalization" by own theatres and "business stealing" by rivals respectively.

Davis (2006) also estimated a potential "market expansion" effect by modeling (using a separate equation), the aggregate revenue across all theatre in a market as a function of total number of screens. More specifically, the total revenue for all theatres in market m, at time t (denoted as R_{mt}) is given by:

$$R_{mt} = \alpha_1 screens_{mt} + \alpha_2 screens_{mt}^2 + \mu_m + \tau_t + \varepsilon_{mt} \qquad (13.19)$$

where μ_m and τ_t are random effects of market and of time respectively.

After estimating Equations (13.18) and (13.19), the author concluded that both cannibalization and business stealing effects are statistically significant and localized. In particular, he found that business stealing, i.e., competition by rivals' chains, has a stronger reduction effect on revenue than cannibalization by theatres from its own chain. Further, the author found evidence that there is a significant market expansion effect. That is, new screens tend to increase the overall size of the market and thus increase total revenue.

In a related study, Davis (2005) used a similar modeling approach to study the relationship between market structure (i.e., the number of screen in a local market) and price (i.e., average price per admission ticket). By estimating a reduced form price equation within-industry and across different local markets, he showed that there is a statistically significant relationship between the number of local movie theatres and the price charged. In general, low average ticket prices are associated with areas that contain more theatres. This effect, however, is "economically small" and smaller than previously expected by many researchers and policy makers. The author thus claimed that there is no evidence that actively controlling local ownership structure will lead to lower ticket prices.

13.2.2.2 Scheduling Movies in Theatrical Facilities

Every week, an exhibitor has to decide which movie(s) to play, and which ones, if any, to discontinue. Since the number of screens is limited, the exhibitor must exercise sound judgment in selecting movies to play in order to maximize its profit. This problem presents a considerable challenge for exhibitors because of the short life cycles of movies, the changing level of demand over time, the scarcity of screens, and the complex revenue sharing contract between the exhibitor and the distributor.

Swami et al. (1999) developed a decision support system called SilverScreener to tackle this movie scheduling problem, by relating it to the "parallel machine problem" (Baker 1993) considered in operations research. In their analogy, screens are *machines*, and movies are *jobs*. The problem of assigning a specific movie to play on each screen can thus be viewed as analogous to the problem of assigning jobs to machines. Although there are a number of differences between the two problems, this powerful analogy allowed Swami et al. (1999) to set up a formal mathematical programming model to solve for the optimal (dynamic) allocation of movies to screen. While readers are encouraged to refer to the original paper for full mathematical details, we briefly outline the key modeling approach here. The objective function that the exhibitor seeks to maximize is the total profit over the planning horizon, taking into account the revenue sharing contract between the exhibitor and the distributor. The action space is the movies to show and how long to keep each of the selected movies on screen. The objective function is maximized subject to two key constraints, as follows:

(i)   A movie must be played only on consecutive weeks. For example, a movie cannot be shown on week 1, withdrawn on week 2, and subsequently re-introduced in week 3.

(ii) The total number of movies scheduled in any week of the planning horizon has to equal to the total number of screens in the multiplex.

Given these two constraints, this mathematical program was then solved using integer programming techniques to recommend an optimal schedule. Thus, SilverScreener is able to help select and schedule movies for a multiple-screens theater over a fixed planning horizon to optimize the exhibitor's cumulative profit.

To demonstrate the applicability of their model, Swami et al. (1999) provided various ex-post analyses of optimal versus actual decision making, based on publicly available data for a specific theater in New York City. Although the modelers did not collaborate with the management of that theater, their analyses provided a number of important insights:

(i)   Based on SilverScreener's recommendations, the exhibitor can achieve substantially higher cumulative profit.

(ii) The improvement over actual decisions in terms of profitability appears to result from a combination of both *better selection* and *improved scheduling* of the movies.

(iii) The general structure of the exhibitor's normative decision as compared to current practice is: *choose fewer "right" movies and run them longer*.

A more extensive testing of the SilverScreener system was undertaken by Eliashberg et al. (2001) (henceforth ESWW), who implemented SilverScreener in collaboration with the Pathé theaters chain in Holland. They presented comparative results for the movie theater in which managers used the Silver-Screener model and for two comparable theaters which did not. They found that the "SilverScreener theater" outperformed the other two theatres in 9 out of 12 weeks, the length of the implementation period. Further, the researchers reported that the use of decision support systems was increasingly valued by managers over time; at the end of the study, the exhibitor asked the authors to develop a revised model for use in a new major multiplex. Later in Section 13.3, we will discuss the details of the implementation and key lessons learned.

A critical portion of the SilverScreener model is the forecasts for each week's movie attendance, in each theater that is under consideration. Thus, the problem of movie scheduling is closely related to the revenue forecasting models discussed in the previous section. See ESWW and Section 13.3 for a discussion of how both objective and subjective elements were incorporated into the decision support system designed for Pathé.

13.2.3 Models for the Home Video Market

The total revenue from the U.S. home video market (including both the sale and rental of videos, which encompasses both DVDs and video tapes) exceeds that of theatrical distribution by a wide margin. For instance, in 2005, the home video market generated around $23.8 billion in total revenues (Standard and Poor's 2006) , while tickets from theatrical distribution only generated around $9.0 billion (http://www.mpaa.org). Despite its economic importance, the home video market has received surprisingly little attention from marketing research-ers. This may be because published data on the home video market are, in general, more difficult to obtain than data for the theater market, or perhaps, because most researchers view theatrical release as the "glamour" industry. Among the handful of published models in this area, three major aspects of decision making have been investigated: (i) the timing of video release (how long after the theatrical release of the movie should the video be released), (ii) the revenue sharing arrangement between the video distributor and the video retailer, and (iii) the video retailer's decision on price and quantity.

13.2.3.1 Home Video Release Timing

Once a movie is released, one of the most important questions is how long to wait before issuing the corresponding video, in the so-called video "window." If the video is released too long after the movie, then the excitement and hype surrounding the movie's release may dissipate. On the other hand, if the video window is too short, movie fans may feel that it is not worthwhile to go to the movie theater and instead just wait to see the video. In other words, to what extent does the movie serves as a promoter of the video, and to what extent does the video cannibalizes box office revenues? Lehmann and Weinberg (2000) and Prasad et al. (2004) addressed this question from two different perspectives.

Lehmann and Weinberg (2000) approached the modeling task from the viewpoint of a distributor who needs to decide when to release the video. They developed a descriptive statistical model of a movie's box office revenue and home video revenue over time. Consistent with previous work that we reviewed earlier in this chapter, they used an exponential model to characterize the declining box-office ticket sales over time for a movie, and then extended the same functional form to the video rental market. Formally, let t_2 be the release time of the video, $M(t)$ and $V(t, t_2)$ be the revenue of the theatre and video over time respectively. The authors specified that

$$M(t) = \begin{cases} m_1^B e^{-m_2 t} & 0 \le t < t_2 \\ m_1^A e^{-m_2 t} & \text{otherwise} \end{cases}$$

and

$$V(t, t_2) = v_1 e^{-v_2^B t_2} e^{-v_2^A (t-t_2)} \tag{13.21}$$

where $m_1^B > m_2^A \ge 0$. The difference between the two decay rates m_1^B and m_1^A thus represents the degree of cannibalization of theatre revenue by the introduction of home video, which is also depicted graphically in Fig. 13.6. As can be seen, the revenue from movie theatre is assumed to drop once the video is introduced. The extent of the drop, i.e., cannibalization, is then estimated from actual data.

To obtain analytical results to guide management thinking, Lehmann and Weinberg (2000) made two critical assumptions in their model. First, when the video of a movie is released, all of the corresponding theater revenue is assumed

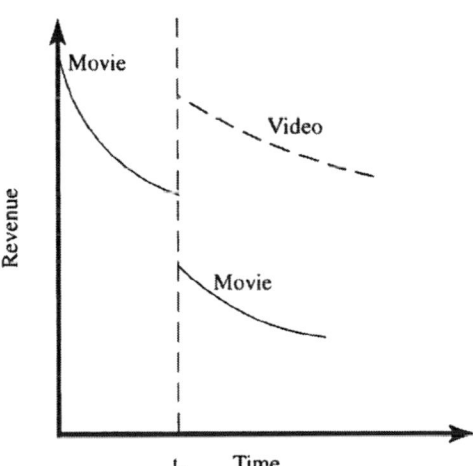

Fig. 13.6 Cannibalization effect of video on movie in Lehmann and Weinberg (2000)'s model

to be cannibalized. Second, the opening strength of a video is assumed to depend on the opening strength and decay rate of the movie's box office, and the length of the video window; typically, a longer video window often leads to a lower opening strength for the home video.

Lehmann and Weinberg (2000) then incorporated their empirical model into a normative framework in order to determine the optimal time to release a video. They solved for the optimal release time of the video using a backward analysis algorithm, which consists of two steps. In the first step, the retailer's optimal order quantity for videos is derived. This optimal quantity is then used in the second step to derive the optimal "window" between the release of the movie and the video. The researchers applied their model to a dataset of 35 movies. For each movie, they collected information on the weekly box office revenue, the marketing activities (e.g., pricing strategy) for the video, and the weekly rentals of the video. They reported a good fit for their model, and suggested two recommendations for distributors. First, using movie ticket sales to forecast video revenues will lead to better predictive accuracy. Second, distributors may adjust the release timing of the video to maximize their profit margins. While the optimal release time varies for each movie, in most cases the analysis suggested that a shorter window between the movie and the video's release is preferred. In particular, the researchers reported that studios may increase their profits on average by 37% if they follow the release timing recommended by the model.

Prasad et al. (2004) studied the issue of optimal release timing of the video from a different perspective. They explored the issue using a theoretical framework and did not offer any empirical test for their model. The focus of their work, therefore, is on understanding how altering various model assumptions will lead to different analytical conclusions under their analytical framework. A key contribution of their model is that they focus on the role of consumer expectation, which is not considered in Lehmann and Weinberg (2000). That is, consumers anticipate the time of a video's release based on their past experience with video rentals. In conjunction with Lehmann and Weinberg (2000), their model gives us a more complete understanding about the issue and competitive dynamics surrounding the home video market. Both papers conclude that for most movies, earlier release of the video is a more profitable strategy.

Papers in this area typically assume that the decisions when to release a movie and when to release a video are independent; however, a broader view may be required. The decision may better be framed as a joint one of when the movie and the video should be released (see Krider and Weinberg 1998), allowing for the decision to be updated after weekly movie revenues are observed.

13.2.3.2 Channels Contractual Arrangements

The contractual agreement between an independent manufacturer and an independent retailer has long been an important area of study in industrial organization, and has been applied to many marketing settings (e.g., Jeuland

and Shugan 1983; McGuire and Staelin 1983). The basic underlying problem is that the retailer, driven by its own profit incentive, may take actions that deviate from those preferred by the manufacturer. These deviations may reduce profits for the channel as a whole. In the case of the video rental industry, the retailer has to make two key decisions, the number of copies of a video placed in stocks, and the rental price. To make these decisions, retailers need to allow for demand uncertainty and the cost of stock out. As video demand declines over time, a special feature of the models is that the retailer orders the video only once, making the problem a variant of what is called the "news vendor" problem in the operations research literature.

One reason that this problem has drawn the attention of researchers is that since the late 1990s, the terms of the contract between the distributor and the video store have changed dramatically. Prior to 1998, most videos were sold to retailers by distributors at a flat price of about \$70. After that, the contract for many movies switched to a two-part tariff: retailers were typically charged a price of about \$5 per video, but had to remit more than 50% of the rental income back to the distributor (see Mortimer 2006 for more details). This provides a fertile testing ground for the theoretical development and empirical examination of contract theories.

Dana and Spier (2001) is representative of the theoretical approach taken by economists to study this problem. Since the theoretical derivations in their paper are fairly involved, we only provide an overview of their model set up, the assumptions, and the key results. Interested readers are encouraged to refer to the original paper for the full mathematical details. The channel set up in Dana and Spier (2001) consists of a monopolistic studio distributor, who produces each unit of output with cost $c > 0$, and retailers whose cost of renting out a movie is $d > 0$. The retailing market is assumed to be perfectly competitive, and each consumer is assumed to have unit valuation $V > d + c$. To mimic the situation in the video rental market, the researchers make a number of assumptions. First, consumer demand is assumed to be uncertain, with the uncertainty captured by allowing the number of consumers to be drawn from a generic distribution $F(.)$. Second, a planning horizon of only one period is considered. Third, retailer can set both the rental price and the quantity to order.

With these assumptions, Dana and Spier (2001) showed that a "revenue sharing contract" $\left\{ \left(\frac{d}{1+d} \right) c, \left(\frac{1-d}{1+d} \right) \right\}$ will optimally "coordinate" the channel, i.e., obtain an outcome equivalent to that of a vertically integrated channel. A revenue sharing contract denoted by $\{t,r\}$ means that the retailer pays an upfront fee of t per unit, and on top of that pays a fraction, denoted by r, of his/her rental revenue to the distributor. While this theoretical result is, like in many other studies, dependent upon many simplifying assumptions which abstract away from the real world, the primary message has powerful managerially implications. It shows that revenue sharing contracts solve the coordination problems generated by vertical separation, demand uncertainty, and downstream competition, and thus lead to improved results for manufacturers. With the use of revenue sharing contracts, retailers will tend to increase their inventory holding, and to be involved in less intense price competition. Finally, Dana and Spier (2001) compared revenue sharing contracts with other mechanisms for channel coordination, including return policies, resale price maintenance, and two-part tariffs, and found that revenue sharing contracts avoid many potential problems associated with the other mechanisms. In particular, revenue sharing contracts typically involve lower transaction cost and logistical burden; thus, Dana and Spier (2001) recommended their use in the video industry.

From a theoretical standpoint such as Dana and Spier (2001), a two-part tariff (and other mechanisms such as revenue sharing) leads to better channel coordination, and thus higher profits, than a fixed price contract. Demonstrating such effect empirically, however, requires a detailed dataset and an econometric methodology that adequately controls for the endogeneity of the retailer's contract choice. Mortimer (2006) presents an empirical test of the impact of the two-part tariffs now implemented in the video industry. Her main goal is to compare the difference in profits, both for the upstream distributor and the downstream retailer, that results from a fixed price contract versus a two-part tariff. In addition, she also investigated the effect of the introduction of two-part tariff on social welfare.

Mortimer (2006) began by constructing a theoretical model of firms' behavior. Assuming a linear demand function, she derived the profit maximizing conditions for a retailer who maximizes his expected profit by first choosing a contractual form, and then an inventory level. She then derived the equilibrium choice of level of inventory and of contract. This theoretical model is then calibrated with actual data by a structural econometrical model at the store-title level, using the Generalized Method of Moments (GMM) approach. Her estimation approach is based on a set of six moment conditions, which jointly incorporates consumers' demand, retailers' inventory and profit maximization considerations, and the relationship between rentals and inventory.

The dataset used is very rich and disaggregated; it contains weekly information, such as price, inventory, rentals, for each title in each store. While her results vary for specific titles and settings, her results are well represented by her own summary statement: For popular movies, both distributor's and retailer's profits are improved by about 10% under two-part tariff. This improvement in profit is even larger for unpopular titles.

We believe that work such as Mortimer (2006) is a key step forward towards applying theory to practice, and is thus particularly important for both researchers and for decision makers. For researchers, this paper contributes to the academic literature by presenting an empirical test for the theoretical predictions with a rich dataset in the context of the video market. It also complements the previous theoretical studies (e.g., Dana and Spier 2001) that have examined the adoption of revenue sharing contracts in the video rental industry. As for decision makers, while such work does not provide information to distributors at the tactical level to suggest the amount of fixed fee and the specific revenue sharing terms to set for a specific movie, it does provide overall strategic guidance as to the type of contracts that should be used, and provides incentives for distributors to consider in changing current practice.

13.2.3.3 Home Video Retailer's Decision on Price and Quantity

While the above cited contracting papers model some aspects of the retailer's decision with regard to ordering policy (rental price and order quantity), the retailer's decision is usually not the primary focus. In this section, we briefly mention literature that studied the price and quantity decisions from a retailer's standpoint.

The video rental industry has been studied by many researchers in operations management (e.g., Drezner and Pasternack 1999; Lariviere and Cachon 2002). In particular, Gerchak et al. (2006) provided the link between this section and the previous section on contract agreements. In this paper, the researchers took the view of a retailer who has to decide how many copies of a specific video to order and how long to keep it on the shelf in the face of uncertain demand that is exponentially declining, on average, over time. With decreasing demand, the retailer needs to balance the costs of holding inventory and of lost sales in choosing the optimal policy. The authors derived the optimal recommendations for the order quantity and the time to hold a video for the retailer, and showed that it depends upon the nature of the contract offered by the distributor. Referring back to the previous section, the authors showed that when order quantity and shelf-retention timing is considered, even a two-part tariff may not be sufficient to coordinate the channel. Instead, a third term, a license fee (or subsidy) per movie title may be required to achieve channel coordination.

This last result raises an important modeling challenge, i.e., how complexly by a model should be specified. Obviously, more complicated models will be able to better capture reality and generate more detailed recommendations on managerial policies; however, they are also more susceptible to unrealistic assumptions. In addition, the policies recommended may be too difficult for managers to implement, especially as managers need to contend with a number of real world limitations as well. The appropriate level of model complexity, therefore, is a delicate issue that must be considered carefully and should be tailored to the specific application at hand. In the next section, we will discuss the application issues faced when the SilverScreener system was implemented.

13.3 Application Issues and Implementation Experience

Many marketing models have been successfully implemented in industry, and marketing researchers have recently placed more emphasis on the impact of their models on industry practice. With the increased attention to real-life applications (e.g., the commencement of the ISBM Practice Prize), we expect to see more successful implementation of marketing models in the near future.

To date, the most prominent application of marketing decision models has been in the area of sales-force models. For instance, Sinha and Zoltners (2001) reported on a long history of successful models in that area; Lodish (2001) discussed the successful use of CallPlan and other models. Outside the sales-force area, however, there has still been relatively little work that discusses the application of decision models, as many cases remained unreported in the existing literature. The movie industry, in particular, is far less receptive to the idea of applying quantitative decision models. Two of the authors of this chapter (Eliashberg and Weinberg) jointly with Sanjeev Swami and Berend Wierenga were involved in that implementation. For expositional convenience, the term "we" is used in this section to refer to the members of the implementation team. In particular, to encourage the use of decision models in this area, we report our experience obtained from the implementation of SilverScreener in Holland and the United States. By sharing the lessons learned during the implementation process, we hope to provide a useful guide to future researchers who may wish to apply their models in the movie industry.

SilverScreener, as discussed in Section 13.2.2, is a mathematical programming routine (used in conjunction with a weekly revenue forecast system) that recommends which movies an exhibitor should show in each week. ESSW described the first implementation of SilverScreener in detail and carefully specified the measures of implementation success. Our implementation was guided by Wierenga et al. (1999) systematic framework for decision support system implementation, which requires a careful match between decision makers and the decision making environment. In the discussion below, we highlight the key lessons learned from the implementation process.

Lesson 1: Managers Are Often Reluctant to Give Predictions

At first, we hoped to use managerial assessment as an input to the forecasting system in SilverScreener. However, we learned that managers are often reluctant to provide predictions due to at least two reasons: First, providing weekly forecast for each movie for each theatre requires a lot of effort; sometimes, managers just use very simple heuristics to guide their decisions. Second, a manager may prefer not to make forecast because of the worry that potential loss in revenue due to forecast error would be held against them personally.

Since the goal of a decision support system is to help managers make better decisions, it must be designed with the end user in mind according to his/her personal preferences. In our case, the implementation of a decision support system should depend on the manager's willingness to provide forecasting inputs. If the manager is reluctant to provide forecasts, a system should be developed with minimal managerial involvement. In contrast, if a manager provides detailed information and forecasts based on domain knowledge, this information should be incorporated as much as possible into the decision support system.

Lesson 2: A Successful Decision Support System Must Take into Account the Degree of Centralization in the Organization

In the exhibition sector, decision making is usually very centralized: One booker typically makes the scheduling decisions for all the chain's screens. It is unlikely that this person, even if he/she is highly motivated, will have the basis for developing judgmental forecasts for the box office performance of each movie, in each of the local theaters. In our assessment, although the local theater manager may be more aware of the needs of the local clientele, he/she is not the person who is asked to provide forecasts for our system. This situation is in sharp contrast with the traditional retailing industry where decentralized decision making is more common and there is more local control. For example, two chain stores located in the same city may carry very different assortments, depending on the local clientele and the local manager's familiarity with the store patrons' preferences. We believe that for a decision support system to be successful, it must take into account the degree of centralization in the decision making mechanism in the target organization.

Lesson 3: Researchers Should Use All Available (and Appropriate) Data When Building a Decision Support System

Even when a field is data rich like the movie industry, managers may not use all the data available when they make decisions on a daily basis. For example, SilverScreener utilizes data that managers had access to but did not regularly use. These data included detailed box office reports and the results of market research on upcoming movies. Sometimes, the data that managers focused on are different from the data required by the decision support system. For instance, managers we spoke to typically pay more attention to gross box office revenues than to net revenues (which includes the effects of concessions and the deduction of sliding scale payments to distributors) although the latter is more directly linked to profitability.

In addition, presumably due to the need to make multiple decisions within a short horizon, managers often base their decision on heuristics rather than on data. This is precisely why models are valuable: though computationally intense at times, they can overcome some heuristic biases by forcing managers to take a hard look at the data available, and thus confront their decisions quantitatively and objectively. Therefore, it is important for modelers to identify and use all available data, even if such data are not regularly used by managers.

Lesson 4: The Goal of a Decision Support System is to Assist in, but not Automate, Decision Making. Thus, Researchers Must Carefully Balance Complexity and Parsimony

Researchers must keep in mind that models are only incomplete maps of the world, and many factors still remain outside the model. Such factors may occur too rarely to be included, and thus would add much complexity with little managerial gain; they may be unexpected and only revealed after the model was completed, perhaps because the manager or modeler may not want to reveal certain information. For example, in one instance, a manager chose not to show a movie that SilverScreener recommended because a distributor for another movie wanted a movie shown now, with the implicit bargain that when a very popular movie was available later on, this manager would have access to that movie. This "contract" is not considered by the SilverScreener system.

SilverScreener also involves several simplifying assumptions. For instance, it does not explicitly consider the seating capacities of the different screening rooms. Since sellouts rarely occur, this simplifying assumption may be justifiable even if it does not correspond exactly to the real world. This raises an important question: how complex should a model be, and how closely should the manager follow the model's recommendations, given that it is an abstract of the actual situation? In one of our implementations, managers followed our recommendations of which movies to play in which screens about 60% of the time; this is consistent with Blattberg and Hoch's (1990) recommendation that a 50-50 weighting between model and expert judgment is a reasonable balance. In any case, in an area as complex as movie scheduling, we believe that the goal is to assist the managers in making decisions, rather than to completely automate the decision process.

Lesson 5: Researchers Should Keep the Managers Involved During the Model Building Process

From our experience, most progress is made when managers stay involved in the model building and testing process. While implementing models is time consuming on the part of the manager, it is necessary to continually monitor the process by which inputs and outputs are provided, identify new factors that may emerge, or even take into account changes in the management structure. In addition, perhaps due to the background of the managers in the movie industry, the managers with whom we interacted were more interested in the outputs of the model than the process by which models were generated. However, we think that managerial involvement is vital not only when we interpret output, but also during model development. Since not all managers are naturally inclined towards the use of analytical procedures, it is critical to make sure that models maintain face validity and adapt to changing circumstances, so that the model will continue to be useful for managers over time. Nevertheless, as the organizational history deepens, there is less need for continual contact over time and the burden on the managers will be reduced.

Lesson 6: It Is Important to Evaluate the Model's Performance After Its Implementation

Finally, managers appear to be reluctant to set up a systematic review in order to judge the level of model improvement. In our experience, managers have been quite willing to put time and effort into the modeling process and have shared extensive internal data, but it has been our initiative to set up a control design in order to evaluate the system. As a result, the evaluation system described in ESWW was entirely developed by the researchers. Yet, we feel that evaluation is a crucial step both for managers and for researchers. For managers, we believe that this is the best way to judge whether the model has led to a profit improvement. In fact, we believe that the demonstrated success reported in ESWW was critical to our continuing work with Pathé. For us as researchers, our interest is in improving the quality of our models. Both diagnostic and performance data are needed in order to improve the models that are provided.

13.4 What Models Are Still Missing: Opportunities for Further Research

While there has been considerable progress in modeling and addressing various managerial issues in the movie industry, many issues are still open for future research. Some of these issues arise because of the recent trends in the movie industry. We provide a list of some of these emerging trends below. While this list is by no means exhaustive, we believe that it provides a valuable guideline for future researchers.

- Increased focus on bottom line performance in movie production decision making
- Availability of multiple distribution outlets (e.g., digital cinema/movies)
- Decline in the U.S. theatrical movie attendance
- Competition from other forms of media
- Increased worldwide focus: Globalization of both supply and demand in the entertainment industry

We now explore the implications of some of these trends for modelers.

13.4.1 Increased Focus on Bottom Line Performance

Over the decades, the motion picture industry has been transformed from one dominated by entrepreneurial studio heads who relied on their own intuitive judgments, to one in which executives and companies focused predominantly on bottom line performance. Few studios are independent entities; most are a part of conglomerates with a multitude of interests inside and outside the entertainment industry. While few would argue that a systematic model will ever replace the art involved in producing a great movie, many decisions are still subject to analytical scrutiny. This provides great opportunities for modelers. To illustrate, as described in *The Wall Street Journal* (April 29–30, 2006), the idea of investing in the production of movies has attracted investors such as hedge funds and other money managers who, in the 2004–2006, have provided more than $4 billion in movie financing to the major film studios. As noted in the article, "armed with computer-driven investment simulations and sophisticated database analysis, [investors] think that they can pick movies with the right characteristics to make money." This represents an opportunity for collaboration between industry and academics where new models, capable of assessing, screening, and forecasting the commercial performance of movies based on the descriptors (e.g., scripts) that are available at each point of decision-making (e.g., green-lighting). An interesting question is: to what level can the uncertainty about movies' performances be reduced? We do not believe that the movie making process should be completely random, and it would be interesting and important for investors to quantify the associated uncertainties as precisely as possible.

13.4.2 Multiple Distribution Outlets

The number of distribution outlets for movies have increased dramatically in the recent years. Besides traditional outlets of theatres and home videos, movies can now be distributed in electronic devices (e.g., iPod, cell phones) and over the Internet (e.g., movielink.com). This leads to a number of new managerial questions that deserve modeling attention. Modelers may study the extent to which these different outlets cannibalize each other and whether, by contrast, they reinforce each other. They may also study what type of movie and content is most appropriate for large screen (i.e., theater) movie, small-screen (i.e., home TV set), and even micro-screen (i.e., cell-phone) entertainment. More generally, one may try to match movie characteristics with distribution channels, by considering the distinct segments of consumers who engage in consuming movies in different outlets. The existence of multiple channels also encourages researchers to jointly model the multi-stage life cycle process that films go through, perhaps even starting with the "buzz" prior to a film's release[4] (e.g., Liu 2006). One particularly important and interesting question, for instance, is how word of mouth (WOM) information and the buzz surrounding a movie affect its performance in each of the distribution outlets. Already, researchers have studied the extent to which WOM drives box office performance (e.g., Eliashberg et al. 2000; Liu 2006; Zufryden 2000); extending their research to consider a multi-channel setting, and hence develop them into decision models, may appear to be a natural next step. This may also add to the long stream of research in marketing that is concerned with the modeling of new products (e.g., the very first article in *Marketing Science*, BBD&O's News model by Pringle et al. (1982) concerned new product management). The changes in the movie industry provide both an opportunity to empirically test and implement existing approaches, and a challenge for researchers to develop new approaches.

13.4.3 Decline in the U.S. Theatrical Movie Attendance

Modeling opportunities are increasingly generated as managers turn from a focus on the domestic box office market to multiple distribution channels and a worldwide perspective. Such changes increase complexity and make it more difficult for managers to rely primarily on intuition to make decisions, and increase the value of models to managers. As we discussed earlier, we do not expect such models to completely automate decision making, but rather to serve as an aid to decision makers. To date, the modeling literature has largely studied movies distributed in theaters, leaving opportunities for more focused models.

Marketing analysts have a long history of separating out the characteristics of primary and secondary demand using sophisticated estimation methods. Such approaches should help answer the important question of whether the decline in North American movie attendance in the recent years is due to a change in people's viewing tastes and habits, to a slippage in quality, or to the employment of suboptimal marketing strategies. Similarly, as movies increasingly become vehicles for product placement, models which have helped media and media buyers to develop advertising programs can be adapted to the context of motion pictures (and other entertainment products such as video games). The impact of

---

[4] We thank Fred Zufryden for this suggestion.

product placement on the quality of movies produced and their appeal to audiences is an important issue that deserves more research attention.

13.4.4 Competition from Other Forms of Media

There is a need for models that address the modeling of competition from "outside sources" to the movie industry. Researchers have considered the competitive aspects of different movies titles in the prediction of film market shares and life cycle (e.g., Krider and Weinberg 1998; Ainslie et al. 2005). The next step forward, we believe, is to model the "higher-level" threats to the film industry from related industries such as video games. More specifically, we believe that different models are needed to capture the "passive" movie watchers' and the "active" entertainment consumers' behavior. Such models are likely to help in identifying fundamental differences that will have significant implications on both the appropriate content provision as well as on the marketing strategy. An important concern for managers and policy makers is the threat of piracy to the economics of the movie industry and current practice. Only limited work has been done in this area.

13.4.5 Increased Worldwide Focus

Much of the work reviewed in this chapter has focused on the United States and on the theater market. As we have already noted, this is where research attention has focused. However, as Weinberg (2005) and others have pointed out, the non-theater market accounts for more revenues than the theater market, and revenues from outside North America are approximately 50% higher than those in North America. An important challenge is determining what modeling structures will be most useful as the North American box office becomes a smaller portion of the overall market. At present, Hollywood studios—or the conglomerates that control them—continue to dominate the world wide market. One may wonder whether there are strategies, both from producers and distributors standpoints, that will allow this dominance to continue. It is too early to determine whether the development of such sites as youtube.com which allow originators to provide their content directly to users will lead to a fundamental shift in movie distribution or just another alternative to the current arrangements.

Finally, consistent with the view of other authors in this volume, we want to emphasize the importance, challenge, and the enjoyment of working with managers to apply marketing models in industry. While the literature reports on relatively few implemented models, we strongly encourage other researchers to examine for themselves whether there is "nothing as practical as a good theory". We hope that this chapter will serve as a useful guide for future researchers in the movie industry.

Reference

Ainslie, A., X. Dreze, F. Zufryden. 2005. Modeling Movie Life Cycle and Market Share. *Marketing Science* **24**(3) 508–517.

Baker, K.R. 1993. *Elements of Sequencing and Scheduling.* Dartmouth College, Hanover, NH.

Bass, F.M. 1969. A New Product Growth Model for Consumer Durables. *Management Science* **15** 215–227.

Blattberg, R.C., S.J. Hoch. 1990. Database Models and Managerial Intuition: 50% Models and 50% Manager. *Management Science* **38**(8) 887–899.

Dana, J.D. Jr., K.E. Spier. 2001. Revenue Sharing in the Video Rental Industry. *Journal of Industrial Economics* **49**(3) 223–245.

Davis, P. 2005. The Effect of Local Competition on Retail Prices: The U.S. Motion Picture Exhibition Market. *Journal of Law and Economics* **48**(2) 677–707.

Davis, P. 2006. Measuring the Business Stealing, Cannibalization and Market Expansion Effects Of Entry in the Motion Picture Exhibition Market. *Journal of Industrial Economics* **54**(3) 293–321.

Drezner, Z., B.A. Pasternack. 1999. The Videotape Rental Model. *Journal of Applied Mathematics and Decision Sciences* **3** 163–170.

Easingwood, C.J., V. Mahajan, E. Muller. 1983. A Nonuniform Influence Innovation Diffusion Model of New Product Acceptance. *Marketing Science* **2**(3) 273–295.

Einav, L. 2007. Seasonality in the U.S. Motion Picture Industry. *RAND Journal of Economics* **38**(1) 127–145.

Elberse, A., J. Eliashberg. 2003. Demand and Supply Dynamics for Sequentially Released Products in International Markets: The Case of Motion Pictures. *Marketing Science* **22**(3) 329–354.

Eliashberg, J., A. Elberse, Mark A.A.M. Leenders. 2006. The Motion Picture Industry: Critical Issues in Practice, Current Research, and New Research Directions. *Marketing Science* **25**(6) 638–661.

Eliashberg, J., S.K. Hui, J.Z. Zhang. 2007. From Storyline to Box Office: A New Approach for Green-Lighting Movie Scripts. *Management Science* **53**(6) 881–893.

Eliashberg, J., J.-J. Jonker, M.S. Sawhney, B. Wierenga. 2000. MOVIEMOD: An Implementable Decision-Support System for Prerelease Market Evaluation of Motion Pictures. *Marketing Science* **19**(3) 226–243.

Eliashberg, J., S. Swami, C.B. Weinberg, B. Wierenga. 2001. Implementation and Evaluation of SilverScreener: A Marketing Management Support System for Movie Exhibitors. *Interfaces: Special Issue on Marketing Engineering* **31**(3) S108–S127.

Gerchak, Y., R.K. Cho, S. Ray. 2006. Coordination of Quantity and Shelf-Retention Timing in the Video Movie Rental Industry. *IIE Transactions* **38** 525–536.

Hennig-Thurau, T., M.B. Houston, S. Sridhar. 2006). Can Good Marketing Carry a Bad Product? Evidence from the Motion Picture Industry. *Marketing Letters* **17** 205–219.

Jeuland, A., S. Shugan. 1983. Managing Channel Profits. *Marketing Science* **2**(3) 239–272.

Jones, J.M., C.J., Ritz. 1991. Incorporating Distribution into New Product Diffusion Models. *International Journal of Research in Marketing* **8** 91–112.

Krider, R.E., C.B. Weinberg. 1998. Competitive Dynamics and the Introduction of New Products: The Motion Picture Timing Game. *Journal of Marketing Research* **35**(1) 1–15.

Krider, R.E., T. Li, Y. Liu, C.B. Weinberg. 2005. The Lead-Lag Puzzle of Demand and Distribution: A Graphical Method Applied to Movies. *Marketing Science* **24**(4) 635–645.

Lariviere, M.A., G.P. Cachon. 2002. Supply Chain Coordination with Revenue Sharing Contracts. *Management Science* **51**(1) 30–44.

Lehmann, D.R., C.B. Weinberg. 2000. Sales Through Sequential Distribution Channels: An Application to Movies and Videos. *Journal of Marketing* **64** 18–33.

Lilien, G.L., A. Rangaswamy. 2005. *Marketing Engineering.* Trafford Publishing.

Litman, B.R., H. Ahn. 1998. Predicting Financial Success of Motion Pictures: The Early '90s Experience. Litman B.R., Ed.. *The Motion Picture Mega-Industry*. Needham Heights, MA: Allyn & Bacon.

Liu, Y. 2006. Word of Mouth for Movies: Its Dynamics and Impact on Box Office Revenue. *Journal of Marketing* **70**(3) 74–89.

Lodish, L. 2001. Building Marketing Models that Make Money. *Interfaces: Special Issue on Marketing Engineering*. **31**(3), Part 2 S45–S55.

McGuire, T., R. Staelin. 1983. An Industry Equilibrium Analysis of Downstream Vertical Integration. *Marketing Science* **2**(2) 161–192.

Mortimer, J.H. 2006. Vertical Contracts in the Video Rental Industry. Working Paper, Harvard Department of Economics.

Moul, C.C. 2005. *A Concise Handbook of Movie Industry Economics*. Cambridge University Press, Cambridge, UK.

Prasad, A., V. Mahajan, B.J. Bronnenberg. 2004. Product Entry Timing in Dual Distribution Channels: The Case of the Movie Industry. *Review of Marketing Science*: Vol. 2, Article 4. http://www.bepress.com/romsjournal/vol2/iss1/art4

Pringle, L., R.D. Wilson, E.J. Brody. 1982. NEWS: A Decision Analysis Model for New Product Analysis and Forecasting. *Marketing Science* **1**(1) 1–30.

Ravid, S.A. 1999. Information, Blockbusters, and Stars: A Study of the Film Industry. *Journal of Business* **72**(4) 463–492.

Sawhney, M.S., J. Eliashberg. 1996. A Parsimonious Model for Forecasting Gross Box-Office Revenues of Motion Pictures. *Marketing Science* **15**(2) 113–131.

Silk, A., G.L. Urban. 1978. Pre-test Market Evaluation of New Packaged Goods: A Model and Measurement Methodology. *Journal of Marketing Research* **15**(2) 171–179.

Sinha, P., A. Zoltners. 2001. Sales-Force Decision Models: Insights from 25 Years of Implementation. *Interfaces: Special Issue on Marketing Engineering* **31**(3), Part 2 S108–S127.

Standard and Poor's. 2006. *Industry Surveys: Movies and Home Entertainment*. McGraw-Hill.

Swami, S., J. Eliashberg, C.B. Weinberg. 1999. SilverScreener: A Modeling Approach to Movie Screens Management. *Marketing Science* **18**(3) 352–372.

Variety. 2004. H'w'd Vexed by Plex Success: Newly Healthy Chains Dueling for Better Film Rental Terms. May 17.

Vogel, H.L. 2001. *Entertainment Industry Economics: A guide for Financial Analysis*, 6th Ed. Cambridge University Press, Cambridge, UK.

Wall Street Journal. 2006. Creative Financing: Defying the Odds, Hedge Funds Bet Billions on Movies. April 29–30.

Waterman, D. 2005. *Hollywood's Road to Riches*. Harvard University Press, Cambridge, MA.

Weinberg, C.B. 2005. Profits Out of the Picture: Research Issues and Revenue Sources Beyond the North American Box Office. Moul, C. Ed. *A Concise Handbook of Movie Industry Economics*. Cambridge University Press, Cambridge, UK.

Wierenga, B., G.H. Van Bruggen, R. Staelin. 1999. The Success of Marketing Management Support Systems. *Marketing Science* **18**(3) 196–207.

Zufryden, F.S. 1996. Linking Advertising to Box Office Performance of New Film Releases: A Marketing Planning Model. *Journal of Advertising Research* July–August 29–41.

Zufryden, F.S. 2000. New Film Website Promotion and Box-Office Performance. *Journal of Advertising Research* **40**(1) 55–64.

Chapter 14
Strategic Marketing Decision Models for the Pharmaceutical Industry

Venkatesh Shankar

14.1 Introduction

The healthcare industry is one of the largest industries worldwide. Healthcare expenditures constitute about 8–15% of the gross domestic product (GDP) of most developed countries. For example, in the United States of America (U.S.), healthcare expenditures made up about 15.3% of the GDP in 2003. Over the past 45 years, these expenditures have grown 2.7% faster than the U.S. GDP.[1]

The pharmaceutical industry forms a critical portion of the healthcare industry. The pharmaceutical industry comprises "companies that research, develop, produce, and sell chemical or biological substances for medical or veterinary use, including prescription, generic and OTC drugs; vitamins and nutritional supplements; drug delivery systems and diagnostic substances; and related products, equipment, and services, including distribution and wholesale" (Hoover's 2006). In 2006, sales of pharmaceutical products in the U.S. were $274 billion. Today, about 10 cents of every health care dollar spent in the U.S. are spent on pharmaceuticals.[2]

Given the importance of the pharmaceutical industry, strategic marketing decisions such as those relating to research and development (R&D), product management, market entry, growth, and reaction strategies are critical to the success of brands and firms in the industry. The influence of product development

---

The author thank Jeff Meyer and Marie Hollinger for their help as graduate assistants.

[1] *White Book – U.S. Healthcare: A Mess Central Planning in Capitalism's Backyard*; May 2005, pp. 9-14, 6p <Business Source Complete> http://search.ebscohost.com.ezproxy.tamu.edu:2048/login.aspx?direct=true&db=bth&AN=18535978&site=bsi-live

[2] Pharmaceutical Industry Profile 2007. Pharmaceutical Research and Manufacturers of America. 2007 < http://www.phrma.org/files/Profile%202007.pdf> Page 25

V. Shankar
Mays Business School, Texas A&M University, College Station, Texas 77845, USA
e-mail: vshankar@mays.tamu.edu

B. Wierenga (ed.), *Handbook of Marketing Decision Models*,
DOI: 10.1007/978-0-387-78213-3_14, © Springer Science+Business Media, LLC 2008

and marketing efforts on the success of pharmaceutical products is growing. In 2006, pharmaceutical companies spent roughly $83 billion or about 30% of revenues in R&D and marketing related expenditures. Given this substantial level of spending, there is an increasing use of and need for analytic and data-driven models for strategic marketing decisions in this industry. Rich R&D, sales and marketing data exist for most developed countries from such sources as PhRMA, International Management Systems (IMS) audits and Scott Levin syndicated data. R&D, product, aggregate and physician level sales data are available for most brands and categories. Such proliferation of rich data has led to the development of use of several strategic marketing decision models. The formulation and implementation of newer strategic marketing models is growing.

It is unsurprising, therefore, that there is a growing body of research on the strategic marketing of pharmaceutical products. As this research proliferates and as the industry grows rapidly, a broad review of this body of research is in order.

14.2 Overview of the Pharmaceutical Industry

In the US, the drug development process goes through the following stages over an average span of 15 years: drug discovery, preclinical trials, clinical trials comprising Phases I, II, and III, Federal Drug Authority (FDA) review, and large-scale manufacturing/Phase IV (PhRMA 2007). For every 5,000–10,000 compounds tested, about 250 compounds make it to the preclinical phase. At this stage, an IND application is submitted by the firm. About five of these 250 compounds qualify for the clinical trials. In Phase I trial, each compound is tested on about 20–100 volunteers, in Phase II, about 100–500 volunteers, and in Phase III, about 1000–5000 volunteers. After the Phase III trial, the firm submits an NDA. After the FDA reviews the application, it will likely approve one out of the five drugs. This process is captured by Fig. 14.1 (PhRMA 2007).

The major drug therapeutic areas are: central nervous system, anti-infective/antibacterial, oncology/hematology, cardiovascular, metabolic/endocrine, immune and vaccines, musculoskeletal, respiratory, reproduction/genitor-urinary, and gastrointenstinal (Caciotti and Shew 2006). The U.S. leads the world in biopharmaceutical development with about 2900 clinically pre-registered compounds in 2005 (PhRMA 2007). The European Union had about 1300 such compounds and Japan had about 600 compounds in 2005 (PhRMA 2007). Over the past few years, the US' lead over the rest of the world in compound development has been growing (PhRMA 2007, see Fig. 14.2).

In 2006, the sales of pharmaceutical products in North America totaled $274 billion, growing by 8.3% from 2005.[3] Retail pharmaceutical sales totaled $197.3

---

[3] Agovina, Teresa. "Global Pharmaceutical Sales Up 7 Pct." Associated Press. 2007 Mar 20 <http://www.forbes.com/feeds/ap/2007/03/20/ap3535773.html>

Fig. 14.1 The pharmaceutical
R&D process
Source: PhRMA (2007)

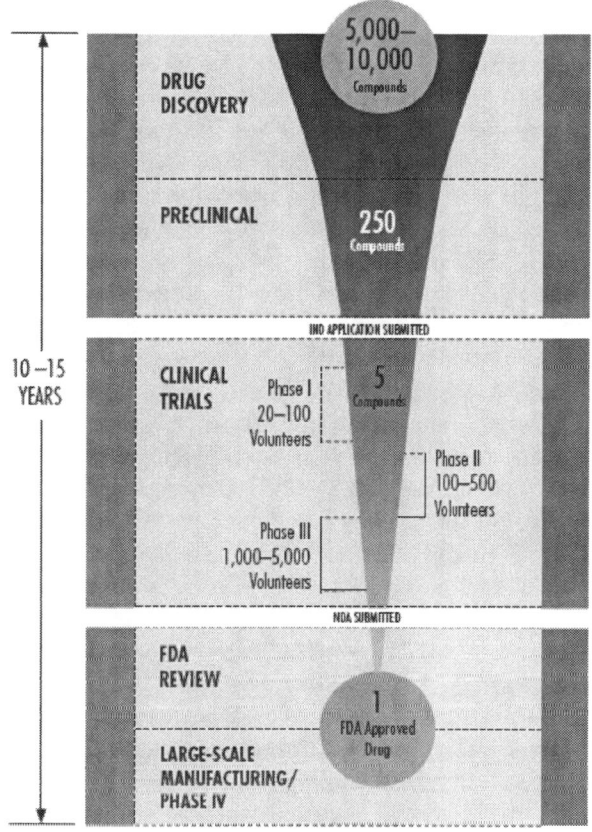

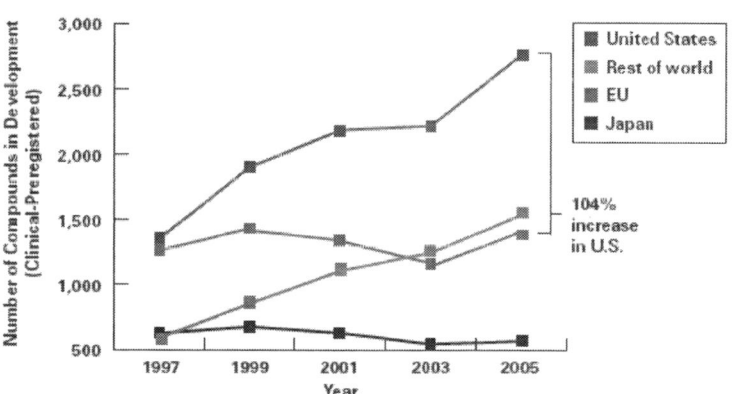

Fig. 14.2 Pharmaceutical drug development outputs of US, EU, Japan and rest of the world
Source: PhRMA (2007)

billion in the U.S. and Canada during the 12 months prior to March 2006. About 40% of the market growth in 2005 was fueled by new products. There were 94 Blockbuster drugs (drugs each with annual worldwide sales of $1 billion and above) with Lipitor, the largest brand, having 2005 sales of $12.9 billion worldwide (IMS Health 2006). The 2006 R&D expenditures by North American companies were $55.2 billion or 19.4% of sales (PhRMA 2007).[4] By comparison, the marketing expenditures in 2006 by North American companies were $27.3 billion or about 10% of sales. Of the total marketing spending in 2006, $23.1 billion were spent on professional physician marketing efforts (samples, detailing and journal advertising), and $4.2 billion in direct-to-consumer (DTC) advertising (IMS Health 2006). In 2001, approximately 185 prescriptions were consumed for every 1,000 people. By 2005, however, that figure rose to nearly 245 for every 1,000 people.[5]

The pharmaceutical industry is growing rapidly in the rest of the world. In Europe, healthcare expenditures averaged around 8% of GDP in 2006.[6] Japan is a huge market with $60 billion in sales in 2005.[7] The rest of Asia, dominated by China and India, is a major contributor to the surge in global growth ($4.5 billion in sales in 2005).[8] Latin America is also a growing regional market ($5.7 billion in sales in 2005).[9] Data, however, are not as freely and completely available in Asia and Latin America as they are for North America and Western Europe, so decision models based on these data are not as common as they are for North America and Western Europe.

There are two types of pharmaceuticals: traditional pharmaceuticals and biopharmaceuticals. Traditional pharmaceutical drugs are small chemical molecules that target or treat the symptoms of a disease or illness. Biopharmaceuticals are large biological molecules or proteins that target the underlying mechanisms and pathways of a medical problem. Biopharmaceuticals are typically made through biotechnology. Biotechnology in the medical context refers to technology that uses biological systems, living organisms, or any of their derivatives to make or modify any products or processes for medicinal purposes.

---

[4] Pharmaceutical Industry Profile 2007. Pharmaceutical Research and Manufacturers of America. 2007 <http://www.phrma.org/files/Profile%202007.pdf>
[5] *White Book - U.S. Healthcare: A Mess Central Planning in Capitalism's Backyard*; May2005, pp. 9-14, 6p <Business Source Complete> http://search.ebscohost.com.ezproxy.tamu.edu:2048/login.aspx?direct = true&db = bth&AN = 18535978&site = bsi-live
[6] Economic Intelligence Unit. "Regional and Country Data." 3/27/2006 <Business Source Complete> http://search.ebscohost.com.ezproxy.tamu.edu:2048/login.aspx?direct = true&db = bth&AN = 20396424&site = bsi-live
[7] http://www.jpma.or.jp/english/library/index.html, Pharmaceutical Industry Profile 2007. Pharmaceutical Research and Manufacturers of America. 2007 <http://www.phrma.org/files/Profile%202007.pdf>
[8] Pharmaceutical Industry Profile 2007. Pharmaceutical Research and Manufacturers of America. 2007 <http://www.phrma.org/files/Profile%202007.pdf>
[9] Pharmaceutical Industry Profile 2007. Pharmaceutical Research and Manufacturers of America. 2007 <http://www.phrma.org/files/Profile%202007.pdf>

The traditional pharmaceutical industry has four major tiers: the super heavyweights (annual revenues of $21 billion and above), the heavyweights (revenues of $11–20 billion), middleweights (revenues of $8–10 billion), and lightweights (revenues of $7 billion and below) (Agarwal et al. 2001). The superheavyweight tier is dominated by big players like Pfizer ($45 billion revenues), GlaxoSmithKline (GSK), Sanofi-Aventis, Johnson & Johnson (J&J), and Merck (Trombetta 2007). In the biopharmaceutical industry, the major players, also known as the big biotechs, are Amgen, Genentech and Biogen.

Among traditional pharmaceutical companies, Pfizer leads the pack in R&D spending, followed by GSK and J&J. Among the biotech companies, Amgen spends the most in R&D. In general, biotechs spend more on R&D as a percentage of sales than do traditional pharmaceutical companies.

The gross margins for biotechs are also higher than those for traditional pharmaceutical companies. In 2006, Biogen had the highest gross margin (89%) among all biotech companies, while Pfizer had the highest gross margin (86%) among all traditional pharmaceutical companies (Trombetta 2007). In 2006, the average percentage earnings before interest, taxes, depreciation and amortization (EBITDA) attributable to intangible assets such as innovation, brands, and human capital for pharmaceutical companies was about 85 percent. Sanofi-Aventis, Forest, GSK, and J&J rank among the highest on this very important metric.

14.3 Strategic Marketing Decisions and Types of Models

The key strategic marketing decisions in this industry can be classified into three groups: (1) R&D, new product development (NPD), and product management strategy, (2) market entry and growth strategy, and (3) defensive or reaction strategy. Models on R&D and new product development strategy include those on the cost of R&D and returns to R&D spending. Product management strategy models range from product selection to product portfolio models. Market entry and growth strategy models include those on the order and timing of entry, on forecasting, and on new product introduction. Models on defensive strategy comprise competitor reaction or incumbent response models. A framework containing these decisions appears in Fig. 14.3.

A summary of the key studies reviewed in this chapter appears in Table 14.1. This summary organized by the three groups of decisions, includes the model type, data, key insights or contributions and key limitations.

We discuss the strategic marketing decision models in the next three sections. We describe the models used in representative studies, summarize the findings from these studies, and delineate the strengths and weaknesses of the models. Models that capture strategic marketing decisions include those at the therapeutic category level as well as at the brand level. Category level models are

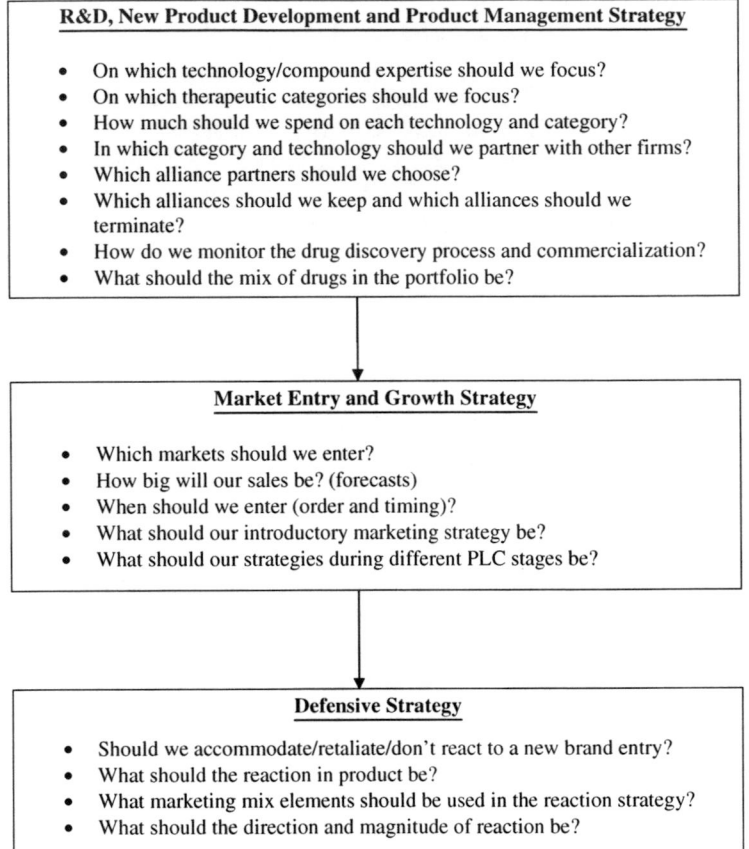

Fig. 14.3 Strategic marketing decision framework in the pharmaceutical industry

typically used to capture product category effects such as diffusion while brand level models are used to examine brand strategy and understand competitor effects. Most models are developed at the brand or category or firm level and rarely at the industry level.

In this chapter, we do not discuss tactical marketing decisions such as those on individual elements in the marketing mix because such a discussion is outside the scope of the paper. Such tactical decision models, nevertheless, are relevant in the pharmaceutical industry and include marketing mix response models (e.g., Rangaswamy and Krishnamurthi 1991), models of returns to marketing expenditures (Dekimpe and Hanssens 1999), sales force structuring and territory models (Mantrala et al. 1994; Rangaswamy et al. 1990), detailing and marketing communication effects models (e.g., Chintagunta and Desiraju 2005; Manchanda and Chintagunta 2004; Manchanda and Honka 2005; Manchanda et al. 2004; Mizik and Jacobsen 2004; Narayanan et al. 2004,

Table 14.1 Summary of selected strategic marketing decision models in the pharmaceutical industry

Paper	Model type	Data	Key findings/contribution	Key limitations
R&D, New Product Development, and Product Management Strategy				
Grabowski et al. (2002)	CAPM and option pricing model	118 new drugs into market during 1990–94	Distribution of returns to R&D highly skewed. Estimated return is 11.5%. R&D costs increased significantly compared to 19980 values.	Limited generalizability of findings due the sample being from a short time window. Does not include all potential drivers of returns.
DiMasi et al. (2003)	Weighted multistage probabilistic model	68 drugs from 10 companies	The development cost of a new drug is about $802 million.	Non-random sample of companies, potential overrepresentation of self-originated new chemical entities.
Sorescu et al. (2003)	Abnormal financial returns model	255 innovations from 66 firms during 1991–2000 from NDA pipeline	Dominant pharmaceutical firms introduce more radical innovations. Financial value of radical innovation increases significantly with marketing and technology support.	Non-dominant firms may not have resources to spend simultaneously on multiple innovative ideas.
Ding and Eliashberg (2002)	Probabilistic normative model	Seven NPD pipeline data	Leading firms underspend on new drug development throughout the clinical trials relative to the normative levels implied by their model. Firms need different NPD pipelines for different new drug development problems and that the shapes of the pipelines are also quite distinctive for different cases.	Assumes same probability of success and cost for all approaches at all stages; different approaches are probabilistically independent; products are identical.
Grewal et al. (2006)	Regression model	308 firms in the Pharmaprojects database	Both early and late stage products-dominated portfolios are significantly positively	Omission of R&D intensity, advertising expenditures and growth rate. Drawbacks of cross-sectional analysis.

Table 14.1 (continued)

Paper	Model type	Data	Key findings/contribution	Key limitations
			associated with their financial values.	
Danzon et al. (2005)	Logistic model of R&D productivity	Alliance data for 900 firms during 1988–2000	A new product developed through an alliance has a greater probability of success, at least during the Phase II and Phase III trials, particularly, if the license is a large firm.	Left and right censored data. Alliance formation and experience may be causally related.
Kalaignanam et al. (2007)	Proportional hazard model with heterogeneity	401 NPAs from 24 firms during 1990–2005	NPA terminations are influenced by the composition of the firm's product portfolio and NPA portfolio.	Non-normative model. Incumbent's internal R&D efforts in other markets not considered.
Market Entry and Growth Strategy				
Lilien et al. (1981)	Repeat purchase diffusion model	IMS data on two ethical drugs	A reliable model for optimal marketing policies can be developed with limited past data.	Omission of non-detailing marketing instruments. Subjective estimation of market size.
Rao and Yamada (1988)	Repeat purchase forecasting diffusion model	19 drugs from IMS database	The forecasting model that improves upon the previous models. Detailing effectiveness is greater for more innovative drugs. Competitive detailing is most effective for frequently prescribed drugs.	Subjective estimation of market potential. Validation inconclusive.
Gaitgnon et al. (1990)	Regression model	68 brands of new drugs from 39 firms during 1978–1982	Resources drive the level of launch communication efforts. Market growth rate moderates the effectiveness of detailing of market share.	No dynamics of competition or longitudinal data. Interaction of firm capabilities with environment not considered.

Table 14.1 (continued)

Paper	Model type	Data	Key findings/contribution	Key limitations
Hahn et al. (1994)	Multisegment repeat purchase diffusion model	IMS data on 21 drugs from 7 categories during 1981–1984	The effectiveness of marketing mix on trial is related primarily to quality and market growth, whereas that of word-of-mouth is associated with product class characteristics and market competitiveness.	Does not capture competitor diffusion effects.
Shankar et al. (1998)	Trial, repeat generalized Bass model	13 brands from two categories from IMS database	Innovative late movers can enjoy advantage through greater market potential, higher repeat rate, and faster growth than the pioneer. They can also slow the growth and marketing effectiveness of the pioneer.	Only two product categories analyzed.
Shankar et al. (1999)	Dynamic sales response model	IMS data on 29 brands from six categories	Growth state entrants reach asymptotic sales faster than pioneers or mature stage entrants. Buyers are more responsive to pioneer's marketing spending. Mature stage entrants are most disadvantaged.	The categories covered did not have failed brands.
Shankar (1999)	Rational expectations simultaneous equation model	23 new brands in six markets	New product introduction spending is significantly influenced by incumbent reaction.	Product categories did not exhibit market exits.
Fischer et al. (2005)	Relative market share model	73 brands in two categories from eight European markets	Late movers can reduce order of entry penalty by entering large countries in a sequential manner.	US market not included in the data.

Table 14.1 (continued)

Paper	Model type	Data	Key findings/contribution	Key limitations
Ding and Eliashberg (2007)	Dynamic (Markovian transition probability) competitive model	Proton pump inhibitors and Statins	Both physician and patient influences on new prescriptions are significant.	DTC advertising omitted. Not an individual model. No pre-launch forecasting.
Shankar (2008)	Market response model	40 brands from eight markets	Marketing expenditures are moderated by the stage in the PLC. Dominant brands shift allocation to sales force over the PLC.	R&D decision not considered.
Defensive Strategy				
Gatignon et al. (1989)	Regression model	Two new entries in the OTC-gyn. category	Competitors retaliate (accommodate) with their most (least) effective marketing weapons.	Incumbent elasticities were not significantly altered by the new entrant. Uncertainty, firm's perceptions not included in analysis.
Shankar (1997)	New empirical industrial organization model	A large drug product category	Pioneers who adopt a follower (leader) role in a marketing mix variable in a static (growing) market and whose elasticity is decreased (increased) should accommodate (retaliate) against a new entry. Pioneers should accommodate (retaliate) with its competitively low (high) elastic variable.	Repositioning reactions not considered. Decoupled response function.
Shankar (1999)	Relative spending model	59 incumbent responses to entries in six categories	Higher spending by a new brand and multimarket contact result in weaker incumbent response	Product and pricing reactions not studied.

2005), promotion effect models (Gönül and Srinivasan 2001; Montgomery and Silk 1972; Neslin 2001), and DTC advertising effect models (Berndt 2006; Wosinska 2005). Some of these models are covered in other chapters in this Handbook. We also do not address issues uniquely relevant to the contexts of countries other than the U.S. and some western European countries as they are beyond the scope of this chapter.

14.4 R&D, New Product Development, and Product Management Strategy Models

The issues of R&D, new product development (NPD) and product management are important in the pharmaceutical industry. Models in this regard include those relating to product innovation (e.g., DiMasi et al. 2003; Sorescu et al. 2003), R&D project selection, structuring new product pipeline (e.g., Ding and Eliashberg 2002; Grabowski and Vernon 1990; Lee 2003), product portfolio (e.g., Grewal et al. 2006), and new product development (NPD) alliance (e.g., Danzon et al. 2005; Kalaignanam et al. 2007).

The R&D process starts with drug discovery as outlined in Fig. 14.1. An example of an organizational structure for drug discovery is shown in Fig. 14.4. At the second level of hierarchy is the type of technology or compounds used in R&D (e.g., small molecules or proteins or antibodies). At the third level are the therapeutic categories (e.g., cardiovascular, nervous system, and oncology). Within each therapeutic category, the R&D efforts are organized by specific diseases (e.g., hypertension under the cardiovascular therapeutic category) for which a cure is targeted by the firm.

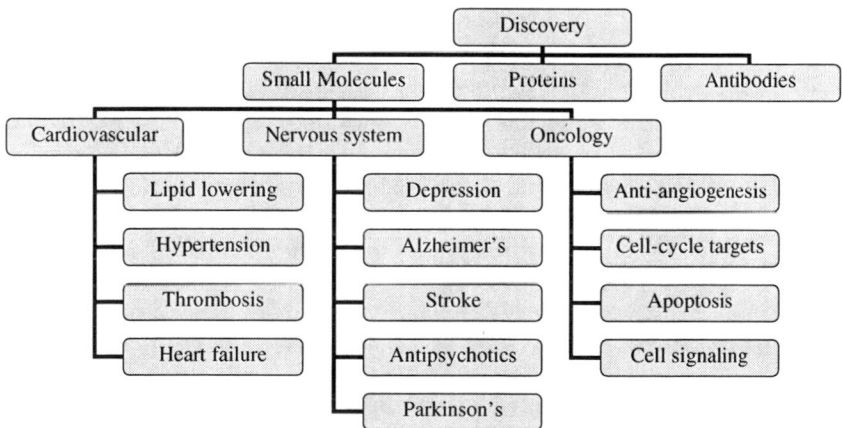

Fig. 14.4 Drug discovery structure in a sample organization
Source: Agarwal et al. (2001)

DiMasi et al. (2003) develop a simple weighted multistage probabilistic model to estimate the average pre-approval cost of a drug based on the R&D costs of 68 randomly selected new drugs from 10 pharmaceutical firms. They conclude that the average pre-approval cost of a drug is $802 million (2000 dollars), including out-of-pocket costs of about $403 million. This study was the first to come up with a rigorous estimate of the pre-approval cost of a new drug. This estimate, however, has been challenged by several authors. One study by Bain & company concludes that if the cost of failed prospective drugs are factored, the actual cost of discovering, developing and launching a new drug is about $1.7 billion and that this cost has risen by 55% during 1995–2000 (Singh and Henske 2003).

Grabowski et al. (2002) use a standard capital asset pricing model (CAPM) to study the returns to R&D spending for drugs introduced in the 1990s. They conclude that the returns are highly skewed with a mean industry internal rate of return of 11.5%, modestly above the cost of capital. They also find that the R&D costs, number of new drugs, sales and contribution margins in 1990s were significantly higher than those in the 1980s. While this is one of the first studies to propose a rate of return on R&D efforts, it does not address the impact of product innovation on firm or shareholder value. Nor does it examine potential differences in returns between incremental and radical innovations.

Sorescu et al. (2003) estimate the following model of financial returns to radical innovations by pharmaceutical companies.

$$NPV_{ikt} = \beta_0 + \beta_1 DOM_{it} + \beta_2 PSUP_{it} + \beta_3 PSC_{it} + \beta_4 RI_{kt} + \beta_5 MB_{kt}$$
$$+ \beta_6 LIC_{kt} + \beta_7 WACC_{it} + \beta_8 CNTRY_i + \beta_9 NRI_{it} + \gamma \mathbf{YEAR}$$
$$+ \lambda \mathbf{CAT} + \varsigma_i + \eta_{it} \tag{14.1}$$

where NPV_{ikt} is net present value, DOM_{it} is dominance (a function of sales, assets, and profits), $PSUP_{it}$ is product support (a function of sales force, sales calls, detailing dollars, number of new products, and advertising expenditures), PSC_{it} is product scope (entropy × number of new products), RI_{kt} is a dummy variable that takes the value 1 if the product is a radical innovation, MB_{kt} is a dummy variable that takes the value 1 if the product is a market breakthrough, LIC_{kt} is a dummy variable that takes the value 1 if the product was invented by the firm that introduced it, $WACC_{it}$ is the cost of capital, CNTRY is a dummy variable that takes the value 1 if the firm introducing the drug is head-quartered in the US, NRI_{it} is the number of breakthrough innovations, **YEAR** is a matrix of dummies for the year in which the innovation was introduced, **CAT** is a matrix of dummies for the therapeutic class to which the drug belongs, ς_i is the unobserved firm-specific effect, and i, k, and t represent firm, therapeutic category, and time, respectively.

They find that dominant firms introduce more radical innovations even after accounting for the source of the innovation (in-house versus acquired) and that they also introduce more market breakthroughs and technological break-throughs. Their results show that the financial value of a radical innovation significantly increases with greater product marketing and technology support and product scope and that it is significantly greater than the financial value of market breakthroughs or technological breakthroughs, but there is no significant difference between the values of market breakthroughs and technological breakthroughs.

The model and results of Sorescu et al. (2003) provide important insights on financial returns of radical innovations, but they do not address the risks associated with such innovations as well as incremental innovations. Firms are interested in such issues as they decide on the number and mix of products in their NPD pipeline.

Ding and Eliashberg (2002) propose the following normative model for deciding the number of new drugs to have on the market.

$$E[\pi] = \sum_{o=1}^{O} q_o \pi_o$$

$$\text{where } \pi_o = \sum_{t=1}^{T} \frac{s(t) \times (1 - \alpha) \times C}{(1 + \beta)^t}$$

$$\text{where } s(t) = MSize(t) \times [1 - CTC(t - 1)]$$

$$\times \frac{t_r}{n(t)} + MSize(t) \times CT(t - 1) \times r_r \qquad (14.2)$$

where $E[\pi]$ is expected gross profit, π_o is gross profit under scenario o, O is the total number of possible competitive scenarios, q_o is the probability of having a particular competitive scenario o, T is the product life, $s(t)$ are revenues from the drug during period t, α is the tax rate, C is the contribution rate, β is the cost of capital, $MSize(t)$ is the market size (\$) during period t, $CTC(t$-$1)$ is the cumulative proportion of the market that has tried any new drugs up to period t-1, $CT(t$-$1)$ is the cumulative proportion of the market that has tried the drug of interest up to period t-1, t_r is the probability of trying the new drugs for the first time in one period, r_r is the probability of getting a repeat prescription for the same drug after trial, and $n(t)$ is the number of new drugs available during period t.

They estimate their model using data from several pharmaceutical product portfolios. Their results show that leading firms underspend on new drug development throughout the clinical trials relative to the normative levels implied by the model. They also suggest that firms need different NPD pipelines for different new drug development problems and that the shapes of the pipelines are also quite distinctive for different cases.

Ding and Eliashberg (2002) offer a valuable decision model for deciding the size of the product portfolio but do not address the composition of the portfolio. It is important for firms to also know the optimal composition of its product portfolio and its relationship with the financial value of the portfolio.

Grewal et al. (2006) relate the choice products in the product portfolio based on the stage of new product development to the financial value of the portfolio. Their descriptive model is given by:

$$TQ_f = \alpha_0 + \alpha_1 INC + \alpha_2 CR + \alpha_3 DE + \sum_{s=1}^{4} \alpha_{4s} CMP_s$$

$$+ \sum_{s=1}^{4} \alpha_{5s} MP_s + \sum_{s=1}^{4} \alpha_{6s} NG_s + \sum_{s=1}^{4} \alpha_{7s} NI_s$$

$$+ \sum_{s=1}^{4} \alpha_{8s} CCV_s + \varepsilon_f \tag{14.3}$$

where TQ, INC, CR, DE, CMP, MP, NG, NI, and CCV are Tobin's Q, net income, current ratio, debt-to-equity ratio, competitor's new product portfolio market potential, the firm's new product portfolio market potential, number of therapeutic areas, number of diseases, and cross-category variance, respectively. α_{0-8} are parameters, ϵ is a disturbance term, f is firm, and s is the stage of development. They estimate this model with data from the product portfolios of 308 firms in the *PharmaProjects* database.

They find empirical support for both early and late stage products-dominated portfolios to be significantly and positively associated with their financial values. Their model, however, does not include potentially relevant variables such as R&D intensity, advertising expenditures and growth rate due non-availability of data. Furthermore, cross-sectional analysis that they use may not be able to fully capture the differences in effects as products move from one stage to the next stage over time.

The above studies have primarily examined internal R&D and NPD situations. Many pharmaceutical companies undertake NPD through alliances with smaller, younger firms, particularly, biotechnology firms. The formation, management, and termination of NPD alliances (NPA) with partner firms are key decisions for many executives.

Danzon et al. (2005) develop a logistic model of R&D productivity for new products developed internally and through alliances. They estimate it using data from 908 firms. They find that a new product developed through an alliance has a higher probability of success, at least during the Phase II and Phase III trials, particularly, if the licensee is a large firm. Their study is perhaps the first to rigorously examine the probability of success through NPAs and offer fresh insights on the issue. Their data, however, are both left- and right-censored and their model may not account for the potential causal relationship between alliance formation and firm experience. Furthermore, it does not address the issue of termination of NPAs—an important strategic decision issue for pharmaceutical executives.

Kalaignanam et al. (2007) develop a model of NPA termination using the Cox's proportional hazard specification that accounts for the unobserved heterogeneity of firms with multiple NPAs (through gamma distributed frailty effects) and for competing risks and ties among NPA duration times (using Efron approximation). In their model, the hazard of NPA termination for NPA i involving incumbent j and partner k conditional on a shared frailty effect v_j can be written as:

$$h(t|X_{ijk}, v_j) = v_j h_o(t) \exp(x_{ijk}\beta) \tag{14.4}$$

where $h_o(t)$ is the baseline hazard at time t, X_{ijk} is a vector of covariates, β is a parameter vector, and the vs are independent and identically distributed gamma variates with density

$$g(v) = \frac{v^{\theta/\theta-1} \exp(-v/\theta)}{\Gamma(1/\theta)\theta^{1/\theta}} \tag{14.5}$$

where θ represents the heterogeneity among firms with higher values of θ representing greater unobserved heterogeneity among sub-groups of firms and $\theta = 0$ implying no unobserved heterogeneity.

They estimate their model using data from 401 NPAs of 24 pharmaceutical firms during the period 1990–2005.

Their results suggest that NPA terminations are influenced by the composition of the firm's product portfolio and NPA portfolio. Their results relating to firm portfolio characteristics suggest that while firms with greater product category focus have lower hazards of NPA termination, firms with greater technology focus have higher hazards of NPA termination. In addition, they find that the hazard of NPA termination is lower for firms with aging portfolios. Their findings relating to product-market factors suggest that in highly competitive product-markets, firms tend to continue their NPAs. Their results relating to partner-specific factors suggest that alliance partner value has a U-shaped effect on the hazard of NPA termination such that the hazard of NPA termination is lowest at moderate levels of alliance partner value.

The model and results of Kalaignanam et al. (2007) provide important results on the factors associated with NPA termination, enabling pharmaceutical managers to better understand and manage alliances. They, however, do not offer a normative model and do not address NPAs in conjunction with internal NPD efforts.

Taken together, research work in this aspect of the pharmaceutical industry offers some useful generalizations. The cost of drug development and commercialization is high ($800 million–$1.7 billion), but the returns to innovation are high as well (average of 11.5%), particularly for radical innovations. Product portfolios with early and late-stage development drugs are associated with high firm values. New products developed through alliances reduce the costs of development and are associated with a higher probability of success. Some of the NPAs, however, are terminated due to several factors which include the composition and age of firms' product portfolios and NPA portfolios, market competitiveness, and partner alliance value.

Existing research and emerging managerial challenges highlight interesting opportunities for future research. First, we need more research on the cost and pay-offs to both incremental and radical innovations. The estimates we have are based on data belonging to the 1990s. Second, we need more models on resource allocation across therapeutic categories and brands. We need to better understand the drivers of allocation and the sensitivity of optimal allocation to these drivers. Third, some of the results are apparently inconsistent. Large firms typically underspend during different stages of clinical trials (Ding and Eliashberg 2002) but also appear to produce many radical innovations that are typically associated with high levels of spending (Sorescu et al. 2003). More research is needed to reconcile these apparently contradictory results. Fourth, although prior research suggests that alliances are a more effective route to new product development, it also shows that many NPAs are terminated. Future research could focus on the optimal combination of internal and alliance-driven NPD strategies. Fifth, while models exist for returns to product innovation, we need more models to help us better understand the risks associated with innovation in the pharmaceutical industry. Finally, although there are a number of models for this and other strategic decision issues for the pharmaceutical industry, there is a dearth of useful decision support systems (DSS) in this industry. A well-designed DSS is an important managerial tool that a good model should help create for successful implementation in the industry (Wierenga et al. 1999).

14.5 Market Entry and Growth Strategy Models

Market entry strategy involves decisions on the following questions: Which markets should a brand enter and what growth strategy should it follow? When should a brand enter a particular market or country (order and timing of entry) and with what introduction strategy and degree of innovativeness? What is the predicted or forecasted sales for a new brand? In the international context, which countries should a new product or brand enter? How (in what order and with what marketing support) does or should the brand enter multiple countries?

Entry strategy decisions in the pharmaceutical industry have some distinctive characteristics. First, brands need to obtain approval from the regulatory authority in each market before being able to launch it in that market. The approval process is different in different countries. Some countries will consider a brand's prior approval in another country to be a favorable factor in the approval of that brand in those countries. Second, some countries or markets have governmental price control regulations that a brand may have to satisfy to compete in the market. Third, different countries or markets may have different rules for prescription and dispensation of drugs. For example, in most developed countries, an ethical drug cannot be obtained from pharmacies without a physician prescription. In some developing countries, however, the same drug may be purchased from pharmacies without a prescription.

Such distinctive features of the pharmaceutical industry across international markets have important implications for entry strategy. Firms will have to carefully plan their international entry strategy over the long-term and need to map out the scope and sequence of entry across international markets before it enters the first few markets. They also have to take into account the differences in the adoption processes across countries before formulating their entry strategies.

Among sales forecasting models of new drugs, only a few models capture both the first and repeat purchases of a new brand of drug in its diffusion process. Lilien et al. (1981) propose a repeat purchase diffusion model (the LRK model) that uses Bayesian estimation with priors to incorporate the effect of marketing variables such as detailing and word-of-mouth effects. The Bayesian procedure, developed on other, similar products, to permit parameter estimates earlier in the life of the product, differs from judgmental methods in that it: (1) specifically and systematically accounts for information available in similar product areas; (2) allows for updating of parameter estimates for purposes of forecasting and control, gradually improving the parameter estimates as new data are collected; and (3) allows for calculation and dynamic updating of optimal marketing decisions at a point in a product's life when sufficient historical data are not available to make clear inferences.

The LRK model can be written out as:

$$C_2(t+1) = C_2(t) + \lambda_1(d(t))C_1(t) + \lambda_2(\Delta C_2(t))C_1(t) - \lambda_3(\bar{d}(t))C_2(t) \quad (14.6)$$

where $C_1(t)$ is the number of doctors not prescribing at time t, $C_2(t)$ is the number of doctors prescribing at t, $\bar{d}(t)$ is competitor detailing, $d(t)$ is own detailing, $\lambda_1(d(t))$ is own detailing effectiveness, $\lambda_2(\Delta C_2(t))$ is word of mouth impact, and $\lambda_3(d(t))$ is competitive detailing effect.

The LRK model does a good job of forecasting sales when limited past data are available. The model, however, does not include marketing variables other than detailing and its estimation of market potential for the brand is subjective.

Rao and Yamada (1988) develop a methodology for forecasting the sales of an ethical drug based on the LRK model. Their model is a function of marketing efforts and forecasts sales before any sales data are available. The model conceptualizes the drug adoption process as a repeat purchase diffusion model in which sales are expressed as a function of a drug's own competitive marketing efforts and word of mouth. Rao and Yamada test the model on data from 19 drugs prescribed by three types of physicians, including data on a number of attributes (e.g., effectiveness, range of ailments for which appropriate). They find that the model results are intuitive, but inconclusive and that the identification of the market potential parameter is somewhat problematic.

Hahn et al. (1994) develop a four segment repeat purchase diffusion model (the HPLZ model) that addresses some limitations of the LRK and the Rao and Yamada models. The HPLZ model includes marketing mix effects and assumes a constant repeat purchase rate. Their full model is given by:

$$s_{2t} = [b_0 + b_1 ln(x_{2t}/(x_{1t} + x_{2t})) + b_2(s_{2(t-1)}/m)][m - q_{t-1}] + \rho q_{t-1} + \varepsilon_t \quad (14.7)$$

where s is sales normalized by the growth rate, x is the marketing effort, q is the growth rate-normalized cumulative sales, m is market potential, ρ is repeat rate, b_0-b_2 are parameters, ϵ is an error term, t is time, 2 is the competing drug, and 1 is the focal new drug. They estimate this model on 21 new drugs from seven pharmaceutical categories launched during 1981–1984.

They find that the effectiveness of marketing mix on trial is related primarily to quality and market growth, whereas that of word-of-mouth is associated with product class characteristics and market competitiveness.

While the HPLZ predicts sales better than the previous models and offers valuable insights into the relationship of sales with marketing and other variables, it does not cover competitor diffusion effects that could be important in predicting a new drug's sales. Furthermore, the model's focus is on sales forecasting and not on decisions relating to order and timing of entry, which are important for pharmaceutical companies.

To primarily address the effects of order of entry and innovativeness on a brand's sales, Shankar et al. (1998) extend Hahn et al. (1994) by developing a brand level repeat purchase diffusion model with competitor diffusion effects. Their model is given by:

$$S_{it} = T_{it} + \rho_i CT_{it} \quad (14.8)$$

where S_{it} is the sales of brand i at time t, T_{it} is trials of brand i at time t, ρ_i is the repeat purchase rate of brand i, and CT_{it} = cumulative trials of brand i at the beginning of time t. The trials follow a generalized Bass model and are a function of innovative and non-innovative competitor cumulative sales and total marketing expenditures of the various brands. The final sales model can be written out as:

$$S_{it} = (a_i + b_i CT_{it} + c_{iI} CS_{iIt} + c_{iN} CS_{iNt})\{M_i - CT_{it}\} TM_{it}^{\beta_{i0} + \beta_{iI} CS_{iIt} + \beta_{iN} CS_{iNt}}$$
$$+ \rho_i CT_{it} + \varepsilon_{it} \quad (14.9)$$

where CS is cumulative competitor sales, TM is the total marketing expenditures, I is innovative competitor, N is non-innovative competitor, M is market potential, c is the coefficient of competitor influence, ϵ is an error term, and the other terms are as defined earlier.

They estimate the model using data on 13 brands from two ethical drug categories. Their results show that innovative late entrant brands can surmount pioneering advantage by enjoying a higher market potential and a higher repeat rate than the pioneer or non-innovative late movers, growing faster than the pioneer, slowing the growth of the pioneer, and reducing the pioneer's marketing mix effectiveness.

The Shankar et al. (1998) model and their results provide deep insights into the order and timing of market entry and its trade-offs with innovativeness. Their model assumes that physician is the decision maker for adoption of a brand by a patient. There is a growing role for patients to influence drug prescription which is facilitated by the DTC advertising efforts of firms.

Ding and Eliashberg (2007) extend the HPLZ and Shankar et al. (1998) models by incorporating the dual influences of physicians and patients on adoptions. Their dynamic model uses transition probability matrices and is applicable for a general situation involving multiple new drugs. Their model is given by:

$$MS_t^k = \frac{P_t^k}{\sum_{d=1}^{K} P_t^d} \tag{14.10}$$

where MS is the market share, P is the unconditional prescription probability of a drug, K is the total number of drugs in the market, k is new drug k, and t is time. P is a function of the influences of both the physician and the patient and uses a parameter that represents the patient's influence. Furthermore, using transition probability matrices, the authors express P as the sum of different conditional probabilities depending on the transition states. They test their hypotheses using data from two drug categories, proton pump indicators and statins.

Their results show that both the influences of the physicians and patients on a new drug's sales are significant, so models of new drug forecasting should include the dyadic decision-making aspect. Their model, however, does not include DTC advertising, which is the primary source of patient influence. It also does not analyze the influence at the patient level and is not meant for pre-launch forecasting.

While all the previously discussed models capture the effects of innovativeness, order and timing of entry, and marketing efforts on the sales of a new drug, they do not explicitly address the issue of a brand's introduction strategy. Gatignon et al. (1990) specify a set of hypotheses about brand introduction strategies and identify the conditions under which a given marketing mix (excluding price) is more effective than another for continuous product innovations. They use the following market share regression model.

$$m_{ij} = \beta_{0i} + \beta_1 P_{ij} + \beta_{2ij} d_{ij} + \beta_3 C_{ij} + \beta_4 MF_{ij} + \beta_5 FS_{ij} + u_{it} \tag{14.11}$$

where m is market share of the brand size (of therapeutic category) at time of entry j in product class i, m is market share, P is relative product quality, d is detailing minutes share, C is concentration ratio, MF is the number of brands (experience) in product class, FS is sales in dollars of firm introducing the brand, β is the parameter vector, and u is a disturbance term. They also express detailing and the parameter associated with it as functions of exogenous variables such as market growth rate, market size. They estimate the model on cross-sectional data from 68 new drugs from 39 firms that were introduced during 1978–1982.

They find that the amount of communication efforts used to introduce a brand depends on the availability of financial resources. Their empirical analysis supports the importance of market growth and superior quality of the new product relative to existing products. It also shows that the competitive structure of the market is extremely important, supporting the need for competitive analysis.

Their model and results were the first to shed light into an important phenomenon, but they did not analyze longitudinal data that are important in capturing the dynamic effects of launch strategies. They also do not capture the roles of order and stage of brand entry on sales into the launch strategy of a brand.

Shankar et al. (1999) examine the effect of the stage of the product life cycle in which a brand enters on its sales through brand growth and market response, after controlling for the effects of order-of-entry and time-in-market. Their model is given by:

$$\ell n S_{it} = \alpha_1 + \sum_{k=2}^{N} \alpha_k I_k + \theta \ell n O_i - \{\phi_P + \phi_G G_i + \phi_M M_i\}/T_{it}$$
$$+ \{\psi_P + \psi_G G_i + \psi_M M_i\} CS_{it} + \{\beta_P + \beta_G G_i + \beta_M M_i\} \ell n Q_{it}$$
$$+ \{\gamma_P + \gamma_G G_i + \gamma_M M_i\} \ell n M K_{it} + \delta \ell n\, CM_{it} + \varepsilon_{it} \qquad (14.12)$$

where $\ell n\, S_{it}$ is the log sales of brand i at time t, α_k is a category-specific parameter for category k, I_k is a dummy variable for category k (1 if category is k, 0 otherwise), θ is the order of entry parameter, $\ell n\, O_i$ is the log of order of entry of brand i, ϕ is the brand growth parameter, T_{it} is time-in-market for brand i *until* time t, ψ is the competitor diffusion parameter, CS_{it} is cumulative sales of the competitor(s) for brand i until time t, β is the perceived product quality parameter, $\ell n\, Q_{it}$ is the log of perceived product quality of brand i at time t, γ is the marketing spending parameter, $\ell n\, MK_{it}$ is the log of marketing mix expenditures of brand i, δ is cross elasticity of competitors' marketing mix, $\ell n\, CM_{it}$ is the log of total marketing mix expenditures of competitors, G_i and M_i are dummy variables indicating entry of brand i during the growth stage and mature stage, respectively, and ε_{it} is the error term assumed to be distributed normal independent with mean 0 and variance σ_i^2.

Estimating a dynamic brand sales model using 29 brands from six pharmaceutical markets, they report that the brand growth rate follows an inverted V pattern. They find that growth-stage entrants grow faster than pioneers and mature-stage entrants; competitor diffusion hurts the pioneer, has no effect on growth-stage entrants, and helps mature-stage entrants; growth stage entrants enjoy greater response to perceived product quality than pioneers and mature-stage entrants; pioneers enjoy higher advertising and sales force response than growth-stage entrants, which in turn, have higher response than mature-stage entrants. They did not find a direct effect of order of entry or pioneering advantage.

These insights are useful for pharmaceutical firms planning their entry and introduction strategies. Their data, however, did not include failed entries or exits from the market. Moreover, none of the previously discussed models consider the anticipated reactions of incumbents in deciding the launch strategy of a brand.

Shankar (1999) includes anticipated incumbent reactions in his model of the drivers of brand introduction strategy through an integrated framework that includes the determinants of both new product introduction and incumbent response strategies. His joint model focuses on the interrelationship between new product introduction and incumbent response strategies and on the role of multimarket contact in these strategies. His new product introduction model is given by:

$$MV_{ijt} = \alpha_{0j} + \alpha_{1j}L_{ij} + \alpha_{2j}FS_i + \alpha_{3j}PQ_i + \alpha_{4j}ME_i + \alpha_{5j}ALIR_{ijt}$$
$$+ \alpha_{6j}ASIR_{ijt} + \alpha_{7j}MMC_i + \alpha_{8j}MS_i + \alpha_{9j}MG_{it} + \varepsilon_{ijt} \qquad (14.13)$$

where MV_{ijt} is the expenditure of new brand i on marketing mix variable j at time t after launch (t is the number of months following entry, $t \in \{1,2,..,6\}$ for short-term introduction and $t \in \{7,8,..,12\}$ for medium-term introduction), L_{ij} is a dummy variable denoting if entrant i is a leader or follower in marketing mix variable j, FS_i is the size of entrant i in the market of entry, PQ_i is the relative quality of new brand i, ME_i is the market experience of entrant i, $ALIR_{ijt}$ and $ASIR_{ijt}$ are the anticipated reactions or marketing spending in variable j of large and small incumbent firms, respectively, at time t after brand i's entry, MMC_i represents the multimarket contact of brand i with incumbent firms during entry, MS_i is the size of the market at the time of brand i's entry, and MG_{it} is the market growth rate at time t after brand i's entry. $MV_{ijt} \in \{A_{it}, D_{it}\}$ where A_{it} and D_{it} are the advertising and sales force spending, respectively of brand i at time t after the launch. ϵ_{ijt} is an error term assumed to be normal, independent with mean 0, and α_{0j}-α_{9j} are the parameters. His incumbent reaction model is:

$$RM_{kijt} = \beta_{0j} + \beta_{1j}ME_i + \beta_{2j}MV_{ijt} + \beta_{3j}SE_i + \beta_{4j}SE_i^2 + \beta_{5j}PQ_i + \beta_{6j}ID_{ki}$$
$$+ \beta_{7j}IE_{kij} + \beta_{8j}L_{kj} + \beta_{9j}MMC_{ki} + \beta_{10j}MS_i + \beta_{11j}MG_{it} + \mu_{kijt} \qquad (14.14)$$

where RM_{kijt} is incumbent k's ratio of spending in marketing variable j at time periods t after and before the entry of brand i, SE_i is the scale of entry of brand i, ID_{ki} is the brand dominance of incumbent k at the time of entry of brand i, IE_{kij} is the estimated elasticity of incumbent k in variable j after entry of brand i, and the rest of the terms are as defined earlier. μ_{kijt} is an error term assumed to be normal i.i.d. with mean 0, independent of ϵ_{ijt}, and β_{0j}-β_{11j} are parameters associated with the independent variables.

He tests his model using U.S. market data from several prescription drug categories. His findings show that new product introduction strategy is influenced significantly by incumbent reaction strategy and vice versa. His results show that the relationship of a new product's marketing spending to the anticipated incumbent reaction differs across incumbents by size–anticipated reactions from large incumbents lead to low entrant spending while anticipated reactions from small incumbents do not pose a threat to a new brand's spending. He finds that greater market experience helps reduce uncertainty about the effectiveness of marketing variables and contributes to greater entrant spending.

By incorporating anticipated incumbent reactions, Shankar (1999) offers a powerful model of new brand introduction strategy and important results. His data, however, include neither the performances of the brands over time nor the market exits. All the studies discussed thus far do not address decisions involving multiple international markets or countries. Such a context is very often the case for most pharmaceutical companies, which are multinational corporations.

With regard to international market entry decisions, there are two major decision variables: scope (extent of exposure across markets) and speed (how fast) of entry, leading to two possible strategies, namely, sprinkler (fast rollout) and waterfall (steady rollout) strategies. An example of a model of market entry strategy across international markets is a relative market share model with endogenous entry and marketing mix variables (Fischer et al. 2005). This model captures the moderating effects of international market scope and speed of rollout of late mover brands on their market shares relative to the pioneer in the focal country or market. Their full model can be written out as:

$$
\begin{aligned}
\ln RMS_{hijt} =\ & \alpha_0 + \alpha_1/TIM_{hijt} + \alpha_2 \ln OE_{hij} + \alpha_3 \ln CME_{hijt} + \alpha_4 \ln PR_{hijt} \\
& + \alpha_5 \ln Q_{hij} + \alpha_6 \ln CCoME_{hijt} + \alpha_7 \ln CCpME_{hijt} \\
& + \alpha_8 \ln ISCOPE_{hijt} + \alpha_9 \ln ISPEED_{hij} + \alpha_{10} \ln INC_{hijt} \\
& + \alpha_{11} \ln SIZE_{hijt} + \alpha_{12} \ln OE_{hij} *ISCOPE_{hijt} \\
& + \alpha_{13} \ln OE_{hij} *ISPEED_{hij} + \alpha_{14} \ln OE_{hij} *INC_{hijt} \\
& + \alpha_{15} \ln OE_{hij} *SIZE_{hijt} + \alpha_{16} \ln CME_{hijt} *ISCOPE_{hijt} \\
& + \alpha_{17} \ln CME_{hijt} *ISPEED_{hij} + u_{hijt}
\end{aligned}
\tag{14.15}
$$

$$u_{hijt} = \mu_{hij} + \nu_{hijt} + \varepsilon_{hijt}, \nu_{hijt} = \omega_{2hijt} \ln OE_{hij} + \omega_{3hijt} \ln CME_{hijt}, \text{ and}$$

$$\varepsilon_{hijt} = \rho \varepsilon_{hijt-1} + \eta_{hijt}$$

where

RMS_{hijt} = Ratio of market share of the focal brand to share of the pioneer (daily dosages)

TIM_{hijt} = Time-in-market for the focal brand since launch until period t

OE_{hij} = Order of entry of the focal brand

CME_{hijt} = Ratio of cumulative marketing expenditures of the focal brand to the pioneer's

PR_{hijt} = Ratio of price of the focal brand to price of the pioneer

Q_{hij} = Ratio of quality of the focal brand to quality of the pioneer

$CCoME_{hijt}$ = Ratio of cumulative marketing expenditures by firms co-marketing the focal brand to those by firms co-marketing the pioneer's brand

$CCpME_{hijt}$ = Cumulative marketing expenditures by competitors of the focal brand, including the pioneer (excluding co-marketing firms)

$ISCOPE_{hijt}$ = Scope of international market coverage of the focal brand

$ISPEED_{hij}$ = Speed of international rollout of the focal brand

INC_{hijt} = Ratio of net income of the parent company of the focal brand to the pioneer's

$SIZE_{hijt}$ = Ratio of size of the parent company of the focal brand to the pioneer's

α = parameter vector

P = parameter

$u, \mu, \nu, \varepsilon, \omega, \eta$ = Error terms

h = Category subscript, 1, ..., H (number of categories)

i = Brand subscript, 1, ..., I (number of brands)

j = Country subscript, 1, ..., J (number of countries)

t = Time subscript, 1, ..., T (number of periods)

They estimate the model by accounting for the endogeneity of international market entry strategy, order of entry, resources, quality, and other decision variables, as well as for unobserved effects, using pharmaceutical data on 73 brands from two product categories in eight European markets during 1987–1996. Their results show that broader international market scope is associated with a lower late entry penalty and a greater marketing spending efficacy for late mover brands. They find that speed of rollout, however, is unrelated to late entry penalty, but a waterfall rollout strategy is associated with a greater marketing spending efficacy. They argue that late mover brands that sequentially enter many large international markets can challenge the market pioneer in a country more effectively than other late mover brands.

The model and findings of Fischer et al. (2005) are the first to offer some insights into international market entry strategies for pharmaceutical firms. Their data, however, do not contain the US market, the largest market for many ethical drugs. Moreover, all the previously discussed models focus on market entry. Pharmaceutical firms also need to better understand market growth strategies.

As a brand goes through different stages in the PLC, its strategic marketing decisions determine its growth. Shankar (2007) develops the following model to examine the effects of the PLC stages on a brand's strategic marketing decisions.

$$
\ln ME_{it} = \alpha_{01t} + \sum_{k=2}^{K} \alpha_{0k} I_{ik} + \alpha_{1t} \ln(PQ_{i(t-1)} + 1) + \alpha_{2t} \ln(CONR_{i(t-1)} + 1)
$$

$$
+ \alpha_{3t} MMC_{i(t-1)} + \alpha_{4t} NE_{i(t-1)} + \alpha_{5t} \ln DCOMPEX_{i(t-1)}
$$

$$
+ \alpha_{6t} \ln FCOMPEX_{i(t-1)} + \alpha_7 \ln S_{it} + \alpha_8 MLDR_i + \alpha_9 \ln OME_{it} + \varepsilon_{it}
$$

$$
(14.16)
$$

where ME_{it} = strategic spending in the focal marketing variable (advertising or sales force) of brand i at time t, I_{ik} = a dummy variable denoting whether brand i is in category k, K = the total number of categories, PQ_{it} = the relative product quality of brand i at time t, $CONR_{it}$ = the market concentration in the market with brand i at time t, MMC_{it} = the multimarket contact of brand i with other brands in the market at time t, NE_{it} = a dummy variable denoting whether there was a new entry in the last six months preceding t in brand i's market, $DCOMPEX_{it}$ and $FCOMPEX_{it}$ = the total marketing expenditures of dominant and weak competitors, respectively, of brand i at time t, S_{it} = the sales of brand i at time t, $MLDR_i$ = a dummy variable denoting whether brand i is a leader in the focal marketing variable (advertising or sales force), and OME_{it} = strategic spending in the other marketing variable (sales force or advertising) of brand i at time t.

He shows that a pharmaceutical brand's strategic marketing (pull vs. push or emphasis on advertising vs. sales force expenditures) is moderated by its market position and the stage it is in the PLC. His results show that dominant brands significantly shift their resource allocation toward push strategy or sales force while moving from the growth to the mature stages of the PLC, while weak brands shift their allocation toward pull strategy or advertising from the growth to the mature stages. He also finds that the impact of the strategies of dominant and weak brands on each other is asymmetric and that dominant brands have a significant effect on weak brand spending, but weak brands have no effect on dominant brand spending. Furthermore, his results show that the effect of dominant brands on weak brand spending differs from the early to the late stages of the PLC.

Shankar (2008) offers a comprehensive view of the effects of brand dominance and the PLC on a brand's sales growth. His data cover the largest therapeutic categories over long periods of time, making the analysis empirically generalizable. Nevertheless, the data do not include R&D expenditures.

Taken together, the models offer some useful insights for effective decision making in the pharmaceutical industry. A brand's decision to enter a new market or country is based not only on the sales potential for that drug in that market, but also on the overall sales potential across multiple markets or countries and the regulatory processes in the different markets. A market pioneer grows faster, and enjoys greater repeat purchase rates than me-too late movers. Innovative late entrants, however, can grow faster than the pioneer and slow the pioneer's growth and marketing spending effectiveness. For a late mover, a strategy of entering the largest markets sequentially (waterfall strategy) may potentially reduce its late entry penalty. Robust sales forecasting models can predict both trials and repeat purchases of new brands in the presence of competitive effects. A dominant (fringe) brand shifts its strategic resource allocation toward a push (pull) strategy as it moves from the growth to the mature stages of the PLC.

There are some areas that need further research and decision models as well. First, there is scant research on market exits. Why do some brands exit markets while others survive? When does a brand exit a market and why? How should brands plan to exit the market before their patent protections expire? Both descriptive and normative models on these issues will provide useful managerial insights.

Second, the effect of synergy across the brands of a firm on their market entry decisions merits future investigation. If a firm has multiple brands within and across therapeutic categories that are related through overlapping technologies or customer segments, how should the firm plan their entry decisions in the relevant markets? Models that incorporate such dependencies across brands can better guide managerial decision making.

Third, more research is required on repeat purchase and brand diffusion models. Should repeat purchases models be different for pharmaceutical products with different interpurchase times? Should biotechnology products be modeled differently than other pharmaceutical products? Are diffusion parameters inherently different for different brands within a product category or across categories and countries? What factors determine the differences in the diffusion parameters at a brand, category, and country level?

Fourth, product life cycle curves are different for different product pharmaceutical categories. Not all product categories exhibit smooth life cycle curves that have readily identifiable introduction, take-off, early and late growth, maturity, and decline stages. Are product life cycles getting shorter? There is a belief among some managers of pharmaceutical products that their product life cycles are getting compressed. We need more empirical analyses across different product categories and different time periods to study these issues.

Fifth, not much is known about the evolution of markets for pharmaceutical innovations that are introduced in multiple countries in different periods of time. How do new pharmaceutical products evolve across countries, continents, and cultures both at the category level and the brand level? What new product introduction strategies are effective when a pharmaceutical innovation is rolled out across countries? What factors determine an effective rollout strategy across countries? More research is needed on market evolution for new products and brands across countries.

14.6 Defensive Strategy Models

Competitor response to new product entry plays an important role in determining the evolution of the market. Both normative and descriptive models have been developed for response to new product entry. Several normative or game theoretic models of incumbent response have been developed.

Descriptive models of competitor response to new entry have used econometric analyses of data from several industries. Gatignon et al. (1989) address how established competitors in an oligopoly react to a new product entry in their market. They estimate an econometric model of demand response functions and reaction functions with data from the market for an over-the-counter gynecological product. Their model is given by:

$$m_{it} = e^{\beta_0} m_{i(t-1)}^{\beta_1} a_{it}^{\beta_2} \prod_{k=1}^{3} e^{\beta_3 D_{kt}} e^{u_{it}} \tag{14.17}$$

where m is the market share of brand i at time t, a is the advertising share, D is a dummy variable for entry of brand 1, 2, or 3, β are response function parameters, and u is a disturbance term. They estimate the model with data from reactions to two new entries in an over-the-counter gynecological (OTC-Gyn) product market.

They argue that reaction time can be better understood and predicted by observing the effectiveness of a current competitor's marketing mix instruments. They find that incumbent firms react positively (retaliate) with their elastic marketing weapons and cut back (withdraw) with their inelastic marketing mix instruments.

Gatignon and his co-authors were the first provide insightful guidelines on defensive strategies of incumbents in pharmaceutical markets. Their model and data contain some assumptions that need to be relaxed to get deeper insights into the topic. In their data, incumbent elasticities were not significantly altered by the new entrant.

Shankar (1997) develops a decoupled multiplicative sales response model in which a late mover brand enters the market occupied by the pioneer and alters the pioneer's elasticity. The model after the late mover's entry is specified as follows:

$$S_{it} = e^{a_{it}} A_{it}^{b_i} A_{jt}^{c_i} D_{it}^{d_i} D_{jt}^{f_i} P_{it}^{-g_i} P_{jt}^{h_i}, \text{ with } a_{it} = \alpha_i - \frac{\phi_i}{T_{it}}, \tag{14.18}$$

where S_{it} is units sales, A_{it} is the advertising spending, D_{it} is the sales force spending, P_{it} is the unit price and T_{it} is the "time in market" of brand i in period t. The terms a-h, α, and ϕ are parameters to be estimated, and j is the new entrant. Maximizing the profit function, Π, with respect to advertising, sales force spending and price:

$$\underset{A,D,P}{Max} \ \Pi_{it} = m_{it}S_{it} - A_{it} - D_{it} - F_{it}, \tag{14.19}$$

where m_{it} denotes the contribution margin and F is other fixed costs. He derives the following equilibrium levels of spending for advertising and sales force, respectively:

$$A_{it}^* = b_i m_{it} S_{it}$$
$$D_{it}^* = d_i m_{it} S_{it} \tag{14.20}$$

This result holds if both the pioneer and the late mover play a Nash game in all marketing instruments or if the late mover is a Stackelberg-follower in one or all of the marketing instruments. He develops equilibrium reactions under Nash and different leader-follower games and empirically illustrates the analytical results with empirical analysis of data from a large pharmaceutical market.

Based on these results and the assumptions, he explains the pioneer's reactions and predicts its shift in marketing mix allocation upon new entry using empirical analysis of simultaneous and sequential games. He finds that the type of competitive game and the anticipated impact of the late mover on the pioneer's margin and elasticities are two critical factors that significantly affect the pioneer's decisions, in addition to the pioneer's characteristics and the market conditions considered by prior research. His results show that a follower (leader) role in a marketing mix variable, a static (growing) market, a decrease (increase) in own elasticity and margin generally lead to accommodation (retaliation) in that variable. He also highlights cases in which general reactions don't hold and points out that it is necessary to look not only at one factor at a time, but examine the combination of all the factors. He argues that the shift in pioneer's equilibrium marketing mix allocation follows changes in its relative marketing mix effectiveness which depends on the structure of competition, the impact of the late mover on its elasticities and margins, and the competitor's marketing mix.

The model and results of Shankar (1997) offer compelling ways and insights into incumbent reaction strategy. The defensive strategies proposed by his model are both theoretically and empirically driven, so they have important normative implications for pharmaceutical managers. His empirical analysis, however, is based on one product category and his model does not include the role of multimarket contact in formulating the incumbent's defensive strategy.

Shankar's (1999) model, discussed earlier, incorporates the role of multi-market contact in incumbent's reactions. His results show that incumbent reaction is strongly related to new entrant spending. They show that incumbents react mildly to high entrant spending to avoid a competitive spending war and that multimarket contact between the incumbent and the entrant leads to milder incumbent response.

Collectively, these articles offer some generalizable insights in the pharmaceutical industry. When a new brand enters a market, incumbents retaliate with their competitively strong variables and accommodate with their competitively weak variables. An incumbent brand's defensive strategy is related to the entrant's new product introduction strategy and vice versa. An incumbent tends to accommodate a new entrant when a new brand enters with a high level of spending and when they compete in multiple product-markets.

There are many unexplored or underexplored issues relating to defensive marketing strategy that merit attention for further research. First, we do not have a good understanding of the speed of response in pharmaceutical markets to competitor entries and actions. Models of timing or speed of response in other context may have to be modified to accommodate the institutional reality that reactions in product and pricing may need regulatory approval and hence cannot be as fast as they can be in other industries. Models capturing the speed and duration of response will be useful for strategic decision-making.

Second, we do not have models of competitor reactions that capture multimarket competition across international markets. Most big companies in the pharmaceutical industry are multinational corporations that compete in a wide array of countries. They have the ability to attack or accommodate their competitors in different geographic markets.

Third, we need models to capture the reaction strategy of branded drugs when generics are about to enter the market. How long should a brand wait before the anticipate entry of generics before it starts to make some strategic decisions? In what strategic variables should it respond and with what intensity?

14.7 Conclusion

The pharmaceutical industry continues to grow in importance. It offers rich data, enabling the development of good strategic marketing decision models. We have gained a good understanding of some of the strategic marketing issues related to R&D, new product development, product management, market entry and growth and defensive strategies in this industry through carefully developed and tested models. The models range from standard econometric to high-level game theoretic models. The models developed so far have provided some generalizable insights into strategic marketing decisions for the industry. We need more models for international entry, allocation between R&D and marketing expenditures, product portfolio analysis, allocation across own marketing initiatives and strategic alliances, and own spending vs. co-marketing spending, and more decision support systems.

References

Agarwal, S., S. Desai, M.H. Holcomb, A. Oberoi. 2001. Unlocking the Value in Big Pharma. *McKinsey Quarterly* **2** 65–73.

Berndt, E.R. 2006. The United States' Experience with Direct-to-Consumer Advertising of Prescription Drugs: What have we Learned? Chapter 9, in Sloan, F.A., C.-R. Hsieh, *Promoting and Coping with Pharmaceutical Innovation: An International Perspective.* Cambridge University Press, Cambridge MA.

Caciotti, J., B. Shew. 2006. Pharma's Next Top Model. *Pharmaceutical Executive* **26**(3) 82–86.

Chintagunta, P.K., R. Desiraju. 2005. Strategic Pricing and Detailing Behavior in International Markets. *Marketing Science* **24**(1) 67–80.

Danzon P., S. Nicholson, N.S. Pereira. 2005. Productivity in Pharmaceutical-Biotechnology R&D: the Role of Experience and Alliances. *Journal of Health Economics* **24** 317–339.

Dekimpe, M.G., D.M. Hanssens. 1999. Sustained Spending and Persistent Response: A New Look at Long-Term Marketing Profitability. *Journal of Marketing Research* **36**(4) 397–412.

DiMasi, J.A., R.W. Hansen, H.G. Grabowski. 2003. The Price of Innovation: New Estimates of Drug Development Costs. *Journal of Health Economics* 151–185.

Ding, M., J. Eliashberg. 2002. Structuring the New Product Development Pipeline. *Management Science* **48**(3) 343–63.

Ding, M., J. Eliashberg. 2008. A Dynamic Competitive Forecasting Model Incorporating Dyadic Decision-Making. *Management Science* **54**(4) 820–834.

Fischer, M., V. Shankar, M. Clement. 2005. Can a Late Mover Use International Market Entry Strategy to Challenge the Pioneer? *MSI Report No. 05-004*, 25–48. Marketing Science Institute, Cambridge: MA.

Gatignon, H., E. Anderson, K. Helsen. 1989. Competitive Reactions to Market Entry: Explaining Interfirm Differences. *Journal of Marketing Research* **26**(1) 44–55.

Gatignon, H., B. Weitz, P. Bansal. 1990. Brand Introduction Strategies and Competitive Environments. *Journal of Marketing Research* **27**(4) 390 401.

Grabowski, H., J. Vernon. 1990. A New Look at the Returns and Risks to Pharmaceutical R&D. *Management Science* **36**(7) 804–821.

Grabowski, H., J. Vernon, J.A. Dimasi. 2002. Returns on Research and Development for 1990s New Drug Introductions. *Pharmacoeconomics* **20**(3) 11–29.

Grewal, R., M. Ding, J. Liechty. 2006. Evaluating New Product Portfolio Strategies. *Working Paper*. Penn State University, PA.

Gönül, F.F., K. Srinivasan. 2001. Promotion of Prescription Drugs and Its Impact on Physicians' Choice Behavior. *Journal of Marketing* **65**(3) 79–90.

Hahn, M., S. Park, L. Krishnamurthi, A. Zoltners. 1994. Analysis Of New Product Diffusion Using A Four Segment Trial-Repeat Model. *Marketing Science* **13**(3) 224–247.

Hoover's .2006. *Hoover's Index.*

IMS Health 2006. *IMS Retail Drug Monitor.* December.

Kalaignanam, Kartik, V. Shankar, R. Varadarajan. 2007. To End or Extend: An Empirical Analysis of Determinants of New Product Development Alliance Terminations. *Working Paper.* Texas A&M University, TX.

Lee, J. 2003. Innovation and Strategic Divergence: An Empirical Study of the U.S. Pharmaceutical Industry from 1920 to 1960. *Management Science* **49**(2) 143–159.

Lilien, G.L., A.G. Rao, S. Kalish. 1981. Bayesian Estimation And Control Of Detailing Effort In A Repeat Purchase Diffusion Environment. *Management Science* **27**(5) 493–506.

Manchanda, P., P.K. Chintagunta. 2004. Responsiveness of Physician Prescription Behavior to Sales force Effort: An Individual Level Analysis. *Marketing Letters* **15**(2–3) 129–145.

Manchanda, P., P.E. Rossi, P.K. Chintagunta. 2004. Response Modeling with Nonrandom Marketing-Mix Variables. *Journal of Marketing Research* **41**(4) 467–478.

Manchanda, P., P.E. Rossi, P.K. Chintagunta. 2004. Response Modeling with Nonrandom Marketing-Mix Variables. *Journal Of Marketing Research* **41**(4) 467–478.

Manchanda, P., E. Honka. 2005. The Effects and Role of Direct-to-Physician Marketing in the Pharmaceutical Industry: An Integrative Review. *Yale Journal of Health Policy, Law and Ethics* **2** 785–822.

Mantrala, M.K., P. Sinha, A. Zoltners. 1994. Structuring A Multiproduct Sales Quota-Bonus Plan for A Heterogeneous Sales Force: A Practical Model-Based Approach. *Marketing Science* **13**(2) 121–44.

Mizik, N., R. Jacobson. 2004. Are Physicians 'Easy Marks'?: Quantifying the Effects of Detailing and Sampling on New Prescriptions. *Management Science* **50**(12) 1704–1715.

Montgomery, D.B., A.J. Silk 1972. Estimating Dynamic Effects of Market Communications Expenditures. *Management Science* **18**(10) B485–B501.

Narayanan, S., P. Manchanda, P.K. Chintagunta. 2005. Temporal Differences in the Role of Marketing Communication in New Product Categories. *Journal of Marketing Research* **42**(3) 278–290.

Narayanan, S., R. Desiraju, P.K. Chintagunta. 2004. Return on Investment Implications for Pharmaceutical Promotional Expenditures: The Role of Marketing-Mix Interactions. *Journal of Marketing* **68**(4) 90–105.

Neslin, S.A. 2001. ROI Analysis of Pharmaceutical Promotion (RAPP): An Independent Study. Association of Medical Publications, (accessed October 26, 2005), [available at http://www.rxpromoroi.org/rappl/]

PhRMA .2007. *Pharmaceutical Industry Profile* Pharmaceutical Research and Manufacturers of America, http://www.phrma.org/files/Profile%202007.pdf.

Rangaswamy, A., L. Krishnamurthi. 1991. Response Function Estimation Using the Equity Estimator. *Journal of Marketing Research* **28**(1) 72–83.

Rangaswamy, A., P. Sinha, A. Zoltners. 1990. An Integration Model-Based Approach for Sales Force Structuring. *Marketing Science* **9**(4) 279–98.

Rao, A.G., M. Yamada. 1988. Forecasting With A Repeat Purchase Diffusion Model. *Management Science* **34**(6) 734–752.

Shankar, V. 1997. Pioneers' Marketing Mix Reactions to Entry in Different Competitive Games Structures: Theoretical Analysis and Empirical Illustration. *Marketing Science* **16**(4) 271–293.

Shankar, V. 1999. New Product Introduction and Incumbent Response Strategies: Their Interrelationship and the Role of Multimarket Contact. *Journal of Marketing Research* **36**(3) 327–344.

Shankar, V. 2008. The Role of Product Life Cycle and Market Dominance in Marketing Expenditures of Products. *Working Paper*. Texas A&M University, TX.

Shankar, V., G.S. Carpenter, L. Krishnamurthi. 1998. Late Mover Advantage: How Innovative Late Entrants Outsell Pioneers. *Journal of Marketing Research* **35**(1) 54–70.

Shankar, V., G.S. Carpenter, L. Krishnamurthi 1999. The Advantages of Entry in the Growth Stage of the Product Life Cycle: An Empirical Analysis. *Journal of Marketing Research* **36**(2) 269–276.

Singh, A., P. Henske 2003. Has the Pharmaceutical Blockbuster Model Gone Bust? *Bain & Company Report*.

Sorescu, A.B., R.K. Chandy, J.C. Prabhu. 2003. Sources and Financial Consequences of Radical Innovation: Insights from Pharmaceuticals. *Journal of Marketing,* **67**(4) 82–102.

Trombetta, B. 2007. Industry Audit. *Pharmaceutical Executive*, September.

Wierenga, B., G.H. van Bruggen, R. Staelin. 1999. The Success of Marketing Management Support Systems. *Marketing Science* **18**(3) 196–207.

Wosinska, M. 2005. Direct-to-Consumer Advertising and Drug Therapy Compliance. *Journal of Marketing Research* **42**(3) 323–332.

Part VII

Return on Marketing Models

Chapter 15
Models for the Financial-Performance Effects of Marketing

Dominique M. Hanssens and Marnik G. Dekimpe

15.1 Introduction

Several of the preceding chapters have focused on models for different aspects of the marketing mix. From a managerial perspective, such models are important at the functional level, such as the optimal deployment of sales resources, the scheduling of promotional activities, or the configuration of new-product features. The logical "end point" of these models is typically an assessment of the sales or market-share lift that can be attributed to the marketing tactic, followed by a profitability assessment.

The current chapter complements this work by focusing on performance criteria that are relevant to the entire enterprise, not just the marketing function. We use *financial* criteria for that purpose, as they provide metrics that are comparable across the marketing mix (an internal criterion), and also relate well to investors' evaluation of the firm (an external criterion). As such, we treat marketing as an investment in customer value creation and communication that ultimately must create shareholder value as well. The mechanism connecting these two has been referred to as the "chain of marketing productivity" (Rust et al. 2004), depicted in Fig. 15.1.

It is well known that investor or shareholder value is created by expectations of future cash flows. These cash flows are transformed into a present value by using a discount factor that reflects the risk or volatility around these expectations. Therefore, we argue that *marketing performance models should ultimately relate to the creation of these cash flows*. This puts a special condition on the models, i.e. the output variable should be intrinsically linked to financial behavior at the firm level. Compared to the vast array of existing marketing models that explore various aspects of customer and competitor behavior (e.g. choice models, game-theoretic models), financial-performance models tend to be structurally simpler, i.e. they typically have fewer constructs and less behavioral detail. On the other hand, the models must account for temporal patterns

D.M. Hanssens
University of California, Los Angeles, USA
e-mail: dominique.hanssens@anderson.ucla.edu

B. Wierenga (ed.), *Handbook of Marketing Decision Models*,
DOI: 10.1007/978-0-387-78213-3_15, © Springer Science+Business Media, LLC 2008

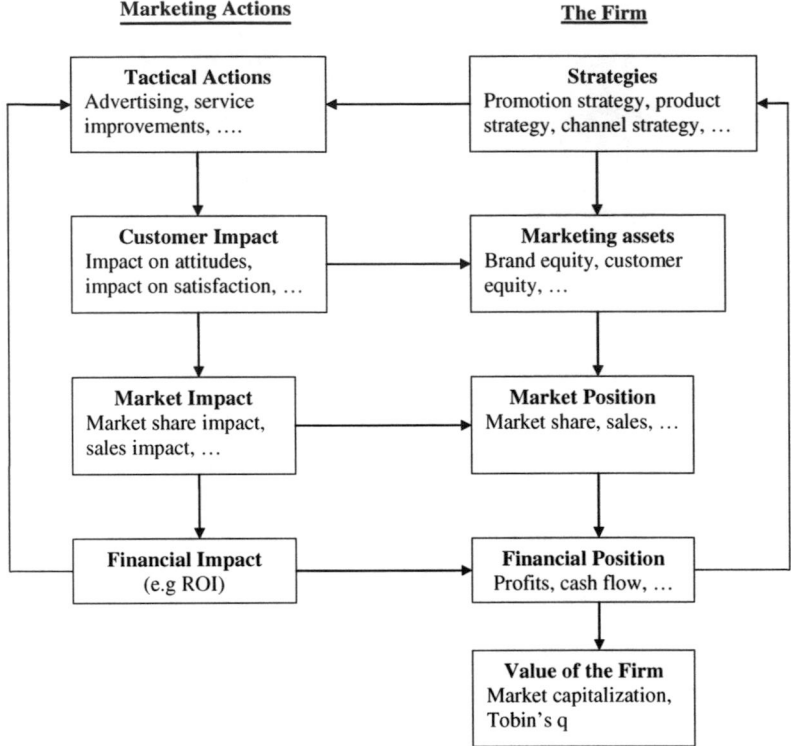

Fig. 15.1 The chain of marketing productivity.
Source: Rust et al. (2004)

such as trends and volatility, and for a substantial forward-looking (expectation) component in the data. Not all marketing models are suitable for that purpose. For example, complex models of brand switching and/or variety seeking may be *cash-flow neutral* if, in any given period, the number of in-switchers vs. out-switchers remains approximately the same. Such models are not discussed in this chapter.

15.2 Marketing and Cash Flows

Shareholder value is driven by a flow metric, i.c. current and anticipated net (or "free") cash flows. According to Srivastava et al. (1998), marketing can enhance shareholder value in three different ways:

- by increasing the magnitude of the net cash flows (i.e. higher profitability)
- by accelerating the cash flows (i.e. faster profitability)
- by lowering the volatility of the cash flows (i.e. safer profitability)

These impacts are often indirect, as marketing's primary role is in creating and stimulating *demand,* which is typically measured by *sales* or *revenues.* Thus, in order to arrive at marketing's role in net cash-flow generation, we must start with models of sales or revenue generation, which are commonly known as market-response models or marketing-mix models (see e.g. Hanssens et al. 2001 for a detailed coverage). Market-response models should then be combined with the *cost* structure of marketing, which may be fixed (e.g. an advertising campaign), variable (e.g. sales commissions), or a combination of both (e.g. the costs of a sales-promotion campaign). Since current accounting standards enforce that marketing actions are expensed, as opposed to capitalized, the profits and cash flows derived from marketing are equivalent. Note that we make abstraction of possible delays between the booking of revenue and the receipt of payments.[1] Therefore "marketing investment spending", such as brand-building advertisements and customer-loyalty-building service enhancements illustrated in Fig. 15.1, is only recognized as "investment" when the fruits of that investment are realized. These benefits may include increased unit sales, higher price premiums and/or a higher revenue base (i.e. the portion of revenue that is realized without marketing effort). Thus the task of quantifying the investment qualities of marketing spending relies on tying financial performance data to these spending levels, which requires the skills of a marketing model builder. The first task in this process is making a careful distinction between *stock* and *flow* performance metrics. This distinction, which originated in the system dynamics literature (e.g. Forrester 1961), is between variables representing accumulations (inventories, or stocks) and changes in these accumulations (flows). A stock in and of itself does not produce cash, but it may enable or enhance future cash flows, and thus plays an important indirect role for financial performance.

The chapter is organized as follows. We begin with a review of financial marketing data and performance metrics, and formulate some criteria for the use of such metrics. Next, we investigate in some detail how key performance metrics are related to marketing activities, using different models as needed. First, we describe how marketing can create cash flows, after which we discuss models that capture how the investment community perceives the firm's marketing actions. In the process, we indicate various areas in need of further research, and discuss managerial implications.

---

[1] By accounting definition, "free" or "net" cash flow is operating profit minus investment. Investment is the net change in the firm's capital. However, "marketing induced capital" such as brand equity or customer equity is currently not recognized on the firm's balance sheet. For example, a $20 million investment in a plant or equipment is recognized as an asset, whereas a $20 million advertising campaign for a brand is not.

15.3 Criteria for Good Performance Metrics

In the spirit of "what you can measure, you can manage", recent years have seen an emergence of marketing performance metrics that help make marketing financially accountable, and that steer marketing resource allocation in a productive direction (see e.g. Ambler 2003). An overview of commonly-used metrics may be found in Fig. 15.2. The figure illustrates that, despite the strategic importance of these metrics, only a subset is routinely reported to the senior levels in the organization. As Srivastava and Reibstein (2005) point out, firms still use a financial jargon at senior levels, and it will take some time before customer- or marketing-oriented metrics become commonplace.

When choosing metrics, we start with the objectives of the measurement process. In marketing there are generally two classes of objectives: evaluation of the impact of past marketing actions, and choice of future marketing actions, i.e. resource allocation (Ambler and Roberts 2006). The former is part of the accounting and control function of the firm, and the latter is part of marketing strategy and planning. In addition, Quelch and McGovern (2006) have formulated desirable properties performance metrics should have from a board-room perspective. We expand on their view by focusing on metrics that are usable in a modeling context as well, and thus are helpful for marketing performance evaluation and resource allocation. We propose the following criteria:

- *Financial relevance*. Firms need to create shareholder value, and therefore any intermediate marketing performance metrics (such as market share, customer satisfaction, etc.) must ultimately be tied to that value.
- *Actionable*. It must be possible, at reasonable cost, to collect data on the performance metric, and to relate it analytically to marketing

Marketing Metric	U.S. (n = 224)	Japan (n = 117)	Germany (n = 120)	U.K. (n = 120)	France (n = 116)	Overall
Market share	73	57	97	80	90	79
Perceived product/ service quality	77	68	84	71	75	77
Customer loyalty/ retention	67	56	69	58	65	64
Customer/segment profitability	73	40	74	65	59	64
Relative price	65	48	84	53	63	63
Actual/potential customer/segment lifetime value	32	35	51	32	58	40
Average	64	51	77	60	68	

Fig. 15.2 Percent of firms reporting various metrics to the board
Source: Barwise and Farley (2003)

investments. This is where a number of empirically-tested models from the marketing-science literature are called for, such as models of trial and repeat purchasing, models of the diffusion of innovations, or models on the creation of brand and/or customer equity.

- *Stable behavior*. Highly volatile metrics are difficult to interpret and manage, and should be avoided where possible. For example, using sufficiently large samples for attitudinal metrics will avoid unduly large sample variation.
- *Reliable long-term guidance*. This is the "leading indicator" aspect of a metric, i.e. are positive movements in the metric indicative of improving health for the brand or firm?

Using these four criteria as a guide, we now turn to marketing models that support various performance metrics. First, we address the *process* perspective, i.e. we describe how marketing can create financial cash flows, along with other antecedents of performance. If a firm understands these causal connections (i.e. marketing evaluation), it is in a stronger position to make productive marketing resource allocation decisions (i.e. marketing planning). However, that does not necessarily imply that the outside world, in particular the investment community, will immediately recognize this know-how (the last arrow in Fig. 15.1). Thus we must also address how investors *perceive* the firm's marketing actions and their impact on its financial outlook. Finally, we make some observations on the linkages between the process and the perception perspective.

15.4 The Process Perspective

15.4.1 The Core Sales-Response Model

We begin with a core sales response model that explains variations in customer demand for the firm's products and services, and which is therefore at the source of cash flow generation. The basic sales response function is the following multiplicative model

$$S_t = e^c \, M_t^\beta \, X_t^\gamma \, Z_t^\delta \, e_t^u, \qquad (15.1)$$

where S_t refers to sales or another performance metric in period t (for example, week t), M_t is marketing support in that week, X_t refers to other firm-controlled variables, Z_t corresponds to uncontrollable (environmental) factors, and u_t is an error term. The core response model may be estimated across time periods t, but could also be specified over cross-sectional units $i = 1, \ldots, I$, or both. We expect $0 < \beta < 1$ in estimation, a condition which results in diminishing returns to scale, or concavity of response.

The base model (15.1) implies that infinite marketing support results in infinite sales. In practice, however, there will be a limit or *ceiling* to sales, usually determined by prevailing market conditions. While there are other ways to represent concavity (see e.g. Hanssens et al. 2001, pp. 100–102), the multi-plicative function is particularly appealing as it recognizes that marketing-mix effects interact with one another, i.e. the marginal sales effect of an incremental marketing dollar depends on the other elements in the equation. In addition, taking logarithms linearizes the model as follows:

$$\ln(S_t) = c + \beta \ln(M_t) + \gamma \ln(X_t) + \delta \ln(Z_t) + u_t, \qquad (15.2)$$

making it easily estimable. Finally, the response parameters are readily inter-preted as response elasticities, which are helpful in making comparisons and deriving empirical generalizations of marketing impact.

In some cases, the response is S-shaped, i.e. there is a minimum or threshold-level of marketing spend below which there is little or no impact, followed by a range of spending with rapidly increasing sales response. At even higher spend-ing levels (i.e. past the inflection point), the usual diminishing returns appear. The core model (15.1) can readily be extended to an "odds" model that allows for S-shaped response, as demonstrated by Johansson (1979):

$$(S_t - I)/(K - S_t) = e^c \, M_t^\beta \, X_t^\gamma \, Z_t^\delta \, e_t^u, \qquad (15.3)$$

where I is the minimum sales level (e.g. the level at zero marketing spend), and K is the ceiling level. For example, if sales is expressed in relative terms (e.g. market share), I could be set at 0% and K at 100%. For marketing response parameters $0 < \beta < 1$, model (15.3) is still concave, but for $\beta > 1$, the function is S-shaped. Johansson (1979) discusses the formal estimation of (15.3) with maximum-likelihood methods, as well as an easy approximation based on ordinary least squares.

For all practical purposes, concavity and S-shape are sufficient functional forms to capture the essence of marketing response.[2] Naturally, the core response model (15.1) will need to be extended in order to accommodate some specific behavioral marketing phenomena. For example, marketing initia-tives often impact demand in time periods after the expenditure has ended. Such lagged effects may be incorporated directly by using a dynamic response func-tion in the lag operator L (i.e. $L^k \, X_t = X_{t-k}$). The response model then generalizes to

$$S_t = e^c \, M_t^{\beta(L)} \, X_t^{\gamma(L)} \, Z_t^{\delta(L)} \, e_t^u, \qquad (15.4)$$

with $\beta(L) = \beta_0 + \beta_1 L + \beta_2 L^2 + \dots$, and similarly for the other dynamic parameters. We will discuss additional extensions to the core response model as needed for incorporating different aspects of cash-flow generation of marketing.

---

[2] We refer to Hanssens, Parsons & Schultz (2001) for a review of other functional specifica-tions that have been used in the literature.

15.4.2 Cash-Flow Generation

How does the core response model generate cash flows ? Assuming a constant profit-margin, the net cash flows (CF) in period t – excluding non-marketing costs – may be expressed as

$$CF_t = S_t \, ^*margin - M_t \qquad (15.5)$$

The return on marketing M, sometimes referred to as ROMI, is then defined as

$$ROMI = [CF(M) - CF(M = 0)]/M \qquad (15.6)$$

Note that ROMI is a ratio, which is useful for an ex-post assessment of the return of a specific marketing campaign or investment. However, ROMI should *not* be used to determine optimal levels of marketing spending. Doing so will often result in under-investing on marketing, because ROMI typically declines monotonically with higher spending (see Ambler and Roberts 2006 for an elaboration). Instead, the optimal marketing spend M* may be derived from maximizing the cash-flow function (15.5) based on the response model (15.4):

$$M^* - [e^{c\,*}\beta(L)\,^*margin]^{1/[1-\beta(L)]}, \qquad (15.7)$$

where we have incorporated the effects of other firm-controlled variables X and environmental conditions Z into the adjusted baseline e^c for ease of exposition.

Importantly, the relationship between marketing spending and cash flow generation depends on (i) the natural size (the baseline) of the business, (ii) the productivity of marketing spending $\beta(L)$, and (iii) the prevailing profit margin. Taken together, they fully determine optimal short-run marketing-resource allocation. At the same time, these determinants are exogenous; for example, it is assumed that more aggressive marketing spending has no impact on either the baseline or marketing effectiveness itself. Thus, the decision rule in (15.7) may be thought of as a harvesting or reactive view of marketing resource allocation.

However, a prevailing belief among practitioners and academics is that well-placed marketing spending not only stimulates sales, but also builds *future assets* for the firm. In order to represent that capability of marketing, we must extend the core response model to account for endogenously created assets that, in turn, will generate future cash flows, as illustrated in Fig. 15.1. This is done by considering *stock metrics* of market performance in addition to cash flows.

15.4.3 Flow and Stock Metrics

The demand or revenue generation process above is naturally expressed as a
flow metric. Similarly, flow metrics are used to express the ongoing cost of
marketing. For example, a firm may routinely spend $2 million a month on
marketing communications, which result in an incremental $3 million in gross
profits. The net monthly cash flow due to marketing communication would be
$1 million, and the ROMI would be $1 million/$2 million = 50% (using
Equation (15.6)).

Ideally, these ongoing marketing expenditures will also create beneficial
cumulative effects, which would be assessed as *stock* metrics. For example,
the cumulative sales of a new technology durable, or installed base, is a stock
variable that is instrumental in convincing other users to adopt the product as
well. Such a stock generates future cash flows without additional marketing
expenditures, which is financially attractive to the firm. Similarly, many attitudinal measures are stock metrics, e.g. the percent of the target market that is
aware of a product, or the overall price image of a retail store. Brand equity and
customer equity, too, are stock measures. From a financial performance perspective, our task is to *gauge the cash flows that are drawn from these stocks,
independent of (or on top of) current marketing expense.*

In what follows, we explore how marketing can create or enhance such stock
metrics, and how the core response model may be extended to capture these
effects. Analytically, this is the case when the *revenue baseline is allowed to
change (grow) over time,* i.e. a higher level of firm revenue is obtained independent of current marketing spending. We identify three sources of such expanded
baseline revenue:

- *External forces:* making strategic choices that expand the scope of the
  business, such as tapping new markets, new segments or distribution channels. Other baseline-driving forces are outside firm control, for example
  rising disposable incomes in the target market or the entry of a new competitor in the category.
- *Experiential quality to the customer.* When the product or service quality is
  high, the resulting customer satisfaction may increase repeat-purchase rates
  and/or word of mouth, even without additional marketing investments. This
  leads to the development of customer equity, i.e. the long-term value of the
  customer to the firm has increased.
- *Brand equity building.* Higher equity brands tend to have higher baseline
  sales, all else (including current marketing expenditures) equal (see e.g.
  Kamakura and Russell 1993). While the sources of brand equity and customer equity may be very different, their financial outcomes for the firm are
  similar, i.e. higher baseline revenue.

"Stock" sources of cash flows are inherently long-run oriented, and strategic
in nature. For example, a brand's quality reputation among customers tends to

lag objective reality by several years, so it takes time for a brand to reap the financial benefits of investments in product quality (Mitra and Golder 2005). By contrast, the optimal marketing spending rule in (15.7) only impacts current (or short-run) flows, either through improved marketing effectiveness (e.g. a better media-mix allocation), which lifts $\beta(L)$, or through more aggressive spending, which lifts M. Improving $\beta(L)$ is the focus of much of the current interest in marketing accountability, as discussed in detail by Ambler (2003). More aggressive spending is naturally limited by the realities of decreasing returns to marketing and competitive reaction. Thus changes in $\beta(L)$ or M are typically more tactical in nature.

Extending the core response model to account for the "stock building" function of marketing allows for a more complete short-run and long-run accountability of marketing activity. We first discuss two models that explicitly account for this stock building potential of marketing: (i) time-varying baseline models (Section 15.4.3.1), and (ii) generalized diffusion models (Section 15.4.3.2). Next, we discuss two stock metrics that have received considerable attention in the recent marketing literature: brand equity (Section 15.4.3.3) and customer equity (Section 15.4.3.4). Finally, we comment on the usefulness of intermediate performance measures (Section 15.4.3.5) in financial-performance models.

15.4.3.1 Time-Varying Baseline Models

Srivastava and Reibstein (2005) make the interesting observation that most market response models assess marketing's influence on sales variations above the baseline, but that the baseline itself does not change. The baseline in revenue is an intuitive measure of brand equity, after adjusting for external determinants such as market size, per capita income and competition. Given sufficiently long time-series data, time-varying parameter models may be used to assess the evolution of baselines, and in particular the evolution that can be attributed to past marketing.[3] The following time-varying market response model for brand i at time t, adapted from Pauwels and Hanssens (2007), and linearized for ease of exposition, captures this process:

$$S_{i,t} = c_{i,t} + {}_k\Sigma\beta_{ki}(L)M_{ki,t} + \varepsilon_{i,t} \tag{15.8}$$

$$c_{i,t} = c_{i,t-1} + {}_k\Sigma\gamma_{ki}(L)M_{ki,t} + \eta_{i,t} \tag{15.9}$$

where the parameters β_{ki} (L) measure the standard sales response effects of marketing instrument k of the brand (M_{ki}), and the parameters γ_{ki} (L) capture

---

[3] Cross-sectional comparisons of brand equity cannot monitor the *formation* of brand strength, only the equilibrium result of the branding process. By contrast, longitudinal data, possibly across several brands or markets, allow us to infer how marketing spending builds brands over time.

the baseline expansion effects of M_{ki} (assuming positive impact). This representation gives rise to the following combinations of demand-generation and brand-building impact of marketing
instrument k:

	$\gamma_{ki}(L) = 0$	$\gamma_{ki}(L) > 0$
$\beta_{ki}(L) = 0$	Ineffective marketing	Marketing builds the brand
$\beta_{ki}(L) > 0$	Marketing generates sales	Marketing generates sales and builds the brand

In the ideal situation, marketing spending offers short-term returns via demand generation, but also builds the brand. In that case, the brand-building effect is a financial bonus or windfall, as the incremental cash flows from demand-stimulation may already be sufficient to generate a positive ROMI.

The more ambiguous scenario is where demand generation is insufficient to generate a positive ROMI, however the sustained marketing spending builds the brand in a "cash-flow invisible" way (behavioral explanations for this scenario exist, but are beyond the scope of our chapter). Such a policy would be a true investment in that short-run losses are incurred for the purpose of increasing long-term benefits. Indeed, as time moves on, an increasing portion of revenue accrues to the firm without marketing spending, and that portion is demonstrably related to previous band-building spending.

From an econometric perspective, the dynamic system of (15.14) and (15.15) may be estimated by state-space methods such as the Kalman filter that provide a time path of brand equity (see Chapter 12 on time-series models for details). Sriram and Kalwani (2007) used a logit-model version of this approach to demonstrate that sales promotions for orange juice brands lift sales revenue, while at the same time eroding brand equity. In a similar vein, Ataman et al. (2007) used dynamic linear modeling to show how marketing activities can be instrumental in building new brands and in managing existing brands for sustainable growth.

15.4.3.2 Generalized Diffusion Models

The notion that marketing expenditures can contribute to an asset or stock which, in turn, generates future cash flows is also reflected in many diffusion models, which may be viewed as special cases of the time-varying baseline models discussed above. The exponential surge in the first-generation sales of consumer and industrial durables such as the fax machine and the iPod cannot be explained by the growth in population or purchasing power alone, nor by the advertising spending patterns in the later stages of the life cycle. Instead, a process of *internal influence* (imitation) from early adopters of the product accounts to a large extent for the exponential growth, even though this imitation effect subsequently dies out as the market reaches maturity. Such a diffusion process can occur spontaneously, but it can also be *accelerated* by marketing spending, as in the model by Bass et al. (1994):

$$S_t = [\text{market size} - Y_{t-1}]^*[p_1 + q_1 Y_{t-1} + p_2{}^*f(M_t)$$
$$+ q_2{}^*Y_{t-1}{}^*f(M_t)]$$

(15.10)

where

Y_{t-1} = installed base at the beginning of period t, i.e. $S_0 + S_1 + S_2 + \ldots + S_{t-1}$
p_1 = the strength of external innovation in the market
p_2 = the impact of marketing on innovation
q_1 = the degree of imitation in the market
q_2 = the impact of marketing on imitation
$f(M)$ = the market response function for innovation and imitation, which could be multiplicative, as in equation (15.1).

This model is sometimes referred to as the "generalized Bass model", as it expands the basic diffusion model due to Bass (1969), which is obtained by setting $p_2 = q_2 = 0$. The spontaneous growth in sales and cash flows comes from the installed base, or stock of cumulative sales (Y_{t-1}) and the strength of consumer imitation (q_1). This factor is largely responsible for the spectacular growth in revenues and earnings in the first decade of high-technology companies such as Microsoft, Dell and Google.

The cash-flow *acceleration* function of marketing comes from two sources: creating awareness of the new product among innovative prospects, and encouraging imitation among imitative customers. However, overall market size is not affected, so these marketing actions *shift forward* a fixed ultimate demand for the product, which is consistent with the cash-flow-acceleration function of marketing in Srivastava et al. (1998). A recurring example of this form of marketing is in the motion-picture industry, where aggressive pre-launch advertising campaigns are often used to attract viewers to the theaters on opening weekend (Elberse and Eliashberg 2003). Other marketing investments are aimed more at increasing the long-run market potential of the innovation, for example by proposing and communicating new usage situations for the product.

The cash-flow implications from the diffusion of innovations are complex, not only because of the nonlinearities involved, but also because the marketing impact may differ in different stages of the life cycle. In addition, profit margins may change with the learning curve and increased competition. Consider, for example, the study by Horksy and Simon (1983) on the impact of advertising on the diffusion of a new electronic banking service. The authors found that life-cycle cash flows for the bank were maximized by initial aggressive advertising for the new product, and then gradually reducing advertising support over time. Moreover, the installed base (or stock) for one technology may positively influence the diffusion of later generations of that product (see e.g. Norton and Bass 1987) and of complementary products (Srinivasan et al. 2004).

15.4.3.3 Brand Equity

Perhaps the most frequently-studied stock metric in the marketing literature is the concept of brand equity. Keller and Lehmann (2001) considered three broad classes of brand-equity measures: customer mindset measures, product-market measures and financial-market based measures. An excellent review is given in Ailawadi et al. (2003), which is not repeated here. These authors propose the *revenue premium* as a financially-relevant measure for the value of a brand in a given industry.

The revenue premium is defined as the difference in revenue realized by branded vs. unbranded competitors, i.e.

$$\text{Revenue premium} = \text{volume}_{\text{brand}} * \text{price}_{\text{brand}}$$
$$- \text{volume}_{\text{non-brand}} * \text{price}_{\text{non-brand}} \tag{15.11}$$

This reflects the idea that brand equity may boost sales volume, allow for a price premium, or both. Put differently, brand-building activities may enhance future cash flows as a result of realizing a higher sales volume, and/or a higher price. The measure is shown to be actionable, stable over time, and to have considerable diagnostic value in terms of the brand's long-run health, thereby conforming to our earlier criteria. Interestingly, Ailawadi et al. (2003) also demonstrate how branded products exhibit asymmetric up- and downward price elasticities. Using data from a variety of consumer-packaged products, they derive that low-revenue premium brands have an average down price elasticity of –1.195, and an average up elasticity of –0.921. High-equity brands, in contrast, have an average down elasticity of –0.747, and an up elasticity of only –0.183. Hence, brands with a higher revenue premium gain considerable share when they reduce their prices, but lose relatively little share when they increase their price. As such, brand equity is a stock metric that enhances future cash flows through three different routes described earlier: higher baseline sales (volume premium), higher profit margins (price premium), and increased marketing effectiveness (differential $\beta(L)$).

Note that some marketing activity may deteriorate brand equity. For example, Mela, Gupta and Lehmann (1997) used time-varying response models to demonstrate that increasing the frequency of sales promotions may increase customers' price sensitivity to the brand. As a result, either a smaller percent of sales is generated at full price, or the brand's price premium is lowered. Both scenarios result in damage to the brand's equity.

From a model building perspective, the revenue premium that captures brand equity in (11) is typically estimated using the sales-response model (15.4) for different brands in a category, and examining differences in the intercept and slope parameters. The time-varying model (15.8) (15.9) may also be used in this context.

15.4.3.4 Customer Equity

While brand equity focuses on the supply side, i.e. the offerings of the firm, customer equity (CE) is an asset valued on the demand side, with specific reference to the firm's customer base. Customer lifetime value (CLV) is generally defined as the present value of all future profits obtained from a customer over his/her life of relationship with a firm (Gupta et al. 2004):

$$CLV = \sum_{t=0}^{T} \frac{(p_t - c_t)r_t}{(1 + i)^t} - AC \tag{15.12}$$

where p_t = revenue generated by a consumer at time t,

$\quad c_t$ = direct cost of servicing the customer at time t,
$\quad\ i$ = discount rate or cost of capital for the firm,
$\quad r_t$ = probability of customer repeat buying or being "alive" at time t,
$\ AC$ = customer acquisition cost,
$\quad\ T$ = time horizon for estimating CLV.

Customer equity (CE) is the sum of the firm's customers' lifetime values. CLV and CE measure "net present value" from a customer asset perspective, and thus speak to both shareholder value and customer value.

Marketing spending may impact customer equity in several ways: through acquiring new customers (at a cost AC per customer), through retaining existing customers (at a servicing cost c_t in each period) and through increasing per-customer revenue, which is sometimes referred to as 'share of wallet'. Different models elaborate on different aspects of marketing's role in customer equity building, see Chapters 9 and 10 for details.

In order to connect customer equity with financial-performance models, we must aggregate customer-specific records and link them with firm performance. In relationship businesses such as insurance and financial services, this can be done through direct counting of customers and aggregation of their CLVs. In that case, the models developed in Chapters 8 and 9 are appropriate representations of the financial performance impact of different marketing investments.

In most cases, however, the direct-count approach is not feasible or practical, and we should infer marketing's impact on customer equity at a more aggregate level (see e.g. Rust et al. 2004). This may be achieved by examining marketing's role in *purchase reinforcement,* i.e. using an existing sale to create more future sales from that customer. Purchase reinforcement modeling applies mainly in frequently purchased product and service categories, where consumers have reason to expect a similar-quality experience between one purchase occasion and the next. Givon and Horsky (1990) developed a market-share model that contrasts the impact of purchase experience (β) relative to marketing-induced retention (λ) as follows:

$$\text{Share}_t = \alpha(1 - \lambda) + (\beta + \lambda)\,\text{Share}_{t-1} - \beta\lambda\,\text{Share}_{t-2} + \gamma M_t + e_t \tag{15.13}$$

This model is a special case of the dynamic core response function (15.5) with two-period dynamics. Thus it lends itself to calculations of the cash-flow impact (and therefore return) of investments in marketing vs. customer service provision. In their empirical investigation of four frequently purchased product categories, the authors reported that $\beta > \lambda$, i.e. the impact of purchase experience exceeds that of marketing spending. As such, even without renewed instantaneous marketing support, a stock effect is at work that results in future sales.

Since then, more complex models have been developed that infer movements in customer equity from sales transactions data and brand-related marketing actions, for consumer durables such as automobiles, as well as frequently purchased products (Yoo and Hanssens 2006, 2007). Customer equity has, in various studies, been found to be an actionable and stable metric, which offers reliable guidance and an explicit linkage to financial performance (see e.g. Gupta and Lehmann 2005 for a review).

It would be useful to develop formal links between brand equity building and customer equity building. Some links are conceptually straightforward. For example, in industries dominated by brand prestige, customer loyalty (and therefore customer equity) may increase with brand appeal, regardless of customer service levels. As an illustration, the more prestigious the ownership of a Rolls Royce, the longer a prospective customer may be willing to wait for product delivery. In other cases, however, there will be tradeoffs between building brand and building customer equity, and we need new marketing models to address these important issues.

15.4.3.5 Intermediate Performance Variables and Marketing Dashboards

Financial performance models have a shareholder-value orientation that may be outside the decision perimeter of most functional marketing decision makers. Marketing dashboards may be used to represent intermediate results that are directly relevant for these functional managers, and to provide the "big picture" of performance evolution for top management. A detailed discussion of marketing dashboards may be found in Lehmann and Reibstein (2006). They note that a complete dashboard should integrate the impact of marketing spending on the *interim marketing metrics* and their impact on the financial consequences. In addition, dashboards should show both the short-term as well as the long-term impact of marketing, i.e. they should be not only historical but forward looking as well. Most corporate dashboards, however, have not yet advanced to this stage.

In the present modeling context, we are mainly concerned with the usefulness of intermediate metrics such as brand awareness and customer satisfaction in evaluating marketing's financial performance.[4] From an econometric

---

[4] An excellent review on the link between perceptual marketing metrics and financial performance is given in Gupta and Zeithaml (2006; see e.g. their Table 1).

perspective, an intermediate metric is *redundant* if it does not add predictive power above and beyond that provided by the core response model (15.1) or its extension. We illustrate this condition with the intermediate variable brand awareness (A). The core response model in implicit form, and omitting time subscripts and error terms for ease of exposition, is:

$$S = f(M), \tag{15.14}$$

and the intermediate response model is

$$A = g(M), \tag{15.15}$$

which could be a standard awareness model discussed in an advertising context in Mahajan, Muller and Sharma (1984). The integrated financial response model

$$S = h(A, M) \tag{15.16}$$

may be compared to the core model (15.14), for example on the basis of its residual mean squared error in a forecast sample. If model (15.16) is superior, then the intermediate metric A should be tracked and included in the dashboard, as it contains financially valuable information above and beyond that already reflected in revenue and marketing spending. This may occur, for example, when advertising-induced-awareness is persistent, thus creating a stock that facilitates demand creation.

If model (15.16) fails the comparison test, the intermediate metric A may still be valuable at the functional level (assuming equation (15.15) produces strong results), but it need not be incorporated in the financial valuation of marketing. This may occur when advertising-induced-awareness loses its relevance quickly due to frequent product innovation, for example in high-technology categories.

In conclusion, we propose that the important question of how many intermediate performance metrics to include in a marketing dashboard be addressed using the notion of *incremental predictive capability*, for which good analytical criteria exist.

15.5 The Investor Perspective

Thus far, we discussed how marketing can create cash flows for the firm, either directly (through the current and lagged effects in the core response model (15.4)), or by contributing to stock variables that result in future cash flows even when new marketing expenditures are absent. The question remains, however, to what extent marketing's contribution to these cash flows is recognized by an important external audience, the shareholder or investor. More specifically, we consider to what extent this contribution is reflected in (changes in) the firms' market value.

The valuation of public firms is captured in their stock price, or market capitalization (stock price times shares outstanding). The movement of these stock prices produces *stock returns*, which is the conventional profit measure for investors. We use *stock-return response modeling* to assess the degree to which marketing actions and industry conditions improve the outlook on a firm's cash flows and thereby lift its valuation. A separate set of financial models deals with the valuation of brands as intangible assets, specifically the portion of a firm's overall market capitalization that may be attributed to brand equity. These models are outside the scope of our review, and we refer the interested reader to Madden et al. (2006) for a comprehensive discussion. Similarly, the relationship between customer equity and market capitalization is discussed in Gupta and Zeithaml (2006).

Stock-return response models are similar to the internal market response models discussed previously, with one important point of difference: the dependent variable is *future* or *expectations* oriented. Indeed, stock prices may be viewed as *consensus forecasts* that react only to *new* information that is deemed relevant. Thus, the basic value assessed by internal financial performance models may already be contained in the firm's existing stock price. As such, stock- return response modeling establishes whether the information contained in one or more marketing actions is associated with changes in expectations of future cash flows and, hence, stock price and returns (we refer to Mizik and Jacobson (2004) and Srinivasan and Hanssens (2007) for a detailed review). We will discuss two approaches to stock-return modeling that have been used to date: a single-equation method based on the efficient markets hypothesis, and a system's (vector-autoregressive) approach.

15.5.1 Single-Equation Approach

The stock-market valuation of a firm depicts the consensus expectation of its discounted future cash flows. The efficient market hypothesis (EMH) developed in the finance literature implies that stock prices follow random walks: the current price reflects all known information about the firm's future earnings prospects (Fama and French 1992). For instance, investors may expect the firm to maintain its usual level of advertising and price promotions. Developments that positively affect cash flows result in increases in stock price, while those negatively affecting cash flows result in decreases. In our context, regressing stock returns on changes in the marketing mix provides insights into the stock market's expectations of the associated long-term changes in cash flows. In particular, we test for *incremental* information content, that is the degree to which marketing actions explain stock price movements above and beyond the impact of current accounting measures such as revenue and earnings.

Stock-return models are highly specific to the marketing and industry characteristics of each firm. We illustrate the principles in the context of the automobile sector, in particular the role of product innovation, advertising and sales promotions (Srinivasan et al. 2009). However, the models all start with a benchmark return model, based on the Capital Asset Pricing Model (CAPM) developed in the finance and accounting literature. Following Fama and French (1992, 1993), the CAPM model is augmented with firm-specific risk factors that control for the size of the company (assets), its market-to-book ratio, and its momentum (past trends in stock return). Indeed, smaller firms are expected to outperform larger firms, and stocks with lower market-to-book ratios are expected to outperform those with a higher market-to-book ratio. Both of these effects imply that riskier stocks are characterized by higher returns. These factors reflect the *a priori* investor expectations in stock returns that are based on the past operations of the firm, and thus they are lagged in the model. As such, the benchmark model takes on the following form:

$$RET_{i,t} = \alpha_0 + \alpha_1 \ ASSETS_{i,t-1} + \alpha_2 VBR_{i,t-1} + \alpha_3 \ MNT_{i,t}$$
$$+ \alpha_4 \ EARN_{i,t} + \alpha_5 \ SP500_t + \Sigma \alpha_j SEAS_{j,t} + \varepsilon_{it} \quad (15.17)$$

where RET_{it} is the stock return for firm i at time t, $ASSETS_{it-1}$ the firm size at time $t-1$, VBR_{it-1} the market-to-book ratio (in logs) at time $t-1$, MNT_{it} measures the momentum in stock returns, $EARN_{it}$ is the firm income, and ε_{it} is the error term. Additionally, the model may control for macro-economic movements by including covariates such as the S&P 500 Index ($SP500_t$). Depending on the nature of the business, the model may also control for seasonal and holiday dummy variables (SEAS$_{it}$ in this case).

The financial benchmark model (15.17) is subsequently augmented with marketing variables in order to assess hypotheses on their impact on future cash flows. They are expressed in changes or shocks (denoted in (18) through the difference operator Δ), i.e. deviations from past behaviors already incorporated in investors' expectations. Such a model has the following form:

$$RET_{i,t} = \alpha_0 + \alpha_1 \ ASSETS_{i,t-1} + \alpha_2 \ VBR_{i,t-1} + \alpha_3 \ MNT_{i,t} + \alpha_4 \ EARN_{i,t}$$
$$+ \alpha_5 \ SP500_t + \Sigma \ \alpha_j \ SEAS_{j,t} + \beta_1 \ \Delta \ ADVi, t \quad (15.18)$$
$$+ \beta_2 \ \Delta \ PROM_{i,t} + \beta_2 \ \Delta \ INNOV_{i,t} + \varepsilon_{it}$$

where the β-parameters allow to test whether changes in firm i's advertising (ADV), promotional support (PROM) or innovation level (INNOV) have additional explanatory power above and beyond the variables already contained in the benchmark model. Equation (15.18) can be extended to control for other industry-relevant characteristics such as category growth rate or category concentration. Likewise, the set of marketing variables can be expanded to reflect specific firm characteristics (see e.g. Srinivasan et al. 2009). Thus, the stock-return model augments traditional financial valuation models with *changes* in marketing strategy. In the case study above, the stock market was found to react positively to product innovation, especially when combined with advertising spending. Investors were also found to react negatively to sales promotion initiatives.

A special case of the stock-return model is the *marketing event study*. Methodologically, event studies are similar in design, however the input variable is one or more isolated interventions, as opposed to ongoing marketing-mix activities. For example, event studies have been used to measure the impact on stock returns of company name changes (Horsky and Swyngedouw 1987), internet channel additions (Geyskens et al. 2002), new-product announcements (Chaney et al. 1991), foreign-market entries (Gielens et al. 2007), and opening-weekend box office results of motion pictures (Joshi and Hanssens 2008), among others. An in-depth discussion on the use of marketing event studies is given in Srinivasan and Bharadwaj (2004).

15.5.2 Vector-Autoregressive Approach

The Efficient Markets Hypothesis may not always hold, due to incomplete information available to investors and biases in their interpretation. In particular, researchers have questioned the assumption of *immediate* dissemination of all available information. For example, Fornell et al. (2006) found that publicly-available information about firms' customer satisfaction levels is slow to be reflected in stock prices, leaving a substantial arbitrage opportunity. It is even more difficult to gauge the impact of single marketing actions, and therefore one should not expect that they will be fully incorporated in stock prices either. Instead, investors will *update* their evaluation of these actions over time. Therefore, the short-term investor reaction may be adjusted over time until it stabilizes in the long run, and becomes so predictable that it loses its ability to further adjust stock prices. This behavior motivates the use of long-run or persistence models instead of event windows to study the impact of marketing on firm value.

Vector-autoregressive (VAR) models are well suited to measure the dynamic performance response and interactions between performance and marketing variables (Dekimpe and Hanssens 1999). Both performance variables and marketing actions are endogenous, i.e. they are explained by their own past and the past of the other endogenous variables. Specifically, VAR models not only measure direct (immediate and lagged) response to marketing actions, but also capture the performance implications of complex feedback loops. For instance, a successful new-product introduction will generate higher revenue, which may prompt the manufacturer to reduce sales promotions in subsequent periods. The combination of increased sales and higher margins may improve earnings and stock price, and thereby further enhance the over-time effectiveness of the initial product introduction. Because of such chains of events, the full performance implications of the initial product introduction may extend well beyond the immediate effects. We refer to Chapter 11 on time-series models in marketing in this volume for more methodological detail on these models.

We illustrate the use of stock-performance VAR models through a recent example in the automobile sector, described in detail in Pauwels et al. (2004). Following the results of various unit-root tests, a VAR model is specified for each automotive brand j (e.g. Chrevrolet, Saturn and Cadillac) from firm i (General Motors) in category k (e.g. the SUV category):

$$
\begin{bmatrix} \Delta VBR_{i,t} \\ \Delta INC_{i,t} \\ \Delta REV_{i,t} \\ NPI_{ijk,t} \\ SPR_{ijk,t} \end{bmatrix} = C + \sum_{n=1}^{N} Bn \times \begin{bmatrix} \Delta VBR_{i,t-n} \\ \Delta INC_{i,t-n} \\ \Delta REV_{i,t-n} \\ NPI_{ijk,t-n} \\ SPR_{ijk,t-n} \end{bmatrix}
$$

$$
+ \Gamma \times \begin{bmatrix} \Delta S\&P500_t \\ \Delta Construct_t \\ \Delta Exchange_t \\ \Delta EPS_{i,t} \end{bmatrix} + \begin{bmatrix} u_{VBRi,t} \\ u_{INCi,t} \\ u_{REVi,t} \\ u_{NPIijk,t} \\ u_{SPRijk,t} \end{bmatrix}
$$

(15.19)

with B_n, Γ matrices of coefficients, and $[u_{VBRi,t}, u_{INCi,t}, u_{REVi,t}, u_{NPIijk,t}, u_{SPRijk,t}]' \sim N(0,\Sigma_u)$. The B_n matrices contain the autoregressive parameters capturing the dynamic effects among the endogenous variables, while the matrix links the endogenous variables to a set of exogenous control variables. In this system, the first equation explains changes in firm value, operationalized as the ratio of the firm's market value to book value (*VBR*). This variable reflects a firm's potential growth opportunities, and is used frequently for assessing a firm's ability to achieve abnormal returns relative to its investment base. The second and third equations explain the changes in, respectively, bottom-line (*INC*) and top-line financial performance (*REV*) of firm i. The fourth and fifth equations model firm i's marketing actions, i.e. new-product introductions (*NPI*) and sales promotions (*SPR*) for brand j in product category k. The model also includes various exogenous factors, seasonal demand variations (such as Labor Day weekend, Memorial Day weekend ,and the end of each quarter), fluctuations in the overall economic and investment climate (S&P 500, the Construction Cost index and the dollar-Yen exchange rate), and accounts for the impact of stock-market analyst earnings expectations (*EPS*).

Overall, VAR models require extensive time-series data as they contain many more parameters than stock-return models. As the quality of financial and marketing databases increases, we expect these models to be used more frequently in the future (see Dekimpe and Hanssens 2000 for a more extensive discussion). In this particular application, Pauwels and his co-authors found that new-product introductions increased long-term financial performance and firm value, while promotions did not. Moreover, investor reactions to new product introductions were found to grow over time, and to yield the highest stock market benefits for entries into new markets.

15.6 Conclusion

Every year, companies spend a sizeable portion of their revenues on a variety of marketing activities. In the U.S., advertising and sales force expenditures alone sum to more than one trillion dollars, about 10% of the Gross National Product. These activities should be viewed as investments that ultimately return value to the firm's shareholders. Thus the assessment of the financial performance of marketing investments is an important task for marketing scientists and marketing managers alike. This assessment involves both flow metrics and stock metrics.

Our chapter has presented a framework for financial performance models from two perspectives: internal – i.e. describing how marketing creates value to the firm's shareholders – and external – i.e. describing how outside investors react to changes in marketing strategy. Starting from the core market response model, we first derived the standard measure of return of investment to marketing. We also isolated the three determinants of marketing spending that drive cash flows to the shareholders, viz. baseline business revenue, marketing effectiveness and profit margin. We then expanded the value creation of marketing to include *stock* metrics, in particular those created by diffusion of innovation, brand equity and customer equity. Marketing's total financial performance contribution is the sum of its impacts on these stock and flow metrics.

The shareholders' valuation of marketing is driven by their expectations on future cash flows and their perceptions on how marketing influences these cash flows. Investor valuation models should therefore focus on the *new* information contained in various marketing strategies and actions. We have discussed, in turn, the single-equation stock return response model, and the vector-autoregressive system's model as viable alternatives to measure marketing's impact on stock returns. Taken together, process models of value creation and investor valuation models provide a comprehensive and powerful resource to gauge marketing's impact on financial performance.

In terms of managerial implications, two important conclusions emerge. First, there *are* formal links between marketing actions and financial outcomes, and thus the marketing executive can and should participate in decisions that impact the financial outlook of the firm. Second, in so doing, the marketing executive should draw a careful distinction between actions that enhance or protect revenue flow and actions that build brand or customer equity. The latter two are not easily visible in the short run, but the metrics and models we have discussed above provide an implementable framework to answer all-important questions about the financial return on marketing and the role of marketing in the modern enterprise.

References

Ambler, T. 2003. *Marketing and the Bottom Line,* 2nd Edition. FT Prentice Hall, London, U.K.

Ambler, T., J. Roberts. 2006. Beware the Silver Metric: Marketing Performance Measurement Has to Be Multidimensional. *Marketing Science Institute* Report 06-003.

Ailawadi, K.L., D.R. Lehmann, S.A. Neslin. 2003. Revenue Premium as an Outcome Measure of Brand Equity. *Journal of Marketing* 67(October) 1–17.

Ataman, B., H.J. van Heerde, C.F. Mela. 2007. Building Brands. *Working Paper.* Rotterdam School of Management, Erasmus University.

Barwise, P., J.U. Farley. 2003. Which Marketing Metrics are Used and Where. *Marketing Reports* 2, 105–107.

Bass, F.M. 1969. A New Product Growth Model for Consumer Durables. *Management Science* 15(January) 215–27.

Bass, F.M., T.V. Krishnan, D.C. Jain. 1994. Why the Bass Model Fits well without Decision Variables. *Marketing Science* 13(2). 204–223.

Chaney, P.K., T.M. Devinney, R.S. Winer. 1991. The Impact of New Product Introductions on the Market Value of Firms. *Journal of Business* 64(4) 573–610.

Dekimpe, M.G., D.M. Hanssens. 1999. Sustained Spending and Persistent Response: A New Look at Long-Term Marketing Profitability. *Journal of Marketing Research* 36(November) 1–31.

Dekimpe, M.G., D.M. Hanssens. 2000. Time Series Models in Marketing: Past, Present and Future. *International Journal of Research in Marketing* 17(2–3) 183–193.

Elberse, A., J. Eliashberg. 2003. Demand and Supply Dynamics for Sequentially Released Products in International Markets: The Case of Motion Pictures. *Marketing Science* 22(3) 329–354.

Fama, E., K. French. 1992. The Cross-Section of Expected Stock Returns. *Journal of Finance* 47(2) 427–465.

Fama, E., K. French. 1993. Common Risk Factors in the Returns on Stocks and Bonds. *Journal of Financial Economics* 33 3–56.

Fornell, C., S. Mithas, F. Morgeson, M.S. Krishnan. 2006. Customer Satisfaction and Stock Prices: High Returns, Low Risk. *Journal of Marketing* 70(January) 3–14.

Forrester, J.W. 1961. *Industrial Dynamics.* MIT Press, Cambridge.

Geyskens, I., K. Gielens, M.G. Dekimpe. 2002. The Market Valuation of Internet Channel Additions. *Journal of Marketing* 66(April) 102–119.

Gielens, K., L.M. Van de Gucht, J.-B.E.M. Steenkamp, M.G. Dekimpe. 2007. Dancing with a Giant: The Effect of Wal-Mart's Entry into the United Kingdom on the Stock Prices of European Retailers. *Marketing Science Institute.* Report 07–106.

Givon, M., D. Horsky. 1990. Untangling the Effects of Purchase Reinforcement and Advertising Carryover. *Marketing Science* 9(2) 171–187.

Gupta, S., D.R. Lehmann. 2005. *Managing Customers as Investments.* Wharton Publishing/Pearson-Financial Times.

Gupta, S., D.R. Lehmann, J. Ames Stuart. 2004. Valuing Customers. *Journal of Marketing Research.* 41(February) 7–18.

Gupta, S., V. Zeithaml. 2006. Customer Metrics and Their Impact on Financial Performance. *Marketing Science* 25(6) 718–739.

Hanssens, D.M., L.J. Parsons, R.L. Schultz. 2001. *Market Response Models*. 2nd edition. Kluwer Academic Publishers, Boston, MA.

Horsky, D., L.S. Simon. 1983. Advertising and the Diffusion of New Products. *Marketing Science* **2**(Winter) 1–17.

Horsky, D., P. Swyngedouw. 1987. Does It Pay to Change Your Company's Name? A Stock Market Perspective. *Marketing Science* (Fall), 320–335.

Johansson, J.K. 1979. Advertising and the S-Curve: A New Approach. *Journal of Marketing Research*. **16**(August) 346–354.

Joshi, A.M., D.M. Hanssens. 2008. Movie Advertising and the Stock Market Valuation of Studios. Marketing Science, forthcoming.

Kamakura, W.A., G.J. Russell. 1993. Measuring Brand Value with Scanner Data. *International Journal of Research in Marketing*. **10** 9–22.

Keller, K.L., D.R. Lehmann. 2001. The Brand Value Chain: Linking Strategic and Financial Performance. *Working Paper*. Tuck School of Business, Dartmouth College.

Lehmann, D.R., D.J. Reibstein. 2006. *Marketing Metrics and Financial Performance*. Cambridge, MA: Marketing Science Institute, Relevant Knowledge Series.

Madden, T.J., F. Fehle, S. Fournier. 2006. Brands Matter: An Empirical Demonstration of the Creation of Shareholder Value through Branding. *Journal of the Academy of Marketing Science*. **34**(2) 224–235.

Mahajan, V., E. Muller, S. Sharma. 1984. An Empirical Comparison of Awareness Forecasting Models of New product Introduction. *Marketing Science*. **3**(Summer) 179–197.

Mela, C.F., S. Gupta, D.R. Lehmann. 1997. The Long-Term Impact of Promotion and Advertising on Consumer Brand Choice. *Journal of Marketing Research*. **34**(2) 248–261.

Mitra, D., P.N. Golder. 2005. Customer Perceptions of Product Quality: A Longitudinal Study. Cambridge, MA: *Marketing Science Institute*. Report 05–120.

Mizik, N., R. Jacobson. 2004. Stock Return Response Modeling. In Christine M., D.R. Lehmann, *Assessing Marketing Strategy Performance*. Marketing Science Institute, Cambridge, MA.

Norton, J.A., F.M. Bass. 1987. A Diffusion Theory Model of Adoption and Substitution for Successive Generations of High-Technology Products. *Management Science* **33**(September) 1069–1086.

Pauwels, K., D.M. Hanssens. 2007. Performance Regimes and Marketing Policy Shifts. *Marketing Science* **26**(3) 293–311.

Pauwels, K., J. Silva-Risso, S. Srinivasan, D.M. Hanssens. 2004. New Products, Sales Promotions and Firm Value, With Application to the Automobile Industry. *Journal of Marketing* **68**(October) 142–156.

Quelch, J., G.J. McGovern. 2006. Boards Must Measure Marketing Effectiveness. *Directors and Boards*. 53–56.

Rust, R.T., T. Ambler, G.S. Carpenter, V. Kumar, R.K. Srivastava. 2004. Measuring Marketing Productivity: Current Knowledge and Future Directions. *Journal of Marketing* **68**(October) 76–89.

Rust, R.T., K.N. Lemon, V.A. Zeithaml. 2004. Return on Marketing: Using Customer Equity to Focus Marketing Strategy. *Journal of Marketing* **68**(January) 109–127.

Srinivasan, R., S. Bharadwaj. 2004. Event Studies in Marketing Strategy Research. Christine M., D.R. Lehmann, *Assessing Marketing Strategy Performance*. Marketing Science Institute, Cambridge, MA.

Srinivasan, R., G.L. Lilien, A. Rangaswamy. 2004. First in, First out? The Effects of Network Externalities on Pioneer Survival. *Journal of Marketing* **68**(January) 41–58.

Srinivasan, S., D.M. Hanssens. 2007. Marketing and Firm Value. *Working Paper*. UCLA Anderson School of Management, June.

Srinivasan, S., K. Pauwels, J. Silva-Risso, D.M. Hanssens. 2009. Product Innovations, Advertising Spending and Stock Returns. Journal of Marketing, January, forthcoming.

Sriram, S., M.U. Kalwani. 2007. Optimal Advertising and Promotion Budgets in Dynamic Markets with Brand Equity as a Mediating Variable. *Management Science* **53**(1) 46–60.

Srivastava, R., T.A. Shervani, L. Fahey. 1998. Market-Based Assets and Shareholder Value: A Framework for Analysis. *Journal of Marketing* **62**(January) 1–18.

Srivastava, R., D.J. Reibstein. 2005. Metrics for Linking Marketing to Financial Performance. Cambridge, MA: *Marketing Science Institute*. Report 05–200e.

Yoo, S., D.M. Hanssens. 2006. Sales and Customer Equity Effects of the Marketing Mix. *Working Paper*. UCLA Anderson School of Management, April.

Yoo, S., D.M. Hanssens. 2007. Measuring Marketing Effects on Customer Equity for Frequently Purchased Brands. *Working Paper*. UCLA Anderson School of Management, June.

Part VIII

Implementation, Use and Success
of Marketing Models

Chapter 16
Marketing Engineering: Models that Connect with Practice

Gary L. Lilien and Arvind Rangaswamy

Other chapters in this book have demonstrated the wide range of marketing problems and the various analytic approaches implemented in decision models to address those problems. We will elaborate on some of those applications, but our main focus here is on how to make those models relevant and useful in practice. We take the perspective that the glass is both half-full and half-empty. We will sketch the range of marketing problems that marketing decision models have addressed, or can address, and we will provide an overview of some of the most visible applications in our literature that have had measurable impact on practice. That is the glass half full. On the half-empty side, we will document the gap between realized and actual potential for those applications. We will also identify areas for fruitful work by marketing scientists (and marketing engineers), both in terms of future domains of application and mechanisms that can be employed to increase the impact of marketing decision models, using an approach we call marketing engineering.

16.1 Marketing Engineering Accomplishments

16.1.1 What is Marketing Engineering?

Marketing managers make ongoing decisions about product features, prices, distribution options, sales compensation plans, and so on. In making these decisions, managers choose from among alternative courses of action in a complex and uncertain world. Like all decisions that people make, even when extensive data are available, marketing decision making involves judgment calls. Most traditional marketing decision making, while sometimes guided by the concepts of our literature, has been largely based on managers' mental models, intuition, and experience. In many situations, such mental models, perhaps backed up by market research data, may be all that managers need to

G.L. Lilien
Pennsylvania State University
e-mail: GLilien@psu.edu

B. Wierenga (ed.), *Handbook of Marketing Decision Models*,
DOI: 10.1007/978-0-387-78213-3_16, © Springer Science+Business Media, LLC 2008

feel psychologically comfortable with their decisions. Yet, mental models are prone to systematic errors (Bazerman 1998). While we all recognize the value of experience, that experience is unique to every person and can be confounded with responsibility bias: Sales managers might choose lower advertising budgets in favor of higher expenditures on personal selling, while advertising managers might prefer larger advertising budgets.

Consider an alternative approach to the mental model for a decision involving setting advertising expenditures: Managers might choose to build a spreadsheet decision model of how the market would respond to various expenditure levels. They could then use this model to explore the sales and profit consequences of alternative expenditure levels before making a decision. The systematic translation of data and knowledge (including judgment) into a tool that is used for decision support is what we call (traditional) marketing engineering. In contrast, relying solely on the mental model of the particular decision maker without using any support system is what we refer to as conceptual marketing. A third option would be to automate the decision process. Consider, for example a different context: when a user logs on to Amazon.com, he or she is often greeted by a recommendation that is produced in the background based on an analysis of what Amazon knows about the user's demographics and past purchase behavior, and the purchases of people who have made purchases similar to those of the focal user. Such a process is what we call *automated marketing engineering*. Bucklin et al. (1998) outline the opportunities for the computer taking over many of the traditionally human tasks associated with marketing decisions. However, given the intrinsic complexity of marketing problems (many instruments; a large number of environmental factors, including competition; and substantial uncertainty in each of these factors), for many marketing decisions, a combination of marketing support tools and the judgment of the decision maker provides the best results.

We define (traditional) marketing engineering (ME) as *a systematic approach to harness data and knowledge to drive marketing decision making and implementation through a technology-enabled and model-supported interactive decision process*. When human judgment or interaction is not involved, i.e., when the marketing decision is automated, we call that *automated marketing engineering*. Figure 16.1 shows how the ME approach transforms objective and subjective data about the marketing environment into insights, decisions, and actions.

The ME approach relies on the design and construction of decision models and implementing such decision models within organizations in the form of marketing management or marketing decision support systems (MMSSs).[1] As

---

[1] Wierenga and van Bruggen (2000) define MMSS as "Any device combining (1) information technology, (2) analytic capabilities, (3) marketing data and (4) marketing knowledge made available to one or more marketing decision makers to improve the quality of marketing management." This definition represents a "systems" view of decision support for the entire marketing function, whereas marketing engineering is focused more specifically on the analysis methods and processes (i.e., those that have a strong analytic component). MMSS

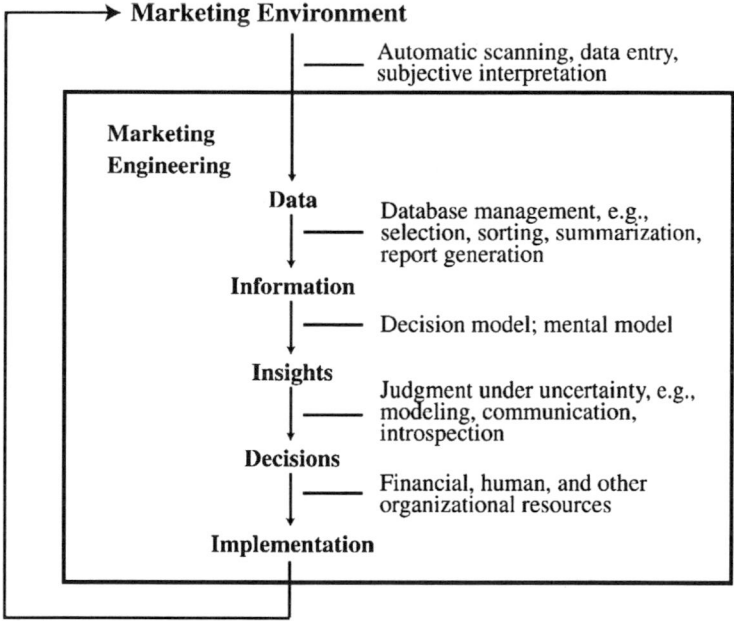

Fig. 16.1 The marketing engineering approach to decision making helps transform objective and subjective data about the marketing environment into decisions and decision implementations

Wierenga et al. (1999) point out, technological and modeling advances have greatly increased the availability and quality of model-based marketing decision support systems (MDSS), a term that is somewhat broader than marketing engineering. Marketing engineering forms the core of those MDSSs that rely on formal or analytical models. Many MDSS's – e.g., database marketing systems, customer relationship management systems, marketing dashboards, pricing decision support systems, sales territory alignment systems – are based on decision models, which have been shown to improve the objective quality of marketing decision making (e.g., McIntyre 1982; Lodish et al. 1988; Hoch and Schkade 1996; Silva-Risso et al. 1999; Eliashberg et al. 2000; Zoltners and Sinha 2005; Divakar et al. 2005), thus improving managerial and organizational performance.

---

and MDSS also incorporate non-analytic processes (e.g., analogizing and creativity enhancement), as well as aspects of the systems architecture, an issue beyond the scope of ME as we define it.

16.1.2 The Benefits of Marketing Engineering

The volume of concepts, tools, and techniques underlying the ME approach is large. The academic world has been producing a great deal of literature on quantitative marketing methods, much of which is focused on marketing decision making. Lehmann (2005) cites the emergence of seven quantitative marketing journals since 1982, before which the field boasted only four; also journals, such as *Marketing Science* have increased the number of issues, and the number of pages per issue. It is fair to say that the rate at which marketing engineering knowledge and tools is being produced and reported in the academic literature, has most likely tripled in the past 25 years.

The models reported in the literature provide a range of benefits: Figure 16.2 illustrates some ways these benefits emerge:

16.1.2.1 Improves Consistency of Decisions

One benefit of models is that they help managers to make more consistent decisions. Consistency is especially desirable in decisions that they make often. Several studies have shown the value of consistency in improving predictions (Table 16.1).

Table 16.2 lists variables experts often use to predict the academic performance of graduate business students (the first row of Table 16.1). Interestingly, the formalized intuition of experts captured in a simple linear decision model outperforms the experts themselves. Accuracy improved from 19% correlation with the actual student performance to 25% correlation. An explanation for

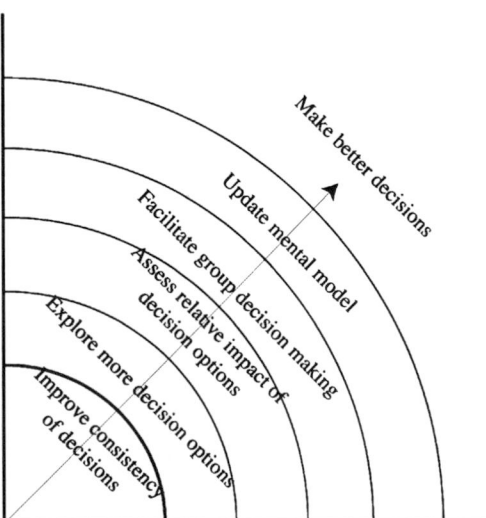

Fig. 16.2 Managers derive a spectrum of benefits from using decision models, leading ultimately to better decisions

Table 16.1 Degree of correlation with the true outcomes of three types of models, showing that even subjective decision models are superior to mental models, but that formal, objective models do far better. Source: Russo and Schoemaker 1989, p. 137

Types of judgments experts had to make	Mental model*	Subjective decision model**	Objective decision model***
Academic performance of graduate students	.19	.25	.54
Life expectancy of cancer patients	−.01	.13	.35
Changes in stock prices	.23	.29	.80
Mental illness using personality tests	.28	.31	.46
Grades and attitudes in psychology course	.48	.56	.62
Business failures using financial ratios	.50	.53	.67
Students' ratings of teaching effectiveness	.35	.56	.91
Performance of life insurance salesman	.13	.14	.43
IQ scores using Rorschach tests	.47	.51	.54
Mean (across many studies)	.33	.39	.64

*Outcomes directly predicted by experts.
**Subjective Decision Model: Outcomes predicted by subjective linear regression model, formalizing past predictions made by experts
***Objective Decision Model: Linear model developed directly from data

this improvement is that humans are inconsistent decision makers while models consistently apply the knowledge of experts in new cases.

The third column in Table 16.1 lists the accuracy of an "objective" linear regression model. For the academic performance study the independent variables for the regression model were the same factors used by the experts, but the dependent variable was a known measure of the academic performance of the graduate students. The predictions in this case were based on a hold-out sample of data to which the objective model was applied. For this model the correlation of the predictions with the true outcomes was 54%. Table 16.1 also shows the average correlations between predictions and true outcomes across several studies. We see that subjective decision models had an average correlation of 39% with true outcomes as compared with 33% for the intuitive mental models. For more details about these studies, see Camerer (1981), Goldberg (1970), and Russo and Schoemaker (1989).

These results point to a few interesting conclusions: (1) When you can build an objective model based on actual data, you will generally make the best predictions. However, in many decision situations we do not have data that show the accuracy or the consequences of past decisions made in the same context. In such cases the next best option is to codify the mental model decision makers use into a formal decision model. The calibrating of response models

Table 16.2 Input data for all three models–namely, mental model, subjective decision model, and objective decision model–used for predicting the performance of graduate students. See first row of Exhibit 1.6

Applicant	Personal essay	Selectivity of undergraduate institution	Undergraduate major	College grade average	Work experience	GMAT verbal	GMAT quantitative
1	Poor	Highest	Science	2.50	10	98%	60%
2	Excellent	Above avg	Business	3.82	0	70%	80%
3	Average	Below avg	Other	2.96	15	90%	80%
⋮	⋮	⋮	⋮	⋮	⋮	⋮	⋮
117	Weak	Least	Business	3.10	100	98%	99%
118	Strong	Above avg	Other	3.44	60	68%	67%
119	Excellent	Highest	Science	2.16	5	85%	25%
120	Strong	Strong	Business	3.98	12	30%	58%

Source: Russo and Schoemaker 1989, p. 132

using the decision calculus method (Little, 1970) is a way to formalize the mental models of decision makers. (2) Among these three types of models, the least accurate is the mental model. However, on average all three types of models had a positive correlation with the truth, whereas a model with random predictions would have zero correlation with the truth. (3) To realize benefits, marketing managers should focus their attention on finding variables useful for prediction but should use decision models to combine the variables in a consistent fashion.

16.1.2.2 Enables Exploration of More Decision Options

In some situations the number of options available to decision makers is so large that it would be physically impossible for them to apply mental models to evaluate each option. For example, in allocating a firm's sales effort across products and market segments, in deciding which media vehicles to use for an advertising campaign, or in pricing the various travel classes and routes of an airline, many thousands of possible options are available to managers. The manager may develop decision heuristics that help cut down the number of options to be evaluated. The use of heuristics helps refine the mental model to incorporate additional considerations that narrow the number of decision options. But such pruning of decision options may lead to worse decisions than considering each of the available options more carefully. An alternative approach is to develop a computer decision model that facilitates the exploration of more options. That computer model is not constrained by the manager's past behavior and can avoid the potential effects of inertia or anchoring. By exploring more options, managers are more likely to move away from their prior dispositions (anchor points). A number of decision models of this type are available to marketing managers, and these have been shown to improve decisions. For example, several salesforce-allocation models have resulted in a 5–10% improvement in profitability with no additional investments (Fudge and Lodish 1977; Rangaswamy et al. 1990; Sinha and Zoltners 2001).

Exploring more decision options often permits the decision maker to calculate the opportunity costs associated with the option(s) he or she chooses, and the potential loss relative to the (economically) "best" option. For example, a manager may choose not to reassign 10 sales representatives to the territories that the model suggests, for an opportunity cost of $200,000. The manager may then argue that the loss of employee and customer goodwill and the organizational disruption associated with such a move does not justify that opportunity cost. In any case, the model provides the means to make that tradeoff calculation.

16.1.2.3 Helps Assess the Relative Impact of Variables

In some situations, the decision options may be few, but the variables that might affect the decision may be numerous. For example, in test marketing a new product a manager may be considering only two decision options—withdraw the product or introduce it in selected markets—but many variables may influence this decision. Such variables as competitor and dealer reactions, consumer trial rates, competitive promotions, the brand equity associated with the brand name, and the availability of the product on the shelf all influence product sales. Here a decision model would provide the manager with a framework to more fully explore each decision option and to understand the impact of each variable on product sales. The model would also serve as a diagnostic tool in helping the manager assess the relative importance of the variables in influencing test market sales of the product. Models such as Assessor have been successfully used in test marketing, and Urban and Katz (1983) report that, on average, the use of the Assessor model offers a 1:6 cost:benefit ratio.

16.1.2.4 Facilitates Group Decision Making

Modeling provides focus and objectivity to group decision making by externalizing ideas and relationships that reside inside the minds of decision makers. In the same way that an explicit agenda helps direct meetings, the model or the results from a modeling effort can help a group deliberate and converge on a decision. For example, discussions on allocating resources tend to degenerate into turf battles, like congressional budget debates. However, if the entire group participates in a decision modeling exercise, then group discussions can be directed toward why someone prefers a particular allocation, rather than focusing simply on what allocation that person prefers. Likewise, if the members of a group agree on a modeling approach, then they may view the model results as unbiased and coming from an external source and therefore favor more rational (less emotional) decision options.

16.1.2.5 Updates Mental Models of Decision Makers

Marketing managers have mental models of how their markets operate. They develop these models through trial and error over years of experience, and these mental models serve as valuable guides in decision making. Yet in forming these mental models they may not take advantage of how managers in other industries have approached similar problems, or they may not incorporate academic research that addresses such problems. When managers are exposed to decision models, they update their own internal mental models in subtle but significant ways. Formal models require that key assumptions be made explicit, or their structure may require new ways of thinking about a familiar problem, resulting in learning that may affect future decisions. Although new learning is an indirect benefit of using models, in many cases it is the most important benefit.

16.1.3 *Examples of Marketing Engineering Success*

Those benefits summarized above and others have been realized in a number of well-documented applications over the years, including:

Gensch et al. (1990): *ABB Electric*, a manufacturer and distributor of power-generation equipment, wanted to increase its sales and market share in an industry that was facing a projected 50 percent drop in demand. By carefully analyzing and tracking customer preferences and actions, it determined which customers to focus its marketing efforts on and what features of its products were most important to those customers. The company used choice modeling to provide ongoing support for its segmentation and targeting decisions, introducing the idea of targeting the "switchable customer. The firm credits its modeling effort as critical for its survival in a declining market.

Wind et al. (1989): *Marriott Corporation* was running out of good downtown locations for new full-service hotels. To maintain its growth, Marriott's management planned to locate hotels outside the downtown area that would appeal to both business travelers and weekend leisure travelers. Marriott used conjoint analysis as the core of its program to design and launch the highly successful Courtyard by Marriott chain, establishing a multi-billion dollar business and creating a new product category.

Smith et al. (1992): *American Airlines* faces the ongoing problem of deciding what prices to charge for its various classes of service on its numerous routes and determining how many seats on each scheduled flight to allocate to each class of service. Too many seats sold at discount prices, overselling seats on a flight, or allowing too many seats to go empty leads to low revenues. Maximizing revenue in a competitive environment is crucial to the successful operation of the firm. It uses a marketing engineering approach, called revenue management, to fill its planes with the right mix of passengers paying different fares, and credits the approach with more than $500 million/year in incremental revenue

Lodish et al. (1988): *Syntex Laboratories* was concerned about the productivity of its salesforce. In particular, managers were unsure whether the size of the salesforce was right for the job it had to do and whether the firm was allocating its salesforce effort to the most profitable products and market segments. The company used judgmentally calibrated market response models and a resource allocation optimization tool to evaluate the current performance of its salesforce and to develop salesforce deployment strategies that were in line with its long-term growth plans. This modeling approach resulted in more than $15 million in additional profit above their original plan.

Zoltners and Sinha (2005). *ZS associates* has implemented various marketing engineering tools to support sales territory alignment decisions, designing sales territories and assigning sales representatives to them for over 500 clients representing 500,000 sales territories in 39 countries They report increased revenues for those firms of more than $10 billion and have saved 14,500 sales-person-equivalents in travel time reduction in the first year of these alignment implementations.

Table 16.3 provides brief descriptions of a sample of the most highly visible recent applications that were either winners or finalists in the INFORMS Society on Marketing Science Practice Prize Competition *http://www.informs. org/article.php?id=613*, which recognize modeling applications for their combination of technical merit and organizational impact. The applications above and in Table 16.3 suggests that the field has been producing highly impactful applications over a long time, several of which embed modeling approaches that can be employed widely. Roberts et al. (2007) provide extensive empirical evidence of the broad impact of marketing engineering on practice at both the conceptual and the operational levels. These developments are good news indeed; so the marketing engineering glass is at least half full.

16.2 Marketing Engineering: Missed Opportunities

As impressive as the current ME applications and reports are, the mere availability, or even the use of a marketing decision model to support decision making, does not guarantee better decisions or the realization of increased value for the firm. Although models can produce significant benefits, many managers are reluctant to use models based just on their objective quality. For example, retail industry analysts report that retailers have been slow to adopt pricing decision models that are known to improve retail performance (Reda 2002, 2003).[2] Sullivan (2005) reports that only 5–6% of retailers use price-optimization models, while most prefer to use their gut-feel for making pricing decisions. As a consequence, "actual retail prices observed over time may differ greatly from model-recommended courses of action" (Nijs et al. 2007). Indeed, according to an Accenture (2002) study, while the Global Fortune 1000 firms collectively spend over $ trillion in marketing, 68% of respondents could not even articulate what was meant by return on marketing investment in their organization, much less measure it.

Wierenga et al. (1999) provide an integrating framework that highlights the many factors that determine the success of marketing decision support systems that can also be applied to marketing engineering. Those factors involve (1) Demand Side issues, involving characteristics of the decision problem, the specific decision maker and the organizational environment in which the decision takes place, matched with (2) Supply Side issues, or characteristics of the system, including the data, the knowledge base, the analytics (or other)

---

[2] The reluctance of decision makers to use decision models even when those models can improve performance is not restricted to marketing.. For example, DSSs significantly improve a doctor's clinical performance in prescribing decisions (Hunt et al. 1998), yet medical professionals are largely unwilling to use such DSSs (Sintchenko et al. 2004; Lapointe and Rivard 2006),

Table 16.3 Recent, documented marketing engineering successes: Marketing science practice prize finalists and winners (W = ISMS Practice Prize Winner F = ISMS Practice Prize Finalist)

Paper	Description	Client	Methodology	Impact/transportability
1. Elsner et al. (2004) W	Model addresses key direct marketing questions: when, how often and who to target with what offers.	Rhenania, German direct mail company	Model involved segmentation, short and long term customer response valuation.	Approach replaced short term optimization approach that was eroding firm's customer base, Firm rose from number 5 to number two market position with increased profitability
2. Roberts et al. (2004) F	Model addresses how best to plan for and react to a new entrant (Optus) into the Australian telecommunications market	Telstra (Australian Telecom Company)	Choice models, diffusion models, market simulations,	Modeling approach lead to new positioning, pricing and resource allocation decisions leading to benefits of over $100 million
3. Foster et al. (2004) F	Model to assess likely takeoff timing for new consumer durable, the Personal Valet	Whirlpool	Diffusion model, takeoff timing model	Modeling lead Whirlpool to modify price targets and market projection, permitting what should be a successful new product the time to develop
4. Zoltners and Sinha (2005) W	Report of a wide range of sales territory design and alignment applications	Over 1500 applications with over 500 companies	Integer, mixed integer and nonlinear programming. Interactive Decision support systems.	Conservative assessment of benefits affecting over 500,000 sales reps in 30 companies amount to $10 billion and the effective savings of 14,500 man-years of sales effort.

Table 16.3 (continued)

Paper	Description	Client	Methodology	Impact/transportability
5. Divakar et al. (2005) F	Sales forecasting model to manage product demand by pack size, region, channel, category and customer account type to plan pricing and promotional strategies.	Pepsico	Econometric models	Company claims conservative benefits of $11 million; DSS integrating the model framework has become operational practice at the firm
6. Sinha et al. (2005) F	The attribute drivers approach permits the use of panel data to support restaging decisions, assessing line extensions/deletions, and pricing and promotion decisions.	Numerous, with Campbell Soup company cited in the paper as example client of IRI, the developer	Choice models, factor analysis	Studies reported at Campbell claimed a return of over $10 million on an investment of under $300,000
7. Tellis et al. (2005) F	An integrated framework to address television advertising copy design, targeting (by channel and time of day) and media weight.	Futuredontics (a dental referral service) and 1-800 Plumber, an a toll-free plumber referral service	Choice models, response models, econometric models	The CEO of Futuredontics reports the ability to maintain or increase response to TV ads with a 25% decrease in advertising spending.
8. Labbi et al. (2007) W	Long run approach to customer lifetime management, jointly developed by Finnair and IBM	Finnair	Choice models, Markovian decision processes, options value	Improved response rates to Finnair's marketing offers by 10%, decreased marketing costs 20% and increased customer satisfaction 10%.

Table 16.3 (continued)

Paper	Description	Client	Methodology	Impact/transportability
9. Ailawadi et al. (2007) F	Decompose promotional sales bump into switching, stockpiling, and primary demand components and estimate its net sales and margin impact, and relate to promotion, brand, category, and market characteristics.	CVS Pharmacy	Econometric models, response models	Results of market tests project to negligible sales loss when optimizing promotions but profit gain of over $50 million annually.
10. Kitts et al. (2005) F (note: no written report, but DVD of presentation is available	Targeting the right customer with the right product at the right time–an innovative approach to online 1:1 marketing via customized emails.	Harborfreight	Hypergeometric distribution tests	Model use resulted in Clickthrough increase by 40%, revenue by 38%, and units sold by 61%.
11. Natter et al. (2007) F	Weekly demand model that incorporates price, reference price effects, seasonality, article availability, features and discounts, integrated into a decision support system	BauMax, an Austrian Do it Yourself Retailer	Econometrics, response functions, optimization, simulation	Baumax reports sales increase associated with use of the model of 2.1% and a profit increase of 8.1%
12. Silva-Risso and Ionava (2008) W	Promotional analysis models to allow auto manufacturers to improve the timing, frequency and selection of promotions, to maintain sales but reduce costs	JD Power clients include major US auto manufacturer	Econometrics, choice models, frontier analysis, optimization	Daimler Chrysler alone attests to $500 million/year in savings; projection for rest of auto industry approximates $2 billion

Table 16.3 (continued)

Paper	Description	Client	Methodology	Impact/transportability
13. Kumar et al. 2008 F	Program to segment the market to optimize the number of touches mid-market customers receive,	IBM field experiment on mid-range business customers (100-999 employees)	Market response modeling, cost-to-serve models, optimization	IBM reports over $20 million in incremental annual returns from the US pilot study alone.
14. Shankar et al. 2008 F	Research to quantify the benefit of corporate branding and allocate that benefit to different business units,	AllState used the approach to set, allocate and evaluate the economic value of its communications expenditures	Choice models, response models, econometrics.	AllState reports transformation from marketing communication as a cost to a strategic investment, with associated cultural change
15. Natter et al. 2008 F	New positioning map as part as segmentation, targeting and positioning program for a new form of wireless phone tariff	Tele.Ring used the approach to identify a new tariff for the Austrian market, and to target that tariff at the appropriate market segments	Cluster analysis, multidimensional scaling, optimization	Tele.Ring reports additional $28 million in profits and market performance five times better than recent competitive entrants.

underlying technology; (3) the design characteristics of the MDSS itself, (4) the Implementation Process, including characteristics and attitudes of the adopting organization and the process used by the system developers and (5) Success Measures, including attitudes toward the system, stakeholder success measures and organizational success measures, both financial and otherwise. The extensive set of factors in this framework suggests that there are many potholes along the way to the success of marketing decision models.

And just how much impact have our most visible models had? While this is a hard question to answer unambiguously, van Bruggen and Wierenga (2001), using self reports from the developers of a sample of these most highly referenced and visible model, report the findings summarized in Table 16.4. If this is a representative report of how the best of the profession's developments are faring, then there seems to be considerable unrealized upside potential.

16.2.1 Reasons for Missed Marketing Engineering Opportunities

We have summarized elsewhere (Lilien and Rangaswamy, 2004) a number of reasons for this lack of adoption, including the following:

16.2.1.1 Mental Models Are Often Good Enough

Human beings are good at reasoning by analogy and recognizing patterns. As long as the situation is similar to past situations, that approach is fine. Indeed, in an experimental study involving forecasting, Hoch and Schkade (1996) find that mental models perform much better in predictable decision environments than in unpredictable environments, where an over reliance on familiar patterns can lead to misleading insights.

Models don't solve managerial problems, people do: It is unrealistic to expect models to directly resolve managerial problems, because by design, they are incomplete. Yet, this is precisely what many managers would like. Realistically, the relevant question is, "what is the role of a model in helping

Table 16.4 Measures of the impact of the most visible marketing models, showing there is still room for improvement

Impact measures	Mean (st. dev.)
Number of companies that implemented the MMSS	46.3 (79.3) (Range: 0–333)
Percentage of companies that still use the MMSS	44.3 (42.2) (Range: 0–100)
Impact of MMSS on actual decisions[a] (small – large)	5.40 (1.33)
Success of implementation of MMSS[a] (not successful – very successful)	5.43 (1.19)
Satisfaction of users[a] (not satisfied – very satisfied)	5.47 (1.07)
Impact Scale (Cronbach $\alpha = 0.80$)	

[a]For these indicators 7-point scale items were applied
(Source: van Bruggen and Wierenga 2001)

users solve a specific problem?", and not, "how can a model solve that problem?" The former requires combining model-based analyses with managerial judgments, which often demands more effort, trained managers, motivation to use models, and the like. If models are to be used in conjunction with a manager's judgments, some managers may legitimately argue, why not rely just on sound judgments? However, this is not a good argument. As Hogarth (1987, p. 199) notes, "When driving at night with your headlights on, you do not necessarily see too well. However, turning your headlights off will not improve the situation." Indeed, as we have often heard said, "All models are wrong; some are useful." We obviously have not been able to demonstrate sufficient utility in situations where substantial benefits can be realized by using models.

16.2.1.2 Managers Do Not Observe the Opportunity Costs of Their Decisions

We believe this is a critical factor that undermines the need for models, Managers observe only the consequences of decisions they have actually made and not the consequences of those they didn't. Therefore they are often unable to judge for themselves whether they could have made better decisions by using decision models. Lilien et al. (2004), show that managers often do not think that their decisions become better when using ME or an MDSS, even when there are objective improvements in outcomes as a consequence of model-supported decisions. Without this ability to observe the value of systematic decision making, many managers continue to do what is intuitively comfortable for them. In some industries, such as mutual funds, managers are rewarded based on their performance compared with that of managers of funds with similar risk portfolios. Here managers can observe indirectly the consequences of decisions they did not make. It is not surprising then that the financial services industry is one of the heaviest users of computer modeling to support decisions (see also Wierenga, van Bruggen, and Althuizen (2007; Section 17.3.1).

16.2.1.3 Models Require Precision

Models require that assumptions be made explicit, that data sources be clearly specified, and so forth. Some managers perceive all this concreteness as a threat to their power base and a devaluation of their positions, particularly middle managers in hierarchical organizations. Using models is analogous to thinking aloud. Many people in traditional organizations may be uncomfortable revealing their thoughts. A typical role of middle managers in traditional organizations has been to gather information from the front lines and structure that information to facilitate top management decision making. However, as information management becomes more computerized and decentralized, middle managers need to focus more on the decision consequences of information. Rarely does information by itself lead to better decisions. Only when decision makers draw insights from information and use those insights as a basis for action does information translate into value for an organization.

16.2.1.4 Models Emphasize Analysis

Managers prefer action. Little (1970) noted this many years ago. In the past, managers could call on corporate support staff whenever they needed help with analysis, so that they could concentrate on what they liked to do best. In today's flatter organizations, support staff is increasingly a luxury that few firms can afford. Managers today operate in a self-help environment which has major implications for the type of decision support they can use. For a discussion of the organizational and personal incentives for increasing model use and impact, see Wierenga et al. (2007; Section 17.3.2).

Delaine Hampton from Procter and Gamble, at a Practitioner-Academic interface session at a Marketing Science conference in June 2004, indicated that she defines model success as change in mental models within the organization. Therefore, for a model to be successful it *either* has to be embedded in an operational system (automated marketing engineering) and integrated into a well-defined operational process (e.g., pricing process, new product development process, customer complaint resolution system), *or*, if it is a non-embedded model (i.e., visible to the decision maker), then users and the organization itself have to effectively change their way of thinking (i.e., their mental models of decision making with respect to those issues).

To understand how to overcome the reluctance of many managers and organizations to deploy Marketing Decision Support Systems, Kayande et al. (2007) explored ways to bridge the gap between the decision model and the mental models of users. The findings are intriguing. They show that a key reason for the lack of positive reactions to even an objectively good marketing engineering model is that such systems are often not designed to help users understand and internalize the underlying factors driving the model results and related recommendations. Thus, there is likely to be a gap between a marketing manager's mental model and the marketing engineering model or MDSS, which reduce the perceived value of the model. A model must not only be objectively good, but it must be designed and implemented in such a way that that gap is reduced. To reduce the gap, we find that a good model must provide feedback on **upside potential** (how much better could we do with a better mental model) as well as feedback on **why and how to change** (that is specific guidance on the prescription for change and associated reasoning). Thus, a good marketing engineering system must *both* encourage more effort for improving decision making and provide ways to channel decision effort toward improved decision making. We elaborate some more on these ideas later in this chapter.

To summarize, the marketing engineering field has produced a rich set of concepts, tools and technologies, many of which have demonstrated remarkable potential and actual positive organizational impact. We have also seen that there is still considerable upside potential for more success in this domain.

While there have been a variety of frameworks developed to help grasp the dimensions of the gap between the perceived and the potential value of marketing engineering, we urge developers in this area to consider three sets of dimensions: (1) *Model Quality*. Is the model objectively good? Does it provide the two necessary types of feedback identified above? Do the financial and objective benefits of using the model (when all costs are considered) provide a sufficient economic return to justify the investment? If the answer to any of these questions is no, then there is no need to go further. No sale. (2) *Organization Incentives*. Does the marketing engineering model or system fit in with the organizational reward system, culture, or metrics for measurement? Is the organization one that embraces or resists/punishes change? Favorable organizational incentives go a long way toward creating the environment and setting the tone for the use of analytics in decision making. Companies in very different industries, such as FedEx, Harrah's Entertainment, Amazon, and Wal-Mart, have taken the lead in providing such organizational incentives. (3) *Personal Incentives*. Assuming the model is of high quality, is there sufficient personal gain (career enhancement, sense of accomplishment, etc.) to overcome the natural inertia we all experience when asked to change the way we have been doing things. Organizational incentives help, but may not be sufficient to overcome personal disinclinations and inertia toward use of analytics in decision making – such inclinations are greater for those individuals either with an inherently large resistance to change, or those who have a greater personal stake in the status quo.

There is thus a great opportunity for more research on the success factors, the potential pitfalls, and the potential for increased use and adoption of marketing engineering.

16.3 A Look Ahead for Marketing Engineering

In this section, we attempt to set the clock forward and take a peek at tomorrow's marketing engineering concepts and tools. What strikes us immediately is that today's marketing engineering is only partially aligned with the evolving decision support needs of managers and customers, and tomorrow's systems must be designed and developed in ways quite different from today's systems. Table 16.5 summarizes the changes we expect to see between marketing engineering frontiers today and the frontiers as they will be in the next 5–10 years. We can already detect some elements of such a transformation in a few examples of ME summarized in Table 16.3: the ME implementations at Rhenania (Elsner et al. 2004), Harborfreight (Kitts et al. 2005), CVS Pharmacy (Ailawadi et al. 2007), Finnair (Labbi et al. 2007), and Baumax (Natter et al. 2007) share some characteristics of the marketing engineering of tomorrow.

The major drivers of the change toward tomorrow's ME are the huge investments that firms are making in information technology infrastructures

Table 16.5 The frontiers of marketing engineering (ME) today, and what it will be in the mid- to long-term future. Marketing models will gradually be woven into the fabric of organizational processes, and become core to enhancing organizational productivity and business model success

	ME frontiers today	ME frontiers tomorrow
Time Scale	Days and weeks, if not months	Moving toward real time in data entry, data access, data analysis, implementation, and feedback
Focus of ME	Support strategic decisions	Support both strategic and operational decisions
Mode of Operation	Individual and PC-centric	Organization and Network centric – support multiple employees in multiple locations on multiple devices
Decision Domain	Marketing	Marketing and other functions, such as Supply Chain and Finance
Company Interface	Loosely coupled to company's IT systems	Woven into IT-supported company's operations and decision processes
ME Intervention Opportunities	Discrete, Problem-driven	Continuous, Process-driven
ME Goal	Support analysis and optimization	Support robust and adaptive organizational decision processes
ME System Design	As a tool to understand information and enhance decisions	As tool to enhance productivity and success of business models
ME System Operation	Interactive (User interacts with model)	Interactive as well as autonomous (embedded)
ME Outputs	Recommended actions; What if analyses	Visualization of markets and their behavior (e.g., Dashboard), Extended reality (e.g., Business model simulation), Explanation (Why?), Automated implementation (e.g., create alerts, automate actions)
ME Implementation Sequence	Intervention Opportunity → Implementation of decisions → Integration with IT Systems	Integration with IT → Intervention Opportunity → Implementation of decisions

linked to communication networks. The digital backbones that exist inside and outside firms today support technologies such as Java that allow computer programs to be executed on any computer connected to a network (e.g., Internet), and XML that allow data of various types and from various sources to be more easily aggregated into self-describing entities. These two developments enable decision makers to tap into vast amounts of computing power and data sources on demand, thereby creating a new environment for the supply and demand for marketing analytics. In this new environment, the digital networks (Internet, Intranet, and Extranet) function essentially as one giant (decentralized) computer, and the data repositories function as one giant filing cabinet. But the vast data and computing resources are just necessary ingredients: by themselves, they do not result in improved decisions, higher productivity, more innovation, faster growth, or competitive gains. Increasingly, firms recognize that one of their most important competitive capabilities is the conversion of information into timely actions (Davenport 2006). We are seeing a trend in marketing toward decision making that is more customer focused and data driven (see also, Wierenga et al. 2007; Section 17.2). And, marketing analytics embedded within Customer Relationship Management (CRM) systems and Dashboards are enabling firms to connect their data and knowledge to intelligent and timely decisions.

Consider the following examples illustrating how Travelocity, Wal-Mart and Amazon.com have converted their IT infrastructure into profits, by facilitating timely decisions and actions:

Travelocity, one of the Web's biggest online travel sites, takes strategic advantage of its Web log data to improve its promotional program. For example, in early 2000, TWA announced a special $360 round-trip fare between Los Angeles and San Juan, Puerto Rico. Typically, a traditional marketing pitch would have notified the whole Hispanic community in the L.A. area, including people with no interest in Puerto Rico. Instead, Travelocity analyzed its data warehouse, and within a few hours it had identified 30,000 customers in L.A. who had inquired about fares to Puerto Rico within the past few days. An e-mail went out to them the next morning, with a remarkable 25 percent of the targeted segment either taking the TWA offer or booking another Caribbean flight (Klebnikov 2001).

Wal-Mart has developed the world's largest commercial data warehouse, reputed to be over 500 terabytes of data. This centralized warehouse includes data on every transaction in every one of its stores for the past 65 weeks, and the inventories carried in each store. This database came in handy on 9/11, when the company detected substantial increases in sales of U.S. flags, decals, as well as guns and ammunition, within hours of the event. For example, flag sales were up 1800% over the same date, previous year, and sales of ammunition increased 100% (Christian Science Monitor 2002). Detecting these changes early enabled Wal-Mart to quickly replenish each store with the appropriate quantities of these items, as well as to place additional orders with its suppliers before most of its competitors. As a result, Wal-Mart not only helped meet customer demand, but was able to do so in a way that conferred it some competitive advantages.

Amazon.com has arguably collected more information about customer decision making process than any other company. According to the company, it has nearly 60 million active customers (those who bought within the past year, ending second quarter 2006) and it collects information on what those customers search, buy, bid, post (e.g., wish lists and guest registries), participate in a contest or questionnaire, or communicate with customer service. Amazon has built ever-more sophisticated recommendation tools for cross-selling that dynamically generates a list of specific products that each individual customer is most likely to want. It uses its database of customer information to make ongoing marketing decisions. For example, when Amazon.com offered the new "Amazon Prime" free shipping club program in 2005, it received mixed reviews among investors. The program offered customers who pay $79 a year unlimited free two-day delivery and discounted next-day delivery on in-stock items. The Prime program enabled the company to differentiate its services – few, if any, retailers would be able to match Amazon on the scope of its product categories, or its scale to tightly manage transportation costs. Jeff Bezos, CEO of Amazon.com, reports (2006 Quarter 2 Earnings Conference Call), that the ongoing analyses of the pre- and post- behaviors of customers who join the Prime program shows that they increased their purchases with the company thereby deepening customer relationships, and increase their customer lifetime value. Further, continuous monitoring and analytics helps Amazon fine-tune its offerings and recommendations to strengthen relationships with these customers.

Such "real-time" marketing analysis and implementation capabilities will become critically important for firms in the years ahead. A key insight from the above examples is that, increasingly, ME applications will be triggered by external events (e.g., customer visits to web sites, 9/11 attack, a customer quote request), or planned "test" events (e.g., price change, free shipping offer), and tied closely to the operational processes of the company. At the same time, there will also be more opportunities for traditional pro-active MDSS applications within the new infrastructure. For example, at NetFlix, about two-thirds of the films rented were automatic recommendations made to subscribers by the recommendation agent (an ME application) available at the web site. These are movies the customers might never have considered themselves. As a result, between 70 and 80 percent of NetFlix rentals come from the company's back catalog of 38,000 films, rather than from recent releases, which allows the company to manage its inventories better (Flynn 2006).

The definition of real-time depends on the context, varying from milliseconds to hours or even days. In the financial services industry, real-time analytics are needed nearly instantaneously to help managers and investors find opportunities (e.g., real-time hedging against interest-rate risks, real-time micro trading); one report suggests that a one millisecond advantage in trade execution can translate into $100 million profit for a major brokerage firm (Information Week 2007). In marketing, the Web has triggered a similar need for near instantaneous support for decision making: a customer coming to amazon.com to purchase a book triggers a complex analytics-supported process that provides product recommendations, credit checks and authorization, inventory checks and release of product from inventory, promotional and customer validation, in addition to updates to inventory, logistics, and the entire supply chain.

The real-time environment is forcing businesses to fundamentally transform the way they make decisions, forcing all employees to make some decisions without waiting for authorizations. For example, in the US, outbound calls to customers have diminished substantially in the last decade as many customers have entered their names in "do not call" lists; according to Mayer (2004) there were 62 million names within a year of launch of this registry. As a result, it has become critical to use inbound calls for marketing, requiring employees receiving inbound calls to be savvier at recognizing customer needs and finding appropriate products and solutions. Such support can be based on background analytical models (e.g., segmentation or targeting models) that are developed via an ongoing model development process, but whose deployment (e.g., customer scores calculated from the model) is made available in real time.

Decision support tools for real-time decision environments require new types of decision models, as well as new ways to make them successful in organizational settings. IT-based marketing analytics, such as the ones summarized above, are typically developed and deployed by IT specialists and computer scientists, and not by marketing modelers. The reason is that marketing modelers often do not have the IT skills for system integration, and have typically focused their attention on marketing engineering models and systems that are designed to address specific strategic problems (segmentation, targeting, new product forecasting, etc.). Traditional ME models are developed and tested for their potential value to resolve the problems before they are implemented within the IT infrastructure of the companies. If initial model tests are successful, the models may then be deployed for broader use by systems specialists who integrate the models into the company's IT architecture. This type of approach characterizes some of the examples summarized in Table 16.3, which follow the sequence: Intervention (i.e., ME development) → Implementation → Integration with IT systems.

In the future, however, ME applications must start with an understanding of the organizational and IT architecture under which the models will be deployed. In many firms, corporate decision environments consist of enterprise-wide systems, such as ERP (Enterprise Resource Planning) and Customer Relationship Management (CRM) systems. To succeed in those environments, ME design and development may have to follow a different sequence: Integration with IT systems → Intervention Opportunity → Implementation. For example, to build an ME application within a Marketing Dashboard, one must begin with an understanding of the company's infrastructure for information gathering and information access, implement the underlying dashboard model to seamlessly interface with the IT infrastructure to obtain the relevant data on an ongoing basis, support various types of ad-hoc managerial queries and analyses based on the dashboard readings, and guide the deployment of corrective actions, as necessary. Thus, the ME intervention enhances management's understanding of the market situation as the basis for actions. This ability to continuously help managers to enhance their "mental models" of customers and markets is the basis for improving the productivity and quality of marketing decision making in the future. As the influential Morgan Stanley economist Stephen Roach notes, "In the end, sustained white-collar productivity enhancement is less about breakthrough technologies and more about newfound efficiencies in the *cerebral production function* of the high value-added knowledge worker" (quoted in IDC report 2002, *italics* added).

16.3.1 Developments Affecting ME Evolution

Several developments described below suggest how we will move from the current model-supported decision environments today to the environments of the future summarized in Table 16.5.

16.3.1.1 Improved Computational Capabilities Available to Decision Makers

The analytical tool most widely used by corporations is the spreadsheet. There are over 400 million copies of Microsoft Excel currently in use (Hamm 2006). With Excel 2007, managers can access and analyze large databases (up to one million rows with the number of columns, which is limited only by available memory). Contrast this with the limit of 64,000 rows and 256 column limits of Excel 2003, the previous version. Excel can also now directly access data from SQL databases (via the command SQL.REQUEST). These and other developments in software and hardware technologies now make it possible to provide decision support using simple interfaces that do not requires users to learn new computer languages (e.g., database query languages) to complete their decision tasks.

16.3.1.2 Models Offered as Web Services

Recently, standards have emerged to support basic Web services architecture that defines interactions between software agents (modeling applications) as exchanges of messages between service requesters and service providers. Requesters are software agents that request the execution of a service (in our case, a model). Providers are software agents that provide a service. For example, a "forecasting service" could provide forecasts to authorized software agents that request such a service. Web services standards enable communication among different software applications running on a variety of platforms and/or with different frameworks. "Discovery services" enable anyone on the web to find the services they are looking for, with the potential for multiple services competing to satisfy a service request. We expect to soon see Web services for marketing analytics, whereby service vendors offer on-demand online access to various types of knowledge resources and application tools (software, data, content, models, back-end analysis, and implementation of results (e.g., email solicitation)).

Web service providers convert knowledge resources into services (e.g., analysis, process control, order management, billing) accessible over the Web, instead of being packaged as products and systems that run as client installations. For example, salesforce.com offers a Web service model for salesforce automation that includes such online services as contact management, forecasting, e-mail communications, customized reports, and synchronization of wireless devices. Google Earth provides the interfaces necessary for anyone to exploit its huge geographic database to provide various value-added services (e.g., bed and breakfast places located in a particular geographic area). It is just a matter of time before model-supported services are appended to the Google database (e.g., what is the forecast for home delivery pizza sales when a snow storm hits a store's target geographies?). Over the next decade, we expect to see an explosion in the availability of customizable, scalable, and (possibly) embedded decision models on the Internet, available anytime, anywhere, for anyone. Lilien and Rangaswamy (2000) discuss in more detail the value and implications of these developments for marketing modeling.

Figure 16.3 summarizes our view of how Web services will influence marketing modeling in the years ahead, and transform marketing models from static decision aids into dynamic real-time tools embedded in systems that are more useable by managers. We classify marketing models along two dimensions: On the horizontal axis (Degree of Integration), we distinguish between standalone models (e.g., supporting a single user for a single task) on one extreme and those that are integrated with organizational processes, databases, and other aspects of the decision environment at the other extreme (e.g., single user, multiple tasks; multiple users, single task). On the vertical axis (Degree of Visibility), we distinguish between models that are embedded inside systems (i.e., a "black box model" that works in the background) requiring few inputs or interactions with the user, and those that are highly interactive and whose structures are visible. We discuss below four categories of models that are at the extremes of these two dimensions and indicate how the emerging networked economy will encourage their use:

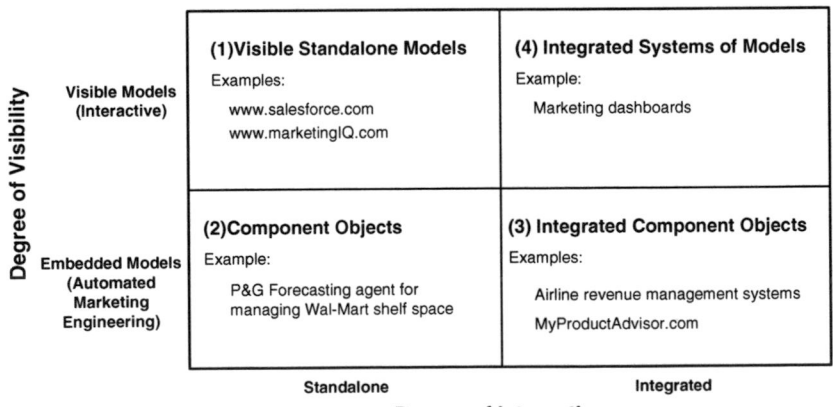

Fig. 16.3 Marketing engineering models classified by degree of integration and degree of visibility that can be deployed on the World Wide Web and accessed over the Internet

Box 1. Visible standalone models can be put on application servers (several Web services already do this—e.g., www.salesforce.com;www.markets-witch.com) and accessed by client browsers. In such an environment, software renditions of marketing models can be maintained in central locations, minimizing costs of updates and distribution. Model users also benefit because they will always have access to the latest versions of the software. Visible models with user interactions can also become more valuable online. For example, applications ranging from simple computational devices, such as a cost-of-living calculator (http://www.homefair.com/homefair/servlet/ActionServlet?pid = 199&cid = moneymag), to sophisticated programs, such as conjoint analysis (www.marketingIQ.com), are available on a 24/7 basis.

Box 2. Component objects (automated marketing engineering) can be deployed more widely on the Internet because they can be structured to continuously monitor and optimize various aspects of how an organization functions. Component objects are designed to support only a few well defined tasks (e.g., assessing whether the caller is a valuable customer), and generally operate in self-contained standalone environments. They are also likely to be deployed in interface systems between companies, where security as well as strategic considerations may prevent deployment of more comprehensive systems. For example, since the late 1980's Proctor and Gamble and Wal-Mart have had a strong IT-enabled collaboration, whereby each company has become an extension of the other for managing merchandising and inventory. Wal-Mart allows P&G to deploy automated models to forecast demand, schedule production and delivery, optimize inventory holdings and even assess the effectiveness of specific promotions. The embedded system has reduced costs, which benefits both companies resulting in lower prices for Wal-Mart customers. The improved availability of product movement data and the associated analytics has provided P&G with rich insights about product sales and customer behavior that helps it improve its product development and sales processes. As evidence of the effectiveness of this decision support system, the total volume of sales between these two companies has grown from $375 million in 1988 to over $10 billion in 2006 (or about 15% of all P&G sales).

Box 3. Integrated component objects (automated integrated marketing engineering) exploit the blurring lines between software, content, services, and applications to deliver more complete decision solutions to managers. Revenue management systems at the world's major airlines dynamically optimize schedules, prices and seat inventories and send messages to targeted customers about new travel opportunities that they might find attractive. And recommender systems such as MyProductAdvisor.com (which uses a Bayesian model), or Amazon's recommender system (which uses collaborative filtering) fall into this category. Although recommender systems are decision support tools used by customers, they are typically developed and deployed by companies to support their marketing activities. To be effective in today's online shopping environments, these systems must link multiple

sources of data and knowledge in automatically generating the recommendations, and they also enable customers to act on those recommendations by
offering them options to purchase products, either at the company Web site,
or with other vendors. Thus, although integrated component objects may be
used by unsophisticated users, the models themselves are likely to be quite
sophisticated (akin to an autopilot for an aircraft) and maintained by highly
skilled modelers.

   Box 4. Integrated systems of models are logically linked sets of models that
share databases and knowledge bases and support common and recurring
decisions (e.g., marketing. planning) for decision makers, who may be in
different locations. Systems of this type in marketing include Dashboards
that integrate multiple sources of data and analyses to provide managers a
detailed view of the entities and activities for which they are responsible.
Examples include GE Capital's Dashboard for senior executives (Whiting
2002) and Harrah's dashboard (Brown 2002) for marketing executives. With
Harrah's dashboard, a marketing executive is able to determine whether a
particular high-value customer would respond better to a promotion offering free meal or a free night in the hotel. More opportunities are emerging for
marketing's use of integrated systems – our description of groupware systems below includes additional details and examples.

16.3.1.3 Intelligent Marketing Systems

Many marketing organizations today generate millions of pieces of data a day.
For example, a firm might distribute 20 products to 10 accounts in each of 300
markets and employ 300 salespeople. The only way it can interpret and use the
large amounts of data it accumulates is by deploying intelligent models that
automate the process of interpreting the data. Several firms are experimenting
with data mining, a process that relies on automated analysis agents to sift
through the data looking for nuggets of insight. Early automatic report gen-
erators in marketing focused on automating the analysis of scanner data (e.g.,
CoverStory, Schmitz et al. 1990). We are now seeing partially-automated
systems (i.e., combination of automated system and human intervention when
the system is unable to make independent judgments) for text analysis of blogs
to sift nuggets from a whole pile of trivia (Bulkeley 2005). An example of such a
system is Nielsen's Buzzmetrics (http://www.nielsenbuzzmetrics.com/).

   Another promising application of data mining is its potential for doing real-
time customization at Web sites, dynamically adjusting the content presented to
users as they interact with the Web site. Among the most important intelligent
marketing systems being developed for marketing are recommendation agents
deployed at Web sites and automated help desk/call center agents. Likewise, we
expect to see automated systems to search the Web to generate customized
reports that help a salesperson prepare for a call, or an intelligent agent

to generate role-specific top-line report for company managers based on recent events.

16.3.1.4 Groupware for Decision Support

Groupware is a general term that describes a variety of computer- and communications-based systems that enhance the efficiency and effectiveness with which a group of people makes decisions, either synchronously or asynchronously. Using groupware, project teams can share information (e.g., reports and presentations) as well as make and record decisions (e.g., online voting). Such systems can circumvent temporal, geographic, and organizational barriers in supporting collaborative work. For example, *Price Waterhouse Coopers* has one of the world's largest installed bases of Lotus Notes to support collaborative decision making. About 40,000 of its employees (consultants) each have a Lotus Notes program with which they access corporate-wide Lotus Notes databases, as well as databases specific to individual projects. With the systems *Price Waterhouse Coopers can* make specialized expertise widely available within the company and quickly put together and support ad hoc teams that make decisions to take advantage of emerging opportunities. Even simple asynchronous groupware that gather, aggregate, and process data from several people can be very useful for decision support.

An interesting application of groupware for marketing modeling involves its value in collecting the judgmental inputs required to support many marketing models. Commercial software such as Groove workspace (www.groove.net) and the workgroup applications built into Microsoft Office 2007 (e.g., SharePoint server) will greatly increase the availability of collaborative decision making tools to a wide range of users, and enable companies to leverage their intellectual assets more broadly within the company and with outside partners. For example, the groupware tool IDEALYST (http://www.ams-inc.com/products/idealyst.htm) is being used to generate and evaluate new product ideas from customers.

16.3.1.5 Improved Model Outputs

As managerial uses of computing increases within firms, the need for user interfaces that operate in an intuitive manner becomes ever more critical. To be successful, decision models have to serve users who have very little time or poor computer skills. Many decision models have failed to attract users because they are incorporated in systems that are difficult to use. For example, several systems for automating lead generation are not meeting their performance goals because they are not designed around familiar and existing sales processes, but embed an imagined notion of how salespeople work or should work.

A useful way to enhance model outputs is via visual representation. Two examples that suggest the potential for such outputs are (i) www.babynamewizard.com, which offers a new way to visually explore the popularity of various baby names from 1880 onwards, and (ii) www.smartmoney.com/maps/?nav= dropTab, which offers an aerial view of 1,000 U.S. and international stocks, all at once, allowing the user both to get the "big picture" as well as to drill down to get details about the current performance of individual stocks. As people get accustomed to these types of better designed software packages, they expect ease of use from every software package they encounter. The best software hides what the novice does not need (covering the engine with a streamlined hood) and highlights those inputs and outputs that are most important to that user at that time.

16.4 Marketing Engineering Development Opportunities and Conclusions

Most developers of marketing models, particularly those in academia, show little concern with issues related to the implementability of their models. Yet, fields as diverse as medicine and architecture demonstrate the value of tight linkages between theory and practice. In medicine, for example, there is a strong tradition of establishing the practical value of theories and methods, i.e., in demonstrating the impact of new insights, procedures, drugs, and tools on extending and improving the quality of life. In a similar vein, more marketing model developers in marketing must become not just cognizant of decision problems faced by practitioners, but also work on developing and refining their models within the types of environments in which their decision models are likely to be used.

16.4.1 Marketing Engineering Development Opportunities

We summarize below some of the ways we think marketing modelers would be able to align their models to the emerging decision support environments.

16.4.1.1 Develop Models that Offer Potential Improvements to Marketing Processes and Operations

Marketing modelers have been successful in building models to help improve discrete decision problems, such as for market segmentation. In the future, standalone models that are not tied to well-defined business processes are not likely to gain the organizational and political clout needed for implementation. Thus, instead of asking how we can further improve segmentation models, we should be asking what kinds of models can help define and improve the complete *segmentation processes* within organizations. Although models are still critical components, we need to think of them as tools for facilitating decision making and implementation within the emerging data-intensive and networked decision environments. There are many well-defined marketing processes that are increasingly the focus of attention in companies, including innovation and new product development, customer relationship management, resource allocation, field sales operations, segmentation, targeting, and positioning, demand generation, and campaign management. Unlike standalone models that typically support individual decision makers, operations-focused models support the whole organization, and will be used by many different decision makers. Although operations-focused models may sometimes be used to support strategic decisions, their real purpose is to provide decision support for routine and recurring questions, such as, how to increase the order pipeline in a particular region, or what incentives to offer a particular segment.

16.4.1.2 Work More Closely with Other Disciplines in Developing Models

In particular, it appears that marketing decisions could be better served if our models are more closely tied to financial metrics, inventory management, and supply chain and fulfillment processes. This perspective calls for working more closely with colleagues in disciplines such as supply chain management, MIS, and Computer Science, in addition to working with economists, statisticians, psychologists, and sociologists.

16.4.1.3 Develop Models for Processing Textual Data

There is now a great deal of customer generated textual data in the form of blogs, product reviews, transactions at social networking sites, and the like. There is also much textual information connected with keyword searches at search engine sites. We need more models that can process such textual data as a basis for management decision making. Perhaps it is time for marketing modelers to work with linguists in formulating formal models for text processing.

16.4.1.4 Design Models to Provide Explanations for Their Results and Recommendations

With the deployment of autonomous decision agents such as recommendations agents and revenue management systems, there is particular need for the embedded models within those systems to be transparent. If a customer is not offered an extra discount, that customer wants to know why. If the recommendation agent recommends a particular camera, the customer wants to know why that particular model was selected. If a market segment did not reach the model projected demand forecast, the manager wants insights to explain the discrepancy.

16.4.1.5 Develop Models for Analysis and Interpretation of Sequence Data

We are seeing more data that capture the sequence of customer activities. For example, Web navigation creates data about customer decision processes and some of the influential factors at different stages of those processes. Likewise, some multichannel retailers now have accumulated data about cross-channel customer behaviors during the course of a specific transaction (e.g., interactions across Web site, call center, and store) as well as over the course of their relationship with the retailer. And spatial data generated by mobile devices, and the spread of word-of-mouth through social networks also offer interesting business opportunities that can be explored and supported by models. For example, identification of influential sources of the spread of word-of-mouth, or the customization of Web pages based on the navigation pattern of a site visitors offer new and interesting opportunities for marketing model builders.

16.4.1.6 Conduct Empirical Analyses of ME Implementations

Many companies are making substantial investments in marketing data and analytics. For example, the global market for on-line analytical processing (OLAP) software, which assists in active decision-support applications such as marketing and sales analysis, direct marketing, and profitability analysis, was estimated to be worth about $4.9 Billion in 2005 (www.olapreport.com/market.htm). However, it is not clear how successful these investments have been. For example, Kale (2004) suggests that 60–80% of CRM investments produce returns much below expectations. Although we have some good case studies demonstrating the positive impact of marketing analytics (see some of the impact metrics summarized in Table 16.4), we need on-going longitudinal studies to identify contexts where marketing analytics will have the most impact, and we need empirical generalizations articulating the nature and magnitude of their impact on firm performance.

16.4.2 Conclusions

Our goal in this chapter has been to develop our glass half full-half empty perspective on marketing engineering and its future. Academic developments over the last 30–40 years have been remarkable and are growing in volume and sophistication. And, we have created and documented a rich range of applications associated with those developments that have produced demonstrable organizational value and impact. We have noted the huge upside potential associated with developing more marketing engineering applications keeping in mind the eventual users of those models, and actually having those applications implemented in practice. We have also summarized the many important ways in which modeling will shape marketing decision making in the future.

Years ago Peter Drucker pointed out that marketing is too important to be left to marketers; that statement is even more true today. Marketing engineering, a bridge between marketing concepts and disciplined marketing decision making and implementation can help integrate marketing thinking and implementation more firmly in the decision making infrastructures of the twenty-first century firm. As of now, however, the potential of marketing engineering remains largely untapped.

References

"9/11 Timeline." *The Christian Science Monitor* (March 11, 2002): p 10.

Accenture Report. 2002. *Insight Driven Marketing*, (January), www.accenture.com.

Ailawadi, K., J. Cesar, B. Harlam, D. Trounce. 2007. Quantifying and Improving Promotion Profitability at CVS, *Marketing Science* (forthcoming).

Bazerman, M. 1998. *Judgment in Managerial Decision Making*. John Wiley and Sons, New York.

Brown, E. 2002. Analyze This. *Forbes* (April 1).

Bucklin, R.E., D.R. Lehmann, J.D.C. Little. 1998. Decision Support to Decision Automation: A 2020 Vision. Marketing Science Institute working paper.

Bulkeley, W.M. 2005. Marketers Scan Blogs For Brand Insights. *Wall Street Journal* (June 23).

Camerer, C. 1981. General Conditions for the Success of Bootstrapping Models. *Organizational Behavior and Human Performance* 27(3) 411–422.

Davenport, T. 2006. Competing on Analytics, Harvard Business Review, 84(1, January) 98–107.

Davenport, T.H., J.G. Harris. 2007. *Competing on Analytics: The New Science of Winning*. Harvard Business School Press, MA: Boston.

Divakar, S., B.T. Ratchford, V. Shankar. 2005. CHAN4CAST: A Multichannel, Multiregion Sales Forecasting Model and Decision Support System for Consumer Packaged Goods. *Marketing Science* 24(3) 334–350.

Eliashberg, J., J.-J. Jonker, M.S. Sawhney, B. Wierenga. 2000. MOVIEMOD: An Implementable Decision-Support System for Prerelease Market Evaluation of Motion Picture. *Marketing Science* 19(3) 226–243.

Elsner, R., M. Krafft, A. Huchzermeier. 2004. Optimizing Rhenania's Direct Marketing Business Through Dynamic Multilevel Modeling (DMLM) in a Multicatalog-Brand Environment. *Marketing Science* 23(2 (Spring)) 192–206.

Flynn, L.J. 2006. Like This? You'll Hate That. (Not All Web Recommendations Are Welcome). *New York Times* (January 23).

Foster, J.A., P.N. Golder, G.J. Tellis. 2004. Predicting Sales Takeoff for Whirlpool's New Personal Valet. *Marketing Science* 23(2(Spring)) 180–191.

Fudge, W.K., L.M. Lodish. 1977. Evaluation of the Effectiveness of a Model Based Salesman's Planning System by Field Experimentation. *Interfaces* 8(1) November 1977 97–0106

Gensch, D.H., N. Aversa, S.P. Moore. 1990. A Choice-Modeling Market Information System that Enabled ABB Electric to Expand its Market Share. *Interfaces* 20(1, January–February) 6–25.

Goldberg, L.R. 1970. Man versus Model of Man: A Rationale Plus Some Evidence for a Method of Improving on Clinical Inferences. *Psychological Bulletin* 73(6) 422–432.

Hamm, S. 2006. More to Life Than the Office. *Business Week* (July 3); No. 3991; p 68.

Hoch, S.J., D.A. Schkade. 1996. A Psychological Approach to Decision Support Systems. *Management Science* 42(1, January) 51–64.

Hogarth, R.M. 1987. *Judgment and Choice, second edition* John Wiley and Sons, New York.

Hunt, D.L., R.B. Haynes, S.E. Hanna, K. Smith. 1998. Effects of Computer-Based Clinical Decision Support Systems on Physician Performance and Patient Outcomes. *J American Med Assoc.*, **280**(15) 1339–1346.

IDC Report. 2002. *The Financial Impact of Business Analytics* (www.idc.com).

Kale, S.H. 2004. CRM Failure and the Seven Deadly Sins. *Marketing Management.* (September/October) **13**(15) 42.

Kayande, U., A. De Bruyn, G.L. Lilien, A. Rangaswamy, G. van Bruggen. 2007. How Feedback Can Improve Managerial Evaluations of Marketing Decision Support Systems. *Working Paper.*

Kitts, B., M. Vrieze, D. Freed. 2005. Product Targeting from Rare Events: Five Years of One to One Marketing at CPI. Presented at the Marketing Science Conference, Atlanta, June 17.

Klebnikov, P. 2001. The Resurrection of NCR. *Forbes* (July 9): p 70.

Kumar, V., D. Beckman, T. Bohling, R. Venkatesan. 2008. The Power of CLV. *Marketing Science* (forthcoming).

Labbi, A., G. Tirenni, C. Berrospi, A. Elisseff, K. Heinonen. 2007. Customer Equity and Lifetime Management (CELM). *Marketing Science* (forthcoming).

Lapointe, L., S. Rivard. 2006. Getting Physicians to Accept New Information Technology: Insights from Case Studies. *Canadian Medical Association Journal.* **174**(11).

Lehmann, D.R. 2005. Journal Evolution and the Development of Marketing. *Journal of Public Policy and Marketing* **24**(1, Spring) 137–142.

Lodish, L.M., E. Curtis, M. Ness, M.K. Simpson. 1988. Sales Force Sizing and Deployment Using a Decision Calculus Model at Syntex Laboratories. *Interfaces* **18** (1, January–February) 5–20.

Lilien, G.L., A. Rangaswamy. 2000. Modeled to Bits: Decision Models for the Digital, Networked Economy. *International Journal of Research in Marketing* **17** 227–235.

Lilien, G.L., A. Rangaswamy. 2004. *Marketing Engineering: Computer-Assisted Marketing Analysis and Planning, Revised Second Edition.* Trafford Press, Victoria, BC, Canada.

Lilien, G.L., A. Rangaswamy, G. van Bruggen, K. Starke. 2004. DSS Effectiveness in Marketing Resource Allocation Decisions: Reality vs. Perception. *Information Systems Research* September **15**(3) 216–235.

Little, J.D.C. 1970. Models and Managers: The Concept of a Decision Calculus. *Management Science* **16**(8, April) B466–B485.

Martin, R. 2007. Data Latency Playing An Ever Increasing Role In Effective Trading. *InformationWeek* (April 23).

Mayer, C.E. 2004. In 1 Year, Do-Not-Call List Passes 62 Million. *Washington Post* (June 24); E05.

McIntyre, S.H. 1982. An Experimental Study of the Impact of Judgment-Based Marketing Models. *Management Science* **28**(1) 17–33.

Natter, M., A. Mild, T. Reutterer, A. Taudes. 2007. An Assortment-Wide Decision-Support System for Dynamic Pricing and Promotion Planning in DIY Retailing. *Marketing Science* **26**(4, August) 576–583.

Natter, M., A. Mild, A. Taudes, U. Wagner. 2008. Planning New Tariffs at Tele.Ring – An Integrated STP Tool Designed for Managerial Applicability. *Marketing Science* (forthcoming).

Nijs, V., S. Srinivasan, K. Pauwels. 2007. Retail-Price Drivers and Retailer Profits. *Marketing Science* **26**(4, August) 473–487.

Rangaswamy, A., P. Sinha, A. Zoltners. 1990. An Integrated Model-Based Approach for Salesforce Restructuring. *Marketing Science* **9**(4, Fall) 279–298.

Reda, S. 2002. Retailers Slow to Adopt Analytics Software. *Stores* **84**(6) 22.

Reda, S. 2003. Despite Early Positive Results, Retailers Haven't Jumped on Analytics Bandwagon. *Stores* **85**(3) 34.

Roberts, J.H., U. Kayande, S. Stremersch. 2007. Impact of Marketing Science on Management Practice European Marketing Academy Annual Conference Proceedings May.

Roberts, J.H., P.D. Morrison, C.J. Nelson. 2004. Implementing a Prelaunch Diffusion Model: Measurement and Management Challenges of the Telstra Switching Study. *Marketing Science* **23**(2, Spring) 180–191.

Russo, J.E., P.J.H. Shoemaker. 1989. *Decision Traps.* Doubleday and Company, New York.

Schmitz, J.D, G.D. Armstrong, J.D.C. Little. 1990. CoverStory: Automated news finding in marketing in *DSS Transactions* ed. Linda Bolinon TIMS College on Information Systems, Providece RI pp 46–54.

Shankar, V., P. Azar, M. Fuller. 2008. BRAN*EQT: A Model and Simulator for Estimating, Tracking, and Managing Multi-Category Brand Equity. *Marketing Science* (forthcoming).

Silva-Risso, J., R.E. Bucklin, D.G. Morrison. 1999. A Decision Support System for Planning Manufacturers' Sales Promotion Calendars. *Marketing Science* **18**(3) 274–300.

Silva-Risso, J., I. Ionova. 2008. Incentive Planning System: A DSS for Planning Pricing and Promotions in the Automobile Industry. *Marketing Science* (forthcoming).

Sinha, A., J. Jeffrey Inman, Y. Wang, J. Park. 2005. Attribute Drivers: A Factor Analytic Choice Map Approach for Understanding Choices Among SKUs. *Marketing Science* **24**(3(Summer)) 351–359.

Sinha, P., A.A. Zoltners. 2001. Salesforce Decision Models: Insights from 25 years of implementation. *Interfaces* **31**(3, Part 2) S8–S44.

Smith, B.C., J.F. Leimkuhler, R.M. Darrow. 1992. Yield Management at American Airlines. *Interfaces* **22**(1, January–February) 8–31.

Sintchenko, V., E. Coiera, J. Iredeli, G.L. Gilbert. 2004. Comparative Impact of Guidelines, Clinical Data, and Decision Support on Prescribing Decisions: An Interactive Web Experiment with Simulated Cases. *Journal of American Medical Informatics Association* **11**(1) 71–77.

Sullivan, L. 2005. Fine-tuned pricing. *Information Week.* Aug. (www.informationweek.com/showArticle.jhtml?articleID = 168601052)

Tellis, G.J., R.K. Chandy, D. MacInnis, P. Thaivanich. 2005. Modeling the Microeffects of Television Advertising: Which Ad Works, When, Where, for How long and Why? *Marketing Science* **24**(3, Summer) 359–366.

Urban, G.L., G.M. Katz. 1983. Pre-Test-Market Models: Validation and Managerial Implications. *Journal of Marketing Research* **20**(3, August) 221–234.

van Bruggen, G.H., B. Wierenga. 2001. Matching Management Support Systems and Managerial Problem-Solving Modes: The Key to Effective Decision Support. *European Management Journal* **19**(3, June) 228–238.

Whiting, R. 2002. GE Capital's Dashboard Drives Metrics To Desktops. *Information Week* (April 22).

Wierenga, B., G.H. van Bruggen. 2000. *Marketing Management Support Systems*, Kluwer Academic Press, Boston, Massachusett.

Wierenga, B., G.H. van Bruggen, R. Staelin. 1999. The Success of Marketing Management Support Systems. *Marketing Science* **18**(3) 196 207.

Wierenga, B., G.H. van Bruggen, N. Althuizen. 2007. Advances in Marketing Management Support Systems. Wierenga, B. Eds. *Handbook of Marketing Decision Models.* Springer Science+Business Media, Boston MA, p 561–592.

Wind, J., P.E. Green, D. Shifflet, M. Scarbrough. 1989. Courtyard by Marriott: Designing a Hotel Facility with Consumer-Based Marketing Models. *Interfaces* 19(1, January–February) 25–47.

Zoltners, A.A., P. Sinha. 2005. Sales Territory Design: Thirty Years of Modeling and Implementation. *Marketing Science* **24**(3, Summer) 313–331.

Chapter 17
Advances in Marketing Management Support Systems

Berend Wierenga, Gerrit H. van Bruggen, and Niek A. P. Althuizen

17.1 Introduction

This chapter discusses recent advances in the field of marketing management support systems (MMSS). We start with a short history of marketing management support systems, with special attention to marketing models, the core topic of this Handbook. In Section 17.2 we describe developments which have improved the quality of MMSS and favor their use for marketing decision making in current marketing practice. Section 17.3 presents our growing know-ledge about the factors that affect the adoption and use of MMSS. In Section 17.4 we discuss developments in a new category of marketing management support systems, i.e. systems that support decision-making for weakly structured marketing problems.

The history of designing systems and models to assist marketers in their decision-making dates back over more than forty years. In 1966, Kotler introduced the concept of a "Marketing Nerve Centre", providing marketing managers with "computer programs which will enhance their power to make decisions." The first of these systems were essentially marketing information systems (Brien and Stafford 1968). At that time, the recently introduced computers in companies produced lots of data, and a systematic approach was needed to make those data available in a way that managers could use them for decision-making. Otherwise, there could be a serious danger of overabundance of irrelevant information (Ackoff 1967). About 10 years later, Little (1979) introduced the concept of marketing decision support systems. He defined a marketing decision support system (MDSS) as a "coordinated collection of data, systems, tools and techniques with supporting software and hardware by which an organization gathers and interprets relevant information from business and environment and turns it into an environment for marketing action" (p. 11). Little's concept of an MDSS was much more than a marketing information system. Important elements were models, statistics, and optimization, and the emphasis was on response analysis;

B. Wierenga
RSM Erasmus University, Rotterdam
e-mail: bwierenga@rsm.nl

B. Wierenga (ed.), *Handbook of Marketing Decision Models*,
DOI: 10.1007/978-0-387-78213-3_17, © Springer Science+Business Media, LLC 2008

for example, how sales respond to promotions. In Little's view, MDSS were suitable for structured and semi-structured marketing problems, had a quantitative orientation and were data-driven.

Almost 2 decades later, Wierenga and Van Bruggen (1997) presented a classification of marketing decision support technologies and tools, and used the term "marketing management support systems" to refer to the complete set of marketing decision aids. They define a marketing management support system (MMSS) as "any device combining (1) information technology, (2) analytical capabilities, (3) marketing data, and (4) marketing knowledge, made available to one or more marketing decision makers, with the objective to improve the quality of marketing management" (p. 28). Marketing management support systems is a comprehensive term which includes the primarily quantitative, data-driven marketing decision support systems (for structured and semi-structured problem areas) as well as technologies that are aimed at supporting marketing decision-making in weakly-structured areas. The latter are primarily qualitative, and knowledge-driven. In this chapter we deal with decision support systems for structured, semi-structured, *and* weakly-structured marketing problems.

17.1.1 Marketing Models as Components of MMSS

From the beginning, marketing models have been a core element of marketing management support systems. They represent the *analytical component* of an MMSS (see the components of MMSS discussed above). A marketing model relates marketing decision variables to the outcomes in the market place (for example sales, market share, profit). A marketing model can be used to find the best decision (optimizing) or to answer so-called "what-if" questions (for example: how will sales respond, if we increase our advertising budget with x percent?). Initially, there was a lot of optimism about the use of marketing models. With marketing models, it seemed, marketing would almost become a scientific activity. Kotler (1971) opens his classical book on marketing models, with the statement: "Marketing operations are one of the last phases of business management to come under scientific scrutiny" (p. 1). It was expected that marketing decision making would just become a matter of formulating a marketing problem as a mathematical programming problem, and then solve it with one of the known techniques of Operations Research. But the harsh reality was that the actual application of marketing models to real-life problems in companies remained far below expectations. This has caused a tradition of complaints in the marketing literature, ranging from "The big problem with marketing science models is, that managers practically never use them" (Little 1970) to (30 years later) "Maybe there is some level of maturity in the technology, but I cannot see much evidence in the application" (Roberts 2000). In this Handbook, Lilien and Rangaswamy (Chapter 16) refer to "the gap between realized and actual potential for the application of marketing models".

In hindsight, for marketers it should not have come as a surprise that the supply of sophisticated marketing models did not automatically generate demand. Marketing models have to be adopted and used by decision-makers in organizations, and marketers are just like other people with their resistance to change and to new ways of doing things. Carlsson and Turban (2002) note that the key issues with decision support systems (DSS) are "people problems". "People *(i)* have cognitive constraints in adopting intelligent systems; *(ii)* do not really understand the support they get and disregard it in favor of past experiences; *(iii)* cannot really handle large amounts of information and knowledge; *(iv)* are frustrated by theories they do not really understand; and *(v)* believe they get more support by talking to other people (even if their knowledge is limited)" (p. 106). Of course, it is not fair to blame only the marketing decision-makers for not using marketing models. In many cases, the models may just not have been good enough or their advantages were not sufficiently clear to the manager.

Given this state of affairs, it became important to have more insight in the role of these "people issues" and, at a more general level, in the factors that can block (or stimulate, for that matter) the adoption and use of marketing management support tools. This gave rise to systematic research (cross-section studies, field studies, lab experiments, field experiments) in these issues. The knowledge acquired can be found in the marketing management support systems literature. "Marketing management support systems" does not just refer to a collection of decision support systems and technologies, but also to a substantive field with an emerging body-of-knowledge about the factors and conditions that affect the adoption, use, and impact of marketing decision support tools in organizations. We will present the most recent insights in Section 17.3 of this chapter. Earlier reviews can be found in books such as Wierenga and Van Bruggen (2000) and Lilien and Rangaswamy (2004), and in Special Issues of academic journals such as *Marketing Science* (Vol. 18, No. 3, 1999) and *Interfaces* (Vol. 31, No. 3, 2001). There are also a substantial number of articles on this topic, many of which are referred to in the previous and the current chapter of this book.

But, as mentioned earlier, we first turn to the advances in the quality of MMSS.

17.2 Advances in the Quality of Marketing Management Support Systems

17.2.1 Better Marketing Management Support Systems

At the time of the early work in marketing models (Bass et al. 1961; Buzzell 1964; Frank et al. 1962; Montgomery and Urban 1969; Kotler 1971), the knowledge about marketing processes was limited. This may sometimes have led to the development of overly simplistic models that were not very usable for marketing practice.[1]

We already observed that the use of marketing models in practice remained behind the initial expectations. Interestingly, a completely different picture has developed in academic research. Marketing model building and the related field of "marketing science" has become one of the dominant areas of research in marketing and has been booming ever since. It looks as though the field of marketing models "retracted" from the battlefield of actual marketing decision-making to the academic halls of science. The purpose of academic marketing models was directed more at developing fundamental insight into marketing phenomena (just like physical models are used to obtain insight in the working of nature) than for immediate decision support. Definitely, this has been a very productive retreat. The modeling approach has produced a wealth of knowledge about marketing processes and the key variables that play a role in these processes. Furthermore, very sophisticated methods and tools for the measurement and analysis of marketing phenomena have been developed. These advances have been documented in a series of books that appeared in intervals of about 10 years: Kotler (1971), Lilien and Kotler (1983), Lilien et al. (1992) and Eliashberg and Lilien (1993). This Handbook describes the state-of-the-art in the first decade of the new Millenium.

Over time, marketing models have become "deeper", in the sense that more relevant variables are included. This has made marketing models more realistic and better adapted to actual marketing problems in practice. Also, the procedures for parameter estimation have become dramatically more sophisticated. We can demonstrate these developments by looking at models for sales promotions. In Kotler's (1971) book the discussion of sales promotions is limited to two pages (47–48), with just one formal model for finding the best sales promotion. In the meantime, researchers have realized that sales promotions is a multi-faceted phenomenon, with aspects such as acceleration, deceleration, cannibalization, category switching, store switching, and many others (see the Chapter [5] van Heerde and Neslin in this book). Similar developments have taken place in the modeling of other phenomena in marketing, such as advertising, sales management, and competition.

So the analytical capabilities component of marketing management support systems, i.e. marketing models, has significantly improved in quality. This is also the case for the information technology component. Using state-of-the-art IT possibilities, most MMSS now have user-friendly interfaces, are easy to use, and are pleasant to work with. As we will see, they are often completely embedded in the IT environment in which a marketing manager works. The situation with respect to another critical component of MMSS, marketing data, has also improved dramatically over time. First, scanner data caused a

---

[1] For example, linear advertising models that were fit for optimization through linear programming, rather than for describing how advertising really works (Engel and Warshaw 1964).

"marketing information revolution" (Blattberg et al. 1994), and more recently this was followed by a second information revolution in the form of enormous amounts of CRM data, clickstream data, and all kinds of interactive marketing data.

The conclusion is that because of better models, more sophisticated information technology, and better data, the quality of marketing management support systems has significantly increased. This is a favorable factor for their use and impact.

17.2.2 MMSS-Favorable User Environments

Thirty years ago, Little (1979, p. 23) observed that computers "are impossible to work with" and he foresaw the need for "marketing science intermediaries", professionals with good technical skills who would entertain the connection between the computer and the manager. Through the spectacular developments in IT, the reality of today is completely different. The computer is now the most intimate business partner of the manager. Whether it is in the form of a PC, a laptop, a terminal in a network or a PDA, the computer is completely integrated in the daily work. A recent study among German managers reported that managers spend on average 10.3 hours per week using information technology (Vlahos et al. 2004), i.e., about 25% of their work time. The comparable figure for the U.S. is 11.1 hours per week and for Greece 9.3 hours (Ferrat and Vlahos 1998). Marketing and sales managers spend on average 8.6 hours per week using the computer (a bit lower than the 10.3 hours overall), which makes it clear that for marketers the computer is now a key element of the job. Today, a marketer typically has several databases and spreadsheet programs available that are used to monitor sales, market shares, distribution, marketing activities, actions of competitors and other relevant items. Such systems are either made in-house, i.e., by the firm's own IT department, or made available by third parties. Providers of syndicated data such as Nielsen or IRI, typically make software available for going through databases, and for specific analyses. For the adoption and use of MMSS it is an important advantage that marketing managers are fully connected to an IT system. When a new MMSS is to be introduced, the "distribution channel" to the marketing manager (i.e., the platform) is already there. In this way, using the MMSS becomes a natural part of the (daily) interaction with the computer. One step further, marketing decision support tools are not separate programs anymore, but have become completely embedded in other IT systems that managers use (see also Lilien and Rangaswamy, Chapter 16).

For the success of MMSS, the relationship between the marketing department and the IT/IS department in a company is critical. There are indications that the power balance between marketing and the firm's overall information department is changing in favor of marketing. In a study among managers of market research in *Fortune 500* companies, Li et al. (2001) concluded that marketing has an increasing influence on the company plan for strategic information resources and that marketing now occupies a "position of power in the organization in terms of computer use with marketing generally calling the shots" (p. 319). This is a big change from the early days of computers in companies, when marketing occupied one of the last places in the IT priority queue, after accounting, finance, production, and operations.

17.2.3 MMSS-Favorable Developments in Marketing

The developments in marketing itself have also been favorable for marketing management support systems. Marketing became an academic discipline around the beginning of the twentieth century. The emerging trend in today's marketing toward customer-centricity follows the eras of marketing as distribution (1900–1960) and marketing as brand management (1960–2000). Marketing as a customer orientation (customer-centric marketing, the third era) emerged toward the end of the twentieth century. Information technology made it increasingly easy to collect and retain information about individual customers. This was not only demographic information (e.g., family status, age, and education) but also information about their purchase history, and their responses to marketing campaigns. This means that individual customers were no longer anonymous but obtained their own identity. With such information a company knows precisely with whom it is dealing, and can figure out the best way of interacting with a particular customer. This is a major shift from the previous era. The individual customer has become central. This does not mean that brands have become obsolete. We can say that after the product had lost its anonymity (and became recognizable as a brand) in the second marketing era, the third marketing era has also given the individual customer an identity. Customer-centric marketing requires new marketing metrics, such as, customer share, customer satisfaction, and customer lifetime value (CLV). Customer-centric marketing also causes a shift in the focus of marketing management support systems, where data are increasingly organized around individual consumers. In the third marketing era a lot of effort is being put in the development of customer data bases, which are the starting points for any interaction with individual customers. According to Glazer (1999) the customer information file (CIF) is the key asset of a corporation. From the perspective of MMSS, the transition to the third marketing era is a tremendous step forward. Individual customer-level data are an enrichment of our information about what is going on in the marketplace. As can be read in several other chapters in this book: Gupta and Lehmann (Chapter 8); Reinartz and Venkatesan (Chapter 9); Bucklin (Chapter 10), these data have also stimulated the development of all kinds of new types of marketing models, which can be used to optimize marketing efforts at the level of the individual customer.

17.2.4 CRM and Interactive Marketing

Customer relationship management (CRM) has been called the "new mantra of marketing" (Winer 2001). Customer relationship management is an enterprise approach aiming at understanding customers and communicating with them in a way that improves customer acquisition, customer retention, customer loyalty and customer profitability (Swift 2001). The basis for doing this is the *CRM system*, a computer system with a data base with data about customers, about company-customer contacts, and data about the customers' purchase history. Recently, companies have been installing CRM systems at a high rate and a large number of companies now have functioning CRM systems in place. Of course, the large scale adoption of CRM systems by companies is directly related to the transition to the third marketing era, described above. CRM systems are basically used for two purposes:

(1) To support and optimize day-to-day interactions with customers. This is called *operational* CRM;
(2) To enable firms to leverage on data and find new marketing opportunities, for example, the need for specific products/services among certain customer groups, opportunities for cross-selling, opportunities for event-driven marketing, etc. This is called *analytical* CRM.

Since the very purpose of a CRM system is to offer decision support for the interaction with customers (operational as well as analytical), every CRM system is a marketing management support system. Hence, the advent of CRM systems implies a quantum leap in the number of MMSS in companies. Interestingly, the companies that are at the forefront of implementing CRM systems are not the same companies that were dominant in the development of MMSS for brand management in the second marketing era. The CRM movement is particularly strong in industries like financial services (e.g., banks and insurance companies), telecommunications, utilities, recreation and travel, whereas in the second marketing era the consumer packaged goods companies were dominant.

There are enormous opportunities for the analysis and optimization of marketing decisions with the data in CRM systems. An example of a frequently employed methodology is data mining. With data mining a prediction model (e.g., a neural net, see Chapter 12 [Hruschka]) is trained to learn the association between customer characteristics (for example, demographic information and purchase history) and interesting dependent variables (for example, whether or not the customer has accepted a specific offer). Once the model has been trained, it can be used to predict whether other customers (with known characteristics) would accept the offer. This technology is typically used in marketing campaigns to select those customers from a database that have a high probability of accepting a particular offer. Data mining can cause large savings, because of a better allocation of expensive marketing resources. As Reinartz and Venkatesan

(Chapter 9) demonstrate, many questions can be answered with the intelligent use of the data in CRM systems, such as: which customers should we acquire, which customers should we retain, and which customers should we grow? Related issues that have been studied recently are how many customers will be "alive" (i.e., still buying) at a certain point in time (Fader et al.2005) and how we can predict customer "churn", i.e., the probability that a customer with a known purchase history will defect (Neslin et al. 2006). Such analyses produce actionable information: if you know which customers have a high probability of defecting, you can selectively take action.

Today, the interaction between companies and their customers is increasingly taking place over the Internet. This has created another source of valuable information: i.e., clickstream data that provide information about how customers behave on websites and about their information acquisition processes. In online marketing settings, companies can produce tailor-made responses to individual customers, advertisement exposure can be individualized through search-engine marketing, and companies can offer Interactive Consumer Decision Aids (see Murray and Häuble, Chapter 3) to help customers with their choices. To support online marketing, new marketing models are needed. For example, models for the attraction of visitors to a site, models for the response to banner ads, models for paid search advertising, and models for site usage and purchase conversion (see Bucklin, Chapter 10).

The most important advances in marketing models and MMSS in the coming years will probably occur in the domain of CRM and interactive marketing.

17.3 Advances in Our Knowledge of the Factors that Drive the Impact of Marketing Management Support Systems

Whatever the nature of MMSS, whether they are brand-oriented (second marketing era) or customer-oriented (third marketing era), the essential question is: how can we make these systems have impact? In this section we discuss the impact of MMSS and we address the following two questions:

1. Do marketing management support systems help marketers to improve the quality of their decision-making?
2. What drives the impact of marketing management support systems?

Because of the high (technical) quality of available MMSS and the evidence that if marketers use these systems they actually do make better decisions, it is critical to make organizations adopt MMSS and decision-makers within these organizations to use these systems. In this Section we present a model that describes the drivers of the use and impact of MMSS. This model advances the work of Wierenga et al. (1999) by taking a dynamic perspective and acknowledging the interdependencies between the various MMSS "Impact" variables.

17.3.1 Do Marketing Management Support Systems Help Marketers to Make Better Decisions?

Relative to other management areas such as finance and operations management, marketing is a domain where human experience and expertise have always played an important role in decision-making. As we have seen, systematically applying analytical support to decision-making in the form of marketing management support systems does not take place on a large scale yet. We have already referred (see Section 17.1) to the rather pessimistic views on the impact of marketing management support systems in practice that have been expressed over time. Bucklin et al. (1998) present a more optimistic view on the impact of decision support systems in marketing, especially with respect to the near future. They argue that a growing proportion of marketing decisions can not only be supported but may also be automated. From a standpoint of both efficiency (e.g., management productivity) and effectiveness (e.g., resource allocation decisions) they find this automation highly desirable. They also foresee that close to full automation can ultimately take place for many decisions about existing products in stable markets. Partial automation could characterize decision-making for new products in stable markets and existing products in unstable markets. In their view, decision support systems (DSS) in marketing will be necessary and successful because of the enormous numbers of decisions that need to be made (where human decision-makers simply lack the time and cognitive resources to make these decisions themselves) and because model-based decision-making is often superior to human decision-making.

Since the early 1970s, various empirical studies have been conducted to systematically study *whether* the use of marketing management support systems improves the quality of decision- making (see Table 17.1 for a summary of these studies).[2] Most of these studies were experimental either in a field setting (e.g., Fudge and Lodish 1977) or in a laboratory environment (e.g., Chakravarti et al. 1979). Most of the DSS were used to support resource allocation decisions, while the DSS in the study of Hoch and Schkade (1996) supported a forecasting task and the DSS in the studies of Van Bruggen et al. (1996) and Van Bruggen, Smidts, and Wierenga (1998) supported decisions about marketing-mix variables.

Analyzing the studies in Table 17.1 leads to a number of observations. First, with the exception of the study of Chakravarti et al. (1979), all other studies show that the use of decision models has a positive impact on the quality of marketing decision-making leading to better organizational performance. The positive impact of these models/systems is probably caused by their high quality

---

[2] Note the difference with Table 3 in Chapter 16 by Lilien and Rangaswamy which presents an overview of Decision Models that were all successful in terms of improving the quality of decision making. All of these award-winning models were "success stories." Table 17.1 is different in that it summarizes studies where the investigation of the effects of the use of MMSS is central.

Table 17.1 Summary of major studies on MMSS impact

Study	Purpose	Decision supported	Study type	Explanatory variables	Outcome (O) and process (P) measures	Key results/comments
(Fudge and Lodish 1977)	Evaluate the effectiveness of a DSS (Decision Calculus model)	Allocation of sales effort at Air cargo services of United Airlines	Field	Availability of the CALLPLAN DSS, including training	*Objective:* Sales	After six months, salespeople who used a DSS had significantly higher sales (+8% on average). DSS users viewed the system as productive.
(Chakravarti et al. 1979)	Evaluate effectiveness of a DSS (Decision Calculus model)	Allocation of ad budget over several periods (includes carry-over effects)	Lab	Availability of the ADBUDG DSS	*Objective:* Profits; Accuracy of parameter estimates of underlying model	Subjects made better decisions before being exposed to the DSS. System use did not lead to improved estimates of parameters (but the simulated dynamic environment seems to be overly complex).
(McIntyre 1982)	Evaluate effectiveness of a DSS (Decision Calculus model)	Allocation of ad budget over several periods (no carry-over effects); sales prediction	Lab	Availability of the CALLPLAN DSS;Task characteristics (size of the problem, noise-to-signal ratio in market); Characteristics of decision makers	*Objective:* Profits; Accuracy in predicting sales; Stability *Subjective:* Confidence in decision	DSS users achieved higher profit levels with less volatility, but they did not do better in predicting sales levels. There was no difference in the perceptions between model users and non-users that the allocations result in profits near to optimal profits. However, decision makers felt more confident when using the DSS.

Table 17.1 (continued)

Study	Purpose	Decision supported	Study type	Explanatory variables	Outcome (O) and process (P) measures	Key results/comments
(Lodish et al. 1988)	Assess effectiveness of a DSS (Decision Calculus model)	Allocation and sizing of sales force (Syntex Laboratories Inc.)	Case study	Actual implementation of DSS (CALLPLAN) in a company.	*Objective:* Sales/Gross Margin	DSS helped Syntex decide to significantly increase its salesforce size and to change its effort allocation to products and market segments. This decision resulted in a documented continuing $25 million – 8% -yearly sales increase.
(Gensch et al. 1990)	Assess effectiveness of a DSS (multi-attribute disaggregate choice model) for segmentation and targeting	Allocation of marketing effort based on model predictions with respect to choice among suppliers of ABB Electric Inc	Case study	Actual implementation of DSS (multi-attribute disaggregate choice model) in a company.	*Objective:* Sales	ABB used the model to segment and target customers. After a year of implementation, total transformer sales for the industry were down 15%. In contrast, ABB sales in the 2 districts using the DSS increased (18% and 12%), whereas its sales in the territory not using the DSS methods were down 10%. The management at ABB Electric felt that the DSS was a competitive advantage that led them to grow market share from 4% to over 40% over a fifteen year period along

Table 17.1 (continued)

Study	Purpose	Decision supported	Study type	Explanatory variables	Outcome (O) and process (P) measures	Key results/comments
						with increased profitability in a highly competitive market.
(Hoch and Schkade 1996)	Evaluate DSS effectiveness in combination with experience (pattern matching efforts)	Forecasting of credit ratings	Lab	Availability of DSS (linear model); Availability of database support (pattern matching support); High/low predictability of environment (credit rating)	*Objective:* Accuracy of forecasting performance	In the? high predictability environment, aided users did better, but not significantly better than unaided users. In the low predictability environment, users with database support (pattern matching) did significantly worse than the? model only or unaided. Users with DSS and database support did best.
(Van Bruggen et al. 1996; Van Bruggen et al. 1998)	Assess the impact of differences in DSS quality	Marketing mix decisions in the MARK-STRAT simulation environment.	Lab	Availability of DSS (what-if model for sales and market share predictions) High/low DSS quality (i.e., the prediction precision) High/low time-pressure	*Objective:* Profit De-anchoring *Subjective:* Perceived usefulness, Decision confidence	DSS users achieved higher profits than non-users. Although users of high-quality DSS outperformed users of lower quality DSS, there was no significant difference in perceived usefulness or decision confidence. DSS users were less susceptible to applying the anchoring and adjustment

Table 17.1 (continued)

Study	Purpose	Decision supported	Study type	Explanatory variables	Outcome (O) and process (P) measures	Key results/comments
						heuristic and, therefore, showed more variation in their decisions in a dynamic environment. Low-analytic subjects and subjects operating under low time pressure benefited most from a DSS.
(Lilien et al. 2004)	Assess how DSS influence decisions	Two different resource allocation tasks: Salesforce allocation (see Lodish et al. 1988) and target segment selection (see Gensch et al. 1990)	Lab	Availability of DSS Task order	*Objective*: Incremental return (profit or sales) Extent of de-anchoring Expert ratings *Subjective*: Complexity, Cognitive effort, Satisfaction, Discussion Quality, Learning, etc.	DSS use improves objective decision outcomes for both DSS models. However, DSS users often do not report better perceptions of outcomes. Expert evaluators had difficulty detecting objective decision quality. Effects of DSS on both process and outcomes may be context and DSS-design specific, with DSS that provide specific feedback having stronger effects both on the process and on the outcomes.

Source: (Lilien et al. 2001)

and the fact that most of these systems were developed for environments that were relatively well-controlled and where it was possible to realize a relatively good match between the system and the decision problem. Second, because of the nature of their design in most of these studies, participants all used the systems that were available because this was part of the (experimental) task. However, in practice, getting decision-makers to *use* these systems is often a problem in itself. If systems are not used, they cannot have impact. Third, most studies only looked at the effects of system use on "objective" organizational variables like sales and profit. However, some studies also investigated the subjective evaluations of system value and impact by the users by measuring variables such as decision confidence and decision satisfaction. It is remarkable that the subjective evaluations of the decisions made when using decision models are not strongly related to the objective results of model-based decision-making (Lilien et al. 2004). Decision-makers seem to have difficulties in recognizing the value of MMSS, or are at least uncertain, about the value these systems add to the quality of decision-making. This hampers the adoption and use of these systems and, consequently, their impact on the quality of decision-making. We discuss ways on how to avoid this later in this chapter.

From the studies summarized in Table 17.1 we conclude that: (i) MMSS generally lead to better decisions if they are used; (ii) MMSS use does not happen automatically; and (iii) that decision- makers have difficulties in recognizing the positive effects of MMSS on the quality of their decisions. So, MMSS do have *potential* impact, but the critical issue is how to realize this impact in practice.

17.3.2 What Drives the Impact of Marketing Management Support Systems?

The Information Systems (IS) research literature has paid quite extensive attention to the impact of information systems and decision support systems in general. The concept of Information System Success is widely accepted throughout IS research as the principal criterion for evaluating information systems (Rai et al. 2002). Rai et al. (2002) state that a problem lies in the ambiguity of the construct and the multiplicity of IS constructs pervading the research.

Indeed, researchers have been using various variables to measure the impact or success of systems. Based on a large review of multiple empirical studies, DeLone and McLean (1992) conclude that IS/DSS success is a multidimensional construct and that it should be measured as such. They also propose a temporal and causal ordering between six IS/DSS success variables. System Quality and Information Quality singularly and jointly affect both System Use and User Satisfaction. Additionally, the amount of System Use affects the degree of User Satisfaction as well as the reverse being true. System Use and

User Satisfaction are direct antecedents of Individual Impact and this Individual Impact should eventually have Organizational Impact. Even though alternative specifications (i.e., Seddon 1997) of the IS success models have been suggested, the Delone and McLean model serves well as the starting point for dealing with the issue of the impact of marketing management support systems. In the impact measurement model that we develop in this chapter, we see Organizational Impact as the key dependent variable which the MMSS aims at maximizing. In our view, the other variables DeLone and McLean (1992) mention are antecedents of this Organizational Impact. We will elaborate on this below.

The main goal of marketing management support systems is to improve the quality of marketing management and marketing decision-making within organizations. This will improve the organization's performance in the market. *Market outcomes* represent the organization's performance in the marketplace (George et al. 2007). This means making the right decisions about whether or not to introduce a new product (and when and in which market), about whether or not to introduce a sales promotion, and about with how much the advertising budget or price level should be changed. Marketing performance is essentially multidimensional and a firm needs at least as many metrics as it has goals, of which short-term survival and long-term growth are the most common (Ambler and Roberts 2006). Organizations will have goals with respect to variables like their profitability, sales, brand awareness etc. The metric that is most appropriate to evaluate the impact of a specific MMSS depends on the goal of that system. The metric can be relatively specific and uni-dimensional in the case of a specific support system. For example, the impact of a system that supports decision-making on advertising decisions may be measured by the extent to which its use leads to advertising decisions that increase brand awareness or brand image. However, for systems that support a broader range of marketing activities and decisions, more general measures like effects on sales, market shares, and profitability can be employed. With the tendency in marketing to target activities at individuals, marketing metrics measured at the individual customer level, such as customer share, become more relevant.

Next to affecting the marketer's performance in the marketplace, it is highly likely that MMSS affect the way decisions are being made, that is they affect the *decision process*. These can be decision processes of the individual marketer or of a decision-making group. If the MMSS is used to improve the quality of decision-making, it leads to a more extensive decision process in which more decision alternatives are being explored and where the outcomes of these alternative are more thoroughly analyzed. This usually also has an effect on the market outcomes of using the MMSS. However, sometimes marketers use the MMSS especially to become more efficient in their decision-making process, which is to spend less time on the process. If this is the case, the impact of the system on market outcomes (at the organizational level) may be limited. Research by Payne et al. (1993) shows that in making decisions, decision-makers constantly trade off making better, more accurate decisions versus putting less cognitive effort into the decision-making process. Research by Todd and Benbasat (1999) has shown that decision-makers often use decision support tools to reduce the amount of cognitive effort they have to spend in the decision-making process rather than optimizing the quality of the decisions. This means that tools are thus used for purposes which are different from those they were designed for, which was to improve market outcomes.

A reason for decision-makers to use MMSS, especially for improving efficiency rather than for increasing decision quality, may be that the effort put into the decision- making process is immediately observable by them. The effects of using MMSS on market outcomes are more difficult to measure directly since they may be more long-term and are realized at the organizational level with several other factors also affecting market outcomes.

To have organizational impact, the ultimate goal of MMSS, one has to ensure that the interests of the organization and the individual are aligned. Therefore, direct feedback of the effects of the MMSS on market outcomes should be presented to the MMSS user. The system should not only propose an optimal decision to its user but also explain why this decision would be best and what its consequences for the market performance of the organization would be (Kayande et al. 2006). Figure 17.1 summarizes the various MMSS Impact variables. We note that the order in which the Decision Process and Market Outcome categories are presented in Fig. 17.1 is opposite to the order in which we introduced them above. The causal ordering between the variables is as presented in Fig. 17.1, which describes the focal dependent variable in our discussion. In a sequence of steps, we will now develop our model of the factors that drive MMSS impact, which will eventually result in the full model depicted in Fig. 17.6.

17.3.2.1 Use of MMSS

To create impact it is necessary for the MMSS to be used by marketers (see Fig. 17.2). More intensive use (i.e., doing more analyses) of MMSS affects both

> **MMSS Impact**
>
> • Decision Process
> (Cognitive Effort Spent, Alternatives Considered, Decision Time, Learning)
>
> • Market Outcome
> (Marketing Metrics: Brand Awareness, Customer Satisfaction, Customer Share, Sales, Market Share, Customer Share, Profit)

Fig. 17.1 MMSS impact

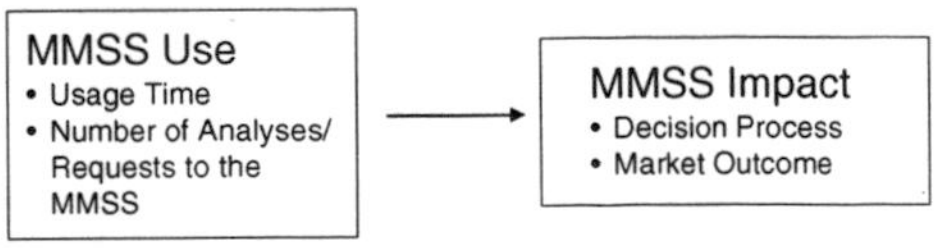

Fig. 17.2 Relationship between MMSS use and MMSS impact

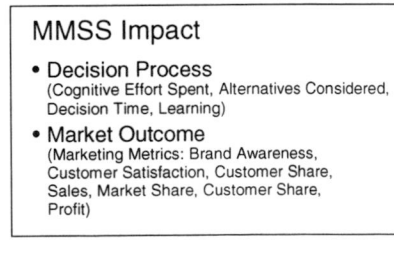

decision processes and market outcomes. These analyses have a quantitative flavor in the case of data- and model-based MMSS, and a qualitative flavor in the case of knowledge-based MMSS, and often concern the analysis of the outcomes of alternative scenarios. The intensity with which the MMSS is used affects the time that marketers allot to working with the MMSS and, consequently, also the amount of time they need to make decisions. However, working with the MMSS will also create a better understanding of the problem at hand and, consequently, lead to higher quality decisions to solve these problems. And, improved understanding will result from learning processes taking place when the decision-maker interactively explores the outcomes associated with alternative courses of action. Thus, more intensive use of the MMSS leads to improved market outcomes. In terms of the effort- accuracy trade-off (Payne et al. 1993) we expect more intensive use of the MMSS to require more cognitive effort but also to lead to better decisions, i.e., improved decision accuracy. Of course, the strength of the relationship between MMSS Use and MMSS Impact can be expected to be moderated by other variables, such as the quality of the MMSS. We discuss potential moderators later.

The decision to use the MMSS is often made by the individual decision-maker. Only in the case of so-called mandatory use, will top management directly affect the intensity of MMSS use. Organizations thus depend on the decisions of individuals to start using systems to obtain effects at the organization levels. However, organizations can affect the decisions of these individuals. The most important way of facilitating the use of MMSSs is by making them available to individual users. At the organizational level, the decision to adopt an MMSS has thus to be made first (see Fig. 17.3).

17.3.2.2 Implementation Characteristics

As shown in Fig. 17.3, the organizational effects of an MMSS (i.e., its effects on market outcomes) are affected by decisions at the organizational level as well as by decisions by and behavior of individuals within these organizations. Of course, the results of decision-making will also depend on the way these decisions are implemented. At the organizational level it is important to create conditions to make sure that individual decisions (to start using MMSS and use it with sufficient intensity) are such that they contribute to obtaining the goals

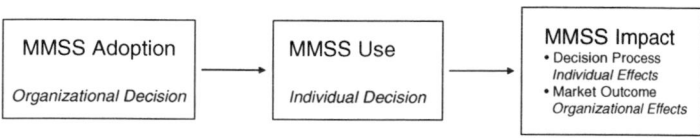

Fig. 17.3 The relationship between MMSS adoption and MMSS impact

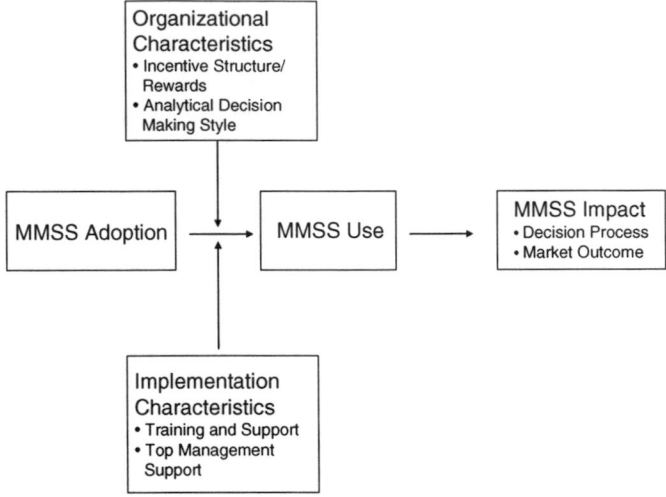

Fig. 17.4 The effects of organizational and implementation characteristics on MMSS impact

of the organization. The characteristics of the organization and of the implementation procedure of the MMSS affect the use of MMSS by individual users
within organizations that have adopted these systems (see Fig. 17.4).

The way the MMSS is implemented in the organization is very important.
There is a large literature in the general IS/DSS field about the effects of
implementation characteristics on the success of IS (e.g., Alavi and Joachimsthaler
1992; DeLone and McLean 1992; Zmud 1979). In the marketing literature, these
implementation variables have also been shown to be important (e.g., Wierenga
and Oude Ophuis 1997; Zinkhan et al. 1987). Two important implementation
characteristics are the amount of training and support users receive after the
MMSS has been adopted by the organization and the extent to which top
management supports individual users in using the system. In the diffusion of
an information system within an organization, users are influenced by training
(Leonard-Barton and Deschamps 1988). In the context of information systems, training refers to the provision of hardware and software skills sufficient
to enable effective interaction with the DSS under consideration (Alavi and
Joachimsthaler 1992). Proper training of end users is an important strategy for
minimizing resistance (Adams et al. 2004). Furthermore, there is strong agreement in the IS literature that top management support is a key factor for
successful IS/DSS implementation and use. A survey on the success of management tools and techniques (Rigby 2001) shows that strong top-down support is
important for a successful implementation of these tools. Leonard-Barton and
Deschamps (1988) note that whether management support or urge is necessary to
make an individual user adopt also depends on the characteristics of the end-
user. We discuss the impact of these variables later.

17.3.2.3 Organizational Characteristics

Next to implementation characteristics, characteristics of the organization affect the extent to which individuals within the organization use the MMSS. First, the incentive structure within an organization affects the way MMSS will be used. The use of appropriate incentives is an important means of keeping people in an organization focused on customers (Day 2003) and having them make decisions that improve the attractiveness of the organization's offerings in the eyes of customers. Reinartz et al. (2004) find that organizational alignment, including rewards for employees for building relationships with customers, shows positive effects on their behavior to accomplish this. If an organization rewards its employees for building relationships with customers, then it becomes instrumental for the employees of that organization to use the MMSS that have been adopted by the organization. That is because this will help them succeed in meeting the goal of improved customer relationships and make them eligible to receive the rewards.

Organizations often have a prevailing attitude and a certain standard approach to doing things (Pettigrew 1979). This approach also concerns the way the organization deals with preparing and supporting its decisions. One can distinguish a more analytical approach using quantitative data and formal analyses to support decision-making from a more heuristic/holistic approach. Data-based MMSS center around data and (quantitative) analysis, and we expect that such MMSS fit best in organizations that have an analytical/ systematical approach towards decision-making and that decision-makers operating in these organizations are more inclined to use the MMSS that has been adopted by the organization.

17.3.2.4 User Characteristics

Next to organizational characteristics and implementation characteristics, we also expect user characteristics and system characteristics to affect the way the MMSS is used (see Fig. 17.5).

17.3.2.5 System Characteristics

System characteristics clearly affect MMSS use and impact. We distinguish two categories of system characteristics. One category, *system quality*, deals with the "content" of the support the system offers (i.e., type, quality and sophistication of models and data, that is the information and insights the system produces) whereas the other category refers to the *interface*, i.e., the "package" through which the user has access to these functionalities of the MMSS. Here we think of user friendliness, flexibility and adaptability of the MMSS.

Regarding the content (*system quality*), Wierenga and Bruggen (1997) and Wierenga et al. (1999) argue that in order to get the system adopted by the user, the way the MMSS provides support should match with the way the marketer

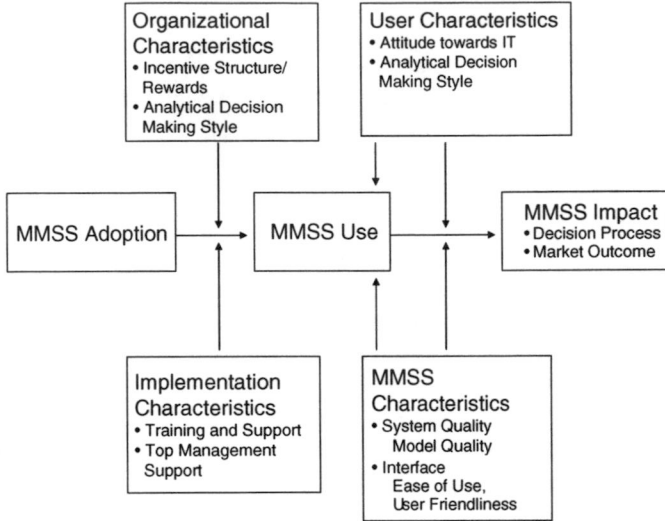

Fig. 17.5 The effects of system and user characteristics on MMSS impact

makes decisions. Wierenga and Oude Ophuis (1997) report a positive relationship between systems sophistication and system impact. Van Bruggen et al. (1996) also find that decision-makers who use better MMSS (i.e., systems that contain better models) make better decisions. More sophisticated, higher quality MMSS moderate the relationship between MMSS Use and MMSS Impact in the sense that a more intensive use of a higher quality system has a more positive effect on its Impact. As we already observed, research in Marketing (Science) over the years has produced a large collection of high-quality models, which can be components of MMSS. This quality of MMSS continues to increase. Unfortunately, there is no evidence that better systems are also used more intensively. The study by Van Bruggen et al. (1996) shows that decision-makers have difficulties in recognizing and valuing the quality of the systems they use and they do not find evidence for a more intensive use of better systems. The lack of a relationship between MMSS quality and MMSS use means that an increase in the quality of systems does not cause the MMSS Impact to increase as much as would be potentially possible.

If we look at the system *interface* or the *packaging* of the MMSS more user-friendly systems are used more intensively. The extent to which a system is perceived to be user-friendly strongly depends on how easy-to-use users perceive the system to be. Research of Davis (1989) indicates that a system's ease of use increases its use. Ease of use is the degree to which a person believes that using an information system would be free of effort. It is one of the "classical" concepts in information systems research (Davis 1989; Sanders and Manrodt 2003; Venkatesh 2000). A significant body of research in information systems cumulatively provides evidence for an effect of perceived ease of use on initial user acceptance and sustained usage of systems (Venkatesh 2000). The Technology Acceptance Model (TAM) (Davis 1989) suggests perceived ease of use to determine one's behavioral intention to use a technology, which is linked to subsequent actual use. TAM also suggests that ease of use influences perceived usefulness because the easier a technology the more useful it is (Venkatesh 2000). Flexibility, also called adaptability, is another critical factor explaining the success of information/ decision support systems (Barki and Huff 1990; Little 1970; Udo and Davis 1992). Flexible systems can be adapted more easily to the changing requirements of the decision situation and the specific needs of its users. This also enhances their use and as a consequence their impact.

17.3.2.6 Feedback Mechanism

MMSS use and the resulting decision-making and market outcomes may lead to revised perceptions of the value of the system, in particular their Perceived Usefulness. Therefore, a model of MMSS Impact should incorporate feedback loops, the importance of learning and the revision of beliefs about the usefulness of MMSS (Seddon 1997). In Fig. 17.6 we present our Model of MMSS Impact which contains these feedback loops. Once decisions have been made and implemented appropriately, (objective) market outcomes will be realized. Decision-makers also have a certain perception of the quality of the decisions they made. This is reflected in the amount of confidence they show in their decisions and their satisfaction with these decisions. Similarly, decision-makers have a perception of the value of the MMSS they used when making their decisions.

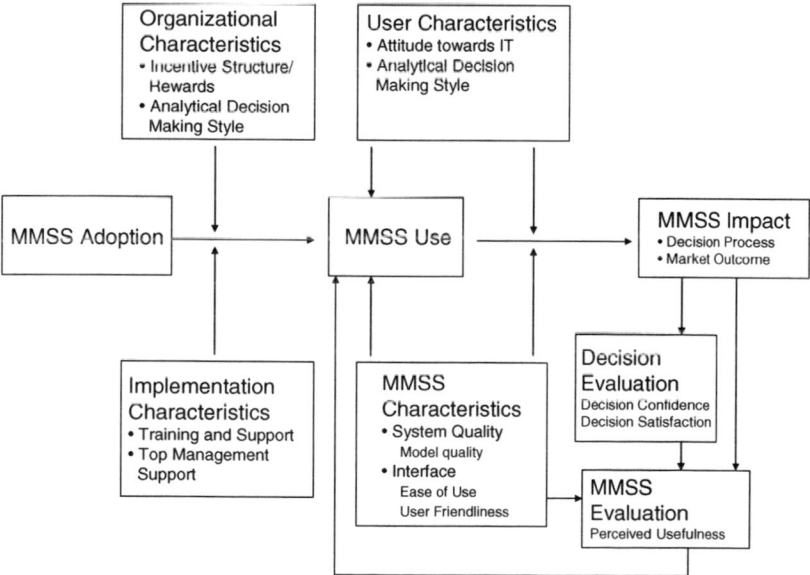

Fig. 17.6 MMSS impact model

This will be reflected in, for example, updating the Perceived Usefulness (Davis 1989) of the system. A relationship between the evaluation of the decisions made and of the use of the MMSS also exists. If decision-makers perceive the quality of their decisions to be good this is (partly) attributed to the MMSS.

Decision-makers who are very satisfied with the decisions they made using the MMSS also evaluate the system more positively. Consequently, these decision-makers are also more inclined to use MMSS again in future decision situations.

17.3.2.7 Discussion

In this Section we have addressed the impact of marketing management support systems. As we have seen, most of the empirical studies on the impact of MMSS show that when these systems are used, they actually improve the quality of decision-making leading to better market outcomes. At the same time, many authors have observed that these systems have not fulfilled their potential. How can we use the model of Fig. 17.6 to solve this discrepancy? *The* key factor for creating MMSS impact is to get these systems used by individuals once they have been adopted by the organization. Several factors stimulate MMSS use. For example, management plays a key role because by rewarding individual decision-makers for using systems and by creating a decision-making style and culture in the organization in which MMSS use is a logical thing to do. Also, they should make sure that a system is not simply "dropped" in the organization but that appropriate implementation procedures are in place. Furthermore, it is also important that the characteristics of the people who are supposed to use the MMSS match with the types of systems that have been implemented in the organization. Either systems should be selected that match with the nature of the decision-making style of the marketers that are employed, or top management should recruit managers that have a decision-making style that matches with the nature of the available MMSS. Furthermore, the systems should be of high quality and the interface should be user friendly.

Getting individual marketers to using MMSS requires endurance. As we have seen earlier, research (Lilien et al. 2004) shows that individual decision-makers have difficulties in recognizing the value of systems. If users do not recognize the quality of MMSS this hampers their impact because systems will not be used as intensively as would be desirable. As Fig. 17.6 shows, especially the intensive use of high-quality systems leads to superior organizational outcomes. Inversely, limited use of such systems leaves a lot of potential unrealized. In order to make decision-makers realize the positive impact of MMSS on the quality of their decision- making a learning process needs to take place. Only by actually using systems and observing the effects of this leads to the realization of their value. Users may not be immediately enthusiastic or certain about the value of MMSS once these have been implemented. By encouraging decision-makers to consider decision alternatives they did not consider before (by enlarging their solution space) is one of the main benefits of MMSS (Van Bruggen et al. 1998). However, doing things differently may create uncertainty. It is important to anticipate this aspect and carefully guide users to make sure that they continue using systems for a longer period of time. Providing decision-makers with feedback about the way the MMSS works and how it adds to the quality of decision-making is essential.

So far, the discussion about marketing management support systems in the literature has focused on decision support for (relatively) structured problems. This also applies to most of the research discussed in the present section. In the next section we turn to weakly-structured marketing problems and discuss how we can support decision-making there.

17.4 Advances in Marketing Management Support Systems for weakly-structured marketing problems

17.4.1 Decision Support for Structured and Weakly-Structured Marketing Problems

In Section 17.1, we briefly discussed the historical development of marketing management support systems. To understand the evolution of decision support in (marketing) management, it is important to explicate the notion of the "structuredness" of managerial problems (Gorry and Scott-Morton 1971). Management problems, including marketing problems, differ in the extent to which they are structured. For example: in sales promotions, a problem can be as structured as determining the optimal consumer price discount in cents per unit and as unstructured as designing a sales promotion campaign with all options open.

The notion of structuredness is directly related to Simon's (1977) distinction between "programmed" and "non-programmed" decisions. For programmed decisions, managerial problem solving is viewed as a fairly systematic process that can be transformed into a mathematical model. However, if problems are "hopelessly qualitative" by nature (Simon 1977, p. 58), then the problem is said to be ill-structured or "non-programmable" (Simon 1977). In marketing we have many problems that are non-programmed or at best weakly structured. Good examples of these are design problems, such as the design of new products, the design of marketing communication campaigns and the design of strategic marketing plans. Design problems are typically constraint problems for which the problem solver has to produce a concrete artifact that satisfies the constraints (Jonassen 2000). Because of the usual under-specification of the design problem – or in Reitman's (1965) terminology, the presence of "open constraints" (i.e., parameters for which the values are left unspecified) – multiple solutions are possible (Voss and Post 1988). Design problems are therefore among the most complex and open-ended type of problems (Goel and Pirolli 1989; Jonassen 2000).

Table 17.2 shows the distinction that Simon made in 1977 between programmed and non-programmed decisions, how both types of decisions are

Table 17.2 "Traditional" and "modern" techniques of decision making

Type of decisions	Decision-making techniques	
	Traditional	Modern
Programmed:	1. Habit	1. Operations Research:
(*i.e., well-structured*)	2. Clerical routine:	– mathematical analysis
Routine, repetitive decisions	– standard operational	– models
Organization develops specific	procedures (SOP's)	– computer simulations
processes for handling them	3. Organization Structure:	2. Electronic Data
	– common expectations	Processing
	– a system of sub goals	
	– well-defined	
	information	
	channels	
Non-programmed:	1. Judgment, intuition,	Heuristic problem-solving
(*i.e., ill-structured*)	and creativity	techniques applied to:
One-shot, ill-structured novel	2. Rules of thumb	(a) training human decision
policy decisions	3. Selection and training of	makers
Handled by general problem-	executives	(b) *constructing heuristic*
solving process		*computer programs*

Source: (Simon 1977)

made in the "traditional" way, and what the "modern" approach would be. If we look at marketing, we can say that at this moment (thirty years after Simon's article), for programmed (i.e., structured) decisions, we have advanced fully to the modern quadrant (upper-right in Simon's table). We have already discussed the progress that has been made in the modeling of marketing phenomena, and this Handbook bundles the most recent advances in marketing modeling in different subfields, such as advertising, sales promotion, sales management, CRM, and e-commerce.

The question now is what has happened to the problems in the lower part of Table 17.2, i.e. non-programmed problems? Are we beyond the traditional approaches based on rules of thumb, or selecting the right executives and relying on their experiences and judgments (see Fig. 17.2)? Or, do we now also have tools to support judgment tasks that involve intuition and creativity? As early as 1958, Simon and Newell argued in their classic paper "Heuristic Problem Solving: The Next Advance in Operations Research" that decision support research should extend its boundaries to cover the class of ill-structured management problems as well (Simon and Newell 1958). Simon and Newell emphasized the huge potential of using computer technology to solve complex, ill-structured problems by simulating human heuristic decision-making.

There has also been progress in these more difficult decision domains as well. Insights from the field of cognitive psychology about managerial decision-making (see, for instance, Hoch and Schkade 1996; Payne et al. 1993; Tversky and Kahneman 1974), combined with advances in the field of Artificial

Intelligence (of which Simon is considered the Founding Father) have led to a second stream of decision support technologies that emerged in the late 1980s/ early 1990s. These have also been applied in marketing. We refer to knowledge-based systems (Rangaswamy 1993), expert systems (McCann and Gallagher 1990; Wierenga 1990) and neural nets (Hruschka, Chapter 12 this book). Especially expert systems technology has been applied in marketing at a considerable scale. Applications can be found in the area of sales promotions (PROMOTOR: Abraham and Lodish 1987)), advertising (ADCAD: Burke et al. 1990) (ADDUCE: Burke 1991), and brand management (BRANDFRAME: Wierenga et al. 2000; Wierenga and Van Bruggen 2001). However, the applicability and success of expert systems is dependent on the structuredness of the problem (i.e., expert systems still require relatively structured problems) and the availability of relevant knowledge, whereas neural nets are dependent on the availability of (large) datasets.

The next advance in decision support for weakly-structured marketing problems is analogical reasoning. Analogical reasoning is a natural and effective problem-solving strategy in complex, weakly-structured decision situations (Gick and Holyoak 1980). A relatively new and promising knowledge-driven decision support technique that is based on the principle of analogical reasoning is Case-Based Reasoning (CBR). With this technique it is possible to put non-codified knowledge, e.g., in the form of cases, into action for supporting managerial decision-making in weakly-structured problem situations. We will discuss the power of analogical reasoning, and the CBR technique, in more detail in the next sections.

17.4.2 Analogical Reasoning

17.4.2.1 The Power of Analogies

Analogical thinking is "the ability to look at specific situations and somehow pull out abstract patterns that may also be found in superficially different situations" (Holyoak and Thagard 1995, p. 19). When confronted with a problem, one of the first things people do is to search their memory for previous, similar experiences (i.e., analogies) that could help to interpret or solve the problem at hand. To put it differently, analogical reasoning is about solving new problems in terms of what is already known (Gregan-Paxton and John 1997).

Analogical reasoning involves accessing, mapping, transferring (and inferring) elements from a familiar problem (the "base") to a new problem (the "target") (Gentner 1983). When a problem is new to a person, that person generally knows a few features of the problem, but does not know how these features are related (Markman and Moreau 2001). Analogical reasoning as a problem-solving strategy excels especially in weakly-structured domains. An analogy helps to impose structure on the problem and provides coherence among the decision elements (the "systematicity" principle: Gentner 1983).

People find analogies a natural way to reason. Architects, physicians, judges, car mechanics, and caterers use it (Leake 1996). The role of analogies in major scientific discoveries, such as the double helix structure of DNA, the wave theory of sound, and the circular structure of benzene, is well documented.[3] In management education, and for solving weakly-structured management problems in particular, the use of cases is ubiquitous. Reflecting on the similarities and differences with previously solved cases can help to interpret the current problem situation, identify successful courses of action, avoid potential failures, and foresee consequences of certain decisions (Jonassen 2000). Learning from previous cases substitutes the experience that novice managers typically lack (Jonassen 2000).

A good deal of marketing problem solving is also a form of analogical reasoning (or "analogizing", see Wierenga and Van Bruggen 1997). Marketers understand a new problem in terms of one that is already familiar, which helps to find a (quick) solution for the new problem. This can be illustrated by the way product managers interpret scanner data. Goldstein (2001) observed this interpretation process and found that product managers organize what they have learned from scanner data into a set of "stories". As soon as a new event (e.g., a new product introduction by a competitor) is identified as being similar to one of the existing stories (patterns) in the head of the manager, the manager "knows" what is happening (and generally also what s/he has to do).

17.4.2.2 Employing Analogical Reasoning as a Decision Support Technology

In order to start the system-supported analogical reasoning process, decision-makers have to be provided with base analogies, which provide the context in which decision options can be considered and evaluated (Markman and Moreau 2001). The base analogies also provide the relational structure (Gentner 1983) to cope with the weak structure of the target problem. This is in line with the theory of "structured imagination" (see Finke et al. 1992). This theory posits that when people come up with solutions for novel problems, these solutions are often inspired by the structure and properties of previous, similar problem-solving experiences (Marsh et al. 1996). Previous experiences are either retrieved from memory or can be provided by, for instance, a decision support system. An excellent technique for providing decision-makers with base analogies is a Case-Based Reasoning (CBR) System. Case-based reasoning is a prominent field in artificial intelligence, founded by Roger Schank (1982), and based on the principle of analogical reasoning (Leake 1996). A CBR system comprises a collection of previous cases from the domain under study and a set of search criteria for retrieving cases for situations that are similar to the new design problem. Solving a problem with the help of a CBR system involves retrieving a previous, similar problem (the base analogy) from its case-base and mapping

---

[3] See for example: "The Analogical Scientist" (Holyoak and Thagard 1995, Chapter 8).

and transferring knowledge from the base analogy to the target (Aamodt and Plaza 1994; Kolodner 1993; Riesbeck and Schank 1989). If necessary, the base solution can be adapted to resolve specific differences between the old and the current problem situation (Kolodner 1993; Riesbeck and Schank 1989).

Analogies have to be brought to mind in order to be effective. The strong point of a CBR system is that it makes analogies available to the decision-maker. Human memory has capacity limitations that a CBR system obviously does not have. Research in laboratory settings has, for instance, shown that it is difficult for people to spontaneously recall relevant analogies (e.g., Gick and Holyoak 1980). A CBR system serves as an external memory that enables directed search for relevant base analogies. CBR systems are also a flexible approach in the sense that it offers decision-makers the freedom to retrieve and select the analogies that *they* find most helpful for constructing a solution from a large set of potential base analogies. We think that analogical reasoning has much potential as a decision support principle for weakly-structured marketing problems, and design problems in particular. This was confirmed in a recent large scale experimental study (n = 120), where participants had to design a sales promotion campaign for a beer brand. The design of a sales promotion campaign is a weakly structured problem with the indefiniteness of open constraints and multiple possible solutions mentioned earlier. It turned out that participants who used a Case-Based Reasoning systems (that contained cases of earlier successful sales promotions) generated sales promotion campaigns that were more creative than participants who did not use a CBR system (Althuizen and Wierenga 2008).

17.5 Conclusions

In this chapter we have discussed recent advances in MMSS. We have argued that the conditions for using MMSS have significantly improved. The quality of marketing management support systems has improved substantially, MMSS can now easily be embedded in the organizational IT infrastructure that managers use. Also, the movement towards individual customer data, especially in the context of CRM and interactive marketing, has created new opportunities for building models that can be used directly to optimize marketing campaigns and marketing actions. We have also presented the actual state of knowledge about the factors that drive the impact of marketing management support systems. For an MMSS to improve decision-making quality it must be good *and* be adopted. A good system that is adopted at a high level will have a greater chance to improve decision quality than a great system that is not adopted. We have summarized the factors that affect MMSS adoption at the company level (organizational and implementation characteristics) and MMSS use by individual decision-makers (user charactcristics and MMSS characteristics). Feedback and learning play an important role in the prolonged use and impact of MMSS. So far, most MMSS are data-driven and deal with relatively structured marketing problems. The last section of this chapter dealt with decision support systems for weakly-structured marketing problems, especially design problems. An important advance in this context is the use of analogical reasoning as a decision support technology. We have shown that providing decision-makers with analogies (in the environment of a Case-Based Reasoning system) helps them to come up with better (i.e., more creative) solutions for marketing design problems.

The field of marketing management support systems keeps moving. Marketing will continue to change, new decision support technologies will emerge, new statistical and optimization techniques will be invented, new data sources will become available, information technology will continue to develop, and we will further expand our knowledge about how to develop and implement MMSS that have impact on the decisions and results of companies. We hope that the account of the recent advances in this chapter is a good vantage point for the developments in MMSS in the years to come.

References

Aamodt, A., E. Plaza. 1994. Case-Based Reasoning: Foundational Issues, Methodological Variations, and System Approaches. *AI Communications* **7**(1) 39–59.

Abraham, M.M., L.M. Lodish. 1987. PROMOTER: An Automated Promotion Evaluation System. *Marketing Science* **6**(2) 101–23.

Ackoff, R.L. 1967. Management Misinformation Systems. *Management Science* **14**(December) 147–156.

Adams, B., E.S. Berner, J. R. Wyatt. 2004. Applying Strategies to Overcome User Resistance in a Group of Clinical Managers to a Business Software Application: A Case Study. *Journal of Organizational and End User Computing* **16**(4) 55–64.

Alavi, M., E.A. Joachimsthaler. 1992. Revisiting DSS Implementation Research: A Meta-Analysis of the Literature and Suggestions for Researchers. *MIS Quarterly* **16**(1) 95–116.

Althuizen, N.A.P., B. Wierenga. 2007. The Value of Analogical Reasoning for the Design of Sales Promotion Campaigns: A Case-Based Reasoning Approach. *ERIM Working Paper*. Erasmus University, 2008.

Ambler, T., J. Roberts. 2006. Beware the Silver Metric: Marketing Performance Measurement Has to Be Multidimensional. *MSI Reports*. Marketing Science Institute.

Barki, H., S.L. Huff. 1990. Implementing Decision Support Systems: Correlates of User Satisfaction and System Usage. *INFOR* **28**(2) 89–101.

Bass, F.M., R.D. Buzzel, M.R. Greene, Eds. 1961. *Mathematical Models and Methods in Marketing*. Homewood, Irwin, IL.

Blattberg, R.C., R. Glazer, J.D.C. Little, Eds. 1994. *The Marketing Information Revolution*. Harvard Business School Press, Boston.

Brien, R.H., J.E. Stafford. 1968. Marketing Information Systems: A New Dimension for Marketing Research. *Journal of Marketing* **32**(3) 19–23.

Bucklin, R.E., D.R. Lehmann, J.D.C. Little. 1998. From Decision Support to Decision Automation: A 2020 Vision. *Marketing Letters* **9**(3) 235–246.

Burke, R.R. 1991. Reasoning with Empirical Marketing Knowledge. *International Journal of Research in Marketing* **8**(1) 75–90.

Burke, R.R., A. Rangaswamy, J. Wind, J. Eliashberg. 1990. A Knowledge-Based System for Advertising Design. *Marketing Science* **9**(3) 212–29.

Buzzel, R.D. 1964. *Mathematical Models and Marketing Management.* Harvard University, Division of Research, Boston.

Carlsson, C., E. Turban. 2002. DSS: Directions for the Next Decade. *Decision Support Systems* **33**(2) 105–110.

Chakravarti, D., A. Mitchell, R. Staelin. 1979. Judgment Based Marketing Decision Models: An Experimental Investigation of the Decision Calculus Approach. *Management Science* **25**(3) 251–263.

Davis, F.D. 1989. Perceived Usefulness, Perceived Ease Of Use, And User Acceptance of Information Technology. *MIS Quarterly* **13**(3) 319–340.

Day, G.S. 2003. Creating a Superior Customer-Relating Capability. *Sloan Management Review* **44**(3) 77–82.

DeLone, W.H., E.R. McLean. 1992. Information Systems Success: The Quest for the Dependent Variable. *Information Systems Research* **3**(1) 60–95.

Eliashberg, J., G.L. Lilien. 1993. *Handbooks in Operations Research and Management Science. Volume 5: Marketing.* Elsevier Science Publishers, Amsterdam.

Engel, J.F., M.R. Warshaw. 1964. Allocating Advertising Dollars by Linear-Programming. *Journal of Advertising Research* **4**(1) 42–48.

Fader, P.S., B.G.S. Hardie, K.K. Lee. 2005. Counting Your Customers the Easy Way: an Alternative to the Pareto/NBD Model. *Marketing Science* **24**(2) 275–284.

Ferrat, T.W., G.E. Vlahos. 1998. An Investigation of Task-Technology Fit for Managers in Greece and the US. *European Journal of Information Systems* **7**(2) 123–136.

Finke, R.A., T.B. Ward, S.M. Smith. 1992. *Creative Cognition: Theory, Research, and Applications.* MIT Press, Cambridge, MA

Frank, R.E., A.A. Kuehn, W.F. Massy, Eds.1962. *Quantitative Techniques in Marketing Analyses.* Irwin, Homewood, IL.

Fudge, W.K., L.M. Lodish. 1977. Evaluation of the Effectiveness of a Model Based Salesman's Planning by Field Experimentation. *Interfaces* **8**(1, Part 2) 97–106.

Gensch, D., N. Arersa, S.P. Moore. 1990. A Choice Modeling Market Information system that Enabled ABB Electric to Expand Its Market Share. *Interfaces* **20**(1) 6–25.

Gentner, D. 1983. Structure-Mapping: A Theoretical Framework for Analogy. *Cognitive Science* **7**(2) 155–70.

George, M., C. Ma, T. Mark, J.A. Petersen. 2007. Marketing Metrics and Financial Performance. *Marketing Science Conference on Marketing Metrics and Financial Performance* Vol. 07-300. MSI., Boston, Massachusetts.

Gick, M.L., K.J. Holyoak.1980. Analogical Problem Solving. *Cognitive Psychology* **12**(3) 306–55.

Glazer, R. 1999. Winning in Smart Markets. *Sloan Management Review* **40**(4) 59–69.

Goel,V., P. Pirolli. 1989. Motivating the Notion of Generic Design Within Information-Processing Theory: The Design Problem Space. *AI Magazine* **10**(1) 19–36.

Goldstein, D.K. 2001. Product Managers' Use of Scanner Data: A Story of Organizational Learning. Deshpande, R. Ed. *Using Market Knowledge.* Sage Publications, Thousand Oaks, CA.

Gorry, G.A., M.S. Scott-Morton. 1971. A Framework for Management Information Systems. *Sloan Management Review* **13**(Fall) 55–70.

Gregan-Paxton, J., D.R. John. 1997. Consumer Learning by Analogy: A Model of Internal Knowledge Transfer. *Journal of Consumer Research* **24**(December) 266–84.

Hoch, S.J., D.A. Schkade. 1996. A Psychological Approach to Decision Support Systems. *Management Science* **42**(1) 51–64.

Holyoak, K.J., P. Thagard. 1995. *Mental Leaps: Analogy in Creative Thought.* MIT Press, Cambridge, MA.

Jonassen, D.H. 2000. Toward a Design Theory of Problem Solving. *Educational Technology Research and Development* **48**(4) 63–85.

Kayande, U., A. De Bruyn, G. Lilien, A. Rangaswamy, G.H. van Bruggen. 2006. *How Feedback Can Improve Managerial Evaluations of Model-based Marketing Decision*

Support Systems. Institute for the Study of Business Markets, Penn State University.

Kolodner, J.L. 1993. *Case-based Reasoning.* Morgan Kaufmann Publishers, Inc., San Mateo, CA.

Kotler, PH. 1966. A Design for the Firm's Marketing Nerve Center. *Business Horizons* **9**(3) 63–74.

Kotler, PH. 1971. *Marketing Decision Making: A Model Building Approach.* Holt, Rinehart and Winston, New York.

Leake, D.B. 1996. CBR in Context: The Present and Future. Leake, D.B. Ed. *Case-Based Reasoning: Experiences, Lessons, and Future Directions.* AAAI Press/MIT Press, Menlo Park.

Leonard-Barton, D., I. Deschamps. 1988. Managerial Influence In The Implementation Of New Technology. *Management Science* **34**(10) 1252–1265.

Li, E.Y, R. McLeod, Jr., J.C. Rogers. 2001. Marketing information systems in *Fortune* 500 companies: a longitudinal analysis of 1980, 1990, and 2000. *Information & Management* **38**(5) 307–322.

Lilien, G.L., PH. Kotler.1983. *Marketing Decision Making: A Model-Building Approach.* Harper & Row, New York.

Lilien, G.L., PH. Kotler, K.S. Moorthy.1992. *Marketing Models.* Prentice-Hall, Englewood Cliffs NJ.

Lilien, G.L., A. Rangaswamy. 2004. *Marketing Engineering: Computer Assisted Marketing Analysis and Planning.* (2nd ed.). PrenticeHall, Upper Saddle River NJ.

Lilien, G.L, A. Rangaswamy, K. Starke, G.H. van Bruggen. 2001. *How and Why Decision Models Influence Marketing Resource Allocations.* University Park, PA. ISBM.

Lilien, G.L., A. Rangaswamy, G.H. Van Bruggen, K. Starke. 2004. DSS Effectiveness in Marketing Resource Allocation Decisions: Reality vs. Perception. *Information Systems Research* **15**(3) 216–35.

Little, J.D.C. 1970. Models and Managers: The Concept of A Decision Calculus. *Management Science* **16** B466–B485.

Little, J.D.C. 1979. Decision Support Systems for Marketing Managers. *Journal of Marketing* **43**(3) 9–26.

Lodish, L.M., E. Curtis, M. Ness, M.K. Simpson. 1988. Sales Force Sizing and Deployment Using a Decision Calculus Model at Syntex Laboratories. *Interfaces* **18**(1) 5–20.

Markman, A.B., C.P. Moreau. 2001. Analogy and Analogical Comparison. Gentner D., K.J. Holyoak, B.N. Kokinov, Eds. *The Analogical Mind: Perspectives from Cognitive Science.* The MIT Press, Cambridge, MA.

Marsh, R.L., J.D. Landau, J.L. Hicks. 1996. How Examples May (and May Not) Constrain Creativity. *Memory & Cognition* **24**(5) 669–80.

McCann, J.M., Gallagher, J.P. 1990. *Expert Systems for Scanner Data Environments.* Kluwer, Boston, MA.

McIntyre, S.H. 1982. An Experimental Study of the Impact of Judgment-Based Marketing Models. *Management Science* **28**(1) 17–33.

Montgomery, D.B., G.L. Urban.1969. *Management Science in Marketing.* Prentice Hall, Englewood Cliffs.

Neslin, S.A, S. Gupta, W. Kamakura, J. Lu, Ch.H. Mason. 2006. Defection Detection: Measuring and Understanding the Predictive Accuracy of Customer Churn Models. *Journal of Marketing Research* **43**(May) 204–211.

Payne, J.W., J. Bettman, E.J. Johnson. 1993. *The Adaptive Decision Maker.* Cambridge University Press, New York.

Pettigrew, A.M. 1979. On Studying Organizational Cultures. *Administrative Science Quarterly* **24**(4) 570–581.

Rai, A., S.S. Lang, R.B Welker. 2002. Assessing the Validity of IS Success Models: An Empirical Test and Theoretical Analysis. *Information Systems Research* **13**(1) 50.

Rangaswamy, A. 1993. Marketing Decision Models: From Linear Programs to Knowledge-based Systems. Eliashberg, J., G.L. Lilien, Eds. *Handbooks in Operations Research and Management Science: Marketing. Vol. 5*. Elsevier Science Publishers, Amsterdam, 733–771.

Reitman, W.R. 1965. *Cognition and Thought*. John Wiley and Sons, New York, NY.

Reinartz, W., M. Krafft, W.D. Hoyer. 2004. The Customer Relationship Management Process: Its Measurement and Impact on Performance. *Journal of Marketing Research* **41**(3) 293–305.

Riesbeck, C.K., R.C. Schank. 1989. *Inside Case-Based Reasoning*. Lawrence Erlbaum, Hillsdale, NJ.

Rigby, D. 2001. Management Tools and Techniques: A survey. *California Management Review* **43**(2) 139–160.

Roberts, J.H. 2000. The Intersection of Modelling Potential and Practice. *International Journal of Research in Marketing* **17**(2/3) 127–134.

Sanders, N.R., K.B. Manrodt. 2003. Forecasting Software in Practice: Use, Satisfaction, and Performance. *Interfaces* **33**(5) 90–93.

Schank, R.C. 1982. *Dynamic Memory*. Cambridge University Press, Cambridge.

Seddon, P.B. 1997. A Respecification and Extension of the Delone and McLean Model of IS Success. *Information Systems Research* **8**(3) 240–253.

Simon, H.A. 1977. *The New Science of Management Decision*, revised edition. Prentice-Hall, Englewood Cliffs, NJ.

Simon, H.A., A. Newell. 1958. Heuristic Problem Solving: The Next Advance in Operations Research. *Operations Research* **6**(January–February) 1–10.

Swift, R.S. 2001. *Accelerating Customer Relationships: Using CRM and Relationship Technologies*. Prentice Hall, Upper Saddle River NJ.

Todd, P., I. Benbasat. 1999. Evaluating the Impact of DSS, Cognitive Effort, and Incentives on Strategy Selection. *Information Systems Research* **10**(4) 356–374.

Tversky, A., D. Kahneman. 1974. Judgment Under Uncertainty: Heuristics and Biases. *Science* **185** 1124–30.

Udo, G.J., J.S. Davis.1992. Factors Affecting Decision Support System Benefits. *Information & Management* **23**(6) 359–371.

Van Bruggen, G.H., A. Smidts, B. Wierenga. 1996. The Impact of the Quality of a Marketing Decision Support System: An Experimental Study. *International Journal of Research in Marketing* **13**(4) 331–343.

Van Bruggen, G.H., A. Smidts, B. Wierenga. 1998. Improving Decision Making by Means of a Marketing Decision Support System. *Management Science* **44**(5) 645–58.

Venkatesh, V. 2000. Determinants of Perceived Ease of Use: Integrating Control, Intrinsic Motivation, and Emotion into the Technology Acceptance Model. *Information Systems Research* **11**(4) 342–365.

Vlahos, G.E., T.W. Ferratt, G. Knoepfle. 2004. The Use of Computer-Based Information Systems by German Managers to Support Decision Making. *Information & Management* **41**(6) 763–779.

Voss, J.F., T.A. Post. 1988. On the Solving of Ill-Structured Problems. Chi, M.T., R. Glaser, M.J. Farr, Eds. *The Nature of Expertise*. Lawrence Erlbaum, New Jersey.

Wierenga, B. 1990. The First Generation of Marketing Expert Systems. *Working Paper*. Marketing Department, The Wharton school, University of Pennsylvania.

Wierenga, B., A. Dalebout, S. Dutta. 2000. BRANDFRAME: A Marketing Management Support System for the Brand Manager. Wierenga, B., G.H. van Bruggen, Eds. *Marketing Management Support System: Principles, Tools, and Implementation*. Kluwer Academic Publisher, Boston, 231–262.

Wierenga, B., P.A.M. Oude Ophuis. 1997. Marketing Decision Support Systems: Adoption, Use, and Satisfaction. *International Journal of Research in Marketing* **14**(3) 275–290.

Wierenga, B., G.H. van Bruggen. 1997. The Integration of Marketing Problem-Solving Modes and Marketing Management Support Systems. *Journal of Marketing* **61**(3) 21.

Wierenga, B., and G.H. van Bruggen. 2000. *Marketing Management Support Systems: Principles, Tools and Implementation*. Kluwer Academic Publishers, Boston.

Wierenga, B., G.H. van Bruggen. 2001. Developing a Customized Decision-Support System for Brand Managers. *Interfaces* **31**(3, Part 2 of 2) S128–S45.

Wierenga, B., G.H. van Bruggen, R. Staelin. 1999. The Success of Marketing Management Support Systems. *Marketing Science* **18**(3) 196–207.

Winer, R.S. 2001. A Framework for Customer Relationship Management. *California Management Review* **43**(Summer) 89–105.

Zinkhan, G.M., E.A. Joachimsthaler, T.C. Kinnear. 1987. Individual Differences and Marketing Decision Support System Usage and Satisfaction. *Journal of Marketing Research* **24**(2) 208–214.

Zmud, R.W. 1979. Individual Differences and MIS Success: A Review of the Empirical Literature. *Management Science* **25**(10) 966–975.

Author Index

Subject Index

Biographies

Editor

Berend Wierenga is Professor of Marketing at Rotterdam School of Management, Erasmus University in Rotterdam. His most important research areas are marketing models, marketing decision making, and marketing management support systems. He has published widely on these topics, in journals such as *Journal of Marketing, Journal of Marketing Research, Marketing Science, International Journal of Research in Marketing, Management Science*, and many others. He has also written several books, most recently: "*Marketing Management Support Systems: Principles, Tools, and Implementation*" (co-author: Gerrit van Bruggen). Berend Wierenga is the founding editor of the *International Journal of Research in Marketing*, one of the leading academic journals in marketing. He is Dean of Fellows of the European Marketing Academy (EMAC). Before joining the Erasmus University, he was a faculty member at Wageningen University, where he also obtained his PhD. He has held visiting positions at Stanford University, INSEAD, and The Wharton School of the University of Pennsylvania. At Rotterdam School of Management, Erasmus University, Berend Wierenga has been Chairman of the Marketing Department, Scientific Director of ERIM (Erasmus Research Institute of Management) and Dean of the School.

Authors

Sönke Albers (Diploma in Business Administration, PhD) is Professor of Innovation, New Media, and Marketing at Christian-Albrechts-University at Kiel, Germany. He was previously Professor of Marketing, and for a year also the first Dean of Otto Beisheim Graduate School of Management (WHU), and further Professor of Marketing at Lüneburg University, both in Germany. He also was a Visiting Scholar or Professor at Stanford University, INSEAD (France), Vienna University and the Australian Graduate School of Management in Sydney. He is chairman of a major research site called "Graduiertenkolleg" with the topic "Business aspects of loosely coupled systems in the age of electronic media" funded by the German Science Foundation (DFG). His research interests are lying in the areas of marketing and sales management, the diffusion of innovations, the planning of new products and electronic business. He is author of about 150 articles in international and German journals such as *Marketing Science, Journal of Marketing Research* and *International Journal of Research* in Marketing and published over 10 books including "Marketing with Interactive Media", "eCommerce", "Product Management", "Salesforce Management", and "The eCommerce Winner", all in German. He currently is chairman of the German association of professors of business administration and serves on the editorial board of several renowned journals.

Niek A.P. Althuizen is Assistant Professor of Marketing at ESSEC Business School Paris. His main research interests are marketing decision making, marketing management support systems, and creativity. Before joining ESSEC, he was a PhD student at RSM Erasmus University Rotterdam, where he worked on decision support systems for weakly-structured marketing problems. He obtained his degree in December 2006. He has presented his research at international marketing conferences, such as Marketing Science and EMAC. He is in the process of preparing several publications based on his dissertation.

Randolph E. Bucklin is the Peter W. Mullin Professor at the UCLA Anderson School. He holds a Ph.D. in Business (Marketing) and an M.S. in Statistics from Stanford University and an A.B. in Economics from Harvard University Professor Bucklin's research interests are in the quantitative analysis of customer purchase behavior. He specializes in choice models using historical records of customer transactions from scanner and Internet data. Using these models, he studies how customers respond to changes in marketing activity (e.g., advertising, price, promotions, distribution), how customers are segmented in their behavior, and how rival brands and stores compete. Professor Bucklin currently serves as co-editor of *Marketing Letters* and is on the editorial boards of the *Journal of Marketing Research, Marketing Science,* and the *International Journal of Research in Marketing*. At UCLA, he teaches courses in sales channels, pricing, and marketing management in the MBA programs. He offers a doctoral seminar on choice models and advises PhD students, chairing seven dissertations to date. He has received five awards for teaching excellence at UCLA, including the Neidorf "Decade" Teaching Award (2001). Professor Bucklin also served as chair of the UCLA Marketing faculty for 2000–2004 and 2005–2007.

Peter J. Danaher is the Coles Myer Chair of Marketing and Retailing at the Melbourne Business School in Australia. He was previously Professor and Chair of the Marketing Department at the University of Auckland in New Zealand. He has also held visiting positions at London Business School, The Wharton School and MIT. He has a PhD in statistics from Florida State University and an MS in statistics from Purdue. His primary research interests are media exposure distributions, advertising effectiveness, television audience measurement and behavior, internet usage behavior, customer satisfaction measurement, forecasting and sample surveys, resulting in many publications in journals such as the *Journal of Marketing Research, Marketing Science, Journal of Marketing, Journal of Advertising Research, Journal of the American Statistical Association, Journal of Retailing, Journal of Business and Economic Statistics* and the *American Statistician.* He serves on the Editorial Boards of the *Journal of Marketing Research, Marketing Science* and *Journal of Marketing* and is an Area Editor for the *International Journal of Research in Marketing.* He has consulted extensively with Telecom, Australia Post, Optus Communications, Unilever, Nielsen Media Research, and other market research companies. He has also been the survey auditor for the television ratings services in New Zealand, Australia and Ireland.

Marnik G. Dekimpe (Ph.D, UCLA) is Research Professor of Marketing at Tilburg University (The Netherlands) and Professor of Marketing, Catholic University Leuven (Belgium). His research has been published in journals as *Marketing Science, The Journal of Marketing Research, The Journal of Marketing, The Journal of Econometrics* and *The International Journal of Research* in Marketing, among others.

Jehoshua Eliashberg is the Sebastian S. Kresge Professor of Marketing and Professor of Operations and Information Management, at the Wharton School of the University of Pennsylvania. His research has addressed various issues including new product development and market analysis, marketing/manufacturing/R&D interface, negotiations and competitive strategies. He has particular interest in the media and entertainment, pharmaceutical, and the hi-tech industries. He has authored numerous articles appearing in journals such as: *Journal of Marketing, Journal of Marketing Research, Management Science, Marketing Science, Manufacturing and Service Operations Management,* and *Optimal Control Applications & Methods.* His work in the entertainment industry has been the subject of articles appearing periodicals such as *Business Week, The Wall Street Journal, The New York Times,* and many others.

He has co-edited the books, *Handbooks in Operations Research and Management Science: Marketing* (with Gary L. Lilien) and *Managing Business Interfaces: Marketing, Engineering, and Manufacturing Perspectives* (with Amiya K. Chakravarty). Professor Eliashberg has held various editorial positions in leading professional journals including: the Marketing Departmental Editor in *Management Science,* an Editorial Board member for *Marketing Science,* the *European Journal of Operational Research, Marketing Letters, and* Senior Editor for *Manufacturing and Service Operations Management*

Philip Hans Franses (1963) is Professor of Econometrics and Professor of Marketing Research, both at the School of Economics of the Erasmus University Rotterdam. He publishes in journals as the *Journal of Econometrics,*

The Journal of Applied Econometrics and in *The Journal of Marketing Research and Marketing Science*. He (co-) authored several books that appeared with Oxford University Press and Cambridge University Press, some of which have been translated into Chinese and Italian. Currently he serves as the Dean of the Erasmus School of Economics.

Sunil Gupta is Edward W. Carter Professor of Business at the Harvard Business School. Before joining Harvard, he taught at Columbia and UCLA. Sunil's research interests include choice models, pricing, and customer management. His articles in these areas have won several awards including the O'Dell (1993, 2002) and the Paul Green (1998, 2005) awards for the *Journal of Marketing Research*, and the best paper awards for the *International Journal of Research in Marketing* (1999) and Marketing Science Institute (1999, 2000 and 2003). Sunil is a co-author of two books. His recent book, *Managing Customers as Investments*, won the 2006 annual Berry-AMA book prize for the best book in marketing. In September 1999, Sunil was selected as the best core course teacher at Columbia Business School. He is an Area Editor for the *Journal of Marketing Research* and serves on the editorial boards of *International Journal of Research in Marketing, Journal of Marketing, Marketing Letters,* M*arketing Science* and *Quantitative Marketing and Economics*. He is a member of the analytical advisory board of Information Resources, Inc.

Dominique M. Hanssens (Ph.D., Purdue University) is the Bud Knapp Professor of Marketing at the UCLA Anderson School of Management. From 2005 to 2007 he served as Executive Director of the *Marketing Science Institute* in Cambridge, Massachusetts. His research focuses on strategic marketing problems, in particular marketing productivity, to which he applies his expertise in econometrics and time-series analysis. Professor Hanssens is currently an associate editor of the *Journal of Marketing Research*. His papers have appeared in the leading academic and professional journals in marketing, economics and statistics. Four of these articles have won Best Paper awards, in *Marketing Science* (1995, 2001, 2002) and *Journal of Marketing Research* (1999, 2007), and three were award finalists. The second edition of his book with Leonard Parsons and Randall Schultz, entitled *Market Response Models* was published in 2001 and translated in Chinese in 2003. In 2003 he was awarded the UCLA Anderson School's Neidorf 'decade' teaching award, and in 2007 he was the recipient of the Churchill Lifetime Achievement Award of the American Marketing Association. He is a partner with MarketShare Partners, a marketing science firm headquartered in Los Angeles.

Gerald Häubl is the Canada Research Chair in Behavioral Science and an Associate Professor of Marketing at the University of Alberta School of Business. His main research interests are consumer decision making, human-information interaction, decision assistance for consumers, and the construction of preference and value. His work has been published in *Marketing Science,* the *Journal of Experimental Psychology: Learning, Memory, and Cognition, The*

Journal of Consumer Research, The Journal of Consumer Psychology, Sloan Management Review, The International Journal of Research in Marketing, Marketing Letters, the *Communications of the Association for Computing Machinery,* and other journals. Gerald is the founding director of the Institute for Online Consumer Studies (IOCS.org). He is a faculty affiliate of the Sloan Center for Internet Retailing and a research fellow of Pennsylvania State University's eBusiness Research Center. He has received the Petro-Canada Young Innovator Award (in 2000) and the inaugural Award for Outstanding Research in Retailing from the University of Alberta (in 2007).

Harald Hruschka holds the Marketing Chair at the University of Regensburg, Germany. His main research interests comprise brand choice and sales response models, direct marketing, semi-parametric models including neural nets, and hierarchical Bayesian models. He has held visiting positions at the University of Massachusetts Amherst, the University of California San Diego , the Vienna University of Business Administration and Economics, the University of Vienna, the Humboldt University Berlin and the University Lille I. He has published in journals such as *Journal of Forecasting, European Journal of Operational Research, OR Spectrum, Marketing Letters, Journal of Retailing and Consumer Services, International Journal of Research in Marketing,* and others. Before joining the University of Regensburg he was associate professor at the Vienna University of Business Administration and Economics, where he also obtained his Ph.D. and his venia docendi. Currently he serves as Dean of the School of Economics at the University of Regensburg.

Sam K. Hui is a Doctoral student in Marketing at the Wharton School at the University of Pennsylvania. His main research interests are models for shopping paths, entertainment industry (movies, DVDs, casinos), spatio-temporal diffusion, and concept maps analyses.

Peter S.H. Leeflang (1946) studied econometrics in Rotterdam, obtaining both his MA, in 1970, and his PhD, in 1974, at Erasmus University. He was appointed in 1975 as Professor of Marketing at the Faculty of Economics, University of Groningen. He has authored or co-authored 20 books including *Mathematical Models in Marketing* (Stenfert Kroese, Leiden, 1974); with Philippe A. Naert: *Building Implementable Marketing Models* (Martinus Nijhoff, The Hague/Boston, 1987); and with Dick Wittink, Michel Wedel, and Philippe Naert: *Building Models for Marketing Decisions* (2000). Other examples of his published work can be found in: *Journal of Marketing, Journal of Marketing Research, International Journal of Research in Marketing, Management Science, Marketing Science, and Quantitative Marketing & Economics.*

In 1978–1979 he was President of the European Marketing Academy and from 1981 to 1990 Vice-President of this Academy. During 1997–2001 he was Dean of the Department of Economics and also Pro-Rector of the University of Groningen. He is Board Member of the European Institute of Advanced Studies in Management (EIASM) in Brussels (Belgium). In 1999 he became a member of the Royal Netherlands Academy of Arts and Sciences. Since 2004 he is also affiliated professor at the Johann Wolfgang Goethe Universität at Frankfurt am Main, Germany. In 2005 he has been appointed at the Frank M. Bass Chair of Marketing at the University of Groningen.

Donald R. Lehmann is George E. Warren Professor of Business at Columbia University Graduate School of Business. He has a B.S. degree in mathematics from Union College, Schenectady, New York, and an M.S.I.A. and PhD from the Krannert School of Purdue University. His research interests include modeling choice and decision making, meta-analysis, the introduction and adoption of innovations, and the measurement and management of marketing assets (customers and brands). He has taught courses in marketing, management, and statistics at Columbia, and has also taught at Cornell, Dartmouth, and New York University. He has published in and served on the editorial boards of *Journal of Consumer Research, Journal of Marketing, Journal of Marketing Research, Management Science, and Marketing Science*, and was the founding editor of Marketing Letters. In addition to numerous journal articles, he has published several books: including Market Research and Analysis, Analysis for Marketing Planning, Product Management, Meta Analysis in Marketing, and Managing Customers as Investments. Professor Lehmann has served as Executive Director of the Marketing Science Institute and as President of the Association for Consumer Research.

Gary L. Lilien is Distinguished Research Professor of Management Science at Penn State and is also co-founder and Research Director of the Institute for the Study of Business Markets. He is the author or co-author of twelve books (including *Marketing Models, Marketing Engineering* and *Principles of Marketing Engineering)*, as well as over 100 professional articles. He was departmental editor for Marketing for, *Management Science*; is on the editorial board of the *International Journal for Research in Marketing*; is functional Editor for Marketing for *Interfaces*, and is Area Editor at *Marketing Science*. He was Editor in chief of *Interfaces* for six years. He is the former President as well as Vice President/Publications for The Institute of Management Sciences. He is VP for External Relations and a Fellow of the European Marketing Academy and is VP External Relations for the INFORMS College on Marketing. He is an Inaugural INFORMS Fellow, was honored as Morse Lecturer for INFORMS and also received the Kimball medal for distinguished contributions to the field of operations research. He has received honorary doctorates from the University of Liege, the University of Ghent and Aston University and is the 2008 AMA/Irwin/McGraw Hill Educator of the year.

Murali Mantrala is Sam. M. Walton Distinguished Professor of Marketing at the University of Missouri-Columbia and an honorary visiting professor of Loughborough University, UK. Previously, he was J.C. Penney Associate Professor of marketing at the University of Florida, Gainesville. He has also taught at Chicago, Duke, Washington-St. Louis, Vanderbilt, Rutgers and

Columbia Universities. Murali holds a PhD in Marketing from the Kellogg School, Northwestern University, and MBAs from the Indian Institute of Management Calcutta and University of Minnesota. Between 2000 and 2003, Murali was a Manager at ZS Associates, Evanston, Illinois, engaged in sales consulting with pharmaceutical, insurance and broadcast industry clients. His current research focuses on sales force incentives, retail pricing, and marketing mix management. He has published articles in the leading marketing journals and is the coauthor of two papers in *Journal of Marketing Research* that have been Finalists for the William O'Dell Award and another in *Marketing Science* that won the ISMS Frank M. Bass Award. He is co-editor of *Retailing in the 21st Century: Current and Emerging Trends* (Springer 2006). He serves on the editorial board of *Marketing Science* and is Sales Force Models Area Editor of the *Journal of Personal Selling and Sales Management*.

Kyle B. Murray is an Assistant Professor of Marketing at the Richard Ivey School of Business. He holds a B.Sc. in Psychology and a Ph.D. in Marketing and Psychology from the University of Alberta. Professor Murray's research focuses on consumer judgment and decision making, with an emphasis on how consumers make choices in electronic environments. His work in this area has been published in journals such as *The Journal of Consumer Research, Organizational Behavior* and *Human Decision Processes, Journal of Consumer Psychology*, MIT Sloan Management Review, and Communications of the Association for Computing Machinery. The results of his research have also been featured in a number of book chapters and newspaper articles. As an educator Dr. Murray has developed and taught undergraduate, MBA, PhD and executive level courses in marketing, consumer behavior, retailing and e-commerce. He has also been active as a consultant for a variety of organizations in fields as diverse as oil and gas, manufacturing, financial services, retailing, and not-for-profit enterprises. Dr. Murray is a Senior Research Fellow at the Institute for Online Consumer Studies (iocs.org) and he is the current Director of Ivey's Behavioural Research Laboratory.

Prasad A. Naik is a Chancellor's Fellow and Professor of Marketing at the University of California Davis. He holds a Ph. D. in Marketing (University of Florida), MBA (Indian Institute of Management Calcutta), and B.S. in Chemical Engineering (University of Bombay). Prior to the doctoral studies, he worked for several years with Dorr-Oliver and GlaxoSmithKline, where he acquired invaluable experience in B2B sales, B2C sales and distribution, and brand management. He develops new models and methods to improve the practice of marketing. He publishes his research in top-tier journals of both the disciplines: Marketing (e.g., *JMR, JM, Marketing Science, and Management Science*) and Statistics (e.g., *JASA, JRSS-B, Biometrika, and Journal of Econometrics*). He serves on the Editorial Boards of *Marketing Science, Marketing Letters*, and *Journal of Interactive Marketing*. He is a recipient of the Doctoral Dissertation Award (AMS), Frank Bass Award (INFORMS), Young Scholar (MSI), AMA Consortium Faculty (2004, 2008), and Professor of the

Year Teaching Award. Besides teaching courses in NPD, IMC and Marketing Management, he led MBA teams to Argentina, Brazil, China, Malaysia, Singapore, and Thailand to learn International Marketing.

Scott A. Neslin is the Albert Wesley Fry Professor of Marketing at the Tuck School of Business, Dartmouth College. Professor Neslin's expertise is in the measurement and analysis of marketing productivity. His focus is on sales promotion and database marketing. In the promotions area, he has investigated issues such as the effect of promotion on consumer stockpiling, brand loyalty, and consumption. In database marketing, he has researched topics such as cross-selling, customer churn, and multichannel customer management. He has published on these and other topics in journals such as *Marketing Science, Journal of Marketing Research, Management Science, Journal of Marketing*, and *Journal of Interactive Marketing*. He is co-author with Robert C. Blattberg and Byung-Do Kim of the book *Database Marketing: Analyzing and Managing Customers*, forthcoming in 2008, to be published by Springer. He is also co-author with Robert C. Blattberg of the book, *Sales Promotion: Concepts, Methods, and Strategies*, published by Prentice-Hall, and author of the monograph *Sales Promotion*, published by the Marketing Science Institute. He is an Area Editor for *Marketing Science*, and on the editorial boards of the *Journal of Marketing Research, Journal of Marketing,* and *Marketing Letters*.

Arvind Rangaswamy is the Anchel Professor of Marketing at Penn State, where he is also the Research Director of the Center for Digital Transformation (www.smeal.psu.edu/cdt). He received a PhD in marketing from Northwestern University, an MBA from the Indian Institute of Management, Calcutta, and a B.Tech from the Indian Institute of Technology, Madras. Professor Rangaswamy has an active research program to develop concepts, methods and models to improve the efficiency and effectiveness of marketing using information technologies. He has published numerous professional articles in leading journals, and has also co-authored a successful book titled, *Marketing Engineering: Computer-Assisted Marketing Analysis and Planning*. He also consults for many companies in the areas of marketing modeling, marketing research, and e-Business, including most recently, Abbott Labs, McNeil Labs (Johnson & Johnson), J.D. Power Associates, UCB, Pfizer, and Unisys. He is an Area Editor for *Marketing Science* and serves on the editorial boards of several other leading journals. He is a Fellow of the IC^2 Institute, co-founder of DecisionPro, Inc., was an IBM Faculty Partner (2000–2001), and is the Chair of the e-Business Section of The Institute for Operations Research and the Management Sciences (INFORMS).

Vithala R. Rao is the Deane Malott Professor of Management and Professor of Marketing and Quantitative Methods, Johnson Graduate School of Management, Cornell University, Ithaca, New York. He received his Ph.D. in applied economics/marketing from the Wharton School of the University of Pennsylvania.

He has published widely on several topics including conjoint analysis and multidimensional scaling, pricing, market structure, corporate acquisition, and brand equity. His current work includes bundle design and pricing, demand estimation and competitive issues for preannounced products, linking branding strategies to financial performance. His papers have appeared in several journals including *Journal of Marketing Research, Marketing Science, Journal of Consumer Research, Decision Science, Management Science, Journal of Marketing, Marketing Letters, and International Journal of Research in Marketing.* He is the co-author of four books, *Applied Multidimensional Scaling, Decision Criteria for New Product Acceptance and Success, New Science of Marketing, and Analysis for Strategic Marketing.*

He currently serves on the editorial boards of *Marketing Science, Journal of Marketing Research, Journal of Marketing,* and *Journal of Business to Business Marketing.* He received the 2000–2001 Faculty Research Award of the Johnson Graduate School of Management at Cornell University and other awards for his papers.

Werner J. Reinartz is a Professor of Marketing at the University of Cologne, Germany. He has been previously the Cora Chaired Professor of Retailing and Management at INSEAD in France. His research interests focuses on the dynamics of the consumer-firm interaction. This interest bridges the areas of customer relationship management, marketing strategy, database marketing, and retailing. He has published in *Journal of Marketing, Journal of Marketing Research, Journal of Consumer Research, Journal of Service Research, Multivariate Behavioral Research, Journal of Retailing, Marketing Letters, Harvard Business Review, California Management Review, and The Economist.* Furthermore, he is a member of the editorial board of *Journal of Marketing* and *Marketing Science.* His research on measuring and managing the lifetime value of customers has received academic awards such as the 1999 AMA Doctoral Dissertation Competition, the 2001 Don Lehmann Award for the Best Dissertation-Based Research Paper to be published in *Journal of Marketing Research* or *Journal of Marketing,* and the 2003 and 2005 MSI/Paul Root Award of the Journal of Marketing. Together with V. Kumar, he coauthored the textbook *Customer Relationship Management: A Databased Approach* (2005). Professor Reinartz holds a Ph.D. in Marketing from the University of Houston (1999).

Venkatesh Shankar is Professor and Coleman Chair in Marketing and PhD Advisor at the Mays Business School, Texas A&M University. His research interests include Branding, Competitive Strategy, Innovation, e-Business, International Marketing, and Retailing. He has a marketing Ph.D. from Kellogg School, Northwestern University. His research has been published in *Journal of Marketing Research, Marketing Science, Management Science, Strategic Management Journal,* and *Journal of Marketing.* He is a winner of the *Clarke* Award for Outstanding Direct Marketing Educator, the *IBM* Faculty Partnership Award, the *Green* Award for the Best Article in *Journal of*

Marketing Research, and the *Lehmann* Award for the Best Dissertation-based Article in an *AMA Journal*. He is co-editor of *Journal of Interactive Marketing* and is/has been on the editorial boards of *Marketing Science, Management Science,* and *Journal of Marketing*. He is an Academic Trustee, *MSI* and President of Marketing Strategy SIG, *AMA*. He is a three-time winner of the *Krowe* Award for Outstanding Teaching and has taught Marketing Management, Digital Business Strategy, Marketing Strategy, Marketing Research, New Product Management, and International Marketing. He has been a visiting faculty at MIT, INSEAD, Singapore Management University, SDA Bocconi, Nanyang Technology University, Indian School of Business, and Chinese European International Business School.

Gerrit H. van Bruggen is Professor of Marketing at Rotterdam School of Management, Erasmus University and ISBM Distinguished Visiting Scholar (Pennsylvania State University). Most of his research addresses the impact of Information Technology on Marketing (Decision) Making. In recent research projects he studied the Adoption and Effectiveness of Marketing Decision Models and the Effectiveness of Virtual Stock Markets for Institutional Forecasting. He co-authored the book *Marketing Management Support Systems: Principles, Tools and Implementation* (Kluwer Academic Publishers) together with Berend Wierenga and published articles in journals such as: *Marketing Science, Management Science, Journal of Marketing Research, Journal of Marketing, International Journal of Marketing, MIS Quarterly and Information Systems Research*.

Harald J. van Heerde is Professor of Marketing at the Waikato Management School, New Zealand. He has a M.Sc. in econometrics (cum laude) and Ph.D. (cum laude) from the University of Groningen, the Netherlands. His research deals with building econometric models in domains such as sales promotions, pricing and loyalty programs, and is branching out into new areas such as building brand equity, private labels, assortment optimization and price wars. Harald's work has appeared in the *Journal of Marketing Research* (*JMR*), *Marketing Science, Quantitative Marketing and Economics,* and the *International Journal of Research in Marketing*. Harald has received the 2004 Paul Green award for the best paper in *JMR* and the 2008 William O'Dell award for most impactful paper in *JMR*. He is an editorial board member of *JMR* and an Area Editor of the *International Journal of Research in Marketing*.

Rajkumar Venkatesan is Associate Professor of Business Administration in the Darden Graduate School of Business Administration at the University of Virginia. He has been on the faculty at the University of Connecticut and received his PhD from the University of Houston. Raj's research focus is on designing marketing strategies that maximize customer profitability, understanding the pricing strategies of online retailers and developing models for forecasting sales of new products. His research has appeared in several journals including *Journal of Marketing, Journal of Marketing Research, Marketing*

Science, and *Harvard Business Review*. Raj's research has been recognized with awards such as the Don Lehmann Award for the Best Dissertation based article published in the *Journal of Marketing* and *The Journal of Marketing Research*, the Marketing Science Institute Alden G. Clayton Award for the best marketing dissertation proposal, and the ISBM outstanding dissertation proposal award.

Charles B. Weinberg is the Presidents of SME Vancouver Professor of Marketing at the Sauder School of Business, University of British Columbia. Before joining UBC, he held faculty positions at New York University, London Business School, and Stanford University. His research focuses on analytical marketing, services, and public & nonprofit marketing and management. His work in the nonprofit sector includes the marketing of safer sex practices, competition among nonprofit organizations, and pricing. For more than 30 years, he has studied the arts and entertainment industry. His early work focused on live entertainment and included the ARTS PLAN model for marketing and scheduling performing arts events. More recently, he has focused on the movie industry with such publications as "Competitive Dynamics and the Introduction of New Products: The Motion Picture Timing Game (*Journal of Marketing Research*), "Sequential Distribution Channels" (*Journal of Marketing*), and "Implementation and Evaluation of SilverScreener" (*Interfaces*). He is a former editor of *Marketing Letters* and area editor of *Marketing Science*. He grew up in New Jersey, but has lived in Vancouver ("Beautiful British Columbia") for more than 25 years. He is the Conference Chairman of the 2008 Marketing Science conference in Vancouver.

Early Titles in the
INTERNATIONAL SERIES IN OPERATIONS RESEARCH & MANAGEMENT SCIENCE

Frederick S. Hillier, Series Editor, *Stanford University*

Printed in the United States
143765LV00001B/26/P